The Writer's World
Readings for College Composition

The Writer's World
Readings for College Composition

Edited by
GEORGE ARMS
University of New Mexico

WILLIAM M. GIBSON
University of Wisconsin—Madison

LOUIS G. LOCKE
James Madison University

St. Martin's Press
New York

Library of Congress Catalog Card Number: 77-086290
Copyright © 1978 by St. Martin's Press, Inc.
All Rights Reserved.
Manufactured in the United States of America.
098
fedcba
For information, write: St. Martin's Press, Inc.,
175 Fifth Avenue, New York, N. Y. 10010
ISBN: 0-312-89433-3

Typography by Arthur Ritter.
Cover design by Mies Hora.
   Moving In, 1961 by Morris Louis. Acrylic on canvas:
   87½" x 41½". Private Collection, New York.

ACKNOWLEDGMENTS

1. INITIATIONS

The College Scene
   "The Football Phenomenon on Campus" by Iver Peterson, from *The New York Times*, Jan. 16, 1974. © 1974 by The New York Times Company. Reprinted by permission.
   "Nothing Is True, Nothing Is False" by J. Mitchell Morse. Reprinted with permission of The Chronicle of Higher Education, April 5, 1976. Copyright © 1976 by Editorial Projects for Education, Inc. Reprinted by permission of the author.
   "Adolescence" by Erik H. Erikson. Reprinted from *Identity, Youth and Crisis* by Erik H. Erikson. By permission of W. W. Norton & Company, Inc. Copyright © 1968 by W. W. Norton & Company, Inc.
   "On Being 17, Bright, and Unable to Read" by David Raymond, from *The New York Times*, April 25, 1976, Special Education Supplement. © 1976 by The New York Times Company. Reprinted by permission.
   "Frustrations of the Gifted" by Norman Murphy, from *The New York Times*, April 25, 1976, Special Education Supplement. © 1976 by The New York Times Company.
   "Should Colleges Retain Tenure?" by Kingman Brewster, Jr. Reprinted with permission of The Wall Street Journal, © Dow Jones & Company, Inc. 1972. All Rights Reserved.

Acknowledgments and copyrights continue at back of the book on pages 497–503, which constitute an extension of the copyright page.

Preface

The title of this anthology, *The Writer's World*, has several meanings. It refers, first, to the astonishing and complex universe of facts, experiences, and ideas in which writers of expository prose may find their subjects. It refers also to the special world to which each writer gives order and shape, according to his or her own vision, through the medium of language. And it refers to the world of the student readers for whom the anthology is intended; we hope they will discover in the writer's world a world of their own—one they, in turn, may share with others in classroom discussion and in their own writing.

These several meanings of our title suggest the principles of selection that have guided us as editors: diversity, quality, and accessibility. There is space in a tolerably brief preface to say only a little about each.

Diversity. The writer's world is a world of variety and excitement. All subjects belong to it. Hence this anthology encompasses an extraordinarily wide range of human activities and concerns: literature, art, music, film, business, politics, education, history, anthropology, medicine, sports, science, religion, philosophy—and more. The writers are as diverse as their subjects. They speak for both popular and unpopular causes. Some write humorously, some in rage. Some make their living as writers, but others are artists, athletes, religious leaders, or scientists. (A few are poets, for we have included a short poem in the anthology here and there, each embodying a theme treated by one or more of the neighboring prose selections.) There is diversity of another kind: although the emphasis in the anthology is distinctly contemporary, writers of the past are often side by side with those of our own day—hence Plato, Ben Franklin, and Mark Twain share these pages with Oriana Fallaci, Leonard Bernstein, and Studs Terkel.

Quality. What the readings clearly demonstrate—some, admittedly, better than others—is that certain qualities of good writing cut across all boundaries of discipline and time. They are present as surely in a first-rate student theme as in a classic essay by George Orwell or James Thurber. From a world in which all subjects are possible, the writers in this anthology have taken subjects that are important to them and about which they have something to say. Because they do care, they write honestly, and so their voices are distinctive. Moreover, they write *for* someone, whether that audience is humankind in the present and in posterity, as it was for Jefferson in the Declaration of Independence, or readers of the Sunday magazine, as in Russell Baker's "Fedgush." Whether they write to inform us, stir us to action, amuse us, or simply allow us to look on as they discover and clarify their own thoughts, they write for a purpose. Finally, they are guided by a conscious concern for language, a wish to be clear, to be understood. In short: a subject, a thesis, a commitment, a sense of audience, a purpose, a concern for language—when all of these are present, as in varying degrees they are in the essays here, we are able to enter the writer's world and so expand our own.

Accessibility. We hope that, from a collection as large and varied as this, instructors will be able to choose just the right combination of readings for a particular class. One might, for example, select readings from all or most of the sections but give particular emphasis to the arts, or to the sciences, or to political, economic, and social issues, or to the religious and philosophical questions raised in the final section. Or one might ignore certain sections entirely.

Most of the readings are relatively brief, though all are either complete works or free-standing selections from longer works. They vary considerably in difficulty; if forced to choose, we have not hesitated to select an exciting but "difficult" piece over a dull but "easy" one. The writer's world, after all, is one of challenge as well as variety and excitement. However, again, given the large number of selections, an instructor might easily, for a particular class, choose an entire semester's reading from among the simpler pieces in the anthology and hope that some students would become sufficiently confident to explore other readings on their own.

Beyond the accessibility of the individual pieces, one may speak of the accessibility of *The Writer's World* as a whole. Students who routinely move in the course of a day from, let us say, English to biology to economics to psychology to computer science will find themselves very much at home in this anthology. Moreover, there is a natural progression from the first section, "Initiations," with its focus on the campus and on the immediate concerns of college students, to the last section, "Final Things," which addresses ultimate concerns of all human beings. The three middle sections, "Society," "The Arts," and "Sciences" afford students a panoramic view of what their world offers, and, not incidentally, represent the living tradition of liberal education.

What appears in *The Writer's World* is offered with the belief that better writing will result from what is read. This can come about in at least three ways: (1) Most of the essays may serve, in whole or in part, as models for student writing, and some of them give direct advice about writing—especially the readings in "Writing, Language, and Style" in the first section. (2) Since most of the essays deal with important ideas worthy of discussion, they will provoke students to respond by writing their own views. A student's response to a selection need not be one of dissent; it may, for instance, expand a certain observation, add information from a different angle, or examine the tone and assumptions of a selection. We believe in the concept of an ongoing dialogue between writers and readers. (3) The Alternate Table of Contents Arranged by Rhetorical Type offers a sequence that some instructors may wish to use for the advantages of exploring rhetorical modes as well as producing unexpected confrontations among essays. We hope that all of this will stimulate students to work to create their own world in writing.

Now to turn to grateful acknowledgments for the help that we have received. It is of course impossible to acknowledge all our many obligations to friends, colleagues, and students of today and yesterday. But we do wish to thank William E. Callahan, Ralph A. Cohen, James Ruff, and William Thomas of James Madison University; Rudolfo A. Anaya, Lynn Z. Bloom, Patrick J. Gallacher, Michael Hogan, Catherine L. Martin, Fern McLean, and Joseph B. Zavadil of the University of New Mexico; Mary Bradish of the University of Wisconsin, Madison; Richard McGuire of MacMurray College; Mary Pulleyn of the University of Toledo; and Edward M. White of California State University, San Bernardino.

We are especially grateful to Professor X. J. Kennedy of Tufts University, who provided the editors with a new and insightful essay especially for this anthology. It deals with the remake of the film *King Kong* and pairs nicely with Kennedy's classic essay about the original movie, "Who Killed King Kong?"

We are also grateful to Peter Phelps and Nancy Perry of St. Martin's Press for their invaluable encouragement, perceptive advice, and careful editing. We also want to thank Frances Ware for her indispensable aid in preparing the manuscript. Our gratitude is likewise extended to the library staffs of the University of New Mexico, the University of Wisconsin, and James Madison University, especially at the latter to Thomas McLaughlin, reference librarian.

1978   G.A., W.M.G., L.G.L.

Contents

Preface v

1 Initiations 1

The College Scene
The Football Phenomenon on Campus, *Iver Peterson* 4
Nothing Is True, Nothing Is False, *J. Mitchell Morse* 8
Adolescence, *Erik H. Erikson* 12
On Being 17, Bright, and Unable to Read, *David Raymond* 15
Frustrations of the Gifted, *Norman C. Murphy* 17
Should Colleges Retain Tenure? *Kingman Brewster, Jr.* 19

Writing, Language, and Style
Learning to Write, *Benjamin Franklin* 24
Language and Thought, *Susanne K. Langer* 26
Politics and the English Language, *George Orwell* 31
Fedgush, *Russell Baker* 41
Baffle-Gab Thesaurus 43
Viable Solutions, *Edwin Newman* 43
The Language Barrier: Why Students Can't Write, *A. Bartlett Giamatti* 48
Being Serious Without Being Stuffy, *Walker Gibson* 53
An Ethic of Clarity, *Donald Hall* 57

Attainment
Animula, *T. S. Eliot* 62
Experience of the Average Girl: Coming of Age in Samoa, *Margaret Mead* 63
Working, *Studs Terkel* 70
Us and Them, *R. D. Laing* 77
Piercing the Veil of the Commonplace, *Charles Frankel* 80
Getting Smart, *Josiah Bunting III* 84
Secrets of the Evergreen People, *Roy Larson* 86
I Think Continually of Those Who Were Truly Great, *Stephen Spender* 88

ix

2 Society 91

Politics and Economics

A Plea for the Freedom of Dissent, *Learned Hand*   94
Declaration of Independence, *Thomas Jefferson*   98
Speech in the Constitutional Convention at the Conclusion of Its Deliberations, September 17, 1787, *Benjamin Franklin*   101
The Bill of Rights   103
The New Inequality, *Peregrine Worsthorne*   104
How a Prince Should Keep His Word, *Niccolò Machiavelli*   106
". . . None Will Sweat But for Promotion . . .," *Michael Korda*   108
Benighted Nations, *Russell Baker*   112
I Have a Dream, *Martin Luther King, Jr.*   114
Looking Backward, 2000–1887, *Edward Bellamy*   117
Somehow, It Has Overcome, *Kenneth J. Arrow*   120
Oh! We've Been Trojan-Horsed! *Peter F. Drucker*   124
Directive, *Robert Frost*   126

War

The Hot Gates, *William Golding*   128
The Persian Version, *Robert Graves*   132
Appomattox, *Bruce Catton*   133
War Memories, *Stephen Crane*   138
The War Prayer, *Mark Twain*   142
A Salutation-Speech from the 19th Century to the 20th, *Mark Twain*   145
On History, Foolishness, and Vietnam, *John Kenneth Galbraith*   145

Sports

Billie Jean King: An Attitude, Instinct, and Sense of Urgency, *Parton Keese*   150
O. J. Simpson: Speed, Balance, and E.S.P., *Gerald Eskenazi*   154
Life on the Run, *Bill Bradley*   157
Why Ali Whipped Patterson, *Muhammad Ali*   162

Minorities

The Grass on the Mountain   165
Wounded Knee, *Dee Brown*   165
The Feast of San Diego at Jemez, *N. Scott Momaday*   170
The Meaning of the Chicano Movement, *Lydia R. Aguirre*   176

The Meaning of July Fourth for the American Negro, *Frederick Douglass* 180
Why I Left the U.S. and Why I Am Returning, *Eldridge Cleaver* 185
As Italian as Apple Pie and Baseball, *Ralph J. Perrotta* 188

Women

A Vindication of the Rights of Woman, *Mary Wollstonecraft* 190
The Stereotype, *Germaine Greer* 192
Rape, But That Has Changed, *Susan Brownmiller* 194
Two-Career Couples, *Alan L. Otten* 197
Why I Never Married, *Oriana Fallaci* 200
Life Without Father, *Ellen Goodman* 202
Planetarium, *Adrienne Rich* 204

3 The Arts 207

Film and Television

Who Killed King Kong? *X. J. Kennedy* 211
The New *King Kong*, or A Great Ape Double-Crossed, *X. J. Kennedy* 214
Henry V, *James Agee* 217
There Are No Mass Media: All We Have Is Television, *Jeffrey Schrank* 220

Music, Painting, and Architecture

Why Don't You Run Upstairs and Write a Nice Gershwin Tune? *Leonard Bernstein* 227
How We Listen, *Aaron Copland* 233
As Picasso Said, Why Assume That To Look Is To See? A Talk Between Malraux and the Master, *André Malraux* 238
The Case for Abstract Art, *Clement Greenberg* 242
The School of "Messy Vitality," *Dennis Farney* 249
Chicago's Stunning Architecture, *Paul Goldberger* 254

Literature

The Macbeth Murder Mystery, *James Thurber* 257
Ars Poetica, *Archibald MacLeish* 260
Sonnet 55: Not marble, nor the gilded monuments, *William Shakespeare* 261
The Use of Poetry, *Harold Bloom* 261

On Reading a Poem, *William M. Gibson* 263
Nat Pine, *Gilbert Millstein* 265
The Keys to Dreamland, *Northrop Frye* 267
The Literary Life: Some Representative Women, *Ellen Moers* 275

Art and Life

Expressiveness, *Susanne K. Langer* 285
Cultural Snobbery, *Arthur Koestler* 292
The Quest for Civilisation, *Kenneth Clark* 299
Ode on a Grecian Urn, *John Keats* 302

4 Sciences 305

Science and Scientists

The Usefulness of Useless Knowledge, *Abraham Flexner* 308
On Albert Einstein, *Robert Oppenheimer* 315
Newton the Man, *John Maynard Keynes* 320

Of Life

The Struggle for Existence, *Charles Darwin* 329
The Territorial Imperative, *Robert Ardrey* 333
The Ladder of Creation, *Jacob Bronowski* 337
Natural Science, *Lewis Thomas* 347
Carbon Monoxide Poisoning, *Claude Bernard* 349
The Music of *This* Sphere, *Lewis Thomas* 351
To a Snail, *Marianne Moore* 355

Ecology

Monsieur Tocqueville! Oh, Get Some Water—He's Fainted! *William W. Serrin* 356
Trying to Restore a Sea of Grass, *Dennis Farney* 359
Bees and Ecology, *Joseph M. Winski* 361
Wilderness, *Aldo Leopold* 364

Some Problems

Why Can't Computers Be More Like Us? *Lewis Thomas* 373
What Physicists Do: Neaten up the Cosmos, *Robert Geroch* 375
Molecular Astronomy: The Great Void Is Alive, *Walter Sullivan* 377

Some Adjustments

Trend Is Not Destiny, *René Dubos*   380
On Growth, *René Dubos*   382
Who Should Control Recombinant DNA? *Cheryl M. Fields*   383
Man's Fourth Adjustment, *Harlow Shapley*   389
The Golden Alphabet, *Loren Eiseley*   392

5 Final Things   401

The Good Life

For Once, Then, Something, *Robert Frost*   404
History as a Moral Science, *Gordon Wright*   404
The Apology of Socrates, *Plato*   408
The Sermon at Benares, *Gautama Buddha*   417
The Sermon on the Mount, *St. Matthew*   422

God and Humankind

Psalm 90: Man and the Providence of God   428
The Upanishads: Svetasvatara   429
Brahma, *Ralph Waldo Emerson*   433
Chanting the Square Deific, *Walt Whitman*   434
God and the Spirit of Man, *Martin Buber*   435

What Is Reality?

Existentialism as a Symptom of Man's Contemporary Crisis, *William C. Barrett*   440
The Allegory of the Cave, *Plato*   447

Death

O Death, Where Is Thy Sting-a-Ling-a-Ling? *Leslie H. Farber*   451
Meditation XVII, *John Donne*   462
Because I Could Not Stop for Death, *Emily Dickinson*   464

What Is Happiness?

What Is Happiness? *William V. Shannon*   465
Myths of Our Time, *L. S. Stavrianos*   467
O Taste and See, *Denise Levertov*   469
A Really New World, *Joseph Wood Krutch*   469

"What Is Man?"

Psalm 8: The Strength and Glory of Man 471
The Stoic Code, *Marcus Aurelius* 471
I Corinthians 13: Love, *St. Paul* 476
The Lowest Animal, *Mark Twain* 477
Know Then Thyself, *Alexander Pope* 484
More Day to Dawn, *Henry D. Thoreau* 484
Ecclesiastes 12:1-8: Remember Now Thy Creator 485
The Divine Image, *William Blake* 486

Notes on Authors 487
Index of Authors and Titles 505

Alternate Table of Contents Arranged by Rhetorical Type

Exposition

Learning to Write, *Benjamin Franklin* 24
Language and Thought, *Susanne K. Langer* 26
Experience of the Average Girl: Coming of Age in Samoa, *Margaret Mead* 63
The Meaning of the Chicano Movement, *Lydia R. Aguirre* 176
Two-Career Couples, *Alan L. Otten* 197
Life Without Father, *Ellen Goodman* 202
On Reading a Poem, *William M. Gibson* 263
The Music of *This* Sphere, *Lewis Thomas* 351
What Physicists Do: Neaten up the Cosmos, *Robert Geroch* 375
Molecular Astronomy: The Great Void Is Alive, *Walter Sullivan* 377

Description

The Feast of San Diego at Jemez, *N. Scott Momaday* 170
Who Killed King Kong? *X. J. Kennedy* 211
The New *King Kong*, or A Great Ape Double-Crossed, *X. J. Kennedy* 214
Henry V, *James Agee* 217
How We Listen, *Aaron Copland* 233
The School of "Messy Vitality," *Dennis Farney* 249
Chicago's Stunning Architecture, *Paul Goldberger* 254
Trying to Restore a Sea of Grass, *Dennis Farney* 359
Wilderness, *Aldo Leopold* 364

Cause and Effect

The Language Barrier: Why Students Can't Write, *A. Bartlett Giamatti* 48
Secrets of the Evergreen People, *Roy Larson* 86
Why I Left the U.S. and Why I Am Returning, *Eldridge Cleaver* 185
Why I Never Married, *Oriana Fallaci* 200

xv

The Use of Poetry, *Harold Bloom* 261
Carbon Monoxide Poisoning, *Claude Bernard* 349

Comparison and Contrast

Us and Them, *R. D. Laing* 77
The New Inequality, *Peregrine Worsthorne* 104
As Italian as Apple Pie and Baseball, *Ralph J. Perrotta* 188
The Case for Abstract Art, *Clement Greenberg* 242
Bees and Ecology, *Joseph M. Winski* 361
Why Can't Computers Be More Like Us? *Lewis Thomas* 373
God and the Spirit of Man, *Martin Buber* 435

Analogy or Exemplum

Looking Backward, 2000–1887, *Edward Bellamy* 117
The Hot Gates, *William Golding* 128
The Allegory of the Cave, *Plato* 447
More Day to Dawn, *Henry D. Thoreau* 484

Definition

Adolescence, *Erik H. Erikson* 12
Should Colleges Retain Tenure? *Kingman Brewster, Jr.* 19
The Bill of Rights 103
Oh! We've Been Trojan-Horsed! *Peter F. Drucker* 124
War Memories, *Stephen Crane* 138
Natural Science, *Lewis Thomas* 347
Existentialism as a Symptom of Man's Contemporary Crisis, *William C. Barrett* 440
I Corinthians 13: Love, *St. Paul* 476

Analysis

The Football Phenomenon on Campus, *Iver Peterson* 4
Politics and the English Language, *George Orwell* 31
Being Serious Without Being Stuffy, *Walker Gibson* 53
An Ethic of Clarity, *Donald Hall* 57
". . . None Will Sweat But for Promotion . . ." *Michael Korda* 108
Somehow, It Has Overcome, *Kenneth J. Arrow* 120
The Keys to Dreamland, *Northrop Frye* 267
Expressiveness, *Susanne K. Langer* 285
Cultural Snobbery, *Arthur Koestler* 292
The Struggle for Existence, *Charles Darwin* 329

The Territorial Imperative, *Robert Ardrey* 333
Man's Fourth Adjustment, *Harlow Shapley* 389
O Death, Where Is Thy Sting-a-Ling-a-Ling? *Leslie H. Farber* 451

Historical Writing

How a Prince Should Keep His Word, *Niccolò Machiavelli* 106
Appomattox, *Bruce Catton* 133
On History, Foolishness, and Vietnam, *John Kenneth Galbraith* 145
Wounded Knee, *Dee Brown* 165
Rape, But That Has Changed, *Susan Brownmiller* 194
The Literary Life; Some Representative Women, *Ellen Moers* 275
The Quest for Civilisation, *Kenneth Clark* 299
Monsieur Tocqueville! Oh, Get Some Water—He's Fainted! *William W. Serrin* 356
Trend Is Not Destiny, *René Dubos* 380
On Growth, *René Dubos* 382
History as a Moral Science, *Gordon Wright* 404
Myths of Our Time, *L. S. Stavrianos* 467

Persuasion

Nothing Is True, Nothing Is False, *J. Mitchell Morse* 8
Getting Smart, *Josiah Bunting III* 84
A Plea for the Freedom of Dissent, *Learned Hand* 94
Speech in the Constitutional Convention at the Conclusion of Its Deliberations, September 17, 1787, *Benjamin Franklin* 101
A Vindication of the Rights of Woman, *Mary Wollstonecraft* 190
The Usefulness of Useless Knowledge, *Abraham Flexner* 308
The Apology of Socrates, *Plato* 408
What Is Happiness? *William V. Shannon* 465
A Really New World, *Joseph Wood Krutch* 469
The Lowest Animal, *Mark Twain* 477
Ecclesiastes 12:1-8: Remember Now Thy Creator 485

Persuasion: Praise and Blame

Piercing the Veil of the Commonplace, *Charles Frankel* 80
The Stereotype, *Germaine Greer* 192
There Are No Mass Media: All We Have Is Television, *Jeffrey Schrank* 220

Nat Pine, *Gilbert Millstein* 265
Who Should Control Recombinant DNA? *Cheryl M. Fields* 383
Psalm 8: The Strength and Glory of Man 471
The Stoic Code, *Marcus Aurelius* 471

Persuasion: Sermon

I Have a Dream, *Martin Luther King, Jr.* 114
The War Prayer, *Mark Twain* 142
The Sermon at Benares, *Gautama Buddha* 417
The Sermon on the Mount, *St. Matthew* 422
Psalm 90: Man and the Providence of God 428
The Upanishads: Svetasvatara 429
Meditation XVII, *John Donne* 462

Persuasion: Ceremonial Essay

Declaration of Independence, *Thomas Jefferson* 98
The Meaning of July Fourth for the American Negro, *Frederick Douglass* 180

Humor and Satire

Fedgush, *Russell Baker* 41
Baffle-Gab Thesaurus 43
Viable Solutions, *Edwin Newman* 43
Benighted Nations, *Russell Baker* 112
A Salutation-Speech from the 19th Century to the 20th, *Mark Twain* 145
The Macbeth Murder Mystery, *James Thurber* 257

Dialogue

Why Don't You Run Upstairs and Write a Nice Gershwin Tune? *Leonard Bernstein* 227
As Picasso Said, Why Assume That To Look Is To See? A Talk Between Malraux and the Master, *André Malraux* 238

Biography and Autobiography

On Being 17, Bright, and Unable to Read, *David Raymond* 15
Frustrations of the Gifted, *Norman C. Murphy* 17
Working, *Studs Terkel* 70
Billie Jean King: An Attitude, Instinct, and Sense of Urgency, *Parton Keese* 150

O. J. Simpson: Speed, Balance, and E.S.P., *Gerald Eskenazi* 154
Life on the Run, *Bill Bradley* 157
Why Ali Whipped Patterson, *Muhammad Ali* 162
On Albert Einstein, *Robert Oppenheimer* 315
Newton the Man, *John Maynard Keynes* 320
The Ladder of Creation, *Jacob Bronowski* 337
The Golden Alphabet, *Loren Eiseley* 392

Poetry

Animula, *T. S. Eliot* 62
I Think Continually of Those Who Were Truly Great, *Stephen Spender* 88
Directive, *Robert Frost* 126
The Persian Version, *Robert Graves* 132
The Grass on the Mountain 165
Planetarium, *Adrienne Rich* 204
Ars Poetica, *Archibald MacLeish* 260
Sonnet 55: Not marble, nor the gilded monuments, *William Shakespeare* 261
Ode on a Grecian Urn, *John Keats* 302
To a Snail, *Marianne Moore* 355
For Once, Then, Something, *Robert Frost* 404
Brahma, *Ralph Waldo Emerson* 433
Chanting the Square Deific, *Walt Whitman* 434
Because I Could Not Stop for Death, *Emily Dickinson* 464
O Taste and See, *Denise Levertov* 469
Know Then Thyself, *Alexander Pope* 484
The Divine Image, *William Blake* 486

1
Initiations

The College Scene

Writing, Language, and Style

Attainment

Going to college is an important initiation in our complex culture, although it is only one of many. In preindustrial cultures the rites of initiation are clearly defined, but in the twentieth century youth might be said to run through countless initiations—going to kindergarten, entering high school, having his or her first date, buying a car, joining a team or a club, finding a job. The list is endless, and adulthood hardly sets a boundary, as we see in Studs Terkel's portrait of the sixty-five-year-old saxophonist Bud Freeman, who needs at least five more years to perfect his playing and wouldn't mind having thirty more.

Our first group of essays, "The College Scene," presents several aspects of the initiation of going to college. Here you'll find a neutral but informed essay on college football by Iver Peterson and a pained outcry on student egocentrism, "Nothing Is True, Nothing Is False," from J. Mitchell Morse. The next three essays—"Adolescence" by Erik H. Erikson, "On Being 17, Bright, and Unable to Read" by David Raymond, and "Frustrations of the Gifted" by Norman C. Murphy—deal with college students and their problems, both the problems that they share with everyone in their age group as well as those peculiar to the gifted and those with learning disabilities. We recall that Freud said, "We are all [neurotically] ill." Perhaps after considering these essays we can say with a like sense of shared human commitment, "We all have dyslexia" or even "We are all gifted." The section concludes with a defense of academic tenure by the former president of Yale University, Kingman Brewster, Jr. At first sight you may be startled to see an article on tenure—what does tenure have to do with us? It's a faculty concern, isn't it? Yet tenure is one of the most salient differences between life on campus and off. We've noticed that when a popular teacher fails to receive tenure, student petitions often pile up on the dean's desk, frequently making invidious comparisons of that teacher's value with what some tenured faculty member has to offer. So the special academic rules of hiring and firing are indeed an important aspect of "The College Scene."

But where does "Writing, Language, and Style," our second group of essays, come into this process of initiation? It comes first perhaps in College Composition, the kind of course in which you probably are reading this book. More importantly, it belongs here because so much of initiation into adulthood depends on expression. As Susanne K. Langer insists, signs will do for animals, but symbols distinguish human beings, for symbols intertwine with ideas and language. Her essay and George Orwell's make up the philosophical core of this group. Benjamin Franklin's "Learning to Write" is an inspiring example of how an ambitious person taught himself to write well. Some of the other essays in the group—those by Russell Baker and Edwin Newman, and the "Baffle-Gab Thesaurus"—are lighthearted, but they are not without serious overtones when you consider how language can confuse ideas just as easily as it can clarify them. However, the last three writers in the group offer some hope: A. Bartlett Giamatti thinks the current situation is terrible but that it can get better; Walker Gibson offers some useful rules (worth comparing with Orwell's); and Donald Hall explains the intimate relationship between clarity and honesty. Of the three, we feel closest to Gibson, who admits his own faults in style (as we admit ours) but can still say, "Keep on trying."

What then happens after the initiations of going to college, staying there, getting out, and going on? We hope that college will be the beginning of a fuller realization of your identity, or that something of the same sort will happen even without college. We've dared to call this last section on initiations "Attainment," though we recognize that attainment is always out of reach and that even getting close isn't easy. These essays tell their own stories with a vividness that we can only touch upon. Reflect on T. S. Eliot's poem "Animula," which has been called the most pessimistic he ever wrote. Compare how young people live in the United States today with Margaret Mead's picture of youth in Samoa half a century ago. Glimpse the challenges and fulfillment two people find in their chosen occupations in Studs Terkel's "Working." Match, if you will, the human situation described by R. D. Laing. See two related but quite different views of liberal education proposed by Charles Frankel and Josiah Bunting III. Examine the wisdom of Roy Larson, who tells us that to remain "evergreen," we somehow must "get ourselves into the habit of saying 'yes' to life." And finally join with Stephen Spender in thinking of "those who were truly great. . . . And left the vivid air signed with their honor." Here in the living tradition of the liberal arts may be our ultimate initiation.

The College Scene

The Football Phenomenon on Campus
IVER PETERSON

Millions of armchair quarterbacks saw some good college football during the annual New Year's Day bowl-game binge, but they probably did not see the best. After all, the University of Oklahoma's Sooners trounced both Cotton Bowl teams—Nebraska and Texas—during the regular season, and tied Southern California, which lost to Ohio State in the Rose Bowl.

The reason for their absence, as college sports fans know, is that the Big Red team from Norman, Okla., is under a two-year ban from playing televised bowl games. The ban was imposed by the National Collegiate Athletic Association [N.C.A.A.] and Oklahoma's Big Eight Conference after the Sooners fielded two players with doctored high school transcripts.

The illegally altered class standings, which made the two players appear eligible for the football scholarships that the University of Oklahoma had pressed upon them, pointed up an important element in the controversy over big time college sports. The intense demand for blue-chip athletes and a winning team has apparently presented too much of a temptation to coaches and players to go beyond the strictly limited inducements for prospective players permitted by the N.C.A.A.—free tuition, room and board, some laundry and book money, and some transportation expenses.

OTHER OFFERS REPORTED

And the college sports scene is rife with reports that many other inducements, including money, cars, clothes and a job, are offered under the table.

"I used to think everything I heard was exaggerated," Darrell Royal, coach of the Texas Longhorns and athletic director of the University of Texas, told *The Chronicle of Higher Education,* "but we've had too many people come here that told us what people have offered them. You're out there trying to sell yourself and your school, and the guy ain't hearing a word you're saying. All he's wondering about is when you're going to start talking money."

To its credit, the University of Oklahoma, like other important sports colleges, acted quickly if not entirely openly to correct these abuses when they were discovered, and the attitude among officials there seems to be that the growing venality of college sports can be contained by good faith and constant vigilance.

But the question that skeptics have long been asking is not just how major colleges should contain the greed and excesses of college sports, but what business does an institution of higher learning have in producing and promoting multimillion-dollar public spectacles in the first place.

A stranger at the University of Oklahoma who poses that question comes away with the realization that probably came to the men who run the country's public colleges and universities a long time ago. It is that, in more ways than just sports, there is a vast gap between the ideals of higher education and the realities of life at a large, state-supported public university.

REALITIES IN AMERICA

The notion that sports should be a pleasant interlude from their studies for energetic young gentlemen has no more to do with these realities in today's America than the Heidelberg and Oxford traditions of turning out refined young men to move smoothly into positions of power have to do with the true goals of American public institutions.

"We are not the linear descendants of Oxford and Heidelberg," said Paul Sharp, president of the University of Oklahoma, in the tone of a man who is tired of explaining the difference. "It is in the context of the realities of American life that we measure the reality on the academic level."

Dr. Sharp and others in his position know that these realities are that American public education has drawn its support from the public by providing what the public needs and wants. Land grant colleges were founded to produce agriculturalists and technicians when intensive farming began after the Civil War; after 1957, campuses produced scientists in response to Sputnik, and today the emphasis is on cheap, informal and easily accessible two-year community colleges. And on sports.

Last season, for example, more than 400 million fans watched nearly 3,000 college football games. About 30 million of the fans paid an estimated $150 million—not including bowl games—to attend in person. The television networks spent another $13.5 million for broadcast rights, and will pay more next season.

And as Wade Walker, the University of Oklahoma's athletic director, points out, sports—and especially football—is a lot more than a game. Being a real fan almost means believing in a particular way of life.

"Athletics is still one of the true free enterprise areas of the American democracy," Mr. Walker said in his friendly Western drawl. "It doesn't make any difference what color your skin is, or what your social status is, because you just got 11 youngsters out there, nose to nose and toes to toes, and the guy who really wants to qualify can make it. That's the way this country began, and this is still one place where a guy can be rewarded by what he does. And it's not like that in any other area anymore."

MORE THAN A GAME

Anyone who has ever watched the Rose Bowl parade or gone through the annual Oklahoma and University of Texas pre-game drinking and partying brawl (278 arrested in 1972) knows that sports is not just a game, that it involves more than a contest between two teams. At the University of Oklahoma, students and faculty members on both sides of the controversy agree that sports—especially football—goes much deeper.

"Football is everything; it's just the life here," said Stephanie Miller, a graduate student in journalism at the University of Oklahoma.

William Maehl, professor of history at the university and president of the Faculty Senate, described the importance of football to Oklahoma in a way that might be applied to many other states, or indeed, to much of the country.

"This is a young state," he said. "It has no real traditions, and football provides a kind of focus of values that is much more important to people here than it would be, perhaps, to people in an Eastern state."

Mr. Walker, the Oklahoma athletic director, sees it clearly:

"If you only had one toy when you were a youngster, but it was a good toy, you could still go out in the neighborhood and stick your chest out and say, 'that's mine!'

"Well, this is a rural state, and our football gives John Doe Q. Public, wherever he lives, something to identify with—it gives him something to stick out his chest about, and say, 'Boy, I'm a Sooner! I'm part of the Big Red!' It gives him something wholesome."

There is nothing abstract in Mr. Walker's view of the connection between sports and American ideals. "We're teachers," he said of himself and his coaching staff. "We teach a philosophy, we teach a skill, and we danged sure also teach a little bit of religion. And we teach discipline—this is one of the last areas where true discipline is taught, where love for the American flag and respect for the American President is taught, through discipline."

Mr. Walker spends most of his time, he said, promoting support for the Sooners by making this kind of appeal and urging fans to "get a piece of the action, be a part of the Big Red." And they respond.

"WE TEACH DISCIPLINE"

Those who can afford the $1,000 annual dues may join the Winning Edge, the university's élite booster club, which raises money for athletic scholarships. By contributing a carcass of beef for the training tables, one can join the Sooner Beef Club. And there are the Sooner Club and the Touchdown Club, established like the others to raise money for the nearly $3 million self-supporting annual athletic budget at the University of Oklahoma.

Last year, these supporters contributed $220,000 toward operating expenses, not including capital gifts, which is a fairly modest sum compared with the more than $800,000 similarly raised last year for the University of North Carolina teams, or the $700,000 contributed to the University of South Carolina athletic program.

Not everyone, of course, shares Wade Walker's view of the wholesomeness of this kind of fan loyalty. Michael Vitt, a senior who is editor of the student-run *Oklahoma Daily*, gave what might be described as the underside of Mr. Wade's explanation for football's popularity at the university.

"If it wasn't for O. U. football," he said, "there wouldn't be anything else that O. U. students could identify with, because in everything else, O. U. is a loser."

What about the nonstudent fans—the alumni and nonalumni boosters who make up most of the team's support?

"When you think about what the history of this state is," Mr. Vitt, a native Oklahoman, said, "you realize it's Indian murders and claim-jumping and people who were so down and out somewhere else that they came here. So if you have a football team that's a winner, well, everybody can identify with a winner. They don't have a damn thing to do with that team going out and winning, but it's something they can be proud of."

Fan loyalty has its pitfalls, however, and officials at big time sports schools have learned that they have to tread gingerly between promoting the enthusiasm of loyal supporters and resisting the demands that seem to accompany the support.

When Chuck Fairbanks ended the 1966–1967 season at Oklahoma with a 6–3–1 record—a disaster for a team that is used to being top or near the top in the country—"Chuck Chuck" stickers appeared on the bumpers of Oklahoma cars, and the coach did leave, to take over the New England Patriots in the National Football League.

Then, when the Big Eight and N.C.A.A. probation was announced, along with a prohibition against the Sooners appearing on television for two seasons, Gov. David Hall of Oklahoma won political points by appealing for a lifting of the TV ban and by threatening to go to court when the appeal failed. The episode made some friends for Governor Hall, but it angered and embarrassed members of the university.

Dr. Sharp, the university's president, said his administration had to resist "constant external pressures to use [football] for political or commercial purposes." He added, "We resist these pressures because we feel that they are an intrusion into the academic purpose of the university."

When he made this comment in an interview just before Christmas, Dr. Sharp was in the midst of a battle with the Oklahoma Legislature and the State Board of Regents for additional funds to cover the university's rising costs. In Oklahoma, student radicalism and the growing popularity of two-year community colleges continue to tempt legislators and regents to give a larger share of public funds for education to community colleges and the more placid Oklahoma State University, formerly called Oklahoma A. & M.

Relations with the Legislature "understandably are eased" when the Sooners have a good season, Dr. Sharp said, but he insisted that success on the gridiron was not all that important in terms of money.

"Relations with the Legislature are always friendlier when we are able to be successful in bringing the state this kind of credit," Dr. Sharp said. "They don't icepick us to death on all the little issues or questions that a legislature could raise if they wanted to." He also said that he would be "more afraid of nit-picking questions of accountability and the management of public funds," rather than questions of funding, if the Sooners started losing.

"But remember, I haven't been through a losing season," he added, "and I would have to go through a losing season before I could make a final judgment on that."

He made it sound like something he would just as soon avoid having to do.

Nothing Is True, Nothing Is False
J. MITCHELL MORSE

Zeus, a stage Irishman in *Finnegans Wake*,[1] gives ambiguous orders to the other gods. To Poseidon he says, "Posidonius O'Fluctuary! Lave that bloody stone as it is!"

Such is the inscrutability of the uncontrollable. All our researches are efforts to control it by making it scrutable, by scrutinizing it; all our frustration comes from the discovery, which we endlessly rediscover but which never satisfies us, that the uncontrollable doesn't stand still for our scrutiny and a formulation of it will last only until the next formulation.

And all our educational efforts are efforts to introduce our students into the confusion without merely confusing them, to make them aware of vanity without filling them with despair. Fortunately, we must begin with comfortable delusions of simplicity and stability. As Maimonides[2] said in *A Guide for the Perplexed*, in the beginning we must simplify the subject, thus unavoidably falsifying it, and later we must sophisticate the falsely simple beginnings away.

This method works well in college for subjects the students have never studied before—*e.g.*, a second foreign language, in which we teach them

---

[1] A novel by James Joyce, published in 1939.—EDS.

[2] Maimonides (1135–1204) was the most famous Jewish philosopher of the Middle Ages.—EDS.

the basic grammar and vocabulary before sending them to Europe to discover that many people speak ungrammatically, that there are regional and local dialects, and so on.

The difficulties of college teaching occur in subjects to which the students have presumably been introduced before they come to us—e.g., the basic processes of arithmetic and the basic grammar and vocabulary of literate English. Because they haven't been introduced to them. A friend in physics tells me that many of his beginning students not only can't handle fractions but don't even know what a fraction is; and in my English classes there are juniors and seniors who write like this:

▶ "He sat in this apt., formally frequented by abandoned societal types. Now, even that's gone. His hair a straggly main, he suffered with haranged senses."

▶ "In Heart of Darkness Marlowe sympathizers in the opressed native's robed of their few possions however he refused in accepting the practices of canonabalism."

▶ "In 'Lady Chatterlys Lover' their is a man called Sir Clifford who was nothing more than a personality. He had lost all contact with his 'mental life.' Sex to him is strictly a sensation one feels with their body but is no way related or involved with your mind. He gave to Conie a mental love which he found lacking to her being. She had no ideniny. I hope I have arisen enough interest to convince the reader."

I was the reader. I was not convinced by any of these writers. All three protested.

"I feel," said the first, "you ought to grade us on content, not the form."

"I feel," said the second, "you are downgrading me because like I was creative and just didn't, like, parrot back what you said."

"I feel," said the third, "that as a consumer I'm entitled to the education I'm paying for. This is the first time I've ever gotten less than a B. When can we go over the paper and see where you went wrong?"

The prevalence of the expression "I feel" is a symptom of the softening effect of a pop Deweyism[3] on our students' brains: a lazy acceptance of the view that since nothing is known with assured finality there are no facts, only opinions, and therefore that one opinion is as good as another.

If we accepted this view with regard to our own disciplines, it would be the death of research, the death of teaching, and the death of our own minds. But our students do accept it with regard to their writing, their literary studies, their aesthetic judgments, and the beliefs they live by. Nothing is true, nothing is false, everything floats, everything is a matter of opinion.

I recently refused to accept, as a topic for a graduate term paper, an

---

[3] The misunderstanding of the educational philosophy of John Dewey (1859–1952) which has widely influenced American education.—EDS.

astrological interpretation of *Ulysses*[4] based on a Ph.D. candidate's own belief in astrology. "Astrology," I said, "implies that the earth is the center of the universe." To which he replied, "I feel that it is." And when I then gave him Copernicus's argument about being on a ship and feeling that the land is moving past us, he said, "Maybe it is. That's just another way of looking at it."

For a moment I felt that I was in the presence of madness; then I thought, *No, he's not insane, he's just a solipsist. This is solipsism, nothing more; take it easy.* But now, on calmer consideration, I think perhaps he *was* having a moment of nuttiness. For solipsism so unquestioning makes rational discourse impossible in the contexts in which it occurs. "I feel that it is so, therefore it is so. For me." But if we are to communicate with others it must also be so for them; and if our communication is to be rational it must stand the tests of such objectivity as we have. At the very least, rational communication requires that we agree on the meaning of words, on the logic of sentences, and tentatively, in the light of available information, on the hypothetical factuality of facts.

As Charles Sanders Peirce[5] said some time ago, for economy of research we must assume that we know certain things. Likewise, for the purpose of making sense we must assume that words mean what they are conventionally supposed to mean in current usage. A conversation between Humpty Dumpty and Mr. Pickwick wouldn't get anywhere. Nevertheless, these two solipsists are English majors now, and they are everywhere. *They* know what they mean, and it's up to us to find out. Here are some examples of their do-it-yourself prose:

▶ "The Congo might very well be the answer for the outcome of Kurtz."

▶ "Molly Bloom was a woman who has lost contact with her once-kept martial oaths."

▶ "Bloom is naïve yet congcience."

▶ "The 'Odysey' is the prototype of romantic literature in the Western world. The book is structured according to the episodes of Homer. Joyce only mastered the basis of structuralization of a book on another. He didn't find a new method of writing or an example but utilized a process."

People who write like that are not in touch with any intellectual reality. They are in a state of intellectual delirium—or, as one of them inadvertently put it, of "confussion." Speaking and writing are efforts to break out of the solitary confinement of subjectivity. These efforts succeed only in proportion as they make use of signals that other people understand. A loud vocal noise made by an unseen person may be interpreted as a yell of joy or a scream of pain or of fear, and the interpretation will be accurate in proportion to the accuracy with which we related the vocal manifestation of a subjective state to something that is not subjective.

---

[4] James Joyce's famous novel, published in 1922.—EDS.

[5] American philosopher (1839–1914) who founded pragmatism.—EDS.

When we speak in words and sentences, we help our hearers to interpret our vocalizations accurately. The shout "Help!" is not likely to be misinterpreted as a shout of joy, although it may have exactly the same musical tone as the shout "Wow!" Both shouts, being words, are intellectualizations—however slight—of subjective states. They are parts of a social code. When we use them we assume, or hope, that there is another person who understands the code.

And when we write we use a purely intellectual code, which does without such elements of the spoken code as gesture, facial expression, and tone of voice, and indicates the tune—which is also part of the spoken code—by punctuation marks. The difference between "Well!" and "Well?" is a difference of tune, hence of meaning.

Likewise, the sentences "John says Joan is sweet" and "John, says Joan, is sweet" have different meanings because they have different tunes, and therefore the presence or absence of the commas is crucial.

But what do you make of the sentences "John, says Joan is sweet" and "John says Joan, is sweet"? It's hard to tell what to make of them. Their meanings are not clear, because their punctuation inadvertently violates the code of musical notation. And when a student writes such a sentence, and defends it by saying, as a student of remedial English did say to me, "It may not mean anything to you, but it means a hell of a lot to me," we then have the task of making him see that subjectivity is not enough. (And we'd better not use the word "subjectivity.")

"I feel." He doesn't want to violate his feeling by intellectualizing it. But *what* does he feel? To the extent that he knows, he has already intellectualized it. Otherwise the feeling would be only a tension of the muscle or a burning sensation in the chest, unidentified and inexpressible except through physical action. He might rape somebody or kill somebody, for example, or simply roll on the ground like a horse in a sunny field. But humanity, for better or worse, involves consciousness and control; and these involve thinking in words. Humanity is verbal or it is nothing.

Therefore, when a senior majoring in English writes, "Authors who succeed in portraying modern situations realistically succeed in portraying we all as victims," I view that "we" as a symptom of a deep disease in our society, a society that is becoming not only non-verbal but anti-verbal.

Some of us are trying to cure it; others are not. The Dewey-eyed Conference on College Composition and Communication has issued an official statement proclaiming that literate English is not the only English, that students have "a right to their own language," and that they are only frustrated and turned off when we correct their misstatements.

I am less pessimistic. I still struggle. If there is any hope, it lies with those of us who struggle. There are more of us than our lack of organization indicates.

Adolescence
ERIK H. ERIKSON

As technological advances put more and more time between early school life and the young person's final access to specialized work, the stage of adolescing becomes an even more marked and conscious period and, as it has always been in some cultures in some periods, almost a way of life between childhood and adulthood. Thus in the later school years young people, beset with the physiological revolution of their genital maturation and the uncertainty of the adult roles ahead, seem much concerned with faddish attempts at establishing an adolescent subculture with what looks like a final rather than a transitory or, in fact, initial identity formation. They are sometimes morbidly, often curiously, preoccupied with what they appear to be in the eyes of others as compared with what they feel they are, and with the question of how to connect the roles and skills cultivated earlier with the ideal prototypes of the day. In their search for a new sense of continuity and sameness, which must now include sexual maturity, some adolescents have to come to grips again with crises of earlier years before they can install lasting idols and ideals as guardians of a final identity. They need, above all, a moratorium for the integration of the identity elements ascribed . . . to the childhood stages: only that now a larger unit, vague in its outline and yet immediate in its demands, replaces the childhood milieu—"society." A review of these elements is also a list of adolescent problems.

If the earliest stage bequeathed to the identity crisis an important need for trust in oneself and in others, then clearly the adolescent looks most fervently for men and ideas to have *faith* in, which also means men and ideas in whose service it would seem worth while to prove oneself trustworthy. At the same time, however, the adolescent fears a foolish, all too trusting commitment, and will, paradoxically, express his need for faith in loud and cynical mistrust.

If the second stage established the necessity of being defined by what one can *will* freely, then the adolescent now looks for an opportunity to decide with free assent on one of the available or unavoidable avenues of duty and service, and at the same time is mortally afraid of being forced into activities in which he would feel exposed to ridicule or self-doubt. This, too, can lead to a paradox, namely, that he would rather act shamelessly in the eyes of his elders, out of free choice, than be forced into activities which would be shameful in his own eyes or in those of his peers.

If an unlimited *imagination* as to what one *might* become is the heritage of the play age, then the adolescent's willingness to put his trust in those peers and leading, or misleading, elders who will give imaginative, if not illusory, scope to his aspirations is only too obvious. By the same token, he objects violently to all "pedantic" limitations on his self-images and will be ready to settle by loud accusation all his guiltiness over the excessiveness of his ambition.

Finally, if the desire to make something work, and to make it work well, is the gain of the school age, then the choice of an occupation assumes a significance beyond the question of remuneration and status. It is for this reason that some adolescents prefer not to work at all for a while rather than be forced into an otherwise promising career which would offer success without the satisfaction of functioning with unique excellence.

In any given period in history, then, that part of youth will have the most affirmatively exciting time of it which finds itself in the wave of a technological, economic, or ideological trend seemingly promising all that youthful vitality could ask for.

Adolescence, therefore, is least "stormy" in that segment of youth which is gifted and well trained in the pursuit of expanding technological trends, and thus able to identify with new roles of competency and invention and to accept a more implicit ideological outlook. Where this is not given, the adolescent mind becomes a more explicitly ideological one, by which we mean one searching for some inspiring unification of tradition or anticipated techniques, ideas, and ideals. And, indeed, it is the ideological potential of a society which speaks most clearly to the adolescent who is so eager to be affirmed by peers, to be confirmed by teachers, and to be inspired by worthwhile "ways of life." On the other hand, should a young person feel that the environment tries to deprive him too radically of all the forms of expression which permit him to develop and integrate the next step, he may resist with the wild strength encountered in animals who are suddenly forced to defend their lives. For, indeed, in the social jungle of human existence there is no feeling of being alive without a sense of identity. . . .

The estrangement of this stage is *identity confusion*. For the moment, we will accept Biff's formulation in Arthur Miller's *Death of a Salesman*: "I just can't take hold, Mom, I can't take hold of some kind of a life." Where such a dilemma is based on a strong previous doubt of one's ethnic and sexual identity, or where role confusion joins a hopelessness of long standing, delinquent and "borderline" psychotic episodes are not uncommon. Youth after youth, bewildered by the incapacity to assume a role forced on him by the inexorable standardization of American adolescence, runs away in one form or another, dropping out of school, leaving jobs, staying out all night, or withdrawing into bizarre and inaccessible moods. Once "delinquent," his greatest need and often his only salvation is the refusal on the part of older friends, advisers, and judiciary personnel to type him further by pat diagnoses and social judgments which ignore the special dynamic conditions of adolescence. It is here . . . that the concept of identity confusion is of practical clinical value, for if they are diagnosed and treated correctly, seemingly psychotic and criminal incidents do not have the same fatal significance which they may have at other ages.

In general it is the inability to settle on an occupational identity which most disturbs young people. To keep themselves together they temporarily overidentify with the heroes of cliques and crowds to the point of an apparently complete loss of individuality. Yet in this stage not even "falling in love" is entirely, or even primarily, a sexual matter. To a considerable extent adolescent love is an attempt to arrive at a definition of one's identity by projecting one's diffused self-image on another and by seeing it thus reflected and gradually clarified. This is why so much of young love is conversation. On the other hand, clarification can also be sought by destructive means. Young people can become remarkably clannish, intolerant, and cruel in their exclusion of others who are "different" in skin color or cultural background, in tastes and gifts, and often in entirely petty aspects of dress and gesture arbitrarily selected as the signs of an in-grouper or out-grouper. It is important to understand in principle (which does not mean to condone in all of its manifestations) that such intolerancy may be, for a while, a necessary defense against a sense of identity loss. This is unavoidable at a time of life when the body changes its proportions radically, when genital puberty floods body and imagination with all manner of impulses, when intimacy with the other sex approaches and is, on occasion, forced on the young person, and when the immediate future confronts one with too many conflicting possibilities and choices. Adolescents not only help one another temporarily through such discomfort by forming cliques and stereotyping themselves, their ideals, and their enemies; they also insistently test each other's capacity for sustaining loyalties in the midst of inevitable conflicts of values.

The readiness for such testing helps to explain the appeal of simple and cruel totalitarian doctrines among the youth of such countries and classes as have lost or are losing their group identities—feudal, agrarian, tribal, or national. The democracies are faced with the job of winning these grim youths by convincingly demonstrating to them—by living it—that a democratic identity can be strong and yet tolerant, judicious and still determined. But industrial democracy poses special problems in that it insists on self-made identities ready to grasp many chances and ready to adjust to the changing necessities of booms and busts, of peace and war, of migration and determined sedentary life. Democracy, therefore, must present its adolescents with ideals which can be shared by young people of many backgrounds, and which emphasize autonomy in the form of independence and initiative in the form of constructive work. These promises, however, are not easy to fulfill in increasingly complex and centralized systems of industrial, economic, and political organization, systems which increasingly neglect the "self-made" ideology still flaunted in oratory. This is hard on many young Americans because their whole upbringing has made the development of a self-reliant personality dependent on a certain degree of choice, a sustained hope for an individual chance, and a firm commitment to the freedom of self-realization.

On Being 17, Bright, and Unable to Read
DAVID RAYMOND

One day a substitute teacher picked me to read aloud from the textbook. When I told her "No, thank you," she came unhinged. She thought I was acting smart, and told me so. I kept calm, and that got her madder and madder. We must have spent 10 minutes trying to solve the problem, and finally she got so red in the face I thought she'd blow up. She told me she'd see me after class.

Maybe someone like me was a new thing for that teacher. But she wasn't new to me. I've been through scenes like that all my life. You see, even though I'm 17 and a junior in high school, I can't read because I have dyslexia. I'm told I read "at a fourth-grade level," but from where I sit, that's not reading. You can't know what that means unless you've been there. It's not easy to tell how it feels when you can't read your homework assignments or the newspaper or a menu in a restaurant or even notes from your own friends.

My family began to suspect I was having problems almost from the first day I started school. My father says my early years in school were the worst years of his life. They weren't so good for me, either. As I look back on it now, I can't find the words to express how bad it really was. I wanted to die. I'd come home from school screaming, "I'm dumb. I'm dumb—I wish I were dead!"

I guess I couldn't read anything at all then—not even my own name—and they tell me I didn't talk as good as other kids. But what I remember about those days is that I couldn't throw a ball where it was supposed to go, I couldn't learn to swim, and I wouldn't learn to ride a bike, because no matter what anyone told me, I knew I'd fail.

Sometimes my teachers would try to be encouraging. When I couldn't read the words on the board they'd say, "Come on, David, you know that word." Only I didn't. And it was embarrassing. I just felt dumb. And dumb was how the kids treated me. They'd make fun of me every chance they got, asking me to spell "cat" or something like that. Even if I knew how to spell it, I wouldn't; they'd only give me another word. Anyway, it was awful, because more than anything I wanted friends. On my birthday when I blew out the candles I didn't wish I could learn to read; what I wished for was that the kids would like me.

With the bad reports coming from school, and with me moaning about wanting to die and how everybody hated me, my parents began looking for help. That's when the testing started. The school tested me, the child-guidance center tested me, private psychiatrists tested me. Everybody knew something was wrong—especially me.

It didn't help much when they stuck a fancy name onto it. I couldn't pronounce it then—I was only in second grade—and I was ashamed to talk about it. Now it rolls off my tongue, because I've been living with it for a lot of years—dyslexia.

All through elementary school it wasn't easy. I was always having to do things that were "different," things the other kids didn't have to do. I had to go to a child psychiatrist, for instance.

One summer my family forced me to go to a camp for children with reading problems. I hated the idea, but the camp turned out pretty good, and I had a good time. I met a lot of kids who couldn't read and somehow that helped. The director of the camp said I had a higher I.Q. than 90 percent of the population. I didn't believe him.

About the worst thing I had to do in fifth and sixth grade was go to a special education class in another school in our town. A bus picked me up, and I didn't like that at all. The bus also picked up emotionally disturbed kids and retarded kids. It was like going to a school for the retarded. I always worried that someone I knew would see me on that bus. It was a relief to go to the regular junior high school.

Life began to change a little for me then, because I began to feel better about myself. I found the teachers cared; they had meetings about me and I worked harder for them for a while. I began to work on the potter's wheel, making vases and pots that the teachers said were pretty good. Also, I got a letter for being on the track team. I could always run pretty fast.

At high school the teachers are good and everyone is trying to help me. I've gotten honors some marking periods and I've won a letter on the cross-country team. Next quarter I think the school might hold a show of my pottery. I've got some friends. But there are still some embarrassing times. For instance, every time there is writing in the class, I get up and go to the special education room. Kids ask me where I go all the time. Sometimes I say, "to Mars."

Homework is a real problem. During free periods in school I go into the special ed room and staff members read assignments to me. When I get home my mother reads to me. Sometimes she reads an assignment into a tape recorder, and then I go into my room and listen to it. If we have a novel or something like that to read, she reads it out loud to me. Then I sit down with her and we do the assignment. She'll write, while I talk my answers to her. Lately I've taken to dictating into a tape recorder, and then someone—my father, a private tutor or my mother—types up what I've dictated. Whatever homework I do takes someone else's time, too. That makes me feel bad.

We had a big meeting in school the other day—eight of us, four from the guidance department, my private tutor, my parents and me. The subject was me. I said I wanted to go to college, and they told me about colleges that have facilities and staff to handle people like me. That's nice to hear.

As for what happens after college, I don't know and I'm worried about that. How can I make a living if I can't read? Who will hire me? How will I fill out the application form? The only thing that gives me any courage is the fact that I've learned about well-known people who couldn't read or had other problems and still made it. Like Albert Einstein, who didn't talk until he was 4 and flunked math. Like Leonardo da Vinci, who everyone seems to think had dyslexia.

I've told this story because maybe some teacher will read it and go easy on a kid in the classroom who has what I've got. Or, maybe some parent will stop nagging his kid, and stop calling him lazy. Maybe he's not lazy or dumb. Maybe he just can't read and doesn't know what's wrong. Maybe he's scared, like I was.

Frustrations of the Gifted

NORMAN C. MURPHY

Most people assume that gifted children—because they are so obviously intelligent—can more or less take care of themselves in school. My own experiences as a child identified as gifted in the 1950's suggests that the very opposite is often true.

As a baby I was first labeled retarded. My 14-year-old mother, living in poverty in the mountains of Idaho, delivered me herself. I was malnourished. My mother, realizing she could not provide for me, decided on the advice of an elderly couple who had befriended her to allow me to be adopted by a young couple known to her friends.

The first indication that I might be above average in intellectual ability appeared when at three and a half years of age I began to read the school lessons of family friends. My ability to read and learn quickly created many problems for me in the lower grades.

My teachers saw me as a behavior problem, a child who always wanted to stay in the classroom and read. I was forced to go out to recess, where I usually stayed to myself or got into discussions with school staff members. The other children were constantly reminded of my difference, both by teachers and by my daily work in the classroom. While other students seemed to be interested in their textbooks, I was bored and getting into trouble by talking, not paying attention to the classroom work or daydreaming.

From grades one through six, I went to twelve different schools in six states. In second grade, school authorities asked my parents to allow me to be moved into the next grade. But I had read an article in *Redbook* on advance placement. I took it to my parents and we decided since I was a bit small for my age and not doing too well with other children socially that it would not be in my best interest to make a grade change. The teacher then promoted me de facto by having me work with students in the upper grades of the two-room school and by asking me to help children my age with their studies. While this treatment was most flattering, I soon found it did not help me to get along with other students. It was not uncommon to be followed home with taunts of "teacher's pet, smarty, smarty, smarty, teacher's pet."

My parents and teachers were first told that I was a gifted child by the College of the Pacific child study clinic. Psychologists there said that I was capable of the most sophisticated university work and could use special class assignment to reduce my boredom and behavior problem.

One particular teacher at the Davis School in Stockton, California, was exceptional in her ability to help me develop without increasing the apparent distance between me and my classmates. I wrote articles for the school newspaper and plays for my classmates. I was then reading the Harvard Classics.

Walking home from school one afternoon, I found a torn copy of Kafka's *In the Penal Colony*. When I began to discuss the bizarre story with a teacher, she told me no one would write a book like that; it must be a part of my active imagination. On another occasion while [I was] "listening" to Strauss waltzes in my mind, the teacher asked me what I was doing. When I told her, she told me that was impossible since I could not read music.

It was not uncommon for me to be taken out of the classroom for special testing. On one such occasion in sixth grade, I returned to the classroom just as the teacher was announcing to the class that they had a "genius" in their midst. If there had been questioning and wondering about me before, the teacher's lack of finesse created open dislike.

Grades seven through nine were spent mostly in a classroom combining all three grades. I was assigned the task of cataloging the school library, by a teacher desperate to keep me busy. While it was interesting, it did not necessarily augment my learning.

These experiences were pretty well universal in the public schools I attended. Had my parents not made a big financial sacrifice to place me in fine preparatory schools run by the Lutheran Church Missouri Synod, it is doubtful I could have received the educational background and study habits necessary for college.

In fact, had I stayed with my natural mother, I doubt very much that I would have received much more than a high-school diploma. If the problems of the middle-class gifted child are difficult, the problems of the poor but gifted child—particularly in remote rural areas—must be exceptionally frustrating. In some cases educators must be treating them with a carelessness that borders on criminal neglect.

Should Colleges Retain Tenure?[1]
KINGMAN BREWSTER, JR.

Of all the folkways of university life, perhaps "tenure" is least comprehensible to those whose professional or executive life involves the staffing of other forms of organized activity—business, finance, government, or nonprofit service. In prosperous times the tradition of academic tenure evokes puzzlement. In times when colleges and universities are struggling for financial survival, tenure is challenged with increasing frequency.

How, it is asked, can we talk glibly about the knowledge explosion or the exponential rate of change—with all its risks of rapid intellectual obsolescence—and at the same time lock ourselves into lifetime obligations to people in their mid-thirties? Not only do we risk becoming stuck with the obsolete, but we remove the most popularly understood incentive to higher levels of performance. Furthermore, since even in financially easy times university resources are finite, every "slot" mortgaged for a full professor's lifetime blocks the hope for advancement by some promising members of oncoming generations. When resources are so tight that the faculty must be pruned, because of tenure most of the pruning is at the expense of the junior faculty. Many juniors are more up to date in their command of new methods and problems in fast-moving fields, and many of them are more talented than are some of the elders.

THE AAUP'S POSITION

The Association of American University Professors [AAUP]—the organized guardian of academic freedom and tenure—has recently taken some pains to make it clear that tenure is not an absolute protection against dismissal. They say that a person can be fired for gross misconduct or neglect of duty. They assert that even a person with tenure may be terminated for financial reasons. Such termination is permissible in their eyes, however, only by a process which puts the burden of proof upon the university and in which the victim's faculty peers are both judge and jury, subject to final disposition by the trustees.

The practical fact in most places, and the unexpected rule at Yale, is that tenure is for all normal purposes a guarantee of appointment until retirement age. Physical or mental incapacity, some chronic disability, some frightful act of moral turpitude, or persistent neglect of all university responsibilities have on a very few occasions in the past resulted in "negotiated" termination settlements. However, even in extreme circumstances there is a deep reluctance to compromise the expectations of tenure.

[1] This selection is a major section of President Brewster's annual report for 1971–1972.—EDS.

The defense of tenure usually falls into two categories: the need for job security, in order to draw good people into underpaid academic life; and the need to protect the academic freedom of the faculty.

Both of these points are valid; but put this simply, both grossly understate the significance of tenure to the quality of a first-rate university.

The argument based on the recruitment of faculty is underscored by the simple fact that as long as most institutions grant tenure then any single institution must go along in order to remain competitive.

The job security argument arose when university faculty were grossly underpaid in comparison with other professional callings. They were even more disadvantaged when compared with the marts of trade and finance. This is still true, especially at both ends of the ladder: the bottom rungs of starting salaries and the higher rungs of top management compensation. In the middle range, however, academic salaries at a place like Yale are not grossly lower than the earnings of other professional callings. So, the use of job security as bait to persuade people to take a vow of "academic poverty" is not a sufficient argument. (It still has persuasive merit, however, for those institutions which pay sub-standard salaries. Such institutions are the proper concern of not only the AAUP but should be the concern of a society which has an enormous stake in attracting a sufficient number of people into careers devoted to the higher education of the young and the advancement of knowledge and understanding.)

The rationale of academic tenure, however, is somewhat different from job security in the industrial world, especially in an institution which wants its teachers to be engaged in pushing forward the frontiers of learning. This lies in the fact that contributions to human knowledge and understanding which add something significant to what has gone before involve a very high risk and a very long-term intellectual investment. This is true especially of those whose life is more devoted to thought, experimentation and writing than it is to practice.

TEACHERS AS SCHOLARS

If teaching is to be more than the retailing of the known, and if research is to seek real breakthroughs in the explanation of man and the cosmos, then teachers must be scholars, and scholarship must be more than the refinement of the inherited stock of knowledge. If scholarship is to question assumptions and to take the risk of testing new hypotheses, then it cannot be held to a timetable which demands proof of pay-out to satisfy some review committee.

I think that even with their privileges and immunities our academic communities are often too timid in their explorations. The fear of failure in the eyes of the peerage inhibits some of our colleagues, even when they do have tenure. Too many seek the safe road of detailed elaboration of accepted truth rather than the riskier paths of true exploration, which might defy conventional assumptions. Boldness would suffer if the research and scholarship of a mature faculty were to be subject to periodic scorekeeping, on the pain of dismissal if they did not score well. Then what should be a venture in creative discovery would for almost everyone degenerate into a safe-sided devotion to riskless footnote gathering. Authentication would replace discovery as the goal. The results might not startle the world, but they would be impressive in quantitative terms and invulnerable to devastating attack.

Purely economic connotations of "job security" greatly understate the distinctive aspect of the academic calling. At its best the university expects a person literally to make a lifetime investment in his special way of looking at the human and natural experience, in the hope that he will contribute something of permanence to the understanding of some corner of the universe.

The second, and most highly touted, rationale for tenure is academic freedom. This concern, traditionally, has focused on the privilege of immunity from "outside" interference. Within the memory of those still active, "McCarthyism" is the most telling nightmare.

Of course there are corrupting influences, financial, institutional and professional. By and large, however, of all the types of institutions which gather people together in a common effort, the university remains the least inhibiting to variety in ideas, convictions, styles and tastes. It encourages its members to pursue doggedly any idea in which they have confidence. Progress in the world of thought depends on people having enough freedom and serenity to take the risk of being wrong.

This struggle to preserve the integrity of the institution and the freedom of its faculty members from external coercion is never over. However, despite the winds of controversy in a troubled time, whetted occasionally by demagogic desire to make academia the scapegoat for society's ills, the ability of a strong university to give its faculty convincing protection against such threats will depend more on the steadfastness of the institution as a whole than it will on tenure.

The dramatic image of the university under siege from taxpayers, politicians, or even occasional alumni is a vivid but not the most difficult aspect of the pressures which tend to erode academic freedom. The more subtle condition of academic freedom is that faculty members, once they have proved their potential during a period of junior probation, should not feel beholden to *anyone*, especially Department Chairmen, Deans, Provosts, or Presidents, for favor, let alone for survival. In David Riesman's phrase teachers and scholars should, insofar as possible, be truly "inner directed"— guided by their own intellectual curiosity, insight and conscience. In the development of their ideas they should not be looking over their shoulders either in hope of favor or in fear of disfavor from anyone other than the judgment of an informed and critical posterity.

In strong universities assuring freedom from intellectual conformity coerced *within* the institution is even more of a concern than is the protection of freedom from external interference.

This spirit of academic freedom within the university has a value which goes beyond protecting the individual's broad scope of thought and inquiry. It bears crucially upon the distinctive quality of the university as a community. If a university is alive and productive, it is a place where colleagues are in constant dispute; defending their latest intellectual enthusiasm, attacking the contrary views of others. From this trial by intellectual combat emerges a sharper insight, later to be blunted by other, sharper minds. It is vital that this contest be uninhibited by fear of reprisal. Sides must be taken only on the basis of the merits of a proposition. Jockeying for favor by trimming the argument because some colleague or some group will have the power of academic life or death in some later process of review would falsify and subvert the whole exercise.

I have not been able to devise, nor have I heard of, any regime of periodic review with the sanction of dismissal which would not have disastrous effect. It would both dampen the willingness to take long-term intellectual risks and inhibit, if not corrupt, the free and spirited exchanges upon which the vitality of a community of scholars depends. This, not the aberrational external interference, is the threat to the freedom of the academic community which tenure seeks to mitigate.

Also, I do not think the costs of tenure are very high for a first-rate university. Those who gain tenure at Yale do not rest in happy security on their professorial laurels. Indeed, in my relatively brief experience, almost without exception it is the elders who are productive up to and well beyond retirement. They are the ones affected with the migraine headaches and other forms of psychosomatic traumae, lest their life should ebb away without the completion of their great work.

A LIFETIME COMMITMENT

As a practical matter of personnel policy, the very fact that the professorial promotion is a lifetime commitment of university resources makes the departmental and committee process of promotion to tenure much more rigorous and hard-headed than it otherwise would be. If there were a confident feeling that mistakes in judgment could be rectified by some later review process we would all go soft and give colleagues of whom we are personally fond an excessive benefit of all doubt. Realization that the commitment is for keeps helps to hold the standards high. So, I would venture that whatever gains might be made by reserving the right to a second guess would be more than offset by the laxity which would come to soften the first guess. In short, we would not have as good a senior faculty as we now do, if tenure were not the consequence of promotion to senior rank.

Such a pragmatic calculation, however, is nothing compared to the value to the university of trying to maintain the ideal of the independence of the individual in his own intellectual pursuit.

When I assumed my office (in 1963) I said that:

> there is a common ethic which draws some men to a university in preference to any of the many other groups which are now publicly and privately organized to discover as well as apply knowledge. Affluence often, prestige sometimes, is foregone in order to be able to spend one's time and energy and mind upon whatever seems to him most intriguing and exciting; not to be directed by what some client or customer may request, or by what some absentee bureaucrat is willing to support.

In the light of intervening reflection, I would now add that this "common ethic" also requires broad protection from administrators and the colleagues within the community, no more and no less than from the "absentee bureaucrats" in Washington to whom I was then referring.

Tenure, then, is not a luxurious indulgence. Even in times when scarcity of resources threatens the existence of whole departments, I would affirm that our mission requires Yale to give that measure of encouragement to independence which only irrevocable appointment can confer.

Writing, Language, and Style

Learning to Write
BENJAMIN FRANKLIN

From my infancy I was passionately fond of reading, and all the little money that came into my hands was laid out in the purchasing of books. I was very fond of voyages. My first acquisition was Bunyan's[1] works in separate little volumes. I afterwards sold them to enable me to buy R. Burton's[2] historical collections; they were small chapmen's books[3] and cheap, forty or fifty in all. My father's little library consisted chiefly of books in polemic divinity, most of which I read. I have since often regretted that at a time when I had such a thirst for knowledge, more proper books had not fallen in my way, since it was now resolved I should not be bred to divinity. There was among them Plutarch's *Lives*,[4] in which I read abundantly, and I still think that time spent to great advantage. There was also a book of Defoe's called an *Essay on Projects*[5] and another of Dr. Mather's called *Essays to do Good*,[6] which perhaps gave me a turn of thinking that had an influence on some of the principal future events of my life.

This bookish inclination at length determined my father to make me a printer, though he had already one son (James) of that profession. In 1717 my brother, James, returned from England with a press and letters to set up his business in Boston. I liked it much better than that of my father, but still had a hankering for the sea. To prevent the apprehended effect of such an inclination, my father was impatient to have me bound to my brother. I stood out some time, but at last was persuaded and signed the indenture, when I was yet but twelve years old. I was to serve as apprentice till I was twenty-one years of age, only I was to be allowed journeyman's wages during the last year. In a little time I made a great progress in the business and became a useful hand to my brother. I now had access to better books. An acquaintance with the apprentices of booksellers enabled me sometimes to borrow a small one, which I was careful to return

---

[1] John Bunyan (1628–1688), British author of *Pilgrim's Progress* (1678) and *Grace Abounding to the Chief of Sinners* (1666).—Eds.

[2] Robert Burton (1577–1640), British writer, author of *The Anatomy of Melancholy* (1621).—Eds.

[3] Paper books sold by street peddlers.—Eds.

[4] Plutarch (c. 40–c. 120 A.D.), Greek biographer, author of *Lives of the Noble Grecians and Romans*.—Eds.

[5] Daniel Defoe (1660–1731), British novelist, published this work in 1697.—Eds.

[6] Cotton Mather (1663–1728), American religious writer, published this book in 1710.—Eds.

soon and clean. Often I sat up in my room reading the greatest part of the night, when the book was borrowed in the evening and to be returned early in the morning, lest it should be found missing or wanted.

After some time a merchant, an ingenious, sensible man, Mr. Matthew Adams, who had a pretty collection of books and who frequented our printing house, took notice of me, invited me to see his library, and very kindly proposed to lend me such books as I chose to read. I now took a fancy to poetry and made some little pieces. My brother, supposing it might turn to account, encouraged me and induced me to compose two occasional ballads. One was called the "Lighthouse Tragedy," and contained an account of the shipwreck of Capt. Worthilake with his two daughters; the other was a "Sailor's Song on the Taking of the Famous *Teach*, or Blackbeard, the Pirate." They were wretched stuff, in street ballad style; and when they were printed, he sent me about the town to sell them. The first sold prodigiously, the event being recent and having made a great noise. This success flattered my vanity, but my father discouraged me by ridiculing my performances and telling me verse-makers were generally beggars. Thus I escaped being a poet and probably a very bad one. But as prose writing has been of great use to me in the course of my life and was a principal means of my advancement, I shall tell you how in such a situation I acquired what little ability I may be supposed to have in that way.

There was another bookish lad in the town, John Collins by name, with whom I was intimately acquainted. We sometimes disputed, and very fond we were of argument, and very desirous of confuting one another—which disputatious turn, by the way, is apt to become a very bad habit, making people often extremely disagreeable in company, by the contradiction that is necessary to bring it into practice; and thence besides souring and spoiling the conversation, it is productive of disgusts and perhaps enmities where you may have occasion for friendship. I had caught it by reading my father's books of dispute on religion. Persons of good sense, I have since observed, seldom fall into it, except lawyers, university men, and men of all sorts who have been bred at Edinburgh. A question was once somehow or other started between Collins and me on the propriety of educating the female sex in learning and their abilities for study. He was of opinion that it was improper and that they were naturally unequal to it. I took the contrary side, perhaps a little for dispute sake. He was naturally more eloquent, having a greater plenty of words, and sometimes, as I thought, I was vanquished more by his fluency than by the strength of his reasons. As we parted without settling the point and were not to see one another again for some time, I sat down to put my arguments in writing, which I copied fair and sent to him. He answered and I replied. Three or four letters on a side had passed, when my father happened to find my papers and read them. Without entering into the subject in dispute, he took occasion to talk with me about my manner of writing, observed that though

I had the advantage of my antagonist in correct spelling and pointing[7] (which I owed to the printing house) I fell far short in elegance of expression, in method, and in perspicuity—of which he convinced me by several instances. I saw the justice of his remarks and thence grew more attentive to my manner of writing, and determined to endeavour to improve my style.

About this time I met with an odd volume of the *Spectator*.[8] It was the third. I had never before seen any of them. I bought it, read it over and over, and was much delighted with it. I thought the writing excellent and wished if possible to imitate it. With that view, I took some of the papers, and making short hints of the sentiment in each sentence, laid them by a few days, and then without looking at the book, tried to complete the papers again by expressing each hinted sentiment at length and as fully as it had been expressed before, in any suitable words that should occur to me. Then I compared my *Spectator* with the original, discovered some of my faults, and corrected them. But I found I wanted a stock of words or a readiness in recollecting and using them, which I thought I should have acquired before that time if I had gone on making verses; since the continual search for words of the same import but of different length to suit the measure, or of different sound for the rhyme would have laid me under a constant necessity of searching for variety, and also have tended to fix that variety in my mind, and make me master of it. Therefore I took some of the tales in the *Spectator* and turned them into verse, and after a time, when I had pretty well forgotten the prose, turned them back again. I also sometimes jumbled my collections of hints into confusion, and after some weeks endeavoured to reduce them into the best order before I began to form the full sentences and complete the paper. This was to teach me method in the arrangement of the thoughts. By comparing my work afterwards with the original, I discovered many faults and corrected them; but I sometimes had the pleasure of fancying that in certain particulars of small import I had been lucky enough to improve the method or the language, and this encouraged me to think that I might possibly in time come to be a tolerable English writer, of which I was extremely ambitious.

Language and Thought
SUSANNE K. LANGER

A symbol is not the same thing as a sign; that is a fact that psychologists and philosophers often overlook. All intelligent animals use signs; so do we. To them as well as to us sounds and smells and motions are signs

[7] Punctuation.—EDS.
[8] *The Spectator*, a famous periodical published in 1711–1712 in London, was written by essayists Joseph Addison (1672–1719) and Richard Steele (1672–1729).—EDS.

of food, danger, the presence of other beings, or of rain or storm. Furthermore, some animals not only attend to signs but produce them for the benefit of others. Dogs bark at the door to be let in; rabbits thump to call each other; the cooing of doves and the growl of a wolf defending his kill are unequivocal signs of feelings and intentions to be reckoned with by other creatures.

We use signs just as animals do, though with considerably more elaboration. We stop at red lights and go on green; we answer calls and bells, watch the sky for coming storms, read trouble or promise or anger in each other's eyes. That is animal intelligence raised to the human level. Those of us who are dog lovers can probably all tell wonderful stories of how high our dogs have sometimes risen in the scale of clever sign interpretation and sign using.

A sign is anything that announces the existence or the imminence of some event, the presence of a thing or a person, or a change in the state of affairs. There are signs of the weather, signs of danger, signs of future good or evil, signs of what the past has been. In every case a sign is closely bound up with something to be noted or expected in experience. It is always a part of the situation to which it refers, though the reference may be remote in space and time. In so far as we are led to note or expect the signified event we are making correct use of a sign. This is the essence of rational behavior, which animals show in varying degrees. It is entirely realistic, being closely bound up with the actual objective course of history—learned by experience, and cashed in or voided by further experience.

If man had kept to the straight and narrow path of sign using, he would be like the other animals, though perhaps a little brighter. He would not talk, but grunt and gesticulate and point. He would make his wishes known, give warnings, perhaps develop a social system like that of bees and ants, with such a wonderful efficiency of communal enterprise that all men would have plenty to eat, warm apartments—all exactly alike and perfectly convenient—to live in, and everybody could and would sit in the sun or by the fire, as the climate demanded, not talking but just basking, with every want satisfied, most of his life. The young would romp and make love, the old would sleep, the middle-aged would do the routine work almost unconsciously and eat a great deal. But that would be the life of a social, superintelligent, purely sign-using animal.

To us who are human, it does not sound very glorious. We want to go places and do things, own all sorts of gadgets that we do not absolutely need, and when we sit down to take it easy we want to talk. Rights and property, social position, special talents and virtues, and above all our ideas, are what we live for. We have gone off on a tangent that takes us far away from the mere biological cycle that animal generations accomplish; and that is because we can use not only signs but symbols.

A symbol differs from a sign in that it does not announce the presence of the object, the being, condition, or whatnot, which is its meaning, but merely *brings this thing to mind.* It is not a mere "substitute sign" to which we react as though it were the object itself. The fact is that our reaction to hearing a person's name is quite different from our reaction to the person himself. There are certain rare cases where a symbol stands directly for its meaning: in religious experience, for instance, the Host is not only a symbol but a Presence. But symbols in the ordinary sense are not mystic. They are the same sort of thing that ordinary signs are; only they do not call our attention to something necessarily present or to be physically dealt with—they call up merely a conception of the thing they "mean."

The difference between a sign and a symbol is, in brief, that a sign causes us to think or act *in face of* the thing signified, whereas a symbol causes us to think *about* the thing symbolized. Therein lies the great importance of symbolism for human life, its power to make this life so different from any other animal biography that generations of men have found it incredible to suppose that they were of purely zoological origin. A sign is always embedded in reality, in a present that emerges from the actual past and stretches to the future; but a symbol may be divorced from reality altogether. It may refer to what is *not* the case, to a mere idea, a figment, a dream. It serves, therefore, to liberate thought from the immediate stimuli of a physically present world; and that liberation marks the essential difference between human and nonhuman mentality. Animals think, but they think *of* and *at* things; men think primarily *about* things. Words, pictures, and memory images are symbols that may be combined and varied in a thousand ways. The result is a symbolic structure whose meaning is a complex of all their respective meanings, and this kaleidoscope of *ideas* is the typical product of the human brain that we call the "stream of thought."

The process of transforming all direct experience into imagery or into that supreme mode of symbolic expression, language, has so completely taken possession of the human mind that it is not only a special talent but a dominant, organic need. All our sense impressions leave their traces in our memory not only as signs disposing our practical reactions in the future but also as symbols, images representing our *ideas* of things; and the tendency to manipulate ideas, to combine and abstract, mix and extend them by playing with symbols, is man's outstanding characteristic. It seems to be what his brain most naturally and spontaneously does. Therefore his primitive mental function is not judging reality, but *dreaming his desires.*

Dreaming is apparently a basic function of human brains, for it is free and unexhausting like our metabolism, heartbeat, and breath. It is easier to dream than not to dream, as it is easier to breathe than to refrain from breathing. The symbolic character of dreams is fairly well established. Symbol mongering, on this ineffectual, uncritical level, seems to be instinctive, the fulfillment of an elementary need rather than the purposeful exercise of a high and difficult talent.

The special power of man's mind rests on the evolution of this special activity, not on any transcendently high development of animal intelligence. We are not immeasurably higher than other animals; we are different. We have a biological need and with it a biological gift that they do not share.

Because man has not only the ability but the constant need of *conceiving* what has happened to him, what surrounds him, what is demanded of him—in short, of symbolizing nature, himself, and his hopes and fears—he has a constant and crying need of *expression*. What he cannot express, he cannot conceive; what he cannot conceive is chaos, and fills him with terror.

If we bear in mind this all-important craving for expression we get a new picture of man's behavior; for from this trait spring his powers and his weaknesses. The process of symbolic transformation that all our experiences undergo is nothing more nor less than the process of *conception*, which underlies the human faculties of abstraction and imagination.

When we are faced with a strange or difficult situation, we cannot react directly, as other creatures do, with flight, aggression, or any such simple instinctive pattern. Our whole reaction depends on how we manage to conceive the situation—whether we cast it in a definite dramatic form, whether we see it as a disaster, a challenge, a fulfillment of doom, or a fiat of the Divine Will. In words or dreamlike images, in artistic or religious or even in cynical form, we must *construe* the events of life. There is great virtue in the figure of speech, "I can *make* nothing of it," to express a failure to understand something. Thought and memory are processes of *making* the thought content and the memory image; the pattern of our ideas is given by the symbols through which we express them. And in the course of manipulating those symbols we inevitably distort the original experience, as we abstract certain features of it, embroider and reinforce those features with other ideas, until the conception we project on the screen of memory is quite different from anything in our real history.

Conception is a necessary and elementary process; what we do with our conceptions is another story. That is the entire history of human culture—of intelligence and morality, folly and superstition, ritual, language, and the arts—all the phenomena that set man apart from, and above, the rest of the animal kingdom. As the religious mind has to make all human history a drama of sin and salvation in order to define its own moral attitudes, so a scientist wrestles with the mere presentation of "the facts" before he can reason about them. The process of *envisaging* facts, values, hopes, and fears underlies our whole behavior pattern; and this process is reflected in the evolution of an extraordinary phenomenon found always, and only, in human societies—the phenomenon of language.

Language is the highest and most amazing achievement of the symbolistic human mind. The power it bestows is almost inestimable, for without it anything properly called "thought" is impossible. The birth of language is the dawn of humanity. The line between man and beast—between the highest ape and the lowest savage—is the language line.

Whether the primitive Neanderthal man was anthropoid or human depends less on his cranial capacity, his upright posture, or even his use of tools and fire, than on one issue we shall probably never be able to settle—whether or not he spoke.

In all physical traits and practical responses, such as skills and visual judgments, we can find a certain continuity between animal and human mentality. Sign using is an ever evolving, ever improving function throughout the whole animal kingdom, from the lowly worm that shrinks into his hole at the sound of an approaching foot, to the dog obeying his master's command, and even to the learned scientist who watches the movements of an index needle.

This continuity of the sign-using talent has led psychologists to the belief that language is evolved from the vocal expressions, grunts and coos and cries, whereby animals vent their feelings or signal their fellows; that man has elaborated this sort of communion to the point where it makes a perfect exchange of ideas possible.

I do not believe that this doctrine of the origin of language is correct. The essence of language is symbolic, not signific; we use it first and most vitally to formulate and hold ideas in our own minds. Conception, not social control, is its first and foremost benefit.

Watch a young child that is just learning to speak play with a toy; he says the name of the object, e.g.: "Horsey! horsey! horsey!" over and over again, looks at the object, moves it, always saying the name to himself or to the world at large. It's quite a time before he talks to anyone in particular; he talks first of all to himself. This is his way of forming and fixing the *conception* of the object in his mind, and around this conception all his knowledge of it grows. *Names* are the essence of language; for the *name* is what abstracts the conception of the horse from the horse itself, and lets the mere idea recur at the speaking of the name. This permits the conception gathered from one horse experience to be exemplified again by another instance of a horse, so that the notion embodied in the name is a general notion.

To this end, the baby uses a word long before he *asks* for the object; when he wants his horsey he is likely to cry and fret, because he is reacting to an actual environment, not forming ideas. He uses the animal language of *signs* for his wants; talking is still a purely symbolic process—its practical value has not really impressed him yet.

Language need not be vocal; it may be purely visual, like written language, or even tactual, like the deaf-mute system of speech; but it *must be denotative*. The sounds, intended or unintended, whereby animals communicate do not constitute a language, because they are signs, not names. They never fall into an organic pattern, a meaningful syntax of even the most rudimentary sort, as all language seems to do with a sort of driving necessity. That is because signs refer to actual situations, in which things have obvious relations to each other that require only to be noted; but symbols refer to ideas, which are not physically there for inspection, so their connections and features have to be represented. This gives all true language a natural tendency toward growth and development, which seems almost like a life of its own. Languages are not invented; they grow with our need for expression.

In contrast, animal "speech" never has a structure. It is merely an emotional response. Apes may greet their ration of yams with a shout of "Nga!" But they do not say "Nga" between meals. If they could *talk about* their yams instead of just saluting them, they would be the most primitive men instead of the most anthropoid of beasts. They would have ideas, and tell each other things true or false, rational or irrational; they would make plans and invent laws and sing their own praises, as men do.

Politics and the English Language
GEORGE ORWELL

Most people who bother with the matter at all would admit that the English language is in a bad way, but it is generally assumed that we cannot by conscious action do anything about it. Our civilization is decadent, and our language—so the argument runs—must inevitably share in the general collapse. It follows that any struggle against the abuse of language is a sentimental archaism, like preferring candles to electric light or hansom cabs to aeroplanes. Underneath this lies the half-conscious belief that language is a natural growth and not an instrument which we shape for our own purposes.

Now, it is clear that the decline of a language must ultimately have political and economic causes: it is not due simply to the bad influence of this or that individual writer. But an effect can become a cause, reinforcing the original cause and producing the same effect in an intensified form, and so on indefinitely. A man may take to drink because he feels himself to be a failure, and then fail all the more completely because he drinks. It is rather the same thing that is happening to the English language. It becomes ugly and inaccurate because our thoughts are foolish, but the slovenliness of our language makes it easier for us to have foolish thoughts. The point is that the process is reversible. Modern English, especially written English, is full of bad habits which spread by imitation and which can be avoided if one is willing to take the necessary trouble. If one gets rid of these habits one can think more clearly, and to think clearly is a necessary first step towards political regeneration: so that the fight against bad English is not frivolous and is not the exclusive concern of professional writers. I will come back to this presently, and I hope that by that time the meaning of what I have said here will become clearer.

Meanwhile, here are five specimens of the English language as it is now habitually written.

These five passages have not been picked out because they are especially bad—I could have quoted far worse if I had chosen—but because they illustrate various of the mental vices from which we now suffer. They are a little below the average, but are fairly representative samples. I number them so that I can refer back to them when necessary:

> (1) I am not, indeed, sure whether it is not true to say that the Milton who once seemed not unlike a seventeenth-century Shelley had not become, out of an experience ever more bitter in each year, more alien (*sic*) to the founder of that Jesuit sect which nothing could induce him to tolerate.
>
> Professor Harold Laski (Essay in *Freedom of Expression*)

> (2) Above all, we cannot play ducks and drakes with a native battery of idioms which prescribes such egregious collocations of vocables as the Basic *put up with* for *tolerate* or *put at a loss* for *bewilder*.
>
> Professor Lancelot Hogben (*Interglossa*)

> (3) On the one side we have the free personality; by definition it is not neurotic, for it has neither conflict nor dream. Its desires, such as they are, are transparent, for they are just what institutional approval keeps in the forefront of consciousness; another institutional pattern would alter their number and intensity; there is little in them that is natural, irreducible, or culturally dangerous. But *on the other side*, the social bond itself is nothing but the mutual reflection of these self-secure integrities. Recall the definition of love. Is not this the very picture of a small academic? Where is there a place in this hall of mirrors for either personality or fraternity?
>
> Essay on psychology in *Politics* (New York)

> (4) All the "best people" from the gentlemen's clubs, and all the frantic fascist captains, united in common hatred of Socialism and bestial horror of the rising tide of the mass revolutionary movement, have turned to acts of provocation, to foul incendiarism, to medieval legends of poisoned wells, to legalize their own destruction of proletarian organizations, and rouse the agitated petty-bourgeoisie to chauvinistic fervor on behalf of the fight against the revolutionary way out of the crisis.
>
> Communist pamphlet

> (5) If a new spirit *is* to be infused into this old country, there is one thorny and contentious reform which must be tackled, and that is the humanization and galvanization of the B.B.C. Timidity here will bespeak canker and atrophy of the soul. The heart of Britain may be sound and of strong beat, for instance, but the British lion's roar at present is like that of Bottom in Shakespeare's *Midsummer Night's Dream*—as gentle as any sucking dove. A verile new Britain cannot continue indefinitely to be traduced in the eyes, or rather ears, of the world by the effete languors of Langham Place, brazenly masquerading as "standard English." When the Voice of Britain is heard at nine o'clock, better far and infinitely less ludicrous to hear aitches honestly dropped than the present priggish, inflated, inhibited, school-ma'amish arch braying of blameless bashful mewing maidens.
>
> Letter in *Tribune*

Each of these passages has faults of its own, but quite apart from avoidable ugliness, two qualities are common to all of them. The first is staleness of imagery; the other is lack of precision. The writer either has a meaning and cannot express it, or he inadvertently says something else, or he is almost indifferent as to whether his words mean anything or not. This mixture of vagueness and sheer incompetence is the most marked characteristic of modern English prose, and especially of any kind of political writing. As soon as certain topics are raised, the concrete melts into the abstract and no one seems able to think of turns of speech that are not hackneyed: prose consists less and less of *words* chosen for the sake of their meaning, and more and more of *phrases* tacked together like the sections of a prefabricated hen-house. I list below, with notes and examples, various of the tricks by means of which the work of prose-construction is habitually dodged:

Dying metaphors. A newly-invented metaphor assists thought by evoking a visual image, while on the other hand a metaphor which is technically "dead" (e.g., *iron resolution*) has in effect reverted to being an ordinary word and can generally be used without loss of vividness. But in between these two classes there is a huge dump of worn-out metaphors which have lost all evocative power and are merely used because they save people the trouble of inventing phrases for themselves. Examples are: *Ring the changes on, take up the cudgels for, toe the line, ride roughshod over, stand shoulder to shoulder with, play into the hands of, an axe to grind, grist to the mill, fishing in troubled waters, on the order of the day, Achilles' heel, swan song, hotbed.* Many of these are used without knowledge of their meaning (what is a "rift," for instance?), and incompatible metaphors are frequently mixed, a sure sign that the writer is not interested in what he is saying. Some metaphors now current have been twisted out of their original meaning without those who use them even being aware of the fact. For example, *toe the line* is sometimes written *tow the line*. Another example is *the hammer and the anvil*, now always used with the implication that the anvil gets the worst of it. In real life it is always the anvil that breaks the hammer, never the other way about: a writer who stopped to think what he was saying would be aware of this, and would avoid perverting the original phrase.

Operators, or *verbal false limbs.* These save the trouble of picking out appropriate verbs and nouns, and at the same time pad each sentence with extra syllables which give it an appearance of symmetry. Characteristic phrases are: *render inoperative, militate against, prove unacceptable, make contact with, be subjected to, give rise to, give grounds for, have the effect of, playing a leading part* (role) *in, making itself felt, take effect, exhibit a tendency to, serve the purpose of,* etc., etc. The keynote is the elimination of simple verbs. Instead of being a single word, such as *break, stop, spoil, mend, kill,* a verb becomes a phrase, made up of a noun or adjective tacked on to some general-purposes verb such as *prove, serve, form, play, render.* In addition, the passive voice is wherever possible used in preference to the active, and noun constructions are used instead of gerunds (*by examination of* instead of *by examining*). The range of verbs is further cut down by means of the *-ize* and *de-* formations, and banal statements are given an appearance of profundity by means of the *not un-* formation. Simple conjunctions and prepositions are replaced by such phrases as *with respect to, having regard to, the fact that, by dint of, in view of, in the interests of, on the hypothesis that;* and the ends of sentences are saved from anti-climax by such resounding commonplaces as *greatly to be desired, cannot be left out of account, a development to be expected in the near future, deserving of serious consideration, brought to a satisfactory conclusion,* and so on and so forth.

Pretentious diction. Words like *phenomenon, element, individual* (as noun), *objective, categorical, effective, virtual, basis, primary, promote, constitute, exhibit, exploit, utilize, eliminate, liquidate,* are used to dress up simple statements and give an air of scientific impartiality to biased judgments. Adjectives like *epoch-making, epic, historic, unforgettable, triumphant, age-old, inevitable, inexorable, veritable,* are used to dignify the sordid processes of international politics, while writing that aims at glorifying war usually takes on an archaic color, its characteristic words being: *realm, throne, chariot, mailed fist, trident, sword, shield, buckler, banner, jackboot, clarion.* Foreign words and expressions such as *cul-de-sac, ancien régime, deus ex machina, mutatis mutandis, status quo, gleichschaltung, weltanschauung,* are used to give an air of culture and elegance. Except for the useful abbreviations *i.e., e.g.,* and *etc.,* there is no real need for any of the hundreds of foreign phrases now current in English. Bad writers, and especially scientific, political and sociological writers, are nearly always haunted by the notion that Latin or Greek words are grander than Saxon ones, and unnecessary words like *expedite, ameliorate, predict, extraneous, deracinated, clandestine, subaqueous* and hundreds of others constantly gain ground from their Anglo-Saxon opposite numbers.[1] The jargon peculiar to Marxist writing (*hyena, hangman, cannibal, petty bourgeois, these gentry, lackey, flunkey, mad dog, White Guard,* etc.) consists largely of words and phrases translated from Russian, German or French; but the normal way of coining a new word is to use a Latin or Greek root with the appropriate affix and, where necessary, the *-ize* formation. It is often easier to make up words of this kind (*deregionalize, impermissible, extramarital, non-fragmentary* and so forth) than to think up the English words that will cover one's meaning. The result, in general, is an increase in slovenliness and vagueness.

Meaningless words. In certain kinds of writing, particularly in art criticism and literary criticism, it is normal to come across long passages which are almost completely lacking in meaning.[2] Words like *romantic, plastic,*

---

[1] An interesting illustration of this is the way in which the English flower names which were in use till very recently are being ousted by Greek ones, *snap-dragon* becoming *antirrhinum, forget-me-not* becoming *myosotis,* etc. It is hard to see any practical reason for this change of fashion: it is probably due to an instinctive turning-away from the more homely word and a vague feeling that the Greek word is scientific.

[2] Example: "Comfort's catholicity of perception and image, strangely Whitmanesque in range, almost the exact opposite in aesthetic compulsion, continues to evoke that trembling atmospheric accumulative hinting at a cruel, an inexorably serene timelessness . . . Wrey Gardiner scores by aiming at simple bullseyes with precision. Only they are not so simple, and through this contented sadness runs more than the surface bittersweet of resignation." (*Poetry Quarterly.*)

values, human, dead, sentimental, natural, vitality, as used in art criticism, are strictly meaningless, in the sense that they not only do not point to any discoverable object, but are hardly even expected to do so by the reader. When one critic writes, "The oustanding feature of Mr. X's work is its living quality," while another writes, "The immediately striking thing about Mr. X's work is its peculiar deadness," the reader accepts this as a simple difference of opinion. If words like *black* and *white* were involved, instead of the jargon words *dead* and *living*, he would see at once that language was being used in an improper way. Many political words are similarly abused. The word *Fascism* has now no meaning except in so far as it signifies "something not desirable." The words *democracy, socialism, freedom, patriotic, realistic, justice,* have each of them several different meanings which cannot be reconciled with one another. In the case of a word like *democracy,* not only is there no agreed definition, but the attempt to make one is resisted from all sides. It is almost universally felt that when we call a country democratic we are praising it: consequently the defenders of every kind of régime claim that it is a democracy, and fear that they might have to stop using the word if it were tied down to any one meaning. Words of this kind are often used in a consciously dishonest way. That is, the person who uses them has his own private definition, but allows his hearer to think he means something quite different. Statements like *Marshal Pétain was a true patriot, The Soviet Press is the freest in the world, The Catholic Church is opposed to persecution,* are almost always made with intent to deceive. Other words used in variable meanings, in most cases more or less dishonestly, are: *class, totalitarian, science, progressive, reactionary, bourgeois, equality.*

Now that I have made this catalogue of swindles and perversions, let me give another example of the kind of writing that they lead to. This time it must of its nature be an imaginary one. I am going to translate a passage of good English into modern English of the worst sort. Here is a well-known verse from *Ecclesiastes*:

> I returned, and saw under the sun, that the race is not to the swift, nor the battle to the strong, neither yet bread to the wise, nor yet riches to men of understanding, nor yet favor to men of skill; but time and chance happeneth to them all.

Here it is in modern English:

> Objective consideration of contemporary phenomena compels the conclusion that success or failure in competitive activities exhibits no tendency to be commensurate with innate capacity, but that a considerable element of the unpredictable must invariably be taken into account.

This is a parody, but not a very gross one. Exhibit (3), above, for instance, contains several patches of the same kind of English. It will be seen that I have not made a full translation. The beginning and ending of the sentence follow the original meaning fairly closely, but in the middle the concrete illustrations—race, battle, bread—dissolve into the vague phrase "success or failure in competitive activities." This had to be so, because no modern writer of the kind I am discussing—no one capable of using phrases like "objective consideration of contemporary phenomena"—would ever tabulate his thoughts in that precise and detailed way. The whole tendency of modern prose is away from concreteness. Now analyze these two sentences a little more closely. The first contains 49 words but only 60 syllables, and all its words are those of everyday life. The second contains 38 words of 90 syllables: 18 of its words are from Latin roots, and one from Greek. The first sentence contains six vivid images, and only one phrase ("time and chance") that could be called vague. The second contains not a single fresh, arresting phrase, and in spite of its 90 syllables it gives only a shortened version of the meaning contained in the first. Yet without a doubt it is the second kind of sentence that is gaining ground in modern English. I do not want to exaggerate. This kind of writing is not yet universal, and outcrops of simplicity will occur here and there in the worst-written page. Still, if you or I were told to write a few lines on the uncertainty of human fortunes, we should probably come much nearer to my imaginary sentence than to the one from *Ecclesiastes*.

As I have tried to show, modern writing at its worst does not consist in picking out words for the sake of their meaning and inventing images in order to make the meaning clearer. It consists in gumming together long strips of words which have already been set in order by someone else, and making the results presentable by sheer humbug. The attraction of this way of writing is that it is easy. It is easier—even quicker, once you have the habit—to say *In my opinion it is a not unjustifiable assumption that* than to say *I think*. If you use ready-made phrases, you not only don't have to hunt about for words; you also don't have to bother with the rhythms of your sentences, since these phrases are generally so arranged as to be more or less euphonious. When you are composing in a hurry—when you are dictating to a stenographer, for instance, or making a public speech—it is natural to fall into a pretentious, Latinized style. Tags like *a consideration which we should do well to bear in mind* or *a conclusion to which all of us would readily assent* will save many a sentence from coming down with a bump. By using stale metaphors, similes and idioms, you save much mental effort at the cost of leaving your meaning vague, not only for your reader but for yourself. This is the significance of mixed metaphors. The sole aim of a metaphor is to call up a visual image. When these images clash—as in *The Fascist octopus has sung its swan song, the jackboot is thrown into the melting pot*—it can be taken as certain that the writer is not seeing a mental image of the objects he is naming; in other words he is not really thinking. Look again at the examples I gave at the beginning of this essay. Professor Laski (1) uses five negatives in 53 words. One of these is superfluous, making nonsense of the whole passage, and in addition there is the slip *alien* for akin, making further nonsense, and several avoidable pieces of clumsiness which increase the general vagueness. Professor Hogben (2) plays ducks and drakes with a battery which is able to write prescriptions, and, while disapproving of the everyday phrase *put up with*, is unwilling to look *egregious* up in the dictionary and see what it means. (3), if one takes an uncharitable attitude towards it, is simply meaningless: probably one could work out its intended meaning by reading the whole of the article in which it occurs. In (4), the writer knows more or less what he wants to say, but an accumulation of stale phrases chokes him like tea leaves blocking a sink. In (5), words and meaning have almost parted company. People who write in this manner usually have a general emotional meaning—they dislike one thing and want to express solidarity with another—but they are not interested in the detail of what they are saying. A scrupulous writer, in every sentence that he writes, will ask himself at least four questions, thus: What am I trying to say? What words will express it? What image or idiom will make it clearer? Is this image fresh enough to have an effect? And he will probably ask himself two more: Could I put it more shortly? Have I said anything that is avoidably ugly? But you are not obliged to go to all this trouble. You can shirk it by simply throwing your mind open and letting the ready-made phrases come crowding in. They will construct your sentences for you—even think your thoughts for you, to a certain extent—and at need they will perform the important service of partially concealing your meaning even from yourself. It is at this point that the special connection between politics and the debasement of language becomes clear.

In our time it is broadly true that political writing is bad writing. Where it is not true, it will generally be found that the writer is some kind of rebel, expressing his private opinions and not a "party line." Othodoxy, of whatever color, seems to demand a lifeless, imitative style. The political dialects to be found in pamphlets, leading articles, manifestoes, White Papers and the speeches of under-secretaries do, of course, vary from party to party, but they are all alike in that one almost never finds in them a fresh, vivid, home-made turn of speech. When one watches some tired hack on the platform mechanically repeating the familiar phrases—*bestial atrocities, iron heel, bloodstained tyranny, free peoples of the world, stand shoulder to shoulder*—one often has a curious feeling that one is not watching a live human being but some kind of dummy: a feeling which suddenly becomes stronger at moments when the light catches the speaker's spectacles and turns them into blank discs which seem to have no eyes behind them. And this is not altogether fanciful. A speaker who uses that kind of phraseology has gone some distance towards turning himself into a machine. The appropriate noises are coming out of his larynx, but his brain is not involved as it would be if he were choosing his words for himself. If the speech he is making is one that he is accustomed to make over and over again, he may be almost unconscious of what he is saying, as one is when one utters the responses in church. And this reduced state of consciousness, if not indispensable, is at any rate favorable to political conformity.

In our time, political speech and writing are largely the defense of the indefensible. Things like the continuance of British rule in India, the Russian purges and deportations, the dropping of the atom bombs on Japan, can indeed be defended, but only by arguments which are too brutal for most people to face, and which do not square with the professed aims of political parties. Thus political language has to consist largely of euphemism, question-begging and sheer cloudy vagueness. Defenseless villages are bombarded from the air, the inhabitants driven out into the countryside, the cattle machine-gunned, the huts set on fire with incendiary bullets: this is called *pacification*. Millions of peasants are robbed of their farms and sent trudging along the roads with no more than they can carry: this is called *transfer of population* or *rectification of frontiers*. People are imprisoned for years without trial, or shot in the back of the neck or sent to die of scurvy in Arctic lumber camps: this is called *elimination of unreliable elements*. Such phraseology is needed if one wants to name things without calling up mental pictures of them. Consider for instance some comfortable English professor defending Russian totalitarianism. He cannot say outright, "I believe in killing off your opponents when you can get good results by doing so." Probably, therefore, he will say something like this:

> While freely conceding that the Soviet régime exhibits certain features which the humanitarian may be inclined to deplore, we must, I think, agree that a certain curtailment of the right to political opposition is an unavoidable concomitant of transitional periods, and that the rigors which the Russian people have been called upon to undergo have been amply justified in the sphere of concrete achievement.

The inflated style is itself a kind of euphemism. A mass of Latin words falls upon the facts like soft snow, blurring the outlines and covering up all the details. The great enemy of clear language is insincerity. When there is a gap between one's real and one's declared aims, one turns, as it were instinctively, to long words and exhausted idioms, like a cuttlefish squirting out ink. In our age there is no such thing as "keeping out of politics." All issues are political issues, and politics itself is a mass of lies, evasions, folly, hatred and schizophrenia. When the general atmosphere is bad, language must suffer. I should expect to find—this is a guess which I have not sufficient knowledge to verify—that the German, Russian and Italian languages have all deteriorated in the last ten or fifteen years as a result of dictatorship.

But if thought corrupts language, language can also corrupt thought. A bad usage can spread by tradition and imitation, even among people who should and do know better. The debased language that I have been discussing is in some ways very convenient. Phrases like *a not unjustifiable assumption, leaves much to be desired, would serve no good purpose, a consideration which we should do well to bear in mind*, are a continuous temptation, a packet of aspirins always at one's elbow. Look back through this essay, and for certain you will find that I have again and again committed the very faults I am protesting against. By this morning's post I have received a pamphlet dealing with conditions in Germany. The author tells me that he "felt impelled" to write it. I open it at random, and here is almost the first sentence that I see: "[The Allies] have an opportunity not only of achieving a radical transformation of Germany's social and political structure in such a way as to avoid a nationalistic reaction in Germany itself, but at the same time of laying the foundations of a cooperative and unified Europe." You see, he "feels impelled" to write—feels, presumably, that he has something new to say—and yet his words, like cavalry horses answering the bugle, group themselves automatically into the familiar dreary pattern. This invasion of one's mind by ready-made phrases (*lay the foundations, achieve a radical transformation*) can only be prevented if one is constantly on guard against them, and every such phrase anesthetizes a portion of one's brain.

I said earlier that the decadence of our language is probably curable. Those who deny this would argue, if they produced an argument at all, that language merely reflects existing social conditions, and that we cannot influence its development by any direct tinkering with words and constructions. So far as the general tone or spirit of a language goes, this may be true, but it is not true in detail. Silly words and expressions have often disappeared, not through any evolutionary process but owing to the conscious action of a minority. Two recent examples were *explore every avenue* and *leave no stone unturned*, which were killed by the jeers of a few journalists. There is a long list of fly-blown metaphors which could similarly be got rid of if enough people would interest themselves in the job; and it should also be possible to laugh the *not un-* formation out of existence,[3] to reduce the amount of Latin and Greek in the average sentence, to drive out foreign phrases and strayed scientific words, and, in general, to make pretentiousness unfashionable. But all these are minor points. The defense of the English language implies more than this, and perhaps it is best to start by saying what it does *not* imply.

To begin with, it has nothing to do with archaism, with the salvaging of obsolete words and turns of speech, or with the setting-up of a "standard English" which must never be departed from. On the contrary, it is especially concerned with the scrapping of every word or idiom which has outworn its usefulness. It has nothing to do with correct grammar and syntax, which are of no importance so long as one makes one's meaning clear, or with the avoidance of Americanisms, or with having what is called a "good prose style." On the other hand it is not concerned with fake simplicity and the attempt to make written English colloquial. Nor does it even imply in every case preferring the Saxon word to the Latin one, though it

---

[3] One can cure oneself of the *not un-* formation by memorizing this sentence: *A not unblack dog was chasing a not unsmall rabbit across a not ungreen field.*

does imply using the fewest and shortest words that will cover one's meaning. What is above all needed is to let the meaning choose the word, and not the other way about. In prose, the worst thing one can do with words is to surrender to them. When you think of a concrete object, you think wordlessly, and then, if you want to describe the thing you have been visualizing, you probably hunt about till you find the exact words that seem to fit it. When you think of something abstract you are more inclined to use words from the start, and unless you make a conscious effort to prevent it, the existing dialect will come rushing in and do the job for you, at the expense of blurring or even changing your meaning. Probably it is better to put off using words as long as possible and get one's meaning as clear as one can through pictures or sensations. Afterwards one can choose —not simply *accept*—the phrases that will best cover the meaning, and then switch round and decide what impressions one's words are likely to make on another person. This last effort of the mind cuts out all stale or mixed images, all prefabricated phrases, needless repetitions, and humbug and vagueness generally. But one can often be in doubt about the effect of a word or a phrase, and one needs rules that one can rely on when instinct fails. I think the following rules will cover most cases:

(i) Never use a metaphor, simile or other figure of speech which you are used to seeing in print.
(ii) Never use a long word where a short one will do.
(iii) If it is possible to cut a word out, always cut it out.
(iv) Never use the passive where you can use the active.
(v) Never use a foreign phrase, a scientific word or a jargon word if you can think of an everyday English equivalent.
(vi) Break any of these rules sooner than say anything barbarous.

These rules sound elementary, and so they are, but they demand a deep change of attitude in anyone who has grown used to writing in the style now fashionable. One could keep all of them and still write bad English, but one could not write the kind of stuff that I quoted in these five specimens at the beginning of this article.

I have not here been considering the literary use of language, but merely language as an instrument for expressing and not for concealing or preventing thought. Stuart Chase and others have come near to claiming that all abstract words are meaningless, and have used this as a pretext for advocating a kind of political quietism. Since you don't know what Fascism is, how can you struggle against Fascism? One need not swallow such absurdities as this, but one ought to recognize that the present political chaos is connected with the decay of language, and that one can probably bring about some improvement by starting at the verbal end. If you simplify your English, you are freed from the worst follies of orthodoxy. You cannot speak any of the necessary dialects, and when you make a stupid remark its stupidity will be obvious, even to yourself. Political language—and with variations this is true of all political parties, from Conservatives to Anarchists—is designed to make lies sound truthful and murder respectable, and to give an appearance of solidity to pure wind. One cannot change this all in a moment, but one can at least change one's habits, and from time to time one can even, if one jeers loudly enough, send some worn-out and useless phrase—some *jackboot, Achilles' heel, hotbed, melting pot, acid test, veritable inferno* or other lump of verbal refuse—into the dustbin where it belongs.

Fedgush
RUSSELL BAKER

Cummings who is finicky about the language, burst into the office and stood aghast. I sat aglectricked, for I sensed that he had just watched a Congressman strangling the English language with his bare tongue, and was outraged.

"Define 'energy crunch,'" Cummings said.

"A breakfast cereal. Tasty, invigorating, packed full of wholesome goodness. Keeps you going hours after higher-priced antiperspirants have quit keeping you safe twice as long."

"Then how can an 'energy crunch' be 'down the road,'" he demanded.

"It can't. It can only be at your grocer's (2 cents off), on the table, or down your gullet."

"Exactly," said Cummings, turning red with rage, white with anger, purple with fury, and slipping into a blue funk. I wanted to turn green with envy at his ability to run the spectrum, but couldn't, so stayed puce with indifference.

I told him to quit mincing words, get to the point, and give me the thrust of his argument. He said he couldn't possibly mince words because he had lost his mincer, and had sent his saber and foil to the cleaner, which left him without a point or a thrusting device to bear his argument.

"Quit trying to speak sensibly and talk like everybody else," I screamed. "Tell me about the breakfast cereal down the road."

"It is going to hit us right between the eyes," Cummings said.

"Get out of here, Cummings."

"It is not only going to hit us right between the eyes, but it is also going to shake us to the roots."

I expressed incredulity, which inflamed Cummings because he believes incredulity travels faster if air-freighted. After smothering the flames, I pushed him toward the door. He was a fire hazard and an alarmist.

I told him there was no breakfast cereal down the road, and even if there were it couldn't possibly hit me right between the eyes, much less shake me to the roots, since I had just had my annual root checkup and been assured that they were as sound as a two-month-old dandelion's.

"Congressman Al Ullman says differently," Cummings replied.

Suddenly, the scales fell from my eyes. Cummings pounced on them and weighed himself. "You need new scales," he said. "These things are eight pounds off."

I was not going to be sidetracked to the hardware store that easily, for everything had become clear. "Congressman Ullman," I explained to Cummings, "is the powerful chairman of the powerful House Ways and Means Committee, which handles oil law. As a Congressman, he does not speak English. He speaks munchy, crunchy, down-the-road, right-between-the-eyes, root-shaking Fedgush."

Cummings cringed and whined when the word "Fedgush" rasped across his word ends, but I showed him no mercy. "In the Federal center of civilization, Cummings, speech has been superseded by gush. Speech became a dangerous tool down there, because it made it too easy for people to understand what Government people were talking about. So they moved up to gush, and now they can't even tell what they're talking about themselves."

"Ghastly," Cummings ghasted.

"Not necessarily. As long as no two of them understand each other, it's harder for them to gang up against us."

"Energy crunch isn't a breakfast cereal?" Cummings asked.

"Probably not. In Fedgush 'energy' usually means 'oil.' 'Crunch' can mean almost anything except 'crunch,' and 'down the road' can mean 'next week' or 'next century.' When Ullman says there is an 'energy crunch down the road,' he probably means the oil problem is going to get worse next week or 25 years from now. All the rest about being hit right between the eyes and shaking us to the roots is added only to make the sentence more musical with ridiculous metaphor. Fedgush relies heavily on ridiculous metaphor to heighten the confusion."

Cummings wept. "Energy crunch," he sobbed. "Down the road. Hit us right between the eyes. Shake us to the roots."

"Don't take on so, Cummings. All it means is what it always means in Washington. Things are going to get worse."

Cummings's spirit was broken, so I put the pieces in a plastic bag for him, told him he was going through a spirit crunch and asked him to come see me down the road if it didn't hit him right between the eyes with root-shaking consequences.

He tried to hit me right between the eyes, but there wasn't enough space left, what with all the other crunches already lodged there.

Baffle-Gab Thesaurus

As any self-respecting bureaucrat knows, it is bad form indeed to use a single, simple word when six or seven obfuscating ones will do.

But where is the Washington phrasemaker to turn if he is hung up for what Horace called "words a foot and a half long"? Simple. Just glance at the Systematic Buzz Phrase Projector, or S.B.P.P.

The S.B.P.P. has aptly obscure origins but appears to come from a Royal Canadian Air Force listing of fuzzy phrases. It was popularized in Washington by Philip Broughton, a U.S. Public Health Service official, who circulated it among civil servants and businessmen. A sort of mini-thesaurus of baffle-gab, it consists of a three-column list of 30 overused but appropriately portentous words. Whenever a GS-14 or deputy assistant secretary needs an opaque phrase, he need only think of a three-digit number—any one will do as well as the next—and select the corresponding "buzz words" from the three columns. For example, 257 produces "systematized logistical projection," which has the ring of absolute authority and means absolutely nothing.

Broughton's baffle-gab guide:

	A	B	C
0)	Integrated	Management	Options
1)	Total	Organizational	Flexibility
2)	Systematized	Monitored	Capability
3)	Parallel	Reciprocal	Mobility
4)	Functional	Digital	Programming
5)	Responsive	Logistical	Concept
6)	Optional	Transitional	Time-Phase
7)	Synchronized	Incremental	Projection
8)	Compatible	Third-Generation	Hardware
9)	Balanced	Policy	Contingency

Viable Solutions
EDWIN NEWMAN

The day is not far off when someone about to join his family will excuse himself by saying that he does not want to keep his microcluster of structured role expectations waiting.

True, I came upon this gem of social-scientific jargon in London, but that only shows how far our influence has spread and how determined the British are to join the Americans at the kill when the English language finally is done to death. Asphyxiation will be the cause, with the lethal agent gas. This is the gas which, added to evidence, produces evidentiary material, and which, escaping from a Secret Service spokesman—how can you have a spokesman for a secret service?—turned President Ford and *his* microcluster of structured role expectations into protectees.

At that, protectee is better than a similar government word, escapee, which is used—misused—to mean somebody who escaped.

"To what do you attribute your escape?" (It is, by the way, becoming fashionable to say successful escape.)

"I am a fast runnee."

The chief current protectee of the Secret Service is not a gross offender—or offendee—against the language, and when he does offend, it is more often out of naïveté than self-importance. He has identified inflation as "the universal enemy of one hundred percent of our people" and has noted that in trying to deal with that enemy, we went through a "long process of economic summit." Others less fortunately placed were going through a long process of economic valley.

Mr. Ford is enthusiastic about the virtues of dialogue. He has called for a new dialogue with the nations of Latin America, though most of those nations were not aware that the old dialogue had ended, or even begun. In one of his first speeches as President, Mr. Ford said he wanted to have "a deepening dialogue" with the nations of Latin America. Until then, I had thought that took place when two men talked to each other while digging a hole.

Last February, twelve Senators and seventy Representatives asked President Ford for a serious, unemotional dialogue on getting the United States out of Indochina. They should have asked for eighty-two dialogues.

It is curious, this devotion to dialogue. An Army officer involved in the amnesty program, Major General Eugene Forrester, was quoted as saying that he and his nineteen-year-old son had had an "extremely volatile dialogue over the war in Vietnam." He evidently meant that they shouted at each other.

General Forrester, the eighty-two members of Congress and President Ford, bent on dialogue though they may be, might well blanch at the prospect of engaging in one with Alan Greenspan, chairman of the Council of Economic Advisers. How would anyone hold up his end after hearing Greenspan say this:

"Thus, once the inflation genie has been let out of the bottle, it is a very tricky policy problem to find the particular calibration and timing that would be appropriate to stem the acceleration in risk premiums created by falling income without prematurely aborting the decline in the inflation-generated risk premiums. This is clearly not an easy policy path to traverse, but it is the path that we must follow."

If that is the path that we must follow, I hope we are able to find it before it (another Greenspanism) obsoletes.

Greenspan was speaking in Washington, a city where a scarcity of money is routinely referred to as a tight resource environment and where, after an experiment with fish in which all the fish died, the Atomic Energy Commission said that "The biota exhibited one hundred percent mortality response." There is a reason for this verbiage. In a tight resource environment, money is more likely to be forthcoming if whatever the money is wanted for can be made to sound abstruse and important. This is why money itself is rarely called money nowadays. It is called funding.

A reader sent me a report by the Youth Services Agency of the New York City Board of Education on the Board's summer program in 1974. The report concluded with the Y.S.A.'s opinion that the program should have more workers and more money, i.e., that it "should be considered for expanded allotments of enrollee personnel and more supportive measures from its own direct funding source."

The same report spoke of employees who had been held up after drawing their paychecks, listed precautions that had been taken, and concluded: "These precautions appeared to be quite successful in dissuading potential individuals with larcenous intent."

Now for a thrust:

"The major thrust of Y.S.A.'s recommendations to maximize the quality and efficiency of services rendered revolve around the necessity for more phone channels. Two additional phone channels would compensate greatly for both communicative and space difficulties and such implementation is strongly urged as an immediate necessity."

Revolve should be revolves, and such implementation also is urged as an immediate necessity, but no matter. A revolving major thrust is hard to match. Indeed, it is hard to find. However, the non-revolving species is spotted fairly often. It was seen at the 1975 convention of the American Booksellers Association, where a press release noted that the major thrust of the convention was (I ask myself whether this really happened) to "foster dialogue."

Major thrusts, unless met by major parries, may be fatal, but almost any thrust can be dangerous. A dean of a university department of home economics (no longer called home economics but family resources and consumer sciences) told an interviewer that in her previous job, in the Office of Education in Washington, most of her work had been in "conceptualizing new thrusts in programming." Beware the conceptualized thrust. There is a verified instance of one that went berserk. It took six strong men to hold it down.

Conceptualizing thrusts, or articulating them, is what we have come to expect from the social sciences. In that world, a sociologist will feel that he has advanced the cause of knowledge by classifying murder and assault as escalated interpersonal altercations; an applicant for a grant for technical training will write that "A quality void in technical capacity constrains achievement"; teachers who encourage children will be said to emit reinforcers; and an economist will be concerned about the adverse effect on the countercyclical dimension that would come from opening the Pandora's box of micro-goals.

It was a social scientist who wrote that knowledge that is transmitted from person to person *qua* knowledge is called intersubjectively transmissible knowledge or, for the sake of brevity, transmissible knowledge. Making knowledge something of a bridge over the river *qua*.

Words like funding, ongoing, constituency, thrust and viable can be worth millions in foundation grants. I received an appeal for money from an organization at Princeton University dedicated to finding viable solutions to international problems. We used to look for solutions and were pleasantly surprised on the rare occasions that we found them. Solutions are no longer sufficient. Viability is now required.

And if not viability, effectiveness. The Committee for Economic Development put out a statement of policy in which it said that a new generation of complex problems demanded fresh and effective solutions. A solution not effective would by definition not be a solution. Nor is there any reason that a solution must be fresh. Old solutions do the job and also have the advantage of experience.

But I stray. I recently came across a phrase that may be worth as much as funding, ongoing and viable put together. It was in a paper advocating the setting of behavioral objectives in schools. Behavioral objectives, so far as I can make out, mean nothing whatever, but it was claimed that they would enable teachers to "provide students with a pharmacy of learning alternatives matched to the objectives and tailored to the individual characteristics of each student." A pharmacy of learning alternatives. The proper reaction is wonder and veneration.

I do not wish to overlook the contribution of business to wrecking the language. B. Altman, in New York, has issued this invitation: "Sparkle your table with Cape Cod classic glassware." As it happened, I did not have time to sparkle my table because I was busy following instructions given in another advertisement and was accessorizing my spacious master bedroom with oil paintings and, in the words of another advertisement that appeared in *The New Yorker*, "making beautiful happen to [my] window treatments with Levolor Rivieras." Some days, I wish I could just make clean happen to my window treatments.

Saks Fifth Avenue, also in New York, has offered to sell men a magnificient—magnificient—glacé leather trench coat collared and lined with natural muskrat. Unnatural muskrat is a muskrat of doubtful sexual proclivities. An advertising executive I have been told of wrote to a client: "This will enable us to direct the most maximally impactful advertising toward the small and medium size dog owner."

I have seen advertisements for a recording of *Così Fan Tutte*[1] that was "totally complete," and for a California Riesling that was "regretfully

---

[1] An opera composed by Mozart in 1790.—Eds.

available only in very limited quantities." The latter is the hopefully disease spreading, though no variation is likely to approach the sheer majesty of the president of the Green Bay Packers saying, when discussing the hiring of a new coach, "We hope to have an announcement before the end of the week, hopefully before that." The wine is regretfully available only in limited quantities. You may have a vision of the Riesling sobbing itself to sleep over its inadequacy.

The Chesapeake and Potomac Telephone Company has something called a single payment gift plan. Under the plan, the customer may pay for a year in advance, and then he receives no other bills until the year is over. That's a gift. In Pompano Beach, Florida, condominium apartments have been offered in which the bedroom is a sleeping chamber, the kitchen is a culinary center, and the dining room is the place de dinner. That last would have been an appropriate place for a dish served at a book-and-author luncheon sponsored in the Athens of America by the *Boston Herald-American*: crepes a la seafood. Both the *Herald* and the condominium promoters may have received advice from the Biltmore Hotel in New York which, for the benefit of foreign visitors, has a sign outside a men's lavatory that reads not only "Gentlemen" but "Monsieurs."

Let us return to Britain, where the locals—quick learners—are having major confrontations, consulting in depth, satisfying targets, giving the score situation instead of the score, flaunting instead of flouting, making an effort to try, calling for legislation that will galvanize a new sense of opportunity and partnership, and describing the way people talk as their conversation culture, and swimming pools and playing fields as leisure complexes.

Remnants of Britain's sturdy conversation culture do survive. At a meeting of shareholders of the British Leyland Motor Corporation, the chairman, Lord Stokes, explaining the disasters that had befallen the company, found his explanation being drowned out by slow handclapping.

Said Lord Stokes, sarcastically, "Well, thank you for your support."

Said one of the shareholders, "There is only one support you want because you are a bloody big rupture all the way through."

It was a little too long to be ideal, but it undoubtedly enlivened the dialogue situation.

The British, in any case, are not as resourceful as the Americans when it comes to making language mushy and boneless. The playwright William Douglas-Home, writing to *The Times* of London, said that the Conservative party "should be plugging, day in, day out, the true facts about taxation." True facts are, of course, the only kind of facts available, but see what a press release for an American television program does with them: "The facts hew to actuality." True facts. The facts hew to actuality. No contest.

But don't cheer, folks.

Soon, also, no language.

The Language Barrier: Why Students Can't Write
A. BARTLETT GIAMATTI

Today's college students—the former grammar and high school students of the late 1960's and early '70's—have lost touch with the language. These were the children nobody remembered when The Movement was moving, when the rest of us were being liberated. These were the genuine young.

They are the products of the anti-structures of that time. They have come and are coming out of the "open classroom," vertical grouping, modular buildings with 50 pupils to a room. They have come out of the "new math" and its concepts, its lego's and blocks and set theory, not knowing how to multiply. They have come out of "individualized instruction" and "elective systems," not knowing how to listen to anyone else, not knowing how to take a direction.

They have come out of the sentimental '60's, where "repressive" and "arbitrary" grades were done away with, not able to take the pressure of grading. They have come out of a primary and secondary world where "personal development" was said to be worth more than achievement, where "creativity" was the highest goal and was often completely divorced from one of its essential components: discipline. And they are arriving in college often completely at a loss about how to cope with their work, with their time, with themselves.

But most of all, these present college students, and those now in junior high and high school, cannot handle the English language, particularly as it is written.

That this is so is no secret. *The New York Times* recently reported that, in the 10 years since 1964, the verbal and math scores on the scholastic achievement tests (SAT's) have been steadily declining, and that the average test scores for 1975 high school graduates declined by 10 points on the verbal portion and by 8 points on the math portion since 1974. This was the largest single drop in the past 12 years.

This decline tells us something real and terrifying about the state of the English language, just as a recent article on course enrollments in foreign languages—in *The Chronicle of Higher Education*—tells us something about literacy and the state of foreign languages. The Modern Language Association reports a drop of 6.2 percent in undergraduate enrollments in foreign languages from 1972 to 1974, with sharpest declines of 14 percent in German, 13.4 percent in French, 11.6 percent in Russian, and slighter declines in Italian and Spanish. This, the article said, reflects a trend that has been apparent since the late 1960's.

Obviously the inclination to immerse oneself in any language is on the wane, and the ability to *use* language is withering rapidly. Ask anyone who reads student writing—or hires recent graduates. Last fall the Yale English Department voted to reinstate English 10, a composition course, because so many Yale students cannot handle English—cannot make a sentence or a paragraph, cannot organize a paper, cannot follow through—well enough to do college work.

Yale is not unique. To take a university different in every respect except quality, Berkeley has just created the Bay Area Writing Project, bringing together college, junior college and high school teachers in the San Francisco area to work on each other to work on student writing. Why? Because where seven years ago only about 25 percent of Berkeley students had to take "Subject A," Berkeley's required basic composition course for entering freshmen, now the number is around 50 percent. Berkeley saw the quality of writing declining sharply and decided to invest its energies in the student's earlier years by going back into the high schools. From the Free Speech Movement to the Bay Area Writing Project in just 10 years.

Never mind the statistics. Ask the students. They will tell you how badly they need help with their language. Last year at Yale, 185 students applied for 12 places in one small college seminar on expository writing—nothing fancy, just a course on how to write. This is typical of the students' desperate wish to be taught how to handle the fundamental medium in which we live.

What has happened? I believe that of all the institutions attacked in the past dozen years—governmental, legal and educational—the one that suffered most was the institution of language itself, that massive, living system of signs which on the one hand limits us and, on the other hand, allows us to decide who we are. This institution—language—was perceived as being repressive. It was thought to be the agent of all other repressive codes—legal, political and cultural. Language was the barrier that blocked—blocked access to pure feeling, blocked true communal experience of the kind that flowered at Woodstock, blocked the restoration of Eden.

Language was what was circumvented by drugs and music—those agents of higher states whose main virtue was that they were not verbal but visual or aural, the pure association of pure shape or sound unencumbered by words—which is to say by distinctions, which is to say by meaning. Language disassociated us from primitive impulses. It polluted us with ambiguity; it was not pure. Language impeded freedom.

The first shot in the revolution in 1964 was the Free Speech Movement.[1] It was intended not only to free speech from middle-class constraints about uttering obscenities, for instance. It was also intended to free us from the shackles of syntax, the racism of grammar, the elitism of style. All those corrupt and corrupting elements in American society, those signs that we had fallen from paradise, could be located in an aspect of language. The Free Speech Movement was where we first began to hear language mediated through the bullhorn into the formulaic chant of a crowd.

This reductiveness would soon be extended to all kinds of systems that

[1] It began at the University of California at Berkeley.—EDS.

asserted differentness or pluralism as essential to their workings. But language was where it was first applied. The slogan—like the picket sign, the bumper sticker, the single name by which so many people in The Movement went (surnames being invidious)—all were part of an effort to compress language to a single unambiguous medium of exchange, a coin of the realm that could not be counterfeited or abused. Because what was being sought was not the protean leap of language, but unity of feeling—complete integration of desire and fulfillment.

And here is where language was more of an enemy than anything else. For while language may be a medium for sentimentality, it will not finally yield to it. Try as you can, you can neither wholly avoid words nor wholly make them mean only what you feel. Words resist. But Abbie Hoffman[2] says it better than I can. I quote from Hoffman's speech on the warm evening of May 1, 1970, in the courtyard of Ezra Stiles College at Yale, on the occasion of one of the last great campus gatherings of The Movement:

"Don't listen to people who say we got to be serious, responsible. Everybody's responsible and serious but us. We gotta redefine the ——— language. Work—W-O-R-K—is a dirty four-letter word. . . . We need a society in which work and play are not separate. We gotta destroy the Protestant ethic as well as capitalism, racism, imperialism—that's gotta go too. We want a society in which dancin' in the streets isn't separate from cuttin' sugar cane. . . . We have picked the Yale lock."

Fascinating. Because the Protestant ethic, capitalism, racism and imperialism are almost forgotten, almost mere afterthoughts, as Hoffman proclaimed what he really wants: a garden world where nothing is separate, work and play, cutting cane and dancing, where the togetherness will come by "redefining the language." If only he could redefine the language as easily as he could manipulate a crowd. But language won't change its essential shape for anyone. If you engage it, you must honor its deep tides. The most that Abbie Hoffman can do is make it do tricks, and the pun at the end is his trick.

Abbie Hoffman's attitude to language was fundamentally sentimental—language was a medium for expressing his feelings. It wasn't really a rhetorical instrument, to be used to persuade others, or a weapon, used to flay others. It was like everything else to him and to those like him—good as long as it made you feel good.

This sentimentality, corrosive as acid, was true of all those for whom books became talismans and fetishes, helpful for inducing states and sensations. This is how the novels of Herman Hesse, awash in sentiment, were used, and the novels of Kurt Vonnegut, Jr. Vonnegut was a culture hero because he seemed to be grinning through exquisite pain, the result of his extraordinary moral sensitivity. As Robert Alter has suggested, the young

---

[2] A prominent radical activist of the 1960s.—EDS.

loved his sense of resignation and the fact that his America was glistening with corruption and guilt and failure. They also loved him because his zany cartoons masqueraded as tragic complexities and therefore massaged their prejudices without requiring them to think. This was the perfect writer for people who felt that words were crowding them, impeding them: people for whom Zen, the occult, Indians, organic gardening, Transcendental Meditation, the "I Ching"—the whole frozen dinner of the new primitivism—were superior to words.

The only texts to be trusted were Eastern ones that might lead to trance or offered no resistance to it. This accounts for the prodigious sales of that poisonous sweetmeat, *The Prophet*, by Kahlil Gibran. For, like Rod McKuen, Gibran continued to satisfy the sentimental longings for absorption of those for whom real politics or drugs were either too dangerous or too distant.

Throughout the 1960's the sentimental mode implied a fundamental attitude to language. Language at best was good only for getting past language. The fact that language has its own laws and imperatives, its own polity, was precisely why it was the most cunning, the most resourceful, the last enemy. And although Abbie Hoffman didn't say so, he might have said "Shut it down to open it up." If language is a city, let it fall. Let the garden of green feeling grow—sweet like the sugar cane, wordless like the dance.

This essential sentimentality, this deep distrust of the restrictions of language, this desire to level its distinguishing features, is at the heart of why young people today can't write, can't shape themselves through words. And it is why so many of the cultural edifices that we raise through words are equally in disrepair.

It is this sentimental attitude, now running throughout our system, that led the editor of *English Today*, the organ of the National Council of Teachers of English, to write an article last April deriding the call from colleges for more "fundamentals" at the high school level. "The English teaching profession—for the most part—has progressed," he wrote, "well beyond thinking of writing instruction solely or principally in terms of basic skills instruction."

This is the very accent of the attitude I am describing. "Skills" is a code word for discipline, for work, for language in its particularity. The editor, a professor at Michigan State University, assures his high school clientele that that is all behind them. He would rather, judging by the titles of two suggestions for courses in his journal—"Creative Writing Without Words" and "A Visual Approach to Writing"—have students create sounds on a tape recorder, or "free-associate" from pictures, because words are dense and recalcitrant, stone that is hard to shape into statues. He would rather have students avoid meaning and grope for feeling. He would urge them not to face the reality of language, though, of course, the consequence is that they will not face or find the reality of themselves.

For that is what is at stake. That is what the neo-primitivism and sentimentality really mean—that all complexity can be avoided in the name of communality and desire. And I claim that this attitude persists because of what we are doing to language.

I believe that all of us are what we say we are—that as individuals and as a people we define through language what we have, and what we will be, and that a group of people who cannot clearly and precisely speak and write will never be a genuine society. We shape ourselves and our institutions, and we and our institutions are shaped, through those individual acts of negotiation between ourselves and our language. Without a respect for its awesome power we can never find out who we are, and thus never have to leave the child's garden of feeling and enter the city—that is, become citizens.

To deny language is finally to deny history, and that is what frightens me most about young people who can't write, particularly those who don't know it or don't care. They have been duped. By thinking that language can be denied, in order to achieve full access to feeling, they have of course become blocked and stunted and frustrated—and at the most important level. It is a sad irony. High school and college students have been encouraged to believe that language does not require work—that if they wait they will suddenly blossom and flower in verbal mastery; that if they transcribe what they feel about anything it will somehow turn into what they think.

Clearly, to have been told all these things—and millions of school children were and are told these things—is to have been lied to. It is also to have been robbed of the only thing that everyone *does* share, the only thing that connects us each to each. Language is the medium in which the race lives, it is what we have brought from our past, and it is what has brought us from the past—our link with who we were and who we want to be.

Being Serious Without Being Stuffy
WALKER GIBSON

It struck him abruptly that a woman whose only being was to "make believe" . . . was a kind of monster.
—The Tragic Muse

Which is it best to be—a Tough or a Sweet or a Stuffy Talker? While many would perhaps not object to being labeled Tough—possibly remembering William James' honorific use of the word—few would want to be called either Sweet or Stuffy. Actually, all three extremes are dangerous. Though it is clearly possible to write very well within the limits of the Tough style, it is easy to write badly too, to sound not simply curt but moronic. Every cheap who-dunit will testify to the indulgence in mindlessness and ego that the Tough style makes easy. As for Sweet Talk and Stuffy Talk, it is difficult to imagine first-rate writing composed strictly within those manners, except as parody. At least I have found no extreme Sweet or Stuffy passage that I can also admire as literature. . . .

I submit, then, that all three of our styles are dangers in modern prose, in ascending order of peril. As a Tough Talker, it is all too easy to sound egocentric, or simpleminded, or plain vulgar. As a Sweet Talker, it is hard to avoid sounding chummy in a way to make most discriminating readers recoil. And as a Stuffy Talker it is almost impossible *not* to sound as if you didn't care about your reader at all.

These difficulties are pervasive in modern American writing, perhaps in any writing. They are apparent, for example, in the styles of those who pontificate on style itself. Let us try a few . . . passages . . . from the discourse of language experts talking about language.

In the last few years there have appeared on the textbook market a number of anthologies of essays about language and usage. These have been extraordinarily similar in purpose, they have been aimed at an identical audience, and they share current fashionable attitudes of the modern linguistic scholar. They provide us, therefore, with something of a laboratory situation for measuring difference in style. What kinds of voice can we identify in the styles of the anthologists themselves? How do they share the difficulties of self-expression that [can be observed] in novelists, journalists, adwriters, and committee spokesmen? All we need, for a tentative answer, is a look at the first hundred words or so of their prefaces.

Here is one:

> From the early grades through the first year of college, the textbooks in grammar and usage scarcely change. The repetition is well meant and apparently necessary: if they won't learn what's good for them, make them do it again. Certainly habits are formed and re-formed by repetitive drill, but it is clear from the record that repetition is not enough.
>
> This book is based on the conviction that knowledge must be added to drill so that repetition may open into growth. Everyone aims at this, at confidence and pleasure in the use of language rather than at anxiety about being correct; the problem has been to get the liberating knowledge, which is scattered through books and journals, into the hands of the students.

A reader who thinks first about details of grammar, and only second of his impression of the whole voice, may too quickly assume that we have a Stuffy Talker here. The reader . . . might tick off those verbs in the passive voice and say, There it is—Stuffy. For there they are: *is well meant, are formed and re-formed, is based, must be added, is scattered*. Nevertheless, as any sensible reader will point out, this is *not* a Stuffy voice at all—quite the contrary. Perhaps it is almost too breezy. In any case the barrage of passive verbs here is simply not enough to overcome all the other stylistic tricks in this passage which propel the tone in quite another direction, toward Toughness and Sweetness.

What are they? For one thing, the wry half-quotation, *if they won't learn what's good for them* . . . , with its colloquial flavor, serves to disarm the reader in the very second sentence. The willingness to include such talk, in a kind of jocular spirit, is part of a general modesty on the part of the speaker, who is at pains to remind us that there is something to be said for the opposition. "The repetition is well meant," he acknowledges. "Everyone aims at this, at confidence and pleasure in the use of language"—not just I in my wisdom. In sum, the voice here is not that of a Stuffy lecturer at all, but represents some mixture of my three styles.

A short time after the anthology prefaced in this manner appeared, another similar collection was published whose preface began as follows:

> The basic premise of this collection of essays is that language in and of itself is an important subject for study. The second, and equally important, premise is that one can learn about language by reading a variety of essays oriented to the best that modern scholars have thought and said about it.
>
> Because the study of English is often atomized, it is effectively divorced from the broad and scholarly concerns that it is uniquely able to illuminate. In his study of language under the guise of composition, grammar, rhetoric, or poetics, the student is seldom made to think about the nature of language itself.

I hope my reader may sense the difference in that voice, before he stops to take notes of details that may account for the difference. The voice here, as I hope we may agree, is less brisk, more removed from the reader, with an academic manner of address that suggests some lack of excitement about what it's saying. If that judgment is at all fair, we may then ask, where does this manner come from? Why is this man so different, even though in realistic fact he is attempting to talk to the same audience for an almost identical purpose?

There are plenty of concrete differences; some of them may be persuasive. The vocabulary of our second speaker is more pretentious, with more longer words and far fewer monosyllables. There are fewer independent verbs, resulting in more subordination, both clauses and other dependent structures. (Half the passage occurs inside subordinate clauses.) There is a tendency to interrupt normal sentence patterns, to make the reader wait for further modification. "The basic premise *of this collection of essays is* . . ." "The second, *and equally important,* premise is . . ." The tag about the best thought and said may be deliberately ironic, but it's a tired tag for all that. These and other habits of speech may partially justify our feeling that the second anthologist is more dryly professorial (if not plain duller) than the first.

Now here is a third, introducing still another collection of similar essays, aimed at the same audience. It may be his sense of the competition that makes this writer speak as he does.

The growth of interest in language study, in linguistics, has been one of the interesting intellectual developments of the twentieth century. Linguistics must now be viewed as an established and independent branch of study. Under the circumstances it would be odd if there were not a number of books issued to introduce this study to the general public and to the university undergraduate. Many excellent collections of language articles and selections for the undergraduate—especially for the freshman—have appeared in recent years. The compiler of still another collection is consequently obliged to indicate why he adds his product to the number available.

Anyone who begins a book by telling us that "the growth of interest" in something is an "interesting development" cannot himself be overwhelmingly interested in what he has to say. In any event, those rhetorical habits of Stuffiness that we associate with a remoteness from both subject and audience are here apparent. The vocabulary is now even more multisyllabic. There are fewer finite verbs, with consequent subordination of much of the language. Passive verbs are actually less frequent than in our first passage, but other significant habits appear—for instance the noun adjunct. We have *language study, university undergraduates, language articles*—clear hints that we are approaching the jargon of officialese. The interrupted sentence patterns are interesting; here the writer habitually places modifying phrases between his subject and verb, letting his reader wait patiently until he is all through qualifying. The writer's reference to himself as "the compiler of still another collection" may be taken as a symptom of his nervous self-consciousness. His reaction to his nervousness is withdrawal.

The paragraph I have quoted is followed by a sentence beginning "It is hoped that this book may be welcome for three main reasons . . ." It is to be wondered who's doing the hoping. Could it be by any chance the author himself? Is there then some good reason why he shouldn't say so? This man seems to be running scared.

The major fault in modern prose generally is Stuffiness. It is true that Sweetness too can be very offensive; witness the overlays of Sweetness on Toughness that . . . [are] observable in the contemporary novel. The excess of Sweetness in journalism . . . speaks for itself. For most people, though, in most situations, in the writing of everyday serious expository prose, it is the Stuffy voice that gets in the way. The reason it gets in the way, I submit, is that the writer is scared. If this is an age of anxiety, one way we react to our anxiety is to withdraw into omniscient and multisyllabic detachment where nobody can get us.

No book . . . can remove a person's anxiety for him. But it may be that, through a study of style, one might remove some *symptoms* of anxiety from one's prose. Therefore it may not be utterly useless to offer a little Practical Advice, most of it fairly obvious, for avoiding the symptoms of Stuffiness. To follow such advice may amount to little more than taking aspirin: it may reduce the headache without touching the anxiety. And yet, if anxiety is found in the style of our language, perhaps changing our style may be the best thing we can do. In any case, here are some Rules . . . for avoiding the Stuffy voice . . .

HOW TO AVOID BEING STUFFY

1. Make about two-thirds of your total vocabulary monosyllabic; keep words of three syllables or more down to under 20 per cent.
2. Try making some of the subjects of your verbs *people*, not neuter nouns.
3. Manage a *finite verb* about every ten words, on the average. (Which is more than that sentence does.)
4. Don't overuse the *passive voice*. (But don't avoid it altogether either.)
5. Keep down the *noun adjuncts*.
6. Keep the average length of *subordinate clauses* down to ten words or so, and see to it that the total proportion of subordinate clauses runs to no more than a third of the whole.
7. Most marks of *punctuation* (except commas and semi-colons) serve to lighten tone. Consider question marks, parentheses, italics, dashes, and of course exclamations.
8. Don't *interrupt* subject and verb with intervening subordinate constructions and modifiers.
9. If really desperate, try a *contraction* or two, or a *fragment* (verbless sentence).
10. Whatever you do, *don't obey all these rules at once,* for to do so would be to emerge with something disastrously cute, probably on the Sweet side. The careful writer, in fact, carefully *dis*obeys some of these rules, precisely to avoid the pose of sickly Sweetness. He includes a passive verb, now and then, a lengthy subordinate clause, an elegant interruption between subject and verb. Perhaps his skill in making such choices is what we mean by a *balanced style.*

It remains to say a word about the moral side of rhetoric. The three styles I have been trying to describe can be called ways of making believe. Any style, any way of thinking, can be regarded as a make-believe performance, and it is always possible to take comfort by distinguishing between the performance on the one hand and the Real Person that stands behind all the play-acting on the other. That's not me, that's just my voice of the moment. But such a distinction breaks down very soon; even in the writing of fiction . . . it produces difficulties. And in the course of our day-to-day lives, we have to live with the effects of our performances. The voices I choose are mine, my responsibility, and the belief I own up to is the make-believe I have made. Serious play-acting. The world is not a stage, nor ever was.

Put that way, all three styles I have been examining are, as I have said, dangerous. Exceedingly common as they are in modern American life, they suggest three ways in which Americans upstage one another. One can talk

Tough, beating the hairy chest, and make a spectacle of one's ostentatious simplicity. See how true and humble I am, more true and humble than you are. (And sometimes, furthermore, I really Know!) Or one can talk Sweet, leaping into the lap of one's listener, however unwanted there. See how nice I am to you, you boob. Or one can talk Stuffy, laying down the law as if one were Moses and all the world were a wandering tribe looking for the Word. In each case the rhetoric, all too often, creates a character who is ill-mannered, to say no worse of him. He has lost forbearance and restraint, a regard for the feelings of his listeners. The result is that in our time we are fairly surrounded by voices that are not much fun to be with.

... Our sense of a person, in an ordinary social introduction, is not simply a matter of words, but a matter of many different physical impressions. Gesture and grimace, voicebox and eyelid are all rich with meaning. In written prose, though, it is all words, and the business of the modern day is performed, much of it, with written words. For some people, actions in written language are the principal actions of their lives—at least of their professional lives. Handsome is as handsome writes. But how few of us write handsomely! Instead, the characters we create for ourselves, the characters we become, are too often egocentric and ill-mannered. We push one another around. (Examples abound, I know, in the style of this book, this chapter, this sentence.) And the ill manners can be produced by, among other things, an excessive Toughness, or Sweetness, or Stuffiness, particularly the latter two.

The excesses are understandable. In the very act of addressing someone we acknowledge a wish to push him around, and in our zeal to push a little harder, it is no wonder our voices begin to sound strident. It is with style that we try to behave like a decent person, one who ruefully concedes his drive for power while remaining aware of his reader's well-chosen resistance. Thus style is our way of becoming a person worth listening to, worth knowing.

A moral justification for the study of rhetoric lies right here. We improve ourselves by improving the words we write. We make our performance less monstrous, by *acting* like human beings. Just what comprises a satisfactory human performance is every man's complicated decision. But at least, by looking at rhetoric, we may begin to know more about who it is we are making believe we are. And then, perhaps, we can do something about it.

An Ethic of Clarity

DONALD HALL

In the expression "good writing" or "good style," the word "good" has usually meant "beautiful" or "proficient"—like a good Rembrandt or a good kind of soap. In our time it has come to mean honest as opposed to fake. Bad writing happens when the writer lies to himself, to others, or to both. Probably, it is usually necessary to lie to oneself in order to lie to others; advertising men use the products they praise. Bad writing may be proficient; it may persuade us to buy a poor car or vote for an imbecile, but it is bad because it is tricky, false in its enthusiasm, and falsely motivated. It appeals to a part of us that wants to deceive itself. I am encouraged to tell myself that I am enjoying my favorite beverage when, really, I am only getting sloshed.

"If a man writes clearly enough any one can see if he fakes," says Hemingway. Orwell[1] reverses the terms: "The great enemy of clear language is insincerity. . . . When there is a gap between one's real and one's declared aims, one turns as it were instinctively to long words and exhausted idioms, like a cuttlefish squirting out ink." Pound[2] talks about the "gap between one's real and one's declared aims" as the distance between expression and meaning. In "The New Vocabularianism," Thurber[3] speaks of the political use of clichés to hide a "menacing Alice in Wonderland meaninglessness."

As Robert Graves[4] says, "The writing of good English is thus a moral matter." And the morality is a morality of truth-telling. Herbert Read[5] declares that "the only thing that is indispensable for the possession of a good style is personal sincerity." We can agree, but we must add that personal sincerity is not always an easy matter, nor is it always available to the will. Real aims, we must understand, are not necessarily conscious ones. The worst liars in the world may consider themselves sincere. Analysis of one's own style, in fact, can be a test of one's own feelings. And certainly, many habits of bad style are bad habits of thinking as well as of feeling.

There are examples of the modern attitude toward style in older writers. Jonathan Swift,[6] maybe the best prose writer of the language, sounds like George Orwell when he writes:

> Our English tongue is too little cultivated in this kingdom, yet the faults are nine in ten owing to affectation, not to want of understanding. When a man's thoughts are clear, the properest words will generally offer themselves first, and his own judgment will direct him in what order to place them, so as they may be best understood.

Here Swift appears tautological; clear thoughts only *exist* when they are embodied in clear words. But he goes on: "When men err against this

---

[1] George Orwell, British novelist and essayist. The quotation is from "Politics and the English Language," reprinted on pages 31–41. See "Notes on Authors" at the end of this book.—EDS.

[2] Ezra Pound (1885–1972), American poet.—EDS.

[3] James Thurber (1894–1961), American humorist and essayist. See "Notes on Authors" at the end of this book.—EDS.

[4] Robert Graves (1895–   ), British poet and novelist. See "Notes on Authors" at the end of this book.—EDS.

[5] Herbert Read (1893–1968), British art critic and author.—EDS.

[6] Jonathan Swift (1667–1745), author of *Gulliver's Travels*.—EDS.

method, it is usually on purpose," purposes, we may add, that we often disguise from ourselves.

Aristotle[7] in his *Rhetoric* makes a case for plainness and truth-telling. "The right thing in speaking really is that we should be satisfied not to annoy our hearers, without trying to delight them: we ought in fairness to fight our case with no help beyond the bare facts." And he anticipates the modern stylist's avoidance of unusual words: "Clearness is secured by using the words . . . that are current and ordinary." Cicero attacks the Sophists[8] because they are "on the lookout for ideas that are neatly put rather than reasonable."

Yet, when we quote Cicero, the master rhetorician, on behalf of honest clarity, we must remember that the ancients did not really think of style as we do. Style until recent times has been a division of rhetoric. To learn style, one learned the types of figures of speech and the appropriateness of each to different levels of discourse—high, middle, and low. The study of style was complex, but it was technical rather than moral. For some writers, Latin was high and the vernacular low, but in the Renaissance the vernacular took in all levels. It is only in modern times that style divorces itself from rhetoric—rhetoric belongs to the enemy, to the advertisers and the propagandists—and becomes a matter of ethics and introspection.

Ezra Pound, like some French writers before him, makes the writer's function social. "Good writers are those who keep the language efficient. That is to say, keep it accurate, keep it clear." We must ask why this idea of the function of good style is so predominantly a modern phenomenon. Pound elsewhere speaks of the "assault," by which he means the attack upon our ears and eyes of words used dishonestly to persuade us, to convince us to buy or to believe. Never before have men been exposed to so many words—written words, from newspapers and billboards and paperbacks and flashing signs and the sides of buses, and spoken words, from radio and television and loudspeakers. Everyone who wishes to keep his mind clear and his feelings his own must make an effort to brush away these words like cobwebs from the face. The assault of the phoney is a result of technology combined with a morality that excuses any technique which is useful for persuasion. The persuasion is for purposes of making money, as in advertising, or winning power, as in war propaganda and the slogans of politicians. Politicians have always had slogans, but they never before had the means to spread their words so widely. The cold war of rhetoric between communism and capitalism has killed no soldiers, but the air is full of the small corpses of words that were once alive: "democracy," "freedom," "liberation."

---

[7] Aristotle (384–322 B.C.), Greek philosopher and literary critic.—EDS.

[8] Marcus Tullius Cicero (106–43 B.C.), Roman author, orator, and rhetorician. The Sophists professed to teach reasoning, but often were more concerned with clever, specious reasoning than with sound logic.—EDS.

It is because of this assault, primarily, that writers have become increasingly concerned with the honesty of their style to the exclusion of other qualities. Concentration on honesty is the only way to exclude the sounds of the bad style that assault us all. These writers are concerned finally *to be honest about what they see, feel, and know.* For some of them, like William Carlos Williams,[9] we can only trust the evidence of our eyes and ears, our real knowledge of our immediate environment.

Our reading of good writers and our attempt to write like them can help to guard us against the dulling onslaught. But we can only do this if we are able to look into ourselves with some honesty. An ethic of clarity demands intelligence and self-knowledge. Really, the ethic is not only a defense against the assault (nothing good is ever merely defensive), but is a development of the same inwardness that is reflected in psychoanalysis. One cannot, after all, examine one's motives and feelings carefully if one takes a naïve view that the appearance of a feeling is the reality of that feeling. . . .

The style is the man. Again and again, the modern stylists repeat this idea. By a man's metaphors you shall know him. When a commencement orator advises students to enrich themselves culturally, chances are that he is more interested in money than in poetry. When a university president says that his institution turned out 1,432 B.A.s last year, he tells us that he thinks he is running General Motors. The style is the man. Rémy de Gourmont[10] used the analogy that the bird's song is conditioned by the shape of the beak. And Paul Valéry[11] said, ". . . what makes the style is not merely the mind applied to a particular action; it is the whole of a living system extended, imprinted and recognizable in expression." These statements are fine, but they sound too deterministic, as if one expresses an unalterable self and can no more change the style of that self than a bird can change the shape of its beak. Man is a kind of bird that can change his beak.

A writer of bad prose, to become a writer of good prose, must alter his character. He does not have to become good in terms of conventional morality, but he must become honest in the expression of himself, which means that he must know himself. There must be no gap between expression and meaning, between real and declared aims. For some people, some of the time, this simply means *not* telling deliberate lies. For most people, it means learning when they are lying and when they are not. It means learning the real names of their feelings. It means not saying or thinking, "I didn't *mean* to hurt your feelings," when there really existed a desire to hurt. It means not saying "luncheon" or "home" for the purpose of

---

[9] William Carlos Williams (1883–1963), American poet and short-story writer.—Eds.

[10] Rémy de Gourmont (1858–1915), French novelist and literary critic.—Eds.

[11] Paul Valéry (1871–1945), French poet and philosopher.—Eds.

appearing upper-class or well-educated. It means not using the passive mood to attribute to no one in particular opinions that one is unwilling to call one's own. It means not disguising banal thinking by polysyllabic writing or the lack of feeling by clichés that purport to display feeling.

The style is the man, and the man can change himself by changing his style. Prose style is the way you think and the way you understand what you feel. Frequently, we feel for one another a mixture of strong love and strong hate; if we call it love and disguise the hate to ourselves by sentimentalizing over love, we are thinking and feeling badly. Style is ethics and psychology; clarity is a psychological sort of ethic, since it involves not general moral laws, but truth to the individual self. The scrutiny of style is a moral and psychological study. . . . Editing our own writing, or going over in memory our own spoken words, or even inwardly examining our thought, we can ask *why* we resorted to the passive in this case or to clichés in that. When the smoke of bad prose fills the air, something is always on fire somewhere. If the style is really the man, the style becomes an instrument for discovering and changing the man. Language is expression of self, but language is also the instrument by which to know that self.

Attainment

Animula[1]
T. S. ELIOT

"Issues from the hand of God, the simple soul"
To a flat world of changing lights and noise,
To light, dark, dry or damp, chilly or warm;
Moving between the legs of tables and of chairs,
Rising or falling, grasping at kisses and toys,
Advancing boldly, sudden to take alarm,
Retreating to the corner of arm and knee,
Eager to be reassured, taking pleasure
In the fragrant brillance of the Christmas tree,
Pleasure in the wind, the sunlight and the sea;
Studies the sunlit pattern on the floor
And running stags around a silver tray;
Confounds the actual and the fanciful,
Content with playing-cards and kings and queens,
What the fairies do and what the servants say.
The heavy burden of the growing soul
Perplexes and offends more, day by day;
Week by week, offends and perplexes more
With the imperatives of "is and seems"
And may and may not, desire and control.
The pain of living and the drug of dreams
Curl up the small soul in the window seat
Behind the *Encyclopædia Britannica*.
Issues from the hand of time the simple soul
Irresolute and selfish, misshapen, lame,
Unable to fare forward or retreat,
Fearing the warm reality, the offered good,
Denying the importunity of the blood,
Shadow of its own shadows, spectre in its own gloom,
Leaving disordered papers in a dusty room;
Living first in the silence after the viaticum.

Pray for Guiterriez, avid of speed and power,
For Boudin, blown to pieces,

---

[1] Little soul (Latin).—EDS.

For this one who made a great fortune,
And that one who went his own way.
Pray for Floret,[2] by the boarhound slain between the yew trees,
Pray for us now and at the hour of our birth.

Experience of the Average Girl: Coming of Age in Samoa
MARGARET MEAD

All of these children had seen birth and death. They had seen many dead bodies. They had watched miscarriage and peeked under the arms of the old women who were washing and commenting upon the undeveloped fœtus. There was no convention of sending children of the family away at such times, although the hordes of neighbouring children were scattered with a shower of stones if any of the older women could take time from the more absorbing events to hurl them. But the feeling here was that children were noisy and troublesome; there was no desire to protect them from shock or to keep them in ignorance. About half of the children had seen a partly developed fœtus, which the Samoans fear will otherwise be born as an avenging ghost, cut from a woman's dead body in the open grave. If shock is the result of early experiences with birth, death, or sex activities, it should surely be manifest here in this postmortem Cæsarian where grief for the dead, fear of death, a sense of horror and a dread of contamination from contact with the dead, the open, unconcealed operation and the sight of the distorted, repulsive fœtus all combine to render the experience indelible. An only slightly less emotionally charged experience was the often witnessed operation of cutting open any dead body to search out the cause of death. These operations performed in the shallow open grave, beneath a glaring noon-day sun, with a frightened, excited crowd watching in horrified fascination, are hardly orderly or unemotional initiations into the details of biology and death, and yet they seem to leave no bad effects on the children's emotional makeup. Possibly the adult attitude that these are horrible but perfectly natural, non-unique occurrences, forming a legitimate part of the child's experience, may sufficiently account for the lack of bad results. Children take an intense interest in life and death, and are more proportionately obsessed by it than are their adults who divide their horror between the death of a young neighbour in childbed and the fact that the high chief has been insulted by some breach

---

[2] In a letter to Ethel M. Stevenson, Eliot wrote that Floret "may suggest . . . certain folklore memories" and that Guiterriez and Boudin represent "different types of career, the successful person of the machine age and someone who was killed in the last war." See Grover Smith, *T. S. Eliot's Poetry and Plays* (1956), p. 130.—EDS.

of etiquette in the neighbouring village. The intricacies of the social life are a closed book to the child and a correspondingly fascinating field of exploration in later life, while the facts of life and death are shorn of all mystery at an early age.

In matters of sex the ten-year-olds are equally sophisticated, although they witness sex activities only surreptitiously, since all expressions of affection are rigorously barred in public. A couple whose wedding night may have been spent in a room with ten other people will never the less shrink in shame from even touching hands in public. Individuals between whom there have been sex relations are said to be "shy of each other," and manifest this shyness in different fashion but with almost the same intensity as in the brother and sister avoidance. Husbands and wives never walk side by side through the village, for the husband, particularly, would be "ashamed." So no Samoan child is accustomed to seeing father and mother exchange casual caresses. The customary salutation by rubbing noses is, of course, as highly conventionalised and impersonal as our handshake. The only sort of demonstration which ever occurs in public is of the horseplay variety between young people whose affections are not really involved. This romping is particularly prevalent in groups of women, often taking the form of playfully snatching at the sex organs.

But the the lack of privacy within the houses where mosquito netting marks off purely formal walls about the married couples, and the custom of young lovers of using the palm groves for their rendezvous, makes it inevitable that children should see intercourse, often and between many different people. In many cases they have not seen first intercourse, which is usually accompanied by greater shyness and precaution. With the passing of the public ceremony, defloration forms one of the few mysteries in a young Samoan's knowledge of life. But scouring the village palm groves in search of lovers is one of the recognised forms of amusement for the ten-year-olds.

Samoan children have complete knowledge of the human body and its functions, owing to the custom of little children going unclothed, the scant clothing of adults, the habit of bathing in the sea, the use of the beach as a latrine and the lack of privacy in sexual life. They also have a vivid understanding of the nature of sex. Masturbation is an all but universal habit, beginning at the age of six or seven. There were only three little girls in my group who did not masturbate. Theoretically it is discontinued with the beginning of heterosexual activity and only resumed again in periods of enforced continence. Among grown boys and girls casual homosexual practices also supplant it to a certain extent. Boys masturbate in groups but among little girls it is a more individualistic, secretive practice. This habit seems never to be a matter of individual discovery, one child always learning from another. The adult ban only covers the unseemliness of open indulgence.

The adult attitude towards all the details of sex is characterised by this view that they are unseemly, not that they are wrong. Thus a youth would think nothing of shouting the length of the village, "Ho, maiden, wait for me in your bed to-night," but public comment upon the details of sex or of evacuation were considered to be in bad taste. All the words which are thus banished from polite conversation are cherished by the children who roll the salacious morsels under their tongues with great relish. The children of seven and eight get as much illicit satisfaction out of the other functions of the body as out of sex. This is interesting in view of the different attitude in Samoa towards the normal processes of evacuation. There is no privacy and no sense of shame. Nevertheless the brand of bad taste seems to be as effective in interesting the young children as is the brand of indecency among us. It it also curious that in theory and in fact boys and men take a more active interest in the salacious than do the women and girls.

It seems difficult to account for a salacious attitude among a people where so little is mysterious, so little forbidden. The precepts of the missionaries may have modified the native attitude more than the native practice. And the adult attitude towards children as non-participants may also be an important causal factor. For this seems to be the more correct view of any prohibitions which govern children. There is little evidence of a desire to preserve a child's innocence or to protect it from witnessing behaviour, the following of which would constitute the heinous offence, *tautala laititi* ("presuming above one's age"). For while a pair of lovers would never indulge in any demonstration before any one, child or adult, who was merely a spectator, three or four pairs of lovers who are relatives or friends often choose a common rendezvous. (This, of course, excludes relatives of opposite sex, included in the brother and sister avoidance, although married brothers and sisters might live in the same house after marriage.) From the night dances, now discontinued under missionary influence, which usually ended in a riot of open promiscuity, children and old people were excluded, as non-participants whose presence as uninvolved spectators would have been indecent. This attitude towards non-participants characterised all emotionally charged events, a women's weaving bee which was of a formal, ceremonial nature, a house-building, a candle-nut burning —these were activities at which the presence of a spectator would have been unseemly.

Yet, coupled with the sophistication of the children went no preadolescent heterosexual experimentation and very little homosexual activity which was regarded in native theory as imitative of and substitutive for heterosexual. The lack of precocious sex experimentation is probably due less to the parental ban on such precocity than to the strong institutionalised antagonism between younger boys and younger girls and the taboo against any amiable intercourse between them. This rigid sex dichotomy may also be operative in determining the lack of specialisation of sex feeling in adults. Since there is a heavily charged avoidance feeling towards brother and cousins, and a tendency to lump all other males together as the enemy who will some day be one's lovers, there are no males in a girl's age group whom she ever regards simply as individuals without relation to sex....

The general preoccupation with sex, the attitude that minor sex activities, suggestive dancing, stimulating salacious conversation, salacious songs and definitely motivated tussling are all acceptable and attractive diversions, is mainly responsible for the native attitude towards homosexual practices. They are simply *play*, neither frowned upon nor given much consideration. As heterosexual relations are given significance not by love and a tremendous fixation upon one individual, the only forces which can make a homosexual relationship lasting and important, but by children and the place of marriage in the economic and social structure of the village, it is easy to understand why very prevalent homosexual practices have no more important or striking results. The recognition and use in heterosexual relations of all the secondary variations of sex activity which loom as primary in homosexual relations are instrumental also in minimising their importance. The effects of chance childhood perversions, the fixation of attention on unusual erogenous zones with consequent transfer of sensitivity from the more normal centres, the absence of a definite and accomplished specialisation of erogenous zones—all the accidents of emotional development which in a civilisation, recognising only one narrow form of sex activity, result in unsatisfactory marriages, casual homosexuality and prostitution, are here rendered harmless. The Samoan puts the burden of amatory success upon the man and believes that women need more initiating, more time for the maturing of sex feeling. A man who fails to satisfy a woman is looked upon as a clumsy, inept blunderer, a fit object for village ridicule and contempt. The women in turn are conscious that their lovers use a definite technique which they regard with a sort of fatalism as if all men had a set of slightly magical, wholly irresistible, tricks up their sleeves. But amatory lore is passed down from one man to another and is looked upon much more self-consciously and analytically by men than by women. Parents are shy of going beyond the bounds of casual conversation (naturally these are much wider than in our civilisation) in the discussion of sex with their children, so that definite instruction passes from the man of twenty-five to the boy of eighteen rather than from father to son. The girls learn from the boys and do very little confiding in each other. All of a man's associates will know every detail of some unusual sex experience while the girl involved will hardly have confided the bare outlines to any one. Her lack of any confidants except relatives towards whom there is always a slight barrier of reserve (I have seen a girl shudder away from acting as an ambassador to her sister) may partly account for this.

The fact that educating one sex in detail and merely fortifying the other sex with enough knowledge and familiarity with sex to prevent shock produces normal sex adjustments is due to the free experimentation which is permitted and the rarity with which both lovers are amateurs. I knew of only one such case, where two children, a sixteen-year-old boy and a fifteen-year-old girl, both in boarding schools on another island, ran away together. Through inexperience they bungled badly. They were both expelled from school, and the boy is now a man of twenty-four with high intelligence and real charm, but a notorious *moetotolo*, execrated by every girl in his village. Familiarity with sex, and the recognition of a need of a technique to deal with sex as an art, have produced a scheme of personal relations in which there are no neurotic pictures, no frigidity, no impotence, except as the temporary result of severe illness, and the capacity for intercourse only once in a night is counted as senility.

Of the twenty-five girls past puberty, eleven had had heterosexual experience. Fala, Tolu, and Namu were three cousins who were popular with the youths of their own village and also with visitors from distant Fitiuta. The women of Fala's family were of easy virtue; Tolu's father was dead and she lived with her blind mother in the home of Namu's parents, who, burdened with six children under twelve years of age, were not going to risk losing two efficient workers by too close supervision. The three girls made common rendezvous with their lovers and their liaisons were frequent and gay. Tolu, the eldest, was a little weary after three years of casual adventures and professed herself willing to marry. She later moved into the household of an important chief in order to improve her chances of meeting strange youths who might be interested in matrimony. Namu was genuinely taken with a boy from Fitiuta whom she met in secret while a boy of her own village whom her parents favoured courted her openly. Occasional assignations with other boys of her own village relieved the monotony of life between visits from her preferred lover. Fala, the youngest, was content to let matters drift. Her lovers were friends and relatives of the lovers of her cousins and she was still sufficiently childlike and uninvolved to get almost as much enjoyment out of her cousins' love affairs as out of her own. All three of these girls worked hard, doing the full quota of work for an adult. All day they fished, washed, worked on the plantation, wove mats and blinds. Tolu was exceptionally clever at weaving. They were valuable economic assets to their families; they would be valuable to the husbands whom their families were not over anxious to find for them.

In the next village lived Luna, a lazy good-natured girl, three years past puberty. Her mother was dead. Her father had married again, but the second wife had gone back to her own people. Luna lived for several years in the pastor's household and had gone home when her stepmother left her father. Her father was a very old chief, tremendously preoccupied with his prestige and reputation in the village. He held an important title; he was a master craftsman; he was the best versed man in the village in ancient lore and details of ceremonial procedure. His daughter was a devoted and efficient attendant. It was enough. Luna tired of the younger girls who had been her companions in the pastor's household and sought instead two young married women among her relatives. One of these, a girl who had deserted her husband and was living with a temporary successor came to live in Luna's household. She and Luna were constant companions, and Luna, quite easily and inevitably took one lover, then two, then a third—all casual affairs. She dressed younger than her years, emphasised that she was still a girl. Some day she would marry and be a church member, but now: *Laititi a'u* ("I am but young"). And who was she to give up dancing.

Her cousin Lotu was a church member, and had attended the missionary boarding school. She had had only one accepted lover, the illegitimate son of a chief who dared not jeopardise his very slender chance of succeeding to his father's title by marrying her. She was the eldest of nine children, living in the third strictly biological family in the village. She showed the effects of greater responsibility at home by a quiet maturity and decision of manner, of her school training in a greater neatness of person and regard for the nicety of detail. Although she was transgressing, the older church members charitably closed their eyes, sympathising with her lover's family dilemma. Her only other sex experience had been with a *moetotolo*, a relative. Should her long fidelity to her lover lead to pregnancy, she would probably bear the child. (When a Samoan woman does wish to avoid giving birth to a child, exceedingly violent massage and the chewing of kava is resorted to, but this is only in very exceptional cases, as even illegitimate children are enthusiastically welcomed.) Lotu's attitudes were more considered, more sophisticated than those of the other girls of her age. Had it not been for the precarious social status of her lover, she would probably have been married already. As it was, she laboured over the care of her younger brothers and sisters, and followed the routine of relationship duties incumbent upon a young girl in the largest family on the island. She reconciled her church membership and her deviation from chastity by the tranquil reflection that she would have married had it been possible, and her sin rested lightly upon her.

In the household of one high chief lived the Samoan version of our devoted maiden aunts. She was docile, efficient, responsible, entirely overshadowed by several more attractive girls. To her were entrusted the newborn babies and the most difficult diplomatic errands. Hard work which she never resented took up all her time and energy. When she was asked to dance, she did so negligently. Others dancing so much more brilliantly, why make the effort? Hers was the appreciative worshipping disposition which glowed over Tolu's beauty or Fala's conquests or Alofi's new baby. She played the ukulele for others to dance, sewed flower necklaces for others to wear, planned rendezvous for others to enjoy, without humiliation or a special air of martyrdom. She admitted that she had had but one lover. He had come from far away; she didn't even know from what village, and he had never come back. Yes, probably she would marry some day if her chief so willed it, and was that the baby crying? She was the stuff of whom devoted aunts are made, depended upon and loved by all about her. A *malaga* to another village might have changed her life, for Samoa boys sought strange girls merely because they were strangers. But she was always needed at home by some one and younger girls went journeying in her stead.

Perhaps the most dramatic story was that of Moana, the last of the group of girls who lived outside the pastors' households, a vain, sophisticated child, spoiled by years of trading upon her older half-sister's devotion. Her amours had begun at fifteen and by the time a year and a half had passed, her parents, fearing that her conduct was becoming so indiscreet as to seriously mar her chances of making a good marriage, asked her uncle to adopt her and attempt to curb her waywardness. This uncle, who was a widower and a sophisticated rake, when he realised the extent of his niece's experience, availed himself also of her complacency. This incident, not common in Samoa, because of the great lack of privacy and isolation, would have passed undetected in this case, if Moana's older sister, Sila, had not been in love with the uncle also. This was the only example of prolonged and intense passion which I found in the three villages. Samoans rate romantic fidelity in terms of days or weeks at most, and are inclined to scoff at tales of life-long devotion. (They greeted the story of Romeo and Juliet with incredulous contempt.) But Sila was devoted to Mutu, her stepfather's younger brother, to the point of frenzy. She had been his mistress and still lived in his household, but his dilettantism had veered away from her indecorous intensity. When she discovered that he had lived with her sister, her fury knew no bounds. Masked under a deep solicitude for the younger girl, whom she claimed was an innocent untouched child, she denounced Mutu the length of the three villages. Moana's parents fetched her home again in a great rage and a family feud resulted. Village feeling ran high, but opinion was divided as to whether Mutu was guilty, Moana lying to cover some other peccadillo or Sila gossiping from spite. The incident was in direct violation of the brother and sister taboo for Mutu was young enough for Moana to speak of him as *tuagane* (brother). But when two months later, another older sister died during pregnancy, it was necessary to find some one stout-hearted enough to perform the necessary Cæsarian postmortem operation. After a violent family debate, expediency triumphed and Mutu, most skilled of native surgeons, was summoned to operate on the dead body of the sister of the girl he had violated. When he later on announced his intention of marrying a girl from another island, Sila again displayed the most uncontrolled grief and despair, although she herself was carrying on a love affair at the time.

The lives of the girls who lived in the pastor's household differed from those of their less restricted sisters and cousins only in the fact that they had no love affairs and lived a more regular and ordered existence. For the excitement of moonlight trysts they substituted group activities, letting the pleasant friendliness of a group of girls fill their lesser leisure. Their interest in salacious material was slightly stronger than the interest of the girls who were free to experiment. They made real friends outside their relationship group, trusted other girls more, worked better in a group, were more at ease with one another but less conscious of their place in their own households than were the others.

Working
STUDS TERKEL

DOLORES DANTE

She has been a waitress in the same restaurant for twenty-three years. Many of its patrons are credit card carriers on an expense account—conventioneers, politicians, labor leaders, agency people. Her hours are from 5:00 P.M. to 2:00 A.M., six days a week. She arrives earlier "to get things ready, the silverware, the butter. When people come in and ask for you, you would like to be in a position to handle them all, because that means more money for you.

"I became a waitress because I needed money fast and you don't get it in an office. My husband and I broke up and he left me with debts and three children. My baby was six months. The fast buck, your tips. The first ten-dollar bill that I got as a tip, a Viking guy gave to me. He was a very robust, terrific atheist. Made very good conversation for us, 'cause I am too.

"Everyone says all waitresses have broken homes. What they don't realize is when people have broken homes they need to make money fast, and do this work. They don't have broken homes because they're waitresses."

I have to be a waitress. How else can I learn about people? How else does the world come to me? I can't go to everyone. So they have to come to me. Everyone wants to eat, everyone has hunger. And I serve them. If they've had a bad day, I nurse them, cajole them. Maybe with coffee I give them a little philosophy. They have cocktails, I give them political science.

I'll say things that bug me. If they manufacture soap, I say what I think about pollution. If it's automobiles, I say what I think about them. If I pour water I'll say, "Would you like your quota of mercury today?" If I serve cream, I say, "Here is your substitute. I think you're drinking plastic." I just can't keep quiet. I have an opinion on every single subject there is. In the beginning it was theology, and my bosses didn't like it. Now I am a political and my bosses don't like it. I speak *sotto voce*. But if I get heated, then I don't give a damn. I speak like an Italian speaks. I can't be servile. I give service. There is a difference.

I'm called by my first name. I like my name. I hate to be called Miss. Even when I serve a lady, a strange woman, I will not say madam. I hate ma'am. I always say milady. In the American language there is no word to address a woman, to indicate whether she's married or unmarried. So I say milady. And sometimes I playfully say to the man milord.

It would be very tiring if I had to say, "Would you like a cocktail?" and say that over and over. So I come out different for my own enjoyment. I would say, "What's exciting at the bar that I can offer?" I can't say, "Do you want coffee?" Maybe I'll say, "Are you in the mood for coffee?" Or, "The coffee sounds exciting." Just rephrase it enough to make it interesting for me. That would make them take an interest. It becomes theatrical and I feel like Mata Hari and it intoxicates me.

People imagine a waitress couldn't possibly think or have any kind of aspiration other than to serve food. When somebody says to me, "You're great, how come you're *just* a waitress?" *Just* a waitress. I'd say, "Why, don't you think you deserve to be served by me?" It's implying that he's not worthy, not that I'm not worthy. It makes me irate. I don't feel lowly at all. I myself feel sure. I don't want to change the job. I love it.

Tips? I feel like Carmen. It's like a gypsy holding out a tambourine and they throw the coin. (Laughs.) If you like people, you're not thinking of the tips. I never count my money at night. I always wait till morning. If I thought about my tips I'd be uptight. I never look at a tip. You pick it up fast. I would do my bookkeeping in the morning. It would be very dull for me to know I was making so much and no more. I do like challenge. And it isn't demeaning, not for me.

There might be occasions when the customers might intend to make it demeaning—the man about town, the conventioneer. When the time comes to pay the check, he would do little things, "How much should I give you?" He might make an issue about it. I did say to one, "Don't play God with me. Do what you want." Then it really didn't matter whether I got a tip or not. I would spit it out, my resentment—that he dares make me feel I'm operating only for a tip.

He'd ask for his check. Maybe he's going to sign it. He'd take a very long time and he'd make me stand there, "Let's see now, what do you think I ought to give you?" He would not let go of that moment. And you knew it. You know he meant to demean you. He's holding the change in his hand, or if he'd sign, he'd flourish the pen and wait. These are the times I really get angry. I'm not reticent. Something would come out. Then I really didn't care. "Goddamn, keep your money!"

There are conventioneers, who leave their lovely wives or their bad wives. They approach you and say, "Are there any hot spots?" "Where can I find girls?" It is, of course, first directed at you. I don't mean that as a compliment, 'cause all they're looking for is females. They're not looking for companionship or conversation. I am quite adept at understanding this. I think I'm interesting enough that someone may just want to talk to me. But I would philosophize that way. After all, what is left after you talk? The hours have gone by and I could be home resting or reading or studying guitar, which I do on occasion. I would say, "What are you going to offer me? Drinks?" And I'd point to the bar, "I have it all here." He'd look blank and then I'd say, "A man? If I need a man, wouldn't you think I'd have one of my own? Must I wait for you?"

Life doesn't frighten me any more. There are only two things that relegate us—the bathroom and the grave. Either I'm gonna have to go to the bathroom now or I'm gonna die now. I go to the bathroom.

And I don't have a high opinion of bosses. The more popular you are, the more the boss holds it over your head. You're bringing them business, but he knows you're getting good tips and you won't leave. You have to worry not to overplay it, because the boss becomes resentful and he uses this as a club over your head.

If you become too good a waitress, there's jealousy. They don't come in and say, "Where's the boss?" They'll ask for Dolores. It doesn't make a hit. That makes it rough. Sometimes you say, Aw hell, why am I trying so hard? I did get an ulcer. Maybe the things I kept to myself were twisting me.

It's not the customers, never the customers. It's injustice. My dad came from Italy and I think of his broken English—*injoost*. He hated injustice. If you hate injustice for the world, you hate more than anything injustice toward you. Loyalty is never appreciated, particularly if you're the type who doesn't like small talk and are not the type who makes reports on your fellow worker. The boss wants to find out what is going on surreptitiously. In our society today you have informers everywhere. They've informed on cooks, on coworkers. "Oh, someone wasted this." They would say I'm talking to all the customers. "I saw her carry such-and-such out. See if she wrote that on her check." "The salad looked like it was a double salad." I don't give anything away. I just give myself. Informers will manufacture things in order to make their job worthwhile. They're not sure of themselves as workers. There's always someone who wants your station, who would be pretender to the crown. In life there is always someone who wants somebody's job.

I'd get intoxicated with giving service. People would ask for me and I didn't have enough tables. Some of the girls are standing and don't have customers. There is resentment. I feel self-conscious. I feel a sense of guilt. It cramps my style. I would like to say to the customer, "Go to so-and-so." But you can't do that, because you feel a sense of loyalty. So you would rush, get to your customers quickly. Some don't care to drink and still they wait for you. That's a compliment.

There is plenty of tension. If the cook isn't good, you fight to see that the customers get what you know they like. You have to use diplomacy with cooks, who are always dangerous. (Laughs.) They're madmen. (Laughs.) You have to be their friend. They better like you. And your bartender better like you too, because he may do something to the drink. If your bartender doesn't like you, your cook doesn't like you, your boss doesn't like you, the other girls don't like you, you're in trouble.

And there will be customers who are hypochondriacs, who feel they can't eat, and I coax them. Then I hope I can get it just the right way from the cook. I may mix the salad myself, just the way they want it.

Maybe there's a party of ten. Big shots, and they'd say, "Dolores, I have special clients, do your best tonight." You just hope you have the right cook behind the broiler. You really want to pleasure your guests. He's selling something, he wants things right, too. You're giving your all. How does the steak look? If you cut his steak, you look at it surreptitiously. How's it going?

Carrying dishes is a problem. We do have accidents. I spilled a tray once with steaks for seven on it. It was a big, gigantic T-bone, all sliced. But when that tray fell, I went with it, and never made a sound, dish and all (softly) never made a sound. It took about an hour and a half to cook that steak. How would I explain this thing? That steak was salvaged. (Laughs.)

Some don't care. When the plate is down you can hear the sound. I try not to have that sound. I want my hands to be right when I serve. I pick up a glass, I want it to be just right. I get to be almost Oriental in the serving. I like it to look nice all the way. To be a waitress, it's an art. I feel like a ballerina, too. I have to go between those tables, between those chairs . . . Maybe that's the reason I always stayed slim. It is a certain way I can go through a chair no one else can do. I do it with an air. If I drop a fork, there is a certain way I pick it up. I know they can see how delicately I do it. I'm on stage.

I tell everyone I'm a waitress and I'm proud. If a nurse gives service, I say, "You're a professional." Whatever you do, be professional. I always compliment people.

I like to have my station looking nice. I like to see there's enough ash trays when they're having their coffee and cigarettes. I don't like ash trays so loaded that people are not enjoying the moment. It offends me. I don't do it because I think that's gonna make a better tip. It offends me as a person.

People say, "No one does good work any more." I don't believe it. You know who's saying that? The man at the top, who says the people beneath him are not doing a good job. He's the one who always said, "You're nothing." The housewife who has all the money, she believed housework was demeaning, 'cause she hired someone else to do it. If it weren't so demeaning, why didn't *she* do it? So anyone who did her housework was a person to be demeaned. The maid who did all the housework said, "Well, hell, if this is the way you feel about it, I won't do your housework. You tell me I'm no good, I'm nobody. Well, maybe I'll go out and be somebody." They're only mad because they can't find someone to do it now. The fault is not in the people who did the—quote—lowly work.

Just a waitress. At the end of the night I feel drained. I think a lot of waitresses become alcoholics because of that. In most cases, a waiter or a waitress doesn't eat. They handle food, they don't have time. You'll pick at something in the kitchen, maybe a piece of bread. You'll have a cracker, a little bit of soup. You go back and take a teaspoonful of something. Then maybe sit down afterwards and have a drink, maybe three, four, five. And bartenders, too, most of them are alcoholics. They'd go out in a group. There are after-hour places. You've got to go release your tension. So they go out before they go to bed. Some of them stay out all night.

It's tiring, it's nerve-racking. We don't ever sit down. We're on stage and the bosses are watching. If you get the wrong shoes and you get the wrong stitch in that shoe, that does bother you. Your feet hurt, your body aches. If you come out in anger at things that were done to you, it would only make you feel cheapened. Really I've been keeping it to myself. But of late, I'm beginning to spew it out. It's almost as though I sensed my body and soul had had quite enough.

It builds and builds and builds in your guts. Near crying. I can think about it . . . (She cries softly.) 'Cause you're tired. When the night is done, you're tired. You've had so much, there's so much going . . . You had to get it done. The dread that something wouldn't be right, because you want to please. You hope everyone is satisfied. The night's done, you've done your act. The curtains close.

The next morning is pleasant again. I take out my budget book, write down how much I made, what my bills are. I'm managing. I won't give up this job as long as I'm able to do it. I feel out of contact if I just sit at home. At work they all consider me a kook. (Laughs.) That's okay. No matter where I'd be, I would make a rough road for me. It's just me, and I can't keep still. It hurts, and what hurts has to come out.

POSTSCRIPT: *"After sixteen years—that was seven years ago—I took a trip to Hawaii and the Caribbean for two weeks. Went with a lover. The kids saw it—they're all married now. (Laughs.) One of my daughters said, 'Act your age.' I said, 'Honey, if I were acting my age, I wouldn't be walking. My bones would ache. You don't want to hear about my arthritis. Aren't you glad I'm happy?' "*

BUD FREEMAN

He is sixty-five years old, though his appearance and manner are of William Blake's "golden youth." He has been a tenor saxophone player for forty-seven years. Highly respected among his colleagues, he is a member of "The World's Greatest Jazz Band." It is a cooperative venture, jointly owned by the musicians, established jazz men.

"I'm with the young people because they refuse to be brainwashed by the things you and I were brainwashed by. My father, although he worked hard all his life, was very easy with us. Dad was being brainwashed by the people in the neighborhood. They'd come in every day and say, 'Why don't your boys go to work?' So he made the mistake of awakening my brother at seven thirty. I pretended to be asleep. Dad said, 'You're going to get up, go out in the world *and get jobs and amount to something.' My brother said, 'How dare you wake us up before the weekend?' (Laughs.) I don't recall ever having seen my father since." (Laughs.)*

I get up about noon. I would only consider myself outside the norm because of the way other people live. They're constantly reminding me I'm abnormal. I could never bear to live the dull lives that most people live, locked up in offices. I live in absolute freedom. I do what I do because I want to do it. What's wrong with making a living doing something interesting?

I wouldn't work for anybody. I'm working for me. Oddly enough, jazz is a music that came out of the black man's oppression, yet it allows for great freedom of expression, perhaps more than any other art form. The jazz man is expressing freedom in every note he plays. We can only please the audience doing what *we* do. We have to please ourselves first.

I know a good musician who worked for Lawrence Welk. The man must be terribly in need of money. It's regimented music. It doesn't swing, it doesn't create, it doesn't tell the story of life. It's just the kind of music that people who don't care for music would buy.

I've had people say to me: "You don't do this for a living, for heaven's sake?" I was so shocked. I said, "What other way am I going to make a living? You want to send me a check?" (Laughs.) People can't understand that there are artists in the world as well as drones.

I only know that as a child I was of a rebellious nature. I saw life as it was planned for most of us. I didn't want any part of that dull life. I worked for Lord and Taylor once, nine to five. It was terribly dull. I lasted six weeks. I couldn't see myself being a nine-to-five man, saving my money, getting married, and having a big family—good God, what a way to live!

I knew when I was eight years old that I wasn't going to amount to anything in the business world. (Laughs.) I wanted my life to have something to do with adventure, something unknown, something involved with a free life, something to do with wonder and astonishment. I loved to play— the fact that I could express myself in improvisation, the *unplanned*.

I love to play now more than ever, because I know a little more about music. I'm interested in developing themes and playing something creative. Life now is not so difficult. We work six months a year. We live around the world. And we don't have to work in night clubs night after night after night.

Playing in night clubs, I used to think, When are we going to get out of here? Most audiences were drunk and you tended to become lazy. And if you were a drinker yourself, there went your music. This is why so many great talents have died or gotten out of it. They hated the music business. I was lucky—now I'm sixty-five—in having played forty-seven years.

If jazz musicians had been given the chance we in this band have today— to think about your work and not have to play all hours of the night, five or six sets—God! Or radio station work or commercial jingle work—the guys must loathe it. I don't think the jazz man has been given a fair chance to do what he really wants to do, to work under conditions where he's not treated like a slave, not subject to the music business, which we've loathed all our lives.

I've come to love my work. It's my way of life. Jazz is a luxurious kind of music. You don't play it all day long. You don't play it all night long. The best way to play it is in concerts. You're on for an hour or two and you give it everything you have, your best. And the audience is sober. And I'm not in a hurry to have the night finish. Playing night clubs, it was endless.

If you're a creative player, something must happen, and it will. Some sort of magic takes place, yet it isn't magic. Hundreds of times I've gone to work thinking, Oh my God, I hate to think of playing tonight. It's going to be awful. But something on a given night takes place and I'm excited before it's over. Does that make sense? If you have that kind of night, you're not aware of the time, because of this thing that hits you.

There's been a lot of untruths told about improvisation. Men just don't get up on the stage and improvise on things they're not familiar with. True improvisation comes out of hard work. When you're practicing at home, you work on a theme and you work out all the possibilities of that theme. Since it's in your head, it comes out when you play. You don't get out on the stage and just improvise, not knowing what the hell you're doing. It doesn't work out that way. Always just before I play a concert, I get the damn horn out and practice. Not scales, but look for creative things to play. I'll practice tonight when I get home, before I go to work. I can't wait to get at it.

I practice because I want to play better. I've never been terribly interested in technique, but I'm interested in facility. To feel comfortable, so when the idea shoots out of my head I can finger it, manipulate it. Something interesting happens. You'll hear a phrase and all of a sudden you're thrown into a whole new inspiration. It doesn't happen every night. But even if I have a terrible night and say, "Oh, I'm so tired, I'll go to sleep and I'll think of other things," the music'll come back. I wasn't too happy about going to work last night because I was tired. It was a drag. But today I feel good. Gonna go home and blow the horn now for a while.

Practicing is no chore to me. I love it. I really do love to play the horn alone. They call me the narcissistic tenor (laughs), because I practice before the mirror. Actually I've learned a great deal looking in the mirror and playing. The dream of all jazz artists is to have enough time to think about their work and play and to develop.

Was there a time when you were altogether bored with your work?

Absolutely. I quit playing for a year. I met a very rich woman. We went to South America to live. We had a house by the sea. I never realized how one could be so rich, so unhappy, and so bored. It frightened me. But I did need a year off. When I came back, I felt fresh.

The other time was when I had a band of my own. I had a name, so I no longer worked for big bands. I was expected to lead one of my own. But I can't handle other people. If I have a group and the pianist, let's say, doesn't like my playing, I can't play. I don't see how these band leaders do it. I can't stand any kind of responsibility other than the music itself. I have to work as a soloist. I can be the custodian only of my own being and thinking.

I had this band and the guys were late all the time. I didn't want to have to hassle with them. I didn't want to mistreat them, so I said, "Fellas, should we quit?" I wouldn't let them go and stay on myself. We were good friends. I'd say I'd quit if they didn't come on time. They started to come on time. But I wasn't a leader. I used to stand by in the band! A bit to the side. (Laughs.) Now we have a cooperative band. So I have a feeling I'm working for myself.

I don't know if I'll make it, but I hope I'll be playing much better five years from now. I oughta, because I know a little bit more of what I'm doing. It takes a lifetime to learn how to play an instrument. We have a lot of sensational young players come up—oh, you hear them for six months, and then they drop out. The kid of the moment, that's right. Real talent takes a long time to mature, to learn how to bring what character you have into sound, into your playing.[1] Not the instrument, but the style of music you're trying to create should be an extension of you. And this takes a whole life.

I want to play for the rest of my life. I don't see any sense in stopping. Were I to live another thirty years—that would make me ninety-five—why not try to play? I can just hear the critics: "Did you hear that wonderful note old man Freeman played last night?" (Laughs.) As Ben Webster[2] says, "I'm going to play this goddamned saxophone until they put it on top of me." It's become dearer to me after having done it for forty-seven years. It's a thing I need to do.

Us and Them

R. D. LAING

Gossip and scandal are always and everywhere elsewhere. Each person is the other to the others. The members of a scandal network may be unified by ideas to which no one will admit in his own person. Each

---

[1] Mme. Lotte Lehmann often spoke of art and age. She recalled a wistful conversation with Maestro Bruno Walter. In his eighties, he reflected on the richness and wisdom of the aged artist and of the long way the young virtuoso had to go—"but he's less tired." It is said that Arturo Toscanini, in his last years, often was thus reflective.

[2] The eminent tenor sax man whose highly creative years were with Duke Ellington.

person is thinking of what he thinks the other thinks. The other, in turn, thinks of what yet another thinks. Each person does not mind a colored lodger, but each person's neighbor does. Each person, however, is a neighbor of his neighbor. What They think is held with conviction. It is indubitable and it is incontestable. The scandal group is a series of others which each serial number repudiates in himself.

It is always the others and always elsewhere, and each person feels unable to make any difference to Them. I have no objection to my daughter marrying a Gentile *really*, but we live in a Jewish neighborhood after all. Such collective power is in proportion to each person's creation of this power and his own impotence. . . .

Now the peculiar thing about Them is that They are created only by each one of us repudiating his own identity. When we have installed Them in our hearts, we are only a plurality of solitudes in which what each person has in common is his allocation to the other of the necessity for his own actions. Each person, however, as other to the other, is the other's necessity. Each denies any internal bond with the others; each person claims his own inessentiality: "I just carried out my orders. If I had not done so, someone else would have." "Why don't you sign? Everyone else has," etc. Yet although I can make no difference, I cannot act differently. No single other person is any more necessary to me than I claim to be to Them. But just as he is "one of Them" to me, so I am "one of Them" to him. In this collection of reciprocal indifference, of reciprocal inessentiality and solitude, there appears to exist no freedom. There is conformity to a *presence* that is everywhere *elsewhere*.

The being of any group from the point of view of the group members themselves is very curious. If I think of you and him as together with me, and others again as not with me, I have already formed two rudimentary syntheses, namely, *We* and *They*. However, this private act of synthesis is not in itself a group. In order that *We* come into being as a group, it is necessary not only that I regard, let us say, you and him and me as *We*, but that you and he also think of us as *We*. I shall call such an act of experiencing a number of persons as a single collectivity, an act of rudimentary group synthesis. In this case *We*, that is each of Us, me, you and him, have performed acts of rudimentary group synthesis. But at present these are simply three private acts of group synthesis. In order that a group really jell, I must realize that you think of yourself as one of Us, as I do, and that he thinks of himself as one of Us, as you and I do. I must ensure furthermore that both you and he realize that I think of myself with you and him, and you and he must ensure likewise that the other two realize that this We is ubiquitous among us, not simply a private illusion on my, your or his part, shared between two of us but not all three. . . .

Under the form of group loyalty, brotherhood and love, an ethic is introduced whose basis is my right to afford the other protection from my violence if he is loyal to me, and to expect his protection from his violence if I am loyal to him, and my obligation to terrorize him with the threat of my violence, if he does not remain loyal.

It is the ethic of the Gadarene swine,[1] to remain true, one for all and all for one, as we plunge in brotherhood to our destruction.

Let there be no illusions about the brotherhood of man. My brother, as dear to me as I am to myself, my twin, my double, my flesh and blood, may be a fellow lyncher as well as a fellow martyr, and in either case is liable to meet his death at my hand if he chooses to take a different view of the situation....

The group becomes a machine—and that it is a man-made machine in which the machine is the very men who make it is forgotten. It is quite unlike a machine made by men, which can have an existence of its own. The group is men themselves arranging themselves in patterns, strata, assuming and assigning different powers, functions, roles, rights, obligations and so on.

The group cannot become an entity separate from men, but men can form circles to encircle other men. The patterns in space and time, their relative permanence and rigidity, do not turn at any time into a natural system or a hyperorganism, although the fantasy can develop, and men can start to live by the fantasy that the relative permanence in space-time of patterns and patterns of patterns is what they must live and die for.

It is as though we all preferred to die to preserve our shadows.

For the group can be nothing else than the multiplicity of the points of view and actions of its members, and this remains true even where, through the interiorization of this multiplicity as synthesized by each, this synthesized multiplicity becomes ubiquitous in space and enduring in time.

It is just as well that man is a social animal, since the sheer complexity and contradiction of the social field in which he has to live is so formidable. This is so even with the fantastic simplifications that are imposed on this complexity, some of which we have examined above.

Our society is a plural one in many senses. Any one person is likely to be a participant in a number of groups, which may have not only different memberships, but quite different forms of unification.

Each group requires more or less radical internal transformation of the persons who comprise it. Consider the metamorphoses that one man may go through in one day as he moves from one mode of sociality to another—family man, speck of crowd dust, functionary in the organization, friend. These are not simply different roles: each is a whole past and present and future, offering differing options and constraints, different degrees of change of inertia, different kinds of closeness and distance, different sets of rights and obligations, different pledges and promises.

I know of no theory of the individual that fully recognizes this. There is every temptation to start with a notion of some supposed basic personality,

---

[1] See Mark 5:1–17.—Eds.

but halo effects are not reducible to one internal system. The tired family man at the office and the tired businessman at home attest to the fact that people carry over, not just one set of internal objects, but *various internalized social modes of being*,[2] often grossly contradictory, from one context to another.

Nor are there such constant emotions or sentiments as love, hate, anger, trust or mistrust. Whatever generalized definitions can be made of each of these at the highest levels of abstraction, specifically and concretely, each emotion is always found in one or another inflection according to the group mode it occurs in. There are no "basic" emotions, instincts or personality, outside of the relationships a person has within one or another social context.[3]

There is a race against time. It is just possible that a further transformation is possible if men can come to experience themselves as "One of Us." If, even on the basis of the crassest self-interest, we can realize that We and They must be transcended in the totality of the human race, if we in destroying them are not to destroy us all.

As war continues, both sides come more and more to resemble each other. The uroborus eats its own tail. The wheel turns full circle. Shall we realize that We and They are shadows of each other? We are They to Them as They are They to Us. When will the veil be lifted? When will the charade turn to carnival? Saints may still be kissing lepers. It is high time that the leper kissed the saint.

Piercing the Veil of the Commonplace[1]
CHARLES FRANKEL

The liberal arts exist in our country and in our time with four great indictments against them. First, they are held to reflect a myth: the myth of man's independent rational mind, the myth that it's in the use of his mind that his true happiness and highest virtue consists.

Second, they're authoritarian. They're imposed on students. They represent the views of a small, tradition-bound clique about what's good for people, views that have been adopted without democratic consultation or popular vote.

Third, they're useless. You don't need the liberal arts to be a statistician or a market analyst or a surgeon or a banker. You certainly don't need them

[2] See "Individual and Family Structure," in *Psychoanalytic Studies of the Family*, edited by P. Lomasz (London: Hogarth Press, 1966).

[3] This [selection], in particular, owes a great deal to *Critique de la Raison Dialectique* (1960) by J.-P. Sartre. It is summarized in *Reason and Violence* (London: Tavistock Publications, 1964), by R. D. Laing and David Cooper.

[1] Adapted from a speech the author gave at the University of Akron.—EDS.

to be a business man or an adviser to Presidents. They waste time, they waste money, they waste words.

Fourth, and probably worst of all, the liberal arts are elitist. Whether the subject is philosophy or grammar, literature or history, if an individual learns something about them, and learns, above all, to pursue them and use them in the formation of his opinions and the expression of his thoughts, then that individual will have drawn away from the opinion that is spoken every day and the language in common use. He will think differently and he will be different. And he will not be different in a way that everyone can understand and respect—like a seven-foot basketball center or a successful folk singer. He will be different in a way that implies that the popular taste is fundamentally wrong. His ideas and his standards will be an insult to the wisdom of the people.

But then, why, with these serious and popular indictments standing against them, do the liberal arts manage to survive at all? Well, one reason is that they do what they have always done. People who are certified as having studied them can escape working with their hands if they wish.

The motivation to escape the necessity of manual labor is a very strong motivation—so strong that immense numbers of people, in response to it, are willing to subject themselves even to the liberal arts.

But of course it isn't the *content* of the liberal arts that leads them to study these subjects; nor does the content of the liberal arts prepare them in any identifiable way, so far as they can see, for the careers they intend to pursue. The liberal arts are hurdles to be jumped, dues to be paid, fraternity hazings to be endured. You get into the club that way: you receive the permit not to have to work with your hands.

Why does the club have these odd entrance requirements? You mustn't ask. They won't let you in the club if you do. It's a conservative club. The people who makes the rules always point to the fact that they go back a long way—to the medieval quadrivium and trivium, even. And of course it's very plain why they're not going to change the rules. They have a vested interest in them. They get their jobs out of them. Teachers of philosophy aren't going to tell you that philosophy does no good for accountants.

That, I think, is a very considerable part of the feeling with which many people now submit to instruction in the liberal arts, and I fear that those who give the instruction, in some considerable number, do not know quite what to say in response. This is not because they don't have answers in their minds; it is because they are embarrassed to state these answers; they feel they will be misunderstood or derided or read out of the fraternity of decent, democratic citizens if they do. They know they have to face the awful charges against the liberal arts—their intellectuality, their authoritarianism, their uselessness, their elitism.

And a defense against such charges, even when perfectly sound, is likely to leave the person who makes the defense permanently scarred. He'll simply be put down as stubborn and assertive in his prejudices. For it ought to be plain that the liberal arts are as anachronistic in the year 1976 as corsets. Indeed, they share similar origins, and have about the same functions—to stifle and conceal.

And yet—and yet, here we are, rededicating ourselves to the liberal arts. And in every generation, even in this one, despite the popular prejudices against the liberal arts, people come to school and choose to study them, and some enjoy them, and some have their lives made over by them. How do we explain this recurrent miracle? What *are* the liberal arts? Why are they liberal? Why are they arts?

The world of learning in 1976 cannot be neatly arranged in a closed system of subjects hierarchically ordered as were the subjects of the curriculum in the Middle Ages. The reason is not simply that ours is a more democratic age, which doesn't approve of hierarchies. It isn't simply that we're a more practical age. In a sense, we're prepared to have many more useless subjects. The Middle Ages were consumingly practical in their ultimate orientation: the supreme purpose of all the arts and sciences was to save the soul.

The disciplines that compose the contemporary world of learning cannot be conclusively fitted into categories and hierarchies for a more important reason. The reason is that we no longer assume that the essential information we need to understand the universe is in hand—given to us by a Revelation not changeable in its fundamental aspects. Study and research aren't conceived to be simply ways of filling in the details in a picture whose main outlines are certain. On the contrary, new knowledge is subversive of the past and moves into a universe whose boundaries are unknown. Knowledge is progressive and growing, and as it progresses and grows it becomes ever more specialized and develops still newer disciplines. Moreover, not only the natural sciences and the descriptive social sciences answer to this description.

The study of history and literature is taken today to be an enterprise of critical *revision*—re-perception of the past, re-judging of the past, re-sifting of it to see what can be retained and used in the living generation.

So no subject—not theology, and heaven knows not philosophy—can be put at the top of the hierarchy. The insights that will basically change our conception of the universe and of the human situation within it may come from any subject, including subjects whose existence we cannot now foresee. And so all the subjects are equal, more or less. The equality of subjects is like the equality of citizens in a democratic polity. Some, at a given moment, may be brighter, quicker, abler than others; some may simply inherit privileged positions; but juridically, before the law, all shall be treated as equal, for we cannot tell from what quarter something of value may emerge, and we cannot rule out *a priori* any opinion that may seek expression.

What, then, does it mean to speak of the liberal arts? In a sense, I think, it means to speak of a *manner* of teaching and study. A subject becomes liberal when it is taught and studied for the purposes that our medieval forebears saw in the quadrivium and trivium. What does it teach not simply within itself but about ubiquitous and recurrent characteristics of the human scene and human destiny? What does it do to liberate the individual from the parochialisms and the egotisms of time and place and self? The liberal arts are liberal if they pierce the veil of the commonplace, if they lift the student from the domination of what is conventional and near at hand. And most subjects can be taught in this way—provided the teacher and the student are not impatient for quick results, provided they don't suppose that the subjects they are studying are inert collections of facts and theories.

Undoubtedly, some subjects lend themselves more easily to this liberating purpose. They are, in the present state of the learned disciplines, the more seminal subjects—the subjects that seem to generate the ideas that shake up the other disciplines. Physics and mathematics have performed this function for a long part of the modern era. Biology and economics now appear to be performing similar functions. And history, philosophy, and literature—rather like the old trivium of grammar, logic, and rhetoric—still function as crossroads subjects, capable of being used for the organization and illumination of ideas in a vast variety of fields. By convention we call these more central, seminal subjects the "liberal arts." And it is a sensible convention, so long as we recognize that it is a convention. The seminal subjects are capable of being converted into pedantries. And the teaching of business management, engineering, or animal husbandry is not exempt from the requirement to seek liberality.

But why the liberal *arts*? I have already implied my own answer, for what it is worth. A *liberal* subject, insofar as it is liberal, affects an individual's way of seeing and thinking and feeling not simply when he is attending to that subject but when he is going about the rest of his business. If he has read *King Lear*, he can't deal with the problem of aging as though it were just a challenge to build more sunshine colonies for the retired. The liberal studies provide a certain perspective; they introduce an extra dimension into experience. They are *arts* for remaking the materials of the commonplace.

George Santayana[2] said of the Italian poet Leopardi[3] that he arrests, he rebukes, he delivers. This is what the liberal arts can do.

They arrest: They make us stop and ask: What is it that we know? What is it that we see? What is it that we believe?

They rebuke: They remind us that our knowledge is three-quarters ignorance, prejudice, sanctified cant; that what we see is image and illusion; that what we believe is yesterday's fashion or today's piety, today's nostrum.

And they deliver: they take us out of ourselves to facts that are not of

---

[2] American philosopher, novelist, and poet (1863–1952).—Eds.
[3] Count Giacomo Leopardi (1798–1837).—Eds.

our making and that we cannot wish away, to ideas and ideals that have transfigured the human race. The greatest of human arts is that of finding a past that has not only made us its victims but can ennoble us; it is that of envisaging a future with an imagination that is larger because it is liberal and more disciplined and prudent because it is liberal.

In brief, when we speak of the liberal arts, we speak of our hopes that we not be our own stupid slaves. The liberal arts do not promise the transformation of humankind. But they offer those privileged enough to be exposed to them a chance to shape their own lives, and the life around them, with some sense of self and context and purpose. All the buildings, all the activities, in the university would lose their saving grace, therefore, were there not, at its heart, an ultimate dedication to the liberal arts.

Getting Smart
JOSIAH BUNTING III

Senator Roman L. Hruska's remarks, some years ago, about providing suitable representation on the United States Supreme Court for mediocre people—mediocre justices—still evokes the knowing snigger of the American intellectual. Of course it should.

There should be no place on the high court of, say 1995–2015, for men and women whose Law Boards in 1976 sank one iota below 795; who did not, as undergraduates and as law students, win sufficient plate and medals, prizes, guerdons and dollars to make themselves top-heavy with pride and ambition. "More brains, dear God, more brains!" screamed George Meredith.[1] *More brains are what is needed.* That is nonsense.

Yet it is mainly upon that dubious, exclusionary principle that many of the best American colleges and universities continue to fill up their undergraduate ranks—with a leaven of freshmen to salve the consciences of administrators and bursars: young people, let us say, who are not so "bright" but who are either "members of minority groups" (whose only commendation, in some cases, is that they *are* members of minority groups) or freshmen who are maybe a little off the wall: "Geez, this kid built his own pedal-propelled airplane and flew it from Saybrook to Clinton."

There is plenty of room in our best colleges for sedulous conners of what are called textbooks, for hypertensive grade-grubbers, for College Board dazzlers. For the rest, for those whose attainments are not of the sort society rewards, who "rank high" neither in "class standing" nor verbal Scholastic Aptitude Tests, there is nothing but attendance at colleges that are called second-rate, or the "job-market," or, shall we say, the Volunteer Army. And it is precisely from the ranks of "these" young people that will

---

[1] British novelist and poet (1828–1909).—EDS.

come the greater portion of those who will lead and sustain the United States in the year 2000.

Of course it is nonsense to agree with Meredith. We don't need more brains. We have plenty of brains. We need young men and women imbued with the notion of *service*, young people prepared to efface personal egoisms in larger causes, people prepared to do the drudge-work that brings neither lucre nor public recognition, people who can lead because they have been willing to follow, people whose intellectualism is not cynical and overweening, young people who understand that the most overrated decision they shall be called upon to make in their young lives is the decision about where they will go to college. We have plenty of young good minds; we have far fewer tender hearts and brave souls.

Could Picasso ace his math Scholastic Aptitude Test? Could Lincoln recognize the subjunctive voice in Latin? Could Churchill make sense of the differential calculus? Did Martin Luther King know Hopkins from Keats? What's the Latin word for parsley?

Colleges exist for two reasons: to make people think better—and this is paramount—but also to give them the experience of living in a community—an agglomeration of young men and women in which the actions of each touch the lives of all.

And it is in the latter mission, and the process by which those whose contributions to it, in college and after, might be estimable, that those who have not always made successful obeisance before the bitch-goddess of the College Boards too frequently are flipped to the reject pile on the desks of admissions officers.

Evidence to give patient, unrewarded service to their communities should be a critical element upon which admission to colleges is based. Those whose *instinct* so dictates will not uncommonly be found to possess brains, and *those* brains can be cultivated, and those students can be inspired, and it is *those* students who will lead and serve this country later: patiently, honestly, doggedly.

It is among *these* young people that will, more often than not, be found the George Catlett Marshalls,[2] the Sam Rayburns,[3] the Lincolns. And besides, twenty years after they leave college, *they* will not be reading the latest silly best-selling nonfiction palaver on "interpersonal relations," but Burke,[4] and Thucydides,[5] and Sterne[6] and Melville.[7] For their education will not have interfered with their learning.

[2] George Catlett Marshall (1880–1959), American general, secretary of state, and author of the Marshall Plan.—EDS.

[3] Sam Rayburn (1882–1961), longtime Speaker of the U.S. House of Representatives.—EDS.

[4] Edmund Burke (1729–1797), British parliamentary leader, who espoused the cause of the American colonies.—EDS.

[5] Greek historian and general (*c.* 471–*c.* 400 B.C.).—EDS.

[6] Laurence Sterne (1713–1768), British novelist, author of *Tristram Shandy*.—EDS.

[7] Herman Melville (1819–1891), American novelist, short-story writer, and poet; author of *Moby-Dick*.—EDS.

It is not anti-intellectualism to say so. It is plain common sense, which, in the case of our sparkling citadels of what is called higher learning, we have not got. And we'd better get it, fast.

Secrets of the Evergreen People
ROY LARSON

In old age, in a path of beauty, lively may you walk.
—An Indian "wish"

Our party host popped the question: "Is there anyone here who still has a hero?" Sensing that the expected answer was "no," I said "yes."

One of the other guests was polite enough to ask, "Who is it?"

"The wild ass of Arabia," I replied brightly.

It was obvious from their expressions that some of the guests didn't take me seriously. One, however, indulged me by asking, "And where did you meet your hero?"

"In the book of Job," I said. "There the wild ass, also known as the 'swift ass,' is introduced as one who 'searches after everything green.'"

"Why does that make him a hero?" my questioner persisted.

"Because," I went on, "I think the wild ass knows what it takes to stay spiritually alive. He keeps gravitating toward everything that's green and fresh and alive."

At this point the conversation was diverted into a discussion of our unheroic age by our host who ruled me out of court by saying, "Number one, your hero is fictional, not real, and number two, he is from another age."

After that putdown there was nothing left for me to do but sip and sulk. But I still think my nomination was in order. To me, no question in contemporary American culture is more interesting than the question: "What is the secret of those people—those evergreen people—who become more and more alive as they grow older, in contrast to those who experience psychological death at an early age?"

Several years ago novelist John Gardner addressed this question in *No Easy Victories*:

> Perhaps the greatest challenge in education—and the most puzzling one—is to discover what it is that keeps alive in some people the natural spark of curiosity, eagerness, hunger for life and experience, and how we can rekindle that spark when it flickers out. If we ever solve that problem we will be at the threshold of a new era.

It's obvious to anyone with the eyes to see that we still haven't approached that threshold, let alone crossed it. In 1975 Sam Keen was still trying "to discover what it is" in his autobiographical book, *Beginnings Without End*, where he wistfully reported.

> My father is dead. But I have not entirely ceased to long for a benevolent and wise authority who will reveal the laws of reality and tell me what I must do to gain eternal life, achieve satori,[1] or prevent premature senility.

The wisest authorities I know on this subject are those who now are "walking lively" in their old age. In some idle moments recently, I doodled a list of the 10 people I have met who belong in the Wild Asses' Hall of Fame because they have never abandoned the search for "everything green." After making the list, I asked myself: "What characteristics do these people have in common?"

At first I was more impressed by the diversity of my hall-of-famers than their sameness. Some are affluent, a couple have very modest means. One is a bawdy old man, but another is quite pious. Politically some regard themselves as conservatives while others have a liberal self-image.

Nonetheless, further reflection made it clear my candidates do have a number of common traits:

1—They carry their eggs in more than one basket. The meaning of their lives is derived from several sources—family and friends, work and leisure, private interests and public concerns. To borrow the language of Paul Tillich,[2] they do not confuse the relative with the ultimate. Their only god is God.

2—They have a capacity for intimacy. In his apologia for fairy tales in *The New Yorker*, Bruno Bettelheim wrote: "If one has found true adult love, the fairy tales make plain, one doesn't need to wish for eternal life." The only thing, Bettelheim added, which can "take the sting out of recognition of the narrow limits of our time on this Earth [is] forming a truly satisfying bond with another."

3—They are rooted in at least one community where they know how it feels to be "surrounded by a whole circle of approving eyes." Some find this in their neighborhoods; others in churches or synagogs, professional societies or volunteer organizations, "larger families" or clusters of friends.

4—They define prestige and success in terms of vitality, not in terms of social status, financial position or professional achievement. They "walk lively" because they love life, not abstractions like job titles, university degrees, club memberships, proper addresses and the right friends.

5—Instead of allowing their lives to be trivialized, they feel at home in "the dimension of depth." As someone put it, they know you find oil, not by drilling foot-deep holes in scores of places, but by drilling deeply into a few well-chosen spots.

6—They do not try to fashion the rest of the world in their own image,

---

[1] "Sudden enlightenment," a Zen word of Japanese origin.—EDS.
[2] Influential modern theologian (1886–1965).—EDS.

but respect the "otherness of the other" (Martin Buber[3]) and relish human diversity. They are able to enjoy "unselected reality" (Buber) because they have freed themselves from the compulsion to overcontrol their own lives and officiously manage the lives of others.

7—They combine competence with insouciance. No one seems to make it in old age who has not demonstrated somewhere along the way that he or she is good at something worth doing. Once their competence is proved, they are freed from the curse of earnest striving and can develop a talent for taking themselves lightly.

8—They remain in constant communication with their own insides. Without becoming narcissistic, they have learned with Theodore Roethke[4] to "stay alive, both in and out of time, by listening to the spirit's smallest cry."

If someone would say, "OK, that's fine, but how do you get that way?" I would reply: "Each day there is set before us the choice between life and death, vitality and sterility. Somehow we have to get ourselves into the habit of saying 'yes' to life."

I Think Continually of Those Who Were Truly Great
STEPHEN SPENDER

I think continually of those who were truly great.
Who, from the womb, remembered the soul's history
Through corridors of light where the hours are suns,
Endless and singing. Whose lovely ambition
Was that their lips, still touched with fire,
Should tell of the Spirit, clothed from head to foot in song.
And who hoarded from the Spring branches
The desires falling across their bodies like blossoms.

What is precious, is never to forget
The essential delight of the blood drawn from ageless springs
Breaking through rocks in worlds before our earth.
Never to deny its pleasure in the morning simple light
Nor its grave evening demand for love.
Never to allow gradually the traffic to smother
With noise and fog the flowering of the Spirit.

---

[3] Jewish theologian and philosopher (1878–1965). See section five of this book, "Final Things," for his "I-Thou" essay ("God and the Spirit of Man").—Eds.

[4] Contemporary American poet (1907–1963).—Eds.

Near the snow, near the sun, in the highest fields,
See how these names are fêted by the waving grass
And by the streamers of white cloud
And whispers of wind in the listening sky.
The names of those who in their lives fought for life,
Who wore at their hearts the fire's centre.
Born of the sun, they travelled a short while toward the sun,
And left the vivid air signed with their honor.

2
Society

Politics and Economics

War

Sports

Minorities

Women

The essays in this section concern themselves with notions of the *Good Society*. Has a good society been realized? Can we realize it at some time in the future? Or is humanity condemned to live in a society more bad than good? Is the life of people in a natural condition always, as Thomas Hobbes phrased it in 1651, "solitary, poor, nasty, brutish, and short"? Can we possibly create a world of material well-being where people are kind, generous, relaxed, humane, and long-lived? If we do, it will come partly from a recognition of current problems and those of the past.

In the first essay, Judge Learned Hand gives the premise for the search for this better society when he remarks, "All discussion, all debate, all dissidence tends to question and in consequence to upset existing convictions; that is precisely its purpose and its justification." In their quest for the Good Society, the citizens of the United States debated the Declaration of Independence, the Bill of Rights, and the Constitution. Today Kenneth Arrow finds that although capitalism contains contradictions, it is not doomed. Peter F. Drucker, however, observes that the Trojan horse of invested money has already begun to produce a pension-fund socialism that is far more effective than the doctrinaire socialism of Edward Bellamy.

But this scenario, with its rosy ending, overlooks much that is suggested in the cynical observations of Machiavelli, the sinister advice on modern corporate life of Michael Korda, and most of all the essays on war—from "The Hot Gates" of William Golding to the even hotter ones of the Americans' late venture into Vietnam. Though it is hard to find much debate today on the general proposition that war is hell, Golding recognizes in the immediate failure of Leonidas the seed somehow sown for the Golden Age of Greece; and both he and Stephen Crane discern a tragic dignity amid the meaninglessness and squalor of battle.

If we can envision an end to war, the growing interest in athletic activities may offer sports as a kind of "moral equivalent of war," proposed long ago by the philosopher William James. Though professional sports and even organized athletics have not often been held in high esteem by intellectuals, a growing recognition of sports as a poetry of the body and of the community has emerged. We have already seen in section one (in "The Football Phenomenon on Campus") that for many people football is "more than a game." Studies here of some extraordinary athletes bring into focus many dimensions and facets of sports beyond athletic prowess. Rhodes scholar Bill Bradley's thoughtful observations about his own basketball career, about winning and losing, and about "those few years of intensified youth" that belong to the professional athlete strike a universal note. For men and for women, Billie Jean King has brought a greater sense of meaning to tennis and to sport; and for whites as well as blacks, Muhammad Ali has given boxing a spiritual dimension. It may be that sports needs no formal defense.

We end the section with some representative comments on two of the most pressing problems that face society today—the injustices directed toward ethnic minorities and those directed toward women. Neither problem is new, as the account of the massacre at Wounded Knee and the challenge of Mary Wollstonecraft make clear. Neither is without its joys, as N. Scott Momaday's remembrance of a Pueblo feast and Oriana Fallaci's personal solution of her lifestyle remind us. And in the midst of the individual frustrations and social dislocations, we have heard compelling voices of hope in the dreams of Martin Luther King, Jr., and in the sensitive, honest poetry of Adrienne Rich. All of these remind us again of Judge Hand's observation that discussion, debate, and dissidence are the powerful and necessary agents for knowing the truth about ourselves and about the world we live in.

Politics and Economics

A Plea for the Freedom of Dissent
LEARNED HAND

What do we mean by "principles of civil liberties and human rights"? We cannot go far in that inquiry until we have achieved some notion of what we mean by Liberty; and that has always proved a hard concept to define. The natural, though naive, opinion is that it means no more than that each individual shall be allowed to pursue his own desires without let or hindrance; and that, although it is true that this is practically impossible, still it does remain the goal, approach to which measures our success. Why, then, is not a beehive or an anthill a perfect example of a free society? Surely you have been a curious and amused watcher beside one of these.

In and out of their crowded pueblo the denizens pass in great number, each bent upon his own urgent mission, quite oblivious of all the rest except as he must bend his path to avoid them. It is a scene of strenuous, purposeful endeavor in which each appears to be, and no doubt in fact is, accomplishing his own purpose; and yet he is at the same time accomplishing the purpose of the group as a whole. As I have gazed at it, the sentence from the Collect of the Episcopal prayerbook has come to me: "Whose service is perfect freedom."

Why is it, then, that we so positively rebel against the hive and the hill as a specimen of a free society? Why is it that such prototypes of totalitarianisms arouse our deepest hostility? Unhappily it is not because they cannot be realized, or at least because they cannot be approached, for a substantial period. Who can be sure that such appalling forecasts as Aldous Huxley's *Brave New World* or Orwell's *1984*[1] are not prophetic? Indeed, there have often been near approaches to such an order.

Germany at the end of 1940 was probably not far removed from one, and who of us knows that there are not countless persons today living within the boundaries of Russia and perhaps of China who are not willing partners, accepting as their personal aspirations the official definitions of the good, the true and the beautiful? Indeed, there have been, and still are, in our own United States large and powerful groups who, if we are to judge their purposes by their conduct, see treason in all dissidence and

---

[1] Huxley's and Orwell's anti-utopias appeared, respectively, in 1932 and 1949.—EDS.

would welcome an era in which all of us should think, feel and live in consonance with duly prescribed patterns.[2]

Human nature is malleable, especially if you can indoctrinate the disciple with indefectible principles before anyone else reaches him. (I fancy that the Janissaries[3] were as fervent Mohammedans as the authentic Turks.) Indeed, we hear from those who are entitled to an opinion that at times the abject confessions made in Russia by victims who know that they are already marked for slaughter are not wrung from them by torture or threats against their families. Rather, they come from partisans, so obsessed with the faith that when they are told that the occasion calls for scapegoats and that they have been selected, recognize and assent to the propriety of the demand and cooperate in its satisfaction. It is as though, when the right time comes, the drones agreed to their extinction in the interest of the hive.

Nor need we be surprised that men so often embrace almost any doctrines, if they are proclaimed with a voice of absolute assurance. In a universe that we do not understand, but with which we must in one way or another somehow manage to deal, and aware of the conflicting desires that clamorously beset us, between which we must choose and which we must therefore manage to weigh, we turn in our bewilderment to those who tell us that they have found a path out of the thickets and possess the scales by which to appraise our needs.

Over and over again such prophets succeed in converting us to unquestioning acceptance; there is scarcely a monstrous belief that has not had its day and its passionate adherents, so eager are we for safe footholds in our dubious course. How certain is any one of us that he, too, might not be content to follow any fantastic creed, if he was satisfied that nothing would ever wake him from the dream? And, indeed, if there were nothing to wake him, how should he distinguish its articles from the authentic dictates of verity?

Remember, too, that it is by no means clear that we are happier in the faith we do profess than we should be under the spell of an orthodoxy that was sage against all heresy. Cruel and savage as othodoxies have always proved to be, the faithful seem able to convince themselves that the heretics, as they continue to crop up, get nothing worse than their due, and to rest with an easy conscience.

In any event, my thesis is that the best answer to such systems is not so much in their immoral quality—immoral though they be—as in the fact that they are inherently unstable because they are at war with our only trustworthy way of living in accord with the facts. For I submit that it is

---

[2] Judge Hand probably refers primarily to the investigations of supposed Communist infiltration into government conducted by Senator Joseph R. McCarthy in 1953–1954: they were preceded and followed by a widespread feeling of "treason in all dissidence." —Eds.

[3] An elite corps of Turkish troops.—Eds.

only by trial and error, by insistent scrutiny and by readiness to re-examine presently accredited conclusions that we have risen, so far as in fact we have risen, from our brutish ancestors, and I believe that in our loyalty to these habits lies our only chance, not merely of progress, but even of survival.

They were not indeed a part of our aboriginal endowment: Man, as he emerged, was not prodigally equipped to master the infinite diversity of his environment. Obviously, enough of us did manage to get through; but it has been a statistical survival, for the individual's native powers of adjustment are by no means enough for his personal safety any more than are those of other creatures. The precipitate of our experience is far from absolute verity, and our exasperated resentment at all dissent is a sure index of our doubts. Take, for instance, our constant recourse to the word, "subversive," as a touchstone of impermissible deviation from accepted canons.

All discussion, all debate, all dissidence tends to question and in consequence to upset existing convictions: that is precisely its purpose and its justification. He is, indeed, a "subversive" who disputes those precepts that I most treasure and seeks to persuade me to substitute his own. He may have no shadow of desire to resort to anything but persuasion; he may be of those to whom any forcible sanction of conformity is anathema; yet it remains true that he is trying to bring about my apostasy, and I hate him just in proportion as I fear his success.

Contrast this protective resentment with the assumption that lies at the base of our whole system that the best chance for truth to emerge is a fair field for all ideas. Nothing, I submit, more completely betrays our latent disloyalty to this premise to all that we pretend to believe than the increasingly common resort to this and other question-begging words. Their imprecision comforts us by enabling us to suppress arguments that disturb our complacency and yet to continue to congratulate ourselves on keeping the faith as we have received it from the Founding Fathers.

Heretics have been hateful from the beginning of recorded time; they have been ostracized, exiled, tortured, maimed and butchered; but it has generally proved impossible to smother them, and when it has not, the society that has succeeded has always declined. Façades of authority, however imposing, do not survive after it has appeared that they rest upon the sands of human conjecture and compromise.

And so, if I am to say what are "the principles of civil liberties and human rights," I answer that they lie in habits, customs—conventions, if you will—that tolerate dissent and can live without irrefragable certainties; that are ready to overhaul existing assumptions; that recognize that we never see save through a glass, darkly,[4] and that at long last we shall succeed only so far as we continue to undertake "the intolerable labor of thought"—that most distasteful of all our activities.

If such a habit and such a temper pervade a society, it will not need in-

---

[4] Cf. I Corinthians 13:12.—EDS.

stitutions to protect its "civil liberties and human rights"; so far as they do not, I venture to doubt how far anything else can protect them: whether it be Bills of Rights, or courts that must in the name of interpretation read their meaning into them.

This may seem to you a bleak and cheerless conclusion, too alien to our nature to be practical. "We must live from day to day"—you will say—"to live is to act, and to act is to choose and decide. How can we carry on at all without some principles, some patterns to meet the conflicts in which each day involves us?" Indeed, we cannot, nor am I suggesting that we should try; but I *am* suggesting that it makes a vital difference—*the* vital difference—whether we deem our principles and our patterns to be eternal verities, rather than the best postulates so far attainable.

Was it not Holmes[5] who said: "The highest courage is to stake everything on a premise that you know tomorrow's evidence may disprove"? "Ah"—you will reply—"there's the rub. That may be the highest courage, but how many have it? You are hopelessly wrong if you assume the general prevalence of such a virtue; ordinary men must be given more than conjectures if they are to face grave dangers."

But do you really believe that? Do you not see about you every day and everywhere the precise opposite? Not alone on the battlefield but in the forest, the desert and the plain; in the mountains, at sea, on the playing field, even in the laboratory and the factory—yes (do not laugh), at the card table and the racetrack—men are forever putting it "upon the touch to win or lose it all." Without some smack of uncertainty and danger, to most of us the world would be a tepid, pallid show.

Surely, like me, you have all felt something of this when you have looked on those pathetic attempts to depict in paint or stone the delights of paradise. I own that the torments of hell never fail to horrify me; not even the glee of the demons in charge is an adequate relief, though the artist has generally been successful in giving a veracious impression of the gusto with which they discharge their duties.

But when I turn to the Congregation of the Blessed, I cannot avoid a sense of anticlimax; strive as I may, the social atmosphere seems a bit forced; and I recalled those very irreverent verses of Lowes Dickinson[6]:

> Burning at first no doubt would be worse,
> But time the impression would soften,
> While those who are bored with praising the Lord,
> Would be more bored with praising him often.

By some happy fortuity man is a projector, a designer, a builder, a craftsman; it is among his most dependable joys to impose upon the flux that passes before him some mark of himself, aware though he always must be

---

[5] Oliver Wendell Holmes, Jr., associate justice of the U.S. Supreme Court, 1902–1932.—Eds.

[6] British man of letters (1862–1932).—Eds.

of the odds against him. His reward is not so much in the work as in its making; not so much in the prize as in the race. We may win when we lose, if we have done what we can; for by so doing we have made real at least some part of that finished product in whose fabrication we are most concerned—ourselves.

And if at the end some friendly critic shall pass by and say, "My friend, how good a job do you really think you have made of it all?" we can answer, "I know as well as you that it is not of high quality, but I did put into it whatever I had, and that was the game I started out to play."

It is still in the lap of the gods whether a society can succeed, based on "civil liberties and human rights," conceived as I have tried to describe them; but of one thing at least we may be sure: the alternatives that have so far appeared have been immeasurably worse, and so, whatever the outcome, I submit to you that we must press along. Borrowing from Epictetus,[7] let us say to ourselves: "Since we are men we will play the part of a Man," and how can I better end than by recalling to you the concluding passage of "Prometheus Unbound"?[8]

> To suffer woes which Hope thinks infinite;
> To forgive wrongs darker than death or night;
> To defy Power, which seems omnipotent
> To love, and bear; to hope till Hope creates
> From its own wreck the thing it contemplates;
> Neither to change, nor falter, nor repent;
> This, like thy glory, Titan, is to be
> Good, great and joyous, beautiful and free;
> This is alone Life, Joy, Empire and Victory.

Declaration of Independence[1]
THOMAS JEFFERSON

When, in the course of human events, it becomes necessary for one people to dissolve the political bands which have connected them with another, and to assume among the powers of the earth the separate and equal station to which the laws of nature and of nature's God entitle them, a decent respect to the opinions of mankind requires that they should declare the causes which impel them to the separation.

We hold these truths to be self-evident: That all men are created equal;

---

[7] Greco-Roman Stoic philosopher (c. 50–120 A.D.).—EDS.
[8] Percy Bysshe Shelley's verse drama, IV, lines 569–577.—EDS.

[1] The unanimous declaration of the thirteen United States of America, in Congress, July 4, 1776.

that they are endowed by their Creator with certain inalienable rights; that among these are life, liberty, and the pursuit of happiness. That, to secure these rights, governments are instituted among men, deriving their just powers from the consent of the governed; that, whenever any form of government becomes destructive of these ends, it is the right of the people to alter or to abolish it, and to institute a new government, laying its foundation on such principles, and organizing its powers in such form, as to them shall seem most likely to effect their safety and happiness. Prudence, indeed, will dictate that governments long established should not be changed for light and transient causes; and accordingly all experience hath shown that mankind are more disposed to suffer, while evils are sufferable, than to right themselves by abolishing the forms to which they are accustomed. But when a long train of abuses and usurpations, pursuing invariably the same object, evinces a design to reduce them under absolute despotism, it is their right, it is their duty, to throw off such government and to provide new guards for their future security. Such has been the patient suffering of these colonies, and such is now the necessity which constrains them to alter their former systems of government. The history of the present king of Great Britain is a history of repeated injuries and usurpations, all having in direct object the establishment of an absolute tyranny over these states. To prove this, let facts be submitted to a candid world.

He has refused his assent to laws the most wholesome and necessary for the public good.

He has forbidden his governors to pass laws of immediate and pressing importance, unless suspended in their operation till his assent should be obtained, and, when so suspended, he has utterly neglected to attend to them.

He has refused to pass other laws for the accommodation of large districts of people, unless those people would relinquish the right of representation in the legislature—a right inestimable to them and formidable to tyrants only.

He has called together legislative bodies, at places unusual, uncomfortable, and distant from the repository of their public records, for the sole purpose of fatiguing them into compliance with his measures.

He has dissolved representative houses repeatedly for opposing with manly firmness his invasions on the rights of the people.

He has refused for a long time after such dissolutions to cause others to be elected; whereby the legislative powers, incapable of annihilation, have returned to the people at large for their exercise: the state remaining, in the meantime, exposed to all the dangers of invasion from without and convulsions within.

He has endeavored to prevent the population of these states; for that purpose obstructing the laws for naturalization of foreigners; refusing to pass others to encourage their migration hither, and raising the conditions of new appropriations of lands.

He has obstructed the administration of justice by refusing his assent to laws for establishing his judiciary powers.

He has made judges dependent on his will alone for the tenure of their offices and the amount and payment of their salaries.

He has erected a multitude of new offices and sent hither swarms of officers to harass our people and eat out their substance.

He has kept among us, in times of peace, standing armies without the consent of our legislatures.

He has affected to render the military independent of and superior to the civil power.

He has combined with others to subject us to a jurisdiction foreign to our constitutions and unacknowledged by our laws, giving his assent to their acts of pretended legislation:

For quartering large bodies of armed troops among us;

For protecting them by a mock trial from punishment for any murders which they should commit on the inhabitants of these states;

For cutting off our trade with all parts of the world;

For imposing taxes on us without our consent;

For depriving us in many cases of the benefits of trial by jury;

For transporting us beyond seas to be tried for pretended offenses;

For abolishing the free system of English laws in a neighboring province, establishing therein an arbitrary government, and enlarging its boundaries so as to render it at once an example and fit instrument for introducing the same absolute rule into these colonies;

For taking away our charters, abolishing our most valuable laws, and altering fundamentally the forms of our government;

For suspending our own legislatures and declaring themselves invested with power to legislate for us in all cases whatsoever.

He has abdicated government here by declaring us out of his protection and waging war against us.

He has plundered our seas, ravaged our coasts, burnt our towns and destroyed the lives of our people.

He is at this time transporting large armies of foreign mercenaries to complete the work of death, desolation, and tyranny already begun, with circumstances of cruelty and perfidy scarcely parallelled in the most barbarous ages and totally unworthy the head of a civilized nation.

He has constrained our fellow citizens taken captive upon the high seas to bear arms against their country, to become the executioners of their friends and brethren, or to fall themselves by their hands.

He has excited domestic insurrection amongst us, and has endeavored to bring on the inhabitants of our frontiers the merciless Indian savages, whose known rule of warfare is an undistinguished destruction of all ages, sexes, and conditions.

In every stage of these oppressions we have petitioned for redress, in the most humble terms; our repeated petitions have been answered only by repeated injury. A prince whose character is thus marked by every act which may define a tyrant is unfit to be the ruler of a free people.

Nor have we been wanting in attention to our British brethren. We have warned them, from time to time, of attempts by their legislature to extend an unwarrantable jurisdiction over us. We have reminded them of the circumstances of our emigration and settlement here. We have appealed to their native justice and magnanimity; and we have conjured them by the ties of our common kindred, to disavow these usurpations, which would inevitably interrupt our connections and correspondence. They, too, have been deaf to the voice of justice and consanguinity. We must, therefore, acquiesce in the necessity which denounces our separation, and hold them, as we hold the rest of mankind, enemies in war; in peace, friends.

We, therefore, the representatives of the United States of America, in general congress assembled, appealing to the Supreme Judge of the World for the rectitude of our intentions, do, in the name and by the authority of the good people of these colonies, solemnly publish and declare that these united colonies are, and of right ought to be, free and independent states; that they are absolved from all allegiance to the British crown, and that all political connection between them and the state of Great Britain is, and ought to be, totally dissolved; and that as free and independent states they have full power to levy war, conclude peace, contract alliances, establish commerce, and to do all other acts and things which independent states may of right do. And for the support of this declaration, with a firm reliance on the protection of Divine Providence, we mutually pledge to each other our lives, our fortunes, and our sacred honor.

Speech in the Constitutional Convention at the Conclusion of Its Deliberations, September 17, 1787

BENJAMIN FRANKLIN

Mr. President,

I confess, that I do not entirely approve of this Constitution at present; but, Sir, I am not sure I shall never approve it; for, having lived long, I have experienced many instances of being obliged, by better information or fuller consideration, to change opinions even on important subjects, which I once thought right, but found to be otherwise. It is therefore that, the older I grow, the more apt I am to doubt my own judgment of others. Most men, indeed, as well as most sects in religion, think themselves in possession of all truth, and that wherever others differ from them, it is so far error. Steele,[1] a Protestant, in a dedication, tells the Pope, that the only

[1] Richard Steele (1672–1729), best known for his essays in *The Tatler* (1709–1711) and *The Spectator* (1711–1712, 1714).—Eds.

difference between our two churches in their opinions of the certainty of their doctrine, is, the Romish Church is *infallible,* and the Church of England is *never in the wrong.* But, though many private persons think almost as highly of their own infallibility as of that of their sect, few express it so naturally as a certain French lady, who, in a little dispute with her sister, said, "But I meet with nobody but myself that is *always* in the right." *"Je ne trouve que moi qui aie toujours raison."*

In these sentiments, Sir, I agree to this Constitution, with all its faults—if they are such; because I think a general government necessary for us, and there is no *form* of government but what may be a blessing to the people, if well administered; and I believe, further, that this is likely to be well administered for a course of years, and can only end in despotism, as other forms have done before it, when the people shall become so corrupted as to need despotic government, being incapable of any other. I doubt, too, whether any other convention we can obtain, may be able to make a better constitution; for, when you assemble a number of men, to have the advantage of their joint wisdom, you inevitably assemble with those men all their prejudices, their passions, their errors of opinion, their local interests, and their selfish views. From such an assembly can a *perfect* production be expected? It therefore astonishes me, Sir, to find this system approaching so near to perfection as it does; and I think it will astonish our enemies, who are waiting with confidence to hear, that our counsels are confounded like those of the builders of Babel, and that our States are on the point of separation, only to meet hereafter for the purpose of cutting one another's throats. Thus I consent, Sir, to this Constitution, because I expect no better, and because I am not sure that it is not the best. The opinions I have had of its *errors* I sacrifice to the public good. I have never whispered a syllable of them abroad. Within these walls they were born, and here they shall die. If every one of us, in returning to our constituents, were to report the objections he has had to it, and endeavour to gain partisans in support of them, we might prevent its being generally received, and thereby lose all the salutary effects and great advantages resulting naturally in our favor among foreign nations, as well as among ourselves, from our real or apparent unanimity. Much of the strength and efficiency of any government, in procuring and securing happiness to the people, depends on *opinion,* on the general opinion of the goodness of that government, as well as of the wisdom and integrity of its governors. I hope, therefore, for our own sakes, as a part of the people, and for the sake of our posterity, that we shall act heartily and unanimously in recommending this Constitution, wherever our influence may extend, and turn our future thoughts and endeavors to the means of having it *well administered.*

On the whole, Sir, I cannot help expressing a wish, that every member of the convention who may still have objections to it, would with me on this occasion doubt a little of his own infallibility, and, to make *manifest* our *unanimity,* put his name to this instrument.

The Bill of Rights[1]

ARTICLE I

Congress shall make no law respecting an establishment of religion, or prohibiting the free exercise thereof; or abridging the freedom of speech, or of the press; or the right of the people peaceably to assemble, and to petition the government for a redress of grievances.

ARTICLE II

A well regulated militia being necessary to the security of a free State, the right of the people to keep and bear arms, shall not be infringed.

ARTICLE III

No soldier shall, in time of peace be quartered in any house, without the consent of the owner, nor in time of war, but in a manner to be prescribed by law.

ARTICLE IV

The right of the people to be secure in their persons, houses, papers, and effects, against unreasonable searches and seizures, shall not be violated, and no warrants shall issue, but upon probable cause, supported by oath or affirmation, and particularly describing the place to be searched, and the persons or things to be seized.

ARTICLE V

No person shall be held to answer for a capital, or otherwise infamous crime, unless on a presentment or indictment of a grand jury, except in cases arising in the land or naval forces, or in the militia, when in actual service in time of war or public danger; nor shall any person be subject for the same offense to be twice put in jeopardy of life or limb; nor shall be compelled in any criminal case to be a witness against himself, nor be deprived of life, liberty, or property, without due process of law; nor shall private property be taken for public use without just compensation.

ARTICLE VI

In all criminal prosecutions, the accused shall enjoy the right to a speedy and public trial, by an impartial jury of the State and district wherein the

[1] Passed by Congress, September 25, 1789; ratified by three-fourths of the states, December 15, 1791.

crime shall have been committed, which district shall have been previously ascertained by law, and to be informed of the nature and cause of the accusation; to be confronted with the witnesses against him; to have compulsory process for obtaining witnesses in his favor, and to have the assistance of counsel for his defense.

ARTICLE VII

In suits at common law, where the value in controversy shall exceed twenty dollars, the right of trial by jury shall be preserved, and no fact tried by a jury shall be otherwise reexamined in any court of the United States, than according to the rules of the common law.

ARTICLE VIII

Excessive bail shall not be required, nor excessive fines imposed, nor cruel and unusual punishments inflicted.

ARTICLE IX

The enumeration in the Constitution of certain rights shall not be construed to deny or disparage others retained by the people.

ARTICLE X

The powers not delegated to the United States by the Constitution, nor prohibited by it to the States, are reserved to the States respectively, or to the people.

The New Inequality
PEREGRINE WORSTHORNE

To most of us it now seems very strange, almost incomprehensible, that for centuries gross hereditary inequalities of wealth, status and power were universally accepted as a divinely ordained fact of life. The lord in his castle, like the peasant at his gate, both believed that this was where God wished them to remain. If anybody had then suggested that such an arrangement was manifestly unfair he would have been dismissed as a little crazed, not to say blasphemous.

Modern man, as I say, finds this awfully difficult to understand. To him it seems absolutely axiomatic that each individual ought to be allowed to make his grade according to merit, regardless of the accident of birth.

All positions of power, wealth and status should be open to talent. To the extent that this ideal is achieved a society is deemed to be just.

If our feudal forebears thought it perfectly fair that the lord should be in his castle and the peasant at his gate, their liberal successors—which means most of us—have tended to believe it to be fair enough that the man of merit should be on top and the man without merit should be underneath. Anybody who challenged this assumption was thought a little crazed.

Much of the current political and social malaise springs, in my view, from the increasing evidence that this assumption should be challenged. The ideal of a meritocracy no longer commands such universal assent.

It used to be considered manifestly unjust that a child should be given an enormous head-start in life simply because he was the son of an earl, or a member of the landed gentry. But what about a child today born of affluent, educated parents whose family life gets him off to a head-start in the educational ladder? Is he not the beneficiary of a form of hereditary privilege no less unjust than that enjoyed by the aristocracy?

It used to be assumed that a system of universal public education would eventually overcome this difficulty. But all the recent evidence suggests that this is an illusion. Family life is more important than school life in determining brain power, and children from poor, uneducated homes will do worse than children from affluent, educated homes, even if they are sent to better schools, let alone comparable schools.

So much is beginning to become inescapably obvious. Educational qualifications are today what armorial quarterings were in feudal times. Yet access to them is almost as unfairly determined by accidents of birth as was access to the nobility. Clearly this makes a nonsense of any genuine faith in equality of opportunity.

It is the realization of this that accounts for the current populist clamor to do away with educational distinctions such as exams and diplomas, since they are seen as the latest form of privilege which, in a sense, they are.

It is perfectly true, of course, that in theory socialism has always been critical of the ideal of equality of opportunity. But hitherto, at least in the free world, it has preferred to concentrate its energies on the old injustices which stemmed from the feudal past and the capitalist present rather than to address itself to the injustices of the future.

For these purposes the ideal of equality of opportunity has been exploited as at least a way of moving in the right, that is to say the Left, direction. But today, for the first time, a new school of radical thinkers is becoming acutely aware that equality of opportunity may be a dead end instead of the thin end of the egalitarian wedge—more a buttress behind which a new form of privilege has taken shelter than a slippery slope down which hereditary privilege is moving to its doom.

And up to a point they are right in this conclusion. If equality of opportunity, as at present practiced, is assumed to be the basis for a just society, then this cannot fail to legitimize inequality in ways that we are only now beginning to discover.

But there is a problem here for the Right quite as much as for the Left. It seems to me certain that there will be a growing awareness in the coming decades of the unfairness of existing society, of the new forms of arbitrary allocation of power, status and privilege. Resentment will build up against the new meritocracy just as it built up against the old aristocracy and plutocracy.

The task of the Right must be to devise new ways of disarming this resentment, without so curbing the high-flyers, so penalizing excellence, or so imposing uniformity as to destroy the spirit of a free and dynamic society.

What will be required of the new meritocracy is a formidably revived and re-animated spirit of *noblesse oblige*,[1] rooted in the recognition that they *are* immensely privileged and must, as a class, behave accordingly, being prepared to pay a far higher social price, in terms of taxation, in terms of service, for the privilege of exercising their talents.

This is not an easy idea for a meritocracy to accept. They like to think that they deserve their privileges, having won them by their own efforts. But this is an illusion, or at any rate a half truth. The other half of the truth is that they are terribly lucky and if their luck is not to run out they must be prepared to pay much more for their good fortune than they had hoped or even feared.

How a Prince Should Keep His Word[1]
NICCOLÒ MACHIAVELLI

How praiseworthy it is for a prince to keep his word and live by honesty and not deceit, everyone knows; nevertheless we see, by what goes on in our own times, that those princes who have accomplished great things are the ones who had cared little for keeping promises and who knew how to manipulate the minds of men with shrewdness; and in the end they won out over those who founded themselves on loyalty.

You should know, then, that there are two ways of fighting: one with the law, the other with force: the first way is peculiar to man, the other to beasts; but since the first in many instances is not enough, it becomes necessary to resort to the second. Therefore, a prince must know how to make good use of the beast and the man. This role was taught to princes

---

[1] The obligations of nobility or, more generally, of the upper class (French).—EDS.

[1] Published in 1532.—EDS.

indirectly by the ancient writers, who wrote how Achilles and many other ancient princes were given to Chiron the Centaur[2] to be brought up and trained under his direction. This can only mean, having as a teacher a half-beast and half-man, that a prince ought to know how to make use of both natures; and the one without the other cannot endure.

Since a prince must know how to make good use of the beast, he should choose then the fox and the lion; for the lion has no protection from traps, and the fox is defenseless against the wolves. It is necessary, therefore, to be a fox in order to know the traps, and a lion to frighten the wolves. Those who live by the lion alone do not understand matters. And so, a wise ruler cannot, nor should he, keep his word when doing so would be to his disadvantage and when the reasons that led him to make promises no longer exist. And if all men were good, this principle would not be good; but since men are a contemptible lot, and would not keep their promises to you, you too need not keep yours to them. To a prince legitimate reasons to break promises are never lacking. Of this an infinite number of present-day examples could be noted, indicating how many peace treaties, how many promises have been made null and void by the unfaithfulness of princes: and he who has known best how to use the fox has come to a better end. But one must know how to disguise this nature well, and how to be a fine liar and hypocrite; and men are so simple-minded and so dominated by their present needs that one who deceives will always find one who will allow himself to be deceived.

There is one of these recent examples I do not wish to be silent about. Alexander VI[3] did nothing else, he thought about nothing else, except to deceive men, and he always found the occasion to do it. And never was there a man more forceful in his assertions, and who affirmed a thing with more promises who kept his word less; nevertheless, the deceits he planned were always successful, because he was well acquainted with this facet of life.

It is not necessary, then, for a prince to have all of the qualities mentioned above, but it is certainly necessary that he appear to have them. In fact, I would go so far as to say this, that having them and observing them at all times, they are harmful; and appearing to have them, they are useful; for example, appearing to be compassionate, faithful, humane, upright, religious, and being so; but his mind should be disposed in such a way that should it become necessary not to be so, he will be able and know how to change to the contrary. And it must be understood that a prince, and in particular a new prince, cannot observe all those things by which men are considered good, for it is often necessary, in order to maintain the state,

---

[2] A Greek mythological figure, half horse and half man, he was the son of Saturn and the nymph Philyra.

[3] A member of the House of Borgia and pope from 1492 to 1503. Unscrupulous, he succeeded in his political and ecclesiastical aims.—EDS.

to act against your word, against charity, against kindness, against religion. And so, he must have a mind ready to turn itself according as the winds of fortune and the fluctuation of things command him, and, as I said above, he must not separate himself from the good, if he is able, but he must know how to take up evil, should it become necessary.

A prince, therefore, should take great care never to say a single thing that is not infused with the five qualities mentioned above; he should appear, when seen and heard, to be all compassion, all faithfulness, all integrity, all kindness, all religion. And nothing is more essential than to appear to have this last quality. And men, in general, judge more according to their eyes than their hands; since everyone is in a position to observe, just a few to touch. Everyone sees what you appear to be, few touch what you are; and those few do not dare oppose the opinions of the many who have the majesty of the state defending them; and with regard to the actions of all men, and especially with princes where there is no court of appeal, we must look at the final result. Let a prince, then, conquer and maintain the state; his methods will always be judged honorable and they will be praised by all; because the ordinary people are always taken by the appearance and the outcome of a thing; and in the world there is nothing but ordinary people; and there is no room for the few while the many have a place to lean on.

"... None Will Sweat But for Promotion ..."[1]
MICHAEL KORDA

"I like the Garter; there is no damned merit in it,"[2] Lord Melbourne once said about the most ancient and exclusive of English honors, a view which applies to promotions in general. Almost everybody in the world feels that they deserve to be promoted to some higher estate, no matter how high they may already have risen. Since the number of positions declines as the level of power increases, most of the world is automatically doomed to live in disappointment and envy. This system has many advantages, chief among them the fact that if it were not for the hope of rising, few people would do any more work than is necessary for survival. It is important for people to believe that work will lead to promotion, but, as Melbourne pointed out, merit is in fact something that most people in power dislike.

From above, merit merely confuses the issue: the reasons for promoting

---
[1] From Robert Graves, *The Greek Myths* (1957).
[2] From Harold Nicholson, *Good Behavior* (1955). (Melbourne was prime minister in 1834 and 1835–1841, supported by Whigs and moderate Tories.—Eds.)

someone that have nothing to do with merit are always the most persuasive ones, if only because they're easier to notice and remember. Those who hang on, get up. Most promotions are based on a system of rewards for faithfulness, rather than on any real attempt to assess merit. It has to be remembered that nobody can be promoted to a job until the person who occupies it has left, a fact which is simple, but often forgotten. If that person is about to be fired, then it is sensible to make yourself as different as you can from him; if he is about to be promoted, then it makes sense to pattern your behavior on his; if he is about to retire, you're on your own. After all, if he is in danger of being fired, then his superiors will be looking for "somebody different"; if they're thinking of promoting him, they will be looking for someone as much like him as possible, not only because they think highly of him, but also because as "promotion material" he will be asked for his advice on replacing him, and will naturally recommend someone like himself; in the case of someone who is about to be retired, the management will be unable to decide what they want, and may even be willing to consider the dangerous expedient of "bringing someone in from the outside." It never does to forget that managements, like individuals, get bored with what they have, and since they are not anxious to replace themselves for the sake of change, they can only change by shaking things up below them. As one executive said of another, "He likes to stir the pot from time to time, just to show he owns the spoon."

To those in power, promoting people is second only to firing them as an exercise in the use of power. As games go, it has the advantage of involving many people—after all, you can only fire one person at a time, as a general rule, but there may be a dozen people who want to be promoted to a given job. The opportunities for playing one person off against another are endless. What is more, such occasions present an excellent chance to gauge the loyalties of those beneath one. As the aged Emperor Franz Josef of Austro-Hungary[3] said, when a minister was recommended for promotion on the grounds that he was a patriot, "Yes, but is he a patriot for *me*?" When people are being interviewed with a view to promotion, the person doing the interviewing, like the old Emperor, is looking for *personal* loyalty, trying to determine the extent to which the interviewee will be obligated, in the event he or she gets the job. This is normally a delicate dialogue; very few people can bring themselves to say, "I'll swing the job your way if you'll agree to join my camp," yet the underlying rationale of promotion is much the same as that of medieval vassalage, each executive trying to build up a small army of supporters who owe their livelihood to him. These people comprise his feudal levy in time of need, and the higher up he is, the more of them he will want; but the more of them there are, the harder it is to support them. Like a medieval army, they must be clothed, fed, housed and provided with rewards and booty.

[3] Emperor from 1848 to 1916.—Eds.

Their leader belongs to them as much as they belong to him, and his obligations to them are as demanding as theirs to him. These groups exist in every corporation, and the urgent need to provide them with promotions, titles, work they can do and raises explains much of the endless activity and intrigue that make office life so fascinating. Since there is always pressure from below, and the need on the part of every executive to build up his ranks of loyalists, the temptation to create openings at every level is always strong, and naturally leads to a good deal of the unnecessary firing and job-changing that characterize corporate life.

A good rule for those who have the power to promote others is to ensure that they maintain absolute control over the process. Many executives insist on being the bearers of good news, with sound reason, and not a few are addicted to creating false rumors, building people's hopes and generally fogging up the issue, in order to keep everyone in suspense and dramatize the final decision. The more nervous people are about getting a promotion, the more they will appreciate it if they do, and many people are flattered at even being included in the rumors. By giving the maximum number of people the chance to believe they may be selected for a job, even if you have already selected the person for it in your mind, you can focus everyone's attention on your power while at the same time making an exciting event of a one-horse race. Besides, as a management friend says, "You don't want a guy to become too cocky, even if he's the only logical choice for a job. Make him sweat a little. He'll be just that much more grateful when he gets it, and it gives you a chance to show him who's boss."

For those who want to be promoted, there are certain rules worth observing. In the first place, propinquity helps. If you can move your office closer and closer to that of the person whose job you want, he or she will not only feel threatened (or that you are the logical successor for the job), but you will also create a certain feeling of inevitability in the minds of the people who will decide on your promotion. It is, therefore, always worthwhile to move from where you are toward the corner of power you covet. By the time you have taken the office next to the one you want, most people will assume that the next step is yours by right of succession. Ordinarily, the executive nearest to the one who has to be replaced will be first in line, so every opportunity should be taken to move in the right direction. Power people walking in and out of an executive's corner office will see you sitting next door, and will naturally assume that you are being "groomed" as the executive's successor, whereas the person who is most qualified to succeed to the job (in other words, the one with merit) may be four offices down, and thus comparatively invisible.

A promotion should always involve a change of office, if it's to do you any good in the larger scheme of things. It does little good to change jobs or receive a new title if you stay in the same office, no matter how important your new responsibilities are. To stay put always seems static.

Shifting offices, by contrast, gives people around you a sense of dramatic change, as if by moving sideways you were in fact moving upward. Even for the most important and successful players, the promotion that means the most to them is likely to be the one that involved a major change of office (to a corner or to the "executive" floor, for example), however many new titles and promotions they may have acquired afterward. It is the *geographical* change that gets celebrated, because it is both visible and symbolic. A promotion may be an important move in a person's career, but if it merely involves ordering new cards and stationery, its effect on most other people will be minimal. What counts is a new office. Few people know or care what an executive's new title is, or can work out what it means in terms of power, whereas a new office can be compared to other people's in terms of size, desirability and decoration. I know of one man who worked his way up the ladder of promotion, eventually reaching quite a high position and title, without ever acquiring any real power over other people, or being taken seriously by his colleagues. Unfortunately for him, he had inherited a large and comfortable office early in his career, when he was not strictly entitled to two windows, a tufted leather couch and a designer desk in Jacaranda veneer. Already comfortable enough, he had no desire to move, and in any case there was no larger office to move him to. As a result, all his promotions seemed like empty formalities, and were dismissed by others as meaningless; eventually they even began to seem meaningless to him, and he complained constantly that his career had "bogged down," though in fact his rise in terms of promotion was impressive and swift.

It is quite possible to simulate promotion by moving one's office, provided the move is accompanied by sufficient ceremony, and doesn't look like a midnight flit or mere restlessness. It is as in certain Indian tribes, where the size of one's tepee, and its place in the encampment, determined one's social standing. Some Indians were notorious for attempting to take advantage of each move the tribe made to a new location to alter the place of their tent.

Promotion by side-effect is a more difficult game, but quite effective. This can take many forms, but the most familiar is to work out a specific relationship with another executive, preferably one who is ambitious and bound to rise. If you can establish that your proper relationship to him is one position behind, then you are quite likely to be promoted whenever *he* is, in order to keep the same distance behind him. Thus, if you are able to persuade people that you belong one rung below X on the ladder, you go up one rung whenever he does, your only risk being that X turns out to be a non-starter. A great many promotions are determined by this or other schemes designed to preserve a balance between people, and once locked into them, it is possible to make one's way quietly upward with little or no effort. Nothing is more useful than an ambitious executive, especially one brought in from the outside, since almost everyone will have to be "adjusted" to compensate for what it has been necessary to give him in order to acquire him in the first place. Thus, the arrival of an outsider who has to be given a good title may well lead to the inflation of everyone else's titles, just so that nobody's feelings are hurt. In cases where the turnover of outsiders is high, the people who remain may find themselves promoted upward with dizzying rapidity, until it's hard to even invent new titles for them. One man I know has stayed in the same place for ten years, placidly doing the same job, while the entertainment conglomerate he works for has nervously hired and fired executives in a reflexive, twitchy attempt to create a new image for itself. By now, he has acquired a certain power, being one of the few people who has been there long enough to remember where everything is and just what it is the company manufactures, but with each change of executives, he gets a new and more sonorous title "to keep him happy." "Happy?" he says, "of course I'm happy. What's not to be happy about? Every time they bring in some hotshot, they come to me and they say, 'Listen, we don't want you to worry, we need this guy and we had to give him a title to get him, but just to show we love you, we're making you deputy creative director, or senior vice-president, or whatever.' Everybody says that these are just phoney titles, they don't mean a thing, and in a way it's true, but you can always use them to get an extra thou or two at the end of the year. I mean, they're pretty embarrassed to have to admit that the titles don't count for anything, and they usually figure if they've given you the title, they may as well give you a little cash as well, just to make it okay. Anyway, if they've given you a new, bigger title, it's hard for them to fire you. Somebody would be bound to ask why they made you a vice-president in 1974 if you were doing such a lousy job that you had to be fired in 1975, you know? So you've got them, really. By me, they can bring in people from everywhere, anytime, and promote them over my head. When they come in, I go up one notch without any effort, and if they keep on doing it I can see myself being president and chairman of the board in five years."

The astute power player should be able to make good use of other people's promotions, rather than resenting them, as many people do. Every promotion means another job or title open, and most promotions can be used as a good reason for promoting *you*.

Benighted Nations
RUSSELL BAKER

Russia is terrible. It snows and snows and snows. If you look out the window and say, "It snows too much," a Government machine reports you to the police and they lock you in a madhouse to have your brain altered. Russia is terrible.

Benighted Nations   113

India is not much fun. It is exceedingly hot and rains at odd times. When you say, "India should get a new Government that will do something about this heat," the police come in the night and take you away. India is not much fun.

Northern Ireland is extremely unpleasant. When you go out for a beer they blast you into many separate pieces with high explosives and answer your children's complaints by saying you died for the cause. Yes, an extremely unpleasant place.

Lebanon is simply intolerable. If you take a walk into town, either Moslems or Christians will shoot you down. Though its religious zeal is commendable, Lebanon is simply intolerable.

China is unspeakable. Everyone wears a quilt and behaves with suspicious sincerity. If you speak with wit or asperity, they ship you out to the country where commissars re-educate you in the evils of hilarity, the virtues of party regularity, and the gravity of sex. China is unspeakable.

England is definitely flawed. You can't get there if there's fog. If you do, they fill you with tea and an overpowering sense of your educational inferiority. Though they don't shoot you, jail you or alter your brain, they soak you for weeks without end in the rain. Oh, England is definitely flawed.

Saudi Arabia simply won't do. If the Government catches you having a drink, there is no telling what it might do. And it is extremely dry there, too. Saudi Arabia simply won't do.

Uganda is barbarous. If they don't like your face, your thoughts or your creed, the Government seizes everything you own and ships you to England without a raincoat, although sometimes it offers to shoot you. Bah to you, Uganda. Bah.

France is out of the question. They charge almost as much as Internal Revenue, and if you despair they say they don't care and ask why you don't refuse to pay taxes as they do. What is worse, they say it in French. France is out of the question.

South America is almost acceptable, but only if you have no objection to being kidnapped by guerrillas, although in Chile the Government might extract your fingernails slowly, which hardly seems almost acceptable unless you are not finicky about things like hands.

Bangladesh is not everyone's cup of tea. If the typhoon isn't drowning you, you are either starving to death or being suddenly murdered for not being on the right side of the latest Government upheaval. Even for tastes that are medieval, Bangladesh is not everyone's cup of tea.

Switzerland is much too clean. They rise at dawn every day and polish their money and, because they have so much of it, hardly ever finish before sundown. At sundown they take in the sidewalks to keep them from getting dirty during the night. Afterwards, there is nothing to do but join the rest of the country in taking a bath. On Mondays, they wash their paper money, and on Tuesdays, iron it. Switzerland is much too clean.

Italy is extremely risky. They send the Mafia to cut off your ear and hold you for absurdly high ransom, or alternatively, they haul you off to Pisa or Lucca for a festival and make you dance some tarantella with a lovely young creature whose inamorato will almost surely take it amiss and disfigure your nose with his fist. Italy is extremely risky.

Germany is nothing to cheer. They stuff you with sauerkraut and float you in beer and fit you in ridiculous leather pants and cry, "*Ach*, if only you could have been here in the old days," and cry in their beer for the day when Americans were as rich as they and brought more money then than they do today. Germany is nothing to cheer.

The world as a whole is not worth a visit. They shoot you, or starve you, cut off your ear, or bomb you. They disfigure your nose and jail you for drink, alter your brain if you say what you think; they rain on you, rob you, torture and mob you, and afterwards weep for the world that was. The world is not what it was. It probably never was. As a whole, not worth a visit.

I Have a Dream[1]

MARTIN LUTHER KING, JR.

Five score years ago, a great American, in whose symbolic shadow we stand, signed the Emancipation Proclamation. This momentous decree came as a great beacon light of hope to millions of Negro slaves who had been seared in the flames of withering injustice. It came as a joyous daybreak to end the long night of captivity.

But one hundred years later, we must face the tragic fact that the Negro is still not free. One hundred years later, the life of the Negro is still sadly crippled by the manacles of segregation and the chains of discrimination. One hundred years later, the Negro lives on a lonely island of poverty in the midst of a vast ocean of material prosperity. One hundred years later, the Negro is still languished in the corners of American society and finds himself an exile in his own land. So we have come here today to dramatize an appalling condition.

In a sense we have come to our nation's Capital to cash a check. When the architects of our republic wrote the magnificent words of the Constitution and the Declaration of Independence, they were signing a promissory note to which every American was to fall heir. This note was a promise that all men would be guaranteed the unalienable rights of life, liberty, and the pursuit of happiness.

It is obvious today that America has defaulted on this promissory note

[1] An address given at the Lincoln Memorial in Washington, D.C., on August 28, 1963, climaxing the civil rights demonstration of that day.—EDS.

insofar as her citizens of color are concerned. Instead of honoring this sacred obligation, America has given the Negro people a bad check; a check which has come back marked "insufficient funds." But we refuse to believe that the bank of justice is bankrupt. We refuse to believe that there are insufficient funds in the great vaults of opportunity of this nation. So we have come to cash this check—a check that will give us upon demand the riches of freedom and the security of justice. We have also come to this hallowed spot to remind America of the fierce urgency of *now*. This is no time to engage in the luxury of cooling off or to take the tranquilizing drug of gradualism. *Now* is the time to make real the promises of Democracy. *Now* is the time to rise from the dark and desolate valley of segregation to the sunlit path of racial justice. *Now* is the time to open the doors of opportunity to all of God's children. *Now* is the time to lift our nation from the quicksands of racial injustice to the solid rock of brotherhood.

It would be fatal for the nation to overlook the urgency of the moment and to underestimate the determination of the Negro. This sweltering summer of the Negro's legitimate discontent will not pass until there is an invigorating autumn of freedom and equality. 1963 is not an end, but a beginning. Those who hope that the Negro needed to blow off steam and will now be content will have a rude awakening if the nation returns to business as usual. There will be neither rest nor tranquillity in America until the Negro is granted his citizenship rights. The whirlwinds of revolt will continue to shake the foundations of our nation until the bright day of justice emerges.

But there is something that I must say to my people who stand on the warm threshold which leads into the palace of justice. In the process of gaining our rightful place we must not be guilty of wrongful deeds. Let us not seek to satisfy our thirst for freedom by drinking from the cup of bitterness and hatred. We must forever conduct our struggle on the high plane of dignity and discipline. We must not allow our creative protest to degenerate into physical violence. Again and again we must rise to the majestic heights of meeting physical force with soul force. The marvelous new militancy which has engulfed the Negro community must not lead us to a distrust of all white people, for many of our white brothers, as evidenced by their presence here today, have come to realize that their destiny is tied up with our destiny and their freedom is inextricably bound to our freedom. We cannot walk alone.

And as we walk, we must make the pledge that we shall march ahead. We cannot turn back. There are those who are asking the devotees of civil rights, "When will you be satisfied?" We can never be satisfied as long as the Negro is the victim of the unspeakable horrors of police brutality. We can never be satisfied as long as our bodies, heavy with the fatigue of travel, cannot gain lodging in the motels of the highways and the hotels of the cities. We cannot be satisfied as long as the Negro's basic mobility is from a smaller ghetto to a larger one. We can never be satisfied as long as a

Negro in Mississippi cannot vote and a Negro in New York believes he has nothing for which to vote. No, no, we are not satisfied, and we will not be satisfied until justice rolls down like waters and righteousness like a mighty stream.

I am not unmindful that some of you have come here out of great trials and tribulations. Some of you have come fresh from narrow jail cells. Some of you have come from areas where your quest for freedom left you battered by the storms of persecution and staggered by the winds of police brutality. You have been the veterans of creative suffering. Continue to work with the faith that unearned suffering is redemptive.

Go back to Mississippi, go back to Alabama, go back to South Carolina, go back to Georgia, go back to Louisiana, go back to the slums and ghettos of our northern cities, knowing that somehow this situation can and will be changed. Let us not wallow in the valley of despair.

I say to you today, my friends, that in spite of the difficulties and frustrations of the moment I still have a dream. It is a dream deeply rooted in the American dream.

I have a dream that one day this nation will rise up and live out the true meaning of its creed: "We hold these truths to be self-evident; that all men are created equal."

I have a dream that one day on the red hills of Georgia the sons of former slaves and the sons of former slaveowners will be able to sit down together at the table of brotherhood.

I have a dream that one day even the state of Mississippi, a desert state sweltering with the heat of injustice and oppression, will be transformed into an oasis of freedom and justice.

I have a dream that my four little children will one day live in a nation where they will not be judged by the color of their skin but by the content of their character.

I have a dream today.

I have a dream that one day the state of Alabama, whose governor's lips are presently dripping with the words of interposition and nullification, will be transformed into a situation where little black boys and black girls will be able to join hands with little white boys and white girls and walk together as sisters and brothers.

I have a dream today.

I have a dream that one day every valley shall be exalted, every hill and mountain shall be made low, the rough places will be made plain, and the crooked places will be made straight, and the glory of the Lord shall be revealed, and all flesh shall see it together.

This is our hope. This is the faith with which I return to the South. With this faith we will be able to hew out of the mountain of despair a stone of hope. With this faith we will be able to transform the jangling discords of our nation into a beautiful symphony of brotherhood. With this faith we will be able to work together, to pray together, to struggle together, to go to jail together, to stand up for freedom together, knowing that we will be free one day.

This will be the day when all of God's children will be able to sing with new meaning

> My country, 'tis of thee,
> Sweet land of liberty,
>   Of thee I sing:
> Land where my fathers died,
> Land of the pilgrims' pride,
> From every mountainside
>   Let freedom ring.

And if America is to be a great nation this must become true. So let freedom ring from the prodigious hilltops of New Hampshire. Let freedom ring from the mighty mountains of New York. Let freedom ring from the heightening Alleghenies of Pennsylvania!

Let freedom ring from the snowcapped Rockies of Colorado!

Let freedom ring from the curvacious peaks of California!

But not only that; let freedom ring from Stone Mountain of Georgia!

Let freedom ring from Lookout Mountain of Tennessee!

Let freedom ring from every hill and molehill of Mississippi. From every mountainside, let freedom ring.

When we let freedom ring, when we let it ring from every village and every hamlet, from every state and every city, we will be able to speed up that day when all God's children, black men and white men, Jews and Gentiles, Protestants and Catholics, will be able to join hands and sing in the words of the old Negro spiritual, "Free at last! free at last! thank God almighty, we are free at last!"

Looking Backward, 2000-1887[1]

EDWARD BELLAMY

Dr. Leete[2] ceased speaking, and I remained silent, endeavoring to form some general conception of the changes in the arrangements of society implied in the tremendous revolution which he had described.

Finally I said, "The idea of such an extension of the functions of government is, to say the least, rather overwhelming."

"Extension!" he repeated, "where is the extension?"

---

[1] Chapter six of *Looking Backward, 2000-1887* (1888).—EDS.

[2] A physician in Boston of the year 2000. He explains the new culture to Julian West, a young man who has awakened from a hypnotic sleep that began in 1887.—EDS.

"In my day," I replied, "it was considered that the proper functions of government, strictly speaking, were limited to keeping the peace and defending the people against the public enemy, that is, to the military and police powers."

"And, in heaven's name, who are the public enemies?" exclaimed Dr. Leete. "Are they France, England, Germany, or hunger, cold, and nakedness? In your day governments were accustomed, on the slightest international misunderstanding, to seize upon the bodies of citizens and deliver them over by hundreds of thousands to death and mutilation, wasting their treasures the while like water; and all this oftenest for no imaginable profit to the victims. We have no wars now, and our governments no war powers, but in order to protect every citizen against hunger, cold, and nakedness, and provide for all his physical and mental needs, the function is assumed of directing his industry for a term of years. No, Mr. West, I am sure on reflection you will perceive that it was in your age, not in ours, that the extension of the functions of governments was extraordinary. Not even for the best ends would men now allow their governments such powers as were then used for the most maleficent."

"Leaving comparisons aside," I said, "the demagoguery and corruption of our public men would have been considered, in my day, insuperable objections to any assumption by government of the charge of the national industries. We should have thought that no arrangement could be worse than to entrust the politicians with control of the wealth-producing machinery of the country. Its material interests were quite too much the football of parties as it was."

"No doubt you were right," rejoined Dr. Leete, "but all that is changed now. We have no parties or politicians, and as for demagoguery and corruption, they are words having only an historical significance."

"Human nature itself must have changed very much," I said.

"Not at all," was Dr. Leete's reply, "but the conditions of human life have changed, and with them the motives of human action. The organization of society with you was such that officials were under a constant temptation to misuse their power for the private profit of themselves or others. Under such circumstances it seems almost strange that you dared entrust them with any of your affairs. Nowadays, on the contrary, society is so constituted that there is absolutely no way in which an official, however ill-disposed, could possibly make any profit for himself or any one else by a misuse of his power. Let him be as bad an official as you please, he cannot be a corrupt one. There is no motive to be. The social system no longer offers a premium on dishonesty. But these are matters which you can only understand as you come, with time, to know us better."

"But you have not yet told me how you have settled the labor problem. It is the problem of capital which we have been discussing," I said. "After the nation had assumed conduct of the mills, machinery, railroads, farms, mines, and capital in general of the country, the labor question still remained. In assuming the responsibilities of capital the nation had assumed the difficulties of the capitalist's position."

"The moment the nation assumed the responsibilities of capital those difficulties vanished," replied Dr. Leete. "The national organization of labor under one direction was the complete solution of what was, in your day and under your system, justly regarded as the insoluble labor problem. When the nation became the sole employer, all the citizens, by virtue of their citizenship, became employees, to be distributed according to the needs of industry."

"That is," I suggested, "you have simply applied the principle of universal military service, as it was understood in our day, to the labor question."

"Yes," said Dr. Leete, "that was something which followed as a matter of course as soon as the nation had become the sole capitalist. The people were already accustomed to the idea that the obligation of every citizen, not physically disabled, to contribute his military services to the defense of the nation was equal and absolute. That it was equally the duty of every citizen to contribute his quota of industrial or intellectual services to the maintenance of the nation was equally evident, though it was not until the nation became the employer of labor that citizens were able to render this sort of service with any pretense either of universality or equity. No organization of labor was possible when the employing power was divided among hundreds or thousands of individuals and corporations, between which concert of any kind was neither desired, nor indeed feasible. It constantly happened then that vast numbers who desired to labor could find no opportunity, and on the other hand, those who desired to evade a part or all of their debt could easily do so."

"Service, now, I suppose, is compulsory upon all," I suggested.

"It is rather a matter of course than of compulsion," replied Dr. Leete. "It is regarded as so absolutely natural and reasonable that the idea of its being compulsory has ceased to be thought of. He would be thought to be an incredibly contemptible person who should need compulsion in such a case. Nevertheless, to speak of service being compulsory would be a weak way to state its absolute inevitableness. Our entire social order is so wholly based upon and deduced from it that if it were conceivable that a man could escape it, he would be left with no possible way to provide for his existence. He would have excluded himself from the world, cut himself off from his kind, in a word, committed suicide."

"Is the term of service in this industrial army for life?"

"Oh, no; it both begins later and ends earlier than the average working period in your day. Your workshops were filled with children and old men, but we hold the period of youth sacred to education, and the period of maturity, when the physical forces begin to flag, equally sacred to ease and agreeable relaxation. The period of industrial service is twenty-four years, beginning at the close of the course of education at twenty-one and terminating at forty-five. After forty-five, while discharged from labor, the citizen still remains liable to special calls, in case of emergencies causing a sudden great increase in the demand for labor, till he reaches the age of fifty-five, but such calls are rarely, in fact almost never, made. The fifteenth day of October of every year is what we call Muster Day, because those who have reached the age of twenty-one are then mustered into the industrial service, and at the same time those who, after twenty-four years' service, have reached the age of forty-five, are honorably mustered out. It is the great day of the year with us, whence we reckon all other events, our Olympiad, save that it is annual."

Somehow, It Has Overcome
KENNETH J. ARROW

There is little warrant for the belief that we know the laws of history well enough to make projections of any great reliability. Most of the turning points of history, great and small, were surprises to both their participants and the analysts of the day, whatever their doctrine.

That the capitalist system excels at productive efficiency is not to be denied. In the United States, Western Europe and Japan, at least, the rate of increase in efficiency is much higher now than it was when the authors of the Communist Manifesto included a fulsome panegyric on the productive accomplishments of the bourgeoisie. But no social institution has ever felt justified solely by material product. Moreover, the inequalities in the distribution of this material wealth and in the power and control over the activities by which it is created constitute a steady indictment.

This indictment has, among several different groups of social analysts, taken the empirical form of asserting that the development of capitalism has given rise to "contradictions" which imply its eventual extinction as a matter of historical law. As I have said, I do not believe us capable of discerning inevitable contradictions and, in any case, capitalism has survived long enough in advanced countries to show that the contradictions can hardly be fatal, though they may have been avoided only by the development of new institutions, such as labor unions and government intervention.

It is still useful to list some six of the leading proposed contradictions, for they do all point to real problems for social policy and criticism. No doubt the idea of a contradiction in the capitalist system is Marxian in origin; but some of the following contradictions have been put forward by non-Marxists only, some by both sides.

(1) Ideological weakness: Capitalism relies for its operation on selfish motives. Its prized efficiency depends on the greed of the owners and managers of firms, on their desire for increasing profits. Further, the success of

capitalism depends on careful calculation, on a nice balancing of costs and benefits. The reliance on selfishness is defended as a realistic evaluation of human motivations. But neither selfishness nor calculation are goals for which men are willing to make deep commitments. It is a fear of many conservative thinkers, the late Joseph Schumpeter[1] being perhaps the best known and most thoroughgoing and Irving Kristol[2] being the latest, that the ideological commitment to capitalism is too weak to resist the idealistic appeal of socialism or similar doctrines, which promise a daily contribution to the common good.

(2) Alienation: A closely related critical theme holds that capitalism, with its emphasis on the impersonal exchange relationship, leads to destruction of personal and communal relations. If these are fundamental needs of mankind, then alienation ultimately undermines the social relations which define the capitalist system itself. This thesis, put forward vigorously by conservative and romantic thinkers of the early 19th century, was adopted by Marx but with an added characteristic element: the worker is alienated from the product of his labor; his work becomes merely a means to income, not the satisfaction of a need to be productive. The human relations movement in industry illustrates how the same critique can be put to defend and improve personal hierarchical relations in industry.

(3) Increasing concentration: Marx and many others have argued that competition and technological development force a growing concentration of economic power into fewer and fewer hands. Among other alleged consequences: the size of the class which benefits from capitalism would be steadily shrinking and therefore the system would be more vulnerable, and the transition to a centrally controlled socialist economy would be made easier.

The actual development has revealed some factors which modify these effects. The hypothesis of growing concentration and the two consequences just drawn were based on observations in the industrial sector of the economy. But, the degree of concentration in the industrial sector seems to have reached a stable level and has not changed greatly in fifty years or more; the exercise of control in giant firms itself requires an increasing large fraction of the employees, who become identified in some measure with the directing groups; and the proportion of employment in the industrial sector is decreasing, as rising incomes cause more expenditure on services, which tend to be operated by smaller firms.

(4) Working-class solidarity: The grouping of workers for effective production, as in factories, reinforces the sense of their common position as against the employers. The sense of solidarity gave strength to the tendency

---

[1] Austrian-American economist (1883–1950); author of *Theory of Business Development* (1911) and other books.—EDS.

[2] Social philosopher (1920–   ); a founder and editor of *Public Interest*, and resident scholar at the American Enterprise Institute.—EDS.

to unionization and, in Europe, to the socialist and syndicalist movements. The intensity of feeling in these movements, exemplified in the sit-down strikes in the United States during the late thirties certainly appeared to justify the notion of intense class conflict.

In fact several factors have mitigated the thrust of working-class solidarity: the conflict between unions and employers has become institutionalized and legitimized wherever unions have become strong enough to reach a level of security; not only are the economic conflicts fought out in ways that pose no threat to the social order, but politically organized labor plays a relatively more conservative role than in the past.

There is, however, one unresolved strain in labor relations which has come to surprise us: the determination of wages and working conditions in the public sector. In recent years, we have moved to unions and strikes in this region. We clearly have not come to an institutional equilibrium here; laws against strikes are not enforced, not even in the case of police, where striking has some especially severe consequences. Labor relations in privately owned public utilities pose some of the same special problems. This development can hardly be called a contradiction of capitalism, to be sure.

(5) Unemployment: Over the last 150 years, by far the most serious criticism of and threat to the capitalist economic system has been the recurring cycles of unemployment. Here was a clear malfunctioning of the system itself, not attributable to external causes, and one which imposed misery on its victims. Further, not only was it to be expected that insecurity and patently unnecessary poverty would create resentment and violent antagonism on the part of the working class, but also each depression was accompanied by a destruction of profits, the lifeblood and *raison d'être*[3] of the capitalist system. It seemed a reasonable extrapolation to foresee a collapse of the system, both economically and politically. But no such collapse occurred. Not even the Great Depression caused a serious question to be raised, except perhaps in the special case of Germany. Perhaps the clearly evident growth in the real incomes of all members of the society more than compensated for the recurrent economic disasters.

The new economic ideas of Keynes[4] and his disciples have been translated into policy with almost unprecedented speed. The idea that the state, through its decisions to spend, tax and regulate the supply of money, could reduce unemployment to levels far lower than those in the depths of previous depressions was accepted among both economists and political leaders, and has shown itself to work in practice with great success. In every advanced country, the post–World War II economic record is like that of a new economy. Sophisticated radical economists, such as Paul Baran[5] and

---

[3] Reason for being (French).—EDS.

[4] John Maynard Keynes (1883–1946), British economist.—EDS.

[5] Economist (1910–1964); author of *The Political Economy of Growth* (1957) and other books.—EDS.

Paul Sweezy,[6] quickly recognized that the Keynesian solution would work but argued that in a capitalist system the government could spend enough to insure full employment only on socially wasteful and even destructive ends, such as war and preparations for war. Socially constructive spending would necessarily compete with and eventually undermine the private sector. The example of Japan suggests some reason to doubt this argument, though the Japanese circumstances are somewhat special. At home, it has been found possible over the last decade, to achieve a much higher level of government spending on social purposes and to decrease defense expenditures at least relatively. We do have higher unemployment rates than are desirable, but that is because of inflationary fears rather than a shortage of ways to spend money. There is little reason, therefore, to accept the Baran-Sweezy variation of the unemployment contradiction, though perhaps it is too soon to regard it as definitely controverted.

(6) Inflation: There appears to be this element of truth in the idea of a contradiction: the resolution of any problem always creates a new problem. From the beginning of the Keynesian era, the fear has been expressed that vigorous full-employment policies will lead to inflation. Standard economic theory has been built in large measure about the idea of equilibrium, that an exact balancing of supply and demand on all markets, including the labor market, will lead to steady prices, while an excess of supply leads to a downward pressure. Thus, unemployment ought to lead to wage declines; they manifestly have not done so in recent years. The coexistence of inflation and unemployment is thus an intellectual riddle and an uncomfortable fact.

But in my judgment the contradiction here hardly compares with some of the others to which capitalism has adapted.

First of all, the rates of inflation with which we have had to contend impose no insuperable problem or even major difficulty to the operation of the economic system, nothing comparable to the major depressions of the past. Individuals will learn and have learned to deal with inflation, making their plans to take expected inflation into account. The economic system and the government will create and are creating methods of mitigating the effects, such as variable-annuity plans and cost-of-living clauses in savings bonds. What the future will bring is of course a matter of conjecture. Some analysts feel that inflation will inevitably accelerate, but others will note that in the past peacetime inflations have tapered off. The present rates are historically high but not totally unprecedented; even in peacetime it appears from the record that over the period 1897–1902, prices rose more rapidly than they have in the last five years.

Second, we may have some reasonable hope that economic research and experimentation in policymaking, between them, will evolve more sophisti-

---

[6] Economist (1910–   ); author of *The Theory of Capitalist Development* (1942) and other books.—EDS.

cated means of managing the over-all economy. Research into monetary economics is at an unprecedented level of activity, and better and more abundant data are available than ever before. With the variety of policy instruments now available and better understood, I think it most likely that the reconciliation of full employment and price stability can be significantly improved in the future.

We find that capitalism, like any very complex system, contains within itself contradictory tendencies, but there is no reason to suppose these are fatal, at least in the foreseeable future. We do find implied in these contradictions some social tasks: the completion of the tasks involved in the achievement of macroeconomic stability, the redistribution of income and power to improve the sense of justice in the arrangements of society, by which I mean the inseparable elements of the liberty and equality of individuals, and, perhaps the hardest, the increase in the sense of individual and local control over one's destiny in the workplace and the small society. These aims are mutually reinforcing, not competitive.

Oh! We've Been Trojan-Horsed!
PETER F. DRUCKER

If socialism is defined, the way Marx did, as "ownership of the means of production by the worker," the United States has become a truly socialist country. The pension funds of the employees of America, and especially of American business, own today more than enough to give them control: in excess of one-third of the capital of all large- and medium-base business—whether manufacturers, retailers, banks or insurance companies.

In most of the top 500 corporations, pension funds already own a majority of the stock, since pension funds concentrate their holdings in the largest and most actively traded companies.

Within another ten years, by 1986, employee pension funds will own a majority of all but truly "small" businesses, and may own as much as two-thirds of the big ones. Only farming, in which in this country the "worker" —that is, the family farmer—owns the means of production anyhow, has not shifted ownership to the "institutional investors"—that is, the pension funds.

More than 40 cents out of every dollar of pretax revenue of business goes to pension funds—either to those of the company's own employees or to the "institutional investors," the pension funds of other companies' employees. The Government share is quite a bit less—not much more than 35 cents (though, of course, Federal, state and city governments take another bite through the personal income tax). The shareholders other than pension funds, the people who we still call the "owners," get less than a quarter. And long before 1985, the pension-fund share in corporate revenues before taxes will have passed 50 percent and will still be rising.

Pension fund socialism started a little more than 25 years ago. The General Motors pension fund, established in October 1950, was the first of the new "institutional investors" and set the pattern. Pension-fund investments began to build up rapidly in the early 1960's and have been growing fast ever since, transferring America's economic structure.

The United States has actually brought under worker ownership a larger share of its productive resources than such stalwart Soviet satellites as Poland or Hungary have socialized. But American pension-fund socialism has "socialized" the means of production without "nationalizing" them. Instead of the Government, the agent of socialism is an autonomous nonprofit "trustee," the employee's pension fund.

Almost no one has yet thought much about the consequences, yet they are startling. The distribution of wealth, for instance, has changed greatly. Pension-fund claims are not "property." They can neither be sold nor bought, can neither be mortgaged nor bequeathed. But they are clearly "wealth." Indeed, for the older family—the family with a breadwinner more than 50 years of age—the pension-fund claim is a more valuable asset than the automobile or even the single-family house. And the wealth represented by pension-fund claims is distributed much more equally than any other item of wealth. If pension-fund claims were counted as "personal wealth," which indeed they are, we would at once see that the employed middle class, rather than the "super-rich," "own America."

The most important consequences of pension-fund socialism are still ahead. Managements have yet to think through how they need to relate to the new owners, the beneficiaries of the pension funds, and how they could and should bring this new "ownership interest" into company structure and corporate policy. The pension funds equally will have to think through what rights and obligations they have acquired as the representatives of these new ownership interests. Union leaders will find increasingly that their own members are the "wicked capitalists." And the employees, above all, will increasingly find themselves related to the employer, both as "wage slaves" and as "owners," both with an interest in today's wage income, and an interest in the profits that finance tomorrow's pensions. But the most important fact about America's accomplished pension-fund socialism are not new problems, new relationships and new opportunities. It is that a change of this magnitude has crept up on us without anyone seeing it or noticing it. Pension-fund socialism is a major "revolution" in economic and social structure, yet one that has been totally nonviolent, totally voluntary, and almost totally unseen.

Directive[1]

ROBERT FROST

Back out of all this now too much for us,
Back in a time made simple by the loss
Of detail, burned, dissolved, and broken off
Like graveyard marble sculpture in the weather,
There is a house that is no more a house
Upon a farm that is no more a farm
And in a town that is no more a town.
The road there, if you'll let a guide direct you
Who only has at heart your getting lost,
May seem as if it should have been a quarry—
Great monolithic knees the former town
Long since gave up pretense of keeping covered.
And there's a story in a book about it:
Besides the wear of iron wagon wheels
The ledges show lines ruled southeast northwest,
The chisel work of an enormous Glacier
That braced his feet against the Arctic Pole.
You must not mind a certain coolness from him
Still said to haunt this side of Panther Mountain.
Nor need you mind the serial ordeal
Of being watched from forty cellar holes
As if by eye pairs out of forty firkins.[2]
As for the woods' excitement over you
That sends light rustle rushes to their leaves,
Charge that to upstart inexperience.
Where were they all not twenty years ago?
They think too much of having shaded out
A few old pecker-fretted apple trees.
Make yourself up a cheering song of how
Someone's road home from work this once was,
Who may be just ahead of you on foot
Or creaking with a buggy load of grain.
The height of the adventure is the height
Of country where two village cultures faded

---

[1] Hyde Cox, a close friend of the poet, has reported that Frost regarded the poem as having a number of meanings: "It would be the poet's directive that one must go back to what he believes to be the source; and to the extent that he had saved something aside, removed from worldly experience—unpolluted, he would be able to contribute something himself" (Theodore Morrison, "The Agitated Heart," *Atlantic Monthly*, July 1967).—EDS.

[2] Small wooden containers, often used for butter.—EDS.

Into each other. Both of them are lost.
And if you're lost enough to find yourself
By now, pull in your ladder road behind you
And put a sign up CLOSED to all but me.
Then make yourself at home. The only field
Now left's no bigger than a harness gall.
First there's the children's house of make believe,
Some shattered dishes underneath a pine,
The playthings in the playhouse of the children.
Weep for what little things could make them glad.
Then for the house that is no more a house,
But only a belilaced cellar hole,
Now slowly closing like a dent in dough.
This was no playhouse but a house in earnest.
Your destination and your destiny's
A brook that was the water of the house,
Cold as a spring as yet so near its source,
Too lofty and original to rage.
(We know the valley streams that when aroused
Will leave their tatters hung on barb and thorn.)
I have kept hidden in the instep arch
Of an old cedar at the waterside
A broken drinking goblet like the Grail
Under a spell so the wrong ones can't find it,
So can't get saved, as Saint Mark says they mustn't.[3]
(I stole the goblet from the children's playhouse.)
Here are your waters and your watering place.
Drink and be whole again beyond confusion.

---

[3] Cf. Mark 16:16.—EDS.

War

The Hot Gates
WILLIAM GOLDING

I had lunch in Lamia, a provincial town of Thessaly which lies on the route south to Athens. Most people go through Lamia without stopping, but I was following the route of the Persian invasion, that spectacular combined operation of almost twenty-five hundred years ago. . . .

It was in these parts, in 480 B.C., that the Persian army had been held up for a few days on its way to Athens. South of Lamia, the river Spercheios has cut a valley athwart the invasion route, and the road must crawl round the corner on the other side of the valley between the cliffs and the sea. Sitting beneath a tree, and drinking my Demestica,[1] I thought about Athens and Persia, and the hot springs that bubble out of the cliff where the road is narrowest, so that the Greeks call it the Hot Gates.[2] I thought of myself too—dreaming for twenty years of coming here, poring over ancient maps; and now faced with the duty and the necessity of trying to understand.

I had seen the valley of the Spercheios when I entered Lamia, had glimpsed the vast wall of rock five thousand feet high on the other side of the valley, which lay between me and Athens. Athens was shining Athens, the Athens of history, shining in the mind. Yet when the Persian Xerxes, King of Kings, drove his army at her, she did not shine. At that time she was little but a thorn in his side, a small city which had insisted on running her own affairs—and had an odd knack of encouraging cities which ought to bow to the King of Kings to do the same.

Athens needed thirty years, and then she would shine as no city had shone before or has shone since. For all her faults she would take humanity with her a long, long step—but on that day she was nothing but a pain in the neck of the King of Kings, who had the greatest army in the world poised at her last gate. . . .

At the time of the Persian invasion, when the sea came close to these cliffs, the narrow track had held seven thousand men—Spartans, Thebans, Locrians, Thespians, Phocians—who watched one another as much as they watched the enemy. Greece to the south was in a turmoil as the Persians marched toward it. What to do? Whom to trust? What to believe? The track that summer was thick with dusty messengers bearing appeals for

---

[1] A wine produced in the Peloponnese, or southern Greece.—EDS.
[2] The battle site is more widely known by the Greek name for "hot gates," Thermopylae.—EDS.

help, or accusations, or denials, or prayers to the gods. In any event, with Xerxes only a few miles away, there was a mixed force to hold the track— groups sent by the cities of Greece, and small groups at that. No city dared strip itself of troops. . . .

I drove on to the Hot Gates proper, where once there had been room for no more than one wagon at a time. Sure enough, there was a memorial, level with the place where that mixed force had once stood in the pass, a nineteenth-century monument, grandiose and expensive. When the battle was fought, the place where the monument stands was out in the sea.

Nature has not done her best here for the story of that battle. The Vale of Tempe would have been a better place, and there are a hundred haunted spots in Greece where the setting would be more striking and the drama more obvious. Quiet, crop-fledged fields lie between the cliffs and the sea, with the scar of the motor road on them. The slopes and cliffs, though sprinkled with shrubs and flowers, aromatic in the hot sun, are arid with outcroppings of rock. There is dust everywhere. Little gullies leading back into the cliffs are marked with low stone walls that look ancient but are recent structures made by farmers and goatherds. If you go to the Hot Gates, take some historical knowledge and your imagination with you.

Just at the mouth of one of these gullies, I came across a mound. It was not very imposing to look at. The Greeks have planted it with laurels; but laurels planted recently in Greece never seem to be doing very well. There are some by the Springs of Daphne, some on the field of Marathon, some at Delphi—and they all look sheepish and a bit scruffy. But it was here, by this very mound, that the mixed force led by Leonidas and his three hundred Spartans came to hold the pass.

Standing by the dusty mound on that April afternoon, in the deserted landscape, where the only sound was an occasional clatter from the laurel leaves in a hot gust of wind, I wondered what Leonidas made of it all. He was, like all the Spartans, a dedicated soldier. But what did he think? As he looked north, where Lamia now lies on the hills across the valley, he must have heard the sound of quarrelling at his back. That is the one certain thing—the mixed force was quarrelling.

You can imagine the sullen afternoon lengthening, the ribaldry, the sudden shouts, perhaps even the clash of arms, the mutter of men who had to do as they were told but knew better than their leaders, the cynical laughter of men who had no faith in anything because Greece behind the wall—Athens, Sparta, Thebes and the rest—was at war not only with Persia but with itself. Then there had come a flash and glitter from the flank of the mountain across the valley.

Mark that Leonidas did not know how Athens needed thirty years to blossom.[3] For him, Sparta, that dull, cruel city, shone brighter than Athens.

---

[3] The Age of Pericles approximates Pericles's leadership from 461 B.C. to 429 B.C. Golding's "thirty years" marks the midpoint.—EDS.

But as the Persian army seeped down from a dozen pathways into the valley, and the mixed force fell silent at his back, it must have been some inarticulate and bitter passion for freedom as he knew it that kept him there, sullen and fiercely determined as he gazed across the plain.

No man had ever seen anything like this army before. It was patently unstoppable. It came along the neck of the hills on the banks of the Asopus, from the heights of the mountain and along the coastal track from Alope and Phalara. Lengthening rivers of men—Persians in fish-scale armor, turbaned Cissians, bronze-clad Assyrians, trousered Scythians, Indian bowmen, Caspians, Sarangians in bright cloth and high-heeled boots—came down and spread in a flood that filled the plain. Soon there was nothing to see but rising clouds of white dust, pierced and speckled with the flicker of steel. If each of the seven thousand Greeks should kill his ten men, there would be more than enough to press forward—and this was only the vanguard.

At their back, stretching for league after league by Mounts Pelion and Ossa, back through the narrow gorge of the Peneus to the wide plain beneath Olympus, marched the main body of the Persian war machine: Arabs in robes and Negroes in leopard skins; leather-clad Libyans, Thracians with headdresses of foxpelt, Pisidians with their oxhide shields, Cabalians and Milyans, Moschians, Tibareni, Tacrones and Mossynoeci; Marians, Colchians with their wooden helmets, Alarodians, Saspires and Medes; and horses and oxen and mules. There were eighty thousand mounted bowmen and lancers, and chariots in a swarm no one could count.

When that assembly of nations heaved itself off the earth and marched, the ground shuddered like the head of a drum. When that assembly came to a swift Greek river and halted for miles along the bank to drink, the waters shrank to a few pools of mud. This was the army that seeped and flooded into the valley all day, and halted under its own dust before the narrow entrance of the Hot Gates.

Not a man in the pass could be sure that the rest of Greece really meant to fight. And if those panicky cities on the other side of the wall *did* combine, what could they do against such an army? And who could be sure that these lousy Thebans (or Thespians or Locrians, according to your own nationality) really meant to fight? Only the three hundred Spartans were calm, and even cheerful. They were soldiers, and nothing but soldiers, and this was what they were for.

Xerxes pitched his tent and set up his throne. He sent forward a scout. The Spartans saw the horseman coming but ignored him. They were bathing in the sulphur springs and combing their hair. The horseman came thumping along the plain by the shore. He turned toward them and reined back his horse just out of bowshot. He balanced there on his rearing horse and peered sideways at the pass under his lifted hand. Then he wheeled away in dust and spurts of sand. The men in the pass saw him go to a kind of glittering mound, dismount and make his report.

Xerxes waited four days—and nothing happened. The men in the pass would not recognize the obvious. On the fifth day he sent forward a troop; and the result was a pushover for the Greeks. Every time the Persians thrust them back, the Greeks simply plugged the pass more completely. He sent forward his own bodyguard, the Company of Immortals, his best troops. They were defeated. For two days the Persians attacked, and the Greeks held them.

It is said that Xerxes leaped from his throne three times in terror for his whole army. Modern historians have found this incredible, but I cannot see why. Communications between the wings of his army were primitive. At any moment, rumor could have sent those savage levies scrambling away into the mountains. If the soldiers immediately engaging the Greeks had run away, panic would have spread like a heath fire.

I strolled away from the cliff to where the modern but colossal statue of Leonidas stands on its narrow plinth beside the road. He wears a helmet and sword belt, carries a shield, and threatens the mountains with a spear that quivers slightly in the brassy wind. I thought of the messages he sent during those two days. He needed reinforcements—as many as Greece could find. But that summer the roads were thick with messengers.

And then, of course, the inevitable traitor appeared from the wings.

I moved back and peered up at the cliffs. The traitor had led a Persian force over those cliffs at night, so that with day they would appear in the rear of the seven thousand in the pass. For years I had promised myself that I would follow that track. But I should have come twenty years earlier, with knapsack, no money, and plenty of breath. Yet twenty years ago I was fighting, too, and in as bitter a war. If I could climb cliffs less easily now, it was possible that I could understand war better. . . .

Suddenly, the years and the reading fused with the thing. I was clinging to Greece herself. Obscurely, and in part, I understood what it had meant to Leonidas when he looked up at these cliffs in the dawn light and saw that their fledging of pines was not thick enough to hide the glitter of arms.

It was then—and by the double power of imagination and the touch of rock, I was certain of it—that the brooding and desperate thinking of Leonidas crystallized into one clear idea. The last pass was sold. If the rest of Greece beyond the wall did not unite and make its stand, the game was up. Leonidas knew now that he could make one last plea for that stand—a desperate plea, but one which those dull, dedicated Spartans were eminently fitted to give. I clambered and sweated down the cliffside to the place where he made it. He sent away most of his army but moved the Spartans out into the open, where they could die properly and in due form. The Persians came at them like waves of the sea. The Spartans retreated to make their last stand on a little mound.

To most of the Persian army, this must have meant nothing. There had been, after all, nothing but a small column of dust hanging under the cliffs in one corner of the plain. If you were a Persian, you could not know that this example would lead, next year, to the defeat and destruction of your whole army at the battle of Plataea,[4] where the cities of Greece fought side by side. Neither you nor Leonidas nor anyone else could foresee that here thirty years' time was won for shining Athens and all Greece and all humanity.

The column of dust diminished. The King of Kings gave an order. The huge army shrugged itself upright and began the march forward into the Hot Gates, where the last of the Spartans were still fighting with nails and feet and teeth.

I came to myself in a great stillness, to find I was standing by the little mound. This is the mound of Leonidas, with its dust and rank grass, its flowers and lizards, its stones, scruffy laurels and hot gusts of wind. I knew now that something real happened here. It is not just that the human spirit reacts directly and beyond all argument to a story of sacrifice and courage, as a wine glass must vibrate to the sound of the violin. It is also because, way back and at the hundredth remove, that company stood in the right line of history. A little of Leonidas lies in the fact that I can go where I like and write what I like. He contributed to set us free.

Climbing to the top of that mound by the uneven, winding path, I came on the epitaph, newly cut in stone. It is an ancient epitaph though the stone is new. It is famous for its reticence and simplicity—has been translated a hundred times but can only be paraphrased:

"Stranger, tell the Spartans that we behaved as they would wish us to, and are buried here."

The Persian Version

ROBERT GRAVES

Truth-loving Persians do not dwell upon
The trivial skirmish fought near Marathon.[1]
As for the Greek theatrical tradition[2]
Which represents that summer's expedition
Not as a mere reconnaissance in force

---

[4] At the Battle of Plataea (479 B.C.) the Greeks completely routed the Persians. But immediately after the stand of Leonidas and his men, the Persians had conquered and destroyed Athens.—EDS.

[1] The Battle of Marathon, in which the Greeks achieved a partial victory, took place in 490 B.C., ten years before the heroic stand at the Hot Gates (Thermopylae) about which William Golding writes in the preceding essay.—EDS.

[2] Reference is to *The Persians* by Aeschylus. No Persian account of the battle survives.—EDS.

By three brigades of foot and one of horse
(Their left flank covered by some obsolete
Light craft detached from the main Persian fleet)
But as a grandiose, ill-starred attempt
To conquer Greece—they treat it with contempt;
And only incidentally refute
Major Greek claims, by stressing what repute
The Persian monarch and the Persian nation
Won by this salutary demonstration:
Despite a strong defence and adverse weather
All arms combined magnificently together.

Appomattox

BRUCE CATTON

Until this Palm Sunday of 1865 the word Appomattox had no meaning. It was a harsh name left over from Indian days, it belonged to a river and to a country town, and it had no overtones. But after this day it would be one of the haunted possessions of the American people, a great and unique word that would echo in the national memory with infinite tragedy and infinite promise, recalling a moment in which sunset and sunrise came together in a streaked glow that was half twilight and half dawn.

The business might almost have been stage-managed for effect. No detail had been overlooked. There was even the case of Wilmer McLean, the Virginian who once owned a place by a stream named Bull Run and who found his farm overrun by soldiers in the first battle of the war. He sold out and moved to southern Virginia to get away from the war, and he bought a modest house in Appomattox Court House; and the war caught up with him finally, so that Lee and Grant chose his front parlor—of all the rooms in America—as the place where they would sit down together and bring the fighting to an end.

Lee had one staff officer with him, and in Mr. McLean's front yard a Confederate orderly stood by while the war horse Traveler nibbled at the spring grass. Grant came with half a dozen officers of his own, including the famous Sheridan, and after he and Lee had shaken hands and taken their seats these trooped into the room to look and to listen. Grant and Lee sat at two separate tables, the central figures in one of the greatest tableaus of American history.

It was a great tableau not merely because of what these two men did but also because of what they were. No two Americans could have been in greater contrast. (Again, the staging was perfect.) Lee was legend incarnate—tall, gray, one of the handsomest and most imposing men who ever lived, dressed today in his best uniform, with a sword belted at his waist. Grant was—well, he was U. S. Grant, rather scrubby and undersized, wearing his working clothes, with mud-spattered boots and trousers and a private's rumpled blue coat with his lieutenant general's stars tacked to the shoulders. He wore no sword. The men who were with them noticed the contrast and remembered it. Grant himself seems to have felt it; years afterward, when he wrote his memoirs, he mentioned it and went to some lengths to explain why he did not go to this meeting togged out in dress uniform. (In effect, his explanation was that he was just too busy.)

Yet the contrast went far beyond the matter of personal appearance. Two separate versions of America met in this room, each perfectly embodied by its chosen representative.

There was an American aristocracy, and it had had a great day. It came from the past and it looked to the past; it seemed almost deliberately archaic, with an air of knee breeches and buckled shoes and powdered wigs, with a leisured dignity and a rigid code in which privilege and duty were closely joined. It had brought the country to its birth and it had provided many of its beliefs; it had given courage and leadership, a sense of order and learning, and if there had been any way by which the eighteenth century could possibly have been carried forward into the future, this class would have provided the perfect vehicle. But from the day of its beginning America had been fated to be a land of unending change. The country in which this leisured class had its place was in powerful ferment, and the class itself had changed. It had been diluted. In the struggle for survival it had laid hands on the curious combination of modern machinery and slave labor, the old standards had been altered, dignity had begun to look like arrogance, and pride of purse had begun to elbow out pride of breeding. The single lifetime of Robert E. Lee had seen the change, although Lee himself had not been touched by it.

Yet the old values were real, and the effort to preserve them had nobility. Of all the things that went to make up the war, none had more poignance than the desperate fight to preserve these disappearing values, eroded by change from within as much as by change from without. The fight had been made and it had been lost, and everything that had been dreamed and tried and fought for was personified in the gray man who sat at the little table in the parlor at Appomattox and waited for the other man to start writing out the terms of surrender.

The other man was wholly representative too. Behind him there was a new society, not dreamed of by the founding fathers: a society with the lid taken off, western man standing up to assert that what lay back of a person mattered nothing in comparison to what lay ahead of him. It was the land of the mudsills, the temporarily dispossessed, the people who had nothing to lose but the future; behind it were hard times, humiliation and failure, and ahead of it was all the world and a chance to lift oneself by one's bootstraps. It had few standards beyond a basic unformulated belief in the irrepressibility and ultimate value of the human spirit, and it could tramp with heavy boots down a ravaged Shenandoah Valley or through the embers of a burned Columbia without giving more than a casual thought to the things that were being destroyed. Yet it had its own nobility and its own standards; it had, in fact, the future of the race in its keeping, with all the immeasurable potential that might reside in a people who had decided that they would no longer be bound by the limitations of the past. It was rough and uncultivated and it came to important meetings wearing muddy boots and no sword, and it had to be listened to.

It could speak with a soft voice, and it could even be abashed by its own moment of triumph, as if that moment were not a thing to be savored and enjoyed. Grant seems to have been almost embarrassed when he and Lee came together in this parlor, yet it was definitely not the embarrassment of an underling ill at ease in a superior's presence. Rather it was simply the diffidence of a sensitive man who had another man in his power and wished to hurt him as little as possible. So Grant made small talk and recalled the old days in the Mexican War, when Lee had been the polished staff officer in the commanding general's tents and Grant had been an acting regimental quartermaster, slouching about like the hired man who looked after the teams. Perhaps the oddest thing about this meeting at Appomattox was that it was Grant, the nobody from nowhere, who played the part of gracious host, trying to put the aristocrat at his ease and, as far as might be, to soften the weight of the blow that was about to come down. In the end it was Lee who, so to speak, had to call the meeting to order, remarking (and the remark must have wrenched him almost beyond endurance) that they both knew what they were there for and that perhaps they had better get down to business. So Grant opened his orderly book and got out his pencil. He confessed afterward that when he did so he had no idea what words he was going to write.

He knew perfectly well what he was going to say, however, and with a few pauses he said it in straightforward words. Lee's army was to be surrendered, from commanding general down to humblest private. All public property would be turned over to the United States Army—battle flags, guns, muskets, wagons, everything. Officers might keep their side arms (Grant wrote this after a speculative glance at the excellent sword Lee was wearing) and their horses, but the army and everything it owned was to go out of existence.

It was not, however, to go off to a prison camp. Throughout the war Lincoln had stressed one point: the people of the South might have peace whenever they chose just by laying down their arms and going home. Grant made this official. Officers and men, having disarmed themselves, would simply give their paroles. Then they could go to their homes . . . and here Grant wrote one of the greatest sentences in American history, the sentence that, more than any other thing, would finally make it impossible for any vengeful government in Washington to proceed against Confederate veterans as traitors. Having gone home, he wrote, officers and men could stay there, "not to be disturbed by the United States authorities so long as they observe their paroles and the laws in force where they may reside." When the powerful signature, "U. S. Grant," was signed under that sentence, the chance that Confederate soldiers might be hanged or imprisoned for treason went out the window.

Having written all of this, Grant handed it over for Lee to read.

Lee's part was not easy. He made a business of getting out his glasses, polishing them carefully, crossing his legs, and adjusting himself. Once he borrowed a lead pencil to insert a word that Grant had omitted. When he had finished he raised a point. In the Confederate army, he said, horses for cavalry and artillery were not government issue; the soldiers themselves owned them. Did the terms as written permit these men to take their horses home with them? Grant shook his head. He had not realized that Confederate soldiers owned their steeds, and the terms he had written were explicit: all such animals must be turned in as captured property. Still—Grant went on to muse aloud; the last battle of the war was over, the war itself was over except for picking up the pieces, and what really mattered was for the men of the South to get back home and become civilians again. He would not change the written terms, but he supposed that most of Lee's men were small farmers anxious to return to their acres and get a crop in, and he would instruct the officers in charge of the surrender ceremonies to give a horse or a mule to any Confederate soldier who claimed to own one, so that the men would have a chance "to work their little farms." And in those homely words the great drama of Appomattox came to a close.

The draft of the terms having been agreed on, one of Grant's staff officers took the document to make a fair copy. The United States Army, it appeared, lacked ink, and to write the copy the officer had to borrow a bottle of ink from Lee's staff officer; a moment later, when the Confederate officer sat down to write Lee's formal acceptance, it developed that the Confederate army lacked paper, and he had to borrow from one of Grant's men. The business was finally signed and settled. Lee went out on the porch, looked off over the hills and smote his hands together absently while Traveler was being bridled, and then mounted and started to ride away. Grant and his officers saluted, Lee returned the salute, and there was a little silence while the man in gray rode off to join the pathetic remnant of an army that had just gone out of existence—rode off into mist and legend, to take his place at last in the folklore and the cherished memories of the nation that had been too big for him.

Grant stayed in character. He heard a banging of guns; Union artillerists were firing salutes to celebate the victory, and Grant sent word to have all that racket stopped—those men in gray were enemies no longer but simply fellow countrymen (which, as Grant saw it, was what the war had all been about), and nothing would be done to humiliate them. Instead, wagonloads of Federal hardtack and bacon would start moving at once for the Confederate camp, so that Lee's hungry men might have a square meal. Grant himself would return to Washington by the next train, without waiting to observe the actual laying down of arms. He was commanding general of the nation's armies, the war was costing four million dollars a day, and it was high time to start cutting expenses. Back in the Federal camp, Grant sat down in front of his tent to wait for the moment of departure. He seemed relaxed and in a mood to talk, and his officers gathered around him to hear what he would say about the supreme moment he had just been through. Grant addressed one of them, who had served with him in the Mexican War . . . "Do you remember that white mule old so-and-so used to ride, down in Mexico?" The officer nodded, being just then, as he confessed later, in a mood to remember the exact number of hairs in the mule's tail if that was what Grant wanted. So Grant chatted about the Mexican War, and if he had great thoughts about the piece of history he had just made he kept them to himself. Meanwhile the Army of the Potomac was alerted to be ready to move on if necessary. It was just possible it might have to march down into North Carolina and help Sherman take care of Joe Johnston.

But this would not be needed. Lee was the keystone of the arch, and when he was removed the long process of collapse moved swiftly to its end. Johnston himself had no illusions. Much earlier he had confessed himself unable to do more against Sherman than annoy him. Now he was ready to do as Lee had done. What remained of the Confederate government—Jefferson Davis and his iron determination, Cabinet ministers, odds and ends of government papers and funds—was flitting south, looking in vain for some refuge where it could start all over again, but there was no place where it could go. Far down in Alabama, General Wilson's cavalry had taken Selma, the last remaining munitions center, had dismantled its productive apparatus with smooth, disciplined effectiveness, and had gone on to occupy Montgomery, where Davis once stood before a great crowd and heard an orator proclaim: "The man and the hour have met!" Mobile had been surrendered, and the Confederate troops in Mississippi and Alabama would lay down their arms as soon as the Federals could catch up with them. Beyond the Mississippi there still existed a Confederate army, but it might as well have been in Siberia. As an obvious matter of inescapable fact, the war was over.

War Memories[1]

STEPHEN CRANE

"But to get the real thing!" cried Vernall, the war correspondent. "It seems impossible! It is because war is neither magnificent nor squalid; it is simply life, and an expression of life can always evade us. We can never tell life, one to another, although sometimes we think we can."

When I climbed aboard the despatch-boat at Key West the mate told me irritably that, as soon as we crossed the bar, we would find ourselves monkey-climbing over heavy seas. It wasn't my fault, but he seemed to insinuate that it was all a result of my incapacity. There were four correspondents in the party. The leader of us came aboard with a huge bunch of bananas, which he hung like a chandelier in the centre of the tiny cabin. We made acquaintance over, around, and under this bunch of bananas, which really occupied the cabin as a soldier occupies a sentry box. But the bunch did not become really aggressive until we were well at sea. Then it began to spar. With the first roll of the ship, it launched its bulk at McCurdy and knocked him wildly through the door to the deck-rail, where he hung cursing hysterically. Without a moment's pause, it made for me. I flung myself head-first into my bunk and watched the demon sweep Brownlow into a corner and wedge his knee behind a sea-chest. Kary gave a shrill cry and fled. The bunch of bananas swung to and fro, silent, determined, ferocious, looking for more men. It had cleared a space for itself. My comrades looked in at the door, calling upon me to grab the thing and hold it. I pointed out to them the security and comfort of my position. They were angry. Finally the mate came and lashed the thing so that it could not prowl about the cabin and assault innocent war correspondents. You see? War! A bunch of bananas rampant because the ship rolled. . . .

One day, our despatch-boat found the shores of Guantanamo Bay flowing past on either side. It was at nightfall, and on the eastward point a small village was burning, and it happened that a fiery light was thrown upon some palm-trees so that it made them into enormous crimson feathers. The water was the color of blue steel; the Cuban woods were sombre; high shivered the gory feathers. The last boatloads of the marine battalion were pulling for the beach. The marine officers gave me generous hospitality to the camp on the hill. That night there was an alarm, and, amid a stern calling of orders and a rushing of men, I wandered in search of some other man who had no occupation. It turned out to be the young assistant-surgeon, Gibbs. We foregathered in the centre of a square of six

---

[1] Excerpts from a longer article in *Wounds in the Rain* (1900). First appearing in the *Anglo-Saxon Review* in December 1899, the story reflects Crane's experience as a reporter in Cuba in 1898 during the Spanish-American War.—EDS.

companies of marines. There was no firing. We thought it rather comic. The next night there was an alarm; there was some firing; we lay on our bellies; it was no longer comic. On the third night the alarm came early; I went in search of Gibbs, but I soon gave over an active search for the more congenial occupation of lying flat and feeling the hot hiss of the bullets trying to cut my hair. For the moment I was no longer a cynic. I was a child who, in a fit of ignorance, had jumped into the vat of war. I heard somebody dying near me. He was dying hard. Hard. It took him a long time to die. He breathed as all noble machinery breathes when it is making its gallant strife against breaking, breaking. But he was going to break. He was going to break. It seemed to me, this breathing, the noise of a heroic pump which strives to subdue a mud which comes upon it in tons. The darkness was impenetrable. The man was lying in some depression within seven feet of me. Every wave, vibration, of his anguish beat upon my senses. He was long past groaning. There was only the bitter strife for air which pulsed out into the night in a clear penetrating whistle, with intervals of terrible silence in which I held my own breath in the common unconscious aspiration to help. I thought this man would never die. I wanted him to die. Ultimately he died. At the moment, the adjutant came bustling along erect amid the spitting bullets. I knew him by his voice. "Where's the doctor? There's some wounded men over there. Where's the doctor?" A man answered briskly: "Just died this minute, sir." It was as if he had said: "Just gone around the corner this minute, sir." Despite the horror of this night's business, the man's mind was somehow influenced by the coincidence of the adjutant's calling aloud for the doctor within a few seconds of the doctor's death. It—what shall I say?— It interested him, this coincidence. . . .

Then came the night of the first of July. A group of correspondents limped back to El Paso. It had been a day so long that the morning seemed as remote as a morning in a previous year. But I have forgotten to tell you about Reuben McNab. Many years ago I went to school at a place called Claverack in New York State, where there was a semi-military institution. Contemporaneous with me as a student was Reuben McNab, a long, lank boy, freckled, sandy-haired—an extraordinary boy in no way, and yet, I wager, a boy clearly marked in every recollection. Perhaps there is a good deal in that name. Reuben McNab. You can't fling that name carelessly over your shoulder and lose it. It follows you like the haunting memory of a sin. At any rate, Reuben McNab was identified intimately in my thought with the sunny irresponsible days at Claverack, when all the earth was a green field and all the sky was a rainless blue. Then I looked down into a miserable huddle at Bloody Bend, a huddle of hurt men, dying men, dead men. And there I saw Reuben McNab, a corporal in the 71st New York Volunteers, and with a hole through his lung. Also several holes through his clothing. "Well, they got me," he said in greeting. Usually they said that. There were no long speeches. "Well, they got me."

That was sufficient. The duty of the upright, unhurt man is then difficult. I doubt if many of us learned how to speak to our own wounded. In the first place one had to play that the wound was nothing; oh, a mere nothing; a casual interference with movement, perhaps, but nothing more; oh, really nothing more. In the second place, one had to show a comrade's appreciation of this sad plight. As a result I think most of us bungled and stammered in the presence of our wounded friends. That's curious, eh? "Well, they got me," said Reuben McNab. I had looked upon five hundred wounded men with stolidity, or with a conscious indifference which filled me with amazement. But the apparition of Reuben McNab, the schoolmate lying there in the mud with a hole through his lung, awed me into stutterings, set me trembling with a sense of terrible intimacy with this war which theretofore I could have believed was a dream—almost. Twenty shot men rolled their eyes and looked at me. Only one man paid no heed. He was dying; he had no time. The bullets hummed low over them all. Death, having already struck, still insisted upon raising a venomous crest. "If you're goin' by the hospital, step in and see me," said Reuben McNab. That was all. . . .

On the morning of July 2, I sat on San Juan Hill and watched Lawton's division come up. I was absolutely sheltered, but still where I could look into the faces of men who were trotting up under fire. There wasn't a high heroic face among them. They were all men intent on business. That was all. It may seem to you that I am trying to make everything a squalor. That would be wrong. I feel that things were often sublime. But they were *differently* sublime. They were not of our shallow and preposterous fictions. They stood out in a simple, majestic commonplace. It was the behavior of men on the street. It was the behavior of men. In one way, each man was just pegging along at the heels of the man before him, who was pegging along at the heels of still another man who—— It was that in the flat and obvious way. In another way it was pageantry, the pageantry of the accomplishment of naked duty. One cannot speak of it—the spectacle of the common man serenely doing his work, his appointed work. It is the one thing in the universe which makes one fling expression to the winds and be satisfied to simply feel. Thus they moved at San Juan—the soldiers of the United States Regular Army. One pays them the tribute of the toast of silence.

Lying near one of the enemy's trenches was a red-headed Spanish corpse. I wonder how many hundreds were cognizant of this red-headed Spanish corpse? It arose to the dignity of a landmark. There were many corpses, but only one with a red head. This red head. He was always there. Each time I approached that part of the field I prayed that I might find that he had been buried. But he was always there—red headed. His strong simple countenance was a malignant sneer at the system which was for ever killing the credulous peasants in a sort of black night of politics, where the peasants merely followed whatever somebody had told them was lofty and good. But nevertheless, the red-headed Spaniard was dead. He was irrevocably dead. And to what purpose? The honor of Spain? Surely the honor of Spain could have existed without the violent death of this poor red-headed peasant? Ah well, he was buried when the heavy firing ceased and men had time for such small things as funerals. The trench was turned over on top of him. It was a fine honorable soldierly fate—to be buried in a trench, the trench of the fight and the death. Sleep well, red-headed peasant. You came to another hemisphere to fight because—because you were told to, I suppose. Well, there you are, buried in your trench on San Juan Hill. That is the end of it. Your life has been taken—that is a flat, frank fact. And foreigners buried you expeditiously while speaking a strange tongue. Sleep well, red-headed mystery. . . .

Very soon after this the end of the campaign came for me. I caught a fever. I am not sure to this day what kind of a fever it was. It was defined variously. I know, at any rate, that I first developed a languorous indifference to everything in the world. . . .

I was almost well, and had defeated the yellow-fever charge which had been brought against me, and so I was allowed ashore among the first. And now happened a strange thing. A hard campaign, full of wants and lacks and absences, brings a man speedily back to an appreciation of things long disregarded or forgotten. In camp, somewhere in the woods between Siboney and Santiago, I happened to think of ice-cream-soda. I had done very well without it for many years; in fact I think I loathe it; but I got to dreaming of ice-cream-soda, and I came near dying of longing for it. I couldn't get it out of my mind, try as I would to concentrate my thoughts upon the land crabs and mud with which I was surrounded. It certainly had been an institution of my childhood, but to have a ravenous longing for it in the year 1898 was about as illogical as to have a ravenous longing for kerosene. All I could do was to swear to myself that if I reached the United States again, I would immediately go to the nearest soda-water-fountain and make it look like Spanish Fours. In a loud, firm voice, I would say, "Orange, please." And here is the strange thing; as soon as I was ashore I went to the nearest soda-water-fountain, and in a loud, firm voice I said, "Orange, please." I remember one man who went mad that way over tinned peaches, and who wandered over the face of the earth saying plaintively, "Have you any peaches?"

Most of the wounded and sick had to be tabulated and marshalled in sections and thoroughly officialized, so that I was in time to take a position on the verandah of Chamberlain's Hotel and see my late shipmates taken to the hospital. The verandah was crowded with women in light, charming summer dresses, and with spruce officers from the Fortress. It was like a bank of flowers. It filled me with awe. All this luxury and refinement and gentle care and fragrance and color seemed absolutely new. Then across the narrow street on the verandah of the hotel there was a similar bank of flowers. Two companies of volunteers dug a lane through the great crowd in the street and kept the way, and then through this lane there passed a curious procession. I had never known that they looked like that. Such a gang of dirty, ragged, emaciated, half-starved, bandaged cripples I had never seen. Naturally there were many men who couldn't walk, and some of these were loaded upon a big flat car which was in tow of a trolley-car. Then there were many stretchers, slow-moving. When that crowd began to pass the hotel the banks of flowers made a noise which could make one tremble. Perhaps it was a moan, perhaps it was a sob— but no, it was something beyond either a moan or a sob. Anyhow, the sound of women weeping was in it.—The sound of women weeping.

And how did these men of famous deeds appear when received thus by the people? Did they smirk and look as if they were bursting with the desire to tell everything which had happened? No they hung their heads like so many jail-birds. Most of them seemed to be suffering from something which was like stage-fright during the ordeal of this chance but supremely eloquent reception. No sense of excellence—that was it. Evidently they were willing to leave the clacking to all those natural born major-generals who after the war talked enough to make a great fall in the price of that commodity all over the world.

The episode was closed. And you can depend upon it that I have told you nothing at all, nothing at all, nothing at all.

The War Prayer[1]

MARK TWAIN

It was a time of great and exalting excitement. The country was up in arms, the war was on, in every breast burned the holy fire of patriotism; the drums were beating, the bands playing, the toy pistols popping, the bunched firecrackers hissing and spluttering; on every hand and far down the receding and fading spread of roofs and balconies a fluttering wilderness of flags flashed in the sun; daily the young volunteers marched down the wide avenue gay and fine in their new uniforms, the proud fathers and mothers and sisters and sweethearts cheering them with voices choked with happy emotion as they swung by; nightly the packed mass-meetings listened, panting, to patriot oratory which stirred the deepest deeps of their hearts, and which they interrupted at briefest intervals with cyclones of applause, the tears running down their cheeks the while; in the churches the pastors preached devotion to flag and country, and invoked the God of Battles, beseeching His aid in our good cause in outpourings of fervid eloquence which moved every listener. It was indeed

[1] Written in 1904–1905 but not published until after Mark Twain's death.—Eds.

a glad and gracious time, and the half dozen rash spirits that ventured to disapprove of the war and cast a doubt upon its righteousness straightway got such a stern and angry warning that for their personal safety's sake they quickly shrank out of sight and offended no more in that way.

Sunday morning came—next day the battalions would leave for the front; the church was filled; the volunteers were there, their young faces alight with martial dreams—visions of the stern advance, the gathering momentum, the rushing charge, the flashing sabres, the flight of the foe, the tumult, the enveloping smoke, the fierce pursuit, the surrender!—then home from the war, bronzed heroes, welcomed, adored, submerged in golden seas of glory! With the volunteers sat their dear ones, proud, happy, and envied by the neighbors and friends who had no sons and brothers to send forth to the field of honor, there to win for the flag, or, failing, die the noblest of noble deaths. The service proceeded; a war-chapter from the Old Testament was read; the first prayer was said; it was followed by an organ-burst that shook the building, and with one impulse the house rose, with glowing eyes and beating hearts and poured out that tremendous invocation—

> God the all-terrible! Thou who ordainest,
> Thunder thy clarion and lightning thy sword![2]

Then came the "long" prayer. None could remember the like of it for passionate pleading and moving and beautiful language. The burden of its supplication was, that the ever-merciful and benignant Father of us all would watch over our noble young soldiers, and aid, comfort, and encourage them in their patriotic work; bless them, shield them in the day of battle and the hour of peril, bear them in His mighty hand, make them strong and confident, invincible in the bloody onset, help them to crush the foe, grant to them and to their flag and country imperishable honor and glory—

An aged stranger entered, and moved with slow and noiseless step up the main aisle, his eyes fixed upon the minister, his long body clothed in a robe that reached to his feet, his head bare, his white hair descending in a frothy cataract to his shoulders, his seamy face unnaturally pale, pale even to ghastliness. With all eyes following him and wondering, he made his silent way; without pausing, he ascended to the preacher's side and stood there, waiting. With shut lids the preacher, unconscious of his presence, continued his moving prayer, and at last finished it with the words, uttered in fervent appeal, "Bless our arms, grant us the victory, O Lord our God, Father and Protector of our land and flag!"

---

[2] The first lines of a hymn by Henry Fothergill Chorley (1842), sung to the majestic tune of the old Russian national anthem. In present-day hymnals the text has been modernized to read: "God the Omnipotent." The stanza concludes, "Give to us peace in our time, O Lord."—Eds.

The stranger touched his arm, motioned him to step aside—which the startled minister did—and took his place. During some moments he surveyed the spell-bound audience with solemn eyes, in which burned an uncanny light; then in a deep voice he said—

"I come from the Throne—bearing a message from Almighty God!" The words smote the house with a shock; if the stranger perceived it he gave it no attention. "He has heard the prayer of His servant your shepherd, and will grant it if such shall be your desire after I, His messenger, shall have explained to you its import—that is to say, its full import. For it is like unto many of the prayers of men, in that it asks for more than he who utters it is aware of—except he pause and think.

"God's servant and yours has prayed his prayer. Has he paused, and taken thought? Is it one prayer? No, it is two—one uttered, the other not. Both have reached the ear of Him who heareth all supplications, the spoken and the unspoken. Ponder this—keep it in mind. If you would beseech a blessing upon yourself, beware! lest without intent you invoke a curse upon a neighbor at the same time. If you pray for the blessing of rain upon your crop which needs it, by that act you are possibly praying for a curse upon some neighbor's crop which may not need rain and can be injured by it.

"You have heard your servant's prayer—the uttered part of it. I am commissioned of God to put into words the other part of it—that part which the pastor—and also you in your hearts—fervently prayed silently. And ignorantly and unthinkingly? God grant that it was so! You heard these words: 'Grant us the victory, O Lord our God!' That is sufficient. The *whole* of the uttered prayer is compacted into those pregnant words. Elaborations were not necessary. When you have prayed for victory you have prayed for many unmentioned results which follow victory—*must* follow it, cannot help but follow it. Upon the listening spirit of God the Father fell also the unspoken part of the prayer. He commandeth me to put it into words. Listen!

"O Lord, our Father, our young patriots, idols of our hearts, go forth to battle—be Thou near them! With them—in spirit—we also go forth from the sweet peace of our beloved firesides to smite the foe. O Lord, our God, help us to tear their soldiers to bloody shreds with our shells; help us to cover their smiling fields with the pale forms of their patriot dead; help us to drown the thunder of the guns with the shrieks of their wounded, writhing in pain; help us to lay waste their humble homes with a hurricane of fire; help us to wring the hearts of their unoffending widows with unavailing grief; help us to turn them out roofless with their little children to wander unfriended the wastes of their desolated land in rags and hunger and thirst, sport of the sun-flames of summer and the icy winds of winter, broken in spirit, worn with travail, imploring Thee for the refuge of the grave and denied it—for our sakes who adore Thee, Lord, blast their hopes, blight their lives, protract their bitter pilgrimage, make heavy their steps, water their way with their tears, stain the white snow with the blood of their wounded feet! We ask it, in the spirit of love, of Him Who is the Source of Love, and Who is the ever-faithful refuge and friend of all that are sore beset and seek His aid with humble and contrite hearts. Amen."

[*After a pause.*] "Ye have prayed it; if ye still desire it, speak!—The messenger of the Most High waits."

It was believed afterwards, that the man was a lunatic, because there was no sense in what he said.

A Salutation-Speech from the 19th Century to the 20th[1]
MARK TWAIN

A Salutation-Speech from the 19th Century to the 20th, taken down in short-hand by Mark Twain: I bring you the stately matron named Christendom, returning bedraggled, besmirched & dishonored from pirate-raids in Kiao-Chou, Manchuria, South Africa & the Philippines,[2] with her soul full of meanness, her pocket full of boodle, & her mouth full of pious hypocrisies. Give her soap & a towel, but hide the looking-glass.

On History, Foolishness, and Vietnam[1]
JOHN KENNETH GALBRAITH

In these last weeks I've come to wonder if historians are not the needed resource in our time. We've been treating our misfortunes in Vietnam as though they were a peculiarly modern and American disaster. They are, in fact, merely the last in a long and remarkably consistent historical experience.

It is now just under 900 years since Trans-Alpine Europeans began extending the beneficence of their presence to the lesser races without the law. Then, as still, they saw themselves as the custodians of higher civilized values and the progenitors and evangelists of these values.

---

[1] First published in the New York *Herald*, December 30, 1900.—EDS.

[2] Domination of Kiao-Chou by the Germans and Manchuria by the Russians led to the Boxer Rebellion of 1900. England made war on the South African Boers in 1899, the same year that the United States began to "pacify" the Philippines.—EDS.

---

[1] Excerpts from an address given in 1975 at Memphis State University in Tennessee. —EDS.

The first effort was, of course, the First Crusade, the beginning of an enterprise which continued, though with diminishing enthusiasm, for nearly 400 years. Repeatedly it was reported back to Rome that there was light at the end of that tunnel. The Kingdom of Jerusalem, so quickly gained and so soon lost, would be redeemed. Since 1096, Austrians, Spaniards, French, British, Dutch, Belgians, Swedes, Danes, Russians, Germans, Portuguese and Italians have answered the call to a civilizing mission beyond their borders. The urge among non-Europeans has been shared by Arabs, Mongols, Turks, Japanese and Americans.

All of these efforts over all of these nine centuries have had three features in common. All have avowed some religious, cultural, moral, legal or other spiritual benefit for the people toward whom the effort was directed. All have involved, often with some tactful disguise, some element of economic interest for the country extending the benefit. All have ended in failure.

The combination of high purpose and lower economic interest has been especially constant. The Crusades, as every schoolchild knows, were to protect the Eastern Christians from the Turks and to redeem Jerusalem from the infidel. But Urban II, preaching the First Crusade in Clermont in 1095, did not omit to mention that there was a lot of excellent land in that part of the world only awaiting occupation by the Christians. As men knelt to take the cross, there was a companion obeisance to the thought of good real estate.

The Spaniards combined a concern for extending the sway of the holy Catholic Church with an even more compelling interest in increasing their cash flow of silver and gold. The British sought to bring the rule of law, the benefits of sound government to Indians and Africans while bringing the trade of these peoples to London, Liverpool and Bristol. The American aim in Puerto Rico and the Philippines was deemed wholly selfless and benign and exclusively to assist subject peoples suddenly, almost accidentally, liberated from Spain. But it is not without importance that these islands were soon extensively covered with sugar plantations, mostly under continental ownership.

Except by a sycophantic minority that allied itself socially, politically or culturally with the paramount power, this civilizing effort was rarely appreciated; this was true even when the motives were exceptionally pure or the rule better by some standard than what preceded it.

India, in the last century, was an exceedingly well-governed country. In efficiency, honesty, stability, safety of person and property the British administration was a quantum step on from the contentious, corrupt and predacious despotisms that it replaced. To this day what was British India —that governed directly by the British Raj—is perceptibly more prosperous than that which was governed indirectly through the princes—the Nabobs, the Nizam, the Rajahs and the Maharajahs. This did not save British rule.

One must assume that the Soviets, after World War II, had a moral interest in extending socialism. This did not make them more welcome in Yugoslavia, China, Czechoslovakia, Algeria, Albania, Ghana and Egypt.

We did not, after World War II, seek directly to govern people distant from our shores. Like the Soviets we were too wise for that. Like the Soviets we proclaimed our aversion to colonial rule. But no less than other powers we sought to guide the political and economic development of other lands. No less than the colonial powers we sought to shape these developments to our own preference, which is to say our own image.

Our technique, in fact, bore a marked resemblance to that of Britain in the princely states of India—to what, in a less ambiguous age, was called indirect rule.

In Indochina, happily the extreme case, we supported rulers of our preference if not our choice. We worried, as did the British, about their behavior. On occasion as the paramount power we dismissed them if they were too bad. (Our standards were, however, more tolerant than those of the Raj; once in Junagadh state in western India it dismissed an animal-loving Nabob for staging an unduly elaborate wedding between two dogs named Roshana and Bobby. About 50,000 attended the ceremony, not counting the dogs.)

We surrounded our Nabobs with advisers—Lodge, Taylor, Bunker, Graham Martin.[2] These were the modern, though perhaps more permissive, equivalent of the British Resident at the princely court. We armed our men against their indigenous enemies and like the British supplied supporting force of our own. We further sought their fealty, if not in the case of General Thieu[3] their enduring gratitude, by providing massive subsidies. We did depart from the British model in one respect. They spoke of colonialism; we said always that we were securing the independence of the people in question.

As also over the 900-year history there was the admixture of idealism and economic interest. Freedom—freedom from the discipline and the coercion that few doubt is a feature of Communist administration—was the motivating ideal.

I've never thought that the companion economic interest was the direct profit of American corporations. They were doing quite well without the war. The stock market invariably went up on news of peace. I spent much of 1968 raising money for the antiwar campaign of Eugene McCarthy. By far the largest part of our support came from businessmen, the largest contributions being from Wall Street.

But Americans were moved by the belief that to preserve free enterprise in the United States we had to act to preserve it everywhere else. Let one country succumb and more would be threatened. It was a proposition that was without merit. What happens in Vietnam has no appreciable bearing

---

[2] Henry Cabot Lodge, Maxwell D. Taylor, Ellsworth Bunker, and Graham A. Martin —successive U.S. ambassadors to South Vietnam.—EDS.

[3] Nguyen Van Thieu, president of South Vietnam, 1967–1975.—EDS.

on what happens in Europe or the United States. Whether a poor, rural society calls itself Communist or capitalist makes little difference. It is a poor, rural society in either case. Only a very sensitive ideologist, walking through a Laotian jungle, can tell whether it is a free-enterprise jungle or a socialist jungle. But this was not the point. We had persuaded ourselves of this interest.

In keeping with all the history we were rejected. In light of the history we should hardly be surprised.

You will ask why, in relation to Hanoi, the Chinese and Russians did better. One answer is that they were wiser: No Chinese or Russian troops were sent; no great body of advisers debouched; there was a Pentagon East but no Kremlin East. To this day we do not know which country, China or the Soviet Union, was more influential in North Vietnam. They weren't thrown out because they weren't there.

We do know that where the Soviet influence and presence have been strong the experience has been similar to our own. In Yugoslavia, China, Algeria, Egypt, the Soviets have been thrown out. I once asked a Soviet journalist what they did with their failed Yugoslav, Albanian, Chinese and Egyptian strategists. Did they, following our humane practice, send them back to teach wisdom to the young? Were they available for thoughtful seminars at some Bolshevist equivalent of the Council on Foreign Relations? Did they explain how it was all for the best on the Op-Ed Page of *Pravda*? He replied only: "We have them."

Voltaire killed off Dr. Pangloss rather early in his academic career;[4] it was a wise decision, and we should deplore the recent efforts to revive him and put him on the White House payroll. But there are two aspects of our Indochina experience which are not altogether dark.

There is a well-articulated view that what happened in Indochina is inevitable under capitalism. It reflects an uncontrollable imperialist drive—for markets, for outlets for investment, for justification for military spending and power. We see that an inability to be guided by historical experience was far more plausibly the cause.

The Vietnam policy was made by men of limited vision who did not know the limits of their vision. They were themselves an historical accident. Some were holdovers from the time when foreign policy was the only proper public profession for a gentleman. Others were members of the legal, business or academic Establishment who had discovered that foreign policy was a source of personal prestige—that the aura of American power in the years of success after World War II reflected luminously on those in its service.

Few could perceive the great historical current against which they were proceeding. Almost none could grasp the most elementary of political

[4] In Voltaire's *Candide* (1759), the optimistic philosopher Pangloss survived a series of harrowing adventures; however, he had lost his job as tutor early in the novel.—EDS.

propositions which is that men will not die to sustain the greed and graft of others. I speak with some personal animus here. There were individuals who made this case. We were dismissed with that contempt which is so marvelously the manner of those who do not understand, do not wish to understand.

Foolishness, even stupidity, to which I attribute blame is not a minor problem in our time. But, unlike the imperialist dynamic, it is not inherent in the system. It could be remediable. In the case of Vietnam there was a remedy. It came out of the good sense of the country as a whole. It is in this that we can justly take the satisfaction.

When before has a great country stopped in the middle of a war, assessed the wisdom of its participation, decided it was wrong, asserted the judgment against all of the chauvinist tendencies aroused by armed conflict, dismissed from power those responsible and brought its participation to an end?

The answer is never, for unlike the French before us we had a choice. The country corrected the error of its leaders on Vietnam. It was not a defeat but a triumph of good sense. Surely our critics abroad might take more note of this achievement. Does it not say something for democracy?

However, let us not make the presence of this remedial power a license for any more such mistakes.

Sports

Billie Jean King: An Attitude, Instinct, and Sense of Urgency
PARTON KEESE

For raw power, Margaret Court has more. Virginia Wade's bullet serve is faster. Rosemary Casals could probably run rings around her. For grace of movement and beauty of swing, Evonne Goolagong wins hands down. And for steadiness, Chris Evert invented the word. But if it came down to one tennis tournament, one final match, one last set or one deciding game, Billie Jean King in her prime would be the overwhelming choice to win.

Why Billie Jean? How could a stubby, 5 foot 4½ inch woman with 20/400 eyesight dominate such a dynamic group of tennis players over the years? What was the secret that allowed her to capture nineteen Wimbledon titles and four United States singles championships on four different surfaces, to be ranked No. 1 nationally seven times and to become the first woman athlete to earn more than $100,000 in a season?

In short, what was the secret that thrust her into the select circle of athletes who outshine, outdraw and outplay the others in the virtuoso manner of Tom Seaver, Muhammad Ali, O. J. Simpson, Kareem Abdul-Jabbar, Angel Cordero, Jr., Phil Esposito and a few others?[1]

"Attitude," replies the 32-year-old Mrs. King, "plus a sense of urgency that made me work and sweat and hit tennis balls day in and day out forever and love every minute of it."

"Single-mindedness," says her former coach, Frank Brennan. "A pride that drove her to succeed at all costs, and a stubborn will not to be humbled, especially in front of a crowd. She's a ham. The more people watching the better Billie Jean becomes."

"Ego," adds an opponent. "It's what Billie Jean is made of, and it's what has made her what she is today. Combined with the inexhaustible energy of a marmot, it compels her to become the best in anything she touches."

"Let's face it," Billie Jean insists, "the game of tennis is mental. Anybody at the top can serve an ace, rifle a forehand crosscourt, a backhand down the line or smash an overhead into oblivion if they practice enough. All the stars can do it.

"It's when you walk out on the court, knowing you and your opponent

---

[1] Champions, respectively, in baseball, boxing, football, basketball, horse racing, and hockey.—EDS.

both have all the shots, that something else must determine the edge. More often than not, it's psychology that takes over, a self-awareness that makes you understand the pressure situations and gives you the confidence to produce the right shot at the key points of the match."

But it has to be almost automatic, instinctive to a player, she believes.

"It's like when a big bear chases you in the forest," she says. "You don't stop to figure it out; you just get the hell out of there."

According to Billie Jean, there are certain moments in every match that become the turning points or the keys to winning or losing. It's different every time, but when you know they occur and you can raise your game at the right time, you can usually win the match.

"I play better under a pressure situation," she reflects. "I eat it up. I thrive on tension. It raises my game to its supreme height. That's the real reason for my success."

Billie Jean concedes that when she lost to Miss Goolagong at Wimbledon in 1971, she "waited 365 days to get even with Evonne." She psyched herself up to a frenzy.

"That's what makes her one of the greatest players in history," Miss Goolagong observes. "She can get herself worked up to the sky. Ask Bobby Riggs[2] about that if you don't believe me."

"IT SETS THE TEMPO"

What are the key moments of a match? Billie Jean believes they can be the first game ("It sets the tempo of the whole match") or picking the right time to go to the net ("When you succeed, it can throw your opponent's whole thinking off") or just overcoming fear ("Champions are afraid to lose when most others are afraid to win").

Billie Jean, who carried out her promise last year to capture the Wimbledon singles title before giving up such competition, doesn't discount technique, however.

"If you don't have the shots or the ability to put the ball where you want it at the time you want to," she says, "then it doesn't matter how much confidence, stubbornness or willpower you've got. You're not going to do the job."

Billie Jean has always seemed to own a sufficient supply of confidence to go with her ability. In early childhood when her parents persuaded her to switch from football and softball to the more ladylike pastime of tennis, she made the brash prediction that she would be No. 1.

"Secretly, I was terrified," she admits. "It's bad enough when you silently think about becoming No. 1, but when you tell everybody, you suddenly feel that perhaps you're not going to make it."

---

[2] Bobby Riggs (1918–   ) has won twenty-nine U.S. national tennis championships. In 1973 he promoted the Bobby Riggs vs. Billie Jean King tennis match.—Eds.

Her training was intense. For about seven years she learned the art from Clyde Walker[3] on the public courts; under the tutelage of Alice Marble, one of the greatest players; and later from Brennan, a taskmaster who taught her not only what she was doing right and wrong, but also why certain things worked and others didn't. All this culminated in a three-month crash course at the hands of Mervyn Rose, a former Australian Davis Cup star, who combined physical endurance and technical craftsmanship into a thinking-woman's game.

The results of this exhausting course are written in the record book. In her own book, *Tennis to Win*, Billie Jean recounted:

SHORTER AND LIGHTER

"Unless you happen to be extremely gifted, there is no such thing as instant gratification in tennis. Most of us can tee up a golf ball and hit it with a club, maybe not very far or very straight, but at least with some immediate tangible result. Or most of us can take a bowling ball and after a few tries knock down a few pins.

"But hitting a moving object while you yourself are moving takes a pretty fair amount of coordination. And more yet is needed to hit a ball back across a net, 36 inches high at its lowest point, into a singles court that is 39 feet long and 27 feet wide."

Another obstacle Billie Jean had to overcome was her physique. Though born with quickness and coordination, she usually gave away a lot to her opponents in the tale of the tape. Mrs. Court is 6 inches taller, for instance; Martina Navratilova outweighs her by 30 or more pounds, and Miss Wade, lankier and taller, has the sinewy arms and legs of an athlete.

"But compare me on the court," Mrs. King says. "Evonne's forehand, same as mine. Backhand, I apply myself better. Maneuverability, she's smoother. Net game, I'm steadier.

"Compare me with Court. She's long, bigger physically with a better reach, better first serve, more power. But she's not so good under pressure and not as good in the hands nor in speed and agility.

"Rosie is fast, no doubt about it. But the secret of speed is in the first two steps. I'm pretty quick off the mark. In school, I always won the short races, against boys or girls.

"As for Virginia, her serve is terrific. But you win on your second serve. And mine is the best.

"I guess I'm the shortest person to win so much, though. Most champion players have been 5–7 or more. My legs are my strength, short as they are. My upper body is the weak part. But when you're small, you must put the ball away quicker. You have to. If you're small, you better be a winner."

---

[3] Walker was named athletic director at the University of Kansas in 1973.—EDS.

"She's a hell of an athlete," says Arthur Ashe.[4] That's the most important thing for a woman. Forget the strokes; if you can move on your feet, you can win."

And you better be in shape, Billie Jean adds: "Look at Martina and Chris. Martina has it all over Chris in size, strength, quickness and even coordination. But who wins all the time? It's how Chris applies herself. It's psychology and how you adapt that count, not size."

Billie Jean can cite the two most difficult drawbacks in her life: weak eyes and bad knees.

"I've had to wear glasses since I was 12," she says. "Nearsighted. I tried contact lenses for three years but gave them up. They irritated me. If I wore them six hours one day, I couldn't wear them at all the day after. But I still see the ball well, which amazes me. My reflexes make up for it, plus footwork and balance."

As for her knees, she's had two painful operations, in 1968 and 1970—"Deterioration of the patella, some big fancy medical term," she remembers. "That set me back. I had to recover first and then play myself back into competitive shape. It was rough.

"The secret is to stay in shape. My ideal playing weight is 138 pounds. I try to keep my body low in fats, too, at 10 percent or under. Martina's body fat is way up there. She's got to stop those big eating sprees."

Asked to analyze her own play, Billie Jean says she is stumped: "It's difficult for a player to analyze herself when she rarely gets a chance to see herself play. I'd love to see me on film. If I could watch myself play, I could figure out how to beat me.

"I guess flexibility may be the key to the whole business of winning when you reach the top. I am a more flexible player than the others. I'm also very emotional. I can give 100 percent. I can set a goal and get myself psyched up, such as Wimbledon. When I have a meaningful goal, I'm tough to beat.

"A tennis match is like life," she theorizes. "There are so many ups and downs. You can be down to where you think there's no way possible you can win a match. But you just keep trying step by step and finally you win. You've got to have the right attitude. Give me attitude over style any day. In the long run, that will beat out a great serve, a fantastic net game, mobility, anything."

---

[4] Arthur Ashe (1943–   ) was ranked in the United States Lawn Tennis Association's top ten from 1964 to 1970.—Eds.

O. J. Simpson: Speed, Balance, and E.S.P.
GERALD ESKENAZI

In a darkened room, the football coaches huddle around a 16-millimeter projector and stare at the wall.

Click.

The film begins. O. J. Simpson receives the ball and heads for a hole. Suddenly, the hole is clogged. He pirouettes and finds another opening.

Click.

The shot is replayed again. And again. Each time the coaches shake their heads.

"We had him," one coach says. "We cut off his routes. But the guy's so good, he can find a secondary opening, just like that. No wasted motion."

That is one reason why O. J. Simpson is the most productive runner in the history of the National Football League [N.F.L.]—and why he performs in the small circle of the elite of professional sports, like Tom Seaver, Muhammad Ali, Kareem Abdul-Jabbar, Billie Jean King, Angel Cordero, Jr., Phil Esposito and a few others.[1]

The 23 touchdowns he amassed this season for the Buffalo Bills broke a 10-year record. He is still the only player to rush for 2,000 yards in a season.

"Simpson is in a different category from any runner who played this game," contends the coach of the New York Jets' defensive backs, Sam Rutigliano, who spends a fair amount of his time trying to figure out ways to contain Orenthal James Simpson.

Nice words. For O.J., though, there may be a mystical reason for his success. He cannot explain himself just by conventional explanations. Instead, he says: "I have a certain amount of extrasensory perception."

And what good does that do in the National Football League? To which he replies: "I have a feeling for where everyone is."

Some people, though, believe that E.S.P. has nothing to do with it—people like the Buffalo team trainer, Eddie Abramoski, who suggests: "He's bow-legged. That gives him balance."

To O.J., though, being bow-legged has its compensations: "It may present some type of optical illusion to my opponents. I look funny. They don't know where to grab me."

So O.J. is bow-legged and perhaps he does indeed have some extrasensory perception, and he can bounce off people and find new openings. But why is it so? How does he do it? And what can be done about it?

Simpson possesses a combination of extraordinary traits—physical, mental, emotional—that a psychologist would have insisted upon if he

---

[1] Champions, respectively, in baseball, boxing, basketball, tennis, horse racing, and hockey.—EDS.

were to create the perfect football player. In Simpson's case, form follows function.

A running back in pro football must be strong enough to withstand 20 or more tackles a game by a variety of players, many weighing more than 250 pounds. The runner must be quick enough to pierce a hole and escape the 250-pound linemen. Then he must be brave and tough enough to collide with hellbent linebackers on the run, and agile and fast enough to elude the secondary, which is usually composed of the fastest players on defense.

Simpson at 28 years of age stands 6 feet 1 inch tall and weighs 207 pounds. He may be the fastest running back in the N.F.L., with a time of 4.45 seconds for a 40-yard sprint. In fact, he's the fastest player on his club, a rarity for anyone who isn't a receiver or a defensive back.

The average running back does the 40—not the same as a track-and-field-meet 40—in 4.6 seconds. Coaches smile especially wide when they have a back who does 4.55. If they get one who runs it in 4.5, they know their job is secure.

"Our offense is geared to get me into the secondary," says Simpson. "Much of my success when I get past the line of scrimmage is based on two factors. One: I'm usually faster than the secondary. Two: I'm usually bigger than they are."

So Simpson has the ability to either run over, or run past, defensive backs.

"You look at him," says Abramoski, the trainer, "and he doesn't seem like 207. You'd say he was 190. He's well-proportioned. His muscles are well-defined. And he can run as fast in a football uniform as out of one. We had the Big-Ten dash champion, Willmer Fowler. He could run a 9.3 in the 100, but he couldn't run in a uniform. But O.J. You remember that Superstars competition on television? He ran the 100 in 9.6. In sneakers."

Beyond O.J.'s speed, size and quickness, there is another quality he possesses. The opposition marvels at it. The trainer of the Jets, Jeff Snedeker, a long-time student of the body, calls Simpson's special quality "kinesthetic awareness."

"He knows where he is in relation to his body, and what his body must do," Snedeker observes.

"HE WAITS AND SEES"

This attribute enables Simpson to change plans even while an enemy linebacker is sailing in on him alone. It enabled Simpson, in the first game this season, to gain 174 yards on 32 carries against the Jets—with 70 more yards called back on Buffalo penalties.

"Yet," contends Rutigliano, "90 percent of his yardage that game was made through secondary holes. We had the primary hole sewed up. But he is unique, his forte is that he waits and sees. He doesn't always go to the predetermined play. He bounces, so to speak."

It appears as if Simpson takes in the complete scene in front of him. He must evaluate the primary situation by looking at 11 men, seven of them his own, who are spaced along the line of scrimmage about 10 yards across from end to end. This is the line he must cross. Then the contest begins.

"It's like being a jet pilot," explains O.J. "He's got to think what's 3 miles ahead of him."

Simpson employs his kinesthetic awareness like "the $6 million man," Steve Austin, looking through bionic eyes.[2] Simpson checks off the possibilities in an instant, some part of his mind calculating the speed of an onrushing linebacker, while determining just what it would take to get to a certain point on the field before the linebacker does. Students have failed calculus over simpler problems.

"I have viable powers," Simpson says. "I have very good peripheral vision. I also study the movies and I know where everyone is supposed to be."

Unlike other running backs who study movies and moves of opposing linemen, as well as other members of the defense, Simpson concentrates only on the linebackers and defensive backs.

"I don't worry about the other linemen," he reports. "My men are supposed to clear them out of the way for me. So on the films I watch the other guys for tendencies—if they tackle better with their right shoulder or their left shoulder. If a safety tends to tackle low, say, I pick up my feet. If a linebacker takes a block from my other back, you go outside."

The philosophy of every team that plays the Bills is simply this: pursue Simpson with a lot of people.

"The main thing with Simpson is to get the first guy to slow him down," says Billy Newsome, the Jets' left end, who has been facing Simpson since 1970. "Then the other guys have to bring him down. You can't expect one guy to be in position to take him down."

LIFE IN THE OPEN FIELD

Newsome has faced Simpson more than most people, probably because running backs like to run to the right, which is the side of the field that Newsome patrols. What are some secrets Newsome learned?

"You see, most linemen want to hurt a runner," he replies. "But you can't do that with O.J. I try never to hurt him. I try to take him down. That's why he's never hurt. You can only hurt a guy when you put all your energy into taking him down. But if you don't leave yourself an extra move, he's past you. The reason is, he's never extended in such a position that he can't make another move."

---

[2] The bionic man, a miracle man who can see through solid objects and break down walls with his arm, is a popular television hero.—EDS.

Newsome attempts to "just aim for him—you have to look at him, not his feet or his eyes, so I just look at him."

Newsome has had fairly good luck against Simpson. Until Newsome joined the Jets, every team he played for beat the Bills. He talks proudly of keeping Simpson to 69 yards when he was with the New Orleans Saints.

"He never just takes off," Newsome says. "He gets the ball and he looks. But he fooled me once in New Orleans. It was a play up the middle. I knew from past experience not to kill him. I figured he would give me a fake, and I was ready just to take a piece of him. A small piece. And that play he came right at me, right up the middle. And he was gone."

Despite the bow-leggedness, that was no optical illusion sailing past the startled Newsome. Yet, Simpson doesn't realize how lucky he is: His skill is part of an astounding circle of attributes that constantly meet.

For example, there is the opposition's reluctance to hit him too hard on the first pop. That has preserved his health. On the other hand, he also has stayed healthy because he is bow-legged. Not only does the parenthetic shape of his knees give him balance by distributing his weight as if over an arch, it also lessens the impact of tackles.

"He's less prone to injury," explains Snedeker. "Most knee injuries occur from a lateral hit combined with rotation. A man gets hit from the side and his knee turns. But Simpson's bow-leggedness lessens the effect of the hit and prevents rotation."

Simpson has never studied films of his style. He contends that he is not quite sure what he does. Indeed, when pressed for an explanation, he gave two incompatible answers. Then again, maybe the mystery is his ultimate success.

"What separates a good runner from a crazy runner?" he asks. "The great runner I call the crazy runner. That is, he runs with his mind."

Life on the Run
BILL BRADLEY

With Phil Jackson's substitution, the Knicks seem revitalized. He blocks two shots, steals three passes, and over a span of four minutes gets six rebounds. Walt Frazier hits four jumpers and we tie the score. Chicago seems befuddled. Jackson hits a hook across the middle and then takes a lead pass from Dave DeBusschere and dribbles the length of the floor for a reverse lay-up. Dick Barnett smiles and shakes his head, unable to comprehend how, despite his apparent awkwardness, Phil can get the job done. On the last series of plays in the first half, Jackson blocks his man from a rebound, only to see the ball bounce to a Chicago guard, who attempts a drive for a lay-up. Phil leaves his man, lunges across the lane as if out of control, and swats away the ball just as it is about to hit the backboard. Goal tending is not called. The buzzer sounds. The Knicks are up by three at the half.

I believe that basketball, when a certain level of unselfish team play is realized can serve as a kind of metaphor for ultimate cooperation. It is a sport where success, as symbolized by the championship, requires that the dictates of community prevail over selfish personal impulses. An exceptional player is simply one point on a five-pointed star. Statistics—such as points, rebounds, or assists per game—can never explain the remarkable range of human interaction that takes place on a successful pro team. Personal conflicts between team members will never surface if there is a strong enough agreement on the community's values and goals. Members of the Budapest String Quartet disliked each other personally, but collectively still made exquisite music. They did so in part because they had a rigid score that limited the range of personal interpretation. The cooperation in basketball is remarkable because the flow of action always includes a role for creative spontaneity; the potential for variation is unlimited. Players improvise constantly. The unity they form is not achieved at the expense of individual imagination. That creative freedom highlights the game's beauty and its complexity, making the moment when the ideal is realized inspiring for the players, thrilling for the fans. . . .

Phil Jackson says you can tell more about a person when he loses. Some players don't care about winning and make excuses because they're interested only in themselves, not team victory. Other players, like me, learn only reluctantly to accept defeat as part of the life. My second game in the NBA [National Basketball Association], I scored 25 points but threw the ball away with nine seconds left. The other team then scored and won in overtime. I took the defeat hard and afterwards didn't speak to anyone, I was so depressed. Later that night in the hotel, Dick Barnett ended up as my roommate. We had exchanged about ten words since I joined the team. I had replayed the game about fifteen times when he walked into the room, looked at me, soaked in a hot tub for ten minutes, then got into bed. Before he turned over to sleep he picked up a statistics sheet of the game and read my line of points, assists, rebounds, free throws, field goals, and minutes played. Looking first at the sheet and then at me, he finally uttered his only comment of the night, putting the game in perspective. "Forty-six minutes—that's a whole lotta' minutes."

When the game is over, the most important thing is the next game. A player must be able to recuperate from a loss within twenty-four hours. Such resiliency is not a bad character trait to take away from the sport. But like so many of "sport's lessons" it becomes oversimplified and even leads to insensitivity when applied to life. Once, for example, I heard an old basketball man say that a coach had a bad year, as if to say a bad season. The coach's wife had died and he had lost a large lawsuit. There are some things for which there will not be another season.

Yet winning and losing is all around us. From the high school level on, athletes are prepared to win and they in turn convey to a larger public what it is to be a winner. Locker-room champagne, humility in victory, and irrefutable knowledge of a favorable, clear-cut resolution are what championships resemble from the outside. The winning team like the conquering army claims everything in its path and seems to say that only winning is important. Yet like getting into a college of your choice or winning an election or marrying a beautiful mate victory is fraught with as much danger as glory. Victory has very narrow meanings and, if exaggerated or misused, can become a destructive force. The taste of defeat has a richness of experience all its own.

Toward the end of the third quarter we begin to make our move against Milwaukee. DeBusschere hits from the corner. I hit on a jumper from the key and Earl Monroe scores on a drive. The next three times down the floor Earl makes a move for a basket. Once, he jumps, changes the position of the ball three times, and floats the ball just over the outstretched hand of Kareem Abdul-Jabbar. The next two times he drives directly at his man, then spins to the left, takes two more dribbles and shoots from the baseline. Earl Monroe plays like a man whose body was assembled through a mail order catalog. Each part seems to move independently yet is controlled from a single command center. He has an uncanny skill for gauging the distance between himself and anyone who can block his shot. When his timing is off, as it is when he is returning from an injury, his shots are often blocked. When he is healthy, he can loft the ball over anyone's outstretched hand. Sometimes the defensive man misses a block by a foot, sometimes by an inch, but when Earl is right no one can stop him. He is one of the few players who openly challenges Kareem with a drive. Seventy percent of the time, Earl finds a way to get a shot off: He shoots it hard against the backboard; he goes straight for the rim; he steps back, jumps, tucks the ball in and then shoots it between Kareem's arm and his head....

Agents have told me that by choosing not to do endorsements I lose fifty thousand dollars every year I play professionally. I have had some unusual offers, and a few times I was close to agreeing to a deal, but when it came down to the crunch I said no. Perhaps I wanted no part of an advertising industry which created socially useless personal needs and then sold a product to meet those needs. Maybe I felt that endorsement offers came to me because I was a great white hope for some people and not because I was a great player, and that offended my sensibilities. Chalk one up for America's two favorites: original sin and guilt. More probably, I wanted to keep my experience of basketball pure, as innocent and unpolluted by commercialism as possible. For many years basketball was my only passion in life. I was immune to the normal profusion of interests that accompany adolescence. I pressed my physical and emotional life into basketball alone, and it made for a very intense feeling. I felt about the court, the ball, and playing, the way people feel about friends. Playing for money compromised me enough. Taking money for hocking products demeaned my experience of the game. I cared about basketball. I didn't give a damn about perfumes, shaving lotions, clothes, or special foods. . . .

There is terror behind the dream of being a professional ballplayer. It comes as a slow realization of finality and of the frightening unknowns which the end brings. When the playing is over, one can sense that one's youth has been spent playing a game and now both the game and youth are gone, along with the innocence that characterizes all games which at root are pure and promote a prolonged adolescence in those who play. Now the athlete must face a world where awkward naiveté can no longer be overlooked because of athletic performance. By age thirty-five any potential for developing skills outside of basketball is slim. The "good guy" syndrome ceases. What is left is the other side of the Faustian bargain: To live all one's days never able to recapture the feeling of those few years of intensified youth. In a way it is the fate of a warrior class to receive rewards, plaudits, and exhilaration simultaneously with the means of self-destruction. When a middle-aged lawyer moves more slowly on the tennis court, he makes adjustments and may even laugh at his geriatric restrictions because for him there remains the law. For the athlete who reaches thirty-five, something in him dies; not a peripheral activity but a fundamental passion. It necessarily dies. The athlete rarely recuperates. He approaches the end of his playing days the way old people approach death. He puts his finances in order. He reminisces easily. He offers advice to the young. But, the athlete differs from an old person in that he must continue living. Behind all the years of practice and all the hours of glory waits that inexorable terror of living without the game.

I have often wondered how I will handle the end of my playing days. No one really knows until that day comes. DeBusschere says that as long as one doesn't puff up with the unnatural attention given a pro athlete, and keeps a few good friends, the adjustment should be easy. I don't know if he really believes it. Tom Heinsohn says you don't realize how much you love the game until you miss it. Forced into a premature retirement by injury, he yearned for the life again so much that he took a 75 percent cut in salary to coach the Celtics. One retired player told me he noticed the end at home in his relationship with his wife. The fears and resentment that were formerly projected into the team now fall on wife and children, making life miserable for all. "Red" Holzman says that he never regretted the end, for when it came he had had enough basketball and wanted out. In my case, I've been preparing for the end since my first year, but even so I can only hope that I will manage easily the withdrawal from what Phil Jackson calls "my addiction."

When DeBusschere announced his retirement after getting a ten-year contract to become General Manager of the New York Nets, many newspapers said that he was retiring at his best. Once, after a speech I gave, a man came up to me and said, "Retire while you're still at the top. Whizzer White did it. Jim Brown did it. Bill Russell did it." DeBusschere talks about how sad he felt for Willie Mays struggling at the end of his brilliant career. He calls Mays' play embarrassing. He also says of several players that they played one year too long.

In the same way that it is difficult to watch your father grow old, it's difficult to watch your favorite player become increasingly unable to do the small things that made you admire him. But unless a man has a better opportunity, why should he stop doing something he loves? Fans want stars to retire on top in part to protect their fantasies. That makes no sense; consider Jerry West or Oscar Robertson, whose last two years of struggle didn't diminish the twelve previous years of achievement. In a way it made them more likable than if they had sought to retain an heroic level through early retirement. The decline is sad but human, for it is the one thing that strikes ineluctably in professional sports. To miss it makes a pro's experience incomplete.

The end of a player's career is the end of the big money and big publicity, and at that point the future depends on past prudence and levelheadedness. The specter of Joe Louis or Sugar Ray Robinson haunts many players. DeBusschere believes that of all the Knicks Frazier will have the most difficulty adjusting to the post-playing days. I'm not so sure. "My biggest motivation not to go broke," says Frazier, "doesn't come from the example of Sugar Ray or Joe Louis, but from my father. When he lost all of his money, he lost everything. The new 'Caddies' and other presents that used to arrive at the house stopped coming. I hold back spending too much money more than I would if I hadn't been around when something happened to my father." Frazier clearly has thought about the change of living standard but DeBusschere wonders also whether Clyde can adjust to a life of less publicity after nearly ten years in the New York spotlight. Though his life seemingly focuses on externals, and remains naively vulnerable to the quixotic taste of strangers, I believe Clyde does seem to understand the precarious path he treads and he confidently prepares for the end with little concern for the potential terror. Maybe no fall can be as hard and damaging as that which he witnessed his father take many years before.

Perhaps the last word on the end of a player's career comes from Danny Whelan. "When the fan is kissing your ass and telling you that you're the greatest," says Danny, "he hates you. They want to get you down on their level and they can't when you're on the top. After you retire just go to that guy who was buying you drinks when you were a player and ask him for a job. He'll show you the door. The fan likes to step on a player after he's finished playing if he gets a chance. A good example is Sweetwater Clifton. Just the other night some guy says he remembers Sweets with the Knicks and asks me if I know what he's doing. I shut up. If I had told him that he's driving a cab in Chicago the guy would have got his nuts off. Players would be better off to change their names and start anew."

Why Ali Whipped Patterson
MUHAMMAD ALI

I had not seen Floyd Patterson[1] since our fight in Las Vegas, but when I came across an article he'd written for a national magazine, saying some honest things about the "loser," the admiration I'd had for him during my amateur days returned and I accepted an invitation to go out to his farm.

"The losing fighter loses more than just his pride in the fight," Patterson had said in the article. "He loses part of his future. He's a step closer to the slum he came from." Then, turning his attention to me, "I'm sure that before each fight Cassius Clay also goes through the mental torture and doubt. He knows how happy thousands of Americans would be if he got beaten bad, and maybe that's why Clay has to say, 'I'm the greatest. I'm the greatest.' He wants people to say, 'You're not,' and then he's forced to meet the challenge. Put himself in a do-or-die frame of mind. Go a little crazy, maybe, crazy with some ferocious fear. So far it has worked for him. What he will be like if he loses, I do not know."

So Floyd wants to know how I'd take a loss, I thought, as I flew out to his place in New York. He greeted me warmly and introduced me to his family. It had been a long time since I had been with a competitor, free from the artificial "hate" promoters and the press use to divide two opponents, and we began to discover and like each other.

We lounged around, talking about the future—his fight plans, my possible jail sentence[2]—and I told him I'd read what he'd written about "losers." "I know the feeling," I said.

He surprised me with his sudden coldness. "You don't know what you're talking about."

"I do," I told him.

But he turned away. "You've been lucky. You've never lost," he said with what I thought was a touch of regret.

His chilliness caught me by surprise. Plainly, the bitterness of our fight in Vegas had not been washed far enough down the drain so that we could

---

[1] Floyd Patterson (1935–   ) was heavyweight champion from 1956 to 1959 and 1960 to 1961. Ali knocked out Patterson in Las Vegas in 1965.—Eds.

[2] Dropped by the World Boxing Association for draft evasion in 1967, Ali was cleared by the Supreme Court in 1970.—Eds.

become buddies. "I've been on the brink," I said. "Man, I've looked down in that pit. I know."

"But as an amateur," he said spitefully. "You don't know until someone knocks you down from the top."

For a quick second I had the impression he was still in that ring in Las Vegas. How could I explain to him what drove me on to whip him so thoroughly and totally? What I was doing in the ring with Patterson that night in Vegas was directly related to what had been going on outside the ring. The rage and uproar over me becoming a Muslim was still at a fever pitch.

Looking at Floyd now, quiet and happy here at home with his wife and children, I felt he still didn't understand what happened that night and I wanted to tell him. I wanted to say, "Floyd, when I became a Muslim, you announced in all the papers you were out to 'bring the title back to America.' You said this was the main reason you wanted to beat me. It was then that I said, 'What do you mean, bring it back to America? It's already in America!' Floyd, I'm the Heavyweight Champion of the World, and I'm an American. I stand for the people, the black people, the poor people, the poor people in ghettos, both black and white.

"When you were Champion, Floyd, whenever you took a picture you'd either be picking up a little white boy or hugging a little white girl, which was all right, but I never saw you pick up little black children and pose with them. You came from the black, the poor, the oppressed, the denied, but you always catered to the whites, the privileged. Even then, I kept my peace until you made the statement that you wanted to bring the title back to America. You let the whites goad you into attacking me because I'd become a follower of the Honorable Elijah Muhammad,[3] this black man who preached unity and progress, who had taken thousands of hopeless dope addicts off the streets and changed their lives, gave them purpose and programs. What he wanted was freedom, justice and equality for black people. You told the white press you'd never call me by my Muslim name, Muhammad Ali. You said, 'I'm gonna call him Cassius Clay, because that's the way he was born.'

"Then I said I was gonna give you a whipping. I said, 'I'm gonna give you a whipping until you call me Muhammad Ali'. I challenged you. I said, 'If you whip me, I'll go and join the Catholic Church, and if I whip you, you come and join the Honorable Elijah Muhammad and be a Muslim.' You never answered me on that. All the white press was backing you, all the Catholics, all the white Protestants. And even though Sonny Liston[4] had destroyed you twice, they revived you just so you could get to me. The

---

[3] Elijah Muhammad (1897–1975) was leader of the Black Muslims from 1946 until his death.—EDS.

[4] Sonny Liston (c. 1932–1970) knocked out Patterson in 1962 and again in a rematch.—EDS.

only reason they gave you a chance at a title fight was they wanted to see you perform a miracle. They wanted to see a nice Catholic boy defeat a Black Muslim.

"You told them Elijah Muhammad was taking all my money, which was untrue, because actually I was borrowing money from the Nation of Islam. They hadn't taken a quarter from me. You said when I lost the title the Muslims would drop me like a hot potato, so I wanted to take all this out on you, but not really on you—on your white supporters.

"And when the fight was on, whenever you'd get in a blow the crowd would roar: 'Ooooooohhh! Aaaaaaahhh!' But whenever I'd throw blows on you, things were quiet. So for thirteen rounds, things were mostly very quiet, because I was doing the whipping. I didn't see myself fighting you, Floyd. I didn't see myself hitting Floyd Patterson. I was fighting the white reporters behind you, the Jimmy Cannons, and the white celebrities, the Frank Sinatras, the Jim Bishops, the Arch Wards, the Dick Youngs,[5] and when it was over they talked about how cruel I was. I don't regret what I did. The trouble was, they wanted to see something cruel happen to me.

"But it's not true when they say I carried you, that I could have knocked you out, gotten you out of your misery. That's not true. Although I didn't really press the fight until after the eighth round, I never saw a time when I felt you were going to fall. I hit you so many times my hands were in pain and I could hardly move them, but you wouldn't fall. You kept taking it. You stood in there and kept taking it. You took everything I threw and you still had punches to throw back at me. You were good. You had guts and heart. You were greater than those egging me on.

"Like the next morning when you went to see Frank Sinatra, what did he do? When you went to see him to apologize for the poor showing? You went up to his room and he turned his back on you and hardly spoke to you, and you came out with tears in your eyes. But it was not you that I was trying to beat and knock out. It was those backing you. I was talking back to them. I was saying, 'I am America. Only I'm the part you won't recognize. But get used to me. Black, confident, cocky; my name, not yours; my religion, not yours; my goals my own—get used to me! I can make it without your approval! I won't let you beat me and I won't let your Negro beat me!'"

---

[5] Except for Sinatra, sports editors and writers.—EDS.

Minorities

The Grass on the Mountain[1]

Oh, long long
The snow has possessed the mountains.

The deer have come down and the big-horn,
They have followed the sun to the south
To feed on the mesquite pods and the bunch grass.
Loud are the thunder drums
In the tent of the mountains.
Oh, long, long
Have we eaten *chia*[2] seeds
And dried deer's flesh of the summer killing.
We are wearied of our huts
And the smoky smell of our garments.

We are sick with desire of the sun
And the grass on the mountain.

Wounded Knee
DEE BROWN

There was no hope on earth, and God seemed to have forgotten us. Some said they saw the Son of God; others did not see Him. If He had come, He would do some great things as He had done before. We doubted it because we had seen neither Him nor His works.

The people did not know; they did not care. They snatched at the hope. They screamed like crazy men to Him for mercy. They caught at the promise they heard He had made.

The white men were frightened and called for soldiers. We had begged for life, and the white men thought we wanted theirs. We heard that soldiers were coming. We did not fear. We hoped that we could tell them our troubles and

---

[1] From the Paiute; translated by Mary Austin. The Paiute Indians live in California, Nevada, Arizona, and Utah.—Eds.
[2] Of the genus *Salvia* (a kind of sage).—Eds.

get help. A white man said the soldiers meant to kill us. We did not believe it, but some were frightened and ran away to the Badlands.

—RED CLOUD[1]

Had it not been for the sustaining force of the Ghost Dance religion, the Sioux in their grief and anger over the assassination of Sitting Bull[2] might have risen up against the guns of the soldiers. So prevalent was their belief that the white men would soon disappear and that with the next greening of the grass their dead relatives and friends would return, they made no retaliations. By the hundreds, however, the leaderless Hunkpapas fled from Standing Rock, seeking refuge in one of the Ghost Dance camps or with the last of the great chiefs, Red Cloud, at Pine Ridge. In the Moon When the Deer Shed Their Horns (December 17) about a hundred of these fleeing Hunkpapas reached Big Foot's Minneconjou camp near Cherry Creek. That same day the War Department issued orders for the arrest and imprisonment of Big Foot. He was on the list of "fomenters of disturbances."

As soon as Big Foot learned that Sitting Bull had been killed, he started his people toward Pine Ridge, hoping that Red Cloud could protect them from the soldiers. En route, he fell ill of pneumonia, and when hemorrhaging began, he had to travel in a wagon. On December 28, as they neared Porcupine Creek, the Minneconjous sighted four troops of cavalry approaching. Big Foot immediately ordered a white flag run up over his wagon. About two o'clock in the afternoon he raised up from his blankets to greet Major Samuel Whitside, Seventh U.S. Cavalry. Big Foot's blankets were stained with blood from his lungs, and as he talked in a hoarse whisper with Whitside, red drops fell from his nose and froze in the bitter cold.

Whitside told Big Foot that he had orders to take him to a cavalry camp on Wounded Knee Creek.[3] The Minneconjou chief replied that he was going in that direction; he was taking his people to Pine Ridge for safety.

Turning to his half-breed scout, John Shangreau, Major Whitside ordered him to begin disarming Big Foot's band.

"Look here, Major," Shangreau replied, "if you do that, there is liable to be a fight here; and if there is, you will kill all those women and children and the men will get away from you."

---

[1] Red Cloud (1822–1909) was a chief of the Ogalala Sioux and leader of Red Cloud's War, 1866–1868.—EDS.

[2] Sitting Bull (c. 1834–1890) was a chief of the Hunkpapa Sioux who, in his final months, was converted to the Ghost Dance religion and was assassinated. Although the Ghost Dance religion was Christian in derivation, the white army and agents feared it. —EDS.

[3] Wounded Knee is in southern South Dakota. South Dakota was admitted as a state in 1889.—EDS.

Whitside insisted that his orders were to capture Big Foot's Indians and disarm and dismount them.

"We better take them to camp and then take their horses from them and their guns," Shangreau declared.

"All right," Whitside agreed. "You tell Big Foot to move down to camp at Wounded Knee."

The major glanced at the ailing chief, and then gave an order for his Army ambulance to be brought forward. The ambulance would be warmer and would give Big Foot an easier ride than the jolting springless wagon. After the chief was transferred to the ambulance, Whitside formed a column for the march to Wounded Knee Creek. Two troops of cavalry took the lead, the ambulance and wagons following, the Indians herded into a compact group behind them, with the other two cavalry troops and a battery of two Hotchkiss guns bringing up the rear.

Twilight was falling when the column crawled over the last rise in the land and began descending the slope toward Chankpe Opi Wakpala, the creek called Wounded Knee. The wintry dusk and the tiny crystals of ice dancing in the dying light added a supernatural quality to the somber landscape. Somewhere along this frozen stream the heart of Crazy Horse[4] lay in a secret place, and the Ghost Dancers believed that his disembodied spirit was waiting impatiently for the new earth that would surely come with the first green grass of spring.

At the cavalry tent camp on Wounded Knee Creek, the Indians were halted and children counted. There were 120 men and 230 women and children. Because of the gathering darkness, Major Whitside decided to wait until morning before disarming his prisoners. He assigned them a camping area immediately to the south of the military camp, issued them rations, and as there was a shortage of tepee covers, he furnished them several tents. Whitside ordered a stove placed in Big Foot's tent and sent a regimental surgeon to administer to the sick chief. To make certain that none of his prisoners escaped, the major stationed two troops of cavalry as sentinels around the Sioux tepees, and then posted his two Hotchkiss guns on top of a rise overlooking the camp. The barrels of these rifled guns, which could hurl explosive charges for more than two miles, were positioned to rake the length of the Indian lodges.

Later in the darkness of that December night the remainder of the Seventh Regiment marched in from the east and quietly bivouacked north of Major Whitside's troops. Colonel James W. Forsyth, commanding Custer's former regiment, now took charge of operations. He informed Whitside that he had received orders to take Big Foot's band to the Union Pacific Railroad for shipment to a military prison in Omaha.

---

[4] Crazy Horse (c. 1849–1877) was a chief of the Minneconjou branch of the Ogalala Sioux. He was active in Red Cloud's War and the War for the Black Hills in which Custer was killed.—EDS.

After placing two more Hotchkiss guns on the slope beside the others, Forsyth and his officers settled down for the evening with a keg of whiskey to celebrate the capture of Big Foot.

The chief lay in his tent, too ill to sleep, barely able to breathe. Even with their protective Ghost Shirts and their belief in the prophecies of the new Messiah, his people were fearful of the pony soldiers camped all around them. Fourteen years before, on the Little Bighorn, some of these warriors had helped defeat some of these soldier chiefs—Moylan, Varnum, Wallace, Godfrey, Edgerly—and the Indians wondered if revenge could still be in their hearts.

"The following morning there was a bugle call," said Wasumaza, one of Big Foot's warriors who years afterward was to change his name to Dewey Beard. "Then I saw the soldiers mounting their horses and surrounding us. It was announced that all men should come to the center for a talk and that after the talk they were to move on to Pine Ridge agency. Big Foot was brought out of his tepee and sat in front of his tent and the older men were gathered around him and sitting right near him in the center."

After issuing hardtack for breakfast rations, Colonel Forsyth informed the Indians that they were now to be disarmed. "They called for guns and arms," White Lance said, "so all of us gave the guns and they were stacked up in the center." The soldier chiefs were not satisfied with the number of weapons surrendered, and so they sent details of troopers to search the tepees. "They would go right into the tents and come out with bundles and tear them open," Dog Chief said. "They brought our axes, knives, and tent stakes and piled them near the guns."

Still not satisfied, the soldier chiefs ordered the warriors to remove their blankets and submit to searches for weapons. The Indians' faces showed their anger, but only the medicine man, Yellow Bird, made any overt protest. He danced a few Ghost Dance steps, and chanted one of the holy songs, assuring the warriors that the soldiers' bullets could not penetrate their sacred garments. "The bullets will not go toward you," he chanted in Sioux. "The prairie is large and the bullets will not go toward you."

The troopers found only two rifles, one of them a new Winchester belonging to a young Minneconjou named Black Coyote. Black Coyote raised the Winchester above his head, shouting that he paid much money for the rifle and that it belonged to him. Some years afterward Dewey Beard recalled that Black Coyote was deaf. "If they had left him alone he was going to put his gun down where he should. They grabbed him and spinned him in the east direction. He was still unconcerned even then. He hadn't his gun pointed at anyone. His intention was to put that gun down. They came on and grabbed the gun that he was going to put down. Right after they spun him around there was the report of a gun, was quite loud. I couldn't say that anyone was shot, but following that was a crash."

"It sounded much like the sound of tearing canvas, that was the crash," Rough Feather said. Afraid-of-the-Enemy described it as a "lightning crash."

Turning Hawk said that Black Coyote "was a crazy man, a young man of very bad influence and in fact a nobody." He said that Black Coyote fired his gun and that "immediately the soldiers returned fire and indiscriminate killing followed."

In the first seconds of violence, the firing of carbines was deafening, filling the air with powder smoke. Among the dying who lay sprawled on the frozen ground was Big Foot. Then there was a brief lull in the rattle of arms, with small groups of Indians and soldiers grappling at close quarters, using knives, clubs, and pistols. As few of the Indians had arms, they soon had to flee, and then the big Hotchkiss guns on the hill opened upon them, firing almost a shell a second, raking the Indian camp, shredding the tepees with flying shrapnel, killing men, women, and children.

"We tried to run," Louise Weasel Bear said, "but they shot us like we were a buffalo. I know there are some good white people, but the soldiers must be mean to shoot children and women. Indian soldiers would not do that to white children."

"I was running away from the place and followed those who were running away," said Hakiktawin, another of the young women. "My grandfather and grandmother and brother were killed as we crossed the ravine, and then I was shot on the right hip clear through and on my right wrist where I did not go any further as I was not able to walk, and after the soldier picked me up where a little girl came to me and crawled into the blanket."

When the madness ended, Big Foot and more than half of his people were dead or seriously wounded; 153 were known dead, but many of the wounded crawled away to die afterward. One estimate placed the final total of dead at very nearly three hundred of the original 350 men, women, and children. The soldiers lost twenty-five dead and thirty-nine wounded, most of them struck by their own bullets or shrapnel.

After the wounded cavalrymen were started for the agency at Pine Ridge, a detail of soldiers went over the Wounded Knee battlefield, gathering up Indians who were still alive and loading them into wagons. As it was apparent by the end of the day that a blizzard was approaching, the dead Indians were left lying where they had fallen. (After the blizzard, when a burial party returned to Wounded Knee, they found the bodies, including Big Foot's, frozen into grotesque shapes.)

The wagonloads of wounded Sioux (four men and forty-seven women and children) reached Pine Ridge after dark. Because all available barracks were filled with soldiers, they were left lying in the open wagons in the bitter cold while an inept Army officer searched for shelter. Finally the Episcopal mission was opened, the benches taken out, and hay scattered over the rough flooring.

It was the fourth day after Christmas in the Year of Our Lord 1890. When the first torn and bleeding bodies were carried into the candelit church, those who were conscious could see Christmas greenery hanging from the open rafters. Across the chancel front above the pulpit was strung a crudely lettered banner: PEACE ON EARTH, GOOD WILL TO MEN.

I did not know then how much was ended. When I look back now from this high hill of my old age, I can still see the butchered women and children lying heaped and scattered all along the crooked gulch as plain as when I saw them with eyes still young. And I can see that something else died there in the bloody mud, and was buried in the blizzard. A people's dream died there. It was a beautiful dream . . . the nation's hoop is broken and scattered. There is no center any longer, and the sacred tree is dead.

—BLACK ELK[5]

The Feast of San Diego at Jemez
N. SCOTT MOMADAY

The activity in the pueblo reached a peak on the day before the Feast of San Diego, November twelfth. It was on that day, an especially brilliant day in which the winter held off and the sun shone like a flare, that Jemez[1] became one of the fabulous cities of the world. In the preceding days the women had plastered the houses, many of them, and they were clean and beautiful like bone in the high light; the strings of chilies at the vigas had darkened a little and taken on a deeper, softer sheen; ears of colored corn were strung at the doors, and fresh cedar boughs were laid about, setting a whole, wild fragrance on the air. The women were baking bread in the outdoor ovens. Here and there men and women were at the woodpiles, chopping, taking up loads of firewood for their kitchens, for the coming feast. Even the children were at work: the little boys looked after the stock, and the little girls carried babies about. There were gleaming antlers on the rooftops, and smoke arose from all the chimneys.

About midday the Navajos began to arrive. And they seemed *all* to come, as a whole people, as if it was their racial destiny to find at last the center of the world, the place of origin, older than *tsegi*,[2] among the rocks. From the yard of the day school I looked southward, along the road to San Ysidro, and there was a train of covered wagons, extending as far as I could see. All afternoon the caravan passed by, shimmering in the winter

---

[5] Black Elk (1863–1950) was one of the chiefs who has left an autobiographical record, *Black Elk Speaks*, edited by John G. Neihardt (1961).—EDS.

[1] The parents of Scott Momaday taught for many years at the Jemez (New Mexico) Day School, beginning in 1946.—EDS.

[2] Sacred ground; or, literally, "place among the rocks" (Navajo).—EDS.

light, its numberless facets gleaming, the hundreds of wagon wheels turning in the dust, in slow and endless motion. Never have the Navajos seemed a more beautiful people to me, for they bore about them the cherished memories of my childhood.[3] This old man, had he not once told us the way to Klagetoh? That beautiful woman, had she not been a schoolgirl at Chinle? They were resplendent. The old people and the children peered out from beneath the canopies, dark-skinned and black-eyed, nearly tentative in the shadows, beautiful in the way that certain photographic negatives are beautiful, dimly traced with light. The outriders were men and women and youths on handsome horses in glossy leather trappings and rich saddle blankets, the men in big hats and fine boots and bright silk and satin shirts, the women in velveteen blouses, long, pleated skirts, and red moccasins. They all wore silver and turquoise and coral—concha belts, necklaces, bracelets, and rings which flashed and glinted and gleamed in the sun. And their voices, as I hear them even now—the singing and the laughter—carried along the train like a long, rising and falling woodwind music; it is a sound that I have heard among bristlecones, or upon the walls of the old ruin of Giusewa. A dog or two followed after each of the wagons, keeping closely in place. The Navajo dogs are solitary creatures. I believe that they assume very early the reserve and nobility of the people with whom they live and they consist in that assumption. They are shepherds, and they know their sheep in the way that an eagle knows its nest; and when they have not their sheep they concentrate themselves in the shadows of the wagons.

Some of the men of Jemez rode out to meet the Navajos. John Cajero was one of them. He was then a man in his prime, a Tanoan[4] man, agile and strong in his mind and body, and he was a first-rate horseman. He was mounted on a good-looking gray quarter horse, which he handled closely and well, and he cut a fine figure upon it in his blue shirt and red headband, his manner easy and confident. He singled out old friends among the Navajos, and soon there was a cluster of riders holding up on the side of the road, convened in a high mood of fellowship and good humor— and a certain rivalry. Then John Cajero was holding the coils of a rope in his hands, shaking out a loop. Suddenly he leaned forward and his horse bolted into the road between two of the wagons, nearly trampling over a dog; the dog lunged away with a yelp and ran at full speed, but the horse was right upon it, bunched in motion, and the rope flashed down and caught the dog up around its hips and set it rolling and twisting in the sand, jerking it up then into the air and slamming it down hard, as the horse squatted, jamming its hooves in the earth, its whole weight cracking against the bit. And John Cajero played out a little of the rope from his

---

[3] Between 1936 and 1943 the Momadays lived on the Navajo reservation.—EDS.
[4] A former Pueblo group. Tanoan is still one of the languages.—EDS.

saddle, and the dog slithered out of the noose and ran ahead, its tail between its legs, and went crouching and wary under its wagon. John Cajero laughed, and the others, too, though their laughter was brittle, I thought, and the Navajos watched evenly the performance, the enactment of a hard joke, and considered precisely what it was worth. There was a kind of trade in this, a bartering of nerve and arrogance and skill, of elemental pride. Then, getting down from his horse, John Cajero drew a dollar bill from his pocket, folded it once lengthwise, and stuck it down in the sand. He gestured to the others; it was a beckoning, an invitation, but I did not understand at first what he meant them to do. He swung himself up into the saddle and gestured again, pointing down to the money on the ground. No one moved; only they were watchful, and he urged his horse away, prancing, a little distance. Then he turned the horse around and set it running—or loping, rather, not fast, but easily, evenly—and reached down from the saddle for the dollar bill. It seemed that his fingers brushed it, but he could not take hold of it, for the stride of the horse was broken slightly at the crucial moment. It was the barest miss—and a beautiful, thrilling thing to see—and he was upright in the saddle again, his motion and the motion of the horse all of a piece. I was watching him so intently that I did not at first see the girl. She came from nowhere, a lithe, lovely Navajo girl on a black horse. She was coming up fast in John Cajero's dust, faster than he had come, and her horse was holding steady in a long, loping stride, level and low. When I saw her she was already hanging down nearly the whole length of her arm from the saddle horn, her knee cocked and her long back curved like a bow, her shoulders close against the deep chest of the horse; she swung her left arm down like a scythe, and up, holding the dollar bill with the tips of her fingers until it was high over her head, and she was standing straight in the stirrups, and her horse did not break stride. And in that way she rode on, past John Cajero, along the wagon train and into the village, having stolen the show and the money, too, going in beauty, trailing laughter. Later I looked for her among the camps, but I did not find her. I imagined that her name was Desbah Yazzie and that she looked out for me from the shadows.

Later in the dusky streets I walked among the Navajo camps, past the doorways of the town, from which came the good smells of cooking, the festive sounds of music, laughter, and talk. The campfires rippled in the crisp wind that arose with evening and set a soft yellow glow on the ground, low on the adobe walls. Mutton sizzled and smoked above the fires; fat dripped into the flames; there were great black pots of strong coffee and buckets full of fried bread; dogs crouched on the rim of the light, the many circles of light; and old men sat hunched in their blankets on the ground, in the cold shadows, smoking, giving almost nothing—only a vague notion—of themselves away. Long into the night the fires cast a glare over the town, and I could hear the singing, until it seemed that one by one the voices fell away, and one remained, and then there was none. On the very edge of sleep I heard coyotes in the hills.

The next day, November twelfth, began with mass at the Pueblo Church. It seemed that the whole town, and all of the visitors, were there, packed into the pews, in the aisle, spilling out of the doors, standing in the *campo santo*.[5] The bright sunlight streamed into the windows, and everyone was dressed in bright colors. The candles on the altar were bright and shone on the bright gilt of the old *santos* and *retablos*.[6] And outside the windows and walls of the church and the village were bright, and the air of the valley was bright as glass, and it was a deep, bright day in the bright November of New Mexico. And after mass the governor spoke in the door of the church, and all of the people formed a procession and moved in a bright throng through the streets to the plaza, to the dancing of the Pecos horse, to the high, constant rattle of a drum.

The street on the north side of the plaza had become a trade fair. There were beautiful things to see: Navajo blankets and silverwork and turquoise, Zia and Santa Ana pottery, Jicarilla baskets; and especially brisk was the trade in perishables; the Jemez people traded their sweet, heavy loaves of *sotobalough* for mutton from Torreon, for apples and melons from Cañon, San Ysidro, and Vallecitos.

As my parents and I wandered along this old north street, observing all that was going on, we were invited to feast in the home of Joe R. Toya, who was to become our close friend and whose children and grandchildren were to graduate from the day school during my parents' tenure there. It is the custom at Jemez that, on the feast days, all of the houses are open to guests; anyone might enter and be welcome—and eat his fill—whether he has been formally invited or not; nonetheless it is a considerable honor to be invited especially, and so it was with us; we were treated royally. The house was immaculate, the earthen floors swept clean as a bone, with everything in its place. A little, long-fingered fire burned evenly in the corner fireplace of the front room. Almost at once we were ushered into the kitchen, where there was a large table laden with food, around which there sat four or five guests, all from out of town, according to their dress, all congenial to us, and shy. Places were made straight away for us, and we were bidden to eat. The food, which was kept hot and unendingly replenished before us, was quite wonderful to see, to smell, and to taste. There were three principal dishes, traditional in the pueblos, stews of rich and distinctive flavor. The first of these was a mild corn stew, that which

---

[5] Cemetery; or, literally, "sacred ground" (Spanish).—EDS.
[6] Statues of wood (strictly speaking, *bultos*) and paintings on wood (Spanish).—EDS.

is called *posole*, made with dried corn (something like hominy), pork bones, and a small amount of chili; the soup of this stew is thin and delicious, and it is among the dishes that I like best in the world. There is no Christmas but that I crave this spicy, smoking Indian *posole*. The second was a thicker soup of chili and beef, brick red in color and decidedly hotter to the taste. And the third was made also of chili and beef and was essentially a deep red chili paste, *con carne*, that burned the mouth and caused perspiration to rise from all the pores of the brow. When I first ate of this dish my whole being cried out for water—I should have given anything for even a spoonful of cold water—but there was none; rather there was only coffee, and it was so hot that it scalded my tongue. Thus did I learn once and for all to eat at the Jemez feasts in the Jemez style, to take bread and dip it into the fiery food and to taste of it delicately, with deliberation and particular respect. I believe that the good, substantial *sotobalough* exists to this very purpose; the moist, sweet, hard-crusted, soft-centered and porous bread is a sop than which there is none better. In addition there was on the table a great variety of canned fruits, breads and *biscochitos*, pies and cakes. Mrs. Toya baked excellent apple pies. We were admonished again and again to "eat good," and that we did. But later, when we went outside again, we were invited to feast in another home, then another, and another, and it seemed that in the interest of diplomacy we could not refuse. In the years at Jemez we were required to negotiate many times an apparent hunger, to exercise fine discretions and deceits. And in this much there was salvation, at least propriety and reprieve. In one of the homes there was a wedding that day. Mary Fragua, the daughter of our housekeeper, Avelina, and a singularly beautiful girl, was married to a young, good-looking man of the pueblo. An old Spanish man of Cañon appeared there in a rumpled black suit and made a sweet, squeaking music on his little violin. Mary wore the traditional manta and white leggings, and she was tall and slender for a pueblo girl, and her deep eyes were dark and dancing and her face was round and radiant, and there grew up in me an admiration for her that was strung between love and lust, and I was full of benevolence and misery.

Through the afternoon the dance went on in the universe. The plaza was thronged with people of every description; they clung there to the adobe walls, looking on; they stood on the housetops, high against the winter sky; and they gave themselves up to the motion and the music of the holy world which was centered there. The dancers came forth in long files of concentrated men and women, first one and then the other of the great Jemez clans, the Turquoise and the Squash, their bodies blue and yellow, taut and tethered to the drums, their feet shaking the hard earth. In them was unspeakable calm and intensity, and these were, I thought and think, unaccountable and unaccountably the same thing. They described every impulse, the whole rhythm of the turning of the earth, the returning of time upon it forever.

Dusk was falling at five o'clock, when the dancing came to an end, and on the way home alone I bought a Navajo dog. I bargained for a while with the thin, wary man whose dog it was, and we settled on a price of five dollars. It was a yellow, honest-to-goodness, great-hearted dog, and the man gave me a bit of rope with which to pull it home. The dog was not large, but neither was it small. It was one of those unremarkable creatures that one sees in every corner of the world. If there were only thirty-nine dogs in Creation, this one would be the fourth, or the thirteenth, or the twenty-first, the archetype, the common denominator of all its kind. It was full of resistance, and yet it was ready to return in full measure my deep, abiding love. I could see that. It needed only, I reasoned, to make a small adjustment in its style of life, to shift the focus of its vitality from one frame of reference to another, in order to be perfectly at home with me. Even as it was nearly strangled on the way, it wagged its bushy tail happily all the while. That night I tied the dog up in the garage, where there was a warm, clean pallet, wholesome food, and fresh water, and I bolted the door. And the next morning the dog was gone, as in my heart of hearts I knew it would be, I believe. I had read such a future in its eyes. It had gnawed the rope in two and squeezed through a vent in the door, an opening much too small for it, as I had thought. But, sure enough, where there is a will there is a way, and the Navajo dog was possessed of one indomitable will. I was crushed at the time, but strangely reconciled, too, as if I had perceived some truth beyond billboards. The dog had done what it had to do, had behaved exactly as it must, had been true to itself and to the sun and moon. It knew its place in the order of things, and its place was away out there in the tracks of a wagon, going home. In the mind's eye I could see it at the very moment, miles away, plodding in the familiar shadows, its tail drooping a little after the harrowing night, but wagging, in its dog's mind contemplating the wonderful ways of mankind.

And on that same harrowing night I saw witches. Some children came to tell us that the witches were about. "Come, we will show you," they said, and they led us outside and pointed with their chins into the night. There, at ground level and far away, were lights, three or four, moving here and there, back and forth. The children watched very solemnly, without alarm, and I understood at once that they were not playing tricks; neither did they care one way or another what I thought of what I saw; only they imagined that I might find it interesting to see witches. You are deceived, I thought; there are men with flashlights, running around in the distance, that is all. But then one of the lights flew suddenly into the air and, like a shooting star, moved across the whole dome of the sky. After midnight Mary Fragua, or whatever her name had become that day, came banging on the door and screaming, "My husband is going to kill me! My husband is going to kill me!" My father let her in and calmed her down, and she went presently to sleep on the divan in our living room. All night long I made trips to the bathroom, that I might switch on the light and see in the flood of it her reclining, foreshortened form, barefooted, beautiful and forsaken, rising and falling, rising and falling.

And the next year there were fewer covered wagons, fewer men and women on horseback. And the next there was relatively little to see on the old wagon road, but the people came in on the high road in cars and trucks. And I think often and with great longing of that first Feast of San Diego in my life at Jemez, that pageant that happened upon me like a dream: say that it was good to see, that it will not be seen again.

The Meaning of the Chicano Movement[1]
LYDIA R. AGUIRRE

Let me start by saying that the Chicano is an extremely diversified "individual." We are as heterogeneous as our history. Without that background of history, it is difficult to understand us. *No somos Mexicanos.*[2] We are citizens of the United States with cultural ties to Mexico and in some instances to Spain, but, within our ties of language and culture, we have developed a culture that is neither Spanish nor Mexican. *Entre nosotros habemos quien habla un español puro, pero también entre nosotros habemos los "batos" que no pueden conseguir "jale" por la razón que sea.*[3]

We are bilingual. We are doctors, university professors, lawyers, and congressmen as well as farm laborers, maids, housewives, plumbers, mailmen, and engineers. There are some Mexican Americans who are *tío-tacos*,[4] those who ride the fence and *cuando se les aprieta el cinto, nos dan en la torre.*[5] But then, there are some Mexican Americans who would readily turn Chicano when they are scratched a little. By that I mean when they understand the true value of this our diversified Chicano movement.

---

[1] This article is subtitled "Extracts from a Letter to a Journalist in Mexico . . ."—EDS.

[2] We are not Mexicans. (Translations of the Chicano Spanish are not always literal but are intended to convey the idiomatic sense.)—EDS.

[3] Among us are those who speak a more correct Spanish, but also among us are those who cannot get a job because they can't.—EDS.

[4] Sellouts.—EDS.

[5] When things get tough, they take it out on us.—EDS.

About the term Chicano, I can not as yet give you a scholarly explanation. From my adolescence in Edinburg, Texas, I remember Chicano as a derogatory term applied *only by us*, who we then insisted should be called Mexican Americans. We demanded that we be classified as Caucasian. Chicano was a term used self-consciously and degradingly only by ourselves. In his columns in the *Los Angeles Times*, Ruben Salazar attempted to define the term. In one column he wrote, "A Chicano is a Mexican American with a non-Anglo image of himself . . . actually the word Chicano is as difficult to define as 'soul.'" In another instance, he wrote, "For those who like simplistic answers Chicano can be defined as short for Mexicano. For those who prefer complicated answers it has been suggested that Chicano may have come from the word Chihuahua—the name of a Mexican state bordering on the United States. Getting trickier this version contends that Mexicans who migrated to Texas call themselves Chicanos." In a third reference he said, "Chicanos then are merely fighting to become 'Americans'. Yes, but with a Chicano outlook."

As I understand the word Chicano in the Chicano movement, it is this: if there is no lowest of the low and no highest of the high and *each* will wear the label of *Chicano* with pride, he will have personal respect and with it *dignidad y unidad con sus hermanos Chicanos*.[6] He will be proud to assume his heritage guaranteed in the Treaty of Guadalupe Hidalgo and proud to use the language and customs that are his by heritage, treaty, and *corazón*.[7] Chicano power simply means that in the finding of identity— that is, a right to be *as he is*, not Mexican, not Spanish, not speaking either a "pure" English or a "pure" Spanish, but *as he is*, a product of a Spanish-Mexican-Indian heritage and an Anglo-Saxon (American, or, as Mexico says, *Estado Unidense*[8]) influence—he will unite with his brothers in heritage. As he has pride and unity, so will he lose his self-consciousness and self-degradation and thereby will gain status and power.

Collectively, the Chicano in unity can influence the social systems that have perpetuated social injustices. Some say we are in the midst of a social revolution. I prefer to state that we are in the midst of a renaissance. We challenge the educational system to recognize our "differentness." We challenge ourselves to be proud of this differentness. We challenge the educational system to teach Hispanic history, to teach bilingually, and to give us adequate schools where students are largely Chicano. We demand not to be segregated. We demand that others recognize our differentness and work within that differentness rather than make the Chicano suppress his Chicanismo and adopt Anglo-Saxon ideals.

We demand that our side of the story be told. From this demand grew the Ruben Salazar Memorial Scholarship Foundation. Ruben Salazar dared

---

[6] Dignity and unity with his fellow Chicanos.—Eds.
[7] Spirit.—Eds.
[8] United States.—Eds.

to speak the truth. His voice was silenced when he was killed in Los Angeles in the line of duty, covering the 1970 Chicano Moratorium for his paper. Through the mass communications scholarships we are offering, we hope to educate young people in television, radio, and journalism to continue Ruben Salazar's message. Needless to say, the present mass media sometimes distort the truth. What may really be a justified confrontation on a social injustice can be reported as a riotous disruption.

Some of us feel that we need parallel institutions to have real justice. The Ruben Salazar memorial foundation has a long-range goal of establishing or sponsoring a daily newspaper. Later on, who knows—perhaps even Chicano radio and television!

We continue being so terribly diversified, yet we have so many cultural values that unite us. Each area has problems unique to that area. Northern New Mexico is rural and communal. The people there are fighting for their lands and grazing and water rights. Urban areas fight both discrimination and racism. Racism is so difficult to fight because it is so intangible and difficult to pinpoint. Yet it is all around us.

Take, for example, El Paso. People with Spanish surnames number almost half of the population of El Paso. Yet we have very few businessmen proportionately. If we look at executive positions of the major companies, we are lucky to find a sprinkling of Spanish surnames. Many of our educated young people have to leave this community to find jobs. I personally know several young people who looked diligently for jobs for months and either left town or took a menial job. Last week, however, I received a call from an Anglo-Saxon young lady friend of mine who found a good job after only three days of looking in a city strange to her. Were the former just unfortunate incidents and was the latter a fortunate incident?

In approaching the problems facing us, the Chicano uses different methods. Each in his own way is striving to achieve human dignity, self-respect, and just equality. Some Chicanos (and I include myself) attempt to effect change within established systems, and if that does not work, attempt to establish parallel systems. Hence, we have separate newspapers, Chicano conferences, businesses. We attempt to change the educational system to better meet our needs. We demand justice in courts and from police within the established order. Other Chicanos prefer isolationism or brown separatism. These are in the minority. Very few would want a separate nation.

Others, particularly in New Mexico, who brought from Spain and continued the system of an agrarian, communal society into this century, want a return to that system which in that climate and region is almost imperative to survival. It is interesting to note that the Pueblo Indian who lived in that region when the Spaniards arrived had a similar system already in operation.

In our search for identity, we are researching and I feel, perhaps creating the concept of *Aztlan*. Supposedly, we are descendants, through our Indian heritage, of the native peoples of the Southwest. The Aztlan people had a civilization that is still with us in a modified form through Mexican-Spanish influences. Aztlan lives in any land where a Chicano lives: in his mind and heart and in the land he walks. The emblem used extensively in Chicano circles is a black Aztec eagle on a red background.

Carnalismo,[9] a feeling or an allegiance that permeates the movement, means a type of brotherhood within members of La Raza characterized by depth of feeling and allegiance to other *carnales*.[10] It is the type of feeling and allegiance that many blood relatives have for one another. Once a Chicano is your *carnal*, he will stand with you through thick or thin.

In social work circles (I am a social worker by training), we are looking at the aspects of the Chicano (Mexican-American) family that are conducive to mental health. We are attempting to break the stereotypes associated with the Chicano family and show the Chicano family with its healthful components as well as with its harmful components. We are looking at the extended family and at the social welfare institutions that penalize the Chicano for preserving these family ties. In a sense, our culture has retained the "people orientation" lost to many in our materialistic society.

One of our leaders in the movement has been César Chávez with his organization of farm workers. His is a nonviolent movement. From the frustration of the strikes originated the Teatro Campesino (in Delano, California, in 1965). Out of the need for laughter, the strikers began a fast-paced, almost slapstick style of comedy mimicking those pertinent to the strikers: the patron, the contractor, the scab, and so forth. It is now a tremendously effective mode of showing the problems faced by Chicanos. It is raw; it is realistic; it is life itself!

Reies López Tijerina is another leader. His leadership is primarily in Tierra Amarilla in New Mexico. He is a land grant spokesman, although presently imprisoned for destroying federal property in one of the National Forests. Tijerina is a native of southern Texas. He saw his father run off his land in a most humiliating fashion. He was from humble origins, and he drifted around in farm camps. He was an extremely eloquent, fiery speaker for his *Alianza*, fighting for return of lands to land grantees and communal rights, but, most important, for full recognition of the Treaty of Guadalupe Hidalgo. Ranchers have distorted laws in this area to suit their needs.

Rodolfo "Corky" González from Colorado has been a leader in the migratory labor area. He is an ex-boxer, lecturer, poet, political activist, and community organizer, as well as a businessman and philanthropist. He is presently president and director of the Crusade for Justice, a Chicano civil rights organization in Denver. His poem, "Yo Soy Joaquín," should

---

[9] Brotherhood.—EDS.
[10] Brothers.—EDS.

be required reading for everyone. Joaquín's first words poignantly describe the anguish of the Chicano who is confused and lost in the Anglo society.[11]

José Angel Gutierrez of Crystal City, Texas, is a young man who is devoting his most capable energies toward establishing a base of political power in Texas. Chicanos who have become disillusioned with both political parties have created a third party, La Raza Unida.

The Mexican press was a strong ally to the Mexican Americans who fought injustices during and after World War II. We are still fighting these injustices, but now with a better self-concept, with a sustaining and lasting dedication and determination, and with more sophisticated and greater manpower. The dedication is courageous and contagious. We are fighting the vast racism that is rampant in our country and that seems unable to tolerate differentness. We are fighting for the right to be *as we are* —Chicanos. And within our culture we demand the right to be first class citizens within this our United States.

Por mi Raza habla el Espíritu.[12]

The Meaning of July Fourth for the American Negro[1]
FREDERICK DOUGLASS

Fellow-citizens, pardon me, allow me to ask, why am I called upon to speak here to-day? What have I, or those I represent, to do with your national independence? Are the great principles of political freedom and of natural justice, embodied in that Declaration of Independence, extended to us? and am I, therefore, called upon to bring our humble offering to the national altar, and to confess the benefits and express devout gratitude for the blessings resulting from your independence to us?

Would to God, both for your sakes and ours, that an affirmative answer could be truthfully returned to these questions! Then would my task be light, and my burden easy and delightful. For *who* is there so cold, that a nation's sympathy could not warm him? Who so obdurate and dead to the claims of gratitude, that would not thankfully acknowledge such priceless benefits? Who so stolid and selfish, that would not give his voice to swell the hallelujahs of a nation's jubilee, when the chains of servitude had been

[11] The poem begins: "I am Joaquín,/Lost in a world of confusion,/Caught up in a whirl of an Anglo society,/Confused by the rules,/Scorned by attitudes,/Suppressed by manipulations,/And destroyed by modern society."—EDS.
[12] The Spirit speaks through my People.—EDS.

---

[1] Excerpted from *Oration Delivered in Corinthian Hall, July 5, 1852* (Rochester, N.Y., 1852). Reprinted from *My Bondage and My Freedom* (1857).—EDS.

torn from his limbs? I am not that man. In a case like that, the dumb might eloquently speak, and the "lame man leap as an hart."[2]

But such is not the state of the case. I say it with a sad sense of the disparity between us. I am not included within the pale of this glorious anniversary! Your high independence only reveals the immeasurable distance between us. The blessings in which you, this day, rejoice, are not enjoyed in common.—The rich inheritance of justice, liberty, prosperity and independence, bequeathed by your fathers, is shared by you, not by me. The sunlight that brought light and healing to you, has brought stripes and death to me. This Fourth July is *yours,* not *mine. You* may rejoice, *I* must mourn. To drag a man in fetters into the grand illuminated temple of liberty, and call upon him to join you in joyous anthems, were inhuman mockery and sacrilegious irony. Do you mean, citizens, to mock me, by asking me to speak to-day? If so, there is a parallel to your conduct. And let me warn you that it is dangerous to copy the example of a nation whose crimes, towering up to heaven, were thrown down by the breath of the Almighty, burying that nation in irrevocable ruin! I can to-day take up the plaintive lament of a peeled and woe-smitten people!

"By the rivers of Babylon, there we sat down. Yea! we wept when we remembered Zion. We hanged our harps upon the willows in the midst thereof. For there, they that carried us away captive, required of us a song; and they who wasted us required of us mirth, saying, Sing us one of the songs of Zion. How can we sing the Lord's song in a strange land? If I forget thee, O Jerusalem, let my right hand forget her cunning. If I do not remember thee, let my tongue cleave to the roof of my mouth."[3]

Fellow-citizens, above your national, tumultuous joy, I hear the mournful wail of millions! whose chains, heavy and grievous yesterday, are, to-day, rendered more intolerable by the jubilee shouts that reach them. If I do forget, if I do not faithfully remember those bleeding children of sorrow this day, "may my right hand forget her cunning, and may my tongue cleave to the roof of my mouth!" To forget them, to pass lightly over their wrongs, and to chime in with the popular theme, would be treason most scandalous and shocking, and would make me a reproach before God and the world. My subject, then, fellow-citizens, is American slavery. I shall see this day and its popular characteristics from the slave's point of view. Standing there identified with the American bondman, making his wrongs mine, I do not hesitate to declare, with all my soul, that the character and conduct of this nation never looked blacker to me than on this 4th of July! Whether we turn to the declarations of the past, or to the professions of the present, the conduct of the nation seems equally hideous and revolting. America is false to the past, false to the present, and solemnly binds herself to be false to the future. Standing with God and the crushed

[2] Isaiah 35:6.—Eds.
[3] Cf. Psalms 137:5–6.—Eds.

and bleeding slave on this occasion, I will, in the name of humanity which is outraged, in the name of liberty which is fettered, in the name of the constitution and the Bible which are disregarded and trampled upon, dare to call in question and to denounce, with all the emphasis I can command, everything that serves to perpetuate slavery—the great sin and shame of America! "I will not equivocate; I will not excuse";[4] I will use the severest language I can command; and yet not one word shall escape me that any man, whose judgment is not blinded by prejudice, or who is not at heart a slaveholder, shall not confess to be right and just.

But I fancy I hear some one of my audience say, "It is just in this circumstance that you and your brother abolitionists fail to make a favorable impression on the public mind. Would you argue more, and denounce less; would you persuade more, and rebuke less; your cause would be much more likely to succeed." But, I submit, where all is plain there is nothing to be argued. What point in the anti-slavery creed would you have me argue? On what branch of the subject do the people of this country need light? Must I undertake to prove that the slave is a man? That point is conceded already. Nobody doubts it. The slaveholders themselves acknowledge it in the enactment of laws for their government. They acknowledge it when they punish disobedience on the part of the slave. There are seventy-two crimes in the State of Virginia which, if committed by a black man (no matter how ignorant he be), subject him to the punishment of death; while only two of the same crimes will subject a white man to the like punishment. What is this but the acknowledgment that the slave is a moral, intellectual, and responsible being? The manhood of the slave is conceded. It is admitted in the fact that Southern statute books are covered with enactments forbidding, under severe fines and penalties, the teaching of the slave to read or to write. When you can point to any such laws in reference to the beasts of the field, then I may consent to argue the manhood of the slave. When the dogs in your streets, when the fowls of the air, when the cattle on your hills, when the fish of the sea, and the reptiles that crawl, shall be unable to distinguish the slave from a brute, *then* will I argue with you that the slave is a man!

For the present, it is enough to affirm the equal manhood of the Negro race. It is not astonishing that, while we are ploughing, planting, and reaping, using all kinds of mechanical tools, erecting houses, constructing bridges, building ships, working in metals of brass, iron, copper, silver and gold; that, while we are reading, writing and ciphering, acting as clerks, merchants and secretaries, having among us lawyers, doctors, ministers, poets, authors, editors, orators and teachers; that, while we are engaged in all manner of enterprises common to other men, digging gold in California, capturing the whale in the Pacific, feeding sheep and cattle on the hill-side, living, moving, acting, thinking, planning, living in families as husbands,

---

[4] Famous phrase of William Lloyd Garrison in *The Liberator*.—EDS.

wives and children, and, above all, confessing and worshipping the Christian's God, and looking hopefully for life and immortality beyond the grave, we are called upon to prove that we are men!

Would you have me argue that man is entitled to liberty? that he is the rightful owner of his own body? You have already declared it. Must I argue the wrongfulness of slavery? Is that a question for Republicans? Is it to be settled by the rules of logic and argumentation, as a matter beset with great difficulty, involving a doubtful application of the principle of justice, hard to be understood? How should I look to-day, in the presence of Americans, dividing, and subdividing a discourse, to show that men have a natural right to freedom? speaking of it relatively and positively, negatively and affirmatively. To do so, would be to make myself ridiculous, and to offer an insult to your understanding.—There is not a man beneath the canopy of heaven that does not know that slavery is wrong *for him*.

What, am I to argue that it is wrong to make men brutes, to rob them of their liberty, to work them without wages, to keep them ignorant of their relations to their fellow men, to beat them with sticks, to flay their flesh with the lash, to load their limbs with irons, to hunt them with dogs, to sell them at auction, to sunder their families, to knock out their teeth, to burn their flesh, to starve them into obedience and submission to their masters? Must I argue that a system thus marked with blood, and stained with pollution, is *wrong*? No! I will not. I have better employment for my time and strength than such arguments would imply.

What, then, remains to be argued? Is it that slavery is not divine; that God did not establish it; that our doctors of divinity are mistaken? There is blasphemy in the thought. That which is inhuman, cannot be divine! *Who* can reason on such a proposition? They that can, may; I cannot. The time for such argument is passed.

At a time like this, scorching irony, not convincing argument, is needed. O! had I the ability, and could reach the nation's ear, I would, today, pour out a fiery stream of biting ridicule, blasting reproach, withering sarcasm, and stern rebuke. For it is not light that is needed, but fire; it is not the gentle shower, but thunder. We need the storm, the whirlwind, and the earthquake. The feeling of the nation must be quickened; the conscience of the nation must be roused; the propriety of the nation must be startled; the hypocrisy of the nation must be exposed; and its crimes against God and man must be proclaimed and denounced.

What, to the American slave, is your 4th of July? I answer; a day that reveals to him, more than all other days in the year, the gross injustice and cruelty to which he is the constant victim. To him, your celebration is a sham; your boasted liberty, an unholy license; your national greatness, swelling vanity; your sounds of rejoicing are empty and heartless; your denunciation of tyrants, brass fronted impudence; your shouts of liberty and equality, hollow mockery; your prayers and hymns, your sermons and thanksgivings, with all your religious parade and solemnity, are, to Him, mere bombast, fraud, deception, impiety, and hypocrisy—a thin veil to cover up crimes which would disgrace a nation of savages. There is not a nation on the earth guilty of practices more shocking and bloody than are the people of the United States, at this very hour.

Go where you may, search where you will, roam through all the monarchies and despotisms of the Old World, travel through South America, search out every abuse, and when you have found the last, lay your facts by the side of the everyday practices of this nation, and you will say with me, that, for revolting barbarity and shameless hypocrisy America reigns without a rival. . . .

Americans! your republican politics, not less than your republican religion, are flagrantly inconsistent. You boast of your love of liberty, your superior civilization, and your pure Christianity, while the whole political power of the nation (as embodied in the two great political parties) is solemnly pledged to support and perpetuate the enslavement of three millions of your countrymen. You hurl your anathemas at the crowned headed tyrants of Russia and Austria and pride yourselves on your Democratic institutions, while you yourselves consent to be the mere *tools* and *body-guards* of the tyrants of Virginia and Carolina. You invite to your shores fugitives of oppression from abroad, honor them with banquets, greet them with ovations, cheer them, toast them, salute them, protect them, and pour out your money to them like water; but the fugitives from your own land you advertise, hunt, arrest, shoot, and kill. You glory in your refinement and your universal education; yet you maintain a system as barbarous and dreadful as ever stained the character of a nation—a system begun in avarice, supported in pride, and perpetuated in cruelty. You shed tears over fallen Hungary, and make the sad story of her wrongs the theme of your poets, statesmen, and orators, till your gallant sons are ready to fly to arms to vindicate her cause against the oppressor; but, in regard to the ten thousand wrongs of the American slave, you would enforce the strictest silence, and would hail him as an enemy of the nation who dares to make those wrongs the subject of public discourse! You are all on fire at the mention of liberty for France or for Ireland; but are as cold as an iceberg at the thought of liberty for the enslaved of America. You discourse eloquently on the dignity of labor; yet, you sustain a system which, in its very essence, casts a stigma upon labor. You can bare your bosom to the storm of British artillery to throw off a three-penny tax on tea; and yet wring the last hard earned farthing from the grasp of the black laborers of your country. You profess to believe "that, of one blood, God made all nations of men to dwell on the face of all the earth,"[5] and hath commanded all men, everywhere, to love one another; yet you notoriously hate (and glory in your hatred) all men whose skins are not colored like your own. You declare before the world, and are understood by the world to

[5] Cf. Acts 17:26.—EDS.

declare that you *"hold these truths to be self-evident, that all men are created equal; and are endowed by their Creator with certain inalienable rights; and that among these are, life, liberty, and the pursuit of happiness"*; and yet, you hold securely, in a bondage which, according to your own Thomas Jefferson, *"is worse than ages of that which your fathers rose in rebellion to oppose,"* a seventh part of the inhabitants of your country.

Fellow-citizens, I will not enlarge further on your national inconsistencies. The existence of slavery in this country brands your republicanism as a sham, your humanity as a base pretense, and your Christianity as a lie. It destroys your moral power abroad: it corrupts your politicians at home. It saps the foundation of religion; it makes your name a hissing and a byeword to a mocking earth. It is the antagonistic force in your government, the only thing that seriously disturbs and endangers your *Union*. It fetters your progress; it is the enemy of improvement; the deadly foe of education; it fosters pride; it breeds insolence; it promotes vice; it shelters crime; it is a curse to the earth that supports it; and yet you cling to it as if it were the sheet anchor of all your hopes. Oh! be warned! be warned! a horrible reptile is coiled up in your nation's bosom; the venomous creature is nursing at the tender breast of your youthful republic; *for the love of God, tear away*, and fling from you the hideous monster, and *let the weight of twenty millions crush and destroy it forever!*

Why I Left the U.S. and Why I Am Returning
ELDRIDGE CLEAVER

I am often asked why I want to return to the United States. This question never fails to bowl me over, and I find it impossible to answer. I also feel that it is an improper question. In fact, most people who ask are not really interested in that question. What they actually want to know is what will I do if they allow me to return.

I always take the opportunity to explain why I left in the first place. Lots of people believe I left because I preferred to go live in a Communist country, and that now, several years and many Communist countries later, I find the grass not greener on the Communist side of the fence. So now, here I stand, locked outside the gates of the paradise I once scorned, begging to be let back in. Let me clarify.

On April 6, 1968, two days after Dr. Martin Luther King, Jr., was assassinated, there was a gun battle between members of the Black Panther Party and the Oakland Police Department. Bobby Hutton was killed. Warren Wells and I received gunshot wounds. Two policemen were wounded. Eight party members, myself included, were arrested in the area of the gunfight.

After I received emergency treatment, guards from the California Department of Corrections transported me directly to San Quentin State Prison, in the spirit of "Oh, boy, we got you now!" It seemed obvious to them that I had violated my parole.[1] I, along with the others, was indicted by an Alameda County Grand Jury. And although bail was set on all of us, the Corrections Department refused to allow me to go free on bail, claiming jurisdiction over me as a parole violator.

I pleaded not guilty. Without a trial or hearing of any sort, the prison authorities were prejudging my case, declaring me guilty, and, in effect, sentencing me to prison. My attorneys filed a petition for a writ of habeas corpus. A hearing was held before Chief Judge Raymond J. Sherwin of the Solano County Superior Court.

Judge Sherwin ordered me free on bail. I quote . . . from his decision:

The record here is that though the petitioner was arrested and his parole cancelled more than two months ago, hearings before the Adult Authority [the state parole board for male felons] have not even been scheduled.

There is nothing to indicate why it was deemed necessary to cancel his parole before his trial on the pending criminal charges of which he is presumed innocent.

It has to be stressed that the uncontradicted evidence presented to this Court indicated that the petitioner had been a model parolee. The peril to his parole status stemmed from no failure of personal rehabilitation, but from his undue eloquence in pursuing political goals, goals which were offensive to many of his contemporaries.

Not only was there absence of cause for the cancellation of parole, it was the product of a type of pressure unbecoming, to say the least, to the law enforcement paraphernalia of this state.

Judge Sherwin's decision exploded like a bomb inside California legal, political and police circles, because it missed the whole point: From Governor Ronald Reagan down, the politicians wanted me silenced, and here Judge Sherwin was talking about due process of law!

People who supported my fight for my rights posted $50,000 bail, and I was free.

The law-enforcement paraphernalia was not stopped by Judge Sherwin's condemnation, and the Adult Authority moved swiftly to have his ruling reversed in the Appellate Court. The court refused to examine the facts at issue in the case and instead simply affirmed the arbitrary power of the Adult Authority to revoke parole. Because of a technicality in court procedure, the ruling ordering me returned to prison could not become effective for sixty days. I was due to surrender on November 27. That day, I was in Montreal. That was seven years ago.

[1] Cleaver had been paroled in 1968 after having served nine years of a fourteen-year sentence that resulted from his 1958 conviction for assault with intent to kill.—EDS.

History shows that when the American political system is blocked and significant segments of the population are unable to have their will brought to bear on the decision-making process, you can count upon the American people to revolt, to take it out into the streets, in the spirit of the Boston Tea Party.

During the 1960's, the chips were down in a fateful way, uniting the upsurge of black Americans against the oppressive features of the system, and the gargantuan popular opposition to the Indochina wars. It was left to the Nixon Administration to bring the issues to a head. In the end, the system rejected President Nixon and reaffirmed its own basic principles.

A fabulous new era of progress is opening up to the world, and coping with all of the problems unleashed by Watergate has opened up a creative era for American democracy. I believe that every American, regardless of his politics, has a duty to re-examine some of his beliefs.

This is particularly true of those active at both extremes of the political spectrum. Those of us who developed a psychology of opposition must take a pause and sum up our experiences. We must recognize that in a sense we are playing in a brand new ball game. The slogans of yesterday will not get us through the tasks at hand. I believe that for America to deal with problems posed on the world level, a fundamental reorientation in the relationship between the American people is absolutely necessary.

We can not afford to refight battles that have already been either won or lost. If Richard Nixon and his friends had accepted the verdict of the people in 1960, rejecting him at the polls, the nation would have been spared the debacle of Watergate. But the truth is that nations do get the leaders they deserve.

With all of its faults, the American political system is the freest and most democratic in the world. The system needs to be improved, with democracy spread to all areas of life, particularly the economic. All of these changes must be conducted through our established institutions, and people with grievances must find political methods for obtaining redress.

Each generation subjects the world it inherits to severe criticism. I think that my generation has been more critical than most, and for good reason. At the same time, at the end of the critical process, we should arrive at some conclusions. We should have discovered which values are worth conserving. It is the beginning of another fight, the fight to defend those values from the blind excesses of our fellows who are still caught up in the critical process. It is my hope to make a positive contribution in this regard.

As Italian as Apple Pie and Baseball
RALPH J. PERROTTA

One of my earliest recollections, going back to before I started school, is of my mother's references to the two Irish families on our block as "Americans" as distinguished from us "Italians." I remember asking myself, and my mother, why they were any more American than we were. Although she conceded the technical point of my American birth and citizenship (and hers) she nevertheless clung to her sense of our being more Italian than American.

The distinctions were obvious, and I could not gloss them over no matter how hard I tried. "Americans" were fair and "cool," spoke fluent English (albeit with a brogue, but who heard any other kind on my block?) and had a sense of belonging about them that was confirmed by their living in homes of their own. We were mostly brunets (there was one Italian family whose red hair everyone marveled at), passionate and demonstrative, and lived in flats or tenements. Our parents were immigrants who had come here as children with their parents and their English was always less than fluent; how much less depended on how facile they were with words and how old they were when they arrived.

School, for me, was among other things a way to erase these distinctions and become American. Most of the teachers then, in Rhode Island, were Yankees and so even more prototypically American than the Irish families I knew. Their names were of the sort I found in my school books, and their demeanor seemed to convey an assurance about their right to be here that I never saw in my relatives and neighbors. I found myself trying, with some success, to emulate them. Some of my classmates, try though they might, were unsuccessful either for lack of skill or because the gap between them and their models was too wide. Still others never tried to be anything but what they started out: Italian.

All of us paid a psychic price, though it was extracted at different times and in varying measure, and got something in return. Those of us who "assimilated" perhaps made the best bargain. The decision to assimilate added urgency to our efforts to "make it," and when we did the rewards were gratifying not only for their own sake but also because they were—and are—deemed to confer the status and dignity so precious to those uncertain of their place. But our price was a growing unease, generally diffuse and below the surface but periodically becoming focused and breaking through to a conscious level: that we might get too excited, wave our arms too vigorously when we spoke, lose our grip on our speech habits, or otherwise reveal some telltale evidence of our past to American friends.

For those who never assimilated, life was perhaps simpler. There was no ambiguity; they were just alien. Sometimes they created a world of their own within but apart from the larger one, and wreaked their vengeance by exploiting both. But most resigned themselves to living quiet but relatively isolated lives, always on the edge of a world that was not their own, as you or I might if we were dropped, tomorrow, into Peking.

When we were coming here in great tides around the turn of the century, it was perhaps understandable that we would create a sense of insecurity in those who preceded us. What's more, a rapidly growing, newly industrialized society was inevitably a practical society, and the most "practical" solution to the problem of cultural diversity was to eliminate it—or try.

But if diversity was once a luxury we could not afford, now it is a reality we can no longer avoid. Once we acknowledged that black is beautiful we could no longer insist on any one version of what it means to be "American" nor any one vision of what it ought to mean. And if that were not enough, the reappraisal of American values prompted by the Vietnam war and the search for identity and self-awareness taking place at all levels of American society cinched it. We will be revealing more and more of ourselves, to ourselves and others, before we are done, and the challenge will be to make this a wholesome and even healing process for this country and not a divisive and self-destructive one.

Women

A Vindication of the Rights of Woman[1]
MARY WOLLSTONECRAFT

My own sex, I hope, will excuse me, if I treat them like rational creatures, instead of flattering their *fascinating* graces, and viewing them as if they were in a state of perpetual childhood, unable to stand alone. I earnestly wish to point out in what true dignity and human happiness consists—I wish to persuade women to endeavour to acquire strength, both of mind and body, and to convince them that the soft phrases, susceptibility of heart, delicacy of sentiment, and refinement of taste, are almost synonymous with epithets of weakness, and that those beings who are only the objects of pity and that kind of love, which has been termed its sister, will soon become objects of contempt.

Dismissing then those pretty feminine phrases, which the men condescendingly use to soften our slavish dependence, and despising that weak elegancy of mind, exquisite sensibility, and sweet docility of manners, supposed to be the sexual characteristics of the weaker vessel, I wish to shew that elegance is inferior to virtue, that the first object of laudable ambition is to obtain a character as a human being, regardless of the distinction of sex; and that secondary views should be brought to this simple touchstone.

This is a rough sketch of my plan; and should I express my conviction with the energetic emotions that I feel whenever I think of the subject, the dictates of experience and reflection will be felt by some of my readers. Animated by this important object, I shall disdain to cull my phrases or polish my style;—I aim at being useful, and sincerity will render me unaffected; for, wishing rather to persuade by the force of my arguments, than dazzle by the elegance of my language, I shall not waste my time in rounding periods, or in fabricating the turgid bombast of artificial feelings, which, coming from the head, never reach the heart.—I shall be employed about things, not words!—and, anxious to render my sex more respectable members of society, I shall try to avoid that flowery diction which has slided from essays into novels, and from novels into familiar letters and conversation.

These pretty superlatives, dropping glibly from the tongue, vitiate the taste, and create a kind of sickly delicacy that turns away from simple unadorned truth; and a deluge of false sentiments and overstretched feel-

---

[1] A part of the Introduction of the *Vindication*, published in 1792.—Eds.

ings, stifling the natural emotions of the heart, render the domestic pleasures insipid, that ought to sweeten the exercise of those severe duties, which educate a rational and immortal being for a nobler field of action.

The education of women has, of late, been more attended to than formerly; yet they are still reckoned a frivolous sex, and ridiculed or pitied by the writers who endeavour by satire or instruction to improve them. It is acknowledged that they spend many of the first years of their lives in acquiring a smattering of accomplishments; meanwhile strength of body and mind are sacrificed to libertine notions of beauty, to the desire of establishing themselves,—the only way women can rise in the world,—by marriage. And this desire making mere animals of them, when they marry they act as such children may be expected to act:—they dress; they paint, and nickname God's creatures.[2]—Surely these weak beings are only fit for a seraglio!—Can they be expected to govern a family with judgment, or take care of the poor babes whom they bring into the world?

If then it can be fairly deduced from the present conduct of the sex, from the prevalent fondness for pleasure which takes place of ambition and those nobler passions that open and enlarge the soul; that the instruction which women have hitherto received has only tended, with the constitution of civil society, to render them insignificant objects of desire— mere propagators of fools!—if it can be proved that in aiming to accomplish them, without cultivating their understandings, they are taken out of their sphere of duties, and made ridiculous and useless when the short-lived bloom of beauty is over,[3] I presume that *rational* men will excuse me for endeavouring to persuade them to become more masculine and respectable.

Indeed the word masculine is only a bugbear: there is little reason to fear that women will acquire too much courage or fortitude; for their apparent inferiority with respect to bodily strength, must render them, in some degree, dependent on men in the various relations of life; but why should it be increased by prejudices that give a sex to virtue, and confound simple truths with sensual reveries?

Women are, in fact, so much degraded by mistaken notions of female excellence, that I do not mean to add a paradox when I assert, that this artificial weakness produces a propensity to tyrannize, and gives birth to cunning, the natural opponent of strength, which leads them to play off those contemptible infantine airs that undermine esteem even whilst they excite desire. Let men become more chaste and modest, and if women do not grow wiser in the same ratio, it will be clear that they have weaker understandings. It seems scarcely necessary to say, that I now speak of the sex in general. Many individuals have more sense than their male

---

[2] Cf. *Hamlet*, Act III, scene 1, line 148: "You nickname [i.e., travesty] God's creatures . . ."—EDS.

[3] A lively writer, I cannot recollect his name, asks what business women turned of forty have to do in this world?

relatives; and, as nothing preponderates where there is a constant struggle for an equilibrium, without it has naturally more gravity, some women govern their husbands without degrading themselves, because intellect will always govern.

The Stereotype
GERMAINE GREER

    The stereotype is the Eternal Feminine. She is the Sexual Object sought by all men, and by all women. She is of neither sex, for she has herself no sex at all. Her value is solely attested by the demand she excites in others. All she must contribute is her existence. She need achieve nothing, for she is the reward of achievement. She need never give positive evidence of her moral character because virtue is assumed from her loveliness, and her passivity. If any man who has no right to her be found with her she will not be punished, for she is morally neuter. The matter is solely one of male rivalry. Innocently she may drive men to madness and war. The more trouble she can cause, the more her stocks go up, for possession of her means more the more demand she excites. Nobody wants a girl whose beauty is imperceptible to all but him; and so men welcome the stereotype because it directs their taste into the most commonly recognized areas of value, although they may protest because some aspects of it do not tally with their fetishes. There is scope in the stereotype's variety for most fetishes. The leg man may follow miniskirts, the tit man can encourage see-through blouses and plunging necklines, although the man who likes fat women may feel constrained to enjoy them in secret. There are stringent limits to the variations on the stereotype, for nothing must interfere with her function as sex object. She may wear leather, as long as she cannot actually handle a motorbike: she may wear rubber, but it ought not to indicate that she is an expert diver or waterskier. If she wears athletic clothes the purpose is to underline her unathleticism. She may sit astride a horse, looking soft and curvy, but she must not crouch over its neck with her rump in the air.

  Because she is the emblem of spending ability and the chief spender, she is also the most effective seller of this world's goods. Every survey ever held has shown that the image of an attractive woman is the most effective advertising gimmick. She may sit astride the mudguard of a new car, or step into it ablaze with jewels; she may lie at a man's feet stroking his new socks; she may hold the petrol pump in a challenging pose, or dance through woodland glades in slow motion in all the glory of a new shampoo; whatever she does her image sells. The gynolatry of our civilization is written large upon its face, upon hoardings, cinema screens, television, newspapers, magazines, tins, packets, cartons, bottles, all consecrated to the reigning deity, the female fetish. Her dominion must not be thought to entail the rule of women, for she is not a woman. Her glossy lips and mat complexion, her unfocused eyes and flawless fingers, her extraordinary hair all floating and shining, curling and gleaming, reveal the inhuman triumph of cosmetics, lighting, focusing and printing, cropping and composition. She sleeps unruffled, her lips red and juicy and closed, her eyes as crisp and black as if new painted, and her false lashes immaculately curled. Even when she washes her face with a new and creamier toilet soap her expression is as tranquil and vacant and her paint as flawless as ever. If ever she should appear tousled and troubled, her features are miraculously smoothed to their proper veneer by a new washing powder or a bouillon cube. For she is a doll: weeping, pouting or smiling, running or reclining, she is a doll. She is an idol, formed of the concatenation of lines and masses, signifying the lineaments of satisfied impotence.

Her essential quality is castratedness. She absolutely must be young, her body hairless, her flesh buoyant, and *she must not have a sexual organ*. No musculature must distort the smoothness of the lines of her body, although she may be painfully slender or warmly cuddly. Her expression must betray no hint of humor, curiosity or intelligence, although it may signify hauteur to an extent that is actually absurd, or smoldering lust, very feebly signified by drooping eyes and a sullen mouth (for the stereotype's lust equals irrational submission), or, most commonly, vivacity and idiot happiness. Seeing that the world despoils itself for this creature's benefit, she must be happy; the entire structure would topple if she were not. So the image of woman appears plastered on every surface imaginable, smiling interminably. An apple pie evokes a glance of tender beatitude, a washing machine causes hilarity, a cheap box of chocolates brings forth meltingly joyous gratitude, a Coke is the cause of a rictus of unutterable brilliance, even a new stick-on bandage is saluted by a smirk of satisfaction. A real woman licks her lips and opens her mouth and flashes her teeth when photographers appear: *she* must arrive at the premiere of her husband's film in a paroxysm of delight, or his success might be murmured about. The occupational hazard of being a Playboy Bunny is the aching facial muscles brought on by the obligatory smiles.

So what is the beef? Maybe I couldn't make it. Maybe I don't have a pretty smile, good teeth, nice tits, long legs, a cheeky arse, a sexy voice. Maybe I don't know how to handle men and increase my market value, so that the rewards due to the feminine will accrue to me. Then again, maybe I'm sick of the masquerade. I'm sick of pretending eternal youth. I'm sick of belying my own intelligence, my own will, my own sex. I'm sick of peering at the world through false eyelashes, so everything I see is mixed with a shadow of bought hairs; I'm sick of weighting my head with a dead mane, unable to move my neck freely, terrified of rain, of wind, of dancing too vigorously in case I sweat into my lacquered curls. I'm sick of the Powder Room. I'm sick of pretending that some fatuous male's self-important pronouncements are the objects of my undivided attention, I'm sick of going to films and plays when someone else wants to, and sick of having no opinions of my own about either. I'm sick of being a transvestite. I refuse to be a female impersonator. I am a woman, not a castrate.

April Ashley was born male. All the information supplied by genes, chromosomes, internal and external sexual organs added up to the same thing. April was a man. But he longed to be a woman. He longed for the stereotype, not to embrace, but to be. He wanted soft fabrics, jewels, furs, makeup, the love and protection of men. So he was impotent. He couldn't fancy women at all, although he did not particularly welcome homosexual addresses. He did not think of himself as a pervert, or even as a transvestite, but as a woman cruelly transmogrified into manhood. He tried to die, became a female impersonator, but eventually found a doctor in Casablanca who came up with a more acceptable alternative. He was to be castrated, and his penis used as the lining of a surgically constructed cleft, which would be a vagina. He would be infertile, but that has never affected the attribution of femininity. April returned to England, resplendent. Massive hormone treatments had eradicated his beard, and formed tiny breasts: he had grown his hair and bought feminine clothes during the time he had worked as an impersonator. He became a model, and began to illustrate the feminine stereotype as he was perfectly qualified to do, for he was elegant, voluptuous, beautifully groomed, and in love with his own image. On an ill-fated day he married the heir to a peerage, the Hon. Arthur Corbett, acting out the highest achievement of the feminine dream, and went to live with him in a villa in Marbella. The marriage was never consummated. April's incompetence as a woman is what we must expect from a castrate, but it is not so very different after all from the impotence of feminine women, who submit to sex without desire, with only the infantile pleasure of cuddling and affection, which is their favorite reward. As long as the feminine stereotype remains the definition of the female sex, April Ashley is a woman, regardless of the legal decision ensuing from her divorce.[1] She is as much a casualty of the polarity of the sexes as we all are. Disgraced, unsexed April Ashley is our sister and our symbol.

Rape, But That Has Changed
SUSAN BROWNMILLER

The difference between human beings and cows, someone once told me, is that cows may have a genealogy but only human beings have a history. When I first became concerned with rape as a human phenomenon, the idea seized my mind that rape must have a history, too.

---

[1] *Corbett* v. *Corbett* (otherwise Ashley) before Mr. Justice Ormerod (Law Report, February 2, 1970, Probate, Divorce and Admiralty Division). *News of the World*, February 8, 1970; *Sunday Mirror*, February 3, 8, 15, 1970.

Written history records ideas and material changes that are the product of human effort. If rape was something other than a blind act of instinct, if it was, as I came to believe, a deliberate conscious crime of man against woman, then a documented record of its evolution could be pieced together.

For surely a crime that begins in the mind, not in the nether regions of "lust," would have undergone changes in perception, and might undergo further changes, in the story of civilization.

Biblical references to rape provided the first clues. Rape sneaked its way into man's law as a criminal act under very special and restricted circumstances: when the victim had been a betrothed virgin.

The nature of the unpardonable crime was not that it was an act of violence against a young girl's body, but that it was a crime against her father's honor and estate. The heinous act that could not be forgiven was the theft of a father's daughter's virginity, the ruination of her pristine state and, thus, her fair price on the marriage market.

Cases in which a married woman had been forcibly ravished were not considered rape; this was adultery and both participants were deemed equally guilty in the eyes of the Hebrew patriarchs.

Deuteronomy's covenants were echoed in medieval English law. The rape of a high-born, propertied virgin brought penalties like death or blinding and castration, but the law historian Bracton[1] allowed that the rapist could be redeemed in a singular manner: the victim might marry her violator to save him from his awful fate. Such a marriage naturally brought with it a transfer of lands and property from her name to his. Heiress-stealing (forcible abduction and rape) had quite a vogue in the Middle Ages.

Not until the 13th-century Statutes of Westminster did English law formally extend its concept of criminal rape to include the forcible violation of wives, widows, nuns, and even prostitutes.

Under the rule of Edward I, the Crown acknowledged—by taking charge of prosecutions—that the public safety of all women, not merely the protection of landed virgins, had become a matter of state concern. In theory, at least, rape had won its proper place in legal thinking.

The violation could now be seen from the vantage point of its original intent—as an act of physical violence against a female body, and not dependent on such "property" concepts as virginity, chastity and marriage. I did say "in theory."

The history of rape in war has even sorrier origins, for the violating of women after a battle was traditionally justified as the first fruit of victory. "To the victor belongs the spoils." It was perfectly lawful in ancient times to take and use captured women as slave-concubines. Indeed, the relevant passages in Deuteronomy were often cited by upholders of slavery in 18th-

---

[1] Howard de Bracton (d. 1268) was the author of *The Law and Customs of England*, the first complete British treatise of its kind.—Eds.

century America as moral justification for their own systematic sexual abuse of black women.

As late as the 17th century, according to the Dutch jurist Grotius,[2] some nations still permitted their armies to rape freely on enemy territory. But the more civilized nations, he went on, now had rape prohibitions in their military codes.

I'm afraid, however, that the stern injunctions always read better on paper than they worked out in practice. Rape in war has continued unchecked: for instance in Bangladesh, Cyprus and Vietnam. And the legal machinery designed to bring a military rapist to justice functions poorly when the victim is an "enemy" woman who—if she survives the assault—does not speak the language of her aggressor-assailant.

Rape in war is an important part of the anguished, hidden history of women, yet most historians tend to discount or slough off the special fate of female noncombatants when they make their solemn assessments of the times that try men's souls. Rape usually crops up in history books when the author is trying for a little color, a paragraph of bright writing. But documentation of mass rape in warfare has survived despite the historians' lack of interest.

Sworn depositions, eyewitness accounts, medical affidavits and the like have been preserved from conflicts as dimly remembered as the Wars of Religion in France (a Catholic priest sorrowfully described to his diary the gang rape by Catholic soldiers of a Huguenot woman) and the Battle of Culloden[3] (the lairds of Scotland meticulously kept their painful records).

Housed in the National Archives in Washington are six notarized affidavits from women of Hunterdon County, New Jersey, who were raped by British soldiers "sometime in December last past," 1776. The youngest was thirteen years old. Another was "five months and Upwards Advanced in her Pregnancy."

World War II offers an impartial bonanza of rape documentation from Allied and Axis sides. To match depositions from Russian women who were raped by the German Army on the road to Stalingrad there are depositions similar in content, similar in tone, from German women who were raped by the Russian Army on the road to Berlin. Has the Rape of Nanking slipped into metaphor? Read the typed transcripts of the International Military Tribunal for the Far East, held at Tokyo, for an idea of its actual dimensions.

Unpleasant to face, agonizing to come to terms with on an emotional level, the historical record must not be ignored. Accepting the history of rape is the first step toward denying rape a future.

---

[2] Hugo Grotius (1583–1645), author of *De Jure Belli et Pacis* (1625), is regarded as the father of international law.—EDS.

[3] The battle on Culloden Moor (1746) in which the Duke of Cumberland defeated the Young Pretender, Charles Edward Stuart ("Bonnie Prince Charlie").—EDS.

Two-Career Couples

ALAN L. OTTEN

Both husband and wife planned careers in investment banking in New York, but banking firms didn't like the idea of hiring a person whose spouse might be working for a competitor. So she's agreed to look for another type of financial job.

A young professor wanted to stay at Harvard, but his wife couldn't get a teaching post there. So he's switched to a less prestigious university, but one where they both are guaranteed tenure.

Another woman, a Russian expert, ought to live in the Soviet Union a couple of years to further her career. Her husband is a statistical consultant whose contracts and career would be unsettled by going there with her. They haven't yet solved their dilemma.

As these examples suggest, conflicts and potential conflicts between career-seeking marriage partners are becoming common and complex. Expert testimony to this effect—and some helpful hints for easing the conflicts—come from Patricia Light, chief psychologist in the office of career development at the Harvard Business School.

When Mrs. Light took on the job several years ago, she expected to deal chiefly with traditional student difficulties: personality problems, identity crisis, overwork, depression. To her surprise, she found that one of the most common calls for help came from young couples anxious over how they were going to manage to handle separate careers.

"There's absolutely no question that the two-career couple is a direction in which we will continue to go, and probably at an accelerating pace," declares Mrs. Light, herself half of a two-career marriage; her husband teaches at the Harvard School of Education, and they have two small children. Higher education levels, the feminist movement, efforts to limit population growth, and other factors all push the trend to two-career or dual-career marriages, Mrs. Light believes.

And, she warns, business firms are sooner or later going to have to change many personnel policies if they want to compete to hire these bright young men and women.

In most families where both husband and wife work, they labor at more or less routine jobs and chiefly to enlarge family income. In two-career marriages, however, money is rarely the major motivation; each partner, usually well educated, aims to advance steadily in the chosen business or profession, seeking psychological as well as financial satisfaction.

MANY FACETS INVOLVED

The dual-career problem has many facets, of course. One is the issue, still faced chiefly by women, of role conflicts. Despite women's liberation, Mrs.

Light finds, society generally still expects a married career woman to continue to fulfill also the traditional roles of companion, housekeeper, mother, hostess.

"Things are beginning to change," Mrs. Light says, "but very slowly. The burden of proof still falls on the wife if the soufflé for the dinner party falls or if the kids don't have clean clothes for school. Men are for the most part still shielded culturally from this sort of role strain. Typically, unless family needs reach crisis proportions, people just naturally expect the man to put the demands of work first."

Conflict arises in many other ways, too. How much competition will the partners feel with each other? If career opportunities clash, which career gives way? What is each partner prepared to do for the other's career?

Having children intensifies all the strains, of course, yet almost all the young couples Mrs. Light has counselled individually and in special group discussions had definitely decided to have children eventually. Most career wives, though, now plan to have the children later, after their own careers have been firmly launched. Then when they have the children, they figure, they can resume part-time or full-time work more easily.

Even then, though, trials abound: corporate discrimination against women who drop out to have babies, parental guilt feelings that the children will be neglected, arguments over which parent comes home to take the sick child to the doctor.

With problems so perplexing, just what help can Mrs. Light offer? The most important thing, she tells her couples, is to try to think and talk about questions in advance. The woman, for example, should try to figure out whether she really will be able to juggle all the different roles, and find out just what her husband will do to help.

"Talking things over and trying to anticipate trouble spots isn't going to solve all the problems," Mrs. Light declares. "But then at least, they don't come up and hit you in the face with quite the same force." And, she adds, "there are few if any institutional devices that will help two-career couples make it work. Above all, they have to be very creative and flexible."

If one is offered a good opportunity in a city 200 miles from where the other is happily at work, perhaps they can live in between and commute daily in opposite directions. Quite a few couples, she finds, are willing to consider living apart in different cities during the week and just spending weekends together; "they argue that's not so different from the situation where one partner is always traveling and away from home anyhow."

One partner may have to change his or her career goal. A wife who's an expert on international finance ought to be working in Europe or New York, but her engineer husband wants a career with a manufacturing firm in a small Midwestern city. So she's now looking for a teaching job in universities near that city.

More couples, too, Mrs. Light says, "seem to have the idea that they can alternate cycles of opportunity—one partner's career being the prime concern for a few years, and then the other career getting priority." And when a corporation asks a young executive to transfer to another city, the wife's situation is increasingly a factor in his decision. "It's no longer certain," Mrs. Light says, "that a young man with a career wife will automatically accept a transfer to a place that gives the wife a mediocre career opportunity."

Another of Mrs. Light's precepts is the need to be realistic in estimating how much can really be accomplished. She cites "Dottie's fantasy"—the case of a talented, hard-driving young woman clearly headed for the top of a major corporation. Yet Dottie also sees herself sitting on the sofa each night reading bedtime stories to two freshly-scrubbed kids.

"For her, time is elastic," Mrs. Light observes. "She thinks she can have everything, as long as she's willing to work harder and run faster." But that's extremely naive, Mrs. Light believes. To get to the top will require long days and lots of travel—and Dottie's simply not going to have much time for children.

"Two-career couples," Mrs. Light asserts, "must set priorities, make choices, accept tradeoffs."

CAREFUL PLANNING NEEDED

Even more than for most people, time and energy are critically scarce resources for two-career couples, and their use must be carefully planned, Mrs. Light advises. "Spontaneity may be great," she says, "but two-career couples will find that planning ahead helps make things work—that allocating your time and energy carefully keeps you from chasing your tail." This means not only planning flexible work patterns but also planning relaxed time together and even time alone for each partner.

A career couple must be willing, too, to spend their money to save time and energy: to buy labor-saving appliances, to hire people to do household jobs, to employ a reliable and sympathetic person to take care of the children during working hours and to hire baby-sitters frequently to give themselves ample diversion.

They must work out what each partner has to do for the children. Mrs. Light's husband, for example, is on full-time child-caring duty two weekday afternoons, and she's on duty the other three; they usually can trade if an office crisis develops for him or her. Two-career couples with children must also develop a strong relationship with the children's caretaker, Mrs. Light says, so that the caretaker has a clear idea of how the parents want disciplinary and other child-rearing troubles handled.

And they must show creativity in working out relationships with their employers. One acquaintance starts work an hour later than her co-workers, having taken the children to school first. Her husband leaves work for 40 minutes each day at 3:15, to pick up the kids and take them to a baby-sitter. Both husband and wife make up the lost time at the end of the day.

"This isn't the sort of demand you make when you go in for your first personnel interview," Mrs. Light admonishes. "You have to build your relationship with your employers first, so they become confident that you're going to get all your work done, even though you need special arrangements to do it."

Just as two-career couples are going to have to learn to compromise and adjust, so will many companies, Mrs. Light believes.

They'll have to permit some employees to work unusual hours, refrain from penalizing an employe who turns down a transfer, guarantee that women who drop out to have babies can return to their old career levels, and perhaps provide new routes to top management that are easier for a man or woman in a dual-career marriage to follow.

"We're not going to see major change in business attitudes overnight," Mrs. Light concedes. "Many companies will insist that all this simply isn't their problem.

"But more companies are going to recognize that a very different group of young people is coming out of the colleges and universities today, and that corporate policies must accommodate to some extent. Otherwise, they're going to lose out on getting the services of some extremely talented young people."

Why I Never Married

ORIANA FALLACI

For sure, in a past that now seems to me as remote as prehistory, I too thought I would get married. I speak of my fifteenth, my eighteenth years of age. However, it's strange: the more my memory searches that time, the less I find the word "marriage." Even then it gave me a mysterious annoyance, like the words wife, husband, fiancée, betrothed. What I wanted as a girl, I suppose, was a man to love and by whom to be loved forever: as in the fairy tales. Yet I felt a threat in the fairy tale, a mortal risk: what if such a man kidnapped me for life? I have never been a domestic animal. I have never seen myself locked up in the small cosmos of the family. The profession of wife has always filled me with horror. I did not want to play the wife. I wanted to write, to travel, to know the world, to use the miracle of having been born. And, as if this weren't enough, I couldn't stand the idea of giving up my name to take the name of a man. To give it up, why? To annul myself like that, why? I was mine. Though confusedly, unawarely, I think I was at that time a feminist *ante litteram*.[1] In fact, knowing I was a woman in a society invented and

---

[1] Before the word (Latin). But the word *feminist* was commonly used in English, if not precisely in its modern sense, by the 1890s.—EDS.

determined by men never gave me an inferiority complex, never put any limitations on my plans and on my dreams. On the contrary, it provoked and lit them. It was a kind of challenge.

My early youth consumed itself in that challenge. Obsessed by the fear of being ensnared and neutralized by a muzzle, for years I went like a dog without a master. As free and as snarling. I rejected whoever fell in love with me; I prohibited myself from falling in love. And I suffered and made others suffer for this, but I never dropped the anchor. I didn't drop it even when I gave myself to my first love. In any case my first love was not joyful. It was exclusively useful in making me understand that to love means to deliver ourselves up, handcuffed, and that the same verb *to love* is a cheat. This hardened me and I didn't permit anyone, any more, to be my jailer. Planes, trains, were the most faithful accomplices of my flights. Running away didn't cost me too much, often it cost me nothing.

Though celebrated, at times, and respected, the men I knew weren't very worthy, and the day always came when I proved to have more balls than they. In a juvenile novel, *Penelope at War*,[2] I tried to tell this; in the story, the hero cried after having deflowered the heroine, and she consoled him by offering him a handkerchief to blow his nose. Maybe my kind of woman is strangled by the drama of having become, thanks to her own tears, stronger than men.

I am not a man hater, on the contrary. And this is another drama of my kind of woman. If a man lives with someone who can usurp his reputation, I know it isn't his fault if, because of this, he commits abuses and meannesses. In fact, when I love a man, I become as tender as a lamb. As a lamb I sacrifice myself. My reasoning, my maternal instinct, always drive me to absolve him. However, without any illusion. Without letting him convince me that I should drop the anchor. Nobody, I mean nobody, under no circumstances and in no continent, has ever been able to convince me that I am wrong to consider marriage as a prison where the first prisoner is the woman. Isn't the first condition of a marriage cohabitation? Well, there's nothing like cohabitation to make you lose respect for a man. The best man.

In cohabiting with a man, half of your time is lost in consoling him, encouraging him, serving him, protecting him as a capricious and spoiled child. If you are younger than he is, or even if you are of the same age and have the same training, he doesn't ask you to be his companion. He asks you to be his nurse, his secretary, his servant, that is, the mother he gave up while becoming a man. He never forgets his mother, loved or hated as she was by him. He never forgets having been a baby to whom all was permitted and served. And even if you work twice as hard as he does, even if you have responsibilities far larger than his, he expects you to prepare his coffee, his food, to give his underwear to the laundry or to wash

---

[2] The novel appeared in 1962.—Eds.

it, to take care of the house, of the friends, of the infinitesimal problems of life, to stand his bad humor without his standing yours.

If the man is very rich and his mother has been replaced by an official housekeeper or a maid, he asks you to be his toy. And with this toy he plays, immaturely, cruelly. Poor mothers of ours. How many torments they suffered for centuries and thousands of years, since the day they were told that woman was born to get married. My deepest regret at not having had a child is to have missed the occasion to teach him or her a few truths.

Marriage is against nature because sentiments get worn down, like shoes that continuously must be mended, patched up, fixed up. Marriage is against nature because the person to love and to be loved by forever doesn't exist, unless you lie or you bend for convenience and hypocrisy and fear of loneliness. Only companions of travel exist, and the tenuous hope of concluding the travel with the companion chosen and tolerated by your maturity. Your wisdom can only come with your first wrinkles. But even then one must not forget that each of the two belongs to himself or herself only, and can find that self only during pauses of solitude.

When I wave good-bye to the companion chosen and tolerated by my maturity, as I leave or he leaves, my throat is closed by the sorrow of separation. At the same time, however, I feel an exquisite and irresistible and triumphal relief. And I go wagging my tail, as happy and as free as a dog without a master.

Life Without Father
ELLEN GOODMAN

A few seconds after the clock struck 1977, Rosie's baby won the Diaper Derby in Salt Lake City. To her, the firstborn of the year, went the spoils of the Utah merchants: the Pampers and powder, the shampoo and snuggies, and, perhaps, a six-month supply of pacifiers.

Now, none of this would be particularly newsworthy except for the fact that Rosie is what we used to refer to, in hushed tones, as an unwed mother. But in 1977, she didn't lose the diapers, the strained peaches or her self-respect when the news got out.

When asked about her marital status she said simply, "It's a new generation." When asked about her motherhood status she said, "It's the best thing that could happen."

Rosie's tale is indicative of a change in attitude and in reality.

For openers, the odds were better than 1 in 10 that the winner of the Diaper Derby would be the child of an unwed mother. Fourteen out of every hundred babies born in 1975 were, and that is double the rate of 25 years ago. In Washington, D.C., last year more than half the live births were out of wedlock. Nationally, the figures add up to 350,000 babies, 80 percent of them to mothers under 25. And the biggest boost to the statistic has come from an 11 percent rise among single white women.

The fact is that today the women who carry their pregnancies to term, by and large, keep their babies; and it has become increasingly difficult for the rest of us to build a rational case for the long-term difference between becoming a mother in or out of wedlock.

For one thing, wed isn't nearly as locked as it used to be. Many of the single pregnant women cannot understand the pressure to marry in the face of divorce.

Last year the number of divorces topped the million mark. Nationally, 16 percent of all children under 18 are living with only one parent, whether or not there were two present at the time of delivery. Of course, some divorced fathers are a strong presence in their children's lives, but it appears that the majority lose meaningful regular contact.

So it becomes harder to answer the question: What difference does being married make?

Even in cases where divorce is averted the truth is that fathering may be equally absent. The men that Carly Simon sings about, "Fair Weather Fathers" are obvious in so many families. One recent study of middle-class men showed that, on the average, a father spent 20 minutes a day with his one-year-old baby, and only 38 seconds actually interacting with the child.

It is these unhappy realities that have made fathers all too emotionally irrelevant to the life of the Rosies and their babies.

The major, irrefutable difference between single-mother homes and two-parent homes is still in their economic situation. The families of single mothers are far more likely to fall into poverty and remain there, held down by a lack of child care, the economic discrimination against women, and the need of the average family for two incomes. But on the two edges of the economic spectrum—when fathers are unable to adequately support their families or when mothers are able to do so—there is even less measureable difference between family life with or without father.

What we are left with is a deeply rooted belief that, on the whole, it is better for children to be raised by their two caring parents in a stable environment. And, on the other hand, we are left with a sense of how difficult it is to assure those conditions. The vast majority of mothers seem to be in some way, or at some time, effectively the only parent. Similarly, most of the children in the country are somewhat "fatherless."

Of course, there is a core of men who have always connected with their children in a deep and rich way. There is a new core of men determined to share far more than 38 seconds of their time. But a pervasive illness allows so many others to deal with their children as if they were merely warts on the surface of their lives. And to excise them at will.

These are the children of the invisible fathers, the men we call "transparents." No, it isn't just a problem for Rosie's baby.

Planetarium[1]

ADRIENNE RICH

Thinking of Caroline Herschel (1750–1848), astronomer, sister of William;[2] and others.

A woman in the shape of a monster
a monster in the shape of a woman
the skies are full of them

a woman   "in the snow
among the Clocks and instruments
or measuring the ground with poles"
in her 98 years to discover
8 comets

she whom the moon ruled
like us
levitating into the night sky
riding the polished lenses

Galaxies of women, there
doing penance for impetuousness
ribs chilled
in those spaces   of the mind

An eye,

     "virile, precise and absolutely certain"
     from the mad webs of Uranusborg[3]

                  encountering the NOVA[4]

every impulse of light exploding
from the core
as life flies out of us

---

[1] All footnotes are by Barbara C. Gelpi and Albert Gelpi.—EDS.

[2] In helping her brother William (1738–1822), the discoverer of Uranus, Carolyn Herschel became a superb astronomer in her own right.

[3] Uranienborg, "castle in the sky," was the name of the observatory built in 1576 by Tycho Brache (1546–1601), the Danish astronomer.

[4] Brache, on November 11, 1573, discovered the famous "New Star" in the constellation Cassiopeia.

      Tycho whispering at last
      "Let me not seem to have lived in vain"[5]

What we see, we see
and seeing is changing

the light that shrivels a mountain
and leaves a man alive

Heartbeat of the pulsar[6]
heart sweating through my body

The radio impulse
pouring in from Taurus[7]

     I am bombarded yet   I stand

I have been standing all my life in the
direct path of a battery of signals
the most accurately transmitted most
untranslatable language in the universe
I am a galactic[8]   cloud so deep   so involuted that a light wave could take 15
years to travel through me   And has
taken   I am an instrument in the shape
of a woman trying to translate pulsations
into images   for the relief of the body
and the reconstruction of the mind.

---

[5] Tycho Brache's last words.
[6] Any of several very short-period variable galactic radio sources.
[7] A constellation in the Northern Hemisphere near Orion and Aries.
[8] Of, pertaining to, occurring in, or originating in the Milky Way.

3
The Arts

Film and Television

Music, Painting, and Architecture

Literature

Art and Life

This section is designed to give an overview of the arts. The first group of readings concerns film and television, which are emerging as major art forms. Indeed, the first conscious experience of art for most people today may well be either film, now well enough established to have at least one course in most colleges, or the everywhere available television. Next we turn to music, painting, and architecture; then to literature; and finally to some larger considerations that we have entitled "Art and Life."

A definition of art is probably different for everyone. Yet certain major critical approaches have been generally agreed upon. The critic M. H. Abrams once proposed a pattern for literature that has been widely accepted. Some people view literature, Abrams says, as primarily *representing* the universe or things in it; others as *expressing* the author's feeling; others as *affecting* the reader; and still others as knowing the literary work as an *organic entity*.[1] His diagram helps to clarify the relationship:

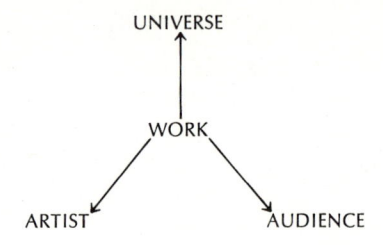

```
              UNIVERSE
                 ↑
                 |
               WORK
              ╱     ╲
             ╱       ╲
          ARTIST    AUDIENCE
```

These interests, given here in a simplified form, do not necessarily exclude one another. And though Abrams applied these four approaches to literature, they can properly be extended to the other arts.

Thus X. J. Kennedy, in his review of the 1933 movie *King Kong*, seems to be most interested in how the movie affected its audience (as we watch King Kong die, we "kill the ape within our bones") and how the character of the great ape retains its hold on them. But in Kennedy's review of the recent remake of the film, his interest shifts

---

[1] See *The Mirror and the Lamp* (1953), pp. 3–29. Our terms are not always those of Abrams.

to the producers' efforts to update the King Kong legend and to imbue it with a modern symbolism. On the other hand, James Agee looks at the film of *Henry V* as an entity in itself with intrinsic "beauty and power." And finally, Jeffrey Schrank discusses television as addiction, ritual, and art.

Landmarks in the group of readings on the traditional fine arts of music, painting, and architecture are provided by Leonard Bernstein and Aaron Copland, both of them composers and conductors, as they explore their special art with breadth and intensity. The conversation between Pablo Picasso and André Malraux, as good studio talk as one can imagine, goes in all sorts of directions—"People *always* begin by not understanding!" And Clement Greenberg puts forward "The Case for Abstract Art," pointing out that the bewilderment sometimes engendered by this genre is often "salutary," as "it expands our capacity for experience." Yet all the selections have the vitality of expression of artists and critics who are in earnest without being stuffy. "You're only a failure. I'm an assistant failure," John Rauch remarks to Robert Venturi on their school of "messy vitality" in architecture.

The largest space in this section is given to literature, for writing and literature go hand in hand. A fine course in technical writing at a major midwestern university was once staffed altogether by poets, because they were the ones who knew best how to "push words around." As a reminder that poets and critics have fun pushing those words around, we've opened the group of readings on literature with a hilarious piece by James Thurber. Yet wit is also present in the poems of Archibald MacLeish and Shakespeare, although it is wit in a more serious context. These poems serve to introduce critical essays that look at literature with the freshness of discovery that every reader ought to share, even though he or she may disagree with the critic's views. Harold Bloom's use of poetry may not be your use, nor his responses yours, but they ought to help define what your use and responses are now and what they may become. Northrop Frye helps us think about the nature of literature in "The Keys to Dreamland," dealing with such fundamentals as the relation of literature to experience and the imagination, the difference between literary and other writing, and the evaluation of literary works. Then we meet two remarkable woman writers in the selection by Ellen Moers. The critic also creates a writer's world.

The final group of selections consider "Art and Life." The opening essay by Susanne K. Langer discusses the underlying unity of the arts, which she finds in their expressiveness, and defines the "work of art" clearly and elegantly. The essay by Arthur Koestler is a witty reflection on originals versus copies and on genuine versus forged paintings; basically, the essay concerns itself with the effect of art on the viewer and takes sidelong glances at other approaches to the enjoyment of art as well. Kenneth Clark is concerned with the "great works of genius" that somehow have produced great moments of civilization. And John Keats's "Ode on a Grecian Urn" is a meditation on an art object that is sufficient in itself to provide meaning and to emphasize the permanence of art. The arts, artists, critics, and audience all contribute to the writer's world.

Film and Television

Who Killed King Kong?

X. J. KENNEDY

The ordeal and spectacular death of King Kong, the giant ape, undoubtedly have been witnessed by more Americans than have ever seen a performance of *Hamlet, Iphigenia at Aulis,* or even *Tobacco Road.* Since RKO-Radio Pictures first released *King Kong,* a quarter-century has gone by; yet year after year, from prints that grow more rain-beaten, from sound tracks that grow more tinny, ticket-buyers by thousands still pursue Kong's luckless fight against the forces of technology, tabloid journalism, and the DAR.[1] They see him chloroformed to sleep, see him whisked from his jungle isle to New York and placed on show, see him burst his chains to roam the city (lugging a frightened blonde), at last to plunge from the spire of the Empire State Building, machine-gunned by model airplanes.

Though Kong may die, one begins to think his legend unkillable. No clearer proof of his hold upon the popular imagination may be seen than what emerged one catastrophic week in March 1955, when New York WOR-TV programmed *Kong* for seven evenings in a row (a total of sixteen showings). Many a rival network vice-president must have scowled when surveys showed that *Kong*—the 1933 B-picture—had lured away fat segments of the viewing populace from such powerful competitors as Ed Sullivan, Groucho Marx and Bishop Sheen.

But even television has failed to run *King Kong* into oblivion. Coffee-in-the-lobby cinemas still show the old hunk of hokum, with the apology that in its use of composite shots and animated models the film remains technically interesting. And no other monster in movie history has won so devoted a popular audience. None of the plodding mummies, the stultified draculas, the white-coated Lugosis[2] with their shiny pinball-machine laboratories, none of the invisible stranglers, berserk robots, or menaces from Mars has ever enjoyed so many resurrections.

Why does the American public refuse to let King Kong rest in peace? It is true, I'll admit, that *Kong* outdid every monster movie before or since in sheer carnage. Producers Merian C. Cooper and Ernest B. Schoedsack crammed into it dinosaurs, headhunters, riots, aerial battles, bullets,

---

[1] Daughters of the American Revolution, a patriotic organization of women who are direct descendants of persons who helped in establishing American independence.—EDS.

[2] Bela Lugosi, an actor in many horror movies; most famous as star of the original film version of *Dracula.*—EDS.

211

bombs, bloodletting. Heroine Fay Wray, whose function is mainly to scream, shuts her mouth for hardly one uninterrupted minute from first reel to last. It is also true that *Kong* is larded with good healthy sadism, for those whose joy it is to see the frantic girl dangled from cliffs and harried by pterodactyls. But it seems to me that the abiding appeal of the giant ape rests on other foundations.

Kong has, first of all, the attraction of being manlike. His simian nature gives him one huge advantage over giant ants and walking vegetables in that an audience may conceivably identify with him. Kong's appeal has the quality that established the Tarzan series as American myth—for what man doesn't secretly image himself a huge hairy howler against whom no other monster has a chance? If Tarzan recalls the ape in us, then Kong may well appeal to that great-granddaddy primordial brute from whose tribe we have all deteriorated.

Intentionally or not, the producers of *King Kong* encourage this identification by etching the character of Kong with keen sympathy. For the ape is a figure in a tradition familiar to moviegoers: the tradition of the pitiable monster. We think of Lon Chaney in the role of Quasimodo,[3] of Boris Karloff in the original *Frankenstein*. As we watch the Frankenstein monster's fumbling and disastrous attempts to befriend a flower-picking child, our sympathies are enlisted with the monster in his impenetrable loneliness. And so with Kong. As he roars in his chains, while barkers sell tickets to boobs who gape at him, we perhaps feel something more deep than pathos. We begin to sense something of the problem that engaged Eugene O'Neill in *The Hairy Ape*: the dilemma of a displaced animal spirit forced to live in a jungle built by machines.

King Kong, it is true, had special relevance in 1933. Landscapes of the depression are glimpsed early in the film when an impresario, seeking some desperate pretty girl to play the lead in a jungle movie, visits souplines and a Woman's Home Mission. In Fay Wray—who's been caught snitching an apple from a fruitstand—his search is ended. When he gives her a big feed and a movie contract, the girl is magic-carpeted out of the world of the National Recovery Act. And when, in the film's climax, Kong smashes that very Third Avenue landscape in which Fay had wandered hungry, audiences of 1933 may well have felt a personal satisfaction.

What is curious is that audiences of 1960 remain hooked. For in the heart of urban man, one suspects, lurks the impulse to fling a bomb. Though machines speed him to the scene of his daily grind, though IBM comptometers ("freeing the human mind from drudgery") enable him to drudge more efficiently once he arrives, there comes a moment when he wishes to turn upon his machines and kick hell out of them. He wants to hurl his combination radio-alarmclock out the bedroom window and listen to its smash. What subway commuter wouldn't love—just for once—to

---

[3] *The Hunchback of Notre Dame* in the novel by Victor Hugo (1831).—EDS.

see the downtown express smack head-on into the uptown local? Such a wish is gratified in that memorable scene in *Kong* that opens with a wide-angle shot: interior of a railway car on the Third Avenue El. Straphangers are nodding, the literate refold their newspapers. Unknown to them, Kong has torn away a section of trestle toward which the train now speeds. The motorman spies Kong up ahead, jams on the brakes. Passengers hurtle together like so many peas in a pail. In a window of the car appear Kong's bloodshot eyes. Women shriek. Kong picks up the railway car as if it were a rat, flips it to the street and ties knots in it, or something. To any commuter the scene must appear one of the most satisfactory pieces of celluloid ever exposed.

Yet however violent his acts, Kong remains a gentleman. Remarkable is his sense of chivalry. Whenever a fresh boa constrictor threatens Fay, Kong first sees that the lady is safely parked, then manfully thrashes her attacker. (And she, the ingrate, runs away every time his back is turned.) Atop the Empire State Building, ignoring his pursuers, Kong places Fay on a ledge as tenderly as if she were a dozen eggs. He fondles her, then turns to face the Army Air Force. And Kong is perhaps the most disinterested lover since Cyrano: his attentions to the lady are utterly without hope of reward. After all, between a five-foot blonde and a fifty-foot ape, love can hardly be more than an intellectual flirtation. In his simian way King Kong is the hopelessly yearning lover of Petrarchan[4] convention. His forced exit from his jungle, in chains, results directly from his single-minded pursuit of Fay. He smashes a Broadway theater when the notion enters his dull brain that the flashbulbs of photographers somehow endanger the lady. His perilous shinnying up a skyscraper to pluck Fay from her boudoir is an act of the kindliest of hearts. He's impossible to discourage even though the love of his life can't lay eyes on him without shrieking murder.

The tragedy of King Kong then, is to be the beast who at the end of the fable fails to turn into the handsome prince. This is the conviction that the scriptwriters would leave with us in the film's closing line. As Kong's corpse lies blocking traffic in the street, the entrepreneur who brought Kong to New York turns to the assembled reporters and proclaims: "That's your story, boys—it was Beauty killed the Beast!" But greater forces than those of the screaming Lady have combined to lay Kong low, if you ask me. Kong lives for a time as one of those persecuted near-animal souls bewildered in the middle of an industrial order, whose simple desires are thwarted at every turn. He climbs the Empire State Building because in all New York it's the closest thing he can find to the clifftop of his jungle isle. He dies, a pitiful dolt, and the army brass and publicity-men cackle over him. His death is the only possible outcome to as neat a tragic dilemma as you can ask for. The machine-guns do him in, while the

---

[4] Petrarch (Francesco Petrarcha, 1304–1374), Italian poet.—EDS.

manicured human hero (a nice clean Dartmouth boy) carries away Kong's sweetheart to the altar. O, the misery of it all. There's far more truth about upper-middle-class American life in *King Kong* than in the last seven dozen novels of John P. Marquand.

A Negro friend from Atlanta tells me that in movie houses in colored neighborhoods throughout the South, *Kong* does a constant business. They show the thing in Atlanta at least every year, presumably to the same audiences. Perhaps this popularity may simply be due to the fact that Kong is one of the most watchable movies ever constructed, but I wonder whether Negro audiences may not find some archetypical appeal in this serio-comic tale of a huge black powerful free spirit whom all the hard-working white policemen are out to kill.

Every day in the week on a screen somewhere in the world, King Kong relives his agony. Again and again he expires on the Empire State Building, as audiences of the devout assist his sacrifice. We watch him die, and by extension kill the ape within our bones, but these little deaths of ours occur in prosaic surroundings. We do not die on a tower, New York before our feet, nor do we give our lives to smash a few flying machines. It is not for us to bring to a momentary standstill the civilization in which we move. King Kong does this for us. And so we kill him again and again, in much-spliced celluloid, while the ape in us expires from day to day, obscure, in desperation.

The New *King Kong,* or A Great Ape Double-Crossed
X. J. KENNEDY

In the bicentennial summer the annunciation came, even before the final scenes were shot and edited. Whole-page newspaper ads heralded Dino De Laurentiis's new production of *King Kong*, to be revealed on 1,500 theater screens just prior to Christmas. Like many another devotee of the 1933 original, I took joy in this fresh proof of the old ape's longevity. Not that the rude beast of Merian C. Cooper and Ernest B. Schoedsack seemed about to be reborn; still, I wanted to see what De Laurentiis could do with the classic legend, seventeen or so million dollars, and some up-to-date technology.

The new *King Kong*, as it turned out, isn't a bad film. Ape-engineer Carlo Rambaldi has managed his new beast expertly, while director John Guillermin has put his human actors through their paces smoothly. Visually, scene after scene is striking and overpowering. Besides, you can't retell a legend, nor echo an archetype, without having powerful forces working in your favor. And yet the new *Kong* seems strangely hollow. Watching it, one beholds some huge machine being grimly manipulated

—some apparatus as cumbersome as the great ape's electronic hand that for all the efforts of its crew kept balking and trying to give Jessica Lange (the new Fay Wray) a squeeze too many.

What set the old *King Kong* apart from other horror movies was its sheer inventive energy—an element hard to reproduce synthetically. Cooper and Schoedsack, I suspect, never did know quite what they were doing, and they ended with a creation greater than they dreamed. ("Escapist entertainment pure and simple," Cooper late in his life called the film, scorning critics who have found implications in it.[1]) Imperfectly comprehending the nature of their feat, the producer-directors were unable to repeat it—as shown by the messes they made of their two later attempts, *Son of Kong* (1933) and *Mighty Joe Young* (1949). Both follow-ups portray good little monkeys, not more than a dozen feet high, who don't covet women, don't protest against city life, don't scare people but come to their rescue, and consequently don't spellbind us as did the original.

Unlike the old unselfconscious *King Kong*, the remake is pretty sophisticated. Clearly the De Laurentiis team studied the original carefully and meditated on it day and night. Even the actor Jeff Bridges, playing a hippie anthropologist, during the filming saw Kong as "a Christ-like symbol of the pure"— or so he is quoted in a paperback history of the production written by Bruce Bahrenburg, the company's "unit publicist."[2] Of course, the remakers could hardly avoid such theorizing in an era when celluloid lapel buttons have proclaimed KING KONG DIED FOR OUR SINS. And to be so painfully aware of all that significance must have made it harder to improve on the original. To work in broad daylight, knowing exactly what you're doing and exactly what it all means, is for any artist the deadliest and most inhibiting of situations. Unluckily, the neoclassical *King Kong* had to be put together deliberately, with the aid of all available slide rules, calculators, and histories of the movies, for nobody spends seventeen or so million dollars without some thought. The flaws of the remake are the kind of flaws that come from thinking excessively.

Take the decision to move the crucifixion of Kong from the Empire State Building to the World Trade Center. Reasoning logically, the remakers must have decided that the twin towers of the Board of Trade, being newer and taller, would not only provide a bigger and better cross but would outnumber the old cross two to one. In making the move, however, they impoverished their film's most basic symbolism. Pointed and hard, uselessly tall, mostly unrentable when opened in the Depression year of 1931, the Empire State Building stands like some hideous monument on the grave of Coolidge prosperity. And its phallic profile, so dear to

---

[1] Quoted by Rudy Behlmer, who talked with Cooper in 1965, in his introduction to *The Girl in the Hairy Paw: King Kong as Myth, Movie, and Monster* (New York: Avon, 1976).

[2] *The Creation of Dino De Laurentiis' King Kong* (New York: Pocket Books, 1976), p. 252.

thoughtful students of the original *King Kong*, remains endlessly meaningful. In a crazy way, the Empire State Building hints at the futility of Kong's love for a woman. When in the end he drops from its tip, he seems the victim both of a social order and of his own quixotic sexual aspirations—cruelly raped himself, and slain in mid-erection. What do we see in the towers of the Board of Trade? A couple of double-blank dominoes.

Like the old version, only with conscious purpose, the new film explores an ailing society. Witness its updating of the entrepreneur who brings Kong to the city, one Fred Wilson, a canny villain who turns the great beast into a commercial for an oil company. (In the old film, you'll recall, the harmless Carl Denham wasn't a villain but a cheerful, well-meaning idiot.) In the person of Wilson the new film embodies its attack on corporate irresponsibility. And its heroine, the lithe and leggy Dwan (who changed her name from Dawn) is a benighted child of a media-dominated age. Fished from the sea, the lone survivor of a Hollywood producer's exploded yacht, she had tried to sleep her way to stardom. As inexorably as a tale by the Marquis de Sade, the rest of the film unfolds her punishment. Although she briefly sours on Hollywood and toys with the notion of marrying the noble hippie Jack Prescott (Bridges), Jack wisely decides he couldn't keep such an expensive woman as a faculty wife. In the end, Dwan's choice of stardom sealed, we last glimpse her drowning beneath a wave of reporters and photographers. Any patron of the film who takes its moral seriously might well feel a pang of guilt from merely sitting in a movie house. But readers of Bahrenburg's book will recall those ads in the New York *Daily News* by which the De Laurentiis company shrewdly recruited some 33,000 unpaid extras; and those invitations to the press and to television soliciting their coverage of the shooting sessions at the World Trade Center; and that long and calculated publicity buildup of the then-unknown Jessica Lange. Then it becomes difficult to trust the film's huffy indignation at corporations and crowds, at media manipulation and star-making. As well go to a Pharisee for a sermon against self-righteousness.

Divided against itself, too, is the character of Dwan: is she helpless innocent or seductress? Your feelings toward her are mixed, unlike your feelings toward Fay Wray's Ann Darrow, that simple cipher. By joining in the capture of Kong, Miss Darrow pursued not stardom but a square meal. Throughout the old film, her reaction to Kong was simply human: to scream for dear life. More sensitive and thoughty, Dwan practically takes the great ape under her well-depilated wing. Atop the towers of the Board of Trade, she implores Kong to hold on to her so that the militiamen won't shoot him down. The remakers have informed Dwan and the other nitwit characters with superfluous personalities and psychologies. But *King Kong* is a true fable, and as fabulists from Aesop to James Thurber have known, characters in fables might just as well be stick figures for all we care. To catch the message of "The Tortoise and the Hare" we don't need to fathom the hare's remorse.

With its jerkily animated dolls and painted backdrops, the 1933 *King Kong* wasn't realistic in the least. In 1976, forty-three years of cinematic progress have enabled the new *Kong* to appear as real as a filmed travelogue or documentary. The size of the new Kong never varies, and his fur displays no handling marks. Mostly represented by a well-trained man in a gorilla suit, he shambles as gorillas are supposed to do. In color, on its wider screen, the new version painstakingly depicts the South Sea jungles that gave Kong birth—long, hazy shots of the beaches of a secret island (actually Hawaii). But the old black-and-white Kong hailed from a never-never land: an island that sported a handmade jungle and miscellaneous dinosaurs and pterodactyls. The remakers give us a literal jungle and leave the dinosaurs out. And somehow, in the showdown between new version and old, it's the deadpan photographic realism of the new that petrifies it and the reckless fantasy of the old that makes it spring alive.

Perhaps there's still another cause for the remake's mildly disappointing performance at the box office. In 1933 the name of Kong was pure nonsense—well, perhaps hinting *Congo*—but in 1976, after years of headlines and telecasts, the name Kong is a terrible pun. The Cong from the jungles of the South Pacific who took on the United States and its military power now seems all too familiar. In an unexpected way, that shadowy monster who skulks through De Laurentiis's graphic jungles disturbingly calls to mind a presence that many Americans would rather forget.

At this writing, the new *King Kong* has yet to be shown on television, but that night will come, as certain as the solstice. Then, I suppose, forty or fifty million screens will glow with its demolition of both Beauty and the Beast; and without a doubt commercials for Dial and Prell and Rave will punctuate its indictment of an acquisitive and media-manipulated society.

Henry V
JAMES AGEE

It seems impertinent to discuss even briefly the excellence of Laurence Olivier's production of Shakespeare's *Henry V* without saying a few words, at least, about the author. If Shakespeare had been no more gifted with words than, say, I am, the depth and liveliness of his interest in people and predicaments, and his incredible hardness, practicality, and resource as a craftsman and maker of moods, rhythms, and points, could still have made him almost his actual equal as a playwright. I had never realized this so well until I saw this production, in which every nail in sight is so cleanly driven in with one blow; and I could watch the film for all that Shakespeare gave it in these terms alone, and for all that in these terms alone is done with what he gave, with great pleasure and gratitude.

But then too, of course, there is the language of a brilliance, vigor, and absoluteness that make the craftsmanship and sometimes the people and their grandest emotions seem almost as negligibly pragmatic as a libretto beside an opera score. Some people, using I wonder what kind of dry ice for comfort, like to insist that *Henry V* is relatively uninteresting Shakespeare. This uninteresting poetry is such that after hearing it, in this production, I find it as hard to judge fairly even the best writing since Shakespeare as it is to see the objects in a room after looking into the sun.

The one great glory of the film is this language. The greatest credit I can assign to those who made the film is that they have loved and served the language so well. I don't feel that much of the delivery is inspired; it is merely so good, so right, that the words set loose in the graciously designed world of the screen, like so many uncaged birds, fully enjoy and take care of themselves. Neither of the grimmest Shakespearian vices, ancient or modern, is indulged: that is to say, none of the text is read in that human, down-to-earth, poetry-is-only-hopped-up-prose manner which is doubtless only proper when a character subscriber to *PM* reads the Lerner editorial to his shop-wise fellow traveler; nor is any of it intoned in the nobler manner, as if by a spoiled deacon celebrating the Black Mass down a section of sewer-pipe. Most of it is merely spoken by people who know and love poetry as poetry and have spent a lifetime learning how to speak it accordingly. Their voices, faces, and bodies are all in charge of a man who has selected them as shrewdly as a good orchestrator selects and blends his instruments; and he combines and directs them as a good conductor conducts an orchestral piece. It is, in fact, no surprise to learn that Mr. Olivier is fond of music; charming as it is to look at, the film is essentially less visual than musical.

I cannot compare it with many stage productions of Shakespeare; but so far as I can they were, by comparison, just so many slightly tired cultural summer-salads, now and then livened, thanks to an unkilled talent or an unkillable line, by an unexpected rose-petal or the sudden spasm of a rattlesnake: whereas this, down to the last fleeting bit of first-rate poetry in a minor character's mouth, was close to solid gold, almost every word given its own and its largest contextual value. Of course nothing prevents this kind of casting and playing on the stage, except talent and, more seriously, the money to buy enough talent and enough time to use it rightly in; and how often do you see anything to equal it on the Shakespearian stage? The specific advantages of the screen are obvious, but no less important for that. Microphones make possible a much more delicate and immediate use of the voice; reactions, in close-up, can color the lines more subtly and richly than on the stage. Thus it is possible, for instance, to get all the considerable excellence there is out of an aging player like Nicholas Hannen, who seemed weak in most scenes when, on the stage, he had to try to fill and dilate the whole Century Theater with unhappy majesty; and the exquisiteness of Renée Asherson's reactions to Olivier's spate of gallantry, in the wooing scene, did as much as he did toward making that scene, by no means the most inspired as writing, the crown of the film. When so much can be done, through proper understanding of these simple advantages, to open the beauties of poetry as relatively extroverted as this play, it is equally hard to imagine and to wait for the explorations that could be made of subtler, deeper poems like *Hamlet, Troilus and Cressida,* or *The Tempest.*

Speaking still of nothing except the skill with which the poetry is used in this film, I could go on far past the room I have. The sureness and seductive power of the pacing alone and its shifts and contrasts, in scene after scene, has seldom been equaled in a movie; the adjustments and relationships of tone are just as good. For just one example, the difference in tone between Olivier's almost schoolboyish "God-a-mercy" and his "Good old Knight," not long afterward, measures the King's growth in the time between with lovely strength, spaciousness, and cleanness; it earns, as craftsmanship, the triumph of bringing off the equivalent to an "impossibly" delayed false-rhyme; and psychologically or dramatically, it seems to me—though my guess may be far-fetched—it fully establishes the King's coming-of-age by raising honorable, brave, loyal, and dull old age (in Sir Thomas Erpingham) in the King's love and esteem to the level of any love he had ever felt for Falstaff.

Olivier does many other beautiful pieces of reading and playing. His blood-raising reply to the French Herald's ultimatum is not just that; it is a frank, bright exploitation of the moment for English ears, amusedly and desperately honored as such, in a still gallant and friendly way, by both Herald and King. His Crispin's Day oration is not just a brilliant bugle-blat; it is the calculated yet self-exceeding improvisation, at once self-enjoying and selfless, of a young and sleepless leader, rising to a situation wholly dangerous and glamorous, and wholly new to him. Only one of the many beauties of the speech as he gives it is the way in which the King seems now to exploit his sincerity, now to be possessed by it, riding like an unexpectedly mounting wave the astounding size of his sudden proud awareness of the country morning, of his moment in history, of his responsibility and competence, of being full-bloodedly alive, and of being about to die.

This kind of branching, nervous interpretive intelligence, so contemporary in quality except that it always keeps the main lines of its drive and meaning clear, never spiraling or strangling in awareness, is vivid in every way during all parts of the film.

It is tantalizing to be able to mention so few of the dozens of large and hundreds of small excellences which Mr. Olivier and his associates have developed to sustain Shakespeare's poem. They have done somewhere near all that talent, cultivation, taste, knowledgeability, love of one's work— every excellence, in fact, short of genius—can be expected to do; and that, the picture testifies, is a very great deal. Lacking space for anything further I would like to suggest that it be watched for all that it does in playing a hundred kinds of charming adventurousness against the incalculably responsive sounding-boards of tradition: for that is still, and will always be, a process essential in most, though not all, of the best kinds of art, and I have never before seen so much done with it in a moving picture. I am not a Tory, a monarchist, a Catholic, a medievalist, an Englishman, or, despite all the good that it engenders, a lover of war: but the beauty and power of this traditional exercise was such that, watching it, I wished I was, thought I was, and was proud of it. I was persuaded, and in part still am, that every time and place has since been in decline, save one, in which one Englishman used language better than anyone has before or since, or ever shall; and that nearly the best that our time can say for itself is that some of us are still capable of paying homage to the fact.

There Are No Mass Media: All We Have Is Television
JEFFREY SCHRANK

> *The problem with television is that the people must sit and keep their eyes glued on a screen; the average American family hasn't time for it. Therefore, the showmen are convinced that for this reason, if for no other, television will never be a serious competitor of broadcasting.*
> —*The New York Times*, March 19, 1939.
> A reporter evaluating a new invention seen at the World's Fair

> "*You might just as well say,*" added the March Hare, "*that 'I like what I get' is the same thing as 'I get what I like.'*"
> —A well-known rabbit speaking to Alice somewhere in Wonderland

Score one for the rabbit in this battle of insight between the March Hare and *The New York Times*. Thirty years after the *Times* reporter dismissed TV as merely another novelty of the 1939 World's Fair, a Gallup poll revealed that Americans rank television as their "favorite evening pastime." In the voting for most popular activity, Americans cast ballots by turning TV knobs and dials and have selected to settle for liking what they get rather than getting what they like.

For the average American (an admittedly elusive creature bearing some resemblance to a unicorn), watching television consumes more time than any other single activity except sleep. In millions of households, bedtime itself is determined by the end of the late night news or the *TV Guide* announcement of who will substitute for Johnny Carson. Even toilet habits are regimented by television, at least according to a discovery made by the Lafayette, Louisiana, water department.

While the rest of the city watches TV, the employees at the water department watch gauges and needles that are far less exciting than even the dullest of programs. Perhaps the boredom of the work gave rise to the introduction of a TV set into the water gauge room. However it happened, someone noticed that the graph used to gauge water pressure took noticeable dips during commercials and at the end of TV shows. The observation gave rise to the waterwork's own version of the Nielsen ratings.

The water department reported that the movie *Airport* produced a record drop of twenty-six pounds per square inch. The department observed that "at approximately 8:30 a bomb exploded in the airplane and from then until 9:00, when the pilot landed safely and the movie ended, almost nobody left their television set to do anything . . . then the 26-pound drop." The regimented toilet break led to twenty-thousand people flushing at the same time, using about eighty thousand gallons of water. The same scene was undoubtedly repeated across the nation as television gave the orders for what resembled a heartless joke played by an all-powerful but unseen dictator.

Synchronized flushing is anything but the most important effect of television on national behavior patterns, but it does illustrate the difficulty of measuring or even realizing how TV influences behavior. We do know that by the time a typical American reaches the deathbed (appropriately placed underneath a TV set in a hospital room), he or she will have spent nearly seven years watching television. Without television, seven years would be added to the average person's activity-life. It is difficult to believe that we have freely chosen to spend so much of a lifetime watching dancing phosphors on a two-dimensional screen. In its young lifetime, television has so dominated American life that the decision to watch has itself become a pseudo-choice.

For millions of regular viewers, television is no longer one option from among a vast array of choices to occupy a weekday night. The option has become *which* programs to watch, not *if* the set should be on. On any given weekday night, year after year, no matter what programs are presented, there is a fairly constant TV audience in about thirty to forty million of the nation's sixty-seven million households. Instead of a freely chosen occasional diversion, televiewing has become a habit, an addiction requiring a nightly fix. In his book, *The Americans*, historian Daniel Boorstin comments on the relation of the citizen to the TV:

> Television watching became an addiction comparable only to life itself. If the set was not on, Americans began to feel that they had missed what was "really happening. . . ." And just as it was axiomatic that it was better to be alive than to be dead, so it became axiomatic that it was better to be watching *something* than to be watching nothing at all. When there was "nothing on TV tonight," there was a painful void.

To call televiewing an addiction is not merely to employ a figure of speech for shock effect. Addiction, normally associated with drug usage, has two necessary components—tolerance and a withdrawal illness or abstinence syndrome. "Tolerance" is the gradual adaption of the body to the drug (or substance) so that more and more is required to produce the same effect previously obtained with a smaller dosage: A "withdrawal illness" is an adverse physical reaction to a complete lack of the addicting substance, while "abstinence syndrome" refers to usually minor symptoms (running nose, sweating, tremors, irritability, etc.) when the normal dosage is delayed or missed.

These two elements of addiction can both be seen in viewing habits. The component of tolerance can be seen in the gradual increase of the "average daily dosage" self-prescribed by viewers over the past eleven years. The average household in 1963 had the set on for five hours and twelve minutes; by 1974 that figure had increased to six hours and fourteen minutes and has remained almost unchanged since then.

The addiction component of withdrawal can be seen in the millions who rush to have the TV set repaired (or rent a replacement) as soon as it breaks and in those who experience boredom and irritation on those evenings when "nothing's on." Perhaps the best illustration of the addictive nature of televiewing can be found in the experiment conducted by the Society for Rational Psychology in Germany. One hundred eighty-four volunteers were paid to give up television for one year. After a brief period during which the subjects reported happily spending more time with their children, reading, visiting relatives and playing more games, the withdrawal symptoms struck. Tension and quarreling increased dramatically, even wife-beating reached a new intensity and the volunteers' sexual activity declined. Not one lasted more than five months in a state of tubelessness. Once the sets were restored, the symptoms disappeared.

Henner Ertel, one of the psychologists who conducted the experiment, attributed the results to the fact that, "Television tends to cover up conflicts between habitual viewers. Many behavior patterns become so closely linked to TV that they are negatively influenced if one takes the set away. The problem is that of addiction." Television, much like marijuana and alcohol, is a kind of addictive buffer. It allows people who have only superficialities in common to be together in a form of peace and seeming contentment. Or, as T. S. Eliot observed, "Television is the medium which permits millions of people to listen to the same joke at the same time and yet remain lonesome."

If television has become the "opiate of the masses," as many of its critics contend, it is no surprise that it should usurp some of the functions traditionally served by religion. Symbolic of the role of TV as electronic religion are several TV towers, two-fifths of a mile high, on the Midwestern prairies. From the towers of Babylon through medieval church steeples and Indian totem poles, cultures have built their tallest structures to demonstrate their deepest beliefs. In the United States, the tallest buildings are those given to business, but the tallest structures are television transmitting towers.

Televiewing is a ritual activity that can be seen as forming part of a common symbolic environment whose true predecessor is religion. The celebrities are the priests of the videosphere, the three networks its denominations (with PBS a mild case of schism and video freaks potential heretics), and the rating system its morality and ethics. The TV sets and antennae are the shrines and altars, and its ritual is the utter regularity of programs viewed at the foot of the glass box shrine. The worship service is outlined as strictly as in any religion by a set of rubrics printed in the weekly *TV Guide*—the nation's largest selling magazine.

Considering television as a partial fulfillment of the need for ritual helps explain the presence of so much repetition in TV series, ads and reruns—repetition is at the heart both of propaganda and of ritual. Perhaps we are like the African tribe who reportedly saw *King Kong* as its first movie. When the film ended there were resounding cheers. The next week they were again shown a movie, but this time they tore down the tent, the screen and attacked the projector because the film was not *King Kong*. Upon hearing this story Robert Goldfarb, then director of program development for CBS, commented, "Maybe people do want to see the same thing week in and week out."

The fact that television series, year after year, are basically the same stories with updated characters and situations supports the belief that TV is watched as a ritual habit. Adventure series celebrate the conquest of evil by the forces of goodness, and the hero with 1001 faces can be seen any night on all the channels. According to Richard Carpenter of the Center for the Study of Popular Culture at Bowling Green State University,

> Such a pattern, repeated night after night in dozens of versions all portraying the same basic theme, implies that the TV audience derives satisfaction from a ritual formalization of ingrained feelings that the evil in the world can be overcome by men working together under the guidance of a leader. The overwhelming complexities of individuals and social problems are simplified and brought within a manageable compass.

Such is the scholarly language of the academic "discipline" of pop culture. An anthropologist might remind us in somewhat simpler language that TV programs reaffirm tribal values. But the most concise statement of the role of TV as religion is media historian Erik Barnouw's reminder that "TV entertainment is propaganda for the status quo."

Further evidence for televiewing as a ritual activity that depends little on which specific programs are shown from year to year is offered by Paul Klein, former vice-president for audience measurement at NBC. He claims that programming is based on the Theory of the Least Objectionable Program. According to the LOP theory, people don't watch particular programs—they watch television. The set is turned on for the same reason people climb mountains—it's there. The program viewed is the one that at that time is the least objectionable. The LOP theory explains why some interesting programs die and stupid ones live on. "Place a weak show against weaker competition, LOP teaches, and it inevitably looks good." Network programmers know that some well-received programs are stupid, but they also know that a program doesn't have to be good, "it only has to be less objectionable than whatever the hell the other guys throw against it." Thus "Marcus Welby" was watched instead of "First Tuesday" because "When a girl has syphilis on 'Welby,' we can expect a happy ending. When the same girl has it on 'First Tuesday,' we can expect to catch it."

Our language further supports Paul Klein's LOP theory in that we read *the* newspaper, listen to *the* radio, read *a* book or *a* magazine but simply watch television. There is some truth buried in this linguistic habit, for we do watch the medium of television and that is significant no matter if the program is opera or mystery.

The Least Objectionable Program theory is another way of saying that televiewing is a pseudo-choice. It should be clear that not every decision to watch TV is a pseudo-choice; but television is so used by society that much, if not most, viewing falls into the pseudo-choice category.

The LOP theory could be adapted and applied to the automobile to produce the LOMT (Least Objectionable Means of Transportation) theory which states that people don't really choose to spend so much time in automobiles, they simply find autos the least objectionable choice available. The Least Offensive Food theory holds that the highly processed "convenience foods" are not chosen for their taste or goodness but because they have been presented as the least offensive.

Pseudo-choice is a kind of psychological Ohm's Law,[1] a tendency to follow the path of least offensiveness. That such choices exist is not a new phenomenon, but that such choices are so widely confused with free choice is a disturbing tendency. Those who consider these choices in autos, food and TV "free choices" need to be reminded by some contemporary version of the March Hare that, "You might as well say that I like what I get is the same thing as I get what I like."

Television watching falls easily into the area of pseudo-choice because it seems such an inconsequential decision. But each choice to watch has hidden consequences implicit. Each decision to watch includes a hidden or pseudo-choice not to engage with living people, not to take part in any other active process, and to allow a handful of corporate executives to assume responsibility for one's own recreation. The decision to watch also contains a secondary choice to subject oneself to a certain kind of value-

---

[1] G. S. Ohm (1787–1854), German physicist, formulated the law which states that "for any circuit the electric current is directly proportional to the voltage and is inversely proportional to the resistance."—EDS.

laden education and conditioning. This educational aspect of *all* television works very slowly but with an inevitability matched only by its invisibility. Perhaps the most important hidden educational function of television is that of emotional education.

Consider television and the situation Plato describes in Book Seven of his *Republic*.[2] Plato presents the parable of the four prisoners chained together in a cave since childhood. They face a wall filled with shadows cast by the light from a fire behind them. All they know of the world is the shadows. One of the prisoners is released and realizes that the shadows he took for the world are only imitations of a far greater reality. He returns to share this discovery with the other prisoners but is rejected as a heretic. The prisoners are incapable of distinguishing between the shadows and reality.

Plato's allegory takes on a new dimension in a society that experiences many emotions in a darkened movie house or the euphemistically named family room where the TV is enthroned. Like the prisoners, we too spend much time watching shadows that flicker across a screen. We too sometimes have problems distinguishing the shadows from reality, depending partly on how much time we spend in the electronic cave.

We have all experienced deep emotions in front of TV screens; we have all learned about the world we will never visit in person or experience "live." We watch television in order to be manipulated into feeling. We want those shadows on the screen to be frightening, to make us cry or howl with laughter, to help us feel vicarious thrills and excitement, to stimulate awe at the ability of others. Our nervous systems do not distinguish between the fear of a mugger lurking ahead on the deserted street at three in the morning or the fear aroused by the midnight creature feature. In both cases our heart throbs, the pulse quickens and the body sensations are real. The feelings are real, only the televised stimulus is lacking a third dimension.

People have always sought out games and theater to experience feelings normally missing from daily life. But when the seeking takes six to eight hours a day it is a sign of an absence of a rich emotional life based on reality. The shadows become substitutes for reality. A Los Angeles soap opera addict explains: "Without these programs going on, I wonder if I would go on. People seem to forget me.... These people are my company. My real friends. I have it [TV] on because I feel people are talking to me."

This woman is an extreme case of TV-as-reality-substitute, but her symptoms are common to millions. By watching television, the feelings and sense of companionship can be enjoyed without responsibility, without the need to share these feelings with others or express them in public or even to "own" them as ours. These TV-generated feelings come from skilled writers and producers and not from within ourselves—they are safe and

---

[2] See "The Allegory of the Cave" on page 447.—Eds.

nonthreatening. Television encourages habitual viewers to abdicate responsibility for their own recreation and feelings of aliveness. Responsibility slips into the willing hands of corporations who control TV content as well as the supply of goods presented as means to "come alive."

True, these same feelings can be experienced by leaving the electronic cave, but risks must be taken to seek them out and their effects must be faced. Inside the cave TV acts upon viewers as a mass, as part of an audience they are objects to be acted upon. The shadows in the cave are projected in order to play upon emotions; they are clear, simple stimuli which demand only those patterned responses we have all learned so well from so much time spent with TV. Time devoted to watching television teaches how to respond to video realities. This is what Marshall McLuhan meant by "the medium is the message." It is not so important *what* we watch, as it is *that* we watch.

Video critic Gene Youngblood contrasts the commercial entertainer with the artist and sheds light on why we watch so much entertainment television:

> By perpetuating a destructive habit of unthinking response to formulas, by forcing us to rely ever more frequently on memory, the commercial entertainer encourages an unthinking response to daily life, inhibiting self-awareness . . . He offers nothing we haven't already conceived, nothing we don't already expect. Art explains, entertainment exploits. Entertainment gives us what we want; art gives us what we don't know we want.

Music, Painting, and Architecture

Why Don't You Run Upstairs and Write a Nice Gershwin Tune?
LEONARD BERNSTEIN

(*Through the windows of the English Grill in Radio City we can see the ice skaters milling about on the rink, inexplicably avoiding collision with one another. One cannot look at them for more than a few seconds, so dazzling are they as they whirl and plummet in the white winter sunlight. The shirred eggs are gone from our plates, and the second cup of coffee offers the momentary escape from the necessity of conversation. My lunch date with P.M. is one of those acid-forming events born of the New York compulsion to have lunch with one's business associates, at all costs, "some time," as if the mere act of eating together for ninety minutes were guaranteed to cement any and all relations, however tenuous.*

P.M. is what is known in the "trade" as a Professional Manager, that unlucky soul whose job it is to see that the music published by his firm actually gets played. This involves his knowing, more or less intimately, an army of musical performers and some composers. He must once have been a large man, I think —powerful and energetic. He must have had young ideas and ideals. He must have gloried in his close association with the giants of the golden age of popular song-writing. But the long years have wearied him, and have reduced his ideas to formulas, his ideals to memories, his persuasive powers to palliatives. Still, he knows and loves two generations' worth of American popular music, and this gives him his warmth, his zeal, his function in life. I like him.

But why has he asked me to lunch? We have ranged all the immediately available subjects, and I feel there must be something in particular he wants to bring up, and can't. Everyone in the Grill seems to be talking, earnestly or gaily; only we remain chained to an axis of interest terminating at one pole in the skating rink and at the other in a cup of coffee. Again the skaters: back to the coffee. Compulsively, I break the silence.)

L.B.: How's business?
(*This is inane, but he looks up gratefully. It must have helped somehow.*)
P.M.: Business? Well, you know. Sheet music doesn't sell the way it did in the old days. It's all records now. The publisher isn't so much a publisher any more. He's an agent. Printing is the least—
L.B. (*Climbing on with excessive eagerness*): But that ought to make good business, oughtn't it? The main thing is owning the music, the rights—

p.m.: Sure, but owning the music doesn't guarantee that we sell it. Take the music from your new show,[1] for instance.

(So this is why he's invited me to lunch. But pretend innocence.)

l.b.: What about the show?

p.m. *(Kindly)*: How's it going?

l.b. *(As though this were just another subject)*: Fine. I caught it two nights ago. Seemed as fresh as ever.

p.m. *(Carefully)*: Very, very strange about that show of yours. It's a big success, the public enjoys it, it's been running for five months, and there's not a hit in it. How do you explain it?

(The bomb has dropped. The pulse has quickened.)

l.b.: How do I explain it? Isn't that your job to know? You're the man who sells the songs to the public. A hit depends on a good selling job. Don't ask me. I'm just the poor old composer.

p.m.: Now don't get excited. If you had been in this business as long as I have, you'd know that there are two sides to everything. There's no point in laying the blame here or there. A hit is the result of a combination of things: a good song, a good singer to launch it, thorough exploitation, and lucky timing. We can't always have all of them together. Now in your case, we've made one of our biggest efforts. I can't remember when we've—

l.b.: All right, I get it. You just weren't handed good material. I don't need a map. I don't write commercial songs, that's all. Why don't you tear up my contract?

p.m.: Really, L.B., you are in a state of gloom today. I didn't ask you to lunch to upset you. We all want to do our best for that score; it's to our mutual advantage. I just thought we might talk a bit about it, quietly and constructively, and maybe come up with something that might—

l.b.: I'm sorry. I'm somewhat sensitive about it. It's just that it would be nice to hear someone accidentally whistle something of mine, somewhere, just once.

p.m.: It's understandable.

l.b.: And I thought there were at least three natural hits in the show. You never hear the songs on the radio or on TV. There are a few forgotten recordings; one is on Muzak, I believe. It's a little depressing, you must admit.

p.m.: Now come on. Think of all the composers who don't have hits, and don't have hit shows either. You're a lucky boy, you know, and you shouldn't complain. Not everyone can write "Booby Hatch" and sell a million records in a month. Why, I remember George always used to say—

l.b.: George who?

p.m.: Gershwin,[2] of course. What other George is there?

l.b.: Ah, but now you're talking about a man who really had the magic

---

[1] Probably *West Side Story*.—Eds.
[2] American composer (1898–1937).—Eds.

touch. Gershwin made hits, I don't know how. Some people do it all the time, like breathing. I don't know.

P.M. *(Plunging in)*: Well, now that you mention it, it might not be a bad idea for you to give a little thought now and then to these things. Learn a little from George. Your songs are simply too arty, that's all. You try too hard to make them what you would call "interesting." That's not for the public, you know. A special little dissonant effect in the bass may make *you* happy, and maybe some of your highbrow friends, but it doesn't help to make a hit. You're too wrapped up in unusual chords and odd skips in the tune and screwy forms: that's all only an amusing game you play with yourself. George didn't worry about all that. He wrote tunes, dozens of them, simple tunes that the world could sing and remember and want to sing again. He wrote for people, not for critics. You just have to learn how to be simple, my boy.

L.B.: You think it's so simple to be simple? Not at all. I've tried hard for years. After all this isn't the first time I'm hearing this lecture. A few weeks ago a serious composer-friend and I were talking about all this, and we got boiling mad about it. Why shouldn't we be able to come up with a hit, we said, if the standard is as low as it seems to be? We decided that all we had to do was to put ourselves into the mental state of an idiot and write a ridiculous hillbilly tune. So we went to work with a will, vowing to make thousands by simply being simple-minded. We worked for an hour and then gave up in hysterical despair. Impossible. We found ourselves being "personal" and "expressing ourselves"; and try as we might we couldn't seem to boil any music down to the bare, feeble-minded level we had set ourselves. I remember that at one point we were trying like two children, one note at a time, to make a tune that didn't even require any harmony, it would be that obvious. Impossible. It was a revealing experiment, I must say, even though it left us with a slightly doomed feeling. As I say, why don't you tear up my contract?

(I drain the already empty coffee cup.)

P.M. *(With a touch of the basketball coach)*: Doom, nothing. I'll bet my next week's salary that you can write simple tunes if you really put your mind to it. And not with another composer, but all by yourself. After all, George was just like you, highbrow, one foot in Carnegie Hall and the other in Tin Pan Alley. He wrote concert music, too, and was all wound up in fancy harmony and counterpoint and orchestration. He just knew when to be simple and when not to be.

L.B.: No, I think you're wrong. Gershwin was a whole other man. No connection at all.

P.M.: You're only being modest, or pretending to be. Didn't that critic after your last show call you a second Gershwin, or a budding Gershwin, or something?

L.B. *(Secretly flattered)*: That's all in the critic's mind. Nothing to do with facts. Actually Gershwin and I came from opposite sides of the tracks, and if we meet anywhere at all it's my love for his music. But there it ends. Gershwin was a songwriter who grew into a serious composer. I am a serious composer trying to be a songwriter. His was by far the more normal way: starting with small forms and blossoming out from there. My way is more confused: I wrote a symphony before I ever wrote a popular song. How can you expect me to have that simple touch that he had?

P.M. *(Paternally)*: But George—did you know him, by the way?

L.B.: I wish I had. He died when I was just a kid in Boston.

P.M. (*A star in his eye*): If you had met him you would have known that George was every inch a serious composer. Why, look at the *Rhapsody in Blue,* the *American in*—

L.B.: Now, P.M., you know as well as I do that the *Rhapsody* is not a composition at all. It's a string of separate paragraphs stuck together—with a thin paste of flour and water. Composing is a very different thing from writing tunes, after all. I find that the themes, or tunes, or whatever you want to call them, in the *Rhapsody* are terrific—inspired, God-given. At least four of them, which is a lot for a twelve-minute piece. They are perfectly harmonized, ideally proportioned, songful, clear, rich, moving. The rhythms are always right. The "quality" is always there, just as it is in his best show tunes. But you can't just put four tunes together, God-given though they may be, and call them a composition. Composition means a putting together, yes, but a putting together of elements so that they add up to an organic whole. *Compono, componere—*[3]

P.M.: Spare us the Latin. You can't mean that the *Rhapsody in Blue* is not an organic work! Why, in its every bar it breathes the same thing, throughout all its variety and all its change of mood and tempo. It breathes America—the people, the urban society that George knew deeply, the pace, the nostalgia, the nervousness, the majesty, the—

L.B.: —the Chaikovsky sequences, the Debussy meanderings, the Lisztian piano-fireworks.[4] It's as American as you please while the themes are going on; but the minute the little thing called development is called for, America goes out the window and Chaikovsky and his friends march in the door. And the trouble is that a composition *lives* in its development.

P.M.: I think I need some more coffee. Waiter!

L.B.: Me too. I didn't mean to get started on all this, and I certainly don't want to tread on your idol's clay feet. He's my idol too, remember. I don't think there has been such an inspired melodist on this earth since Chaikovsky, if you want to know what I really feel. I rank him right up there with Schubert and the great ones. But if you want to speak of a *composer,* that's another matter. Your *Rhapsody in Blue* is not a real composition in the sense that whatever happens in it must seem inevitable,

---

[3] The Latin verb from which the English word *compose* is derived.—EDS.

[4] Peter Ilyich Tchaikovsky (1840–1893), Russian composer; Claude Debussy (1862–1918), French composer; Franz Liszt (1811–1886), Hungarian composer.—EDS.

or even pretty inevitable. You can cut out parts of it without affecting the whole in any way except to make it shorter. You can remove any of these stuck-together sections, and the piece still goes on as bravely as before. You can even interchange these sections with one another, and no harm done. You can make cuts within a section, or add new cadenzas, or play it with any combination of instruments or on the piano alone; it can be a five-minute piece or a six-minute piece or a twelve-minute piece. And in fact all these things are being done to it every day. It's still the *Rhapsody in Blue*.

P.M.: But look here. That sounds to me like the biggest argument yet in its favor. If a piece is so sturdy that whatever you do to it has no effect on its intrinsic nature, then it must be pretty healthy. There must be something there that resists pressure, something real and alive, wouldn't you say?

L.B.: Of course there is: those tunes. Those beautiful tunes. But they still don't add up to a piece.

P.M.: Perhaps you're right in a way about the *Rhapsody*. It was an early work, after all—his first attempt to write in an extended form. He was only twenty-six or so, don't forget; he couldn't even orchestrate the piece when he wrote it. But how about the later works? What about the *American in Paris*? Now that is surely a well-knit, organic—

L.B.: True, what you say. Each work got better as he went on, because he was an intelligent man and a serious student, and he worked hard. But the *American in Paris* is again a study in tunes, all of them beautiful, and all of them separate. He had by that time discovered certain tricks of composition, ways of linking themes up, of combining and developing motives, of making an orchestral fabric. But even here they still remain tricks, mechanisms borrowed from Strauss and Ravel[5] and who knows where else. And when you add it all up together it is still a weak work because none of these tricks is his own. They don't arise from the nature of the material; they are borrowed and applied to the material. Or rather *appliquéed* to it, like beads on a dress. When you hear the piece you rejoice in the first theme, then sit and wait through the "filler" until the next one comes along. In this way you sit out about two thirds of the composition. The remaining third is marvelous because it consists of the themes themselves; but where's the composition?

P.M. (*A bit craftily*): But you play it all the time, don't you?

L.B.: Yes.

P.M.: And you've recorded it, haven't you?

L.B.: Yes.

P.M.: Then you must like it a lot, mustn't you?

L.B.: I adore it. Ah, here's the coffee.

---

[5] Richard Strauss (1864–1949), German composer; Maurice Joseph Ravel (1875–1937), French composer.—EDS.

P.M. *(Sighing)*: I don't understand you. How can you adore something you riddle with holes? Can you adore a bad composition?

L.B.: Each man kills the thing he loves. Yes, I guess you can love a bad composition. For non-compositional reasons. Sentiment. Association. Inner meaning. Spirit. But I think I like it most of all because it is so sincere. It is trying so hard to be good: it has only good intentions.

P.M.: You mean you like it for its faults?

L.B.: No, I don't. But what's good in it is so good that it's irresistible. If you have to go along with some chaff in order to have the wheat, it's worth it. And I love it because it shows, or begins to show, what Gershwin might have done if he had lived. Just look at the progress from the *Rhapsody* to the piano concerto, from the concerto to—

P.M. *(Glowing)*: Ah, the concerto is a masterpiece.

L.B.: That's your story. The concerto is the work of a young genius who is learning fast. But *Porgy and Bess*—there the real destiny of Gershwin begins to be clear.

P.M.: Really, I don't get it. Doesn't *Porgy* have all the same faults? I'm always being told that it's perhaps the weakest composition of all he wrote, in spite of the glorious melodies in it. He intended it as a grand opera, after all, and it seems to have failed as a grand opera. Whenever a production of *Porgy* really succeeds, you find that it's been changed into a sort of operetta. They have taken out all the "in-between" singing and replaced it with spoken lines, leaving only the main numbers. That seems to me to speak for itself.

L.B.: Oh, no. It speaks only for the producers. It's a funny thing about *Porgy*: I always miss the in-between singing when I hear it in its cut form. Perhaps it is more successful that way; it certainly is for the public. It may be because so much of that recitative seems alien to the character of the songs themselves, instead recalling *Tosca* and *Pelléas*.[6] But there's a danger of throwing out the baby with the bath. Because there's a lot of that recitative that *is* in the character of the songs and fits the opera perfectly. Do you remember Bess's scene with Crown on the island? Bess is saying *(Singing)*:

> "It's like dis, Crown,
> I's the only woman Porgy ever had—"

P.M. *(Joining in rapturously)*:

> "An I's thinkin' now,
> How it will be tonight
> When all these other niggers go back to
>   Catfish Row."

---

[6] *La Tosca*, an opera (1900) by Giacomo Puccini; *Pelléas et Mélisande,* an opera (1902) by Claude Debussy based on a play by Maurice Maeterlinck.—EDS.

L.B. and P.M. *(Together, with growing excitement)*:

> "He'll be sittin' and watchin' the big front gate,
> A-countin' 'em off waitin' for Bess.
> An' when the last woman—"

(The restaurant is all eyes and ears.)

P.M. *(In a loud whisper)*: I think we are making a scene.

L.B. *(In a violent whisper)*: But that's just what I mean! Thrilling stuff, isn't it? Doesn't it point the way to a kind of Gershwin music that would have reached its own perfection eventually? I can never get over the horrid fact of his death for that reason. With *Porgy* you suddenly realize that Gershwin was a great, great theater composer. He always had been. Perhaps that's what was wrong with his concert music: it was really theater music thrust into a concert hall. What he would have done in the theater in another ten or twenty years! And then he would still have been a young man! What a loss! Will America ever realize what a loss it was?

P.M. *(Moved)*: You haven't touched your coffee.

L.B. *(Suddenly exhausted)*: It's gotten cold. Anyway, I have to go home and write music. Thanks for lunch, P.M.

P.M.: Oh, thank you for coming. I've enjoyed it. Let's do it again, shall we? We have so much to talk about.

How We Listen
AARON COPLAND

We all listen to music according to our separate capacities. But, for the sake of analysis, the whole listening process may become clearer if we break it up into its component parts, so to speak. In a certain sense we all listen to music on three separate planes. For lack of a better terminology, one might name these: (1) the sensuous plane, (2) the expressive plane, (3) the sheerly musical plane. The only advantage to be gained from mechanically splitting up the listening process into these hypothetical planes is the clear view to be had of the way in which we listen.

The simplest way of listening to music is to listen for the sheer pleasure of the musical sound itself. That is the sensuous plane. It is the plane on which we hear music without thinking, without considering it in any way. One turns on the radio while doing something else and absent-mindedly bathes in the sound. A kind of brainless but attractive state of mind is engendered by the mere sound appeal of the music.

You may be sitting in a room reading this book. Imagine one note struck on the piano. Immediately that one note is enough to change the atmosphere of the room—proving that the sound element in music is a powerful and mysterious agent, which it would be foolish to deride or belittle.

The surprising thing is that many people who consider themselves qualified music lovers abuse that plane in listening. They go to concerts in order to lose themselves. They use music as a consolation or an escape. They enter an ideal world where one doesn't have to think of the realities of everyday life. Of course they aren't thinking about the music either. Music allows them to leave it, and they go off to a place to dream, dreaming because of and apropos of the music yet never quite listening to it.

Yes, the sound appeal of music is a potent and primitive force, but you must not allow it to usurp a disproportionate share of your interest. The sensuous plane is an important one in music, a very important one, but it does not constitute the whole story.

There is no need to digress further on the sensuous plane. Its appeal to every normal human being is self-evident. There is, however, such a thing as becoming more sensitive to the different kinds of sound stuff as used by various composers. For all composers do not use that sound stuff in the same way. Don't get the idea that the value of music is commensurate with its sensuous appeal or that the loveliest sounding music is made by the greatest composer. If that were so, Ravel[1] would be a greater creator than Beethoven. The point is that the sound element varies with each composer, that his usage of sound forms an integral part of his style and must be taken into account while listening. The reader can see, therefore, that a more conscious approach is valuable even on this primary plane of music listening.

The second plane on which music exists is what I have called the expressive one. Here, immediately, we tread on controversial ground. Composers have a way of shying away from any discussion of music's expressive side. Did not Stravinksy[2] himself proclaim that his music was an "object," a "thing," with a life of its own, and with no other meaning than its own purely musical existence? This intransigent attitude of Stravinsky's may be due to the fact that so many people have tried to read different meanings into so many pieces. Heaven knows it is difficult enough to say precisely what it is that a piece of music means, to say it definitely, to say it finally so that everyone is satisfied with your explanation. But that should not lead one to the other extreme of denying to music the right to be "expressive."

My own belief is that all music has an expressive power, some more and some less, but that all music has a certain meaning behind the notes and that that meaning behind the notes constitutes, after all, what the piece is saying, what the piece is about. This whole problem can be stated

---

[1] Maurice Joseph Ravel (1875–1937), French composer.—Eds.

[2] Igor Fedorovich Stravinsky (1882–1971), influential modern Russian composer. —Eds.

quite simply by asking, "Is there a meaning to music?" My answer to that would be, "Yes." And "Can you state in so many words what the meaning is?" My answer to that would be, "No." Therein lies the difficulty.

Simple-minded souls will never be satisfied with the answer to the second of these questions. They always want music to have a meaning, and the more concrete it is the better they like it. The more the music reminds them of a train, a storm, a funeral, or any other familiar conception the more expressive it appears to be to them. This popular idea of music's meaning—stimulated and abetted by the usual run of musical commentator—should be discouraged wherever and whenever it is met. One timid lady once confessed to me that she suspected something seriously lacking in her appreciation of music because of her inability to connect it with anything definite. That is getting the whole thing backward, of course.

Still, the question remains, How close should the intelligent music lover wish to come to pinning a definite meaning to any particular work? No closer than a general concept, I should say. Music expresses, at different moments, serenity or exuberance, regret or triumph, fury or delight. It expresses each of these moods, and many others, in a numberless variety of subtle shadings and differences. It may even express a state of meaning for which there exists no adequate word in any language. In that case, musicians often like to say that it has only a purely musical meaning. They sometimes go further and say that *all* music has only a purely musical meaning. What they really mean is that no appropriate word can be found to express the music's meaning and that, even if it could, they do not feel the need of finding it.

But whatever the professional musician may hold, most musical novices still search for specific words with which to pin down their musical reactions. That is why they always find Tschaikovsky[3] easier to "understand" than Beethoven. In the first place, it is easier to pin a meaning-word on a Tschaikovsky piece than on a Beethoven one. Much easier. Moreover, with the Russian composer, every time you come back to a piece of his it almost always says the same thing to you, whereas with Beethoven it is often quite difficult to put your finger on what he is saying. And any musician will tell you that that is why Beethoven is the greater composer. Because music which always says the same thing to you will necessarily soon become dull music, but music whose meaning is slightly different with each hearing has a greater chance of remaining alive.

Listen, if you can, to the forty-eight fugue themes of Bach's *Well Tempered Clavier*. Listen to each theme, one after another. You will soon realize that each theme mirrors a different world of feeling. You will also soon realize that the more beautiful a theme seems to you the harder it is to find any word that will describe it to your complete satisfaction. Yes, you will certainly know whether it is a gay theme or a sad one. You

---

[3] Peter Ilyich Tchaikovsky (1840–1893), major Russian composer.—EDS.

will be able, in other words, in your own mind, to draw a frame of emotional feeling around your theme. Now study the sad one a little closer. Try to pin down the exact quality of its sadness. Is it pessimistically sad or resignedly sad; is it fatefully sad or smilingly sad?

Let us suppose that you are fortunate and can describe to your own satisfaction in so many words the exact meaning of your chosen theme. There is still no guarantee that anyone else will be satisfied. Nor need they be. The important thing is that each one feel for himself the specific expressive quality of a theme or, similarly, an entire piece of music. And if it is a great work of art, don't expect it to mean exactly the same thing to you each time you return to it.

Themes or pieces need not express only one emotion, of course. Take such a theme as the first main one of the *Ninth Symphony*,[4] for example. It is clearly made up of different elements. It does not say only one thing. Yet anyone hearing it immediately gets a feeling of strength, a feeling of power. It isn't a power that comes simply because the theme is played loudly. It is a power inherent in the theme itself. The extraordinary strength and vigor of the theme results in the listener's receiving an impression that a forceful statement has been made. But one should never try to boil it down to "the fateful hammer of life," etc. That is where the trouble begins. The musician, in his exasperation, says it means nothing but the notes themselves, whereas the nonprofessional is only too anxious to hang on to any explanation that gives him the illusion of getting closer to the music's meaning.

Now, perhaps the reader will know better what I mean when I say that music does have an expressive meaning but that we cannot say in so many words what that meaning is.

The third plane on which music exists is the sheerly musical plane. Besides the pleasurable sound of music and the expressive feeling that it gives off, music does exist in terms of the notes themselves and of their manipulation. Most listeners are not sufficiently conscious of this third plane. . . .

Professional musicians, on the other hand, are, if anything, too conscious of the mere notes themselves. They often fall into the error of becoming so engrossed with their arpeggios and staccatos that they forget the deeper aspects of the music they are performing. But from the layman's standpoint, it is not so much a matter of getting over bad habits on the sheerly musical plane as of increasing one's awareness of what is going on, in so far as the notes are concerned.

When the man in the street listens to the "notes themselves" with any degree of concentration, he is most likely to make some mention of the melody. Either he hears a pretty melody or he does not, and he generally lets it go at that. Rhythm is likely to gain his attention next, particularly if it seems exciting. But harmony and tone color are generally taken for granted, if they are thought of consciously at all. As for music's having

---

[4] Composed by Ludwig van Beethoven (1770–1827) in 1823.—Eds.

a definite form of some kind, that idea seems never to have occurred to him.

It is very important for all of us to become more alive to music on its sheerly musical plane. After all, an actual musical material is being used. The intelligent listener must be prepared to increase his awareness of the musical material and what happens to it. He must hear the melodies, the rhythms, the harmonies, the tone colors in a more conscious fashion. But above all he must, in order to follow the line of the composer's thought, know something of the principles of musical form. Listening to all of these elements is listening on the sheerly musical plane.

Let me repeat that I have split up mechanically the three separate planes on which we listen merely for the sake of greater clarity. Actually, we never listen on one or the other of these planes. What we do is to correlate them—listening in all three ways at the same time. It takes no mental effort, for we do it instinctively.

Perhaps an analogy with what happens to us when we visit the theater will make this instinctive correlation clearer. In the theater, you are aware of the actors and actresses, costumes and sets, sounds and movements. All these give one the sense that the theater is a pleasant place to be in. They constitute the sensuous plane in our theatrical reactions.

The expressive plane in the theater would be derived from the feeling that you get from what is happening on the stage. You are moved to pity, excitement, or gayety. It is this general feeling, generated aside from the particular words being spoken, a certain emotional something which exists on the stage, that is analogous to the expressive quality in music.

The plot and plot development is equivalent to our sheerly musical plane. The playwright creates and develops a character in just the same way that a composer creates and develops a theme. According to the degree of your awareness of the way in which the artist in either field handles his material will you become a more intelligent listener.

It is easy enough to see that the theatergoer never is conscious of any of these elements separately. He is aware of them all at the same time. The same is true of music listening. We simultaneously and without thinking listen on all three planes.

In a sense, the ideal listener is both inside and outside the music at the same moment, judging it and enjoying it, wishing it would go one way and watching it go another—almost like the composer at the moment he composes it; because in order to write his music, the composer must also be inside and outside his music, carried away by it and yet coldly critical of it. A subjective and objective attitude is implied in both creating and listening to music.

What the reader should strive for, then, is a more *active* kind of listening. Whether you listen to Mozart or Duke Ellington, you can deepen your understanding of music only by being a more conscious and aware listener —not someone who is just listening, but someone who is listening *for* something.

As Picasso Said, Why Assume That To Look Is To See?
A Talk Between Malraux and the Master[1]
ANDRE MALRAUX

In the winter of 1944–1945, after the liberation of Paris from the Nazis, André Malraux visited Pablo Picasso in the painter's Grands-Augustin studio.... Here, Malraux recalls the impact of the Picasso paintings, most of which he was seeing for the first time. The two men discussed what the artist strives for in his art—and what the public sees in it....

He spoke very impressively about the pair of spectacles an artist's creation imposes upon the viewer. Not about "nature imitating art," but about the filter one is forced to look through the very moment one's eyes settle on an object; about the preconceived intention which made everybody believe that Marcel Duchamp's bottle-driers was a piece of sculpture because it was shown in an exhibition, and that Negro sculptors were clumsy because everyone had been assured that they wanted to imitate their neighbors or nature.

PICASSO: "Obviously, people must be forced to see painting in spite of nature. But what, exactly, is nature?"

(I remembered an answer he gave, long ago, to the type of reporter who thinks he's so clever and who had asked him: "Monsieur Picasso, should feet be painted rectangular or square?" Picasso replied, "I don't know. There aren't any feet in nature.")

MALRAUX: "Giotto, the shepherd, was very bad at drawing sheep, but when people realized that painters were no longer referring to nature, they weren't pleased at all. Modern art began with Manet's 'Olympia' and 'Olympia' was the first painting that ever needed police protection."

PICASSO: "Are you sure of that?"

MALRAUX: "Absolutely, and it's all the more strange in that the canvas isn't erotic. It has only to do with painting. Now if all those who were so loudly protesting didn't like it, they simply didn't have to buy it. And, indeed, they didn't."

PICASSO: "People have always felt like destroying paintings they hate. And they're right. Funny they didn't do anything against 'Les Demoiselles d'Avignon'... People don't like painting. All they want to know is which painters will be considered good a hundred years from now. They think that if they can make the leap and see ahead, they've won. They should all be art dealers. Yet we have no idea of how painting lives. Or how it dies. No one can talk about painting. I can talk about Van Gogh. Maybe. But not about painting. It makes me do what it wants me to do: to push

---

[1] This article is adapted from the book *Picasso's Mask* (*La Tête D'Obsidienne*) by André Malraux. English translation by June Guicharnaud with Jacques Guicharnaud.

on, to push on further and further, to push on even further than that—and to make it work. . . . But that's the problem!—to make it work in relation to what?

"People aren't pleased," he went on, "because what they want is a painter who, when he thinks about Kazbek [Picasso's dog], makes a copy of Kazbek. But the letters that make up the word 'dog' are not a copy of the dog!"

MALRAUX: "Nor are Chinese characters; at least, they haven't been for a long time."

PICASSO: "They name things. A painter should name things. If I do a nude, people ought to think, 'That's a nude.' Not, 'That's Mrs. So and So.'"

MALRAUX: "Or the goddess So and So. But the art lover wants a Picasso nude."

PICASSO: "It would be one in any case, if I manage to name it a nude. It's hard, of course. It's painting: In painting, things are signs; before the First World War, we called them emblems. What would a painting be if not a sign? A *tableau vivant*? Ah, yes, of course, if one were a professional painter! But when one is merely Cézanne, or poor old Van Gogh, or Goya, then one paints signs."

The cubists had understood very early on that the privileged means of painting is the affective sign. Picasso's personal freedom was rarely willing to free itself from it. It was necessary to his art, for it enabled him to vie with nature, and even to destroy it.

MALRAUX: "In any case, everyone now knows that your signs signify something. But what?"

PICASSO: "It knocks them out. What difference should it make to them? Still, my cubist Harlequins are reproduced in magazines. . . ."

MALRAUX: "Because they're mistakenly thought of as decorations, especially for stage sets. But your Negro period . . . and these canvases here! . . ."

PICASSO: "People *always* begin by not understanding! Afterward, it's only as if they understood! But that's great! Because, personally, I haven't the vaguest idea what they understand. When you're dead, fine. I'm not dead. Is it that they've got used to my work? No, there's more to it than that. Take Apollinaire,[2] for example. He knew nothing about painting, yet he loved the real thing. Poets often have a sense for it."

MALRAUX: "Yes, from that point of view, what about Baudelaire,[3] who wasn't much of a musician but sensed what Wagner was about?"

PICASSO: "But don't you find that funny? When one starts a painting,

---

[2] French poet, of Polish descent (1880–1918). Apollinaire was a leader of the literary and artistic avant-garde, and one of the first to hail cubism.—EDS.

[3] French poet (1821–1867) whose work influenced modern poetry widely. Author of *The Flowers of Evil* (*Les Fleurs du Mal*) (1857), Baudelaire also was an early sponsor of modern art, which in his time was generally rejected.—EDS.

one never knows how it will turn out. When it's finished, one still doesn't know. You might say that painting ripens until it's good enough to eat. Think of Cézanne, of Van Gogh. People don't understand that *I'm* Van Gogh, right? But it doesn't matter—we're in no hurry. . . ."

He sounded as if he were joking; I believe he was only half-joking. He was poking fun—at himself? More probably, at everything, just as he seemed to be jeering at the human forms he gave to some of his figures. . . .

"People can tell me anything they want about a painting which isn't present to me when I look at it; I couldn't care less. Those paintings are for historians; it's like friends: There are those we love and those we're indifferent to. Has my idol become a piece of sculpture? Yes. So has the fetish. Absolutely. And it won't stop with us, right? Sometimes I *see* the studio and everything in it. Just as I see things before I paint them, before I think of using them. What will become of it all? My early canvases have changed a lot. Not the colors: the canvases. The sculptures, too. And I'm alive. Afterwards. . . . And what about Van Gogh? And Cézanne? As I told you: No one knows how painting lives. . . ."

He meant "art," but to him that word was taboo. The most important words in our vocabulary—"love," "death," "God," "revolution"—owe their power to meanings that have been superimposed on them; to Picasso, "painting" belonged to that same category of words.

With the hand in which he was holding the small marble violin,[4] he pointed to his "Woman with Leaves," standing in a corner: "The leaves were mighty surprised to find themselves in my sculpture, right?"

He spoke in the simplest way possible. Without pretension, and not in any way "sick." But he experienced metamorphosis just as mediums experience their trances. When talking about his new canvases, he would say: "They're still coming!" And regarding those he was finishing: "I'm going to leave them just like that." He spoke of his landscapes as if they had first been absorbed within him and had then come out as paintings. After "Les Demoiselles d'Avignon," his works had become one inexhaustible metamorphosis. He literally lived in a state of metamorphosis. When the journalists described Picasso as a sorcerer, they were rather hastily expressing what in fact was the profound and disturbing power he possessed and was perhaps exorcizing. Actually, his works as a whole, given their very nature and their successive periods, are more haunted by metamorphosis than the works of any previous artist. I had not forgotten those cockroaches at the foot of "Guernica."

Ironic wonderment was one of his most frequent facial expressions. . . .

"I always know when I come out a winner. If I make a mistake, the future will choose. That's the future's job, right? To be continued in the next issue. With some canvases, we have children; with others, it's im-

---

[4] A violin-shaped idol from the Cyclades, an ancient sculpture admired by Picasso. —EDS.

possible. Afterward, the good ones become our guides. Canes for our old age! They keep coming and coming! Like pigeons out of a hat. I know, in some vague way, what I want, like when I'm about to start on a canvas. Then what happens is very interesting. I could say: I'm painting my complete works. But for me. . . . When I look at my hand, I know it's fate; it changes as life goes on, right? I want to see my branches grow. That's why I started to paint trees; yet I never paint them from nature. My trees are myself.

"I want to cut the branches, too. What exactly is a painting, or a piece of sculpture? Are they objects? No. What, then? Let's say they're things —that's more like it. Things within which whatever is sculpted or painted meets with its own destruction. The painter takes whatever it is and destroys it. At the same time, he gives it another life. For himself. Later on, for other people. But he must pierce through what the others see—to the reality of it. He must destroy. He must demolish the framework itself."

His irony had disappeared. He was probably summing up a thought that was familiar to him, for he was speaking in an offhand way, and using a precise vocabulary which reflected the lacerated thrust of his paintings. . . .

"Maybe the most important word is the word 'tension.' Lines shouldn't . . . shouldn't even vibrate, shouldn't be able to any longer . . . But there's more to it than the line itself. You have to create as much distance as possible. The head that becomes an egg. That was perfectly understood by the sculptors from the Cyclades—not when they made their violins, but when they made their idols, which are actually oblique eggs anchored down by a neck . . . The body, and plant life. That I did in my 'Woman with Leaves.' Also, you have to confound people. Square heads, for instance, when they ought to be round."

Imperceptibly, his voice took on an ironic tone again—this time, almost to the point of parody. "And to shift things about," he said. "Putting eyes in legs. And to be contradictory. Painting one eye in full view and the other in profile. People always make both eyes the same; have you noticed? Nature does many things the way I do; it hides them! But it has got to confess. When I paint, I skip from one thing to another. All right. But they make a whole. That's why people have to reckon with me. Since I work with Kazbek, I make paintings that bite. Violence, clanging cymbals . . . explosions. At the same time, the painting has to hold up. That's very important. But painters want to please! A good painting—any painting —ought to bristle with razor blades."

A sound of barking came in from the street. "What does that mean—to work? To keep pushing on further and further? To make corrections? But how would you go about it? You lose your spontaneity. Matisse believes in stripping his work bare. When it comes to drawings, the first sketch is always the best. And there's nothing wrong with an unretouched painting. Nothing whatever.

"After all, you can only work against something. Even if it's yourself.

That's very important. Most painters make themselves a little cake-mold; then they make cakes. Always the same cakes. And they're very pleased with themselves. A painter should never do what people expect of him. A painter's worst enemy is style."

"Is it also painting's worst enemy?"

"Painting finds a style once you're dead. Painting always wins out."

The Case for Abstract Art
CLEMENT GREENBERG

Many people say that the kind of art our age produces is one of the major symptoms of what's wrong with the age. The disintegration and, finally, the disappearance of recognizable images in painting and sculpture, like the obscurity in advanced literature, are supposed to reflect a disintegration of values in society itself. Some people go further and say that abstract, nonrepresentational art is pathological art, crazy art, and that those who practice it and those who admire and buy it are either sick or silly. The kindest critics are those who say it's all a joke, a hoax, and a fad, and that modernist art in general, or abstract art in particular, will soon pass. This sort of thing is heard or read pretty constantly, but in some years more often than others.

There seems to be a certain rhythm in the advance in popularity of modernist art, and a certain rhythm in the counter-attacks which try to stem it. More or less the same words or arguments are used in all the polemics, but the targets usually change. Once it was the impressionists who were a scandal, next it was Van Gogh and Cézanne, then it was Matisse, then it was cubism and Picasso, after that Mondrian, and now it is Jackson Pollock.[1] The fact that Pollock was an American shows, in a backhanded way, how important American art has lately become.

Some of the same people who attack modernist art in general, or abstract art in particular, happen also to complain that our age has lost those habits of disinterested contemplation, and that capacity for enjoying things as ends in themselves and for their own sake, which former ages are supposed to have cultivated. This idea has been advanced often enough to convert it into a cliché. I hate to give assent to a cliché, for it is almost always an oversimplification, but I have to make an exception in this case. While I strongly doubt that disinterested contemplation was as unalloyed or as

[1] Vincent Van Gogh (1853–1890) was a Dutch painter; Paul Cézanne (1839–1906) and Henri Matisse (1869–1954) were French painters; Pablo Picasso (1881–1973) was a native of Spain who painted in France; Pieter Cornelis Mondrian (1872–1944) was Dutch, and Jackson Pollock (1912–1956) American.—EDS.

popular in ages past as is supposed, I do tend to agree that we could do with more of it in this time, and especially in this country.

I think a poor life is lived by anyone who doesn't regularly take time out to stand and gaze, or sit and listen, or touch, or smell, or brood, without any further end in mind, simply for the satisfaction gotten from that which is gazed at, listened to, touched, smelled or brooded upon. We all know, however, that the climate of Western life, and particularly of American life, is not conducive to this kind of thing; we are all too busy making a living. This is another cliché, of course. And still a third cliché says that we should learn from Oriental society how to give more of ourselves to the life of the spirit, to contemplation and meditation, and to the appreciation of what is satisfying or beautiful in its own sole right. This last is not only a cliché, but a fallacy, since most Orientals are even more preoccupied than we are with making a living. I hope that I myself am not making a gross and reductive simplification when I say that so much of Oriental contemplative and aesthetic discipline strikes me as a technique for keeping one's eyes averted from ugliness and misery.

Every civilization and every tradition of culture seem to possess capacities for self-cure and self-correction that go into operation automatically, unbidden. If the given tradition goes too far in one direction it will usually try to right itself by going equally far in the opposite one. There is no question but that our Western civilization, especially in its American variant, devotes more mental energy than any other to the production of material things and services; and that, more than any other, it puts stress on interested, purposeful activity in general. This is reflected in our art, which, as has been frequently observed, puts such great emphasis on movement and development and resolution, on beginnings, middles, and endings—that is, on dynamics. Compare Western music with any other kind, or look at Western literature, for that matter, with its relatively great concern with plot and over-all structure and its relatively small concern with tropes and figures and ornamental elaborations; think of how slow-moving Chinese and Japanese poetry is by comparison with ours, and how much it delights in static situations; and how uncertain the narrational logic of non-Western fiction tends to be. Think of how encrusted and convoluted Arabic poetry is by contrast even with our most euphuistic lyrical verse. And as for non-Western music, does it not almost always, and literally, strike us as more monotonous than ours?

Well, how does Western art compensate for, correct, or at least qualify its emphasis on the dynamic—an emphasis that may or may not be excessive? And how does Western life itself compensate for, correct, or at least qualify its obsession with material production and purposeful activity? I shall not here attempt to answer the latter question. But in the realm of art an answer is beginning to emerge of its own accord, and the shape of part of that answer is abstract art.

Abstract decoration is almost universal, and Chinese and Japanese calligraphy is quasi-abstract—abstract to the extent that few occidentals can read the characters of Chinese or Japanese writing. But only in the West, and only in the last fifty years, have such things as abstract pictures and free-standing pieces of abstract sculpture appeared. What makes the big difference between these and abstract decoration is that they are, exactly, pictures and free-standing sculpture—solo works of art meant to be looked at for their own sake and with full attention, and not as the adjuncts, incidental aspects, or settings of things other than themselves. These abstract pictures and pieces of sculpture challenge our capacity for disinterested contemplation in a way that is more concentrated and, I daresay, more conscious than anything else I know of in art. Music is an essentially abstract art, but even at its most rarefied and abstract, and whether it's Bach's or the middle-period Schoenberg's[2] music, it does not offer this challenge in quite the same way or degree. Music tends from a beginning through a middle toward an ending. We wait to see how it "comes out"— which is what we also do with literature. Of course, the *total* experience of literature and music is completely disinterested, but it becomes that only at a further remove. While undergoing the experience we are caught up and expectant as well as detached—disinterested and at the same time interested in a way resembling that in which we are interested in how things turn out in real life. I exaggerate to make my point—aesthetic experience *has* to be disinterested, and when it is genuine it always is, even when bad works of art are involved—but the distinctions I've made and those I've still to make are valid nevertheless.

With representational painting it is something like what it is with literature. This has been said before, many times before, but usually in order to criticize representational painting in what I think is a wrong-headed when not downright silly way. What I mean when I say, in this context, that representational painting is like literature, is that it tends to involve us in the interested as well as the disinterested by presenting us with the images of things that are inconceivable outside time and action. This goes even for landscapes and flower pieces and still lifes. It is not simply that we sometimes tend to confuse the attractiveness of the things represented in a picture with the quality of the picture itself. And it is not only that attractiveness as such has nothing to do with the abiding success of a work of art. What is more fundamental is that the meaning—as distinct from the attractiveness—of what is represented becomes truly inseparable from the representation itself. That Rembrandt[3] confined impasto—thick paint, that is—to his highlights, and that in his later portraits especially these coincide with the ridges of the noses of his subjects is important to the artistic effect of these portraits. And that the effectiveness of the impasto, as impasto—as an abstract element of technique—coincides with its effec-

---

[2] Arnold Schoenberg (1874–1951), Austrian-born composer identified with expressionism.—EDS.

[3] Rembrandt van Rijn (1606–1669), great Dutch painter.—EDS.

tiveness as a means of showing just how a nose looks under a certain kind of light is also genuinely important. And that the lifelike delineation of the nose contributes to the evocation of the personality of the individual to whom the nose belongs is likewise important. And the manner and degree of insight into that individual's personality which Rembrandt exhibits in his portrait is important too. None of these factors can be, or ought to be, separated from the legitimate effect of the portrait as a picture pure and simple.

But once we have to do with personalities and lifelikeness we have to do with things from which we cannot keep as secure a distance for the sake of disinterestedness as we can, say, from abstract decoration. As it happens, the whole tendency of our Western painting, up until the later stages of impressionism, was to make distance and detachment on the part of the spectator as insecure as possible. It laid more of a stress than any other tradition on creating a sculpture-like, or photographic, illusion of the third dimension, on thrusting images at the eye with a lifelikeness that brought them as close as possible to their originals. Because of their sculptural vividness, Western paintings tend to be far less quiet, far more agitated and active—in short, far more explicitly dynamic—than most non-Western paintings do. And they involve the spectator to a much greater extent in the practical and actual aspects of the things they depict and represent.

We begin to wonder what we think of the people shown in Rembrandt's portraits, *as* people; whether or not we would like to walk through the terrain shown in a Corot[4] landscape; about the life stories of the burghers we see in a Steen[5] painting; we react in a less than disinterested way to the attractiveness of the models, real or ideal, of the personages in a Renaissance painting. And once we begin to do this we begin to participate in the work of art in a so-to-speak practical way. In itself this participation may not be improper, but it does become so when it begins to shut out all other factors. This it has done and does, all too often. Even though the connoisseurs have usually been able in the long run to prefer the picture of a dwarf by Velásquez[6] to that of a pretty girl by Howard Chandler Christy,[7] the enjoyment of pictorial and sculptural art in our society has tended, on every other level than that of professional connoisseurship, to be excessively "literary," and to center too much on merely technical feats of copying.

But, as I've said, every tradition of culture tends to try to correct one extreme by going to its opposite. And when our Western tradition of painting came up at last with reservations about its forthright naturalism, these quickly took the form of an equally forthright antinaturalism. These reserva-

---

[4] Jean Baptiste Camille Corot (1796–1875), French landscape painter.—Eds.

[5] Jan Steen (1626–1679), Dutch genre painter.—Eds.

[6] Diego Rodríguez de Silva y Velásquez (1599–1660), great Spanish representative of the naturalistic school of painting.—Eds.

[7] American illustrator and painter (1873–1952).—Eds.

tions started with late impressionism, and have now culminated in abstract art. I don't at all wish to be understood as saying that it all happened because some artist or artists decided it was time to curb the excesses of realistic painting, and that the main historical significance of abstract art lies in its function as an antidote to these. Nor do I wish to be understood as assuming that realistic or naturalistic art inherently needs, or ever needed, such a thing as an antidote. The motivations, conscious and unconscious, of the first modernist artists, and of present modernists as well, were and are quite different. Impressionism itself started as an effort to push naturalism further than ever before. And all through the history of art—not only in recent times—consequences have escaped intentions.

It is on a different, and more impersonal and far more general level of meaning and history that our culture has generated abstract art as an antidote. On that level this seemingly new kind of art has emerged as an epitome of almost everything that disinterested contemplation requires, and as both a challenge and a reproof to a society that exaggerates, not the necessity, but the intrinsic value of purposeful and interested activity. Abstract art comes, on this level, as a relief, an archexample of something that does not have to mean, or be useful for, anything other than itself. And it seems fitting, too, that abstract art should at present flourish most in this country. If American society is indeed given over as no other society has been to purposeful activity and material production, then it is right that it should be reminded, in extreme terms, of the essential nature of disinterested activity.

Abstract art does this in very literal and also in very imaginative ways. First, it does not exhibit the illusion or semblance of things we are already familiar with in real life; it gives us no imaginary space through which to walk with the mind's eye; no imaginary objects to desire or not desire; no imaginary people to like or dislike. We are left alone with shapes and colors. These may or may not remind us of real things; but if they do, they usually do so incidentally or accidentally—on our own responsibility as it were; and the genuine enjoyment of an abstract picture does not ordinarily depend on such resemblances.

Second, pictorial art in its highest definition is static; it tries to overcome movement in space or time. This is not to say that the eye does not wander over a painted surface, and thus travel in both space and time. When a picture presents us with an illusion of real space, there is all the more inducement for the eye to do such wandering. But ideally the whole of a picture should be taken in at a glance; its unity should be immediately evident, and the supreme quality of a picture, the highest measure of its power to move and control the visual imagination, should reside in its unity. And this is something to be grasped only in an indivisible instant of time. No expectancy is involved in the true and pertinent experience of a painting; a picture, I repeat, does not "come out" the way a story, or a poem, or a piece of music does. It's all there at once, like a sudden revelation. This "at-onceness" an abstract picture usually drives home to us with greater singleness and clarity than a representational painting does. And to apprehend this "at-onceness" demands a freedom of mind and untrammeledness of eye that constitute "at-onceness" in their own right. Those who have grown capable of experiencing this know what I mean. You are summoned and gathered into one point in the continuum of duration. The picture does this to you, willy-nilly, regardless of whatever else is on your mind: a mere glance at it creates the attitude required for its appreciation, like a stimulus that elicits an automatic response. You become all attention, which means that you become, for the moment, selfless and in a sense entirely identified with the object of your attention.

The "at-onceness" which a picture or a piece of sculpture enforces on you is not, however, single or isolated. It can be repeated in a succession of instants, in each one remaining an "at-onceness," an instant all by itself. For the cultivated eye, the picture repeats its instantaneous unity like a mouth repeating a single word.

This pinpointing of the attention, this complete liberation and concentration of it, offers what is largely a new experience to most people in our sort of society. And it is, I think, a hunger for this particular kind of experience that helps account for the growing popularity of abstract art in this country: for the way it is taking over in the art schools, the galleries, and the museums. The fact that fad and fashion are also involved does not invalidate what I say. I know that abstract art of the latest variety—that originating with painters like Pollock and Georges Mathieu[8]—has gotten associated with progressive jazz and its cultists; but what of it? That Wagner's[9] music became associated with German ultranationalism and that Wagner was Hitler's favorite composer, still doesn't detract from its sheer quality as music. That the present vogue for folk music started, back in the 1930's, among the Communists doesn't make our liking for it any the less genuine, or take anything away from folk music itself. Nor does the fact that so much gibberish gets talked and written about abstract art compromise it, just as the gibberish in which art criticism in general abounds, and abounds increasingly, doesn't compromise art in general.

One point, however, I want to make glaringly clear. Abstract art is not a special kind of art; no hard-and-fast line separates it from representational art; it is only the latest phase in the development of Western art as a whole, and almost every "technical" device of abstract painting is already to be found in the realistic painting that preceded it. Nor is it a superior kind of art. I still know of nothing in abstract painting, aside perhaps from some of the near-abstract cubist works that Picasso, Braque and Léger[10] executed between 1910 and 1914, which matches the highest achievements of the old

---

[8] French artist (1921–   ).—EDS.

[9] Wilhelm Richard Wagner (1813–1883), famed German composer of operas and other musical works.—EDS.

[10] Georges Braque (1882–1963) and Fernand Léger (1881–1955), French painters. —EDS.

masters. Abstract painting may be a purer, more quintessential form of pictorial art than the representational kind, but this does not of itself confer quality upon an abstract picture. The ratio of bad abstract painting to good is actually much greater than the ratio of bad to good representational painting. Nonetheless, the very best painting, the major painting, of our age is almost exclusively abstract. Only on the middle and lower levels of quality, on the levels below the first-rate—which is, of course, where most of the art that gets produced places itself—only there is the better painting preponderantly representational.

On the plane of culture in general, the special, unique value of abstract art, I repeat, lies in the high degree of detached contemplativeness that its appreciation requires. Contemplativeness is demanded in greater or lesser degree for the appreciation of every kind of art, but abstract art tends to present this requirement in quintessential form, at its purest, least diluted, most immediate. If abstract art—as does happen nowadays—should chance to be the first kind of pictorial art we learn to appreciate, the chances are that when we go to other kinds of pictorial art—to the old masters, say, and I hope we all do go to the old masters eventually—we shall find ourselves all the better able to enjoy them. That is, we shall be able to experience them with less intrusion of irrelevancies, therefore more fully and more intensely.

The old masters stand or fall, their pictures succeed or fail, on the same ultimate basis as do those of Mondrian or any other abstract artist. The abstract formal unity of a picture by Titian[11] is more important to its quality than what that picture images. To return to what I said about Rembrandt's portraits, the whatness of what is imaged is not unimportant —far from it—and cannot be separated, really, from the formal qualities that result from the way it is imaged. But it is a fact, in my experience, that representational paintings are essentially and most fully appreciated when the identities of what they represent are only secondarily present to our consciousness. Baudelaire[12] said he could grasp the quality of a painting by Delacroix[13] when he was still too far away from it to make out the images it contained, when it was still only a blur of colors. I think it was really on this kind of evidence that critics and connoisseurs, though they were almost always unaware of it, discriminated between the good and the bad in the past. Put to it, they more or less unconsciously dismissed from their minds the connotations of Reubens'[14] nudes when assessing and experiencing the final worth of his art. They may have remained aware of the pinkness as a *nude* pinkness, but it was a pinkness and a nudity devoid of most of their usual associations.

Abstract paintings do not confront us with such problems. Or at least the

[11] Tiziano Vecellio (1477–1576), great Italian painter.—EDS.
[12] Charles Pierre Baudelaire (1821–1867), French poet.—EDS.
[13] Ferdinand Victor Eugène Delacroix (1799–1863), French romantic painter.—EDS.
[14] Peter Paul Rubens (1577–1640), Flemish painter.—EDS.

frequenting of abstract art can train us to relegate them automatically to their proper place; and in doing this we refine our eyes for the appreciation of non-abstract art. That has been my own experience. That it is still relatively rare can be explained perhaps by the fact that most people continue to come to painting through academic art—the kind of art they see in ads and in magazines—and when and if they discover abstract art it comes as such an overwhelming experience that they tend to forget everything produced before. This is to be deplored, but it does not negate the value, actual or potential, of abstract art as an introduction to the fine arts in general, and as an introduction, too, to habits of disinterested contemplation. In this respect, the value of abstract art will, I hope, prove far greater in the future than it has yet. Not only can it confirm instead of subverting tradition; it can teach us, by example, how valuable so much in life can be made without being invested with ulterior meanings. How many people I know who have hung abstract pictures on their walls and found themselves gazing at them endlessly, and then exclaiming, "I don't know what there is in that painting, but I can't take my eyes off it." This kind of bewilderment is salutary. It does us good not to be able to explain, either to ourselves or to others, what we enjoy or love; it expands our capacity for experience.

The School of "Messy Vitality"
DENNIS FARNEY

Sometimes, by working very hard, architect Robert Venturi succeeds in designing a truly "dumb" building. This pleases him. What pleases his tongue-in-cheek nature even more, though, is a building that also looks "ugly," "expedient" and "banal."

The rest of the time he and his wife, Denise, an architect and urban planner, seem to work at enraging people. They're succeeding. Other architects, in particular, grow livid when the Venturis explain how "ugly" architecture can be beautiful and "banal" architecture interesting. Or how a billboard can be more beautiful than a tree. Or how a commercial strip, with its neon signs, utility poles and filling stations, looks "almost all right."

The Venturis really do believe all these things, which makes them about as welcome in most architectural circles as a drive-in carwash in the gardens of Versailles. Critics often pan them, and potential clients mostly ignore them. And yet their philosophy and their architecture—architecture they perversely label "ugly and ordinary" although admirers find it neither— have made them among the most influential of U.S. architects today.

For they have emerged as the most articulate champions of an architectural counterrevolution of sorts. It puts the changing tastes of a "third generation" of younger architects against the stern dictates and gee-whiz geometries of the "first generation" of Frank Lloyd Wright and his contemporaries.

SURRENDER TO VULGARITY?

The first generation, considered revolutionary in the 1920s, established the styles and the values that dominate architecture today. Now the counterrevolutionaries are railing against both. If they succeed, architects will have to stop hating, and start learning from, the existing environment of ordinary things made by ordinary people—things like McDonald's hamburger stands and A&P parking lots, Levittown and great big billboards. Indeed, the Venturi school might be called the school of "messy vitality."

The Venturis drew inspiration from one messy element of the ordinary environment, the billboard, when they recently designed a theater for the Hartford Stage Company. As the theater's front facade curves around a corner of the site, the wall peels away and veers off to become a kind of billboard without a message. The Venturis say Las Vegas inspired this feature. The building's exterior is straightforwardly decorated with a checkerboard of gray and reddish panels of porcelain enamel—except for the color, the same kind as used on White Tower hamburger stands, the Venturis point out.

But despite an occasional commission like the one in Hartford, the Venturis and their counterrevolutionary crowd may fail in their aims of changing architectural values. For arrayed against them are phalanxes of architects and architecture critics who believe the counterrevolutionaries advocate nothing less than a surrender to everything that is tasteless and vulgar in contemporary American society.

"A PIECE OF JUNK"

"No matter how long the article or clever the words," an infuriated architect wrote after reading about the mathematics building the Venturis have designed for Yale University, "the building is still a piece of junk." (The Venturis say they made the building determinedly "ordinary" by employing conventional windows and brick curtain-wall construction. To admirers, it defers to its surroundings and therefore helps tie the area together. But to critics, it's so modest that it looks no better than the kind of ordinary office buildings they can see anywhere.)

If the Venturis are avant-garde, another critic said, this is the first time the avant-garde is leading from the rear.

The objects of all this vitriol are a deceptively mild-mannered couple whose idea of a good time runs toward quiet evenings at home with their 2½-year-old son, Jimmy. Robert Venturi, who is 48 but looks a decade younger, is a scholarly man with an ironic sense of humor. Denise, 42, red-haired and pale complexioned, could strike an observer as almost frail. The observer would be making a big mistake.

For when attacked, both Venturis fight back with a fierceness that belies their gentle exteriors. Some years ago, the Washington, D.C., Fine Arts Commission rather curtly vetoed their firm's design for a major office complex as "ugly and ordinary." "The Venturis came in with a building that would have been, shall we say, unnoticed," recalls the commission's most outspoken member at the time, architect Gordon Bunshaft of Skidmore, Owings & Merrill. The Venturis have neither forgotten nor forgiven.

"When you create a fine arts commission," Denise observed recently in her correct British accent, "it's like creating an SS. All the thugs in the world are drawn to it." As for Mr. Bunshaft, her verdict was unequivocal: "a thug," she said.

"LESS IS A BORE"

Denise, a South African who had recently earned degrees in architecture at London's Architectural Association, met Bob when she came to the University of Pennsylvania to study city planning. Bob was teaching architecture there, while working in the office of Philadelphia architect Louis Kahn. Married in 1967, the Venturis collaborate on both architecture and essays. "When our work was first called 'ugly and ordinary' it was very hurting," Denise admits. But then, in a kind of verbal jujitsu, they defiantly appropriated the terms for their own rallying cry.

When they champion "ugly and ordinary" architecture, though, they're deliberately exaggerating to emphasize how their architecture differs from orthodox modern architecture. What they really mean by "ordinary," "dumb," "banal" and "expedient" buildings are relatively modest-looking buildings built by conventional methods, as opposed to spectacular-looking buildings built by revolutionary methods. What they mean by "ugly" buildings are buildings that don't look like a lot of modern architects think buildings ought to look.

The "first generation" believed the architect should try to transform the existing environment and uplift mankind through buildings that awed and inspired. It held that an "honest" building didn't rely on surface decoration for effect. Instead, it expressed itself through such purely architectural elements as its form. First-generation architect Mies van der Rohe, principal designer of New York's steel-and-glass Seagram building, was observing this code when he refined each design down to a kind of irreducible essence—spare, abstract and elegant. As he put it: "less is more."

The "second generation," which currently dominates the profession, has largely devoted itself to adapting the ideas of the first. Enter the third, and the Venturis, who say: "Less is a bore."

Mr. Venturi threw down the gauntlet in a 1966 book, *Complexity and Contradiction in Architecture*. In a sweeping historical analysis that ranged from Michelangelo to Wright, he argued that great architecture has often not been pure and simple like a modern glass skyscraper, but rather impure, complex and even ambiguous. "I am for messy vitality over obvious unity," he declared.

The Venturis argue that in casting out superficial ornamentation, architects have often been tempted to show off their talents by distorting whole buildings into giant ornaments. Not only are these "monuments" expensive, they argue, but rather sterile, too. "Decoration is cheaper" and more interesting. As connoisseurs of "messy vitality," the Venturis found inspiration for their latest book in the glitter and the honky tonk of the Las Vegas Strip.

Learning from Las Vegas argues that urban sprawl is here to stay and that architects might as well learn how to work with it. Pop artist Andy Warhol pointed the way when he painted a giant portrait of a Campbell's soup can, the Venturis suggest. He took a banal object and transformed it into art. The book argues that there is beauty, even a hidden kind of order, in Las Vegas' mélange of casinos, drive-in marriage chapels and utility poles—and a direct and valid kind of communication in neon signs that say things like "Free Aspirin Ask Us Anything."

This is more than many architects can take. "Las Vegas," says New York architect James Stewart Polshek, "is nothing more than a lesion, a sore on the landscape. As far as I'm concerned, the only thing to be learned from the ordinary environment is how to level it. This is beyond me."

AN "ASSISTANT FAILURE"

Nor has the book done much for the Venturi firm. The firm, headquartered in a rather threadbare old townhouse here [Philadelphia], expects to gross little more than $275,000 this year. As partners, the Venturis and John Rauch pay themselves base annual salaries of $25,000 apiece, less than they could make working anonymously for someone else.

"Don't feel too bad," Mr. Rauch consoled Mr. Venturi on a particularly dark day. "You're only a failure. I'm an assistant failure."

But failure is emphatically not the verdict of a small but forceful band of Venturi admirers. "The Venturis have the profession on the run," flatly declares Robert Stern, a New York architect and writer on architecture. "They're the most influential architects practicing in the U.S. What they've done is to free architects to solve each problem as it comes along, rather than to fit it obsessively into some preconceived style."

Another champion is Vincent Scully, the Yale architectural historian and author. He served on a jury that unanimously selected the Venturi and Rauch design for the contemplated Yale mathematics building over 478 other entries. Most other architects, Mr. Scully commented, seemed to be "knocking themselves out with great heroic gestures." In contrast, he called the winning design "absolutely straightforward and pleasingly understated."

Like Dave Brubeck, the Venturis "take ordinary things and build on them," explains architect Charles Moore, whose own work often follows the same approach. Were the Venturis to design, say, a Holiday Inn, "their design would look enough like a Holiday Inn so that whatever emotions Holiday Inns are supposed to stir would be stirred. But it would look enough unlike it so that the building would be making a commentary. Elements would be turned upside down or sideways, or they'd be surprisingly large, so that for the first time you'd notice them."

UGLY AND BEAUTIFUL

This illustration is a good deal easier to understand than the Venturis themselves when they plunge into the subtleties of how ugly can be beautiful. Which they did a few years ago when they designed a beach house in New Jersey.

The site was a drab world of sand, houses and utility poles. A pretty house would merely emphasize the drabness, the Venturis reasoned. So they designed a "kind of bold little ugly banal box." In a paradoxical kind of way, an ugly house in an ugly landscape made the ugly landscape look less ugly, and the ugly house came out looking, well, almost pretty—or so the Venturis reasoned.

Put it another way, one of them explained to an interviewer. The house is "ordinary and extraordinary at the same time. It is like the landscape and not like the landscape, ugly and beautiful. It is the tension between these opposites. We are saying it is like everything else; yet it isn't like everything else, we admit that. It is like everything else in the way that the pop artists make something like a Campbell's soup can. It is like, but it isn't like. See what I mean?"

In a word, no. At least, this is the reaction of some critics, who wonder: Are the Venturis putting us on? Architecture critic Peter Blake, for one, has conceded that Mr. Venturi can be "a very talented architect." But he suspected a big put-on in the Venturis' solemn justifications for things that, in his view, are just plain dumb. Among them is a feature of the house Mr. Venturi designed for his mother—a "nowhere stair" that, predictably enough, goes nowhere.

The stairway goes from the floor to the ceiling of an upstairs room—a "whimsical" touch, Mr. Venturi thinks. Actually, it does serve a purpose when it's time to wash a big clerestory window or paint the wall. And in any event it is a minor feature of a house that is perhaps the most explicitly "complex and contradictory" of any Mr. Venturi has designed.

The outside facade of the Venturi house is a symmetrical rectangle that has been distorted—pushed and pulled out of shape—by the asymmetrical rooms and features inside. Similarly, the fireplace distorts the main stairway that runs behind it at one point, while the stairway distorts the fireplace at another.

Some of the Venturi buildings don't look as bad as the Venturis make them sound, critics concede, and partner John Rauch admits that "we turn a lot of people off with our rhetoric." He goes on: "Ugly and ordinary —that's another academic conceit that has been a mistake."

"Bob and Denise both have academic backgrounds, and they both have a tendency to want to record their innovations for posterity," he says. "But I don't want posterity to remember our innovations. I want posterity to remember us as a large and successful and prosperous firm."

And will this happen? "We ran out in front of the ranks and planted a flag," Mr. Rauch says. "Now we'll have to wait for the ranks to catch up."

Chicago's Stunning Architecture
PAUL GOLDBERGER

"It is a milestone of sorts to be invited from the provinces to America's first city of architecture."

That is how a prominent New York architect began an address to Chicago architects not long ago, and his choice of words underscored how much this city's accomplishments in modern architecture have impressed the world and, indeed, evoked considerable envy in that larger city on the East Coast.

Chicago is the city of Louis Sullivan, Frank Lloyd Wright and John Welborn Root. It is the city of Daniel Burnham and the nation's first attempt at large-scale urban planning. And it is the city of Mies van der Rohe; Skidmore, Owings & Merrill; and the other more recent masters of the glass and steel tower.

It is also a city of passionate architectural interests. The average man on the street here can rattle off architects' names in a way that would bewilder his counterparts in other cities. James I. Freed, the New York architect who moved here last year to head the Mies van der Rohe–designed architecture school at the Illinois Institute of Technology, said, "Buildings are for Chicagoans what the 19th-century novel was to Parisians—everybody can, at least up to a point, talk intelligently about them."

A SINGLE STYLE

But, for all its brilliance, the 19th-century French novel was essentially a single style, and so is architecture in Chicago. This is a city defined by the austere towers of Mies van der Rohe and the newer, bolder glass structures of Skidmore, Owings & Merrill and followers. It is a place of remarkable, even stunning, architectural quality—glass towers as good as the Mies-designed Seagram building, the pride of Park Avenue in New York, are common sights here.

Chicagoans do not theorize about their architecture. But Bruce Graham, the partner in Skidmore, Owings & Merrill who designed both the Sears Tower and the John Hancock Building, said, "In the heartland we believe in a direct relationship between work and thought. We make real buildings; we are not abstract about life, as they are in New York."

In one sense this is nothing new. In the early days of the skyscraper, around the turn of the century, Chicago was making straightforward, structurally honest buildings by such designers as Sullivan and Root that were at the vanguards of modern design, while New York, never willing to be either so direct or so singleminded, was decorating its skyscrapers with historical allusions from dozens of different periods.

TREMENDOUS EFFECT

Lately, however, that quality has come under fire from a number of critics who suggest that it comes at the price of diversity. Earlier this year, a major exhibition at the Institute of Contemporary Art, "100 Years of Architecture in Chicago," celebrated the city's better-known architectural accomplishments. At the same time, a "counter show" was mounted by a group of dissident architects who argued that the structural rationalism of the so-called "Chicago School" was too narrow an architecture.

But if the Miesian era is coming to a close and if Chicago is breaking out of its glass box into a greater diversity, that is another matter. The point right now is that this sort of architecture has had a tremendous effect on this city.

It is not exaggeration to say that, on the average, Chicago has the best downtown commercial buildings in the nation. The fact that they are all much the same in appearance, and are generally products of an ideology that has traditionally been taken as gospel in this city, does not disturb Chicago's partisans. To them, a city is judged by what it builds—and only by that.

But diversity is the price for this quality. It makes Chicago the architectural opposite of New York, a city of dozens of different philosophies, building styles and general attitudes about architecture, a city of talkers, as much as builders. Chicago, on the other hand, prides itself on being tough, pragmatic, and successful. It likes to see itself as a city whose architects like to build before they talk.

The best New York architects build very little on their home turf. Major decisions are left to real-estate developers who tend to hire dull commercial firms.

In Chicago, on the other hand, the tradition of building well in a single style is so strong that the city government itself commissioned Jacques Brownson of C. F. Murphy Associates, a firm of the Miesian school, to design the Civic Center in 1965, a much-acclaimed building with a Picasso sculpture in front.

The Federal Government, at around the same time it was building a mediocre, decorated cracker-box court house on New York's Foley Square, hired Mies van der Rohe himself to design Chicago's Federal Center.

More important, standards of even developer-built buildings are higher here.

"In Chicago, developers wouldn't think of going to anybody but the top firms for a major downtown building," said John Burgee, a former Chicago architect who is now in New York as a partner in the firm of Johnson/Burgee.

There are other comparisons similar to the two Federal projects in the two cities. New York has for years been getting some of the most mediocre luxury housing in the world on the Upper East Side, the result in part of high labor costs but due also to the insistence of developers on adhering to the white-brick Third Avenue formula. Chicago, in 1971, saw completion of Lake Point Tower, a 70-story curved-glass form designed by Schipporeit & Heinreich and based on a sketch by Mies van der Rohe from the 1920's and one of the most daring pieces of commercial housing design in the country.

Literature

The Macbeth Murder Mystery
JAMES THURBER

"It was a stupid mistake to make," said the American woman I had met at my hotel in the English lake country, "but it was on the counter with the other Penguin books—the little sixpenny ones, you know, with the paper covers—and I supposed of course. it was a detective story. All the others were detective stories. I'd read all the others, so I bought this one without really looking at it carefully. You can imagine how mad I was when I found it was Shakespeare." I murmured something sympathetically. "I don't see why the Penguin-books people had to get out Shakespeare plays in the same size and everything as the detective stories," went on my companion. "I think they have different-colored jackets," I said. "Well, I didn't notice that," she said. "Anyway, I got real comfy in bed that night and all ready to read a good mystery story and here I had *The Tragedy of Macbeth*—a book for high-school students. Like *Ivanhoe*,"[1] "Or *Lorna Doone*,"[2] I said. "Exactly," said the American lady. "And I was just crazy for a good Agatha Christie,[3] or something. Hercule Poirot is my favorite detective." "Is he the rabbity one?" I asked, "Oh, no," said my crime-fiction expert. "He's the Belgian one. You're thinking of Mr. Pinkerton, the one that helps Inspector Bull.[4] He's good, too."

Over her second cup of tea my companion began to tell the plot of a detective story that had fooled her completely—it seems it was the old family doctor all the time. But I cut in on her. "Tell me," I said. "Did you read *Macbeth*?" "I *had* to read it," she said. "There wasn't a scrap of anything else to read in the whole room." "Did you like it?" I asked. "No, I did not," she said, decisively. "In the first place, I don't think for a moment that Macbeth did it." I looked at her blankly. "Did what?" I asked. "I don't think for a moment that he killed the King," she said. "I don't think the Macbeth woman was mixed up in it, either. You suspect them the most, of course, but those are the ones that are never guilty—or shouldn't be, anyway." "I'm afraid," I began, "that I—" "But

---

[1] *Ivanhoe* (1819), a novel by Sir Walter Scott.—EDS.

[2] *Lorna Doone, A Romance of Exmoor* (1869), a romantic novel by R. D. Blackmore. —EDS.

[3] Agatha Christie (1890–1976), prolific British author of detective novels; Hercule Poirot is the brilliant detective in a number of her books.—EDS.

[4] Mr. Evan Pinkerton and Inspector J. Humphrey Bull are characters in *The Hammersmith Murders* by David Frome.—EDS.

don't you see?" said the American lady. "It would spoil everything if you could figure out right away who did it. Shakespeare was too smart for that. I've read that people never *have* figured out *Hamlet*, so it isn't likely Shakespeare would have made *Macbeth* as simple as it seems." I thought this over while I filled my pipe. "Who do you suspect?" I asked, suddenly. "Macduff," she said, promptly. "Good God!" I whispered, softly.

"Oh Macduff did it, all right," said the murder specialist. "Hercule Poirot would have got him easily." "How did you figure it out?" I demanded. "Well," she said, "I didn't right away. At first I suspected Banquo. And then, of course, he was the second person killed. That was good right in there, that part. The person you suspect of the first murder should always be the second victim." "Is that so?" I murmured. "Oh, yes," said my informant. "They have to keep surprising you. Well, after the second murder I didn't know *who* the killer was for a while." "How about Malcolm and Donalbain, the King's sons?" I asked. "As I remember it, they fled right after the first murder. That looks suspicious." "Too suspicious," said the American lady. "Much too suspicious. When they flee, they're never guilty. You can count on that." "I believe," I said, "I'll have a brandy," and I summoned the waiter. My companion leaned toward me, her eyes bright, her teacup quivering. "Do you know who discovered Duncan's body?" she demanded. I said I was sorry, but I had forgotten. "Macduff discovers it," she said, slipping into the historical present. "Then he comes running downstairs and shouts, 'Confusion has broke open the Lord's anointed temple' and 'Sacrilegious murder has made his masterpiece' and on and on like that." The good lady tapped me on the knee. "All that stuff was rehearsed," she said. "You wouldn't say a lot of stuff like that, offhand, would you—if you had found a body?" She fixed me with a glittering eye. "I—" I began. "You're right!" she said. "You wouldn't! Unless you had practiced it in advance. 'My God, there's a body in here!' is what an innocent man would say." She sat back with a confident glare.

I thought for a while. "But what do you make of the Third Murderer?" I asked. "You know, the Third Murderer has puzzled *Macbeth* scholars for three hundred years." "That's because they never thought of Macduff," said the American lady. "It was Macduff, I'm certain. You couldn't have one of the victims murdered by two ordinary thugs—the murderer always has to be somebody important." "But what about the banquet scene?" I asked, after a moment. "How do you account for Macbeth's guilty actions there, when Banquo's ghost came in and sat in his chair?" The lady leaned forward and tapped me on the knee again. "There wasn't any ghost," she said. "A big, strong man like that doesn't go around seeing ghosts—especially in a brightly lighted banquet hall with dozens of people around. Macbeth was *shielding somebody!*" "Who was he shielding?" I asked. "Mrs. Macbeth, of course," she said. "He thought she did it and he was going to take the rap himself. The husband always does that when the wife is suspected." "But what," I demanded, "about the sleepwalking scene, then?" "The same thing, only the other way around," said my companion. "That time *she* was shielding *him*. She wasn't asleep at all. Do you remember where it says, 'Enter Lady Macbeth with a taper'?" "Yes," I said. "Well, people who walk in their sleep *never carry lights!*" said my fellow-traveler. "They have a second sight. Did you ever hear of a sleep-walker carrying a light?" "No," I said, "I never did." "Well, then, she wasn't asleep. She was acting guilty to shield Macbeth." "I think," I said "I'll have another brandy," and I called the waiter. When he brought it, I drank it rapidly and rose to go. "I believe," I said, "that you have got hold of something. Would you lend me that *Macbeth*? I'd like to look it over tonight. I don't feel, somehow, as if I'd ever really read it." "I'll get it for you," she said. "But you'll find that I am right."

I read the play over carefully that night, and the next morning, after breakfast, I sought out the American woman. She was on the putting green, and I came up behind her silently and took her arm. She gave an exclamation. "Could I see you alone?" I asked, in a low voice. She nodded cautiously and followed me to a secluded spot. "You've found out something?" she breathed. "I've found out," I said, triumphantly, "the name of the murderer!" "You mean it wasn't Macduff?" she said. "Macduff is as innocent of those murders," I said, "as Macbeth and the Macbeth woman." I opened the copy of the play, which I had with me, and turned to Act II, Scene 2. "Here," I said, "you will see where Lady Macbeth says, 'I laid their daggers ready. He could not miss 'em. Had he not resembled my father as he slept, I had done it.' Do you see?" "No," said the American woman, bluntly, "I don't." "But it's simple!" I exclaimed. "I wonder I didn't see it years ago. The reason Duncan resembled Lady Macbeth's father as he slept is that *it actually was her father!*" "Good God!" breathed my companion, softly. "Lady Macbeth's father killed the King," I said, "and, hearing someone coming, thrust the body under the bed and crawled into the bed himself." "But," said the lady, "you can't have a murderer who only appears in the story once. You can't have that." "I know that," I said, and I turned to Act II, Scene 4. "It says here, 'Enter Ross with an old Man.' Now, that old man is never identified and it is my contention he was old Mr. Macbeth, whose ambition it was to make his daughter Queen. There you have your motive." "But even then," cried the American lady, "he's still a minor character!" "Not," I said, gleefully, "when you realize that he was also *one of the weird sisters in disguise!*" "You mean one of the three witches?" "Precisely," I said. "Listen to this speech of the old man's. 'On Tuesday last, a falcon towering in her pride of place, was by a mousing owl hawk'd at and kill'd.' Who does that sound like?" "It sounds like the way the three witches talk," said my companion, reluctantly. "Precisely!" I said again. "Well," said the American woman, "maybe you're right, but—" "I'm sure I am," I said. "And do you know what I'm going to do now?" "No," she said. "What?" "Buy a copy of *Hamlet*," I said, "and solve *that!*" My companion's eye brightened.

"Then," she said, "you don't think Hamlet did it?" "I am," I said, "absolutely positive he didn't." "But who," she demanded, "do you suspect?" I looked at her cryptically. "Everybody," I said, and disappeared into a small grove of trees as silently as I had come.

Ars Poetica
ARCHIBALD MAC LEISH

A poem should be palpable and mute
As a globed fruit

Dumb
As old medallions to the thumb

Silent as the sleeve-worn stone
Of casement ledges where the moss has grown—

A poem should be wordless
As the flight of birds

A poem should be motionless in time
As the moon climbs

Leaving, as the moon releases
Twig by twig the night-entangled trees,

Leaving, as the moon behind the winter leaves,
Memory by memory the mind—

A poem should be motionless in time
As the moon climbs

A poem should be equal to:
Not true

For all the history of grief
An empty doorway and a maple leaf

For love
The leaning grasses and two lights above the sea—

A poem should not mean
But be.

Sonnet 55
WILLIAM SHAKESPEARE

Not marble, nor the gilded monuments
Of princes, shall outlive this powerful rhyme;
But you shall shine more bright in these contents
Than unswept stone, besmeared with sluttish time.[1]
When wasteful war shall statues overturn,
And broils[2] root out the work of masonry,
Nor Mars his[3] sword nor war's quick fire shall burn
The living record of your memory.
Gainst death and all-oblivious enmity[4]
Shall you pace forth; your praise shall still find room
Even in the eyes of all posterity
That wear this world out to the ending doom.[5]
So, till the judgment that yourself arise,[6]
You live in this, and dwell in lovers' eyes.

The Use of Poetry
HAROLD BLOOM

In a time when nearly every other activity of the mind has suffered a demystification or a de-idealization, the writing (and reading) of poetry has retained a curious prestige of idealism. Curious because the nature of poetry, during the last two hundred years or so, may have changed in ways we scarcely begin to apprehend.

Poetry from Homer through Alexander Pope (who died in 1744) had a subject matter, in the characters and actions of men and women clearly distinct from the poet who observed them, and who described and sometimes judged them.

But from 1744 or so to the present day the best poetry had internalized its subject matter, particularly in the mode of Wordsworth after 1798. Wordsworth had no true subject except his own subjective nature, and very nearly all significant poetry since Wordsworth, even by American poets, has repeated Wordsworth's inward turning.

---

[1] Than in a stone effigy or monument, worn away by time and covered with dust. —Eds.

[2] Disturbances or tumults.—Eds.

[3] *Mars his*—Mars's.—Eds.

[4] The enmity of oblivion; i.e., of being forgotten.—Eds.

[5] The Day of Judgment.—Eds.

[6] Until you rise from the dead on Judgment Day.—Eds.

This no longer seems to be a question of any individual poet's choice, but evidently is a necessity, perhaps a blight of the broad movement that we see now can be called Romanticism *or* Modernism, since increasingly the latter would appear to have been only an extension of the former.

What can be the use of a poetry that has no true subject except the poet's own selfhood? The traditional use of poetry in the Western world has been instruction through delight, where teaching has meant the common truths or common deceptions of a societal tradition, and where esthetic pleasure has meant a fulfillment of expectations founded upon past joys of the same design.

But an individual psyche has its own accidents, which it needs to call truths, and its own necessity for self-recognition, which requires the pleasures of originality, even if those pleasures depend upon a kind of lying against time, and against the achievements of the past. The use of such a poetry demands to be seen in a de-idealized way, if it is to be seen more truly.

The philosopher of modern poetry is the Neapolitan rhetorician Giambattista Vico, who died in 1744, the same year as the poet Pope.

In his *New Science* (1725), Vico strikingly de-idealized the origin and purpose of poetry. Vico believed that the life of our primitive ancestors was itself what he termed "a severe poem."

These giants, through the force of a cruel imagination, defended themselves against nature, the gods, and one another by metaphoric language, with which they "divinated," that is, at once they sought to become immortal gods and also to ward off potential and future dangers from their own lives. For them, the function of poetry was not to liberate, but to define, limit, and so defend the self against everything that might destroy it.

This Vichian or de-idealizing view of poetry is the truth about all poetry, in my judgment, but particularly modern poetry.

The use of poetry, for the reader as for the poet, is at a profound level an instruction in defense. Poetry teaches a reader the necessity of interpretation, and interpretation is, to cite the other great philosopher of modern poetry, Nietzsche, the exercise of the will-to-power over a text.

The strong American poets—Emerson, Whitman, Dickinson, Frost, Stevens, Hart Crane[1]—and the strongest of our contemporaries—Robert Penn Warren, Elizabeth Bishop, A. R. Ammons, and John Ashbery—can give their American readers the best of pragmatic aids in the self-reliance of a psychic self-defense.

In the struggle of the reader both with and against a strong poem, more than an interpretation of a poem becomes the prize. What instruction is

---

[1] Ralph Waldo Emerson (1803–1882); Walt Whitman (1819–1892); Emily Dickinson (1830–1886); Robert Frost (1874–1963); Wallace Stevens (1879–1955); Hart Crane (1899–1932).—Eds.

more valuable than that which shows us how to distinguish real from illusory dangers to the self's survival, and how to ward off the real menaces?

On Reading a Poem
WILLIAM M. GIBSON

You have asked me how I read a poem. I take it you mean how do I as an individual come to understand a particular poem rather than how I think poems should be taught. But I shan't try to separate the two questions because I have been an amateur of poetry and a teacher of literature too long to be able to make useful distinctions between the two.

No theory without particulars. I will answer by talking about a poem of Emily Dickinson, of the "flood" year 1862, number 307 in Thomas Johnson's edition. (One can't get anywhere, of course, without the poet's own text accurately printed.) Poem 307[1] goes this way:

> The One who could repeat the Summer day—
> Were greater than itself—though He
> Minutest of Mankind should be—
>
> And He—could reproduce the Sun—
> At period of going down—
> Tha Lingering—and the Stain—I mean—
>
> When Orient have been outgrown—
> And Occident—become Unknown—
> His Name—remain—

My first answer to your question is that Poem 307 must be read aloud as if it were a piece of music, directly and simply because the tone of the poem is colloquial, but also with a musician's awareness of the subtle, beautiful chiming of *Lingering, Stain, mean, Name,* and *remain.* As one reads the lines aloud, the mood of condition-contrary-to-fact, or potentiality emerges, as well, so that the compressed last line comes to mean, "His, the painter's, name would remain, a long time." Thus one must read with some understanding of the syntax—and in Dickinson an exact sense of the words—in order to understand her short-hand economies. One must read also to discover, consciously or unconsciously, how the phrases and clauses,

---

[1] Reprinted by permission of the publishers and the Trustees of Amherst College from Thomas H. Johnson (ed.), *The Poems of Emily Dickinson,* Cambridge, Mass.: The Belknap Press of Harvard University Press. Copyright 1951, 1955 by the President and Fellows of Harvard College.

or the parts of the poem whatever they may be, work together to make an emotionally and intellectually satisfying whole. So that one regards the poem as a construct, quite as finely balanced and assembled as a 19th-century clipper ship or an Alexander Calder mobile of our own time. Seen in its two parts, the poet asserts: "The person who could film and reshow a summer day would be as great as the day itself; and [may mean *an*, or *if*] were he to paint the afterglow of the sunset, when east and west have gone dark, his name would last." The last line is plainly the rounding off of the construct, as it completes the sense of the second "if" statement after parenthetical phrases and clauses that create suspense. Part 2 is twice as long as Part 1. The exact sound reversal of *Name—(re)main* underlines the finality of the slant rhyme; and—one must still be reading aloud—one's ear with some help from the eye will record an inverted triangle pattern: the first line is five feet long, the next seven lines are four feet, and the last line concludes with two.

Since Dickinson believes that poets "tell all the truth but tell it slant," which is to say metaphorically, one will observe that the basic metaphor is embedded in the two key verbs: to "repeat the Summer day" and to "reproduce the Sun"—variants on the ancient poetic doctrine of "imitation" or of holding up the mirror to nature.

So far I have confined the questions mostly to the elements of the poem itself. But clearly, the more one has read of Dickinson's poetry, all 1775 poems, the better one is prepared to read a particular poem. Poem 307, the reader of Dickinson rather quickly recognizes, is one of many poems having to do with summer and with poetry itself. In Poem 505, she avers that she would not choose to be a painter, or a musician, or especially a poet—only to confess she would feel richly dowered *if* she had the "art to stun myself/With bolts of melody." So too in Poem 307 she dramatizes the difficult aim of the poet, to translate the beauty of the natural world into poetry. But Poem 308,[2] which is closely linked to 307 by time of composition and by subject, takes a different tone entirely:

> I send Two Sunsets—
> Day and I—in competition ran—
> I finished Two—and several Stars—
> While He—was making One—
>
> His own was ampler—but as I
> Was saying to a friend—
> Mine—is the more convenient
> To Carry in the Hand—

[2] From Thomas H. Johnson (ed.), *The Poems of Emily Dickinson.* Reprinted by permission of Little, Brown and Co. Copyright 1914, 1942 by Martha Dickinson Bianchi. Also by permission of the publishers, The Belknap Press of Harvard University Press, and the Trustees of Amherst College. Copyright 1951, 1955 by the President and Fellows of Harvard College.

Dickinson gives this verse the casual tone of a letter enclosing Poem 307 presumably; but she is witty and boastful rather than contemplative and wishful.

Still another kind of question, as difficult to answer as it is rewarding when properly answered, is what does one's knowledge of Dickinson's life add to one's feelings about the poem? For other Dickinson poems, much; for this poem, only a little, in that the reference to "Minutest of Mankind" is a glance by the poet at her own slight figure and small stature. This is of a piece in another poem with her observing her own "narrow hands" which are yet capable, she says, of "gathering Paradise." Still another possibly useful question may involve analogy or source. So, for Poem 308 and *her* sunset, which was more convenient to carry in her hand, she took her idea, it seems probable, from one of Davy Crockett's fabulous adventures on a frigid winter morning. Finding the January sun frozen fast in sweat on its axis at the top of Daybreak Hill, Crockett breaks it loose with the help of hot bear oil, and walks home whistling a tune and "introducin' people to the fresh daylight with a piece of sunrise in my pocket."

I suppose, finally, that in reading this concentrated small poem one may add still further to its dimensions by comparing it to poems in the ancient tradition of the "makers" who hope to achieve immortality in their verse. Or one can show, through this and other of her poems, that Dickinson as transcendentalist and romantic believes that the true poets possess divine power: to "repeat the Summer day" is the prerogative of a god. But it is in its particular images and metaphors, its subtle orchestration of sounds, its elegant structure, and its passionate aspiration that the poem moves me most.

Though Poem 307 is not one of the very best of Dickinson's poems, it is good and characteristic. It also embodies one of her most striking poetic traits—the serious pun, in the manner of Shakespeare, if we see and hear "reproduce . . . Sun" as "reproduce . . . son" (an old quibble in the history of poetry) though Dickinson may not have intended it or been conscious of it.

Nat Pine

GILBERT MILLSTEIN

Nat Pine, the bookseller, is a small darling man of 84, of enormous dignity and serenity and quiet and vigor (one would take him for no more than 65) whose voice sounds like the dry rustling of good paper and the turning of pages. I have done business with him, if you can call it that, for 30 years and I am drawn, irresistibly, to think of him as an article of *vertu*—handset letterpress as opposed to pasted-up phototype. When he talks, it is, so to say, in Caslon or Bodoni or Goudy or Cheltenham, all classic, handsome type faces set in wide margins, with lots of air between the lines. His face is almost unlined (the Great Printer found few corrections to make and no deletions) and he is altogether a rare first edition in mint condition. Octavo. Unpaged. Morocco. Perfect condition.

Nat Pine has been in the book business for 70 years, and I am only another to pay him homage. There is hardly an American writer of any note whom Pine has not known or who has not known him. He has greatly augmented their libraries at low prices, and, he says, in a nakedly reverential way, they have greatly enlarged his life at no expense at all. Saul Bellow to Walter Lippmann. Norman Mailer to Christopher Morley, Isaac Bashevis Singer to Gorham Munson. When the New School for Social Research tried to evict him three years ago in taking over the building in which his shop is located, there was such an uproar in the literary world that the New School turned pale, reversed itself, let him stay and threw a party in the basement, all the while congratulating itself on preserving a cultural resource.

Pine is one of the owners of the Dauber & Pine Bookshops, Inc., on lower Fifth Avenue, across 12th Street from the First Presbyterian Church, which is only 47 years older than Pine and equally well preserved. (The other owner is Murray Dauber, the 67-year-old son of Pine's original partner who reads Thucydides when he isn't selling him.) Actually, there is only one Dauber & Pine bookshop. There once were two over on Fourth Avenue, which used to be the Athens of the secondhand-book business, but the partners, in their dreamy way, never got around to calling themselves anything else when they moved over to Fifth Avenue half a century ago last Christmas.

There are probably only half a dozen or so bookstores like Dauber & Pine left in New York City and, I will swear, no booksellers of the age, tenacity or enthusiasm of Nat Pine. There are about 200,000 books of all ages in the store, about a third of them on the street level (Pine's domain), the remainder in the basement (Dauber's domain). If there is a cataloguing system, I don't know what it is, but either man can lay a hand on anything at any time, however exotic or covered with dust. The place has a marvelous feeling of *brown*. Brooks Atkinson, the drama critic of the *Times* for so many years, once wrote of Dauber & Pine, "It is more bookish than a publisher's office or a writer's study, for it does not manufacture books, which is the seamy side of the scribbling trade. It esteems books for what they are worth."

Not long ago, having received the 695th catalogue put out by the store (who would have imagined so many?), I went around to see Pine to ask him why in God's name he was still at it at his age. He was elliptical, lyrical, divagational. (He told me, among many other things, that his wife and mother of their only child, a daughter, has written 25 books *and* taught school.) Three days after he landed at Ellis Island early in the century (his father didn't fancy fighting in the Russo-Japanese war) he wandered into a bookstore on Fourth Avenue, a bookstore owned by an uncle, Peter Stammer. A few years later, he wandered out and opened one of his own, also on Fourth Avenue. And, a few years after that, he sold the store and wandered out to Chicago, where he wandered into another bookstore and went to work. He uses the word "wander" a good deal. From Chicago he wandered into a bookstore in San Francisco, and from there he wandered back to Fourth Avenue and wandered into the bookstore of Sam Dauber on Fourth Avenue.

"Until then," Pine told me, "I had no *zitzfleisch*. Then I got it. Sam had had a previous miserable experience with Peter Stammer and so we had the same things to commiserate over. There were conversations, discussions, and finally, inevitably, he said, 'Go into business with me.' I suppose he thought a partner couldn't do much harm." But why books, I persisted. "Is there anything else?" Pine asked. He frequently answers a question with a question, in the Talmudic way and all in the elusive accent of an announcer for the BBC.

"Come on Nat," I said. "There's more to it than that." "Well," he said, "when you get into a profession such as books that are the means of life and civilization . . ." "Yes," I said, "go on." "Without the printed word we couldn't have possibly arrived at this civilization, this very life. It is my bloodstream, part of me, my very existence and, as I go on from day to day . . ."

"Yes?" He grew almost shy. "This subject can be elaborated on endlessly, but I'm not writing an essay. These people—writers, people who buy books—are of such a nature that life means a great deal more just meeting them. They are of a special nature—knowledgeable, kind, understanding, thinking of today, yesterday, tomorrow." Excessive? "No, I think I'm correct. I attribute my well being at this age to having been among books all my life. In any other profession, I would not be as actively engaged in the profession of living. I still have the joy, the pleasure, the thrill of meeting people who write and becoming part of their lives. . . ."

And then, *l'envoi*: "I would do it all over again. All over again. All over again. For $3 a week, which I got on my first job from an uncle by marriage. Yes."

The Keys to Dreamland[1]

NORTHROP FRYE

Suppose you're walking down the street of a North American city. All around you is a highly artificial society, but you don't think of it as artificial: you're so accustomed to it that you think of it as natural. But

[1] Chapter 4 in *The Educated Imagination*, 1964.

suppose your imagination plays a little trick on you of a kind that it often does play, and you suddenly feel like a complete outsider, someone who's just blown in from Mars on a flying saucer. Instantly you see how conventionalized everything is: the clothes, the shop windows, the movement of the cars in traffic, the cropped hair and shaved faces of the men, the red lips and blue eyelids that women put on because they want to conventionalize their faces, or "look nice," as they say, which means the same thing. All this convention is pressing toward uniformity or likeness. To be outside the convention makes a person look queer, or, if he's driving a car, a menace to life and limb. The only exceptions are people who have decided to conform to different conventions, like nuns or beatniks. There's clearly a strong force making toward conformity in society, so strong that it seems to have something to do with the stability of society itself. In ordinary life even the most splendid things we can think of, goodness and truth and beauty, all mean essentially what we're accustomed to. As I hinted just now in speaking of female makeup, most of our ideas of beauty are pure convention, and even truth has been defined as whatever doesn't disturb the pattern of what we already know.

When we move on to literature, we again find conventions, but this time we notice that they are conventions, because we're not so used to them. These conventions seem to have something to do with making literature as unlike life as possible. Chaucer represents people as making up stories in ten-syllable couplets. Shakespeare uses dramatic conventions, which means, for instance, that Iago has to smash Othello's marriage and dreams of future happiness and get him ready to murder his wife in a few minutes. Milton has two nudes in a garden haranguing each other in set speeches beginning with such lines as "Daughter of God and Man, immortal Eve"—Eve being Adam's daughter because she's just been extracted from his ribcase. Almost every story we read demands that we accept as fact something that we know to be nonsense: that good people always win, especially in love; that murders are complicated and ingenious puzzles to be solved by logic, and so on. It isn't only popular literature that demands this: more highbrow stories are apt to be more ironic, but irony has its conventions too. If we go further back into literature, we run into such conventions as the king's rash promise, the enraged cuckold, the cruel mistress of love poetry—never anything that we or any other time would recognize as the normal behavior of adult people, only the maddened ethics of fairyland.

Even the details of literature are equally perverse. Literature is a world where phoenixes and unicorns are quite as important as horses and dogs—and in literature some of the horses talk, like the ones in *Gulliver's Travels*. A random example is calling Shakespeare the "swan of Avon"—he was called that by Ben Jonson. The town of Stratford, Ontario, keeps swans in its river partly as a literary allusion. Poets of Shakespeare's day hated to admit that they were writing words on a page: they always insisted that they were producing music. In pastoral poetry they might be playing a flute (or more accurately an oboe), but every other kind of poetic effort was called song, with a harp, a lyre or a lute in the background, depending on how highbrow the song was. Singing suggests birds, and so for their typical songbird and emblem of themselves, the poets chose the swan, a bird that can't sing. Because it can't sing, they made up a legend that it sang once before death, when nobody was listening. But Shakespeare didn't burst into song before his death: he wrote two plays a year until he'd made enough money to retire, and spent the last five years of his life counting his take.

So however useful literature may be in improving one's imagination or vocabulary, it would be the wildest kind of pedantry to use it directly as a guide to life. Perhaps here we see one reason why the poet is not only very seldom a person one would turn to for insight into the state of the world, but often seems even more gullible and simple-minded than the rest of us. For the poet, the particular literary conventions he adopts are likely to become, for him, facts of life. If he finds that the kind of writing he's best at has a good deal to do with fairies, like Yeats, or a white goddess, like Graves, or a life-force, like Bernard Shaw, or episcopal sermons, like T. S. Eliot, or bullfights, like Hemingway, or exasperation at social hypocrisies, as with the so-called angry school, these things are apt to take on a reality for him that seems badly out of proportion to his contemporaries. His life may imitate literature in a way that may warp or even destroy his social personality, as Byron wore himself out at thirty-four with the strain of being Byronic. Life and literature, then, are both conventionalized, and of the conventions of literature about all we can say is that they don't much resemble the conditions of life. It's when two sets of conventions collide that we realize how different they are.

In fact, whenever literature gets too probable, too much like life, some self-defeating process, some mysterious law of diminishing returns, seems to set in. There's a vivid and expertly written novel by H. G. Wells called *Kipps*, about a lower-middle-class, inarticulate, very likeable Cockney, the kind of character we often find in Dickens. Kipps is carefully studied: he never says anything that a man like Kipps wouldn't say; he never sounds the "h" in home or head; nothing he does is out of line with what we expect such a person to be like. It's an admirable novel, well worth reading, and yet I have a nagging feeling that there's some inner secret in bringing him completely to life that Dickens would have and that Wells doesn't have. All right, then, what would Dickens have done? Well, one of the things that Dickens often does do is write *badly*. He might have given Kipps sentimental speeches and false heroics and all sorts of inappropriate verbiage to say; and some readers would have clucked and tut-tutted over these passages and explained to each other how bad Dickens's taste was and how uncertain his hold on character could be. Perhaps they'd be right too. But we'd have had Kipps a few times the way he'd look to himself or the way he'd sometimes wish he could be: that's part of his reality, and the effect would remain with us however much we disapproved of it. Whether I'm right about this book or not, and I'm not at all sure I am, I think my general principle is right. What we'd never see except in a book is often what we go to books to find. Whatever is completely lifelike in literature is a bit of a laboratory specimen there. To bring anything really to life in literature we can't be lifelike: we have to be literaturelike.

The same thing is true even of the use of language. We're often taught that prose is the language of ordinary speech, which is usually true in literature. But in ordinary life prose is no more the language of ordinary speech than one's Sunday suit is a bathing suit. The people who actually speak prose are highly cultivated and articulate people, who've read a good many books, and even they can speak prose only to each other. If you read the beautiful sentences of Elizabeth Bennett's conversation in *Pride and Prejudice*, you can see how in that book they give a powerfully convincing impression of a sensible and intelligent girl. But any girl who talked as coherently as that on a street car would be stared at as though she had green hair. It isn't only the difference between 1813 and 1962 that's involved either, as you'll see if you compare her speech with her mother's. The poet Emily Dickinson complained that everybody said "What?" to her, until finally she practically gave up trying to talk altogether, and confined herself to writing notes.

All this is involved with the difference between literary and other kinds of writing. If we're writing to convey information, or for any practical reason, our writing is an act of will and intention: we mean what we say, and the words we use represent that meaning directly. It's different in literature, not because the poet doesn't mean what he says too, but because his real effort is one of putting words together. What's important is not what he may have meant to say, but what words themselves say when they get fitted together. With a novelist it's rather the incidents in the story he tells that get fitted together—as D. H. Lawrence says, don't trust the novelist; trust his story. That's why so much of a writer's best writing is or seems to be involuntary. It's involuntary because the forms of literature itself are taking control of it, and these forms are what are embodied in the conventions of literature. Conventions, we see, have the same role in literature that they have in life: they impose certain patterns of order and stability on the writer. Only, if they're such different conventions, it seems clear that the order of words, or the structure of literature, is different from the social order.

The absence of any clear line of connection between literature and life comes out in the issues involved in censorship. Because of the large involuntary element in writing, works of literature can't be treated as embodiments of conscious will or intention, like people, and so no laws can be framed to control their behavior which assume a tendency to do this or an intention of doing that. Works of literature get into legal trouble because they offend some powerful religious or political interest, and this interest in its turn usually acquires or exploits the kind of social hysteria that's always revolving around sex. But it's impossible to give legal definitions of such terms as obscenity in relation to works of literature. What happens to the book depends mainly on the intelligence of the judge. If he's a sensible man we get a sensible decision; if he's an ass we get that sort of decision, but what we don't get is a legal decision, because the basis for one doesn't exist. The best we get is a precedent tending to discourage cranks and pressure groups from attacking serious books. If you read the casebook on the trial of *Lady Chatterley's Lover*, you may remember how bewildered the critics were when they were asked what the moral effect of the book would be. They weren't putting on an act: they didn't know. Novels can only be good or bad in their own categories. There's no such thing as a morally bad novel: its moral effect depends entirely on the moral quality of its reader, and nobody can predict what that will be. And if literature isn't morally bad it isn't morally good either. I suppose one reason why *Lady Chatterley's Lover* dramatized this question so vividly was that it's a rather preachy and self-conscious book: like the Sunday-school novels of my childhood, it bores me a little because it tries so hard to do me good.

So literature has no consistent connection with ordinary life, positive or negative. Here we touch on another important difference between structures of the imagination and structures of practical sense, which include the applied sciences. Imagination is certainly essential to science, applied or pure. Without a constructive power in the mind to make models of experience, get hunches and follow them out, play freely around with hypotheses, and so forth, no scientist could get anywhere. But all imaginative effort in practical fields has to meet the test of practicability, otherwise it's discarded. The imagination in literature has no such test to meet. You don't relate it directly to life or reality: you relate works of literature to each other. Whatever value there is in studying literature, cultural or practical, comes from the total body of our reading, the castle of words we've built, and keep adding new wings to all the time.

So it's natural to swing to the opposite extreme and say that literature is really a refuge or escape from life, a self-contained world like the world of the dream, a world of play or make-believe to balance the world of work. Some literature is like that, and many people tell us that they only read to get away from reality for a bit. And I've suggested myself that the sense of escape, or at least detachment, does come into everybody's literary experience. But the real point of literature can hardly be that. Think of such writers as William Faulkner or François Mauriac,[2] their great moral dignity, the intensity and compassion that they've studied the life around them

[2] François Mauriac, French novelist (1885–1970). He won the Nobel Prize for literature in 1952.—Eds.

with. Or think of James Joyce, spending seven years on one book and seventeen on another, and having them ridiculed or abused or banned by the customs when they did get published. Or of the poets Rilke[3] and Valéry,[4] waiting patiently for years in silence until what they had to say was ready to be said. There's a deadly seriousness in all this that even the most refined theories of fantasy or make-believe won't quite cover. Still, let's go along with the idea for a bit, because we're not getting on very fast with the relation of literature to life, or what we could call the horizontal perspective of literature. That seems to block us off on all sides.

The world of literature is a world where there is no reality except that of the human imagination. We see a great deal in it that reminds us vividly of the life we know. But in that very vividness there's something unreal. We can understand this more clearly with pictures, perhaps. There are trick-pictures—*trompe l'oeil*, the French call them—where the resemblance to life is very strong. An American painter of this school played a joke on his bitchy wife by painting one of her best napkins so expertly that she grabbed at the canvas trying to pull it off. But a painting as realistic as that isn't a reality but an illusion: it has the glittering unnatural clarity of a hallucination. The real realities, so to speak, are things that don't remind us directly of our own experience, but are such things as the wrath of Achilles or the jealousy of Othello, which are bigger and more intense experiences than anything we can reach—except in our imagination, which is what we're reaching with. Sometimes, as in the happy endings of comedies, or in the ideal world of romances, we seem to be looking at a pleasanter world than we ordinarily know. Sometimes, as in tragedy and satire, we seem to be looking at a world more devoted to suffering or absurdity than we ordinarily know. In literature we always seem to be looking either up or down. It's the vertical perspective that's important, not the horizontal one that looks out to life. Of course, in the greatest works of literature we get both the up and down views, often at the same time as different aspects of one event.

There are two halves to literary experience, then. Imagination gives us both a better and a worse world than the one we usually live with, and demands that we keep looking steadily at them both. The arts follow the path of the emotions, and of the tendency of the emotions to separate the world into a half that we like and a half that we don't like. Literature is not a world of dreams, but it would be if we had only one half without the other. If we had nothing but romances and comedies with happy endings, literature would express only a wish-fulfillment dream. Some people ask why poets want to write tragedies when the world's so full of them anyway, and suggest that enjoying such things has something morbid or gloating about it. It doesn't, but it might if there were nothing else in literature.

---

[3] Rainer Maria Rilke (1875–1926), German poet.—EDS.
[4] Paul Valéry (1871–1945), French poet and essayist.—EDS.

This point is worth spending another minute on. You recall that terrible scene in *King Lear* where Gloucester's eyes are put out on the stage. That's part of a play, and a play is supposed to be entertaining. Now in what sense can a scene like that be entertaining? The fact that it's not really happening is certainly important. It would be degrading to watch a real blinding scene, and far more so to get any pleasure out of watching it. Consequently, the entertainment doesn't consist in its reminding us of a real blinding scene. If it did, one of the great scenes of drama would turn into a piece of repulsive pornography. We couldn't stop anyone from reacting in this way, and it certainly wouldn't cure him, much less help the public, to start blaming or censoring Shakespeare for putting sadistic ideas in his head. But a reaction of that kind has nothing to do with drama. In a dramatic scene of cruelty and hatred we're seeing cruelty and hatred, which we know are permanently real things in human life, from the point of view of the imagination. What the imagination suggests is horror, not the paralyzing sickening horror of a real blinding scene, but an exuberant horror, full of the energy of repudiation. This is as powerful a rendering as we can ever get of life as we don't want it.

So we see that there are moral standards in literature after all, even though they have nothing to do with calling the police when we see a word in a book that's more familiar in sound than in print. One of the things Gloucester says in that scene is: "I am tied to the stake, and I must stand the course." In Shakespeare's day it was a favorite sport to tie a bear to a stake and set dogs on it until they killed it. The Puritans suppressed this sport, according to Macaulay,[5] not because it gave pain to the bear but because it gave pleasure to the spectators. Macaulay may have intended his remark to be a sneer at the Puritans, but surely if the Puritans did feel this way they were one hundred percent right. What other reason is there for abolishing public hangings? Whatever their motives, the Puritans and Shakespeare were operating in the same direction. Literature keeps presenting the most vicious things to us as entertainment, but what it appeals to is not any pleasure in these things, but the exhilaration of standing apart from them and being able to see them for what they are because they aren't really happening. The more exposed we are to this, the less likely we are to find an unthinking pleasure in cruel or evil things. As the eighteenth century said in a fine mouth-filling phrase, literature refines our sensibilities.

The top half of literature is the world expressed by such words as sublime, inspiring, and the like, where what we feel is not detachment but absorption. This is the world of heroes and gods and titans and Rabelaisian giants, a world of powers and passions and moments of ecstasy far greater than anything we meet outside the imagination. Such forces would not only absorb but annihilate us if they entered ordinary life, but luckily the protecting wall of the imagination is here too. As the German poet

[5] Thomas Babington Macaulay (1800–1859), English historian and essayist.—EDS.

Rilke says, we adore them because they disdain to destroy us. We seem to have got quite a long way from our emotions with their division of things into "I like this" and "I don't like this." Literature gives us an experience that stretches us vertically to the heights and depths of what the human mind can conceive, to what corresponds to the conceptions of heaven and hell in religion. In this perspective what I like or don't like disappears, because there's nothing left of me as a separate person: as a reader of literature I exist only as a representative of humanity as a whole.

No matter how much experience we may gather in life, we can never in life get the dimension of experience that the imagination gives us. Only the arts and sciences can do that, and of these, only literature gives us the whole sweep and range of human imagination as it sees itself. It seems to be very difficult for many people to understand the reality and intensity of literary experience. To give an example that you may think a bit irrelevant: why have so many people managed to convince themselves that Shakespeare did not write Shakespeare's plays, when there is not an atom of evidence that anybody else did? Apparently because they feel that poetry must be written out of personal experience, and that Shakespeare didn't have enough experience of the right kind. But Shakespeare's plays weren't produced by his experience: they were produced by his imagination, and the way to develop the imagination is to read a good book or two. As for us, we can't speak or think or comprehend even our own experience except within the limits of our own power over words, and those limits have been established for us by our great writers.

Literature, then, is not a dream-world: it's two dreams, a wish-fulfillment dream and an anxiety dream, that are focused together, like a pair of glasses, and become a fully conscious vision. Art, according to Plato, is a dream for awakened minds, a work of imagination withdrawn from ordinary life, dominated by the same forces that dominate the dream, and yet giving us a perspective and dimension on reality that we don't get from any other approach to reality. So the poet and the dreamer are distinct, as Keats says. Ordinary life forms a community, and literature is among other things an art of communication, so it forms a community too. In ordinary life we fall into a private and separate subconscious every night, where we reshape the world according to a private and separate imagination. Underneath literature there's another kind of subconscious, which is social and not private, a need for forming a community around certain symbols, like the Queen and the flag, or around certain gods that represent order and stability, or becoming and change, or death and rebirth to a new life. This is the myth-making power of the human mind, which throws up and dissolves one civilization after another.

I've taken my title, "The Keys to Dreamland," from what is possibly the greatest single effort of the literary imagination in the twentieth century, Joyce's *Finnegans Wake*. In this book a man goes to sleep and falls, not into the Freudian separate or private subconscious, but into the deeper dream of man that creates and destroys his own societies. The entire book is written in the language of this dream. It's a subconscious language, mainly English, but connected by associations and puns with the eighteen or so other languages that Joyce knew. *Finnegans Wake* is not a book to read, but a book to decipher: as Joyce says, it's about a dreamer, but it's addressed to an ideal reader suffering from an ideal insomnia. The reader or critic, then, has a role complementing the poet's role. We need two powers in literature, a power to create and a power to understand.

In all our literary experience there are two kinds of response. There is the direct experience of the work itself, while we're reading a book or seeing a play, especially for the first time. This experience is uncritical, or rather pre-critical, so it's not infallible. If our experience is limited, we can be roused to enthusiasm or carried away by something that we can later see to have been second-rate or even phony. Then there is the conscious, critical response we make after we've finished reading or left the theatre, where we compare what we've experienced with other things of the same kind, and form a judgment of value and proportion on it. This critical response, with practice, gradually makes our pre-critical responses more sensitive and accurate, or improves our taste, as we say. But behind our responses to individual works, there's a bigger response to our literary experience as a whole, as a total possession.

The critic has always been called a judge of literature, which means, not that he's in a superior position to the poet, but that he ought to know something about literature, just as a judge's right to be on a bench depends on his knowledge of law. If he's up against something the size of Shakespeare, he's the one being judged. The critic's function is to interpret every work of literature in the light of all the literature he knows, to keep constantly struggling to understand what literature as a whole is about. Literature as a whole is not an aggregate of exhibits with red and blue ribbons attached to them, like a cat show, but the range of articulate human imagination as it extends from the height of imaginative heaven to the depth of imaginative hell. Literature is a human apocalypse, man's revelation to man, and criticism is not a body of adjudications, but the awareness of that revelation, the last judgment of mankind.

The Literary Life: Some Representative Women
ELLEN MOERS

The poet is representative. She stands among partial women for the complete woman. . . . The young woman reveres women of genius, because, to speak truly, they are more herself than she is. . . . For all women live by truth and stand in need of expression.
—Ralph Waldo Emerson

A woman's life is hard in its own way, as women have always known and men have rarely understood. Literary women speak for themselves on this matter, as on every other, with finality. The horrors of the housewife's lot have never been more powerfully evoked than in this letter of 1850, by Harriet Beecher Stowe, about her plumber:

> So this same sink lingered in a precarious state for some weeks, and when I had *nothing else to do*, I used to call and do what I could in the way of enlisting the good man's sympathies in its behalf.
>
> How many times I have been in and seated myself in one of the old rocking-chairs, and talked first of the news of the day, the railroad, the last proceedings in Congress, the probabilities about the millenium, and thus brought the conversation by little and little round to my sink! . . . because, till the sink was done, the pump could not be put up, and we couldn't have any rain-water. Sometimes my courage would quite fail me to introduce the subject, and I would talk of everything else, turn and get out of the shop, and then turn back as if a thought had just struck my mind, and say:—
>
> "Oh, Mr. Titcomb! about that sink?"
>
> "Yes, ma'am, I was thinking about going down street this afternoon to look out stuff for it."
>
> "Yes, sir, if you would be good enough to get it done as soon as possible; we are in great need of it."
>
> "I think there's no hurry. I believe we are going to have a dry time now, so that you could not catch any water, and you won't need a pump at present."
>
> These negotiations extended from the first of June to the first of July, and at last my sink was completed. . . . Also during this time good Mrs. Mitchell and myself made two sofas, or lounges, a barrel chair, divers bedspreads, pillow cases, pillows, bolsters, mattresses; we painted rooms; we revarnished furniture; we—what *didn't* we do?
>
> Then on came Mr. Stowe; and then came the eighth of July and my little Charley. I was really glad for an excuse to lie in bed, for I was full tired, I can assure you. Well, I was what folks call very comfortable for two weeks, when my nurse had to leave me. . . .
>
> During this time I have employed my leisure hours in making up my engagements with newspaper editors. I have written more than anybody, or I myself, would have thought. I have taught an hour a day in our school, and I have read two hours every evening to the children. The children study English history in school, and I am reading Scott's historic novels in their order . . . ; yet I am constantly pursued and haunted by the idea that I don't do anything. Since I began this note I have been called off at least a dozen times; once for the fish-man, to buy a codfish; once to see a man who had brought me some barrels of apples; once to see a book-man; then to Mrs. Upham, to see about a drawing I promised to make for her; then to nurse the baby; then into the kitchen to make a chowder for dinner; and now I am at it again, for nothing but deadly determination enables me ever to write; it is rowing against wind and tide. . . .
>
> To tell the truth, dear, I am getting tired; my neck and back ache, and I must come to a close.

It is a letter to leave one between laughter and tears, probably just the effect Mrs. Stowe intended, for she was already an accomplished writer of sketches and other journalism, the income from which was required by her large family. "Now, Hattie," her sister-in-law wrote, "if I could use a pen as you can, I would write something that would make this whole nation feel what an accursed thing slavery is"; but there was, after all, little Charley, just born, the last of her seven children. "As long as the baby sleeps with me nights I can't do much at anything, but I will do it at last. I will write that thing if I live." The first installment of *Uncle Tom's Cabin, or Life Among the Lowly* did in fact appear a little less than a year after Mr. Titcomb took care of Mrs. Stowe's sink. . . .

But there were some lucky ones, lucky by birth, circumstance, physique, temperament especially: that miracle of temperament which creates its own luck. Two nineteenth-century women stand out in this respect, George Sand[1] and Elizabeth Barrett Browning[2]; what positively miraculous beings they were. A magnetism emanates from their life stories, some compelling power which drew the world to them—and all the goods and blessings of the kind that facilitate and ornament the woman's life in letters. It was not that their lives were without the difficulties that plague other women —hardly; but they made those difficulties into resources with a wave of the magic wand of their—what shall we call it: charm? power? egotism? energy? confidence? pride? genius? or just plain luck? Whatever it was, Elizabeth Barrett always knew it was hers, as we can see from the "Glimpses into My Own Life and Literary Character" that she set down in 1820.

> Perhaps these pages may never meet a human eye—and therefore no EXCESSIVE vanity can dictate them tho a feeling akin to it SELF LOVE may have prompted my not unwilling pen.
> . . . I was always of a determined and if thwarted violent disposition. My actions and temper were infinitely more inflexible at three years old than now at fourteen. At that early age I can perfectly remember reigning in the Nursery and being renowned amongst the servants for self love and excessive passion. . . . At four and a half my great delight was poring over fairy phenomenons and the actions of necromancers. . . . At five I supposed myself a heroine. . . .
> I perfectly remember the delight I felt when I attained my sixth birthday. I enjoyed my triumph to a great degree over the inhabitants of the Nursery, there being no UPSTART to dispute my authority. . . .
> At four I first mounted Pegasus but at six I thought myself privileged to show off feats of horsemanship. In my sixth year for some lines on virtue which I had penned with great care I received from Papa a ten shilling note enclosed in a letter which was addrest to the *Poet Laureat of Hope End*; I mention this because I received much more pleasure from the word *Poet*

---

[1] 1804–1876.—EDS.
[2] 1806–1861.—EDS.

than from the ten shilling note. I did not understand the meaning of the word laureat but it being explained to me by my dearest Mama, the idea first presented itself to me of celebrating our birthdays by my verse. *"Poet Laureate of Hope End"* was too great a title to lose—

. . . . at SEVEN I began to think of *"forming my taste."* . . . I read the History of England and Rome—at 8 I perused the History of Greece. . . .

At nine I felt much pleasure from the effusions of my imagination in the adorned drapery of versification. . . . The subject of my studies was Pope's "Illiad" some passages from Shakespeare & novels which I enjoyed to their full extent.

. . . At ten my poetry was entirely formed by the style of written authors and I read that I might write. . . . At eleven I wished to be considered an authoress. Novels were thrown aside. Poetry and Essays were my studies & I felt the most ardent desire to understand the learned languages—To comprehend even the Greek alphabet was delight inexpressible. Under the tuition of Mr. McSwiney I attained that which I so fervently desired. For 8 months during this year I never remember having diverted my attention to any other object than the ambition of gaining fame . . . and never had a better opinion of my own talents—In short I was in infinite danger of being as vain as I was inexperienced! During this dangerous period I was from home & the fever of a heated imagination was perhaps increased by the intoxicating gaieties of a watering place Ramsgate where we then were and where I commenced my poem "The Battle of Marathon" now in print!!

. . . At twelve I enjoyed a literary life in all its pleasures. Metaphysics were my highest delight. . . . At this age I was in great danger of becoming the founder of a religion of my own. . . . This year I read Milton for the first time *thro* together with Shakespeare & Pope's Homer. . . . I had now attained my thirteenth birthday! . . . I perused all modern authors. . . . I read Homer in the original with delight inexpressible, together with Virgil. . . .

I am now fourteen and since those days of my tenderest infancy my character has not changed—

. . . My admiration of literature, especially of poetical literature, can never be subdued nor can it be extinguished but with life. . . .

My views of every subject are naturally cheerful and light as the first young visions of aerial hope but there have been moments, nay hours when contemplation has been arrayed in sorrows dusky robe. . . . And yet I have not felt miserable even then. . . .

My mind is naturally independant and spurns that subserviency of opinion which is generally considered necessary to feminine softness. But this is a subject on which I must always feel strongly for I feel within me an almost proud consciousness of independance which prompts me to defend my opinions & to yield them only to conviction!!!!!!!

. . . Better oh how much better to be the ridicule of mankind, the scoff of society, than lose that self respect which tho' this heart were bursting would elevate me above misery—above wretchedness & above abasement!!! These principles are irrevocable! It is not—I feel it is not vanity that dictates them! it is not—I know it is not an encroachment on masculine prerogative but it is a proud sentiment which will never allow me to be humbled in my own eyes!!!

And so it went; no one and nothing could resist her. She wanted Greek—there was that tutor; before she was done she read "nearly every word extant in Greek," published her translation of Aeschylus,[3] wrote as a specialist on Byzantine Greek literature, and also learned Latin, Hebrew, French, German, Italian, and Portuguese without ever going to school. She wanted a learned friend with whom to discuss as an equal the technicalities of Greek prosody and such matters; he was provided—it had to be a he—in a shape which permitted long hours of intimate converse without scandal: a blind scholar. She wanted to do nothing but read and write; it has been estimated that her curiously convenient regime as an invalid gave her more time, daily, for those occupations than any other modern young person has ever enjoyed.

Only a woman, perhaps, can fully appreciate the luxurious scholarly idleness of Elizabeth Barrett's life when a young woman, and the female head of a large household (after her mother's death). Her younger sisters and brothers, who all adored her, tiptoed by her door; while full of affection, so devoid of responsibility was she, that she confessed to confusion about their ages. And so protected was she from even the awareness of domestic responsibilities that her own room was cleaned only once a year—a ritual occasion, managed by others so that she need not observe servant industry. Whenever her large family moved house, she herself was transported separately, a precious burden, to the new residence made ready by others for her convenience. Elizabeth Barrett was not to be disturbed.

She wanted fame: published in her teens and twenties, her poetry was hailed round the world, and she was nominated for the laureateship. She wanted a share in the normal masculine literary life, and without unseemly effort on her part, almost without leaving home, she saw that life come to her: epistolary friendships with writers, assignments from the quarterlies, collaborations on a modernization of Chaucer and on a critical assessment of contemporary writers; even appointment as literary executor of an important man she had never met.

She wanted love as well: what poet does not? Her father did not remarry when her mother died, which is extraordinary, for he was only forty-three, and handsome, vigorous, and rich. All his amatory energies (which had produced twelve children) were turned to the worship of his brilliant and pretty eldest daughter, who was merely twenty-one years younger than he. Mr. Barrett comes down to us in legend as a patriarchal tyrant of black religiosity; but what woman can help relishing his style? Those nightly prayers in Elizabeth's room, only the two of them; she stretched on her couch like an invalid queen, and he on his knees before her. . . .

She wanted more love; and it came, it came—

---

[3] Greek dramatist (525–456 B.C.).—EDS.

> O liberal
> And princely giver, who has brought the gold
> And purple of thine heart, unstained, untold,
> And laid them on the outside of the wall . . .

Robert Browning came for Elizabeth Barrett just the way a lover should come for every literary woman, out of the blue, fascinated, enchanted, magnetized by her writing—the two-volume 1844 collection of her poetry. "I love your verses with all my heart, dear Miss Barrett," this unknown lover wrote; and this first letter of his, shot through with critical raptures and sexual metaphors, climaxed with ". . . my feeling rises altogether. I do, as I say, love these books with all my heart—and I love you too. . . ."

The rest of their courtship produced some of the finest love poems and love letters in the language. "My letters!" she wrote—

> My letters! all dead paper, mute and white!
> And yet they seem alive and quivering
> Against my tremulous hands which loose the string
> And let them drop down on my knee tonight.
> This said,—he wished to have me in his sight
> Once, as a friend: this fixed a day in spring
> To come and touch my hand . . . a simple thing,
> Yet I wept for it!—this, . . . the paper's light . . .
> Said, *Dear, I love thee*; and I sank and quailed
> As if God's future thundered on my past.
> This said, *I am thine*—and so its ink has paled
> With lying at my heart that beat too fast.
> And this . . . O Love, thy words have ill availed
> If, what this said, I dared repeat at last!
>
> . . .

Alfred de Musset, young, handsome, and a poet, read George Sand's novel *Indiana*, met her, reread it, wrote her a letter containing much critical admiration and the poem called "After Reading *Indiana*":

> Sand, quand tu l'écrivais, où donc l'avais-tu vue,
> Cette scène terrible où Noun, à demi nue,
> Sur le lit d'Indiana s'enivre avec Raimond?
> Qui donc te la dictait, cette page brulante
> Où l'amour cherche en vain d'une main palpitante
> Le fantôme adoré de son illusion?
>
> . . . .
>
> As-tu rêvé cela, George, ou l'as-tu connu?[4]

---

[4] Sand, when you wrote it, where then had you seen it,
That terrible scene where Noun, a half nude,
On Indiana's bed, is getting drunk with Raimond?
Who then dictated it to you, that burning page
Where love is seeking in vain with a throbbing hand
The adored phantom of his illusion?
 . . . .
Did you dream that, George, or did you experience it? [Editors' translation]

She answered, in part:

> If I write literary criticism in response to your verses, which are so beautiful in thought and feeling, it is because I am very much at a loss as to how to answer the questions of the poet who addresses them to me . . . for I cannot forget that the poet is twenty years old, that he has the good fortune still to doubt, still to inquire, and it would be a bad grace on my part to reveal to him the mournful secrets of my own experience. . . .
>
> When I had the honor of meeting you, I did not dare invite you to come and see me. I still fear that the somberness of my domestic interior may alarm and bore you. However, if on some day of weariness and disgust with the active life, you were tempted to enter the cell of a recluse, you would be received with gratitude and cordiality.

He came.

To Musset, to everyone, she was George Sand—usually Madame George Sand. No one could tell the story of the birth of that pen name better than Sand does herself, in Part IV of the *Histoire de ma vie*, where she interweaves it with the story of her adoption of male dress when she began her literary life in Paris.

> I yearned to deprovincialize myself and became informed about the ideas and the arts of my time . . . ; I was particularly thirsty for the theater.
>
> I was well aware that it was impossible for a poor woman to indulge herself in these delights . . . I took this problem to my mother. . . . She replied: ". . . When I was young and your father was short of money, he had the idea of dressing me as a boy. . . . That meant a saving of half our household budget." . . .
>
> So I had made for myself a *redingote-guérite* [the long, shapeless man's outer coat of the 1830s] in heavy gray cloth, pants and vest to match. With a gray hat and a large woolen cravat, I was a perfect first-year student. I can't express the pleasure my boots gave me: I would gladly have slept with them, as my brother did in his young age, when he got his first pair. With those little iron-shod heels, I was solid on the pavement. I flew from one end of Paris to the other. It seemed to me that I could go round the world. And then, my clothes feared nothing. I ran out in every kind of weather, I came home at every sort of hour, I sat in the pit at the theater. No one paid attention to me, and no one guessed at my disguise. . . .
>
> Myself, I had the Ideal lodged in a corner of my brain . . . I carried it about in the street, my feet on the icy pavement, my shoulders covered with snow, my hands in my pockets, my stomach a bit hollow every now and then, but my head all the more filled with dreams, melodies, colors, shapes, gleams and phantoms. I was no longer a *lady*, but I wasn't a *gentleman* either. . . . No one knew me, no one looked at me, no one found fault with me; I was an atom lost in that immense crowd. No one said to me, as they did in La Châtre: "There's Madame Aurore going by; she's got the same hat and dress on"; nor, as they did in Nohant: "Take a look at our ladyship riding on her big horse; she's got to be crazy to sit a horse that way." In Paris, nobody thought anything of me. . . . I could make up a whole novel as I walked from one side of town to another without running into someone who would say: "What the devil are you thinking about?"

The year was 1831. She was starting out in the world of letters just as all young Frenchmen from the provinces did in those romantic days. That she was a woman writer rather than a man writer is not the most remarkable fact about Sand's literary debut. Something else about it, something so remarkable as to be almost unbelievable, turned out to be the characteristic note of Sand's whole literary career; and that is, its speed.

Before she came to Paris to earn her way as a writer, she had done a little scribbling, but had hardly shown any particular interest in or talent for a writing career. Once in Paris, she made contact with leading editors and writers, joined the staff of *Le Figaro*, and contributed regularly to the *Revue de Paris*. To learn her craft, she wrote alone or in collaboration numerous articles, tales, and novels; some of this apprentice work was never published, some appeared anonymously, some under various pen names. *Rose et Blanche*, a five-volume collaborative novel signed "J. Sand," marked the end of her apprenticeship. Next came *Indiana*, entirely her own work, the novel Musset read as did many others. ("Very brilliant and powerful," said Elizabeth Barrett of *Indiana*, "and eloquent beyond praising.") It established the fame of "George Sand," the pen name she used for the first time for *Indiana*.

The whole business took some fifteen months, only about half of which she was able to spend in Paris or devote to the literary life. She was twenty-six years, six months, and five days old when she came to Paris, and when she was done with her debut—with the contacts and the journalism, the hack fiction and sketches, the thousands of pages and dozens of volumes, and the writing of *Indiana* as well—she was twenty-seven years and nine months old. It took her friend Balzac, that dynamo of literary energy, about ten years to complete a similar apprenticeship in journalism and hack fiction.

There is certainly nothing remarkable about Jules Sandeau, her lover and collaborator during this period. He was a timid, aspiring, unpublished poet of nineteen, from her part of France, when she fell in love with him in 1830. She swept him off with her to Paris the next year, there to mother him, support him, introduce him around, and manage his literary debut while she attended to her own. From Sandeau she took nothing but the first syllable of the pen name she required—for what other name was she to use? Her maiden name was Amantine-Aurore-Lucile Dupin, of which Aurore was the operative first name (fortunately for literature: from "Aurora" Mrs. Browning derived a heavenly host of images for *Aurora Leigh*). Had she used her maiden name, it would have been an offense to her mother, Mme Dupin; and her married name, an outrage to her mother-in-law, the Baronne Dudevant.

Her marriage at eighteen to young Casimir Dudevant, which began as a love match, had in any case long since deteriorated into a marriage of form, with infidelities on both sides; but the form was extremely important. She was the mother of two children and the *châtelaine* of Nohant, her country estate by birth, her husband's property by marriage. They made an unusual separation agreement in 1830 under the terms of which her literary career unfolded. Dudevant made her a very modest allowance (out of her own money) on which to live part of every year in Paris. The rest of the time she would spend at Nohant, still officially a wife, still tied to her beloved countryside, still passionately a mother. But she would have to earn enough by writing to support a Paris establishment including one or both of her children, as their schooling dictated. This she did, with a drive, a speed, a versatility, and a force that can hardly be equaled in literary history. And in addition she supplied herself with an abundance of the goods of this earth which she so relished—lots of sex, lots of travel, lots of friends, lots of wholesome country life, lots of music.

The picture of George Sand that stays most in my mind (because she described it often and brilliantly) is that of her typical country evening at Nohant. At the center sits Madame Sand, with the needlework she loved in her hands, surrounded by a houseful of friends, children, lovers, guests, neighbors. Nohant was a messy household, full of laughter and games and theatricals and family arguments and good intellectual talk and tobacco smoke and music—just like yours and mine. With Sand, in fact, begins a literary life-style distinctly modern in its middle-class informality, and child-centered domesticity, and dominating presence: the efficient, versatile, overworked, modern mother. But there is one old-fashioned detail—live music on the piano, rather than recordings. Sand herself did not play but loved to listen, and what with the frequent visits of her friend Lizst, and the long residence of her lover Chopin, she managed to provide herself with the very best in piano-playing.

How did she do it? It is not the management of Sand's sex life that is baffling (except for one detail: what contraceptive device she relied on) but the management of her working life; for throughout all her years of passions, pleasures, politics, and domestic responsibilities, she went on producing at the rate of at least two long novels a year, and hundreds upon hundreds of pages of other kinds of writing. This is really the interesting question about George Sand, and it has always fascinated literary professionals. "It's taken me a long time to scribble some forty volumes," Colette[5] once wrote.

> So many hours stolen from travelling, idleness, reading, even from healthy feminine stylishness! How the devil did George Sand manage? That sturdy woman of letters found it possible to finish one novel and start another in the same hour. And she did not thereby lose either a lover or a puff of the narghile, not to mention a *Story of my Life* in twenty volumes, and I am overcome by astonishment.[6]

---

[5] French novelist (1873–1954).—EDS.
[6] Translation by David Le Vay from *L'Étoile Vesper*. Unless otherwise indicated, as in this case, all translations are by E.M.

And Henry James,[7] a prolific romancer himself, took a highly professional interest in the mystery of Sand's productivity. "During the five-and-forty years of her literary career," he wrote in one of his eight essays on George Sand,

> she had something to say about most things in the universe; but the thing about which she had least to say was the writer's, the inventor's, the romancer's art. She possessed it by the gift of God, but she seems never to have felt the temptation to examine the pulse of the machine.

James combed the prefaces Sand wrote for the popular edition of her novels (irresistible documents, the writer at her professional best) for clues to Sand's technique for managing time, and came up with what is probably the essence of her secret and of her luck. On the one hand, James saw, George Sand had "an extraordinary physical robustness"; and on the other, "it was her constant practice to write at night, beginning after the rest of the world had gone to sleep." That was it: she was a night worker. This inalterable physiological bias to the night hours probably accounted for more in George Sand's development as a writer than the fact of her sex.

As women writers especially know, there is no better way to stretch the day than by working late at night when human claims upon one's time are still. It was all very well for Sylvia Plath[8] to get up to write her astonishing last poems "at about four in the morning—that still blue, almost eternal hour before the baby's cry, before the glassy music of the milkman, settling his bottles." Poets can manage with an hour or two of writing time, before the baby cries, because they carry their work in their head the rest of the day; but the novelists like James and Colette and Sand need more time for turning out copy, and night is the longest time when a woman's two hands are free to hold pen and paper.

The picture of George Sand that most people remember best is the one that became celebrated after the Musset/Sand love affair ended in great bitterness on his side. Late at night, when he awoke after an exhausting *nuit d'amour*, Alfred de Musset would see George Sand—heartless bitch!—sitting up in her wrapper in their bedroom, scratching, scratching away at the pages with her pen by candlelight.

---

[7] Major American novelist (1843–1916); author of, among other novels, *The American* (1877), *Daisy Miller* (1879), *Washington Square* (1881), and *The Golden Bowl* (1904).—EDS.

[8] American poet (1932–1963).—EDS.

Art and Life

Expressiveness
SUSANNE K. LANGER

When we talk about "Art" with a capital "A"—that is, about any or all of the arts: painting, sculpture, architecture, the potter's and goldsmith's and other designers' arts, music, dance, poetry, and prose fiction, drama and film—it is a constant temptation to say things about "Art" in this general sense that are true only in one special domain, or to assume that what holds for one art must hold for another. For instance, the fact that music is made for performance, for presentation to the ear, and is simply not the same thing when it is given only to the tonal imagination of a reader silently perusing the score, has made some aestheticians pass straight to the conclusion that literature, too, must be physically heard to be fully experienced, because words are originally spoken, not written; an obvious parallel, but a careless and, I think, invalid one. It is dangerous to set up principles by analogy, and generalize from a single consideration.

But it is natural, and safe enough, to ask analogous questions: "What is the function of sound in music? What is the function of sound in poetry? What is the function of sound in prose composition? What is the function of sound in drama?" The answers may be quite heterogeneous; and that is itself an important fact, a guide to something more than a simple and sweeping theory. Such findings guide us to exact relations and abstract, variously exemplified basic principles.

At present, however, we are dealing with principles that have proven to be the same in all the arts, when each kind of art—plastic, musical, balletic, poetic, and each major mode, such as literary and dramatic writing, or painting, sculpturing, building plastic shapes—has been studied in its own terms. Such candid study is more rewarding than the usual passionate declaration that all the arts are alike, only their materials differ, their principles are all the same, their techniques all analogous, etc. That is not only unsafe, but untrue. It is in pursuing the differences among them that one arrives, finally, at a point where no more differences appear; then one has found, not postulated, their unity. At that deep level there is only one concept exemplified in all the different arts, and that is the concept of Art.

The principles that obtain wholly and fundamentally in every kind of art are few, but decisive; they determine what is art, and what is not. Expressiveness, in one definite and appropriate sense, is the same in all art works of any kind. What is created is not the same in any two distinct arts—this is, in fact, what makes them distinct—but the principle of creation is the same. And "living form" means the same in all of them.

A work of art is an expressive form created for our perception through sense or imagination, and what it expresses is human feeling. The word "feeling" must be taken here in its broadest sense, meaning *everything that can be felt*, from physical sensation, pain and comfort, excitement and repose, to the most complex emotions, intellectual tensions, or the steady feeling-tones of a conscious human life. In stating what a work of art is, I have just used the words "form," "expressive," and "created"; these are key words. One at a time, they will keep us engaged.

Let us consider first what is meant, in this context, by a *form*. The word has many meanings, all equally legitimate for various purposes; even in connection with art it has several. It may, for instance—and often does—denote the familiar, characteristic structures known as the sonnet form, the sestina, or the ballad form in poetry, the sonata form, the madrigal, or the symphony in music, the contredance or the classical ballet in choreography, and so on. This is not what I mean; or rather, it is only a very small part of what I mean. There is another sense in which artists speak of "form" when they say, for instance, "form follows function," or declare that the one quality shared by all good works of art is "significant form," or entitle a book *The Problem of Form in Painting and Sculpture*, or *The Life of Forms in Art*, or *Search for Form*. They are using "form" in a wider sense, which on the one hand is close to the commonest, popular meaning, namely just the *shape* of a thing, and on the other hand to the quite unpopular meaning it has in science and philosophy, where it designates something more abstract; "form" in its most abstract sense means structure, articulation, a whole resulting from the relation of mutually dependent factors, or more precisely, the way that whole is put together.

The abstract sense, which is sometimes called "logical form," is involved in the notion of expression, at least the kind of expression that characterizes art. That is why artists, when they speak of achieving "form," use the word with something of an abstract connotation, even when they are talking about a visible and tangible art object in which that form is embodied.

The more recondite concept of form is derived, of course, from the naive one, that is, material shape. Perhaps the easiest way to grasp the idea of "logical form" is to trace its derivation.

Let us consider the most obvious sort of form, the shape of an object, say a lampshade. In any department store you will find a wide choice of lampshades, mostly monstrosities, and what is monstrous is usually their shape. You select the least offensive one, maybe even a good one, but realize that the color, say violet, will not fit into your room; so you look about for another shade of the same shape but a different color, perhaps green. In recognizing this same shape in another object, possibly of another material as well as another color, you have quite naturally and easily abstracted the concept of this shape from your actual impression of the first lampshade. Presently it may occur to you that this shade is too big for your lamp; you ask whether they have *this same shade* (meaning another one of this shape) in a smaller size. The clerk understands you.

But what is *the same* in the big violet shade and the little green one? Nothing but the interrelations among their respective various dimensions. They are not "the same" even in their spatial properties, for none of their actual measures are alike; but their shapes are congruent. Their respective spatial factors are put together in the same way, so they exemplify the same form.

It is really astounding what complicated abstractions we make in our ordinary dealing with forms—that is to say, through what twists and transformations we recognize the same logical form. Consider the similarity of your two hands. Put one on the table, palm down, superimpose the other, palm down, as you may have superimposed cutout geometric shapes in school—they are not alike at all. But their shapes are *exact opposites*. Their respective shapes fit the same description, provided that the description is modified by a principle of application whereby the measures are read one way for one hand and the other way for the other—like a timetable in which the list of stations is marked: "Eastbound, read down; Westbound, read up."

As the two hands exemplify the same form with a principle of reversal understood, so the list of stations describes two ways of moving, indicated by the advice to "read down" for one and "read up" for the other. We can all abstract the common element in these two respective trips, which is called the *route*. With a return ticket we may return only by the same route. The same principle relates a mold to the form of the thing that is cast in it, and establishes their formal correspondence, or common logical form.

So far we have considered only objects—lampshades, hands, or regions of the earth—as having forms. These have fixed shapes; their parts remain in fairly stable relations to each other. But there are also substances that have no definite shapes, such as gases, mist, and water, which take the shape of any bounded space that contains them. The interesting thing about such amorphous fluids is that when they are put into violent motion they do exhibit visible forms, not bounded by any container. Think of the momentary efflorescence of a bursting rocket, the mushroom cloud of an atomic bomb, the funnel of water or dust screwing upward in a whirlwind. The instant the motion stops, or even slows beyond a certain degree, those shapes collapse and the apparent "thing" disappears. They are not shapes of things at all, but forms of motions, or dynamic forms.

Some dynamic forms, however, have more permanent manifestations, because the stuff that moves and makes them visible is constantly replenished. A waterfall seems to hang from the cliff, waving streamers of foam.

Actually, of course, nothing stays there in mid-air; the water is always passing; but there is more and more water taking the same paths, so we have a lasting shape made and maintained by its passage—a permanent dynamic form. A quiet river, too, has dynamic form; if it stopped flowing it would either go dry or become a lake. Some twenty-five hundred years ago, Heracleitos was struck by the fact that you cannot step twice into the same river at the same place—at least, if the river means the water, not its dynamic form, the flow.

When a river ceases to flow because the water is deflected or dried up, there remains the river bed, sometimes cut deeply in solid stone. That bed is shaped by the flow, and records as graven lines the currents that have ceased to exist. Its shape is static, but it *expresses* the dynamic form of the river. Again, we have two congruent forms, like a cast and its mold, but this time the congruence is more remarkable because it holds between a dynamic form and a static one. That relation is important; we shall be dealing with it again when we come to consider the meaning of "living form" in art.

The congruence of two given perceptible forms is not always evident upon simple inspection. The common *logical* form they both exhibit may become apparent only when you know the principle whereby to relate them, as you compare the shapes of your hands not by direct correspondence, but by correspondence of opposite parts. Where the two exemplifications of the single logical form are unlike in most other respects one needs a rule for matching up the relevant factors of one with the relevant factors of the other; that is to say, a *rule of translation*, whereby one instance of the logical form is shown to correspond formally to the other.

The logical form itself is not another thing, but an abstract concept, or better an *abstractable* concept. We usually don't abstract it deliberately, but only use it, as we use our vocal cords in speech without first learning all about their operation and then applying our knowledge. Most people perceive intuitively the similarity of their two hands without thinking of them as conversely related; they can guess at the shape of the hollow inside a wooden shoe from the shape of a human foot, without any abstract study of topology. But the first time they see a map in the Mercator projection—with parallel lines of longitude, not meeting at the poles—they find it hard to believe that this corresponds logically to the circular map they used in school, where the meridians bulged apart toward the equator and met at both poles. The visible shapes of the continents are different on the two maps, and it takes abstract thinking to match up the two representations of the same earth. If, however, they have grown up with both maps, they will probably see the geographical relationships either way with equal ease, because these relationships are not *copied* by either map, but *expressed*, and expressed equally well by both; for the two maps are different *projections* of the same logical form, which the spherical earth exhibits in still another—that is, a spherical—projection.

An expressive form is any perceptible or imaginable whole that exhibits relationships of parts, or points, or even qualities or aspects within the whole, so that it may be taken to represent some other whole whose elements have analogous relations. The reason for using such a form as a symbol is usually that the thing it represents is not perceivable or readily imaginable. We cannot see the earth as an object. We let a map or a little globe express the relationships of places on the earth, and think about the earth by means of it. The understanding of one thing through another seems to be a deeply intuitive process in the human brain; it is so natural that we often have difficulty in distinguishing the symbolic expressive form from what it conveys. The symbol seems to be the thing itself, or contain it, or be contained in it. A child interested in a globe will not say: "This means the earth," but: "Look, this is the earth." A similar identification of symbol and meaning underlies the widespread conception of holy names, of the physical efficacy of rites, and many other primitive but culturally persistent phenomena. It has a bearing on our perception of artistic import; that is why I mention it here.

The most astounding and developed symbolic device humanity has evolved is language. By means of language we can conceive the intangible, incorporeal things we call our *ideas*, and the equally inostensible elements of our perceptual world that we call facts. It is by virtue of language that we can think, remember, imagine, and finally conceive a universe of facts. We can describe things and represent their relations, express rules of their interactions, speculate and predict and carry on a long symbolizing process known as reasoning. And above all, we can communicate, by producing a serried array of audible or visible words, in a pattern commonly known, and readily understood to reflect our multifarious concepts and percepts and their interconnections. This use of language is *discourse*; and the pattern of discourse is known as *discursive form*. It is a highly versatile, amazingly powerful pattern. It has impressed itself on our tacit thinking, so that we call all systematic reflection "discursive thought." It has made, far more than most people know, the very frame of our sensory experience—the frame of objective facts in which we carry on the practical business of life.

Yet even the discursive pattern has its limits of usefulness. An expressive form can express any complex of conceptions that, via some rule of projection, appears congruent with it, that is, appears to be of that form. Whatever there is in experience that will not take the impress—directly or indirectly—of discursive form, is not discursively communicable or, in the strictest sense, logically thinkable. It is unspeakable, ineffable; according to practically all serious philosophical theories today, it is unknowable.

Yet there is a great deal of experience that is knowable, not only as immediate, formless, meaningless impact, but as one aspect of the intricate web of life, yet defies discursive formulation, and therefore verbal expression: that is what we sometimes call the *subjective aspect* of experience, the direct feeling of it—what it is like to be waking and moving, to be drowsy, slowing down, or to be sociable, or to feel self-sufficient but alone; what it feels like to pursue an elusive thought or to have a big idea. All such directly felt experiences usually have no names—they are named, if at all, for the outward conditions that normally accompany their occurrence. Only the most striking ones have names like "anger," "hate," "love," "fear," and are collectively called "emotion." But we feel many things that never develop into any designable emotion. The ways we are moved are as various as the lights in a forest; and they may intersect, sometimes without cancelling each other, take shape and dissolve, conflict, explode into passion, or be transfigured. All these inseparable elements of subjective reality compose what we call the "inward life" of human beings. The usual factoring of that life-stream into mental, emotional, and sensory units is an arbitrary scheme of simplification that makes scientific treatment possible to a considerable extent; but we may already be close to the limit of its usefulness, that is, close to the point where its simplicity becomes an obstacle to further questioning and discovery instead of the revealing, ever-suitable logical projection it was expected to be.

Whatever resists projection into the discursive form of language is, indeed, hard to hold in conception, and perhaps impossible to communicate, in the proper and strict sense of the word "communicate." But fortunately our logical intuition, or form-perception, is really much more powerful than we commonly believe, and our knowledge—genuine knowledge, understanding—is considerably wider than our discourse. Even in the use of language, if we want to name something that is too new to have a name (e.g., a newly invented gadget or a newly discovered creature), or want to express a relationship for which there is no verb or other connective word, we resort to metaphor; we mention it or describe it as something else, something analogous. The principle of metaphor is simply the principle of saying one thing and meaning another, and expecting to be understood to mean the other. A metaphor is not language, it is an idea expressed by language, an idea that in its turn functions as a symbol to express something. It is not discursive and therefore does not really make a statement of the idea it conveys; but it formulates a new conception for our direct imaginative grasp.

Sometimes our comprehension of a total experience is mediated by a metaphorical symbol because the experience is new, and language has words and phrases only for familiar notions. Then an extension of language will gradually follow the wordless insight, and discursive expression will supersede the non-discursive pristine symbol. This is, I think, the normal advance of human thought and language in that whole realm of knowledge where discourse is possible at all.

But the symbolic presentation of subjective reality for contemplation is not only tentatively beyond the reach of language—that is, not merely beyond the words we have; it is impossible in the essential frame of language. That is why those semanticists who recognize only discourse as a symbolic form must regard the whole life of feeling as formless, chaotic, capable only of symptomatic expression, typified in exclamations like "Ah!" "Ouch!" "My sainted aunt!" They usually do believe that art is an expression of feeling, but that "expression" in art is of this sort, indicating that the speaker has an emotion, a pain, or other personal experience, perhaps also giving us a clue to the general kind of experience it is—pleasant or unpleasant, violent or mild—but not setting that piece of inward life objectively before us so we may understand its intricacy, its rhythms and shifts of total appearance. The differences in feeling-tones or other elements of subjective experience are regarded as differences in quality, which must be felt to be appreciated. Furthermore, since we have no intellectual access to pure subjectivity, the only way to study it is to study the symptoms of the person who is having subjective experiences. This leads to physiological psychology—a very important and interesting field. But it tells us nothing about the phenomena of subjective life, and sometimes simplifies the problem by saying they don't exist.

Now, I believe the expression of feeling in a work of art—the function that makes the work an expressive form—is not symptomatic at all. An artist working on a tragedy need not be in personal despair or violent upheaval; nobody, indeed, could work in such a state of mind. His mind would be occupied with the causes of his emotional upset. Self-expression does not require composition and lucidity; a screaming baby gives his feeling far more release than any musician, but we don't go into a concert hall to hear a baby scream; in fact, if that baby is brought in we are likely to go out. We don't want self-expression.

A work of art presents feeling (in the broad sense I mentioned before, as everything that can be felt) for our contemplation, making it visible or audible or in some way perceivable through a symbol, not inferable from a symptom. Artistic form is congruent with the dynamic forms of our direct sensuous, mental, and emotional life; works of art are projections of "felt life," as Henry James called it, into spatial, temporal, and poetic structures. They are images of feeling, that formulate it for our cognition. What is artistically good is whatever articulates and presents feeling to our understanding.

Artistic forms are more complex than any other symbolic forms we know. They are, indeed, not abstractable from the works that exhibit them. We may abstract a shape from an object that has this shape, by disregarding color, weight and texture, even size; but to the total effect that is an artistic form, the color matters, the thickness of lines matters, and the appearance of texture and weight. A given triangle is the same in any position, but to an artistic form its location, balance, and surroundings are not indifferent. Form, in the sense in which artists speak of "significant form" or "expressive form," is not an abstracted structure, but an apparition; and the vital processes of sense and emotion that a good work of art expresses seem to the beholder to be directly contained in it, not symbolized but really presented. The congruence is so striking that symbol and meaning appear as one reality. Actually, as one psychologist who is also a musician has written, "Music sounds as feelings feel." And likewise, in good painting, sculpture, or building, balanced shapes and colors, lines and masses look as emotions, vital tensions and their resolutions feel.

An artist, then, expresses feeling, but not in the way a politician blows off steam or a baby laughs and cries. He formulates that elusive aspect of reality that is commonly taken to be amorphous and chaotic; that is, he objectifies the subjective realm. What he expresses is, therefore, not his own actual feelings, but what he knows about human feeling. Once he is in possession of a rich symbolism, that knowledge may actually exceed his entire personal experience. A work of art expresses a conception of life, emotion, inward reality. But it is neither a confessional nor a frozen tantrum; it is a developed metaphor, a non-discursive symbol that articulates what is verbally ineffable—the logic of consciousness itself.

Cultural Snobbery
ARTHUR KOESTLER

A friend of mine, whom I shall call Brenda, was given for her birthday by one of her admirers a Picasso line drawing in a simple modern frame. It was an admirable and typical sample of Picasso's "classical" period: a Greek youth carrying a girl in his arms, the contours of the two figures somehow mixed up and partly indistinguishable like those of Siamese twins with shared limbs, yet adding up to a charming and harmonious total effect. It looked like a lithograph, but it bore no serial number, so Brenda took it to be a reproduction and hung it, somewhat disappointed with the gift, over her staircase. On my next visit, several weeks later, it was hanging over her drawing room mantelpiece. "I see the Picasso reproduction has been promoted," I said. "*Reproduction!*" she cried indignantly. "It turned out it's an *original*! Isn't it lovely? Look at that line along the girl's hip. . . ." etc.

As a matter of fact, it *was* an original—a shyly understated gift of the mumbling and devoted admirer. But as it was a line drawing consisting of nothing but black contour on white paper, it needed an expert, or at least a good magnifying lens, to decide whether it was an original, a lithograph, or a reproduction. Neither Brenda nor any of her visitors could tell the difference. But they took it for granted, as we all do, that an original deserves a proud display, whereas a reproduction belongs, at best, over the staircase.

I shall now try to analyze, in a pedantic way, the reason for this apparently so natural attitude. The original is of course many times more expensive than a reproduction; but we would indignantly reject the idea of displaying a picture simply because it is expensive; we pretend to be guided in these matters by purely aesthetic considerations. Next, one might surmise that our contempt for reproductions originates in the poor quality and even poorer choice of subjects of the Victorian print. But modern printing techniques have achieved miracles, and some Ganymede reproductions are almost indistinguishable from the original. In the extreme case of the line drawing, we have complete aesthetic equivalence between original and reproduction.

And yet there is something revolting in this equivalence. It even takes a certain courage to admit to oneself that the aesthetic effect of a copy might be indistinguishable from that of the original. We live in an age of stereotyped mass production; and after mass-produced furniture, mass-produced and prefabricated houses, the idea of mass-produced Piero della Francescas is indeed revolting. But then, we have no similar objection to mass-produced gramophone records. Nor to mass-produced books, and yet they too fall into the category of "reproductions." Why then do you prefer, according to your income, a more or less second-rate original picture on the wall to a first-rate reproduction of a masterpiece? Would you rather read a mediocre young poet in manuscript than Shakespeare in a paper-cover edition?

Our argument seems to have become bogged down. Let us find out what Brenda herself has to say to explain her behavior, in a dialogue with the writer:

BRENDA: "I simply can't understand what all this fuss and talk is about. But *of course* my attitude to the drawing has changed since I know that Picasso himself did it. That's nothing to do with snobbery—it's just that I wasn't told before."

K: "Your attitude has changed—but has that thing on the wall changed?"

B: "Of course it hasn't, but now I *see* it differently!"

K: "I would like to understand what it is that determines your attitude to a picture in general."

B: "It's quality, of course."

K: "And what determines its quality?"

B: "Oh, don't be such a pedant. Color, composition, balance, harmony, power, what have you."

K: "So, in looking at a picture, you are guided by purely aesthetic value judgments, depending on the qualities you mentioned?"

B: "Of course I am."

K: "Now, as that picture hasn't changed, and its qualities haven't changed, how can your attitude have changed?"

B: "But I have told you before, you idiot. Of course my attitude to it is now different, since I know it isn't one reproduction in a million, but done by Picasso himself. Can't you see?"

K: "No, I can't; you are contradicting yourself. The rarity of the object, and your knowledge of the manner in which it came into being, do not alter the qualities of that object, and accordingly should not alter your judgment of it, if it were really based on purely aesthetic criteria—as you believe it to be. But it isn't. Your judgment is not based on what you *see*, but on a purely accidental bit of information, which might be right or wrong and is entirely extraneous to the issue."

B: "Wrong? How dare you insinuate that my Picasso isn't an original? And how *dare* you say that the question whether he drew it himself is 'extraneous' to the issue?"

And so it will go on indefinitely. Yet Brenda is not stupid; she is merely confused in believing that her attitude to an object of art is determined by purely aesthetic considerations, whereas in fact it is decisively influenced by factors of a quite different order. She is unable to see her picture isolated from the context of her knowledge of its origin. For, in our minds, the question of origin, authorship, or authenticity, *though in itself extraneous to aesthetic value*, is so intimately and indistinguishably fused with our attitude to the object that we find it well-nigh impossible to isolate the two. Thus, Brenda unconsciously projects one scale of values onto a system of quite different values.

Is Brenda, then, a snob? It depends on the definition of snobbery at which we hope to arrive at the end. But as a working hypothesis, I would like to suggest that this process of unconsciously applying to any given field a judgment derived from an alien system of values constitutes the essence of the phenomenon of snobbery. By these standards Brenda would *not* be a snob if she had said: "The reproduction in this case is just as beautiful as the original. But one gives me a greater thrill than the other for reasons which have nothing to do with beauty." She is an unconscious snob because she is unable to distinguish between the two elements of her experience, unable to name the extraneous cause of her biased aesthetic judgment, or to see that it is biased.

I am aware of pedantically laboring an apparently obvious point. But it will become at once less obvious if we turn to a different yet related problem.

In 1948, a German art restorer named Dietrich Fey, engaged in reconstruction work on Lübeck's ancient St. Marien Church, stated that his workmen had discovered traces of old Gothic wall paintings dating back to the thirteenth century, under a coating of chalk on the church walls. The restoration of the paintings was entrusted to Fey's assistant, Lothar Malskat, who finished the job two years later. In 1950, Chancellor Adenauer presided over the ceremonies marking the completion of the restoration work in the presence of art experts from all parts of Europe. Their unanimous opinion, voiced by Chancellor Adenauer, was that the twenty-one thirteenth-century Gothic saints on the church walls were "a valuable treasure and a fabulous discovery of lost masterpieces."

None of the experts on that or any later occasion expressed doubt as to the authenticity of the frescoes. It was Herr Malskat himself who, two years later, disclosed the fraud. He presented himself on his own initiative at Lübeck police headquarters, where he stated that the frescoes were entirely his own work, undertaken by order from his boss, Herr Fey, and asked to be tried for forgery. The leading German art experts, however, stuck to their opinion: the frescoes, they said, were no doubt genuine, and Herr Malskat was merely seeking cheap publicity. An official Board of Investigation was appointed which came to the conclusion that the restoration of the wall paintings was a hoax—but only after Herr Malskat had confessed that he had also manufactured hundreds of Rembrandts, Watteaus, Toulouse-Lautrecs, Picassos, Henri Rousseaus, Corots, Chagalls, Vlamincks, and other masters, and sold them as originals—some of which were actually found by the police in Herr Fey's house. Without this evidence, it is doubtful whether the German experts would ever have admitted having been fooled.

My point is not the fallibility of the experts. Herr Malskat's exploit is merely the most recent of a number of similarly successful hoaxes and forgeries—of which the most fabulous were probably van Megeeren's false Vermeers. The disturbing question which they raise is whether the Lübeck saints are less beautiful, and have ceased to be "a valuable treasure of masterpieces," simply because they had been painted by Herr Malskat and not by somebody else?

There are several answers to this line of argument, but before going into them I want to continue in the part of *advocatus diaboli* by considering an example of a forgery in a different field: Macpherson's *Ossian*. The case is so notorious that the facts need only be briefly mentioned. James Macpherson (1736–1796), a Scottish poet and adventurer, alleged that in the course of his wanderings, in the Highlands he had discovered some ancient Gaelic manuscripts. Enthusiastic Scottish littérateurs put up a subscription to enable Macpherson to pursue his researches, and in 1761 he published *Fingal, an Ancient Epic Poem in Six Books, together with Several Other Poems composed by Ossian, the Son of Fingal*. Ossian is the legendary third-century hero and bard of Celtic literature. *Fingal* was soon followed by the publication of a still larger Ossianic epic called *Temora*, and this by a collected edition, *The Works of Ossian*. The authenticity of Macpherson's text was at once questioned in England, particularly by Dr. Johnson[1] (whom Macpherson answered by sending him a challenge to a duel), and to his death Macpherson refused, under various unconvincing pretexts, to publish his alleged Gaelic originals. By the turn of the century the con-

---

[1] Samuel Johnson (1709–1784), English essayist, poet, and lexicographer; compiler of the *Dictionary of the English Language* (1755).—Eds.

troversy was settled and it was established that, while Macpherson had used fragments of ancient Celtic lore, most of the "Ossianic" texts were of his own making.

Yet here again the question arises whether the poetic quality of the work itself is altered by the fact that it was written not by Ossian, the son of Fingal, but by James Macpherson? The "Ossianic" texts were translated into many languages, and had a considerable influence on the literature and cultural climate of Europe at the late eighteenth and early nineteenth centuries. This is how the *Encyclopaedia Britannica* sums up its evaluation of Macpherson:

> The varied sources of his work and its worthlessness as a transcript of actual Celtic poems do not alter the fact that he produced a work of art which . . . did more than any single work to bring about the romantic movement in European, and especially in German, literature. . . . Herder and Goethe . . . were among its profound admirers.

These examples could be continued indefinitely. Antique furniture, Roman statuary, Greek tanagra figures, and Italian madonnas are being forged, copied, counterfeited all the time, and the value we set on them is not determined by aesthetic appreciation and pleasure to the eye, but by the precarious and often uncertain judgment of experts. A mediocre but authenticated picture by a known master is held in higher esteem than an artistically superior work of his unknown pupil or "school"—not only by art dealers guided by "investment," but by all of us, including this writer. Are we, then, all snobs to whom a signature, an expert testimonial, or the postmark of a given period is more important than the intrinsic beauty of the object itself?

I now propose to present the case for the defense. It can be summed up in a single sentence: our appraisal of any work of literature or art is never a unitary act, but the result of two independent and simultaneous processes which tend to distort each other.

When we look at an Egyptian fresco, we do not enjoy the painting at its face value, but by means of an unconscious reattunement of the mind to the values of the period. We know, for instance, that the Egyptians had not discovered the technique of perspective in depth. We know that on certain Egyptian murals the size of the figures is determined by their relative social rank. Similarly, we look at every picture through a double frame: the solid frame which isolates it from its surroundings and creates for it a hole in space, as it were; and the unconscious frame of reference in our minds which creates for it a hole in time and locates it in its period and cultural climate. Every time we think that we are making a purely aesthetic judgment based on pure sensory perception, we are in fact judging relative to this second frame or context or mental field.

Any work of art, or literature, or music, can only be appreciated against the background of its period, and that is what we unconsciously do: when we naïvely believe that we are applying absolute criteria, we are in fact applying relative ones. When we contemplate the false Vermeer the first time believing it to be authentic and the second time knowing that it is a fake, our aesthetic experience will indeed completely change, though the picture has remained the same. For it is now seen in a different frame of reference and therefore, in fact, differently. The same considerations apply to the perpetrator of the fake. He may be able to imitate the technique of the seventeenth-century Dutch School, but he could not spontaneously start painting like Vermeer[2]—because his visual organization is different, his perception of reality is different, and because he cannot, except by an artificial effort, erase from his mind the accumulated experience of everything that happened in painting since Vermeer. And if, by a tour de force, a contemporary artist succeeded in reconditioning his own vision to that of the Dutch seventeenth century or the Italian *quattrocento*,[3] he would have to use mass hypnosis to recondition the vision of his customers in a similar manner.

We can add to our knowledge and experience, but we cannot subtract from it. When Picasso decides to disregard the laws of perspective, that means that he has passed through and beyond a certain technique—unlike the Egyptian painter, who has never acquired it. Evolution is an irreversible process; the culture of a period might apparently point into the same direction as an earlier one, but it does so from a different turn of the spiral. A modern primitive is different from a primitive primitive; contemporary classicism is different from any classical classicism; only the mentally insane are able to amputate part of their past.

And yet when we contemplate works of the past, we must perform just such a process of mental subtraction, by attuning our minds to the climate and experience of the period. In order to appreciate them, we must enter into their spirit, by forgetting our modern experience and all that we have learnt since that Homeric epic or Byzantine mosaic was created. We must descend into the past, making our mind a blank; and as we do so, we unconsciously condescend. We close our eyes to crudities of technique, naïveties of perception, prevailing superstitions, limitations of knowledge, factual errors. We make allowances. A little honest introspection will always reveal the element of condescension contained in our admiration for the classics; and part of our enjoyment when listening to the voices of the past is derived from this half-consciously patronizing attitude—"how clever of them to know that at their age." We feel that we have descended a turn of the spiral; we are looking up in awe and wonder at Dante's dreadful Paradise, but at the same time we seem to be bending down, with a tender antiquarian stoop.

[2] Jan Vermeer (1632–1675), Dutch painter.—EDS.
[3] The fifteenth century; used in reference to the art of that time.—EDS.

This legitimate kind of aesthetic double-think degenerates into snobbery at the point where the frame of reference becomes more important than the picture, when the thrill derived from the gesture of bending over the past dominates the aesthetic experience. The result is a widespread confusion of critical judgment—overestimation of the dead and belittlement of the living, indiscriminate reverence for anything that is "classical," "antique," "primitive," or simply old. In its extreme form this tendency prompts people to have their wall brackets and picture frames artificially dirtied to lend them the patina of age; so let us call it the "patina snobbery."

The process that leads to these distortions of judgment is basically the same as outlined before: the projection of one scale of values to a psychologically related but objectively alien field of experience. The essence of snobbery is to assess value according to a wrong type of scale; the snob is always trying to measure beauty with a thermometer or weight with a clock.

The thirteen-year-old daughter of a friend was recently taken to the Greenwich Museum. When she was asked which was the most beautiful thing she had seen in the Museum, she said unhesitatingly: "Nelson's shirt."[4] When asked what was so beautiful about it, she explained: "That shirt with the blood on it was jolly nice. Fancy real blood on a real shirt, which belonged to somebody really historic!"

The child's thrill is obviously derived from the same source as the magic that emanates from Napoleon's inkpot, the lock of hair on the Egyptian mummy's head, the relic of the saint carried in annual procession, the strand of the rope by which a famous murderer was hanged, and from Tolstoi's laundry bill. In the mentality of the primitive, an object which had been in contact with a person is not merely a souvenir: it becomes magically imbued with the substance of that personality and in turn magically emanates something of that substance.

"There is, I am sure, for most of us, a special pleasure in sinking your teeth into a peach produced on the estate of an earl who is related to the Royal Family," a London columnist wrote recently in the *Daily Express*.

Primitive magic survives in the subconscious; the strand of hair carried in the locket, grandmother's wedding dress, the faded fan of the first ball, the regimental badge, all have a half-conscious fetish character. The bobby-soxers who tear shreds off the crooner's garb are the vulgarized twentieth-century version of the worshipers cherishing a splinter from a saint's bone. The value that we set on original manuscripts, on "signed" pieces of furniture, on Dickens' quill and Kepler's[5] telescope, are more dignified mani-

---

[4] Lord Horatio Nelson (1758–1805), British naval hero of the Battle of Trafalgar (1805).—EDS.

[5] Johannes Kepler (1571–1630), German astronomer who discovered the three important laws of planetary motion.—EDS.

festations of the same unconscious tendency. It is, as the child said, "jolly nice" to behold a fragment of a marble by Praxiteles[6]—even if it is battered out of human shape, with a leper's nose and broken ears. The contact with the master's hand has imbued it with a magic quality which has lingered on and radiates at us, conveying the same thrill as "the real blood on Nelson's real shirt."

The change in our attitude—and in the art dealer's price—when it is learned that a cracked and blackened piece of canvas is an "authenticated" work by X has nothing to do with beauty, aesthetics, or what have you—it is the working of sympathetic magic in us. (See Brenda and her Picasso drawing.) The inordinate importance that we attribute to the original, the authenticated, in those borderline cases where only the expert could tell the difference, is a derivative from primitive fetishism. And as every honest art dealer will admit, these borderline cases are so frequent as to be almost the rule. Moreover, it was a general practice in the past for the master to let his pupils assist in the execution of larger undertakings. It is not the eye that guides the average museum visitor, but the magic of names and the magic of age. The bedevilment of aesthetic experience by unconscious fetish worship and patina snobbery is so general that it has become a major factor in our attitude to the art of past epochs—an attitude as remote from spontaneous appreciation as the "Emperor's Clothes" fallacy regarding hyper-modern art forms.

The Quest for Civilisation
KENNETH CLARK

We have no idea where we are going, and sweeping, confident articles on the future seem to me, intellectually, the most disreputable of all forms of public utterance. The scientists who are best qualified to talk have kept their mouths shut. J. B. S. Haldane[1] summed up the situation when he said: "My own suspicion is that the universe is not only queerer than we suppose, but queerer than we can suppose. I saw a new heaven and a new earth, for the old heaven and the old earth had passed away." Which reminds us that the universe so vividly described in the Book of Revelation is queer enough; but with the help of symbols not beyond description. Whereas our universe cannot even be stated symbolically. . . . The incomprehensibility of our new cosmos seems to me, ultimately, to be the reason for the chaos of modern art. I know next to nothing about

---

[6] Greek sculptor of the fourth century B.C.—EDS.

[1] J. B. S. Haldane (1892–1964), British scientist, professor, and prolific author of scientific works, including *New Paths in Genetics* (1941).—EDS.

science, but I've spent my life in trying to learn about art, and I am completely baffled by what is taking place today. I sometimes like what I see, but when I read modern critics I realise that my preferences are merely accidental.

However, in the world of action a few things are obvious—so obvious that I hesitate to repeat them. One of them is our increasing reliance on machines. They have ceased to be tools and have begun to give us directions. And unfortunately machines, from the Maxim gun to the computer, are for the most part means by which a minority can keep free men in subjection.

Our other specialty is our urge to destruction. With the help of machines we did our best to destroy ourselves in two wars, and in doing so we released a flood of evil, which intelligent people have tried to justify with praise of violence, "theaters of cruelty" and so forth. Add to this the memory of that shadowy companion who is always with us, like an inverted guardian angel, silent, invisible, almost incredible—and yet unquestionably there and ready to assert itself at the touch of a button; and one must concede that the future of civilisation does not look very bright.

And yet when I look at the world about me . . . I don't at all feel that we are entering a new period of barbarism. The things that made the Dark Ages so dark—the isolation, the lack of mobility, the lack of curiosity, the hopelessness—don't obtain at all. When I have the good fortune to visit one of our new universities, it seems to me that the inheritors of all our catastrophes look cheerful enough—very different from the melancholy late Romans or pathetic Gauls whose likenesses have come down to us. In fact, I should doubt if so many people have ever been as well-fed, as well-read, as bright-minded, as curious and as critical as the young are today.

Of course there has been a little flattening at the top. But one mustn't overrate the culture of what used to be called "top people" before the wars. They had charming manners, but they were as ignorant as swans. They did know something about literature, and a few had been to the opera. But they knew nothing about painting and less than nothing about philosophy (except for Balfour[2] and Haldane). The members of a music group or an art group at a provincial university would be five times better informed and more alert. Naturally, these bright-minded young people think poorly of existing institutions and want to abolish them. Well, one doesn't need to be young to dislike institutions. But the dreary fact remains that, even in the darkest ages, it was institutions that made society work, and if civilisation is to survive society must somehow be made to work.

At this point I reveal myself in my true colors, as a stick-in-the-mud. I hold a number of beliefs that have been repudiated by the liveliest intellects

---

[2] Arthur James Balfour, First Earl of Balfour (1848–1930), philosopher and prime minister (1902–1905), author of *A Defence of Philosophic Doubt* (1879), *Theism and Humanism* (1915), and *Theism and Thought* (1923).—Eds.

of our time. I believe that order is better than chaos, creation better than destruction. I prefer gentleness to violence, forgiveness to vendetta. On the whole I think that knowledge is preferable to ignorance, and I am sure that human sympathy is more valuable than ideology. I believe that in spite of the recent triumphs of science, men haven't changed much in the last two thousand years; and in consequence we must still try to learn from history. History is ourselves. I also hold one or two beliefs that are more difficult to put shortly. For example, I believe in courtesy, the ritual by which we avoid hurting other people's feelings by satisfying our own egos. And I think we should remember that we are part of a great whole, which for convenience we call nature. All living things are our brothers and sisters. Above all, I believe in the God-given genius of certain individuals, and I value a society that makes their existence possible.

[Our civilisation] has been filled with great works of genius, in architecture, sculpture and painting, in philosophy, poetry and music, in science and engineering. There they are; you can't dismiss them. And they are only a fraction of what western man has achieved in the last thousand years, often after setbacks and deviations at least as destructive as those of our own time. Western civilisation has been a series of rebirths. Surely this should give us confidence in ourselves.

. . . It is lack of confidence, more than anything else, that kills a civilisation. We can destroy ourselves by cynicism and disillusion, just as effectively as by bombs. Fifty years ago W. B. Yeats,[3] who was more like a man of genius than anyone I have ever known, wrote a famous prophetic poem.[4]

> Things fall apart; the centre cannot hold;
> Mere anarchy is loosed upon the world,
> The blood-dimmed tide is loosed, and everywhere
> The ceremony of innocence is drowned;
> The best lack all conviction, while the worst
> Are full of passionate intensity.

Well, that was certainly true between the wars, and it damn nearly destroyed us. Is it true today? Not quite, because good people have convictions, rather too many of them. The trouble is that there is still no center. The moral and intellectual failure of Marxism has left us with no alternative to heroic materialism, and that isn't enough. One may be optimistic, but one can't exactly be joyful at the prospect before us.

---

[3] William Butler Yeats (1865–1939), major poet and leader of the Irish literary revival. Among his books are *Deirdre* (1907), *The Wild Swans at Coole* (1917), *The Winding Stair* (1929), and *Wheels and Butterflies* (1934). He was awarded the Nobel Prize for literature in 1923.—EDS.

[4] The title of the poem is "The Second Coming."—EDS.

Ode on a Grecian Urn[1]
JOHN KEATS

1

Thou still unravished bride of quietness,
  Thou foster child of silence and slow time,
Sylvan[2] historian, who canst thus express
  A flowery tale more sweetly than our rhyme:
What leaf-fringed legend haunts about thy shape
  Of deities or mortals, or of both,
    In Tempe or the dales of Arcady?[3]
What men or gods[4] are these? What maidens loath?
What mad pursuit? What struggle to escape?
    What pipes and timbrels? What wild ecstasy?

2

Heard melodies are sweet, but those unheard
  Are sweeter; therefore, ye soft pipes, play on;
Not to the sensual ear,[5] but, more endeared,
  Pipe to the spirit ditties of no tone:
Fair youth, beneath the trees, thou canst not leave
  Thy song, nor ever can those trees be bare;
    Bold Lover, never, never canst thou kiss,
Though winning near the goal—yet, do not grieve;
    She cannot fade, though thou hast not thy bliss,
  Forever wilt thou love, and she be fair!

3

Ah, happy, happy boughs! that cannot shed
  Your leaves, nor ever bid the Spring adieu;
And, happy melodist, unwearièd,
  Forever piping songs forever new;
More happy love! more happy, happy love!
    Forever warm and still to be enjoyed,
      Forever panting, and forever young;

---

[1] The urn depicts two scenes: young lovers pursuing maidens and a procession from a little town going into the country to sacrifice a heifer. Both scenes are for Keats the perfect correlative for permanence—the permanence of art in the midst of a human world of transience.—EDS.

[2] Woodland.—EDS.

[3] Tempe is a lovely valley in Greece; Arcady, or Arcadia, an actual valley in Greece, has come to symbolize the pastoral ideal in art and literature.—EDS.

[4] The ancient Greeks depicted their gods in human form.—EDS.

[5] The ear of the senses—as opposed to that of the imagination.—EDS.

All breathing human passion far above,
   That leaves a heart high-sorrowful and cloyed,
     A burning forehead, and a parching tongue.

4

Who are these coming to the sacrifice?
   To what green altar, O mysterious priest,
Lead'st thou that heifer lowing at the skies,
   And all her silken flanks with garlands dressed?
What little town by river or sea shore,
   Or mountain-built with peaceful citadel,
     Is emptied of this folk, this pious morn?
And, little town, thy streets for evermore
   Will silent be; and not a soul to tell
     Why thou art desolate, can e'er return.

5

O Attic[6] shape! Fair attitude! with brede
Of marble men and maidens overwrought,[7]
With forest branches and the trodden weed;
   Thou, silent form, dost tease us out of thought
As doth eternity: Cold Pastoral!
   When old age shall this generation waste,
     Thou shalt remain, in midst of other woe
   Than ours, a friend to man, to whom thou say'st,
"Beauty is truth, truth beauty,"[8]—that is all
   Ye know on earth, and all ye need to know.

---

[6] Greek—from *Attica*, name of an ancient region in Greece.—Eds.

[7] Ornamented all over.—Eds.

[8] There is great critical controversy over this statement—does the urn speak these lines? Does Keats speak the remaining lines of the poem? For a full treatment of the various interpretations, see *Keats' Well-Read Urn*, edited by H. T. Lyon (1958).—Eds.

4

Sciences

Science and Scientists

Of Life

Ecology

Some Problems

Some Adjustments

This section, "Sciences," comes between but does not separate the aesthetic and humanistic ideas contained in "The Arts" and "Final Things." Instead of reflecting the too easy view of opposition between the sciences and the humanities, it emphasizes the continuity between them. At the end of his introductory essay on "The Usefulness of Useless Knowledge," Abraham Flexner explicitly groups music, art, and "every other expression of the untrammeled human spirit" with what he has said of science and mathematics.

Without proposing an identity, we would look upon the similarities between the scientific and humanistic imaginations as quite as striking as their differences. Not accidentally Robert Oppenheimer uses the word "beautiful" four times in his biographical sketch of Einstein. Lewis Thomas speaks of the "music" in nature. Robert Geroch makes the point that science is no less full of crosscurrents than poetry or fiction. And to Loren Eiseley "The Golden Alphabet" on a shell symbolizes the inextricability of nature and literature, while Marianne Moore celebrates a snail for its "style."

Still, science has its own domain, and to give glimpses into that domain, especially the rapidly changing and developing life sciences, is the main purpose of the group of essays "Of Life." Charles Darwin's centrality is recognized in our placing first a part of his own *Origin of Species*, in Jacob Bronowski's chapter from his book *The Ascent of Man* (playing on Darwin's title *The Descent of Man*), and in Robert Ardrey's dramatic account of the territorial imperative. Loren Eiseley brings the whole section to a close with his own view of Darwin. But Eiseley also recognizes the astonishing variety and differences among scientists by contrasting Darwin and Thoreau—as we tried to do earlier by including Oppenheimer's thumbnail biography of Albert Einstein and John Maynard Keynes's portrait of Isaac Newton. The condensed, classical account of the mechanism of carbon monoxide poisoning by the French physiologist Claude Bernard may profitably be compared with Geroch's outlining of the zigzag trial-and-error methods of contemporary physicists. Both are valid accounts of scientific method as it is pursued by real scientists.

Other matters are in store. One of them is the despoiling of nature by the misuse of technology emerging from science, yet the possible rescue of nature by even more technology and science. Another is the necessity of ecology. Then we come to some problems that scientists still face. And finally we see a series of "adjustments," a word that we have taken from Harlow Shapley's essay and extended into the whole area of the continual process of testing older concepts and proposing new clarifications.

Perhaps some adjustments may strike readers as too neat or easy or even hazardous. Though René Dubos argues that "Trend Is Not Destiny," he admits that his examples "do not correspond to final solutions." That experimentation with genetic structure may conceivably lead to life forms dangerous to man is a general fear that has been voiced specifically by many of the scientists quoted by Cheryl M. Fields in her article on recombinant DNA studies. One wonders whether like Newton, as described here by Keynes, those scientists suspect that they may become Copernicus and Faustus in one. But of one thing we may be sure. Science never destroys wonder at the beauty and complexity of the world or of life, whether they are seen through the telescope or under the microscope: as Darwin himself believed, science only shifts that wonder higher and deeper.

Science and Scientists

The Usefulness of Useless Knowledge
ABRAHAM FLEXNER

I

Is it not a curious fact that in a world steeped in irrational hatreds which threaten civilization itself, men and women—old and young—detach themselves wholly or partly from the angry current of daily life to devote themselves to the cultivation of beauty, to the extension of knowledge, to the cure of disease, to the amelioration of suffering, just as though fanatics were not simultaneously engaged in spreading pain, ugliness, and suffering? The world has always been a sorry and confused sort of place—yet poets and artists and scientists have ignored the factors that would, if attended to, paralyze them. From a practical point of view, intellectual and spiritual life is, on the surface, a useless form of activity, in which men indulge because they procure for themselves greater satisfactions than are otherwise obtainable. In this paper I shall concern myself with the question of the extent to which the pursuit of these useless satisfactions proves unexpectedly the source from which undreamed-of utility is derived.

We hear it said with tiresome iteration that ours is a materialistic age, the main concern of which should be the wider distribution of material goods and worldly opportunities. The justified outcry of those who through no fault of their own are deprived of opportunity and a fair share of worldly goods therefore diverts an increasing number of students from the studies which their fathers pursued to the equally important and no less urgent study of social, economic, and governmental problems. I have no quarrel with this tendency. The world in which we live is the only world about which our senses can testify. Unless it is made a better world, a fairer world, millions will continue to go to their graves silent, saddened, and embittered. I have myself spent many years pleading that our schools should become more acutely aware of the world in which their pupils and students are destined to pass their lives. Now I sometimes wonder whether that current has not become too strong and whether there would be sufficient opportunity for a full life if the world were emptied of some of the useless things that give it spiritual significance; in other words, whether our conception of what is useful may not have become too narrow to be adequate to the roaming and capricious possibilities of the human spirit.

We may look at this question from two points of view: the scientific and the humanistic or spiritual. Let us take the scientific first. I recall a conversation which I had some years ago with Mr. George Eastman[1] on the subject of use. Mr. Eastman, a wise and gentle farseeing man, gifted with taste in music and art, had been saying to me that he meant to devote his vast fortune to the promotion of education in useful subjects. I ventured to ask him whom he regarded as the most useful worker in science in the world. He replied instantaneously: "Marconi."[2] I surprised him by saying, "Whatever pleasure we derive from the radio or however wireless and the radio may have added to human life, Marconi's share was practically negligible."

I shall not forget his astonishment on this occasion. He asked me to explain. I replied to him somewhat as follows:

"Mr. Eastman, Marconi was inevitable. The real credit for everything that has been done in the field of wireless belongs, as far as such fundamental credit can be definitely assigned to anyone, to Professor Clerk Maxwell,[3] who in 1865 carried out certain abstruse and remote calculations in the field of magnetism and electricity. Maxwell reproduced his abstract equations in a treatise published in 1873. At the next meeting of the British Association Professor H. J. S. Smith of Oxford declared that 'no mathematician can turn over the pages of these volumes without realizing that they contain a theory which has already added largely to the methods and resources of pure mathematics.' Other discoveries supplemented Maxwell's theoretical work during the next fifteen years. Finally in 1887 and 1888 the scientific problem still remaining—the detection and demonstration of the electromagnetic waves which are the carriers of wireless signals—was solved by Heinrich Hertz,[4] a worker in Helmholtz's[5] laboratory in Berlin. Neither Maxwell nor Hertz had any concern about the utility of their work; no such thought ever entered their minds. They had no practical objective. The inventor in the legal sense was of course Marconi, but what did Marconi invent? Merely the last technical detail, mainly the now obsolete receiving device called coherer, almost universally discarded."

Hertz and Maxwell could invent nothing, but it was their useless theoretical work which was seized upon by a clever technician and which has created new means for communication, utility, and amusement by which men whose merits are relatively slight have obtained fame and earned millions. Who were the useful men? Not Marconi, but Clerk Maxwell and Heinrich Hertz. Hertz and Maxwell were geniuses without thought of use. Marconi was a clever inventor with no thought but use.

---

[1] George Eastman (1854–1932) was the American inventor of the Kodak camera and, with Thomas Edison, performed experiments crucial to the development of the moving picture.—Eds.

[2] Guglielmo Marconi (1874–1937), Italian inventor of the wireless telegraph.—Eds.

[3] James Clerk Maxwell (1831–1879), Scottish physicist.—Eds.

[4] Heinrich Rudolf Hertz (1857–1894), German physicist.—Eds.

[5] Hermann Ludwig Ferdinand von Helmholtz (1821–1894), German physicist and physiologist.—Eds.

The mention of Hertz's name recalled to Mr. Eastman the Hertzian waves, and I suggested that he might ask the physicists of the University of Rochester precisely what Hertz and Maxwell had done; but one thing I said he could be sure of, namely, that they had done their work without thought of use and that throughout the whole history of science most of the really great discoveries which had ultimately proved to be beneficial to mankind had been made by men and women who were driven not by the desire to be useful but merely the desire to satisfy their curiosity.

"Curiosity?" asked Mr. Eastman.

"Yes," I replied, "curiosity, which may or may not eventuate in something useful, is probably the outstanding characteristic of modern thinking. It is not new. It goes back to Galileo, Bacon, and to Sir Isaac Newton,[6] and it must be absolutely unhampered. Institutions of learning should be devoted to the cultivation of curiosity and the less they are deflected by considerations of immediacy of application, the more likely they are to contribute not only to human welfare but to the equally important satisfaction of intellectual interest which may indeed be said to have become the ruling passion of intellectual life in modern times."

II

What is true of Heinrich Hertz working quietly and unnoticed in a corner of Helmholtz's laboratory in the later years of the nineteenth century may be said of scientists and mathematicians the world over for several centuries past. We live in a world that would be helpless without electricity. Called upon to mention a discovery of the most immediate and far-reaching practical use we might well agree upon electricity. But who made the fundamental discoveries out of which the entire electrical development of more than one hundred years has come?

The answer is interesting. Michael Faraday's[7] father was a blacksmith; Michael himself was apprenticed to a bookbinder. In 1812, when he was already twenty-one years of age, a friend took him to the Royal Institution where he heard Sir Humphry Davy[8] deliver four lectures on chemical subjects. He kept notes and sent a copy of them to Davy. The very next year, 1813, he became an assistant in Davy's laboratory, working on chemical problems. Two years later he accompanied Davy on a trip to the Continent. In 1825, when he was thirty-four years of age, he became Director of the Laboratory of the Royal Institution where he spent fifty-four years of his life.

Faraday's interest soon shifted from chemistry to electricity and magnetism, to which he devoted the rest of his active life. Important but puzzling work in this field had been previously accomplished by Oersted,

---

[6] Galileo Galilei (1564–1642), Italian physicist and astronomer; Francis Bacon (1561–1626), British writer and philosopher; Isaac Newton (1642–1727), British mathematician and astronomer.—EDS.

[7] Michael Faraday (1791–1867), British chemist and physicist.—EDS.

[8] Sir Humphry Davy (1778–1829), British chemist.—EDS.

Ampere, and Wollaston.[9] Faraday cleared away the difficulties which they had left unsolved and by 1841 had succeeded in the task of induction of the electric current. Four years later a second and equally brilliant epoch in his career opened when he discovered the effect of magnetism on polarized light. His earlier discoveries have led to the infinite number of practical applications by means of which electricity has lightened the burdens and increased the opportunities of modern life. His later discoveries have thus far been less prolific of practical results. What difference did this make to Faraday? Not the least. At no period of his unmatched career was he interested in utility. He was absorbed in disentangling the riddles of the universe, at first chemical riddles, in later periods, physical riddles. As far as he cared, the question of utility was never raised. Any suspicion of utility would have restricted his restless curiosity. In the end, utility resulted, but it was never a criterion to which his ceaseless experimentation could be subjected.

In the atmosphere which envelops the world to-day it is perhaps timely to emphasize the fact that the part played by science in making war more destructive and more horrible was an unconscious and unintended byproduct of scientific activity. Lord Rayleigh,[10] president of the British Association for the Advancement of Science, in a recent address points out in detail how the folly of man, not the intention of the scientists, is responsible for the destructive use of the agents employed in modern warfare. The innocent study of the chemistry of carbon compounds, which has led to infinite beneficial results, showed that the action of nitric acid on substances like benzene, glycerine, cellulose, etc., resulted not only in the beneficent aniline dye industry but in the creation of nitroglycerine, which has uses good and bad. Somewhat later Alfred Nobel,[11] turning to the same subject, showed that by mixing nitroglycerine with other substances, solid explosives which could be safely handled could be produced—among others, dynamite. It is to dynamite that we owe our progress in mining, in the making of such railroad tunnels as those which now pierce the Alps and other mountain ranges; but of course dynamite has been abused by politicians and soldiers. Scientists are, however, no more to blame than they are to blame for an earthquake or a flood. The same thing can be said of poison gas. Pliny[12] was killed by breathing sulphur dioxide in the eruption of Vesuvius almost two thousand years ago. Chlorine was not isolated by scientists for warlike purposes, and the same is true of mustard

---

[9] Hans Christian Oersted (1777–1851), Danish physicist; André-Marie Ampère (1775–1836), French chemist and physicist; William Hyde Wollaston (1766–1828), British chemist.—Eds.

[10] John William Strutt (Lord Rayleigh) (1842–1919), British physicist—Eds.

[11] Alfred Bernhard Nobel (1833–1896), Swedish chemist. Nobel's earnings from his invention of dynamite were donated for Nobel prizes.—Eds.

[12] Gaius Plinius Secundus (23–79 A.D.), Roman scholar who wrote the thirty-seven–volume *Natural History*.—Eds.

gas. These substances could be limited to beneficent use, but when the airplane was perfected, men whose hearts were poisoned and whose brains were addled perceived that the airplane, an innocent invention, the result of long disinterested and scientific effort, could be made an instrument of destruction, of which no one had ever dreamed and at which no one had ever deliberately aimed.

In the domain of higher mathematics almost innumerable instances can be cited. For example, the most abstruse mathematical work of the eighteenth and nineteenth centuries was the "Non-Euclidian Geometry." Its inventor, Gauss,[13] though recognized by his contemporaries as a distinguished mathematician, did not dare to publish his work on "Non-Euclidian Geometry" for a quarter of a century. As a matter of fact, the theory of relativity itself with all its infinite practical bearings would have been utterly impossible without the work which Gauss did at Göttingen.

Again, what is known now as "group theory" was an abstract and inapplicable mathematical theory. It was developed by men who were curious and whose curiosity and puttering led them into strange paths; but "group theory" is today the basis of the quantum theory of spectroscopy, which is in daily use by people who have no idea as to how it came about. . . .

III

I am pleading for the abolition of the word "use," and for the freeing of the human spirit. To be sure, we shall thus free some harmless cranks. To be sure, we shall thus waste some precious dollars. But what is infinitely more important is that we shall be striking the shackles off the human mind and setting it free for the adventures which in our own day have, on the one hand, taken Hale and Rutherford and Einstein[14] and their peers millions upon millions of miles into the uttermost realms of space and, on the other, loosed the boundless energy imprisoned in the atom. What Rutherford and others like Bohr and Millikan[15] have done out of sheer curiosity in the effort to understand the construction of the atom has released forces which may transform human life; but this ultimate and unforeseen and unpredictable practical result is not offered as a justification for Rutherford or Einstein or Millikan or Bohr or any of their peers. Let them alone. No educational administrator can possibly direct the channels in which these or other men shall work. The waste, I admit again, looks prodigious. It is not really so. All the waste that could be summed up in developing the science of bacteriology is as nothing compared to the advantages which have accrued from the discoveries of Pasteur, Koch,

---

[13] Karl Friedrich Gauss (1777–1855), German mathematician.—Eds.

[14] George Ellery Hale (1868–1938), American astrophysicist; Ernest Rutherford (1871–1937), physicist and chemist from New Zealand; Albert Einstein (1879–1955), German-born physicist who developed the theory of relativity.—Eds.

[15] Niels Henrik Bohr (1885–1962), Danish physicist; Robert Millikan (1868–1953), American physicist.—Eds.

Ehrlich, Theobald Smith,[16] and scores of others—advantages that could never have accrued if the idea of possible use had permeated their minds. These great artists—for such are scientists and bacteriologists—disseminated the spirit which prevailed in laboratories in which they were simply following the line of their own natural curiosity.

I am not criticising institutions like schools of engineering or law in which the usefulness motive necessarily predominates. Not infrequently the tables are turned, and practical difficulties encountered in industry or in laboratories stimulate theoretical inquiries which may or may not solve the problems by which they were suggested, but may also open up new vistas, useless at the moment, but pregnant with future achievements, practical and theoretical.

With the rapid accumulation of "useless" or theoretic knowledge a situation has been created in which it has become increasingly possible to attack practical problems in a scientific spirit. Not only inventors, but "pure" scientists have indulged in this sport. I have mentioned Marconi, an inventor, who, while a benefactor to the human race, as a matter of fact merely "picked other men's brains." Edison[17] belongs to the same category. Pasteur was different. He was a great scientist; but he was not averse to attacking practical problems—such as the condition of French grapevines or the problems of beer-brewing—and not only solving the immediate difficulty, but also wresting from the practical problem some far-reaching theoretic conclusion, "useless" at the moment, but likely in some unforeseen manner to be "useful" later. Ehrlich, fundamentally speculative in his curiosity, turned fiercely upon the problem of syphilis and doggedly pursued it until a solution of immediate practical use—the discovery of salvarsan—was found. The discoveries of insulin by Banting for use in diabetes and of liver extract by Minot and Whipple[18] for use in pernicious anemia belong in the same category; both were made by thoroughly scientific men, who realized that much "useless" knowledge had been piled up by men unconcerned with its practical bearings, but that the time was now ripe to raise practical questions in a scientific manner.

Thus it becomes obvious that one must be wary in attributing scientific discovery wholly to any one person. Almost every discovery has a long

---

[16] Louis Pasteur (1822–1895), French chemist and bacteriologist who discovered a method of inhibiting fermentation; Robert Koch (1843–1910), German bacteriologist who developed the basic principles and techniques of modern bacteriology; Paul Ehrlich (1854–1915), German scientist who initiated advances in biomedical research in hematology, immunology, and chemotherapy; Theobald Smith (1859–1934), American microbiologist who worked to discover the causal agent and mode of transmission of Texas cattle fever.—EDS.

[17] Thomas Alva Edison (1847–1931), American inventor of lighting systems.—EDS.

[18] Frederick Grant Banting (1891–1941), Canadian scientist; George Richards Minot (1885–1950), American physician; George Hoyt Whipple (1879–   ), American pathologist. Minot and Whipple received the 1934 Nobel Prize for medicine for this research.—EDS.

and precarious history. Some one finds a bit here, another a bit there. A third step succeeds later and thus onward till a genius pieces the bits together and makes the decisive contribution. Science, like the Mississippi, begins in a tiny rivulet in the distant forest. Gradually other streams swell its volume. And the roaring river that bursts the dikes is formed from countless sources.

I cannot deal with this aspect exhaustively, but I may in passing say this: over a period of one or two hundred years the contributions of professional schools to their respective activities will probably be found to lie, not so much in the training of men who may to-morrow become practical engineers or practical lawyers or practical doctors, but rather in the fact that even in the pursuit of strictly practical aims an enormous amount of apparently useless activity goes on. Out of this useless activity there come discoveries which may well prove of infinitely more importance to the human mind and to the human spirit than the accomplishment of the useful ends for which the schools were founded.

The considerations upon which I have touched emphasize—if emphasis were needed—the overwhelming importance of spiritual and intellectual freedom. I have spoken of experimental science; I have spoken of mathematics; but what I say is equally true of music and art and of every other expression of the untrammeled human spirit. The mere fact that they bring satisfaction to an individual soul bent upon its own purification and elevation is all the justification that they need. And in justifying these without any reference whatsoever, implied or actual, to usefulness we justify colleges, universities, and institutes of research. An institution which sets free successive generations of human souls is amply justified whether or not this graduate or that makes a so-called useful contribution to human knowledge. A poem, a symphony, a painting, a mathematical truth, a new scientific fact, all bear in themselves all the justification that universities, colleges, and institutes of research need or require. . . .

This is not a new idea. It was the idea which animated von Humboldt[19] when, in the hour of Germany's conquest by Napoleon, he conceived and founded the University of Berlin. It is the idea which animated President Gilman[20] in the founding of the Johns Hopkins University, after which every university in this country has sought in greater or less degree to remake itself. It is the idea to which every individual who values his immortal soul will be true whatever the personal consequences to himself.

---

[19] Friedrich Heinrich Alexander von Humboldt (1769–1859), German scientist. —EDS.

[20] Daniel Coit Gilman (1831–1908), American educator and scientist; president of Johns Hopkins University from 1875 to 1901.—EDS.

On Albert Einstein[1]
ROBERT OPPENHEIMER

Though I knew Einstein for two or three decades, it was only in the last decade of his life that we were close colleagues and something of friends. But I thought that it might be useful, because I am sure that it is not too soon—and for our generation perhaps almost too late—to start to dispel the clouds of myth and to see the great mountain peak that these clouds hide. As always, the myth has its charms; but the truth is far more beautiful.

Late in his life, in connection with his despair over weapons and wars, Einstein said that if he had to live it over again he would be a plumber. This was a balance of seriousness and jest that no one should now attempt to disturb. Believe me, he had no idea of what it was to be a plumber; least of all in the United States, where we have a joke that the typical behavior of this specialist is that he never brings his tools to the scene of the crisis. Einstein brought his tools to his crises; Einstein was a physicist, a natural philosopher, the greatest of our time.

What we have heard, what you all know, what is the true part of the myth is his extraordinary originality. The discovery of quanta[2] would surely have come one way or another, but he discovered them. Deep understanding of what it means that no signal could travel faster than light would surely have come; the formal equations were already known; but this simple, brilliant understanding of the physics could well have been slow in coming, and blurred, had he not done it for us. The general theory of relativity which, even today, is not well proved experimentally, no one but he would have done for a long, long time. It is in fact only in the last decade, the last years, that one has seen how a pedestrian and hard-working physicist, or many of them, might reach that theory and understand this singular union of geometry and gravitation; and we can do even that today only because some of the *a priori* open possibilities are limited by the confirmation of Einstein's discovery that light would be deflected by gravity.

Yet there is another side besides the originality. Einstein brought to the work of originality deep elements of tradition. It is only possible to discover in part how he came by it, by following his reading, his friendships, the meager record that we have. But of these deep-seated elements of tradition—I will not try to enumerate them all; I do not know them all—at least three were indispensable and stayed with him.

[1] Lecture delivered at UNESCO (United Nations Educational, Scientific, and Cultural Organization) House in Paris on December 13, 1965.—EDS.

[2] Quanta, the plural of quantum: "One of the very small increments or parcels into which many forms of energy are subdivided and which are always associated directly or indirectly with a frequency v such that the quantum is equal to v multiplied by Planck constant." *Webster's Third New International Dictionary*.—EDS.

The first is from the rather beautiful but recondite part of physics that is the explanation of the laws of thermodynamics in terms of the mechanics of large numbers of particles, statistical mechanics. This was with Einstein all the time. It was what enabled him from Planck's[3] discovery of the law of black body radiation to conclude that light was not only waves but particles, particles with an energy proportional to their frequency and momentum determined by their wave-number, the famous relations that de Broglie[4] was to extend to all matter, to electrons first and then clearly to all matter.

It was this statistical tradition that led Einstein to the laws governing the emission and absorption of light by atomic systems. It was this that enabled him to see the connection between de Broglie's waves and the statistics of light-quanta proposed by Bose.[5] It was this that kept him an active proponent and discoverer of the new phenomena of quantum physics up to 1925.

The second and equally deep strand—and here I think we do know where it came from—was his total love of the idea of a field: the following of physical phenomena in minute and infinitely subdividable detail in space and in time. This gave him his first great drama of trying to see how Maxwell's[6] equations could be true. They were the first field equations of physics; they are still true today with only very minor and well-understood modifications. It is this tradition which made him know that there had to be a field theory of gravitation, long before the clues to that theory were securely in his hand.

The third tradition was less one of physics than of philosophy. It is a form of the principle of sufficient reason. It was Einstein who asked what do we mean, what can we measure, what elements in physics are conventional? He insisted that those elements that were conventional could have no part in the real predictions of physics. This also had roots: for one the mathematical invention of Riemann,[7] who saw how very limited the geometry of the Greeks had been, how unreasonably limited. But in a more important sense, it followed from the long tradition of European philosophy, you may say starting with Descartes[8]—if you wish you can start it in the Thirteenth Century, because in fact it did start then—and leading through the British empiricists, and very clearly formulated, though probably without influence in Europe, by Charles Peirce:[9] One had to ask

---

[3] Max Karl Planck (1858–1947), German theoretical physicist.—EDS.

[4] Louis-César-Victor-Maurice de Broglie (1875–1960), French physicist.—EDS.

[5] Jagadis Chandra Bose (1858–1937), Indian physicist.—EDS.

[6] James Clerk Maxwell (1831–1879), Scottish physicist.—EDS.

[7] Georg Friedrich Riemann (1826–1866), German physicist and mathematician. —EDS.

[8] René Descartes (1596–1650), French mathematician and philosopher.—EDS.

[9] Charles Sanders Peirce (1839–1914), American philosopher and mathematician. —EDS.

how do we do it, what do we mean, is this just something that we can use to help ourselves in calculating, or is it something that we can actually study in nature by physical means? For the point here is that the laws of nature not only describe the results of observations, but the laws of nature delimit the scope of observations. That was the point of Einstein's understanding of the limiting character of the velocity of light; it also was the nature of the resolution in quantum theory, where the quantum of action, Planck's constant, was recognized as limiting the fineness of the transaction between the system studied and the machinery used to study it, limiting this fineness in a form of atomicity quite different from and quite more radical than any that the Greeks had imagined or than was familiar from the atomic theory of chemistry.

In the last years of Einstein's life, the last twenty-five years, his tradition in a certain sense failed him. They were the years he spent at Princeton[10] and this, though a source of sorrow, should not be concealed. He had a right to that failure. He spent those years first in trying to prove that the quantum theory had inconsistencies in it. No one could have been more ingenious in thinking up unexpected and clever examples; but it turned out that the inconsistencies were not there; and often their resolution could be found in earlier work of Einstein himself. When that did not work, after repeated efforts, Einstein had simply to say that he did not like the theory. He did not like the elements of indeterminacy. He did not like the abandonment of continuity or of causality. These were things that he had grown up with, saved by him, and enormously enlarged; and to see them lost, even though he had put the dagger in the hand of their assassin by his own work, was very hard on him. He fought with Bohr[11] in a noble and furious way, and he fought with the theory which he had fathered but which he hated. It was not the first time that this has happened in science.

He also worked with a very ambitious program, to combine the understanding of electricity and gravitation in such a way as to explain what he regarded as the semblance—the illusion—of discreteness, of particles in nature. I think that it was clear then, and believe it to be obviously clear today, that the things that this theory worked with were too meager, left out too much that was known to physicists but had not been known much in Einstein's student days. Thus it looked like a hopelessly limited and historically rather accidentally conditioned approach. Although Einstein commanded the affection, or, more rightly, the love of everyone for his determination to see through his program, he lost most contact with the profession of physics, because there were things that had been learned which came too late in life for him to concern himself with them.

[10] Einstein spent his last years at the Institute for Advanced Study in Princeton, New Jersey.—Eds.
[11] Niels Henrik Bohr (1885–1962), Danish physicist.—Eds.

Einstein was indeed one of the friendliest of men. I had the impression that he was also, in an important sense, alone. Many very great men are lonely; yet I had the impression that although he was a deep and loyal friend, the stronger human affections played a not very deep or very central part in his life taken as a whole. He had of course incredibly many disciples, in the sense of people who, reading his work or hearing it taught by him, learned from him and had a new view of physics, of the philosophy of physics, of the nature of the world that we live in. But he did not have, in the technical jargon, a school. He did not have very many students who were his concern as apprentices and disciples. And there was an element of the lone worker in him, in sharp contrast to the teams we see today, and in sharp contrast to the highly cooperative way in which some other parts of science have developed. In later years, he had people working with him. They were typically called assistants and they had a wonderful life. Just being with him was wonderful. His secretary had a wonderful life. The sense of grandeur never left him for a minute, nor his sense of humor. The assistants did one thing which he lacked in his young days. His early papers are paralyzingly beautiful, but there are many errata. Later there were none. I had the impression that, along with its miseries, his fame gave him some pleasures, not only the human pleasure of meeting people but the extreme pleasure of music played not only with Elizabeth of Belgium but more with Adolf Busch, for he was not that good a violinist. He loved the sea and he loved sailing and was always grateful for a ship. I remember walking home with him on his seventy-first birthday. He said, "You know, when it's once been given to a man to do something sensible, afterward life is a little strange."

Einstein is also, and I think rightly, known as a man of very great good will and humanity. Indeed, if I had to think of a single word for his attitude towards human problems, I would pick the Sanskrit word *Ahinsa*, not to hurt, harmlessness. He had a deep distrust of power; he did not have that convenient and natural converse with statesmen and men of power that was quite appropriate to Rutherford[12] and to Bohr, perhaps the two physicists of this century who most nearly rivaled him in eminence. In 1915, as he made the general theory of relativity, Europe was tearing itself to pieces and half losing its past. He was always a pacifist. Only as the Nazis came into power in Germany did he have some doubts, as his famous and rather deep exchange of letters with Freud showed, and began to understand with melancholy and without true acceptance that, in addition to understanding, man sometimes has a duty to act.

After what you have heard, I need not say how luminous was his intelligence. He was almost wholly without sophistication and wholly without worldliness. I think that in England people would have said that he did not

---

[12] Ernest Rutherford (1871–1937), physicist and chemist from New Zealand.—EDS.

have much "background," and in America that he lacked "education." This may throw some light on how these words are used. I think that this simplicity, this lack of clutter and this lack of cant, had a lot to do with his preservation throughout of a certain pure, rather Spinoza-like, philosophical monism,[13] which of course is hard to maintain if you have been "educated" and have a "background." There was always with him a wonderful purity at once childlike and profoundly stubborn.

Einstein is often blamed or praised or credited with these miserable bombs.[14] It is not in my opinion true. The special theory of relativity might not have been beautiful without Einstein; but it would have been a tool for physicists, and by 1932 the experimental evidence for the interconvertibility of matter and energy which he had predicted was overwhelming. The feasibility of doing anything with this in such a massive way was not clear until seven years later, and then almost by accident. This was not what Einstein really was after. His part was that of creating an intellectual revolution, and discovering more than any scientist of our time how profound were the errors made by men before then. He did write a letter to Roosevelt[15] about atomic energy. I think this was in part his agony at the evil of the Nazis, in part not wanting to harm any one in any way; but I ought to report that that letter had very little effect, and that Einstein himself is really not answerable for all that came later. I believe he so understood it himself.

His was a voice raised with very great weight against violence and cruelty whenever he saw them and, after the war, he spoke with deep emotion and I believe with great weight about the supreme violence of these atomic weapons. He said at once with great simplicity: Now we must make a world government. It was very forthright, it was very abrupt, it was no doubt "uneducated," no doubt without "background"; still all of us in some thoughtful measure must recognize that he was right.

Without power, without calculation, with none of the profoundly political humor that characterized Gandhi,[16] he nevertheless did move the political world. In almost the last act of his life, he joined with Lord Russell[17] in suggesting that men of science get together and see if they could not understand one another and avert the disaster which he foresaw from the arms race. The so-called Pugwash movement, which has a longer name now, was the direct result of this appeal. I know it to be true that it had an essential part to play in the Treaty of Moscow, the limited test-

---

[13] That is, holding the belief that there is only one principle underlying reality.—EDS.

[14] Atomic bombs.—EDS.

[15] Franklin Delano Roosevelt (1882–1945), President of the United States from 1933 to 1945.—EDS.

[16] Mohandas Karamchand (Mahatma) Gandhi (1869–1948), Indian leader noted for his development of passive resistance as a form of civil disobedience.—EDS.

[17] Bertrand Arthur Russell (1872–1970), British mathematician and philosopher. —EDS.

ban treaty, which is a tentative, but to me very precious, declaration that reason might still prevail.

In his last years, as I knew him, Einstein was a twentieth-century Ecclesiastes, saying with unrelenting and indomitable cheerfulness, "Vanity of vanities, all is vanity."[18]

Newton the Man[1]

JOHN MAYNARD KEYNES

It is with some diffidence that I try to speak to you in his own home of Newton *as he was himself*. I have long been a student of the records and had the intention to put my impressions into writing to be ready for Christmas Day 1942, the tercentenary of his birth. The war has deprived me both of leisure to treat adequately so great a theme and of opportunity to consult my library and my papers and to verify my impressions. So if the brief study which I shall lay before you to-day is more perfunctory than it should be, I hope you will excuse me.

One other preliminary matter. I believe that Newton was different from the conventional picture of him. But I do not believe he was less great. He was less ordinary, more extraordinary, than the nineteenth century cared to make him out. Geniuses *are* very peculiar. Let no one here suppose that my object to-day is to lessen, by describing, Cambridge's greatest son. I am trying rather to see him as his own friends and contemporaries saw him. And they without exception regarded him as one of the greatest of men.

In the eighteenth century and since, Newton came to be thought of as the first and greatest of the modern age of scientists, a rationalist, one who taught us to think on the lines of cold and untinctured reason.

I do not see him in this light. I do not think that any one who has pored over the contents of that box which he packed up when he finally left Cambridge in 1696 and which, though partly dispersed, have come down to us, can see him like that. Newton was not the first of the age of reason. He was the last of the magicians, the last of the Babylonians and Sumerians, the last great mind which looked out on the visible and intellectual world with the same eyes as those who began to build our intellectual inheritance rather less than 10,000 years ago. Isaac Newton, a posthumous child born with no father on Christmas Day, 1642, was the

---

[18] Ecclesiastes 1:2.—Eds.

[1] Address read by Mr. Geoffrey Keynes at the Newton Tercentenary Celebrations at Trinity College, Cambridge, on 17 July 1946, and therefore not revised by the author who had written it some years earlier.

last wonder-child to whom the Magi[2] could do sincere and appropriate homage.

Had there been time, I should have liked to read to you the contemporary record of the child Newton. For, though it is well known to his biographers, it has never been published *in extenso*, without comment, just as it stands. Here, indeed, is the makings of a legend of the young magician, a most joyous picture of the opening mind of genius free from the uneasiness, the melancholy and nervous agitation of the young man and student.

For in vulgar modern terms Newton was profoundly neurotic of a not unfamiliar type, but—I should say from the records—a most extreme example. His deepest instincts were occult, esoteric, semantic—with profound shrinking from the world, a paralyzing fear of exposing his thoughts, his beliefs, his discoveries in all nakedness to the inspection and criticism of the world. "Of the most fearful, cautious and suspicious temper that I ever knew," said Whiston, his successor in the Lucasian Chair. The too well-known conflicts and ignoble quarrels with Hooke, Flamsteed, Leibnitz[3] are only too clear an evidence of this. Like all his type he was wholly aloof from women. He parted with and published nothing except under the extreme pressure of friends. Until the second phase of his life, he was a wrapt, consecrated solitary, pursuing his studies by intense introspection with a mental endurance perhaps never equalled.

I believe that the clue to his mind is to be found in his unusual powers of continuous concentrated introspection. A case can be made out, as it also can with Descartes,[4] for regarding him as an accomplished experimentalist. Nothing can be more charming than the tales of his mechanical contrivances when he was a boy. There are his telescopes and his optical experiments. These were essential accomplishments, part of his unequalled all-round technique, but not, I am sure, his *peculiar* gift, especially amongst his contemporaries. His peculiar gift was the power of holding continuously in his mind a purely mental problem until he had seen straight through it. I fancy his pre-eminence is due to his muscles of intuition being the strongest and most enduring with which a man has ever been gifted. Anyone who has ever attempted pure scientific or philosophical thought knows how one can hold a problem momentarily in one's mind and apply all one's powers of concentration to piercing through it, and how it will dissolve and escape and you find that what you are surveying is a blank. I believe that Newton could hold a problem in his mind for hours and days and weeks until it surrendered to him its secret. Then being a supreme mathematical technician he could dress it up, how

---

[2] The Magi were the wise men who brought tribute to the Christ child.—EDS.

[3] Robert Hooke (1635–1703), British physicist; John Flamsteed (1646–1719), British astronomer; Gottfried Wilhelm Leibnitz (1646–1716), German mathematician. —EDS.

[4] René Descartes (1596–1650), French mathematician and philosopher.—EDS.

you will, for purposes of exposition, but it was his intuition which was pre-eminently extraordinary—"so happy in his conjectures," said de Morgan, "as to seem to know more than he could possibly have any means of proving." The proofs, for what they are worth, were, as I have said, dressed up afterwards—they were not the instrument of discovery.

There is the story of how he informed Halley[5] of one of his most fundamental discoveries of planetary motion. "Yes," replied Halley, "but how do you know that? Have you proved it?" Newton was taken aback—"Why, I've known it for years," he replied. "If you'll give me a few days, I'll certainly find you a proof of it"—as in due course he did.

Again, there is some evidence that Newton in preparing the *Principia*[6] was held up almost to the last moment by lack of proof that you could treat a solid sphere as though all its mass was concentrated at the centre, and only hit on the proof a year before publication. But this was a truth which he had known for certain and had always assumed for many years.

Certainly there can be no doubt that the peculiar geometrical form in which the exposition of the *Principia* is dressed up bears no resemblance at all to the mental processes by which Newton actually arrived at his conclusions.

His experiments were always, I suspect, a means, not of discovery, but always of verifying what he knew already.

Why do I call him a magician? Because he looked on the whole universe and all that is in it *as a riddle*, as a secret which could be read by applying pure thought to certain evidence, certain mystic clues which God had laid about the world to allow a sort of philosopher's treasure hunt to the esoteric brotherhood. He believed that these clues were to be found partly in the evidence of the heavens and in the constitution of elements (and that is what gives the false suggestion of his being an experimental natural philosopher), but also partly in certain papers and traditions handed down by the brethren in an unbroken chain back to the original cryptic revelation in Babylonia. He regarded the universe as a cryptogram set by the Almighty—just as he himself wrapt the discovery of the calculus in a cryptogram when he communicated with Leibnitz. By pure thought, by concentration of mind, the riddle, he believed, would be revealed to the initiate.

He *did* read the riddle of the heavens. And he believed that by the same powers of his introspective imagination he would read the riddle of the Godhead, the riddle of past and future events divinely foreordained, the riddle of the elements and their constitution from an original undifferen-

---

[5] Edmund Halley (1656–1742), British astronomer who hypothesized parabolic cometary paths and so predicted the reappearance of "Halley's comet."—Eds.

[6] *Philosophiae Naturalis Principia Mathematica* (*The Mathematical Principles of Natural Philosophy*). In the *Principia*, written during 1684–1685, Newton discusses his theory of the gravitational pull of the earth.—Eds.

tiated first matter, the riddle of health and of immortality. All would be revealed to him if only he could persevere to the end, uninterrupted, by himself, no one coming into the room, reading, copying, testing—all by himself, no interruption for God's sake, no disclosure, no discordant breakings in or criticism, with fear and shrinking as he assailed these half-ordained, half-forbidden things, creeping back into the bosom of the Godhead as into his mother's womb. "Voyaging through strange seas of thought *alone*,"[7] not as Charles Lamb "a fellow who believed nothing unless it was as clear as the three sides of a triangle."

And so he continued for some twenty-five years. In 1687, when he was forty-five years old, the *Principia* was published.

Here in Trinity it is right that I should give you an account of how he lived amongst you during these years of his greatest achievement. The east end of the Chapel projects farther eastwards than the Great Gate. In the second half of the seventeenth century there was a walled garden in the free space between Trinity Street and the building which joins the Great Gate to the Chapel. The south wall ran out from the turret of the Gate to a distance overlapping the Chapel by at least the width of the present pavement. Thus the garden was of modest but reasonable size, as is well shown in Loggan's print of the College in 1690. This was Newton's garden. He had the Fellow's set of rooms between the Porter's Lodge and the Chapel—that, I suppose, now occupied by Professor Broad. The garden was reached by a stairway which was attached to a veranda raised on wooden pillars projecting into the garden from the range of buildings. At the top of this stairway stood his telescope—not to be confused with the observatory erected on the top of the Great Gate during Newton's lifetime (but after he had left Cambridge) for the use of Roger Cotes and Newton's successor, Whiston. This wooden erection was, I think, demolished by Whewell in 1856 and replaced by the stone bay of Professor Broad's bedroom. At the Chapel end of the garden was a small two-storied building, also of wood, which was his laboratory. When he decided to prepare the *Principia* for publication he engaged a young kinsman, Humphrey Newton, to act as his amanuensis (the MS. of the *Principia*, as it went to the press, is clearly in the hand of Humphrey). Humphrey remained with him for five years—from 1684 to 1689. When Newton died his nephew-in-law Conduitt wrote to Humphrey for his reminiscences, and among the papers I have is Humphrey's reply.

During these twenty-five years of intense study mathematics and astronomy were only a part, and perhaps not the most absorbing, of his occupations. Our record of these is almost wholly confined to the papers which he kept and put in his box when he left Trinity for London.

---

[7] "Where the statue stood/Of Newton with his prism and silent face,/The marble index of a mind forever/Voyaging through strange seas of thought, alone." William Wordsworth, *The Prelude*, III (1850).—Eds.

Let me give some brief indications of their subject. They are enormously voluminous—I should say that upwards of 1,000,000 words in his handwriting still survive. They have, beyond doubt, no substantial value whatever except as a fascinating sidelight on the mind of our greatest genius.

Let me not exaggerate through reaction against the other Newton myth which has been so sedulously created for the last two hundred years. There was extreme method in his madness. All his unpublished works on esoteric and theological matters are marked by careful learning, accurate method and extreme sobriety of statement. They are just as *sane* as the *Principia*, if their whole matter and purpose were not magical. They were nearly all composed during the same twenty-five years of his mathematical studies. They fall into several groups.

Very early in life Newton abandoned orthodox belief in the Trinity. At this time the Socinians[8] were an important Arian sect amongst intellectual circles. It may be that Newton fell under Socinian influences, but I think not. He was rather a Judaic monotheist of the school of Maimonides.[9] He arrived at this conclusion not on so-to-speak rational or sceptical grounds, but entirely on the interpretation of ancient authority. He was persuaded that the revealed documents give no support to the Trinitarian doctrines which were due to late falsifications. The revealed God was one God.

But this was a dreadful secret which Newton was at desperate pains to conceal all his life. It was the reason why he refused Holy Orders, and therefore had to obtain a special dispensation to hold his Fellowship and Lucasian Chair and could not be Master of Trinity. Even the Toleration Act of 1689 excepted anti-Trinitarians. Some rumours there were, but not at the dangerous dates when he was a young Fellow of Trinity. In the main the secret died with him. But it was revealed in many writings in his big box. After his death Bishop Horsley was asked to inspect the box with a view to publication. He saw the contents with horror and slammed the lid. A hundred years later Sir David Brewster looked into the box. He covered up the traces with carefully selected extracts and some straight fibbing. His latest biographer, Mr. More, has been more candid. Newton's extensive anti-Trinitarian pamphlets are, in my judgement, the most interesting of his unpublished papers. Apart from his more serious affirmation of belief, I have a completed pamphlet showing up what Newton thought of the extreme dishonesty and falsification of records for which St. Athanasius was responsible, in particular for his putting about the false calumny that Arius died in a privy. The victory of the Trinitarians in England in the latter half of the seventeenth century was not only as

---

[8] Those who followed the doctrines of Fausto Sozzini, a seventeenth-century Italian theologian who developed the rationalist doctrine that denied the tenets of the Trinity, the divinity of Christ, and the total depravity of man.—EDS.

[9] Rabbi Moses ben Maimon (RaMBaM) (1135 or 1138–1204), Spanish philosopher who held that philosophy enables man to attain his final end—the perfection of the intellect.—EDS.

complete, but also as extraordinary, as St. Athanasius's original triumph. There is good reason for thinking that Locke[10] was a Unitarian. I have seen it argued that Milton[11] was. It is a blot on Newton's record that he did not murmur a word when Whiston, his successor in the Lucasian Chair, was thrown out of his professorship and out of the University for publicly avowing opinions which Newton himself had secretly held for upwards of fifty years past.

That he held this heresy was a further aggravation of his silence and secrecy and inwardness of disposition.

Another large section is concerned with all branches of apocalyptic writings from which he sought to deduce the secret truths of the Universe—the measurements of Solomon's Temple, the Book of Daniel, the Book of Revelations, an enormous volume of work of which some part was published in his later days. Along with this are hundreds of pages of Church History and the like, designed to discover the truth of tradition.

A large section, judging by the handwriting amongst the earliest, relates to alchemy—transmutation, the philosopher's stone, the elixir of life. The scope and character of these papers have been hushed up, or at least minimized, by nearly all those who have inspected them. About 1650 there was a considerable group in London, round the publisher Cooper, who during the next twenty years revived interest not only in the English alchemists of the fifteenth century, but also in translation of the medieval and post-medieval alchemists.

There is an unusual number of manuscripts of the early English alchemists in the libraries of Cambridge. It may be that there was some continuous esoteric tradition within the University which sprang into activity again in the twenty years from 1650 to 1670. At any rate, Newton was clearly an unbridled addict. It is this with which he was occupied "about 6 weeks at spring and 6 at the fall when the fire in the elaboratory scarcely went out" at the very years when he was composing the *Principia* —and about this he told Humphrey Newton not a word. Moreover, he was almost entirely concerned, not in serious experiment, but in trying to read the riddle of tradition, to find meaning in cryptic verses, to imitate the alleged but largely imaginary experiments of the initiates of past centuries. Newton has left behind him a vast mass of records of these studies. I believe that the greater part are translations and copies made by him of existing books and manuscripts. But there are also extensive records of experiments. I have glanced through a great quantity of this—at least 100,000 words, I should say. It is utterly impossible to deny that it is wholly magical and wholly devoid of scientific value; and also impossible

---

[10] John Locke (1632–1704), the most important English philosopher of the Age of Reason; he established the importance of science as an object of philosophical analysis. —Eds.

[11] John Milton (1608–1674), English poet.—Eds.

not to admit that Newton devoted years of work to it. Some time it might be interesting, but not useful, for some student better equipped and more idle than I to work out Newton's exact relationship to the tradition and MSS. of his time.

In these mixed and extraordinary studies, with one foot in the Middle Ages and one foot treading a path for modern science, Newton spent the first phase of his life, the period of life in Trinity when he did all his real work. Now let me pass to the second phase.

After the publication of the *Principia* there is a complete change in his habit and way of life. I believe that his friends, above all Halifax, came to the conclusion that he must be rooted out of the life he was leading at Trinity which must soon lead to decay of mind and health. Broadly speaking, of his own motion or under persuasion, he abandons his studies. He takes up University business, represents the University in Parliament; his friends are busy trying to get a dignified and remunerative job for him—the Provostship of King's, the Mastership of Charterhouse, the Controllership of the Mint.

Newton could not be Master of Trinity because he was a Unitarian and so not in Holy Orders. He was rejected as Provost of King's for the more prosaic reason that he was not an Etonian. Newton took this rejection very ill and prepared a long legalistic brief which I possess, giving reasons why it was not unlawful for him to be accepted as Provost. But, as ill-luck had it, Newton's nomination for the Provostship came at the moment when King's had decided to fight against the right of Crown nomination, a struggle in which the College was successful.

Newton was well qualified for any of these offices. It must not be inferred from his introspection, his absent-mindedness, his secrecy and his solitude that he lacked aptitude for affairs when he chose to exercise it. There are many records to prove his very great capacity. Read, for example, his correspondence with Dr. Covell, the Vice-Chancellor, when, as the University's representative in Parliament, he had to deal with the delicate question of the oaths after the revolution of 1688. With Pepys and Lowndes[12] he became one of the greatest and most efficient of our civil servants. He was a very successful investor of funds, surmounting the crisis of the South Sea Bubble,[13] and died a rich man. He possessed in exceptional degree almost every kind of intellectual aptitude—lawyer, historian, theologian, not less than mathematician, physicist, astronomer.

And when the turn of his life came and he put his books of magic back into the box, it was easy for him to drop the seventeenth century behind him and to evolve into the eighteenth-century figure which is the traditional Newton.

[12] Samuel Pepys (1633–1703), English diarist; William Lowndes (1798–1843), English bookseller and bibliographer.—EDS.

[13] A stock market scheme which led to England's first great stock market panic in 1720, in which thousands of investors were ruined.—EDS.

Nevertheless, the move on the part of his friends to change his life came almost too late. In 1689 his mother, to whom he was deeply attached, died. Somewhere about his fiftieth birthday on Christmas Day, 1692, he suffered what we should now term a severe nervous breakdown. Melancholia, sleeplessness, fears of persecution—he writes to Pepys and to Locke and no doubt to others letters which lead them to think that his mind is deranged. He lost, in his own words, the "former consistency of his mind." He never again concentrated after the old fashion or did any fresh work. The breakdown probably lasted nearly two years, and from it emerged, slightly "gaga," but still, no doubt, with one of the most powerful minds of England, the Sir Isaac Newton of tradition.

In 1696 his friends were finally successful in digging him out of Cambridge, and for more than another twenty years he reigned in London as the most famous man of his age, of Europe, and—as his power gradually waned and his affability increased—perhaps of all time, so it seemed to his contemporaries.

He set up house with his niece Catharine Barton, who was beyond reasonable doubt the mistress of his old and loyal friend Charles Montague, Earl of Halifax and Chancellor of the Exchequer, who had been one of Newton's intimate friends when he was an undergraduate at Trinity. Catharine was reputed to be one of the most brilliant and charming women in the London of Congreve, Swift and Pope.[14] She is celebrated not least for the broadness of her stories, in Swift's *Journal to Stella*. Newton puts on rather too much weight for his moderate height. "When he rode in his coach one arm would be out of his coach on one side and the other on the other." His pink face, beneath a mass of snow-white hair, which "when his peruke was off was a venerable sight," is increasingly both benevolent and majestic. One night in Trinity after Hall he is knighted by Queen Anne. For nearly twenty-four years he reigns as President of the Royal Society. He becomes one of the principal sights of London for all visiting intellectual foreigners, whom he entertains handsomely. He liked to have clever young men about him to edit new editions of the *Principia*—and sometimes merely plausible ones as in the case of Fatio de Duillier.

Magic was quite forgotten. He has become the Sage and Monarch of the Age of Reason. The Sir Isaac Newton of orthodox tradition—the eighteenth-century Sir Isaac, so remote from the child magician born in the first half of the seventeenth century—was being built up. Voltaire[15] returning from his trip to London was able to report of Sir Isaac—" 'twas his peculiar felicity, not only to be born in a country of liberty, but in an Age when all scholastic impertinences were banished from the World.

---

[14] William Congreve (1670–1729), English dramatist considered the master of the Restoration comedy; Jonathan Swift (1667–1745), satirist and poet; Alexander Pope (1688–1744), poet and satirist, the leading literary arbiter of his days.—EDS.

[15] Pen name of François Marie Arouet (1694–1778), French satirist, philosopher and poet.—EDS.

Reason alone was cultivated and Mankind cou'd only be his Pupil, not his Enemy." Newton, whose secret heresies and scholastic superstitions it had been the study of a lifetime to conceal!

But he never concentrated, never recovered "the former consistency of his mind." "He spoke very little in company." "He had something rather languid in his look and manner."

And he looked very seldom, I expect, into the chest where, when he left Cambridge, he had packed all the evidences of what had occupied and so absorbed his intense and flaming spirit in his rooms and his garden and his elaboratory between the Great Gate and Chapel.

But he did not destroy them. They remained in the box to shock profoundly any eighteenth- or nineteenth-century prying eyes. They became the possession of Catharine Barton and then of her daughter, Lady Lymington. So Newton's chest, with many hundreds of thousands of words of his unpublished writings, came to contain the "Portsmouth Papers."

In 1888 the mathematical portion was given to the University Library at Cambridge. They have been indexed, but they have never been edited. The rest, a very large collection, were dispersed in the auction room in 1936 by Catharine Barton's descendant, the present Lord Lymington. Disturbed by this impiety, I managed gradually to reassemble about half of them, including nearly the whole of the biographical portion, that is, the "Conduitt Papers," in order to bring them to Cambridge which I hope they will never leave. The greater part of the rest were snatched out of my reach by a syndicate which hoped to sell them at a high price, probably in America, on the occasion of the recent tercentenary.

As one broods over these queer collections, it seems easier to understand—with an understanding which is not, I hope, distorted in the other direction—this strange spirit, who was tempted by the Devil to believe, at the time when within these walls he was solving so much, that he could reach *all* the secrets of God and Nature by the pure power of mind—Copernicus and Faustus[16] in one.

---

[16] Nicolaus Copernicus (1473–1543), Polish astronomer who challenged Ptolemy's astronomical system by proclaiming that the earth is not the center of the universe, but rather that the earth revolves around the sun. Faustus is the legendary figure who sought after all knowledge and in the process damned his immortal soul.—EDS.

Of Life

The Struggle for Existence
CHARLES DARWIN

I must make a few preliminary remarks, to show how the struggle for existence bears on Natural Selection. . . . Amongst organic beings in a state of nature there is some individual variability: indeed I am not aware that this has ever been disputed. It is immaterial for us whether a multitude of doubtful forms be called species or sub-species or varieties; what rank, for instance, the two or three hundred doubtful forms of British plants are entitled to hold, if the existence of any well-marked varieties be admitted. But the mere existence of individual variability and of some few well-marked varieties, though necessary as the foundation for the work, helps us but little in understanding how species arise in nature. How have all those exquisite adaptations of one part of the organisation to another part, and to the conditions of life, and of one organic being to another being, been perfected? We see these beautiful co-adaptations most plainly in the woodpecker and the mistletoe; and only a little less plainly in the humblest parasite which clings to the hairs of a quadruped or feathers of a bird: in the structure of the beetle which dives through the water: in the plumed seed which is wafted by the gentlest breeze; in short, we see beautiful adaptations everywhere and in every part of the organic world.

Again, it may be asked, how is it that varieties, which I have called incipient species, become ultimately converted into good and distinct species, which in most cases obviously differ from each other far more than do the varieties of the same species? How do those groups of species, which constitute what are called distinct genera, and which differ from each other more than do the species of the same genus, arise? All these results . . . follow from the struggle for life. Owing to this struggle, variations, however slight and from whatever cause proceeding, if they be in any degree profitable to the individuals of a species, in their infinitely complex relations to other organic beings and to their physical conditions of life, will tend to the preservation of such individuals, and will generally be inherited by the offspring. The offspring, also, will thus have a better chance of surviving, for, of the many individuals of any species which are periodically born, but a small number can survive. I have called this principle, by which each slight variation, if useful, is preserved, by the term Natural Selection, in order to mark its relation to man's power of selection. But the expression often used by Mr. Herbert Spencer[1] of the Survival of the Fittest is more accurate, and is sometimes equally convenient. We have seen that man by selection can certainly produce great results, and can adapt organic beings to his own uses, through the accumulation of slight but useful variations, given to him by the hand of Nature. But Natural Selection, as we shall hereafter see, is a power incessantly ready for action, and is as immeasurably superior to man's feeble efforts, as the works of Nature are to those of Art. . . .

Complex relations of all animals and plants to each other in the struggle for existence. Many cases are on record showing how complex and unexpected are the checks and relations between organic beings, which have to struggle together in the same country. I will give only a single instance, which, though a simple one, interested me. In Staffordshire, on the estate of a relation, where I had ample means of investigation, there was a large and extremely barren heath, which had never been touched by the hand of man; but several acres of exactly the same nature had been enclosed twenty-five years previously and planted with Scotch fir. The change in the native vegetation of the planted part of the heath was most remarkable, more than is generally seen in passing from one quite different soil to another: not only the proportional numbers of the heath-plants were wholly changed, but twelve species of plants (not counting grasses and carices) flourished in the plantations, which could not be found on the heath. The effect on the insects must have been still greater, for six insectivorous birds were very common in the plantations, which were not to be seen on the heath; and the heath was frequented by two or three distinct insectivorous birds. Here we see how potent has been the effect of the introduction of a single tree, nothing whatever else having been done, with the exception of the land having been enclosed, so that cattle could not enter. But how important an element enclosure is, I plainly saw near Farnham, in Surrey. Here there are extensive heaths, with a few clumps of old Scotch firs on the distant hilltops: within the last ten years large spaces have been enclosed, and self-sown firs are now springing up in multitudes, so close together that all cannot live. When I ascertained that these young trees had not been sown or planted, I was so much surprised at their numbers that I went to several points of view, whence I could examine hundreds of acres of the unenclosed heath, and literally I could not see a single Scotch fir, except the old planted clumps. But on looking closely between the stems of the heath, I found a multitude of seedlings and little trees which had been perpetually browsed down by the cattle. In one square yard, at a point some hundred yards distant from one of the

---

[1] Herbert Spencer (1820–1903), British writer and philosopher who popularized Darwin's theories by synthesizing the accepted science of his day within the framework of evolution.—EDS.

old clumps, I counted thirty-two little trees; and one of them, with twenty-six rings of growth, had, during many years, tried to raise its head above the stems of the heath, and had failed. No wonder that, as soon as the land was enclosed, it became thickly clothed with vigorously growing young firs. Yet the heath was so extremely barren and so extensive that no one would ever have imagined that cattle would have so closely and effectually searched it for food.

Here we see that cattle absolutely determine the existence of the Scotch fir; but in several parts of the world insects determine the existence of cattle. Perhaps Paraguay offers the most curious instance of this; for here neither cattle nor horses nor dogs have ever run wild, though they swarm southward and northward in a feral state; and Azara and Rengger have shown that this is caused by the greater number in Paraguay of a certain fly, which lays its eggs in the navels of these animals when first born. The increase of these flies, numerous as they are, must be habitually checked by some means, probably by other parasitic insects. Hence, if certain insectivorous birds were to decrease in Paraguay, the parasitic insects would probably increase; and this would lessen the number of the navel-frequenting flies—then cattle and horses would become feral, and this would certainly greatly alter (as indeed I have observed in parts of South America) the vegetation: this again would largely affect the insects; and this, as we have just seen in Staffordshire, the insectivorous birds, and so onwards in ever-increasing circles of complexity. Not that under nature the relations will ever be as simple as this. Battle within battle must be continually recurring with varying success; and yet in the long-run the forces are so nicely balanced, that the face of nature remains for long periods of time uniform, though assuredly the merest trifle would give the victory to one organic being over another. Nevertheless, so profound is our ignorance, and so high our presumption, that we marvel when we hear of the extinction of an organic being; and as we do not see the cause, we invoke cataclysms to desolate the world, or invent laws on the duration of the forms of life!

I am tempted to give one more instance showing how plants and animals, remote in the scale of nature, are bound together by a web of complex relations. I shall hereafter have occasion to show that the exotic Lobelia fulgens is never visited in my garden by insects, and consequently, from its peculiar structure, never sets a seed. Nearly all our orchidaceous plants absolutely require the visits of insects to remove their pollen-masses and thus to fertilise them. I find from experiments that humble-bees are almost indispensable to the fertilisation of the heartsease (Viola tricolor), for other bees do not visit this flower. I have also found that the visits of bees are necessary for the fertilisation of some kinds of clover; for instance, 20 heads of Dutch clover (Trifolium repens) yielded 2,290 seeds, but 20 other heads protected from bees produced not one. Again, 100 heads of red clover (T. pratense) produced 2,700 seeds, but the same number of protected heads produced not a single seed. Humble-bees alone visit red clover, as other bees cannot reach the nectar. It has been suggested that moths may fertilise the clovers; but I doubt whether they could do so in the case of the red clover, from their weight not being sufficient to depress the wing petals. Hence we may infer as highly probable that, if the whole genus of humble-bees became extinct or very rare in England, the heartsease and red clover would become very rare, or wholly disappear. The number of humble-bees in any district depends in a great measure upon the number of field-mice, which destroy their combs and nests; and Col. Newman, who has long attended to the habits of humble-bees, believes that "more than two-thirds of them are thus destroyed all over England." Now the number of mice is largely dependent, as every one knows, on the number of cats; and Col. Newman says, "Near villages and small towns I have found the nests of humble-bees more numerous than elsewhere, which I attribute to the number of cats that destroy the mice." Hence it is quite credible that the presence of a feline animal in large numbers in a district might determine, through the intervention first of mice and then of bees, the frequency of certain flowers in that district!

In the case of every species, many different checks, acting at different periods of life, and during different seasons or years, probably come into play; some one check or some few being generally the most potent; but all will concur in determining the average number or even the existence of the species. In some cases it can be shown that widely-different checks act on the same species in different districts. When we look at the plants and bushes clothing an entangled bank, we are tempted to attribute their proportional numbers and kinds to what we call chance. But how false a view is this! Every one has heard that when an American forest is cut down, a very different vegetation springs up; but it has been observed that ancient Indian ruins in the Southern United States, which must formerly have been cleared of trees, now display the same beautiful diversity and proportion of kinds as in the surrounding virgin forest. What a struggle must have gone on during long centuries between the several kinds of trees, each annually scattering its seeds by the thousand; what war between insect and insect—between insects, snails, and other animals with birds and beasts of prey—all striving to increase, all feeding on each other, or on the trees, their seeds and seedlings, or on the other plants which first clothed the ground and thus checked the growth of the trees! Throw up a handful of feathers, and all fall to the ground according to definite laws; but how simple is the problem where each shall fall compared to that of the action and reaction of the innumerable plants and animals which have determined, in the course of centuries, the proportional numbers and kinds of trees now growing on the old Indian ruins!

The dependency of one organic being on another, as of a parasite on its prey, lies generally between beings remote in the scale of nature. This is likewise sometimes the case with those which may be strictly said to struggle with each other for existence, as in the case of locusts and grass-feeding quadrupeds. But the struggle will almost invariably be most severe between the individuals of the same species, for they frequent the same districts, require the same food, and are exposed to the same dangers. In the case of varieties of the same species, the struggle will generally be almost equally severe, and we sometimes see the contest soon decided: for instance, if several varieties of wheat be sown together, and the mixed seed be resown, some of the varieties which best suit the soil or climate, or are naturally the most fertile, will beat the others and so yield more seed, and will consequently in a few years supplant the other varieties. To keep up a mixed stock of even such extremely close varieties as the variously-coloured sweet peas, they must be each year harvested separately, and the seed then mixed in due proportion, otherwise the weaker kinds will steadily decrease in number and disappear. So again with the varieties of sheep; it has been asserted that certain mountain-varieties will starve out other mountain-varieties, so that they cannot be kept together. The same result has followed from keeping together different varieties of the medicinal leech. It may even be doubted whether the varieties of any of our domestic plants or animals have so exactly the same strength, habits, and constitution, that the original proportions of a mixed stock (crossing being prevented) could be kept up for a half-a-dozen generations, if they were allowed to struggle together, in the same manner as beings in a state of nature, and if the seed or young were not annually preserved in due proportion.

The Territorial Imperative
ROBERT ARDREY

At the heart of the territorial principle lies the command to defend one's property, but as close to the heart lies recognition of the next animal's rights. But we may state it in another way, from the viewpoint of the intruder. Fundamental to the territorial principle are two opposing impulses: there is the urge to intrude on the property of one's neighbor, and the urge to avoid it. Out of the basic psychological need for stimulation or the alluring temptation of loot, the balance will be swung in favor of intrusion. But if the life of a species keeps the animal too busy gathering hazelnuts in far-off thickets or provides him with such hazards and natural excitements as abundantly to fill his daily quota of thrills, or if some defensive asset of the proprietor—shocking fangs, appalling claws, a murderous disposition, or the concerted ranks of a biological nation—renders loot unlikely and excitement suicidal, then the balance of innate command will be swung toward avoidance. Animal treaties will be signed. Rights will be not only recognized but honored. Uninvited guests will be few.

There is nothing in the territorial principle to deny peace among nations. The student of man's evolutionary nature may ask his great-aunt to embroider the statement on fine linen, that it may be framed and hung on the wall where once hung the testament HOME SWEET HOME. Nothing in animal example or primate precedent offers any but the conclusion that territory is conservative, that it is invariably defensive, that the biological nation is the supreme natural mechanism for the security of a social group, and that when intrusion becomes maladaptive and no longer of selective value to a species, the territorial imperative will itself command its abandonment.

The question, then, must . . . arise: Why do men intrude? And . . . we must remind ourselves that we are not the descendants of these monkeys and apes which today we so assiduously observe. We are distant, distant cousins with our own ancient line of evolutionary experience and selection. And . . . we must remind ourselves, too, that as man is not all sex, and not all economics, and not all cultural tradition, and not all a pot rounded on environment's wheel, so he is not all territory. We are also predators.

The Miocene was an epoch of world-wide benevolence. Rain was abundant; lakes brimmed. Forests were richly disposed, lending comfort of leaf and fruit to their arboreal inhabitants. Modern grasses took root as never before. Broad were the prairies, green the pastures, fat the grazing creatures who dined thereon. And in this fortunate time the ape that would someday be man spoke his evolutionary farewell to the ape that would someday be chimp or gorilla.

It was a long time ago. The Miocene ended as best we can reckon about twelve million years ago, to give way to the deepening despairs of the drought-ridden Pliocene. Good times had lasted long, however—almost twenty million years. For the human mind to comprehend such spacious vistas of ensuing seasons is a challenge as formidable as the counting of milestones lying between stars. Time and space may yield to our mathematics, but they become as one in their defiance of our perceptions. And yet, with a reality as true as tomorrow or the fall of next autumn's bright leaves, the Miocene passed like infinity's procession through twenty long millions of years. Animals bred, died. Generations of horses and mice and monkeys joined the ancient democracy of death. The advancing shore of life formed new coves, new sea cliffs, or clung to old broad seemly beaches facing out on posterity's unknowable sea.

We went our way. We left our bones on this old mountainside or beside that lake. More and more we lived beneath the open sky, less and less beneath the forest canopy. We were the adventurers, the seekers after farther fields, whereas our cousins of the forest remained the conservators of the arboreal primate traditions. Luck and circumstance combined, here and there, to preserve our bones for a fossil eternity. Rarely in the depths of the forest, amid the rot and disintegration of broken bough and fallen leaf, could the arboreal ape anticipate such immortality. Fragmentary though knowledge of our own history may be, our knowledge of his is less.

Even from these bits and pieces, however, that have come to us from most ancient of days, we may demonstrate or deduce a few fair certainties. When in the midst of the Miocene, twenty or twenty-five million years ago, our hominid line renounced the arboreal way to embrace a life on the ground, we accepted hazards and opportunities, stimulations and social necessities of an order quite different from life in the trees. The ruthless commands of natural selection would press us one way, press the ape of the forest another. We retained the vulnerable primate body, but any mutation favoring survival on the hostile earth would spread through the generations to whole populations, through the ages to entire species. Our feet flattened, our backs straightened, our buttocks strengthened their muscular arrangements to permit us to run. And as more and more we became specialized earthlings, so more and more it became anatomically impossible for us to return to the arboreal life. Such trends take place in an evolving world. A minor alteration of behavior and body, a change of equivocal value, may command that further genetic alteration be of increased specific value until a course is determined, and horses are set upon their way, men upon theirs. Now evolution becomes irreversible.

As important as our anatomical adjustments to the terrestrial life were the psychological changes which such life commanded. Shyness is a luxury permitted the mountain gorilla in his high, remote, cloud-softened bamboo thickets. The modesty once demanded of the tiny, primitive mammal in his monster-dominated times retained a value in the lives of jungle primates with profound green tangles of vine and leaf in which they might vanish. But for the ape of the field in those long-gone Miocene times, hiding places might be far from hand. Not unlike the baboon today, the aggressive spirit became a survival asset. Time and again we had no alternative but to stand and fight. And the social necessity, since the time of the true lemur a primate compulsion, doubled and redoubled its survival value.

So we, the developing hominid, found ourselves committed to a course quite unlike our ever more distant forest cousins. We scratched for a living. Like the baboon we became omnivorous. Apes and monkeys in their forest home might retain their dependence on fruits and shoots. We came to eat anything. In all likelihood, long before the Pliocene presented all primates with a climatic crisis, we developed a certain taste for meat. The savannah chimpanzee, Jane Goodall[1] has learned, will kill a young bushbuck or monkey and devour it with utmost relish. The baboon when fortune presents him with a victim will do the same, and when the season

---

[1] British ethnologist (1934–   ) who lived among the chimpanzees in Tanzania, researching their behavior. She wrote *My Friends, the Wild Chimpanzees* (1967). —EDS.

is right will become a systematic predator. Neither, however, is dependent on meat, and neither, probably, were we—not so long, at least, as the mellow Miocene brought to our table a copious larder.

Millennia passed upon millennia. And something new came into our lives—new in the history of primates—and the new thing was freedom. Our growing adaptation to life on the ground gave us the freedom to move anywhere; our growing independence from any single source of food made us free to adapt to this environment or that; our growingly aggressive spirit gave us the freedom to dare, to explore. It is a quality in animals which ten years ago we should have dismissed with raised scientific eyebrows. But now we know that in countless species there is an innate compulsion to explore, lacking either the pressure of deprivation or the seeking of economic reward. Adventure—there is no other word for it—satisfies the basic need for stimulation. Whether we sought adventure in the old lost golden days, we cannot know. But we were free to. And then came the Pliocene.

The prime time of a good, ripe earth slowly vanished. Seasonal rains on the high African plateaus became shorter and more irregular. Old lakes shrank; rivers became less dependable. Forests diminished, and with them the primate populations imprisoned by forest necessity. Grasslands spread, and impenetrable deserts like the Sahara and the Kalahari made of certain African areas impassable seas of sand. Perhaps these were the days when the ancestral baboon took to the field, and certain monkeys like the patas and vervet found marginal accommodation to terrestrial life. But we do not know anything for sure. So dry became the Pliocene that the fossil record vanished. There was not enough water to provide the lime to turn bone into stone.

We who complain of a drought lasting four or five years, what shall we say of a drought that lasted, with deepening ferocity, for ten or twelve million? And yet it was the time that saw the making of man as we know him. He became a carnivore. The grasslands still teemed with those edible grazing creatures prepared by evolutionary fortune to survive on the Pliocene's scant offerings. Perhaps at first we scavenged the kills of the lion and cheetah and leopard, and we competed with hyena and jackal and vulture for the crumbs of the kills. We retained our omnivorous way, our taste for roots and tubers, when we could find them, and for berries and edible greens; even the chimpanzee when he is consuming a monkey will after each bite eat a leaf, just as man, today, will eat salad. But we became dependent on meat as our main source of sustenance, and sooner or later we became systematic hunters.

When exactly did it happen? Again, we do not know. It was Raymond A. Dart who discovered man's predecessor in the hominid line, southern Africa's small-brained australopithecines, and it was Dart who formulated the theory of the predatory transition from ape to man. And in the past five years—in the same period when, as with a burst of stage lighting, science has illuminated the lives and the dramas of monkeys and apes—

science has likewise gone far to illuminate the hominid stage on which the human drama was prepared. The spectacular discoveries of Louis S. B. Leakey[2] and his family in East African fossil beds have confirmed the theories of Raymond Dart. But they have not informed us as to just when proto-man became a predator, dependent on his hunting life for survival.

The Ladder of Creation
JACOB BRONOWSKI

The theory of evolution by natural selection was put forward in the 1850s independently by two men. One was Charles Darwin; the other was Alfred Russel Wallace. Both men had some scientific background, of course, but at heart both men were naturalists. Darwin had been a medical student at Edinburgh University for two years, before his father who was a wealthy doctor proposed that he might become a clergyman and sent him to Cambridge. Wallace, whose parents were poor and who had left school at fourteen, had followed courses at Working Men's Institutes in London and Leicester as a surveyor's apprentice and pupil teacher.

The fact is that there are two traditions of explanation that march side by side in the ascent of man. One is the analysis of the physical structure of the world. The other is the study of the processes of life: their delicacy, their diversity, the wavering cycles from life to death in the individual and in the species. And these traditions do not come together until the theory of evolution; because until then there is a paradox which cannot be resolved, which cannot be begun, about life.

The paradox of the life sciences, which makes them different in kind from physical science, is in the detail of nature everywhere. We see it about us in the birds, the trees, the grass, the snails, in every living thing. It is this. The manifestations of life, its expressions, its forms, are so diverse that they must contain a large element of the accidental. And yet the nature of life is so uniform that it must be constrained by many necessities.

So it is not surprising that biology as we understand it begins with naturalists in the eighteenth and nineteenth centuries: observers of the countryside, bird-watchers, clergymen, doctors, gentlemen of leisure in country houses. I am tempted to call them, simply, "gentlemen in Victorian England," because it cannot be an accident that the theory of evolution is conceived twice by two men living at the same time in the same culture—the culture of Queen Victoria in England.

Charles Darwin was in his early twenties when the Admiralty was about to send out a survey ship called the *Beagle* to map the coast of South

[2] British anthropologist (1903–1972) who discovered fossil bones of tool-using hominids in the Olduvai Gorge of Tanzania.—EDS.

America, and he was offered the unpaid post of naturalist. He owed the invitation to the professor of botany who had befriended him at Cambridge, though Darwin had not been excited by botany there but by collecting beetles.

> I will give a proof of my zeal: one day, on tearing off some old bark, I saw two rare beetles, and seized one in each hand; then I saw a third and new kind which I could not bear to lose, so that I popped the one which I held in my right hand into my mouth.

Darwin's father opposed his going, and the captain of the *Beagle* did not like the shape of his nose, but Darwin's Wedgwood uncle spoke up for him and he went. The *Beagle* set sail on 27 December 1831.

The five years that he spent on the ship transformed Darwin. He had been a sympathetic, subtle observer of birds, flowers, life in his own countryside; now South America exploded all that for him into a passion. He came home convinced that species are taken in different directions when they are isolated from one another; species are not immutable. But when he came back he could not think of any mechanism that drove them apart. That was in 1836.

When Darwin did hit on an explanation for the evolution of species two years later, he was most reluctant to publish it. He might have put it off all his life if a very different kind of man had not also followed almost exactly the same steps of experience and thought that moved Darwin, and arrived at the same theory. He is the forgotten and yet the vital character, a sort of man from Porlock[1] in reverse, in the theory of evolution by natural selection.

His name was Alfred Russel Wallace, a giant of a man with a Dickensian family history as comic as Darwin's was stuffy. At that time, in 1836, Wallace was a boy in his teens; he was born in 1823, and that makes him fourteen years younger than Darwin. Wallace's life was not easy even then.

> Had my father been a moderately rich man . . . my whole life would have been differently shaped, and though I should, no doubt, have given some attention to science, it seems very unlikely that I should have ever undertaken . . . a journey to the almost unknown forests of the Amazon in order to observe nature and make a living by collecting.

So Wallace wrote about his early life, when he had had to find a way to earn his living in the English provinces. He took up the profession of land-surveying, which did not require a university education, and which

---

[1] The poet Samuel Taylor Coleridge (1772–1834) was interrupted in the midst of a reverie by a man from Porlock and was unable to retrieve the fantasy after the interruption. His poem "Kubla Khan" (1797) remains a poetic fragment as a result of the interruption.—Eds.

his older brother could teach him. His brother died in 1846 from a chill he caught travelling home in an open third-class carriage from a meeting of a Royal Commission committee on rival railway firms.

Evidently it was an open-air life, and Wallace became interested in plants and insects. When he was working at Leicester, he met a man with the same interests who was rather better educated. His new friend astonished Wallace by telling him that he had collected several hundred different species of beetles in the neighbourhood of Leicester, and that there were more to be discovered.

> If I had been asked before how many different kinds of beetles were to be found in any small district near a town, I should probably have guessed fifty . . . I now learnt . . . that there were probably a thousand different kinds within ten miles.

It was a revelation to Wallace, and it shaped his life and his friend's. The friend was Henry Bates, who later did famous work on mimicry among insects.

Meanwhile the young man had to make a living. Fortunately, it was a good time for a land-surveyor, because the railway adventurers of the 1840s needed him. Wallace was employed to survey a possible route for a line in the Neath Valley in South Wales. He was a conscientious technician, as his brother had been and as Victorians were. But he suspected rightly that he was a pawn in a power game. Most of the surveys were only meant to establish a claim against some other railway robber baron. Wallace calculated that only a tenth of the lines surveyed that year were ever built.

The Welsh countryside was a delight to the Sunday naturalist, as happy in his science as a Sunday painter is in his art. Now Wallace observed and collected for himself, with a growing excitement in the variety of nature that affectionately remained in his memory all his life.

> Even when we were busy I had Sundays perfectly free, and used then to take long walks over the mountains with my collecting box, which I brought home full of treasures . . . At such times I experienced the joy which every discovery of a new form of life gives to the lover of nature, almost equal to those raptures which I afterwards felt at every capture of new butterflies on the Amazon.

Wallace found a cave on one of his weekends where the river ran underground, and decided then and there to camp overnight. It was as if unconsciously he was already preparing himself for life in the wild.

> We wanted for once to try sleeping out-of-doors, with no shelter or bed but what nature provided . . . I think we had determined purposely to make no preparation, but to camp out just as if we had come accidentally to the place in an unknown country, and had been compelled to sleep there.

In fact he hardly slept at all.

When he was twenty-five, Wallace decided to become a full-time naturalist. It was an odd Victorian profession. It meant that he would have to keep himself by collecting specimens in foreign parts to sell to museums and collectors in England. And Bates would come with him. So the two of them set off in 1848 with £100 between them. They sailed to South America, and then a thousand miles up the Amazon to the city of Manaus, where the Amazon is joined by the Rio Negro.

Wallace had hardly been further than Wales, but he was not overawed by the exotic. From the moment of arrival, his comments were firm and self-assured. For example, on the subject of vultures, he records his thoughts in his *Narrative of Travels on the Amazon and Rio Negro* five years later.

> The common black vultures were abundant, but were rather put to it for food, being obliged to eat palm-fruits in the forest when they could find nothing else.
>
> I am convinced, from repeated observations, that the vultures depend entirely on sight, and not at all on smell, in seeking out their food.

The friends separated at Manaus, and Wallace set off up the Rio Negro. He was looking for places that had not been much explored by earlier naturalists; for if he was going to make a living by collecting, he needed to find specimens of unknown or at least of rare species. The river was swollen with rain, so that Wallace and his Indians were able to take their canoe right into the forest. The trees hung low over the water. Wallace for once was awed by the gloom, but he was also elated by the variety in the forest, and he speculated how it might look from the air.

> What we may fairly allow of tropical vegetation is, that there is a much greater number of species, and a greater variety of forms, than in the temperate zones.
>
> Perhaps no country in the world contains such an amount of vegetable matter on its surface as the valley of the Amazon. Its entire extent, with the exception of some very small portions, is covered with one dense and lofty primeval forest, the most extensive and unbroken which exists upon the earth.
>
> The whole glory of these forests could only be seen by sailing gently in a balloon over the undulating flowery surface above: such a treat is perhaps reserved for the traveller of a future age.

He was excited and frightened when for the first time he went into a native Indian village; but it is characteristic of Wallace that his lasting feeling was pleasure.

> The ... most unexpected sensation of surprise and delight was my first meeting and living with a man in a state of nature—with absolute uncontaminated savages! ... They were all going about their own work or pleasure which had nothing to do with white men or their ways; they walked with the free step of the independent forest-dweller, and ... paid no attention whatever to us, mere strangers of an alien race.
>
> In every detail they were original and self-sustaining, as are the wild animals of the forests, absolutely independent of civilisation, and who could

and did live their lives in their own way, as they had done for countless generations before America was discovered.

It turned out that the Indians were not fierce but helpful. Wallace drew them into the business of collecting specimens.

> During the time I remained here (forty days), I procured at least forty species of butterflies quite new to me, besides a considerable collection of other orders.
>
> One day I had brought me a curious little alligator of a rare species, with numerous ridges and conical tubercles (*Caiman gibbus*), which I skinned and stuffed, much to the amusement of the Indians, half a dozen of whom gazed intently at the operation.

Sooner or later, amid the pleasures and the labours of the forest, the burning question began to flicker in Wallace's acute mind. How had all this variety come about, so alike in design and yet so changeable in detail? Like Darwin, Wallace was struck by the differences between neighbouring species, and like Darwin he began to wonder how they had come to develop so differently.

> There is no part of natural history more interesting or instructive than the study of the geographical distribution of animals.
>
> Places not more than fifty or a hundred miles apart often have species of insects and birds at the one, which are not found at the other. There must be some boundary which determines the range of each species; some external peculiarity to mark the line which each one does not pass.

He was always attracted by problems in geography. Later, when he worked in the Malay archipelago, he showed that the animals on the western islands resemble species from Asia, and on the eastern islands from Australia: the line that divides them is still called the Wallace line.

Wallace was as acute an observer of men as of nature, and with the same interest in the origin of differences. In an age in which Victorians called the people of the Amazon "savages," he had a rare sympathy with their culture. He understood what language, what invention, what custom meant to them. He was perhaps the first person to seize the fact that the cultural distance between their civilisation and ours is much shorter than we think. After he conceived the principle of natural selection, that seemed not only true but biologically obvious.

> Natural selection could only have endowed savage man with a brain a few degrees superior to that of an ape, whereas he actually possesses one very little inferior to that of a philosopher. With our advent there had come into existence a being in whom that subtle force we term "mind" became of far more importance than mere bodily structure.

He was steadfast in his regard for the Indians, and he wrote an idyllic account of their life when he stayed in the village of Javíta in 1851. At this point, Wallace's journal breaks into poetry—well, into verse.

> There is an Indian village; all around,
> The dark, eternal, boundless forest spreads
> Its varied foliage.
>
> Here I dwelt awhile, the one white man
> Among perhaps two hundred living souls.
>
> Each day some labour calls them. Now they go
> To fell the forest's pride, or in canoe
> With hook, and spear, and arrow, to catch fish;
>
> A palm-tree's spreading leaves supply a thatch
> Impervious to the winter's storms and rain.
>
> The women dig the mandiocca root,
> And with much labour make of it their bread.
>
> And all each morn and eve wash in the stream,
> And sport like mermaids in the sparkling wave.
>
> The children of small growth are naked, and
> The boys and men wear but a narrow cloth.
> How I delight to see those naked boys!
> Their well-form'd limbs, their bright, smooth, red-brown skin,
> And every motion full of grace and health;
> And as they run, and race, and shout, and leap,
> Or swim and dive beneath the rapid stream,
>
> I pity English boys; their active limbs
> Cramp'd and confined in tightly-fitting clothes;
>
> But how much more I pity English maids,
> Their waist, and chest, and bosom all confined
> By that vile torturing instrument called stays!
>
> I'd be an Indian here, and live content
> To fish, and hunt, and paddle my canoe,
> And see my children grow, like young wild fawns,
> In health of body and in peace of mind,
> Rich without wealth, and happy without gold!

The sympathy is different from the feelings that South American Indians aroused in Charles Darwin. When Darwin met the natives of Tierra del Fuego he was horrified: that is clear from his own words and from the drawings in his book on *The Voyage of the Beagle*. No doubt the ferocious climate had an influence on the customs of the Fuegians. But nineteenth-century photographs show that they did not look as beastly as they seemed to Darwin. On his voyage home, Darwin had published a pamphlet with the captain of the *Beagle* at Cape Town to recommend the work that missionaries were doing to change the life of savages.

Wallace spent four years in the Amazon basin; then he packed his collections and started home.

> The fever and ague now attacked me again, and I passed several days very uncomfortably. We had almost constant rains; and to attend to my numerous birds and animals was a great annoyance, owing to the crowded state of the canoe, and the impossibility of properly cleaning them during the rain. Some died almost every day, and I often wished I had nothing whatever to do with them, though, having once taken them in hand, I determined to persevere.
>
> Out of a hundred live animals which I had purchased or had had given to me, there now only remained thirty-four.

The voyage home went badly from the start. Wallace was always an unlucky man.

> On the 10th June we left [Manaus], commencing our voyage very unfortunately for me; for, on going on board, after bidding adieu to my friends, I missed my toucan, which had, no doubt, flown overboard, and not being noticed by any one, was drowned.

His choice of a ship was most unlucky, since she was carrying an inflammable cargo of resin. Three weeks out, on 6 August 1852, the ship caught fire.

> I went down into the cabin, now suffocatingly hot and full of smoke, to see what was worth saving. I got my watch and a small tin box containing some shirts and a couple of old note-books, with some drawings of plants and animals, and scrambled up with them on deck. Many clothes and a large portfolio of drawings and sketches remained in my berth; but I did not care to venture down again, and in fact felt a kind of apathy about saving anything, that I can now hardly account for.
>
> The captain at length ordered all into the boats, and was himself the last to leave the vessel.
>
> With what pleasure had I looked upon every rare and curious insect I had added to my collection! How many times, when almost overcome by the ague, had I crawled into the forest and been rewarded by some unknown and beautiful species! How many places, which no European foot but my own had trodden, would have been recalled to my memory by the rare birds and insects they had furnished to my collection!
>
> And now everything was gone, and I had not one specimen to illustrate the unknown lands I had trod or to call back the recollection of the wild scenes I had beheld! But such regrets I knew were vain, and I tried to think as little as possible about what might have been and to occupy myself with the state of things which actually existed.

Alfred Wallace returned from the tropics, as Darwin had done, convinced that related species diverge from a common stock, and nonplussed as to why they diverged. What Wallace did not know was that Darwin had hit on the explanation two years after he returned to England from his voyage in the *Beagle*. Darwin recounts that in 1838 he was reading the *Essay on Population* by the Reverend Thomas Malthus ("for amusement," says Darwin, meaning that it was not part of his serious reading) and he was struck by a thought in Malthus. Malthus had said that population multiplies faster than food. If that is true of animals, then they must compete to survive: so that nature acts as a selective force, killing off the weak, and forming new species from the survivors who are fitted to their environment.

"Here then I had at last got a theory by which to work," says Darwin. And you would think that a man who said that would set to work, write papers, go out and lecture. Nothing of the kind. For four years Darwin did not even commit the theory to paper. Only in 1842 he wrote a draft of thirty-five pages, in pencil; and two years later expanded it to two hundred and thirty pages, in ink. And that draft he deposited with a sum of money and instructions to his wife to publish it if he died.

"I have just finished my sketch of my species theory," he wrote in a formal letter for her dated 5 July 1844 at Downe, and went on:

> I therefore write this in case of my sudden death, as my most solemn and last request, which I am sure you will consider the same as if legally entered in my will, that you will devote £400 to its publication, and further, will yourself, or through Hensleigh (Wedgwood), take trouble in promoting it. I wish that my sketch be given to some competent person, with this sum to induce him to take trouble in its improvement and enlargement.
>
> With respect to editors, Mr (Charles) Lyell would be the best if he would undertake it; I believe he would find the work pleasant, and he would learn some facts new to him.
>
> Dr (Joseph Dalton) Hooker would be *very* good.

We feel that Darwin would really have liked to die before he published the theory, provided after his death the priority should come to him. That is a strange character. It speaks for a man who knew that he was saying something deeply shocking to the public (certainly deeply shocking to his wife) and who was himself, to some extent, shocked by it. The hypochondria (yes, he had some infection from the tropics to excuse it), the bottles of medicine, the enclosed, somewhat suffocating atmosphere of his house and study, the afternoon naps, the delay in writing, the refusal to argue in public: all those speak for a mind that did not want to face the public.

The younger Wallace, of course, was held back by none of these inhibitions. Brashly he went off in spite of all adversities to the Far East in 1854, and for the next eight years travelled all over the Malay archipelago to collect specimens of the wild life there that he would sell in England. By now he was convinced that species are not immutable; he published an essay *On the Law which has regulated the Introduction of New Species* in 1855; and from then "the question of *how* changes of species could have been brought about was rarely out of my mind."

In February of 1858 Wallace was ill on the small volcanic island of Ternate in the Moluccas, the Spice Islands, between New Guinea and Borneo. He had an intermittent fever, was hot and cold by turns, and thought fitfully. And there, on a night of fever, he recalled the same book by Malthus and had the same explanation flash on him that had struck Darwin earlier.

> It occurred to me to ask the question, Why do some die and some live? And the answer was clearly, that on the whole the best fitted lived. From the effects of disease the most healthy escaped; from enemies, the strongest, the swiftest, or the most cunning; from famine, the best hunters or those with the best digestion; and so on.
> Then I at once saw, that the ever present variability of all living things would furnish the material from which, by the mere weeding out of those less adapted to the actual conditions, the fittest alone would continue the race.
> There suddenly flashed upon me the *idea* of the survival of the fittest.
> The more I thought over it, the more I became convinced that I had at length found the long-sought-for law of nature that solved the problem of the Origin of Species . . . I waited anxiously for the termination of my fit so that I might at once make notes for a paper on the subject. The same evening I did this pretty fully, and on the two succeeding evenings wrote it out carefully in order to send it to Darwin by the next post, which would leave in a day or two.

Wallace knew that Charles Darwin was interested in the subject, and he suggested that Darwin show the paper to Lyell if he thought it made sense.

Darwin received Wallace's paper in his study at Down House four months later, on 18 June 1858. He was at a loss to know what to do. For twenty careful, silent years he had marshalled facts to support the theory, and now there fell on his desk from nowhere a paper of which he wrote laconically on the same day,

> I never saw a more striking coincidence; if Wallace had my MS. sketch written out in 1842, he could not have made a better short abstract!

But friends resolved Darwin's dilemma. Lyell and Hooker, who by now had seen some of his work, arranged that Wallace's paper and one by Darwin should be read in the absence of both at the next meeting of the Linnean Society in London the following month.

The papers made no stir at all. But Darwin's hand had been forced. Wallace was, as Darwin described him, "generous and noble." And so Darwin wrote *The Origin of Species* and published it at the end of 1859, and it was instantly a sensation and a bestseller. . . .

The theory of evolution is no longer a battleground. That is because the evidence for it is so much richer and more varied now than it was in the days of Darwin and Wallace. The most interesting and modern evidence comes from our body chemistry. Let me take a practical example: I am able to move my hand at this moment because the muscles contain a store of oxygen, and that has been put there by a protein called myoglobin. That protein is made up of just over one hundred and fifty amino acids. The number is the same in me and all the other animals that use myoglobin. But the amino acids themselves are slightly different. Between me and the chimpanzee there is just one difference in an amino acid; between me and the bush baby (which is a lower primate) there are several amino acid differences; and then between me and the sheep or the mouse, the number of differences increases. It is the number of amino acid differences which is a measure of the evolutionary distance between me and the other mammals.

It is clear that we have to look for the evolutionary progress of life in a build-up of chemical molecules. And that build-up must begin from the materials that boiled on the earth at its birth. To talk sensibly about the beginning of life we have to be very realistic. We have to ask a historical question. Four thousand million years ago, before life began, when the earth was very young, what was the surface of the earth, what was its atmosphere like?

Very well, we know a rough answer. The atmosphere was expelled from the interior of the earth, and was therefore somewhat like a volcanic neighbourhood anywhere—a cauldron of steam, nitrogen, methane, ammonia and other reducing gases, as well as some carbon dioxide. One gas was absent: there was no free oxygen. That is crucial, because oxygen is produced by the plants and did not exist in a free state before life existed.

These gases and their products, dissolved weakly in the oceans, formed a reducing atmosphere. How would they react next under the action of lightning, electric discharges, and particularly under the action of ultraviolet light—which is very important in every theory of life, because it can penetrate in the absence of oxygen? That question was answered in a beautiful experiment by Stanley Miller in America round about 1950. He put the atmosphere in a flask—the methane, the ammonia, the water, and so on—and went on, for day after day, and boiled and bubbled them up, put an electric discharge through them to simulate lightning and other violent forces. And visibly the mixture darkened. Why? Because on testing it was found that amino acids had been formed in it. That is a crucial step forward, since amino acids are the building blocks of life. From them the proteins are made, and proteins are the constituents of all living things. . . .

Biology has been fortunate in discovering within the span of one hundred years two great and seminal ideas. One was Darwin's and Wallace's theory of evolution by natural selection. The other was the discovery, by our own contemporaries, of how to express the cycles of life in a chemical form that links them with nature as a whole.

Were the chemicals here on earth at the time when life began unique to us? We used to think so. But the most recent evidence is different. Within the last years there have been found in the interstellar spaces the spectral traces of molecules which we never thought could be formed out in those frigid regions: hydrogen cyanide, cyano acetylene, formaldehyde. These are molecules which we had not supposed to exist elsewhere than on earth. It may turn out that life had more varied beginnings and has more varied forms. And it does not at all follow that the evolutionary path which life (if we discover it) took elsewhere must resemble ours. It does not even follow that we shall recognise it as life—or that it will recognise us.

Natural Science
LEWIS THOMAS

The essential wildness of science as a manifestation of human behavior is not generally perceived. As we extract new things of value from it, we also keep discovering parts of the activity that seem in need of better control, more efficiency, less unpredictability. We'd like to pay less for it and get our money's worth on some more orderly, businesslike schedule. The Washington planners are trying to be helpful in this, and there are new programs for the centralized organization of science all over the place, especially in the biomedical field.

It needs thinking about. There is an almost ungovernable, biologic mechanism at work in scientific behavior at its best, and this should not be overlooked.

The difficulties are more conspicuous when the problems are very hard and complicated and the facts not yet in. Solutions cannot be arrived at for problems of this sort until the science has been lifted through a preliminary, turbulent zone of outright astonishment. Therefore, what must be planned for, in the laboratories engaged in the work, is the totally unforeseeable. If it is centrally organized, the system must be designed primarily for the elicitation of disbelief and the celebration of surprise.

Moreover, the whole scientific enterprise must be arranged so that the separate imaginations in different human minds can be pooled, and this is more a kind of game than a systematic business. It is in the abrupt, unaccountable aggregation of random notions, intuitions, known in science as good ideas, that the high points are made.

The most mysterious aspect of difficult science is the way it is done. Not the routine, not just the fitting together of things that no one had guessed at fitting, not the making of connections; these are merely the workaday details, the methods of operating. They are interesting, but not as fascinating as the central mystery, which is that we do it at all, and that we do it under such compulsion.

I don't know of any other human occupation, even including what I have seen of art, in which the people engaged in it are so caught up, so totally preoccupied, so driven beyond their strength and resources.

Scientists at work have the look of creatures following genetic instructions; they seem to be under the influence of a deeply placed human instinct. They are, despite their efforts at dignity, rather like young animals engaged in savage play. When they are near to an answer their hair stands on end, they sweat, they are awash in their own adrenalin. To grab the answer, and grab it first, is for them a more powerful drive than feeding or breeding or protecting themselves against the elements.

It sometimes looks like a lonely activity, but it is as much the opposite of lonely as human behavior can be. There is nothing so social, so communal, so interdependent. An active field of science is like an immense intellectual anthill; the individual almost vanishes into the mass of minds tumbling over each other, carrying information from place to place, passing it around at the speed of light.

There are special kinds of information that seem to be chemotactic. As soon as a trace is released, receptors at the back of the neck are caused to tremble, there is a massive convergence of motile minds flying upwind on a gradient of surprise, crowding around the source. It is an infiltration of intellects, an inflammation.

There is nothing to touch the spectacle. In the midst of what seems a collective derangement of minds in total disorder, with bits of information being scattered about, torn to shreds, disintegrated, deconstituted, engulfed, in a kind of activity that seems as random and agitated as that of bees in a disturbed part of the hive, there suddenly emerges, with the purity of a slow phrase of music, a single new piece of truth about nature.

In short, it works. It is the most powerful and productive of the things human beings have learned to do together in many centuries, more effective than farming, or hunting and fishing, or building cathedrals, or making money.

It is instinctive behavior, in my view, and I do not understand how it works. It cannot be prearranged in any precise way; the minds cannot be lined up in tidy rows and given directions from printed sheets. You cannot get it done by instructing each mind to make this or that piece, for central committees to fit with the pieces made by the other instructed minds. It does not work this way.

What it needs is for the air to be made right. If you want a bee to make honey, you do not issue protocols on solar navigation or carbohydrate chemistry, you put him together with other bees (and you'd better do this quickly, for solitary bees do not stay alive) and you do what you can to arrange the general environment around the hive. If the air is right, the science will come in its own season, like pure honey.

There is something like aggression in the activity, but it differs from other forms of aggressive behavior in having no sort of destruction as the objective. While it is going on, it looks and feels like aggression: get at it, uncover it, bring it out, grab it, it's mine! It is like a primitive running hunt, but there is nothing at the end of it to be injured. More probably, the end is a sigh. But then, if the air is right and the science is going well, the sigh is immediately interrupted, there is a yawping new question, and the wild, tumbling activity begins once more, out of control all over again.

Carbon Monoxide Poisoning
CLAUDE BERNARD

About 1846, I wished to make experiments on the cause of poisoning with carbon monoxide. I knew that this gas had been described as toxic, but I knew literally nothing about the mechanism of its poisoning; I therefore could not have a preconceived opinion. What, then, was to be done? I must bring to birth an idea by making a fact appear, i.e., make another experiment to see. In fact I poisoned a dog by making him breathe carbon monoxide and after his death I at once opened his body. I looked at the state of the organs and fluids. What caught my attention at once was that its blood was scarlet in all the vessels, in the veins as well as the arteries, in the right heart as well as in the left. I repeated the experiment on rabbits, birds and frogs, and everywhere I found the same scarlet coloring of the blood. But I was diverted from continuing this investigation, and I kept this observation a long time unused except for quoting it in my course *a propos* of the coloring of blood.

In 1856, no one had carried the experimental question further, and in my course at the Collège de France on toxic and medicinal substances, I again took up the study of poisoning by carbon monoxide which I had begun in 1846. I found myself then in a confused situation, for at this time I already knew that poisoning with carbon monoxide makes the blood scarlet in the whole circulatory system. I had to make hypotheses, and establish a preconceived idea about my first observation, so as to go ahead. Now, reflecting on the fact of scarlet blood, I tried to interpret it by my earlier knowledge as to the cause of the color of blood. Whereupon all the following reflections presented themselves to my mind. The scarlet color, said I, is peculiar to arterial blood and connected with the presence of a large proportion of oxygen, while dark coloring belongs with absence of oxygen and presence of a larger proportion of carbonic acid; so the idea occurred to me that carbon monoxide, by keeping venous blood scarlet might perhaps have prevented the oxygen from changing into carbonic acid in the capillaries. Yet it seemed hard to understand how that could be the cause of death. But still keeping on with my inner preconceived reasoning, I added: If that is true, blood taken from the veins of animals poisoned with carbon monoxide should be like arterial blood in containing oxygen; we must see if that is the fact.

Following this reasoning, based on interpretation of my observation, I tried an experiment to verify my hypothesis as to the persistence of oxygen in the venous blood. I passed a current of hydrogen through scarlet venous blood taken from an animal poisoned with carbon monoxide, but I could not liberate the oxygen as usual. I tried to do the same with arterial blood; I had no greater success. My preconceived idea was therefore false. But the impossibility of getting oxygen from the blood of a dog poisoned with carbon monoxide was a second observation which suggested a fresh hypothesis. What could have become of the oxygen in the blood? It had not changed with carbonic acid, because I had not set free large quantities of that gas in passing a current of hydrogen through the blood of the poisoned animals. Moreover, that hypothesis was contrary to the color of the blood. I exhausted myself in conjectures about how carbon monoxide could cause the oxygen to disappear from the blood; and as gases displace one another I naturally thought that the carbon monoxide might have displaced the oxygen and driven it out of the blood. To learn this, I decided to vary my experimentation by putting the blood in artificial conditions that would allow me to recover the displaced oxygen. So I studied the action of carbon monoxide on blood experimentally. For this purpose I took a certain amount of arterial blood from a healthy animal; I put this blood on the mercury in an inverted test tube containing carbon monoxide; I then shook the whole thing so as to poison the blood sheltered from contact with the outer air. Then, after an interval, I examined whether the air in the test tube in contact with the poisoned blood had been changed, and I noted that the air thus in contact with the blood had been remarkably enriched with oxygen, while the proportion of carbon monoxide was lessened. Repeated in the same conditions, these experiments taught me that what had occurred was an exchange, volume by volume, between the carbon monoxide and the oxygen of the blood. But the carbon monoxide, in displacing the oxygen that it had expelled from the blood, remained chemically combined in the blood and could no longer be displaced either by oxygen or by other gases. So that death came through death of the molecules of blood, or in other words by stopping their exercises of a physiological property essential to life.

This last example, which I have very briefly described, is complete; it shows from one end to the other, how we proceed with the experimental method and succeed in learning the immediate cause of phenomena. To begin with I knew literally nothing about the mechanism of the phenomenon of poisoning with carbon monoxide. I undertook an experiment to see, i.e., to observe. I made a preliminary observation of a special change in the coloring of blood. I interpreted this observation, and I made an hypothesis which proved false. But the experiment provided me with a second observation about which I reasoned anew, using it as a starting point for making a new hypothesis as to the mechanism, by which the oxygen in the blood was removed. By building up hypotheses, one by one, about the facts as I observed them, I finally succeeded in showing that carbon monoxide replaces oxygen in a molecule of blood, by combining with the substance of the molecule. Experimental analysis, here, has reached its goal. This is one of the cases, rare in physiology, which I am happy to be able to quote. Here the immediate cause of the phenomenon of poisoning is found and is translated into a theory which accounts for all the facts and at the same time includes all the observations and experiments. Formulated as follows, the theory posits the main facts from which all the rest are deducted: Carbon monoxide combines more intimately than oxygen with the hemoglobin in a molecule of blood. It has quite recently been proved that carbon monoxide forms a definite combination with hemoglobin. So that the molecule of blood, as if petrified by the stability of the combination, loses its vital properties. Hence everything is logically deduced: because of its property of more intimate combination, carbon monoxide drives out of the blood the oxygen essential to life; the molecules of blood become inert, and the animal dies, with symptoms of hemorrhage, from true paralysis of the molecules.

The Music of *This* Sphere
LEWIS THOMAS

It is one of our problems that as we become crowded together, the sounds we make to each other, in our increasingly complex communication systems, become more random-sounding, accidental or incidental, and we have trouble selecting meaningful signals out of the noise. One reason is, of course, that we do not seem able to restrict our communication to information-bearing, relevant signals. Given any new technology for transmitting information, we seem bound to use it for great quantities of small talk. We are only saved by music from being overwhelmed by nonsense.

It is a marginal comfort to know that the relatively new science of bioacoustics must deal with similar problems in the sounds made by other animals to each other. No matter what sound-making device is placed at their disposal, creatures in general do a great deal of gabbling, and it requires long patience and observation to edit out the parts lacking syntax and sense. Light social conversation, designed to keep the party going, prevails. Nature abhors a long silence.

Somewhere, underlying all the other signals, is a continual music. Termites make percussive sounds to each other by beating their heads against the floor in the dark, resonating corridors of their nests. The sound has been described as resembling, to the human ear, sand falling on paper, but spectrographic analysis of sound records has recently revealed a high degree of organization in the drumming; the beats occur in regular, rhythmic phrases, differing in duration, like notes for a tympani section.

From time to time, certain termites make a convulsive movement of their mandibles to produce a loud, high-pitched clicking sound, audible ten meters off. So much effort goes into this one note that it must have urgent meaning, at least to the sender. He cannot make it without such a wrench that he is flung one or two centimeters into the air by the recoil.

There is obvious hazard in trying to assign a particular meaning to this special kind of sound, and problems like this exist throughout the field of bioacoustics. One can imagine a woolly-minded Visitor from Outer Space, interested in human beings, discerning on his spectrograph the click of that golf ball on the surface of the moon, and trying to account for it as a call of warning (unlikely), a signal of mating (out of the question), or an announcement of territory (could be).

Bats are obliged to make sounds almost ceaselessly, to sense, by sonar, all the objects in their surroundings. They can spot with accuracy, on the wing, small insects, and they will home onto things they like with infallibility and speed. With such a system for the equivalent of glancing around, they must live in a world of ultrasonic bat-sound, most of it with an industrial, machinery sound. Still, they communicate with each other as well, by clicks and high-pitched greetings. Moreover, they have been heard to produce, while hanging at rest upside down in the depths of woods, strange, solitary, and lovely bell-like notes.

Almost anything that an animal can employ to make a sound is put to use. Drumming, created by beating the feet, is used by prairie hens, rabbits, and mice; the head is banged by woodpeckers and certain other birds; the males of deathwatch beetles make a rapid ticking sound by percussion of a protuberance on the abdomen against the ground; a faint but audible ticking is made by the tiny beetle *Lepinotus inquilinus*, which is less than two millimeters in length. Fish make sounds by clicking their teeth, blowing air, and drumming with special muscles against tuned inflated air bladders. Solid structures are set to vibrating by toothed bows in crustaceans and insects. The proboscis of the death's-head hawk moth is used as a kind of reed instrument, blown through to make high-pitched, reedy notes.

Gorillas beat their chests for certain kinds of discourse. Animals with loose skeletons rattle them, or, like rattlesnakes, get sounds from externally placed structures. Turtles, alligators, crocodiles, and even snakes make various more or less vocal sounds. Leeches have been heard to tap rhythmically on leaves, engaging the attention of other leeches, which tap back, in synchrony. Even earthworms make sounds, faint staccato notes in regular clusters. Toads sing to each other, and their friends sing back in antiphony.

Birdsong has been so much analyzed for its content of business communication that there seems little time left for music, but it is there. Behind the glossaries of warning calls, alarms, mating messages, pronouncements of territory, calls for recruitment, and demands for dispersal, there is redundant, elegant sound that is unaccountable as part of the working day. The thrush in my backyard sings down his nose in meditative, liquid runs of melody, over and over again, and I have the strongest impression that he does this for his own pleasure. Some of the time he seems to be practicing, like a virtuoso in his apartment. He starts a run, reaches a midpoint in the second bar where there should be a set of complex harmonics, stops, and goes back to begin over, dissatisfied. Sometimes he changes his notation so conspicuously that he seems to be improvising sets of variations. It is a meditative, questioning kind of music, and I cannot believe that he is simply saying, "thrush here."

The robin sings flexible songs, containing a variety of motifs that he rearranges to his liking; the notes in each motif constitute the syntax, and the possibilities of variation produce a considerable repertoire. The meadow lark, with three hundred notes to work with, arranges these in phrases of three to six notes and elaborates fifty types of song. The nightingale has twenty-four basic songs, but gains wild variety by varying the internal arrangement of phrases and the length of pauses. The chaffinch listens to other chaffinches, and incorporates into his memory snatches of their songs.

The need to make music, and to listen to it, is universally expressed by human beings. I cannot imagine, even in our most primitive times, the emergence of talented painters to make cave paintings without there having been, near at hand, equally creative people making song. It is, like speech, a dominant aspect of human biology.

The individual parts played by other instrumentalists—crickets or earthworms, for instance—may not have the sound of music by themselves, but we hear them out of context. If we could listen to them all at once, fully orchestrated, in their immense ensemble, we might become aware of the counterpoint, the balance of tones and timbres and harmonics, the sonorities. The recorded songs of the humpback whale, filled with tensions and resolutions, ambiguities and allusions, incomplete, can be listened to as a *part* of music, like an isolated section of an orchestra. If we had better hearing, and could discern the descants of sea birds, the rhythmic tympani of schools of mollusks, or even the distant harmonics of midges hanging over meadows in the sun, the combined sound might lift us off our feet.

There are, of course, other ways to account for the songs of whales. They might be simple, down-to-earth statements about navigation, or sources of krill, or limits of territory. But the proof is not in, and until it is shown that these long, convoluted, insistent melodies, repeated by different singers with ornamentations of their own, are the means of sending through several hundred miles of undersea such ordinary information as "whale here," I shall believe otherwise. Now and again, in the intervals between songs, the whales have been seen to breach, leaping clear out of the sea and landing on their backs, awash in the turbulence of their beating flippers. Perhaps they are pleased by the way the piece went, or perhaps it is celebration at hearing one's own song returning after circumnavigation; whatever, it has the look of jubilation.

I suppose that my extraterrestrial Visitor might puzzle over my records in much the same way, on first listening. The 14th Quartet might, for him, be a communication announcing, "Beethoven here," answered, after passage through an undersea of time and submerged currents of human thought, by another long signal a century later, "Bartok here."[1]

If, as I believe, the urge to make a kind of music is as much a characteristic of biology as our other fundamental functions, there ought to be an explanation for it. Having none at hand, I am free to make one up. The rhythmic sounds might be the recapitulation of something else—an earliest memory, a score for the transformation of inanimate, random matter in chaos into the improbable, ordered dance of living forms. Morowitz[2] has presented the case, in thermodynamic terms, for the hypothesis that a steady flow of energy from the inexhaustible source of the sun to the unfillable sink of outer space, by way of the earth, is mathematically destined to cause the organization of matter into an increasingly ordered state. The resulting balancing act involves a ceaseless clustering of bonded atoms into molecules of higher and higher complexity, and the emergence of cycles for the storage and release of energy. In a nonequilibrium steady state, which is postulated, the solar energy would not just flow to the earth and radiate away; it is thermodynamically inevitable that it must rearrange matter into symmetry, away from probability, against entropy, lifting it, so to speak, into a constantly changing condition of rearrangement and molecular ornamentation. In such a system, the outcome is a chancy kind of order, always on the verge of descending into chaos, held taut against probability by the unremitting, constant surge of energy from the sun.

If there were to be sounds to represent this process, they would have the arrangement of the Brandenburg Concertos[3] for my ear, but I am open to wonder whether the same events are recalled by the rhythms of insects, the long, pulsing runs of birdsong, the descants of whales, the modulated vibrations of a million locusts in migration, the tympani of gorilla breasts, termite heads, drumfish bladders. A "grand canonical ensemble" is, oddly enough, the proper term for a quantitative model system in thermodynamics, borrowed from music by way of mathematics. Borrowed back again, provided with notation, it would do for what I have in mind.

---

[1] Béla Bartók (1881–1945), Hungarian composer.—EDS.
[2] Harold J. Morowitz (1927–   ), American biochemist, Yale University.—EDS.
[3] Celebrated composition by Johann Sebastian Bach (1685–1750), great German composer.—EDS.

To a Snail

MARIANNE MOORE

If "compression is the first grace of style,"[1]
you have it. Contractility is a virtue
as modesty is a virtue.
It is not the acquisition of any one thing
that is able to adorn,
or the incidental quality that occurs
as a concomitant of something well said,
that we value in style,
but the principle that is hid:
in the absence of feet, "a method of conclusions";
"a knowledge of principles,"
in the curious phenomenon of your occipital horn.

---

[1] "The very first grace of style is that which comes from compression." *Demetrius on Style*, translated by W. Hamilton Fyfe (Heinemann, 1932).

Ecology

Monsieur Tocqueville! Oh, Get Some Water—He's Fainted!

WILLIAM W. SERRIN

In July 1831, Alexis de Tocqueville, the French social observer, arrived in Detroit in search of "the extreme limits of European civilization." His was not a simple task. Although this country was only a half-century old, wild areas were disappearing. Forests were falling. Swamps were being drained. Settlements were expanding. Roads were being constructed. Where Tocqueville expected to find solitude, he found the sound of the axe and the tinkle of cow bells.

Even to find where to go was not easy. Tocqueville wrote: "To cross almost impenetrable forests; to swim deep rivers; to encounter pestilential marshes; to sleep exposed to the damp air of the woods;—these are efforts which an American can easily conceive, if a dollar is to be gained. . . . But that a man should take such journeys from curiosity, he cannot understand . . ."

A land agent suggested that he and his companion, Gustave de Beaumont, might venture as far as Pontiac, where, he said, "some pretty fair establishments have lately been commenced." But farther off, he said, "the country is covered by an almost impenetrable forest . . . full of nothing but wild beasts and Indians. . . ." That was the kind of place Tocqueville fervently wished to see. The next morning, the two men, having rented two horses, were off, their hearts as light, Tocqueville wrote in his journal, as schoolboys going home for the holidays.

The 100-mile journey made an important impression upon Tocqueville. He saw an untouched America—thick forests, rolling hills, brawling streams, lakes spread like tablecloths beneath the trees. Tocqueville had climbed in the Alps; these lonely, wild lands, he wrote, were no less enchanting.

The journey today is as instructive as it was for Tocqueville. One senses what America was; one sees where great events took place; one sees what America has become. Always, the contrast with what Tocqueville saw leaves one dumbstruck. Tocqueville journeyed through a paradise; the traveler today journeys through a junkyard.

Tocqueville's trail entered the forest a mile from Detroit. Today, that spot marks the beginning of an ugly slum that runs for miles along Woodward Avenue. Rebuilding occurs at the Detroit Medical Center and Wayne State University. But most of the avenue consists of abandoned buildings, old drug stores, sleazy bars, dime-a-dance parlors. Once-fine movie houses smell of urine and show movies like "Massage Parlor Hookers."

Off neglected Grand Circus Park is a bronze plaque commemorating where Henry Ford on a cold night in December 1896 knocked a hole in his garage and drove his first automobile onto Detroit streets, altering the world. On Woodward, in 1943, blacks and whites fought in the Detroit race riot, then the largest race riot ever in America. In 1967, at a Woodward intersection, a white woman was shot and killed, the first person shot in the nation's newest, largest riot.

On Woodward in Highland Park in January 1913 Henry Ford first manufactured cars on the moving assembly line, adopting a principle used in the abattoirs of Chicago. Just north, in 1909, the first mile of concrete highway was constructed. Highway engineers came from "near and far" to observe this, and concrete roads spread across the nation.

The Bloomfield Hills area, in Detroit's north suburbs, is one of the country's most affluent areas, a white, rich reverse of the black Detroit slums. The men who have lived here are automobile executives whose beliefs and actions are typical of the men who have guided America. Charles S. Wilson. Lee A. Iacocca. John Z. DeLorean. James M. Roche. Thomas A. Murphy. The belief is the common American belief, new things, more things. Has life ever been better than here?

After sunset, Tocqueville reached Pontiac, a community of some twenty "neat and pretty houses . . . well-provided shops, a transparent brook . . ."

Pontiac today is a depressed industrial town dependent on the General Motors Corporation. Its downtown is gutted by abandonment and urban redevelopment. The stream Tocqueville described as transparent, the Clinton River, is heavily polluted; trees are gone, and its sides have been encased in concrete. The affluent have left. It is like cities that exist by the score across America.

North of Pontiac, Tocqueville entered the "flowery wilderness" that he found as enchanting as the Alps. This area today is a shabby place of small businesses, marginal farms, unrestored woodlots. The dismal one- and two-story buildings are scattered for miles along the highway: gas stations, a drive-in movie, a Big Boy, a Colonel Sanders, a motorcycle shop, a boat store, a putt-putt golf course, bars, mobile-home lots, a television repair shop. Public ownership of land is rare, as it is most anywhere in this country.

Tocqueville spent the second night in Flint, a settlement of two or three huts along the violet-colored Flint River.

Today Flint is an ugly manufacturing city dependent on automobiles. Here, the wildcatting entrepreneur William C. Durant transformed a road-cart business into the General Motors Corporation. Here, in January 1937, the auto workers won recognition, and gave impetus to the nation's great union organization drive.

Like almost all American cities, the Flint area has spread without planning. It begins to the south, at Grand Blanc, and ends north, beyond

Mt. Morris. Downtown, merchants are valiantly trying to compete with suburban shopping areas. A covered walkway has been built on Court Street, and there are trees in planters. But the new development is in the suburbs. The river that appeared violet to Tocqueville in the twilight is black with pollutants.

The forest north of Flint was one of the splendid sights Tocqueville observed in America. The tall, thick trees formed a canopy that blotted out the sun. The silence, he wrote, was like that at sea.

Today, this flat area consists of cheap farms, small parcels of land on which workers live in cheap homes, dreary little towns. U.S. 10 was known as the Dixie Highway, for in the postwar years it was the major route to Florida. Today the traffic, the noise, the lights are on I-75. The Dixie is left with abandoned motels and signs: "Vicki's Motel, Good Food."

Tocqueville reached Saginaw on the third night of his journey. It was, he said, an "unknown corner of the earth," comprising five log huts and a population of thirty—Americans, Canadians, Indians and half-castes. He stayed three days. He went fowling, fascinating the Indians with his double-barreled shotgun. He explored the slow-moving Saginaw River by canoe, paddling a wilderness that he called a "delicious, blooming, perfumed, gorgeous dwelling, a living palace made for man."

Saginaw today is a manufacturing town with two large General Motors plants, a steering-gear plant and a foundry. It has a fine greenbelt along one part of the river, and a number of quiet residential neighborhoods. But it faces decay, crime and flight. Blacks live on one side of town, whites on the other. The well-to-do escape to the western suburbs.

Once Saginaw was the center of the American lumber industry. Millions of logs came down the Chippewa, the Tobacco, the Molasses, the Tittabawasee, the Shiawassee, the Flint, to Saginaw. In 1882, Saginaw sawed a billion board feet of lumber and had 112 millionaires.

The lumbermen cleared the forests as though the trees were cleaved with the single stroke of a giant axe. Then fires swept through. No reforestation was begun until the Depression. Today, despite Michigan's reputation as a forest state, thousands of acres are nothing but jackpine forests.

What is wrong? Why do we abandon our cities? Why did we cut our forests and break our prairies with so little thought to what we were doing? Why have we done so little conservation and restoration, although it has been clear for a hundred years that we must conserve and restore? Why do we not plan the use of our land?

Tocqueville, on the steamboat "Superior," reflected: "Use familiarizes all scenes . . . Deserts become villages—villages towns. The American who daily witnesses these marvels . . . considers them laws of nature." We are, he wrote, a "mighty race" devoted to the pursuit of wealth "with a perseverance and contempt for life which might be called heroic if such a term could be applied to any but virtuous efforts."

Trying to Restore a Sea of Grass
DENNIS FARNEY

Wildflowers and grass, rippling in the wind; a landscape in motion beneath the wide Midwestern sky.

That is late spring on the prairie. It is a placid time of meadowlarks singing from sun-splashed hillsides and cattle lowing in a gathering dusk. The prairie then is a gentle landscape, a world of low green hills and little wooded valleys that rolls away toward a far-off horizon.

It seems an unlikely place for anything of significance to be happening. Yet a quiet development hereabouts may tell something about the changing mood of the nation:

People are finally coming to value what Walt Whitman once called "North America's characteristic landscape," the American prairie.

Some think this is a reflection of a deep-felt national anxiety about the dizzying pace of social change in the last decade and a half, a yearning for simple, enduring things. Others think it's just an indication that the environmental movement has matured enough to appreciate unspectacular landscapes as well as spectacular ones. Whatever the reason, there is a growing appreciation for the landscape regarded through most of U.S. history as good only for plowing up or mowing down.

Here in the Kansas Flint Hills, a 50-mile-wide band that runs north-south across the state, environmentalists are struggling to establish a Tallgrass Prairie National Park. It would preserve the kind of prairie the homesteaders crossed and conquered, a sea of grass up to nine feet tall, with a root system so matted that it broke the pioneer plows.

Other types of prairie, which have shorter grasses, still survive in large tracts in the drier parts of the Great Plains. But the tallgrass prairie, which once occupied more humid country from western Ohio to eastern Kansas, has long since vanished beneath the plow. It has become the Corn Belt—except for here where it's protected by a topsoil too thin to plow.

It is a widespread misconception that prairies are always flat; most of them have a pitch and roll. Another misconception is that they are monotonous landscapes of grass and only grass. A virgin prairie sparkles with the color of from 200 to 300 kinds of wildflowers from April to October. But above all else, a prairie is an utterly open landscape, a place of lonely windmills turning in a ceaseless wind, of redtailed hawks circling in an empty sky, of endless distances receding toward infinity.

This openness tends either to invigorate people or to terrify them. "Between that earth and that sky, I felt erased, blotted out," Willa Cather wrote in *My Antonia*, her classic novel on the settlement of the prairie. All through such prairie novels, and the letters and diaries of the early sodbusters, there is an eerie ambivalence: the prairie will enchant you with its solitude and its serenity—if it doesn't devour you with its loneliness, its enervating winds, its blizzards and its broiling sun.

Perhaps it is only now, after the prairie has been conquered by the plow, the air conditioner and the interstate highway, that men can safely appreciate its harsh and sharp-edged beauty. Perhaps that is the reason a new movement of sorts has sprung up in recent years, waxing strongest in those states like Illinois and Iowa where the prairie has all but disappeared. It is the prairie restoration movement, composed of a diverse assemblage of people who are trying, with seeds and infinite patience, to re-create—from plowed ground—a semblance of the virgin prairie.

It is no hobby for those who like their payoffs quick and their results guaranteed. The native prairie grasses are difficult to reestablish and many of the wildflowers are next to impossible. Some scientists estimate it may be possible to create a pretty good facsimile of the original prairie in 300 years. Others think 500 years. It's an inexact science.

And yet the prairie restoration movement continues to grow. Practically every college and university in the Midwest seems to have its own little plot of restored prairie now. More surprisingly, a growing collection of individuals are toiling in prairie plantations—everybody from academic types to retired farmers, from little old ladies to Madison Avenue admen.

Maybe all this is part of a broader phenomenon, being one of many ways that Americans are trying to ward off future shock. This, at least, is the suspicion of one man who is as much an authority on the subject as anybody.

"People long for something that will give them a sense of security and continuity and permanence," ventures Jim Wilson, a sort of philosopher-activist in the prairie restoration movement. He is an ex-saxophone player, ex-explorer (by motorcycle) of the sub-Sahara region, ex-English professor, ex-farmer and now, late in a life well-spent, a writer and seller of grass and wildflower seeds in Polk, Nebraska.

For years Jim Wilson and his wife Alice have been selling prairie grass seed to ranchers and farmers, who have been planting it for the usual utilitarian reasons. In recent years, though, they've been flooded with orders from a new kind of customer—people who seem to be planting prairie grass and wildflowers just for the innate rightness of it. "They think in poetry," explains Jim Wilson, "whereas the agricultural people think in prose."

All those prairie restorations may or may not endure for the 300 years, or 500 years, necessary before nature slowly shapes them into something approaching the prairie that Willa Cather knew. And the proposed Tallgrass Prairie National Park for the Flint Hills of Kansas may or may not make it through the congressional labyrinth. It's snagged right now, as usually happens with national park proposals before they ultimately pass.

But something subtle does seem to be happening in lots of unheralded ways and places, all across the country. It may be no coincidence that, at the same time the prairie restoration movement is booming, manufacturers of old-fashioned Mason jars report they can't keep up with demand. In recent years, it seems, many people have begun home canning again. It may be no coincidence that in city after city, the rush is on to restore old houses and warehouses instead of tearing them down; that handicrafts are more than ever in vogue; that for the first time in decades, there is a modest movement from the cities to the small towns and countryside.

People seem to be searching for authentic, enduring things. They seem to want to do things for themselves. They seem to believe that if the world has fragmented into countless problems, people, acting individually and together in countless small ways, may yet be able to knit it back together again.

No doubt it would be a mistake to read too much into these quiet and ephemeral developments having to do with Mason jars and prairie coneflowers. Yet they are hardly insignificant, or pessimistic, developments either. And, at a time when our political leaders seem increasingly befuddled and disheartened by events, they just may be a truer gauge of the national temper.

Bees and Ecology
JOSEPH M. WINSKI

Remember the old saying about how a horse and rider were lost because somebody neglected to tend to a small matter like a missing horseshoe nail?

Some scientists and agriculturists are worried that the same sort of ballooning consequences may stem from what many people probably consider to be a minor irrelevancy: The nation's honeybees slowly but steadily are being exterminated.

Not on purpose, of course. But as the honeybees forage for pollen and nectar they increasingly are gathering poison also—pesticides that farmers apply to protect their crops from destructive insects.

So there are 20% fewer honeybee colonies in the United States today than there were 10 years ago—about four million versus five million. (A colony contains between 25,000 and 60,000 bees.) In California, the leading bee state, as much as 20% of the state's honeybees have been killed in some recent years—a mortality rate double that of the early 1960s.

"All the indications are that it's going to get a lot worse," says Ward Stanger, an apiculturist at the University of California at Davis. "It's a serious situation," Mr. Stanger says—so serious that he's seeking to have the honeybee declared an endangered species.

It is even more serious in another respect: Nearly 100 crops with a farm value of $1 billion annually depend on honeybees for pollination; another $3 billion worth benefit from bee pollination in terms of higher and better-quality yields. Among these crops are apples, cherries, plums, broccoli, cucumbers, cabbage, melons—indeed, virtually all fruits and berries as well as many vegetables and even some livestock-forage crops such as alfalfa.

Thus, at a time when boosting food production is becoming a global priority, the fate of honeybees takes on some of the significance of the proverbial horseshoe nail.

Floyd Moeller, research leader at the North Central States Bee Laboratory at the University of Wisconsin, says that the economic value of honeybees as pollinators is twenty times their value as honey makers. Far from being an esoteric ecological concern, the dwindling number of honeybees bodes ill for the nation's food supply. "You just can't pollinate as efficiently with fewer bees," Mr. Moeller says.

(Bees pollinate inadvertently by dropping bits of pollen, which they gather for food, as they fly from plant to plant. This cross-pollination, which is also performed by other insects, the wind and hummingbirds, produces crops genetically superior to those produced by self-pollination. Nectar, the bees' other main food, is the one they make honey from.)

Some crops already are threatened by a lack of bees. Most notable is the California almond. Each of the 200,000 acres requires two colonies of bees for pollination, but there are now only 300,000 colonies in the entire state. Last year, almond growers had to import more than 100,000 colonies of bees, some of them hauled from as far away as Montana in big tandem-trailer trucks to pollinate their fields. "This obviously isn't a very practical way to do things," says the University of California's Mr. Stanger. "I just don't know how long we can keep it up."

Researchers almost routinely are uncovering more evidence attesting to the honeybee's contribution. For example, Mr. Moeller and his colleagues at the University of Wisconsin discovered a few years ago that cranberry production could be tripled with efficient bee pollination—whereupon Wisconsin cranberry growers rushed out and rented 2,000 bee colonies and increased the cash value of their crop by $4 million. (Rental fees since have doubled to $30 per colony currently.)

An even more dramatic and significant breakthrough may lie in the potential effect of bee pollination of soybeans, the country's second most important feed crop and a critical source of protein. Some observers expect a new hybrid soybean that would double present yields to be in common use in several years. Unlike present varieties, however, the new hybrid will require honeybees for pollination. With all-out production, about two million colonies of bees—half of the country's present total—would be required for just this one crop.

In a way, it's surprising that honeybees are declining in numbers because they in effect have been a protected species for years. Their protectors have been the dedicated practitioners of the art of beekeeping, a form of animal husbandry whose beginnings are lost in antiquity.

But the economics of beekeeping have taken a turn for the worse in the last 10 years or so, largely because of the sharply increased possibility that a beekeeper's bees could be wiped out by pesticides. Changed farming practices (such as using chemicals for fertilizers instead of plowed-under legumes, which while in blossom are excellent sources of nectar) and the continuing spread of suburbia into what used to be open fields also have contributed. "The bee just doesn't have enough flowers she can visit," says John Root, whose family has been in the beekeeping supplies business in Medina, Ohio, since 1869. Another factor, until the last couple of years, has been a depressed honey market.

"There's just been no incentive for a guy to stay in the business," says Robert Banker, secretary-treasurer of the American Beekeeping Federation in Cannon Falls, Minnesota. The result, he says, has been "a steady decline" of full-time beekeepers to about 3,000 and of all beekeepers, including those with one or two colonies, to about 150,000. A rise in honey prices in the last two years appears to be attracting more people into beekeeping, though so far apparently not in substantial enough numbers to reverse the decline of either bees or beekeepers.

Researchers have suggested various protective measures to beekeepers, such as keeping bees in hives and feeding them pollen supplements when nearby sprayed crops are flowering, installing pollen traps that knock the poison-tainted pollen off the bee when she returns to the hive and even draping colonies with wet burlap when pesticides are being applied.

But there isn't a simple solution to the poisoning problem. "It's a complicated situation," Mr. Banker says. "We want to protect our bees but we fully recognize that a grower has a right to protect his crops" from legitimate threats. "Something's got to be done, but we're not sure what," says a spokesman for the National Wildlife Federation in Washington, D.C. He recalls that "last summer bees were dropping off like flies in Virginia."

All this doesn't mean that the honeybee faces extinction, however. They no doubt will be around as long as there are people who are intrigued by them. "I have several observation hives mounted in windows," says Mr. Root, the Ohio supplier of beekeeping equipment. "I can sit and watch them for hours."

Some people spend lifetimes watching bees. Foremost among them is Karl von Frisch, a professor at the University of Munich who has devoted virtually all of his working years to studying bees and other insects. Last year, Mr. von Frisch received a Nobel Prize for his work; it was the first time the prize was given to an animal behaviorist.

The bees' rigid social order (the females do all the work while the males do nothing but mate with the queen and die soon afterwards) and industry (a bee will make 30,000 trips, averaging up to 800 an hour, to gather enough nectar for a pound of honey) are well documented. But Mr. von Frisch found that bees also have a language facility for communication "which, as far as we know, has no parallel in any other animal."

Specifically, Mr. von Frisch found that a foraging bee can tell others in the hive when she has found food, how much, whether it's near or distant, and if distant how far away and in which direction her fellow workers should fly to find it. She does this by dancing around in circles if the food is close, or with vigorous tail-wagging and varying rhythms if it's far away. (Bees frequently gather food a mile or more away from the hive.)

Later, a student of Mr. von Frisch's, Martin Lindauer, found that bees —again by dancing to communicate—are able to arrive at a community decision on a new home after they swarm from their existing one (usually because of overcrowding). Those bees who have inspected the best potential sites dance more vigorously than those who have examined mediocre spots; this causes more bees to inspect the site of the excited dancers, and if they agree they will return and dance in an equally vigorous manner. Eventually, a consensus is reached wherein the whole swarm is throbbing with ecstasy and they fly off to their new home. One swarm studied by Mr. Lindauer considered 21 possibilities and took two weeks to decide.

Though the research that led to these discoveries was conducted primarily for its scientific interest, the findings may have significant practical benefits. "When some day in the future food grows scarce," Mr. von Frisch writes, "people . . . should recall that in their own language bees can be aroused to greater industry and can be dispatched . . . in accord with the wishes of the beekeeper and the farmer."

Some scientists have pooh-poohed such findings of what might be called intelligence in these "lower animals," as bees are categorized. But Donald R. Griffin, a biologist at Rockefeller University in New York and an early skeptic himself, duplicated the von Frisch experiments and came up with the same conclusions. Mr. Griffin says: "I am willing to entertain the thought that perhaps the bees know what they are doing."

Wilderness

ALDO LEOPOLD

Wilderness is the raw material out of which man has hammered the artifact called civilization.

Wilderness was never a homogeneous raw material. It was very diverse, and the resulting artifacts are very diverse. These differences in the end-product are known as cultures. The rich diversity of the world's cultures reflects a corresponding diversity in the wilds that gave them birth.

For the first time in the history of the human species, two changes are now impending. One is the exhaustion of wilderness in the more habitable portions of the globe. The other is the world-wide hybridization of cultures through modern transport and industrialization. Neither can be prevented, and perhaps should not be, but the question arises whether, by some slight amelioration of the impending changes, certain values can be preserved that would otherwise be lost.

To the laborer in the sweat of his labor, the raw stuff on his anvil is an adversary to be conquered. So was wilderness an adversary to the pioneer.

But to the laborer in repose, able for the moment to cast a philosophical eye on his world, that same raw stuff is something to be loved and cherished, because it gives definition and meaning to his life. This is a plea for the preservation of some tag-ends of wilderness, as museum pieces, for the edification of those who may one day wish to see, feel, or study the origins of their cultural inheritance.

THE REMNANTS

Many of the diverse wildernesses out of which we have hammered America are already gone; hence in any practical program the unit areas to be preserved must vary greatly in size and in degree of wildness.

No living man will see again the long-grass prairie, where a sea of prairie flowers lapped at the stirrups of the pioneer. We shall do well to find a forty here and there on which the prairie plants can be kept alive as species. There were a hundred such plants, many of exceptional beauty. Most of them are quite unknown to those who have inherited their domain.

But the short-grass prairie, where Cabeza de Vaca[1] saw the horizon under the bellies of the buffalo, is still extant in a few spots of 10,000-acre size, albeit severely chewed up by sheep, cattle, and dry-farmers. If the forty-niners are worth commemorating on the walls of state capitols, is not the scene of their mighty hegira worth commemorating in several national prairie reservations?

Of the coastal prairie there is one block in Florida, and one in Texas, but oil wells, onion fields, and citrus groves are closing in, armed to the teeth with drills and bulldozers. It is last call.

No living man will see again the virgin pineries of the Lake States, or the flatwoods of the coastal plain, or the giant hardwoods; of these, samples of a few acres each will have to suffice. But there are still several blocks of maple-hemlock of thousand-acre size; there are similar blocks of Appalachian hardwoods, of southern hardwood swamp, of cypress swamp, and of Adirondack spruce. Few of these tag-ends are secure from prospective cuttings, and fewer still from prospective tourist roads.

One of the fastest-shrinking categories of wilderness is coastlines. Cottages and tourist roads have all but annihilated wild coasts on both oceans, and Lake Superior is now losing the last large remnant of wild

---

[1] Alvar Núñez Cabeza de Vaca (c. 1490–1557), Spanish explorer, whose *Retación* is an account of his North American journey.—EDS.

shoreline on the Great Lakes. No single kind of wilderness is more intimately interwoven with history, and none nearer the point of complete disappearance.

In all of North America east of the Rockies, there is only one large area formally reserved as a wilderness: the Quetico-Superior International Park in Minnesota and Ontario. This magnificent block of canoe-country, a mosaic of lakes and rivers, lies mostly in Canada, and can be about as large as Canada chooses to make it, but its integrity is threatened by two recent developments: the growth of fishing resorts served by pontoon-equipped airplanes, and a jurisdictional dispute whether the Minnesota end of the area shall be all National Forest, or partly State Forest. The whole region is in danger of power impoundments, and this regrettable cleavage among proponents of wilderness may end in giving power the whip-hand.

In the Rocky Mountain states, a score of areas in the National Forests, varying in size from a hundred thousand to half a million acres, are withdrawn as wilderness, and closed to roads, hotels, and other inimical uses. In the National Parks the same principle is recognized, but no specific boundaries are delimited. Collectively, these federal areas are the backbone of the wilderness program, but they are not so secure as the paper record might lead one to believe. Local pressures for new tourist roads knock off a chip here and a slab there. There is perennial pressure for extension of roads for forest-fire control, and these, by slow degrees, become public highways. Idle CCC[2] camps presented a widespread temptation to build new and often needless roads. Lumber shortages during the war gave the impetus of military necessity to many road extensions, legitimate and otherwise. At the present moment, ski-tows and ski-hotels are being promoted in many mountain areas, often without regard to their prior designation as wilderness.

One of the most insidious invasions of wilderness is via predator control. It works thus: wolves and lions are cleaned out of a wilderness area in the interest of big-game management. The big-game herds (usually deer or elk) then increase to the point of overbrowsing the range. Hunters must then be encouraged to harvest the surplus, but modern hunters refuse to operate far from a car; hence a road must be built to provide access to the surplus game. Again and again, wilderness areas have been split by this process, but it still continues.

The Rocky Mountain system of wilderness areas covers a wide gamut of forest types, from the juniper breaks of the Southwest to the "illimitable woods where rolls the Oregon."[3] It is lacking, however, in desert areas,

---

[2] Civilian Conservation Corps, a federal agency set up in 1933 during the Depression to provide training and employment in public conservation work for unemployed young men.—EDS.

[3] "Or lose thyself in the continuous woods/Where rolls the Oregon."—William Cullen Bryant, "Thanatopsis."—EDS.

probably because of that under-aged brand of esthetics which limits the definition of "scenery" to lakes and pine trees.

In Canada and Alaska there are still large expanses of virgin country

> Where nameless men by nameless rivers wander
> and in strange valleys die strange deaths alone.

A representative series of these areas can, and should, be kept. Many are of negligible or negative value for economic use. It will be contended, of course, that no deliberate planning to this end is necessary; that adequate areas will survive anyhow. All recent history belies so comforting an assumption. Even if wild spots do survive, what of their fauna? The woodland caribou, the several races of mountain sheep, the pure form of woods buffalo, the barren ground grizzly, the freshwater seals, and the whales are even now threatened. Of what use are wild areas destitute of their distinctive faunas? The recently organized Arctic Institute has embarked on the industrialization of the Arctic wastes, with excellent chances of enough success to ruin them as wilderness. It is last call, even in the Far North.

To what extent Canada and Alaska will be able to see and grasp their opportunities is anybody's guess. Pioneers usually scoff at any effort to perpetuate pioneering.

WILDERNESS FOR RECREATION

Physical combat for the means of subsistence was, for unnumbered centuries, an economic fact. When it disappeared as such, a sound instinct led us to preserve it in the form of athletic sports and games.

Physical combat between men and beasts was, in like manner, an economic fact, now preserved as hunting and fishing for sport.

Public wilderness areas are, first of all, a means of perpetuating, in sport form, the more virile and primitive skills in pioneering travel and subsistence.

Some of these skills are of generalized distribution; the details have been adapted to the American scene, but the skill is world-wide. Hunting, fishing, and foot travel by pack are examples.

Two of them, however, are as American as a hickory tree; they have been copied elsewhere, but they were developed to their full perfection only on this continent. One of these is canoe travel, and the other is travel by pack-train. Both are shrinking rapidly. Your Hudson Bay Indian now has a put-put, and your mountaineer a Ford. If I had to make a living by canoe or packhorse, I should likely do likewise, for both are grueling labor. But we who seek wilderness travel for sport are foiled when we are forced to compete with mechanized substitutes. It is footless to execute a portage to the tune of motor launches, or to turn out your bell-mare in the pasture of a summer hotel. It is better to stay home.

Wilderness areas are first of all a series of sanctuaries for the primitive arts of wilderness travel, especially canoeing and packing.

I suppose some will wish to debate whether it is important to keep these primitive arts alive. I shall not debate it. Either you know it in your bones, or you are very, very old.

European hunting and fishing are largely devoid of the thing that wilderness areas might be the means of preserving in this country. Europeans do not camp, cook, or do their own work in the woods if they can avoid doing so. Work chores are delegated to beaters and servants, and a hunt carries the atmosphere of a picnic, rather than of pioneering. The test of skill is confined largely to the actual taking of game or fish.

There are those who decry wilderness sports as "undemocratic" because the recreational carrying capacity of a wilderness is small, as compared with a golf links or a tourist camp. The basic error in such argument is that it applies the philosophy of mass-production to what is intended to counteract mass-production. The value of recreation is not a matter of ciphers. Recreation is valuable in proportion to the intensity of its experiences, and to the degree to which it *differs from* and *contrasts with* workaday life. By these criteria, mechanized outings are at best a milk-and-water affair.

Mechanized recreation already has seized nine-tenths of the woods and mountains; a decent respect for minorities should dedicate the other tenth to wilderness.

WILDERNESS FOR SCIENCE

The most important characteristic of an organism is that capacity for internal self-renewal known as health.

There are two organisms whose processes of self-renewal have been subjected to human interference and control. One of these is man himself (medicine and public health). The other is land (agriculture and conservation).

The effort to control the health of land has not been very successful. It is now generally understood that when soil loses fertility, or washes away faster than it forms, and when water systems exhibit abnormal floods and shortages, the land is sick.

Other derangements are known as facts, but are not yet thought of as symptoms of land sickness. The disappearance of plants and animal species without visible cause, despite efforts to protect them, and the irruption of others as pests despite efforts to control them, must, in the absence of simpler explanations, be regarded as symptoms of sickness in the land organism. Both are occurring too frequently to be dismissed as normal evolutionary events.

The status of thought on these ailments of the land is reflected in the fact that our treatments for them are still prevailingly local. Thus when a soil loses fertility we pour on fertilizer, or at best alter its tame flora and fauna, without considering the fact that its wild flora and fauna, which built the soil to begin with, may likewise be important to its maintenance. It was recently discovered, for example, that good tobacco crops depend, for some unknown reason, on the preconditioning of the soil by wild ragweed. It does not occur to us that such unexpected chains of dependency may have wide prevalence in nature.

When prairie dogs, ground squirrels, or mice increase to pest levels we poison them, but we do not look beyond the animal to find the cause of the irruption. We assume that animal troubles must have animal causes. The latest scientific evidence points to derangements of the *plant* community as the real seat of rodent irruptions, but few explorations of this clue are being made.

Many forest plantations are producing one-log or two-log trees on soil which originally grew three-log and four-log trees. Why? Thinking foresters know that the cause probably lies not in the tree, but in the micro-flora of the soil, and that it may take more years to restore the soil flora than it took to destroy it.

Many conservation treatments are obviously superficial. Flood-control dams have no relation to the cause of floods. Check dams and terraces do not touch the cause of erosion. Refuges and hatcheries to maintain the supply of game and fish do not explain why the supply fails to maintain itself.

In general, the trend of the evidence indicates that in land, just as in the human body, the symptoms may lie in one organ and the cause in another. The practices we now call conservation are, to a large extent, local alleviations of biotic pain. They are necessary, but they must not be confused with cures. The art of land doctoring is being practiced with vigor, but the science of land health is yet to be born.

A science of land health needs, first of all, a base datum of normality, a picture of how healthy land maintains itself as an organism.

We have two available norms. One is found where land physiology remains largely normal despite centuries of human occupation. I know of only one such place: northeastern Europe. It is not likely that we shall fail to study it.

The other and most perfect norm is wilderness. Paleontology offers abundant evidence that wilderness maintained itself for immensely long periods; that its component species were rarely lost, neither did they get out of hand; that weather and water built soil as fast or faster than it was carried away. Wilderness, then, assumes unexpected importance as a laboratory for the study of land-health.

One cannot study the physiology of Montana in the Amazon; each biotic province needs its own wilderness for comparative studies of used and unused land. It is of course too late to salvage more than a lopsided system of wilderness study areas, and most of these remnants are far too small to retain their normality in all respects. Even the National Parks, which run up to a million acres each in size, have not been large enough to retain their natural predators, or to exclude animal diseases carried by livestock. Thus the Yellowstone has lost its wolves and cougars, with the result that elk are ruining the flora, particularly on the winter range. At the same time the grizzly bear and the mountain sheep are shrinking, the latter by reason of disease.

While even the largest wilderness areas become partially deranged, it required only a few wild acres for J. E. Weaver to discover why the prairie flora is more drouth-resistant than the agronomic flora which has supplanted it. Weaver found that the prairie species practice "team work" underground by distributing their root-systems to cover all levels, whereas the species comprising the agronomic rotation overdraw one level and neglect another, thus building up cumulative deficits. An important agronomic principle emerged from Weaver's researches.

Again, it required only a few wild acres for Togrediak to discover why pines on old fields never achieved the size or wind-firmness of pines on uncleared forest soils. In the latter case, the roots follow old root channels, and thus strike deeper.

In many cases we literally do not know how good a performance to expect of healthy land unless we have a wild area for comparison with sick ones. Thus most of the early travelers in the Southwest describe the mountain rivers as originally clear, but a doubt remains, for they may, by accident, have seen them at favorable seasons. Erosion engineers had no base datum until it was discovered that exactly similar rivers in the Sierra Madre of Chihuahua, never grazed or used for fear of Indians, show at their worst a milky hue, not too cloudy for a trout fly. Moss grows to the water's edge on their banks. Most of the corresponding rivers in Arizona and New Mexico are ribbons of boulders, mossless, soil-less, and all but treeless. The preservation and study of the Sierra Madre wilderness, by an international experiment station, as a norm for the cure of sick land on both sides of the border, would be a good-neighbor enterprise well worthy of consideration.

In short all available wild areas, large or small, are likely to have value as norms for land science. Recreation is not their only, or even their principal, utility.

WILDERNESS FOR WILDLIFE

The National Parks do not suffice as a means of perpetuating the larger carnivores; witness the precarious status of the grizzly bear, and the fact that the park system is already wolfless. Neither do they suffice for mountain sheep; most sheep herds are shrinking.

The reasons for this are clear in some cases and obscure in others. The parks are certainly too small for such a far-ranging species as the wolf.

Many animal species, for reasons unknown, do not seem to thrive as detached islands of population.

The most feasible way to enlarge the area available for wilderness fauna is for the wilder parts of the National Forests, which usually surround the Parks, to function as parks in respect of threatened species. That they have not so functioned is tragically illustrated in the case of the grizzly bear.

In 1909, when I first saw the West, there were grizzlies in every major mountain mass, but you could travel for months without meeting a conservation officer. Today there is some kind of conservation officer "behind every bush," yet as wildlife bureaus grow, our most magnificent mammal retreats steadily toward the Canadian border. Of the 6,000 grizzlies officially reported as remaining in areas owned by the United States, 5,000 are in Alaska. Only five states have any at all. There seems to be a tacit assumption that if grizzlies survive in Canada and Alaska, that is good enough. It is not good enough for me. The Alaskan bears are a distinct species. Relegating grizzlies to Alaska is about like relegating happiness to heaven; one may never get there.

Saving the grizzly requires a series of large areas from which roads and livestock are excluded, or in which livestock damage is compensated. Buying out scattered livestock ranches is the only way to create such areas, but despite large authority to buy and exchange lands, the conservation bureaus have accomplished virtually nothing toward this end. The Forest Service has, I am told, established one grizzly range in Montana, but I know of a mountain range in Utah in which the Forest Service actually promoted a sheep industry, despite the fact that it harbored the sole remnant of grizzlies in that state.

Permanent grizzly ranges and permanent wilderness areas are of course two names for one problem. Enthusiasm about either requires a long view of conservation, and a historical perspective. Only those able to see the pageant of evolution can be expected to value its theater, the wilderness, or its outstanding achievement, the grizzly. But if education really educates, there will, in time, be more and more citizens who understand that relics of the old West add meaning and value to the new. Youth yet unborn will pole up the Missouri with Lewis and Clark, or climb the Sierras with James Capen Adams, and each generation in turn will ask: Where is the big white bear? It will be a sorry answer to say he went under while conservationists weren't looking.

DEFENDERS OF WILDERNESS

Wilderness is a resource which can shrink but not grow. Invasions can be arrested or modified in a manner to keep an area usable either for recreation, or for science, or for wildlife, but the creation of new wilderness in the full sense of the word is impossible.

It follows, then, that any wilderness program is a rearguard action, through which retreats are reduced to a minimum. The Wilderness Society was organized in 1935 "for the one purpose of saving the wilderness remnants in America."

It does not suffice, however, to have such a society. Unless there be wilderness-minded men scattered through all the conservation bureaus, the society may never learn of new invasions until the time for action has passed. Furthermore a militant minority of wilderness-minded citizens must be on watch throughout the nation, and available for action in a pinch.

In Europe, where wilderness has now retreated to the Carpathians and Siberia, every thinking conservationist bemoans its loss. Even in Britain, which has less room for land-luxuries than almost any other civilized country, there is a vigorous if belated movement for saving a few small spots of semi-wild land.

Ability to see the cultural value of wilderness boils down, in the last analysis, to a question of intellectual humility. The shallow-minded modern who has lost his rootage in the land assumes that he has already discovered what is important; it is such who prate of empires, political or economic, that will last a thousand years. It is only the scholar who appreciates that all history consists of successive excursions from a single starting-point, to which man returns again and again to organize yet another search for a durable scale of values. It is only the scholar who understands why the raw wilderness gives definition and meaning to the human enterprise.

Some Problems

Why Can't Computers Be More Like Us?
LEWIS THOMAS

Everyone must have had at least one personal experience with a computer error by this time. Bank balances are suddenly reported to have jumped from 379 dollars into the millions, appeals for charitable contributions are mailed over and over to people with crazy-sounding names at your address, utility companies write that they're turning everything off—that sort of thing. If you manage to get in touch with someone and complain, you then get instantaneously typed, guilty letters from the same computer, saying, "Our computer was in error, and an adjustment is being made in your account."

These are supposed to be the sheerest, blindest accidents. Mistakes are not believed to be part of the normal behavior of a good machine. If things go wrong, it must be a personal, human error, the result of fingering, tampering, a button getting stuck. The computer, at its normal best, is infallible.

I wonder whether this can be true. After all, the whole point of computers is that they represent an extension of the human brain, vastly improved upon but nonetheless human, superhuman maybe. A good computer can think clearly and quickly enough to beat you at chess, and some of them have even been programmed to write obscure verse. They can do anything we can do, and more besides.

It is not yet known whether a computer has its own consciousness, and it would be hard to find out about this. When you walk into one of those great halls now built for the huge machines, and stand listening, it is easy to imagine that the faint, distant noises are the sound of thinking, and the turning of the spools gives them the look of wild creatures rolling their eyes in the effort to concentrate, choking with information. But real thinking, and dreaming, are other matters.

On the other hand, the evidences of something like an *unconscious*, equivalent to ours, are all around, in every mail. As extensions of the human brain, they have been constructed with the same property of error, spontaneous, uncontrolled, and rich in possibilities.

Mistakes are at the very base of human thought, embedded there, feeding the structure like root nodules. If we were not provided with the knack of being wrong, we could never get anything useful done. We think our way along by choosing between right and wrong alternatives, and the wrong choices have to be made as frequently as the right ones. We get along in life this way. We are built to make mistakes, coded for error.

We learn, as we say, by "trial and error." Why do we always say that? Why not "trial and rightness," or "trial and triumph"? The old phrase puts it that way because that is, in real life, the way it is done.

A good laboratory, like a good bank, or a corporation or a government, has to run like a computer. Almost everything is done flawlessly, by the book, and all the numbers add up to the predicted sums. The days go by. And then, if it is a lucky day, and a lucky laboratory, somebody makes a mistake: the wrong buffer, something in one of the blanks, a decimal misplaced in reading counts, the warm room off by a degree and a half, a mouse out of his box, or just a misreading of the day's protocol. Whatever, when the results come in, something is obviously screwed up, and then the action can begin.

The misreading is not the important error; it opens the way. The next step is the crucial one. If the investigator can bring himself to say, "But even so, look at that!" the new finding, whatever it is, is ready for snatching. What is needed, for progress to be made, is the move based on the error.

Whenever new kinds of thinking are about to be accomplished, or new varieties of music, there has to be an argument beforehand. With two sides debating in the same mind, haranguing, there is an amiable understanding that one is right and the other wrong. Sooner or later the thing is settled, but there can be no action at all if there are not the two sides, and the argument. The hope is in the faculty of wrongness, the tendency toward error. The capacity to leap across mountains of information to land lightly on the wrong side represents the highest of human endowments.

We are at our human finest, dancing with our minds, when there are more choices than two. This process is called exploration and is based on human fallibility. If we had only a single center in our brains, capable of responding only when a correct decision was to be made, instead of the jumble of different, credulous, easily conned clusters of neurons that provide for being flung off into blind alleys, up wrong trees, down dead ends, out into blue sky, along wrong turnings, around bends, we could only stay the way we are today, stuck fast.

The lower animals do not have this splendid freedom. They are limited, most of them, to absolute infallibility. Fish are flawless in everything they do. Individual cells in a tissue are mindless machines, perfect in their performance, as absolutely inhuman as bees.

We should have this in mind as we become dependent on more complex computers for the arrangement of our affairs. Give the computers their heads, I say; let them go their way. Your average good computer can make calculations in an instant that would take a lifetime of slide rules for any of us. Think of what we could gain from the near infinity of precise, machine-made miscomputation that is now so easily within grasp. We could begin the solving of some of our hardest problems. What we need for moving ahead is a set of wrong alternatives much longer and more interesting than the short list of mistaken courses that any of us can think up right now. We need, in fact, an infinite list, and when it is printed out we need the computer to turn on itself and select, at random, the next way to go. If it is a big enough mistake, we could find ourselves on a new level, out in the clear, ready to move again.

What Physicists Do: Neaten up the Cosmos
ROBERT GEROCH

A common misconception among students is that physics is sharp, clear-cut and dried. It probably comes from the way students are trained: One has to do problem 17 and problem 17 has an answer. Maybe that's what's wrong with the way we train people generally: problem 17 has an answer. Physics isn't like that, and life isn't like that.

Students ask questions as if you're going to answer them. And in science you don't normally answer questions—you try to say how one normally thinks about such matters.

How does one think about eight billion light years *ago* or eight billion light years *away*? I think one just gives up. But such distances to a faraway object are made to be comprehensible because the distance is ultimately reduced by a number of steps to something like the distance between here and New Jersey. One studies the solar system, and one can figure out the distance between here and the sun, which is large, but not impossible to work out.

The earth goes around the sun; and so you can see certain stars from a slightly different vantage point at different seasons. You can tell by how the image of the star appears to wiggle how far away it is. Some stars seem to have an oscillating brightness, and it turns out you can correlate the period of the oscillation with how bright the star is. So, for more-distant stars that are so far away you can't see the wiggle as the earth goes around the sun, you can nonetheless see the brightness oscillate and can infer what the real brightnesses are. You can compare that with the brightness you observe, and from that you can determine the distance. And from that you can get the distance to the nearby galaxy and work your way out. In this way such enormous distances are reduced, ultimately, to ordinary everyday distances.

Sixteen billion light years is not the edge of the universe but the beginning of the universe. Think of the universe as a balloon—there are little black spots all over the balloon—and they represent the galaxies. Now let the balloon be blown up. Eight billion light years ago, halfway back through time, the balloon was only half as big.

The balloon is analogous to the universe where the three spatial dimensions of our universe are reduced to two on the balloon. Now on the surface of the balloon you can imagine a little ant that represents a light ray. The ants only travel at a certain speed. This means that if one had strong enough telescopes, one could see to the very beginning—in a manner of speaking.

It's always the same sort of story—there's always some extreme, and the closer you get to the extreme, the more difficult and expensive it is. You never get to the extreme; it is always a question of "how close."

It's like absolute zero—wouldn't it be nice if one could get to absolute zero and see all those very cold things? The fact is, it costs you $1,000 to get halfway and $10,000 to get three-quarters of the way and so on. At any given state of the technology it's only feasible to be so many degrees from absolute zero. And each little bit of a degree costs so much, in terms of either money or effort. And one *always* has that feeling; one just never thinks of reaching such extremes. So you never have all the answers.

It's not just physics—it's the same way with everything. One goes shopping and tries to get the very best buy on soft drinks. But one cannot because in order to get the best buy you have to check out all the stores in the next county, and that's not enough because you didn't consider the possibility of reselling the bottle caps, and you can go on and on. You *never* get the best buy; it's all a question of how much time you have and how much gas you have to drive around and how interested you are.

Physics is like life; there's no perfection. It's never all sewed up. It's all a question of better, better yet, and how much time and interest you have in it. Is the universe really curved? It's not that cut and dried. Theories come and go. A theory isn't right or wrong. A theory has a sort of sociological position that changes as new information comes in.

"Is Einstein's theory correct?" You can take a poll and have a look. Einstein is rather "in" right now. But who knows if it is "true"? I think there is a view that physics has a sort of pristineness, rightness, trueness that I don't see in physics at all. To me, physics is the activity you do between breakfast and supper. Nobody said anything about Truth. Perhaps Truth is "out." One thinks, "Well, this idea looks bad for or looks good for general relativity."

Physics is confusing; like life it would be so easy were it otherwise. It's a human activity and you have to make human judgments and accept human limitations.

This way of thinking implies a greater mental flexibility and a greater tolerance for uncertainty than we tend towards naturally, perhaps.

Molecular Astronomy: The Great Void Is Alive

WALTER SULLIVAN

It may come as a surprise to the distilling industry, but there is a greater reservoir of grain neutral spirits adrift in the constellation Sagittarius than has been produced on earth since alcoholic beverages were discovered.

How is this known? Because the alcohol molecules—billions upon billions of them—have sent radio messages across the great void of the heavens. Such emissions have, in fact, made it clear that, far from being a true void, space between the stars is almost literally alive.

What practitioners of the new science of molecular astronomy are finding, through the use of giant radio telescopes, is that the precursor chemicals of life on earth exist in many regions of space. Such substances occur as molecules formed from highly diverse combinations of atoms.

So striking are the parallels between the chemistry seen in space and that associated with the manner in which life is thought to have originated on earth that there is a temptation to revive the old panspermia hypothesis in modified form. Early in this century, Svante August Arrhenius of Sweden, one of the first Noble laureates, proposed that the spores of life are adrift throughout the universe, ready to populate any planet with a suitable environment. It was thus, he proposed, that life on earth originated.

In the revived version of this concept, germs of life are continuously evolving in suitable regions of space. The requisite molecules are thought to form on grains within dust clouds that help protect them from destructive ultraviolet light, such as that emitted by the sun. The grains would also provide a platform on which atoms could collect and merge.

MINIATURE WORLDS

Some scientists consider the grains to be miniature worlds with, as on earth, an iron-rich core, an envelope of silicates, water (frozen) and a surface coating of organic material. And, some speculate, life itself may have evolved here and there in the distant dust clouds. There is no evidence for this, but if it were true, it might mean that man's most remote ancestry originated far out among the stars.

Radio emissions signal the presence in interstellar space of a growing catalogue of organic molecules. Such molecules are called organic because it was believed in earlier centuries that they could only have been produced by living organisms. The list already includes about 35 varieties.

The spontaneous synthesis of these substances in space appears to parallel the way laboratory evidence now shows molecules on earth evolved into increasingly complex forms and finally into self-supporting reproductive units that were "alive."

While most of the molecular signals have come from within the Milky Way star system, or galaxy, to which earth belongs, some have been detected in other galaxies so distant that their light and radio emissions have taken millions of years to reach earth. Two types that have been detected, for example, are formaldehyde and carbon monoxide.

That processes native to the Milky Way have also occurred in other galaxies (and there are billions of them) is not surprising because it is a basic tenet of science that the physics and chemistry, and perhaps biology, as they are known on earth are applicable everywhere.

What is particularly striking to molecular astronomers is the key role that carbon plays in space chemistry. There has been speculation, by biologists and science-fiction writers alike, that life in other worlds might have evolved a different chemistry—one whose molecules, for example, were based on chains of silicon atoms instead of carbon chains.

EVOLVES SPONTANEOUSLY

It now appears that carbon-based organic chemistry is the one that spontaneously evolves throughout the universe—unless, of course, the other types of molecules are remaining silent and hidden.

The detection of these many molecules has resulted from a combination of laboratory work and highly sensitive scanning with radio telescopes. The molecules in question give off characteristic radio waves as they change their energy states.

The process of absorbing and giving off energy in clearly defined packets (and hence wave lengths) forms the basis of a large proportion of natural phenomena. For instance, each atom or molecule, when heated, gives off characteristic wave lengths of light, enabling astronomers to catalogue the constituents of the most distant stars.

The interstellar molecules, as a rule, are far too cold to glow, but they do change energy states in various ways. Their electrons can move in different orbital patterns involving varying amounts of energy. The molecules can vibrate in various modes, some more energetic than others.

An entire molecule can change its spin axis resulting in a change in spinning energy. When energy is added, its source may be from collision with another molecule or it may be from an electromagnetic wave (such as a light wave or radio wave).

The formaldehyde molecule, for example, is triangular with a carbon atom in the middle and two hydrogen atoms plus an oxygen atom forming the three corners. When it rotates in its flattened plane, like a spinning Frisbee, it carries minimal energy. When it rotates like a Frisbee tumbling over and over, its added energy equals that carried by a radio wave of 4,830 million cycles.

If it switches from this mode to the less energetic one, it therefore gives off a radio wave of that frequency and at a wave length of 6.21 centimeters. Conversely, if radio emissions spanning a broad range of wave lengths pass through a cloud of such molecules, those at this special wave length will be absorbed, stimulating the formaldehyde molecules to flip into the more energetic spin mode.

These two processes of absorption and emission lie at the basis of all molecular observations in space.

It was in this way that astrophysicists identified a previously unknown element in the sun. Because of its presence there they called it helium and only later was it found to exist on earth as well.

Laboratory work has played an important role because the radio "signatures" of these molecules under the conditions of extreme cold and deep vacuum in space were unknown until determined by experiment. Some of the molecules more closely linked to life, such as amino acids, will remain undetectable until their special emissions have also been determined.

Amino acids are the building blocks of all protein. Their synthesis in space, particularly in clouds of dust and gas that are falling together to form a new star, seems probable now that they have been found within a meteorite that is thought to have come from the outer fringes of the solar system.

This, the Murchison meteorite, fell on Australia and was found to contain amino acids clearly different from those found in living organisms on earth. The meteorite is believed to be formed of the primordial material that came together when the solar system was formed.

Both methyl alcohol (the "wood alcohol" that blinds and kills) and ethyl alcohol (the one that intoxicates) have been detected in space, as well as their sister substances formaldehyde and formic acid. It is the latter that produces the bite of a bee sting and takes its name from its presence in ants. It inspired Ogden Nash to write:

> The ant has made itself illustrious
> Through constant industry industrious
> So what?
> Would you be calm and placid,
> If you were full of formic acid?

When those lines were written in 1938 no one suspected the great clouds that obscure the stars of Sagittarius and other constellations to be filled with so earthy a substance.

Some Adjustments

Trend Is Not Destiny
RENÉ DUBOS

In 1575—400 years ago!—the French scholar Louis Le Roy published a learned book in which he voiced despair over the upheavals caused by the social and technological innovations of his time, what we now call the Renaissance. "All is pell-mell, confounded, nothing goes as it should." We, also, feel that our times are out of joint; we even have reason to believe that our descendants will be worse off than we are.

The earth will soon be overcrowded and its resources exhausted. Pollution will ruin the environment, upset the climate, damage human health. The gap in living standards between the rich and the poor will widen and lead the angry, hungry people of the world to acts of desperation including the use of nuclear weapons as blackmail. Such are the inevitable consequences of population and technological growth *if* present trends continue. But what a big *if* this is!

The future is never an extrapolation of the past. Animals probably have no chance to escape from the tyranny of biological evolution, but human beings are blessed with the freedom of social evolution. For us, trend is not destiny. The escape from existing trends is now facilitated by the fact that societies anticipate future dangers and take preventive steps against expected upheavals.

In the past, disasters caught humankind by surprise; now future situations are discussed long before the event, especially if they are likely to be dangerous. One of the fashionable intellectual games of our time consists in imagining the symptoms of "future shock" that people will experience when their ways of life are transformed either by man-made changes or by natural catastrophes. But the very fact that these symptoms have been publicized in advance makes it unlikely that they will occur as described. A few examples will illustrate the range of potentially dangerous situations which modern societies have anticipated and for which they are developing preventive measures.

During the winter of 1917-1918, the Spanish flu spread explosively throughout the world, killing more than 20 million people. The epidemic was unexpected; it was like an apocalyptic visitation of mysterious origin and nothing could be done to stop it. Other outbreaks of influenza have occurred since that time, but any new strains of it, the Hong Kong flu for example, can now be detected early in its spread and steps can be taken to tame its virulence.

During the 1950's, environmental degradation and population growth reached critical levels in many parts of the world. These problems are still with us, but progress is being made toward their control wherever the public realizes the dangers of present trends.

For example, Algeria and continental China are carrying out reforestation programs based on the experience of the Dust Bowl in the United States; population growth has begun to slow down in several industrialized countries.

Urban agglomerations are in a state of crisis, but efforts are being made everywhere to reform urban life. Old cities are rediscovering the value of their ancient buildings and traditions; large new cities are being created, especially in Europe, each with its own economic and cultural identity; even New York City may eventually establish a sounder budgetary basis on which to build its future.

These examples are typical of our times in that they do not correspond to final solutions of problems but rather symbolize a kind of social ferment generated by public concern for the future.

Despite the widespread belief that the world has become too complex for comprehension by the human brain, modern societies have often responded effectively to critical situations.

The decrease in birth rates, the shelving of the supersonic transport, the partial banning of pesticides, the rethinking of technologies for the production and use of energy are but a few examples illustrating a sudden reversal of trends caused not by political upsets or scientific breakthroughs, but by public awareness of consequences.

Even more striking are the situations in which social attitudes concerning future difficulties undergo rapid changes before the problems have come to pass—witness the heated controversies about the ethics of behavior control and of genetic engineering even though there is as yet no proof that effective methods can be developed to manipulate behavior and genes on a population scale.

One of the characteristics of our times is thus the rapidity with which steps can be taken to change the orientation of certain trends and even to reverse them. Such changes usually emerge from grassroot movements rather than from official directives; they are less a result of conventional education than of the widespread awareness of problems generated by the news media.

There is the danger, admittedly, that such awareness is not always sufficient for rapid enough feedback to prevent critical processes from overshooting and causing catastrophes. But hope against the danger of overshooting can be found in the fact that most biological and social systems are extremely resilient. It is this resilience which leads me to reject the myth of inevitability and reaffirm that, wherever human beings are concerned, trend is not destiny.

On Growth
RENÉ DUBOS

Much of contemporary gloom concerning the future originates from the belief that there are "limits to growth"—an expression which has penetrated deeply into the public subconscious from the catchy title of a much-publicized book. One of the themes of this book is that the resources of the Earth are limited and that shortages will soon reach critical levels.

Although the phrase "limits to growth" appears self-explanatory, it is in fact deceptive because it hides assumptions and has static connotations that are incompatible with human behavior.

It implies that growth means producing more and more of what industrial societies have been producing at an obscene rate, and that it will therefore require more of the same kind of resources that were used in the past.

History shows, however, that social evolution continuously drives human activities into new channels and that each age creates the resources it needs.

Resources are not as "natural" as usually assumed. They are derived from raw materials that acquire value only after they have been separated from the earth to serve human purposes.

Gold and copper became resources very early because these metals can be extracted and manipulated by simple techniques. Iron did not become a resource until much later because it requires more complex technologies. Aluminum became a resource only after sophisticated methods had been developed to derive it from bauxite at the turn of the century. And so it goes for other metals.

Agricultural lands, also, had to be created out of the wilderness by human ingenuity and labor. In North America this involved clearing the forests that used to cover a large part of the continent, using the plow "that broke the plains," draining marshes and irrigating semidesert areas. Much of what is called nature was for ages some aspect of wilderness that has been transformed by human efforts.

One kind of growth is simply the exploitation of the materials stored in the earth; another more interesting kind results from the transformation of raw materials into resources through a continuous evolutionary process.

To a large extent, in other words, growth means the evolution of the man-made. The creativeness of social evolution is strikingly evident in the change of attitudes regarding sources of energy.

For millennia, all work was done by human and animal muscles. During the Middle Ages, mechanization began with the use of water mills and windmills. The Industrial Revolution operated its machines first with wood, then with fossil fuels such as coal, petroleum products, and recently uranium.

At present, studies are going on all over the world to determine what sources of energy are best suited for each individual purpose and what are the safe limits in the production and use of energy.

The awareness that the supplies of fossil fuels are limited is now directing thought to renewable sources—for example, nuclear fission and the sun—and to the vital contribution made by the wilderness to the energy balance of the earth.

In any given year, the total amount of energy derived from the sun by the photosynthetic activities of wild vegetation greatly exceeds the total amount used to support human life and to drive technologies. The problem of energy supplies thus leads back to concern about the preservation of nature.

The meaning of the word "growth" has evolved also with regard to human existence. Quantitative growth, for its own sake, is no longer socially acceptable because it threatens the quality of life and of the environment.

In the countries of Western civilization, many members of the upper and middle classes are beginning to recognize the merits of a less-consuming society. Just as this bellwether group led the movement toward smaller families, so it may eventually transmit new social values to the rest of the population.

In matters of growth, the new mentality is more important than advances in science and in technology. The fact that a good environment is now considered one of the "inalienable rights" will probably influence the design of future technologies as much as scientific discoveries have in the past.

Even though the phrase "quality of life" does not define a social philosophy, it symbolizes an attitude that can be contrasted with the following statement from the guidebook prepared for the 1933 Chicago World's Fair: "Science finds, industry applies, man *conforms*."

Today, 40 years after the 1933 World's Fair, no one would dare state that humankind must conform to technological imperatives. The goal is rather to make technology conform to human needs and aspirations.

This involves a kind of qualitative growth for which there are no discernible limits, because social evolution is more inventive than biological evolution and more creative of resources really valuable for human existence.

Who Should Control Recombinant DNA?

CHERYL M. FIELDS

Public and scholarly debate over controversial new genetic studies has produced a surprising consensus among many of the scientists involved—that federal legislation is needed to regulate this form of basic research.

Generally, researchers are strongly opposed to outside interference—especially by the government—in fundamental scientific inquiry. In this case, however, both the supporters and critics of so-called "recombinant DNA" studies say it is time for the government to take firm control of the issue, study the likely long-range impact of the technique, and make policy that will apply to all researchers.

The recombinant DNA studies, which have led to scientific and political controversies in a number of university communities, have been variously described as a potential boon in the search for cures for cancer and other diseases and as a possible forerunner of "genetic engineering" that could make George Orwell's *1984* a reality.

The technique seeks to study the working of heredity by taking genes—composed of DNA, or deoxyribonucleic acid—from the cells of complex organisms and inserting them into simple bacteria, where their functioning can be studied in a less complicated environment.

"We expected a consensus to develop on the need for federal legislation, but we never expected it to develop this quickly," said Stanley B. Jones, staff director of the Senate Subcommittee on Health and Scientific Research, at the close of a recent three-day public forum at the National Academy of Sciences.

Indeed, for many speakers at the forum, the issue was not whether a federal law was needed, but what kind.

The forum, marked by protests from a public-interest group known as the People's Business Commission (formerly the People's Bicentennial Commission), demonstrated the emotions, fears, and frustrations that have become attached to the recombinant-DNA issue, as well as the difficulty of involving members of the public and scientists in mutual discussion of scientific questions.

IGNORING LONG-RANGE ISSUES

Critics, including the People's Commission and a coalition of scientists and representatives of environmental groups, argued that the public controversy over the research had focused on the safety standards necessary for conducting the studies and assuring that bacteria with "foreign" genes inserted do not escape and cause disease or environmental damage.

The debate, they said, has ignored the long-range social and ethical issues of whether the research should be done at all, particularly by pharmaceutical companies and other commercial interests.

"A primary danger is that the deliberate production of 'desirable' changes in certain organisms might result in the disruption of the infinitely complex and delicate balance among living things," said George Wald, professor of biology at Harvard University and a winner of the Nobel Prize.

"The central issue," said Jeremy Rifkin, co-director of the People's Commission, "is the mystery of life itself. It is now only a matter of time until scientists will be able to create new strains of plants, even alter human life."

Considering the potential value of the research for understanding the causes of various diseases and for production of new medical or agricultural substances, countered David Baltimore, professor of microbiology at the Massachusetts Institute of Technology and another Nobel laureate, "it seems inhumane not to do the research. Should we forgo the benefits because the technique has potential for misuse?"

Supporters of the research also insisted that most recombinant experiments that scientists agreed in 1974 to ban until special enfeebled bacteria could be developed to act as "hosts" for foreign genes, had been suspended purely because of "speculative" or "theoretical" dangers—not because of anything that most molecular biologists expected to occur.

FEDERAL LAW SOUGHT

Other recombinant experiments judged to require more routine safety precautions have been carried out all along, with no apparently hazardous organisms being produced, the proponents said.

The upshot of the National Academy debate appeared to be:

▶ Critics of the research believe that Congressional hearings on bills to regulate the studies are a way of insuring greater public scrutiny of the long-range implications.

▶ Supporters believe a federal law setting uniform laboratory standards for all researchers is needed to avert a patchwork of local and state regulations.

In Cambridge, Massachusetts, home of both Harvard and M.I.T., a citizens' review committee decided a few months ago that recombinant research should be conducted under somewhat stricter standards than those issued last summer by the National Institutes of Health [N.I.H.] to cover its grant recipients. Other cities, including Princeton, New Jersey, and Madison, Wisconsin, have also set up local study boards.

Bills have been introduced in both the New York and California state legislatures to license all facilities conducting such research and provide for their inspection.

Although the Cambridge review committee's handling of the complex scientific issues involved in recombinant DNA won high praise from many scientists, some noted that inequity and chaos could result if greatly varying standards or restrictions were applied across the country.

Hearings on federal legislation to regulate the research began last week in the House Subcommittee on Health and Environment, and Senate hearings will begin next month.

Joseph A. Califano, Jr., Secretary of Health, Education, and Welfare, announced last week that his department would draft legislation to regulate the research and license facilities undertaking it. Such legislation, which is expected to cover both academic and commercial research facilities, was recommended by a federal inter-agency committee that included representatives from several departments with an interest in recombinant research.

"CONFUSION AND HYPOCRISY"

"I'm surprised to be saying this, but I support federal legislation. The proliferation of local guidelines can only lead to confusion and hypocrisy," said Norton D. Zinder, a professor in the department of genetics at Rockefeller University.

"It's clear there must be federal legislation because these are not appropriate issues for local regulation," said Robert L. Sinsheimer, chairman of the biology division of the California Institute of Technology. Noting that such a law might be the first example of federal control of basic research, he added, "I'm not happy about it, but we have nothing now," since the N.I.H. guidelines do not technically cover researchers in commercial laboratories and are not backed by any official enforcement mechanism.

"Zinder would have been absolutely opposed to legislation six months ago," Mr. Sinsheimer said, ". . . but there is the feeling that there is no other option."

"SALEM WITCH TRIALS"

David Clem, a member of the Cambridge City Council, said there was a much different reaction among members of the Cambridge citizens' review board to genetic research with insects and other lower animals "than to research with humans."

"If we don't set up a mechanism now to decide what research is safe, what the hazards are with experiments with higher organisms and with human research, in 10 years scientists will be working with humans and the public will ban it. It will be like the Salem witch trials," he said.

"I think a federal law with a federal regulatory mechanism that vests monitoring at the local level is probably the best answer," Mr. Clem said.

Clifford Grobstein, professor of biology and vice-chancellor for university relations at the University of California at San Diego, suggested that a joint commission with representatives of Congress and the executive branch be set up to oversee the research and make an assessment of its long-range impact.

The American Pharmaceutical Association also has submitted proposals calling for federal standards for conducting the research.

Many scientists appeared to assume that any federal legislation would be confined to mechanisms for regulating the research and would pre-empt local controls.

However, Mr. Jones of the Senate health subcommittee said there were "big technical problems" in drafting legislation to pre-empt local authorities when there is a legitimate community interest at stake. In addition, he predicted that at the Senate hearings, at least, "the value debate will be the big one, the issue of the value of the research versus its risk, to what degree the government should encourage the research, the issue of social priorities for spending of public funds."

In fact, observed Roger G. Noll, a professor of economics at the California Institute of Technology, the academy's forum might be the last major public debate of the issue "in which the biologists predominate." He predicted recombinant DNA research would probably become "a minor political issue in which biologists give technical information but will not be the major force behind public policy."

IS IT WORTH IT?

The public initially became involved in the issue because of concern over safety, Mr. Noll said, but since it will be the federal government that sponsors much of the research, "I suspect the question, 'Is this worth buying?' is going to be the real issue."

Whether or not that does become the central question, proponents of the research insisted that, besides basic new knowledge about heredity, scientists could justify proceeding with the research under appropriate safeguards because of its likely impact on the understanding of cancer and a variety of genetically linked diseases, such as sickle-cell anemia.

Paul Berg, professor of biochemistry at the Stanford University Medical Center and a pioneer in the recombinant DNA technique, said, "I firmly believe that the most important practical benefit from recombinant DNA research will be the knowledge acquired about mammalian and human genes and chromosomes. For surely that knowledge will make the diagnosis, prevention, and cure of disease more rational and effective."

"GROSSLY IRRESPONSIBLE"

Critics of the research, such as Ruth Hubbard, professor of biology at Harvard University, rejected that "quick linkage between knowledge and cures." She termed it "grossly irresponsible to claim curative benefits" in arguing for the support of fundamental studies.

"The sources of famine and disease lie much more in social and economic arrangements than in some lack of technological progress," argued Jonathan Beckwith, professor of microbiology and molecular genetics at the Harvard University Medical School. "Major funding goes to genetics research and into viral causes of cancer—and a pittance, for example, to occupational health and safety."

Recombinant DNA research, said Ethan R. Signer, professor of biology at the Massachusetts Institute of Technology, "will eventually tinker with the gene pool of humanity. So the public, like the subject of any experiment, must give its informed consent—but willingly, not by coercion."

However, some scientists at the National Academy forum here were clearly frustrated by the general level of public debate on the DNA issue.

They questioned whether members of Congress, as representatives of the public, might not be the only persons who could give the issue a considered analysis.

Mr. Baltimore, of M.I.T., said he was "appalled by the limited knowledge and poor logic" of the public.

"All of the appropriate fuss being made about the need for socially responsible scientists could well be matched with some concern about a socially responsible public. The future of the recombinant DNA debate will turn on the quality of the dialogue between the scientific community and the public," said Daniel Callahan, director of the Institute of Society, Ethics, and the Life Sciences.

Kurt Mislow, professor of chemistry at Princeton University, said that everyone except molecular biologists must be considered laymen when the debate is over such a complex scientific issue. "Lay opposition is necessarily emotional because it is not based on data. We are operating from a gut feeling, but it would be a tremendous mistake if we ignore it."

"ENORMOUSLY FRUSTRATED"

Members of the public are "enormously frustrated" because of their dependence on scientists for information about scientific questions with potentially broad impact on society, said Mr. Jones of the Senate health subcommittee, who chaired a workshop at the forum on the ways laymen should be involved in decisions on recombinant DNA. Scientists must understand that the development of public understanding will be a slow process, he said.

A fundamental question about public decision-making that emerged from his workshop, he noted, was "What institutions can be trusted to make decisions for the American people, to represent the public's values?" As public distrust of government increases, he said, people want more members of the public involved in those decisions, whether through local referenda, public members on university biohazards committees, local health-planning agencies, or the like.

LOOK 20 YEARS AHEAD

Ted Howard of the People's Business Commission insisted, however, that along with the need for the public to decide whether "we should begin the steps that could lead to genetic alteration of humans," the scientific community "needs to take the responsibility for looking 20 years into the future, because you're starting the process."

Citing the growth in environmental studies and other "research into the inadvertent changes mankind has made in his world," David A. Hamburg, president of the Institute of Medicine of the National Academy of Sciences, responded:

"To some extent, you're pushing on an open door. . . . I think you seriously underestimate the extent to which these concerns are prevalent in society, Congress, and the academy."

"The deliberate production of 'desirable' changes in certain organisms might [disrupt] the infinitely complex and delicate balance among living things."
GEORGE WALD, *Harvard*

Man's Fourth Adjustment
HARLOW SHAPLEY

The scattering of galaxies, the habits of macromolecules, and the astounding abundance of stars are forcing those who ponder such matters to a further adjustment of their concept of the place and functioning of man in the material universe.

In the history of the evolving human mind, with its increasing knowledge of the surrounding world, there must have been a time when the philosophers of the early tribes began to realize that the world was not simply anthropocentric—centered on man himself. The geocentric concept became common doctrine. It accepted a universe centered on the earth. This first adjustment was only mildly deflationary to the human ego, for man appeared to surpass all other living forms.

The second adjustment in the relation of man to the physical universe, that is, the abandonment of the earth-center theory, was not generally acceptable until the sixteenth-century Copernican revolution soundly established the heliocentric concept—the theory of a universe centered on the sun. Man is a stubborn adherent to official dogma. Eventually, however, he accepted the sun as the center not only of the local family of planets, but also of the total sidereal assemblage, and long held that view.

He had slowly given up the earth-center. But why, in spite of increasing evidence, did he then hold so persistently to the heliocentric view? Was it only because of vanity—his feeling, nourished by the unscientific dogmatists, that he is of paramount significance in the world? There were several better reasons for his second delusion. For example, the Milky Way is a great circle, a band of starlight that divides the sky into two nearly equal parts. It is of about the same brightness in all its parts. By implication, therefore, the sun and earth are centrally located. Also, the numbers of stars seemed to the early census-takers to fall off with distance from the sun as though it were central, and such a position for his star among the stellar millions brought to man a dignity of position not at all disagreeable.

The shift from the geocentric to the heliocentric concept doubtless had some philosophical impact in the sixteenth century, but not much. After all, the hot, turbulent, gaseous sun is no place for the delicate biology in which man finds himself at or near the top. Earth-center or sun-center seemed to make little difference to cosmic thinking during the past four centuries. But then, less than forty years ago, came the inescapable need for a third adjustment—one that should have deeply affected and to some extent has disturbed man's thoughts about his place, his career and his cosmic importance.

This shift has dug deeply into man's pride and self-assurance, for it has carried with it the knowledge of the appalling number of galaxies. He could accept rather cheerfully the Darwinian evidence of his animal origin, for that still left him at the summit of all terrestrial organisms. But the abandonment of the heliocentric universe on the authority of the astronomical evidence was certainly deflationary, from the standpoint of man's position in the material world, however flattering it was to the human mind.

The "galactocentric universe" suddenly puts the earth and its life near the edge of one great galaxy in a universe of millions of galaxies. Man becomes peripheral among the billions of stars of his own Milky Way; and according to the revelations of paleontology and geochemistry, he is recent and apparently ephemeral in the unrolling of cosmic time. And here is a somber or happy thought, whichever mood you prefer. There is no retreat! The inquiring human has passed the point of no return. We cannot restore geocentrism or heliocentrism. The apes, eagles and honeybees may be wholly content to be peripheral ephemerals, and thus miss the great vision that opens before us. For them, egocentrism and lococentrism may suffice; for us, no! And since we cannot go back to the cramped but comfortable past (without sacrificing completely our cultures and civilizations), we go forward and find there is more to the story.

The downgrading of the earth and sun, and the elevation of the galaxies, is not the end of this progress of scientific pilgrims through philosophic fields. The need for a further jolting adjustment now appears—not wholly unexpected by workers in science, nor wholly the result of one or two scientific revelations.

Our new problem concerns the spread of life throughout the universe. As unsolicited spokesmen for all the earthly organisms of land, sea and air, we ask the piquant question: Are we alone?

From among the many measures and thoughts that promote this fourth adjustment of *Homo sapiens sapiens* in the galaxy of galaxies (the metagalaxy), I select three phenomena as most demanding of our consideration. The first refers to the number of stars, the second to catastrophes of ancient days, and the third to the origin of self-duplicating molecules.

To the ancients, only a few thousand stars were known; to the early telescopes, however, it was a million; and that astounding number has increased spectacularly with every telescopic advance. Finally, with the discovery that the "extragalactic nebulae" are in reality galaxies, each with its hundreds or thousands of millions of stars, and with our inability to "touch metagalactic bottom" with the greatest telescopes, we are led to accept the existence of more than 10^{20} stars in our explorable universe, perhaps many more.

The significance of this discovery, or rather of this uncovering, is that we have at hand—that is, the universe contains—more than one hundred million million million sources of light and warmth for whatever planets accompany these radiant stars.

The second phenomenon, the expanding metagalaxy, bears on the question: Do planets accompany at least some of the stars that pour forth energy suitable for the complex biological activity that we call life?

We now accept the observational evidence for an expanding universe of galaxies. The rapid expansion of the measurable part of the metagalaxy implies an increasingly greater concentration of these cosmic units (galaxies) as we go back in time. A few thousand million years ago, the average density of matter in space was so great that collisions, near encounters, and gravitational disruptions were of necessity frequent. The crust of the earth, radioactively measured, is also a few thousand million years old, and therefore the earth and the other planets of our sun's system were "born" in those days of turbulence. At that time countless millions of other planetary systems must have developed, for our sun is of a very common stellar variety. (Miss Cannon's catalogue of spectra[1] reports forty thousand sunlike stars in our immediate neighborhood.)

Other ways in which planets may form—other than this primitive process of the early days—are recognized. The contraction of protostars out of the hypothetical primeval gas, giving birth on the way to protoplanets, is an evolutionary process now widely favored. It would imply the existence of countless planets.

The head-on-collision theory of planetary origin has also been considered. But the stars are now so widely dispersed that collisions must be exceedingly rare—so very unlikely, in fact, that we might claim uniqueness for our planetary system and for ourselves if planet birth depended only on such procedure. The expanding universe discovery, however, has shown the crowded conditions when our earth was born.

Passing over details, we state the relevant conclusion: *Millions of planetary systems must exist.* Whatever the method of origin, planets may be the common heritage of all stars except those so situated that planetary materials would be swallowed or cast off through gravitational action. In passing we note that astrophysicists have shown that our kinds of chemistry and physics prevail throughout the explorable universe. There is nothing uncommon here or now.

Remembering our 10^{20} stars and the high probability of millions of planets with suitable chemistry, dimensions and distance from their nutrient stars, we are ready for the question: On some of these planets is there

---

[1] Annie Jump Cannon (1863–1941), American astronomer called "the census taker of the sky," who compiled a bibliography of 200,000 references to stars.—EDS.

actually life; or is that biochemical operation strangely limited to our planet, No. 3 in the family of the sun, which is a run-of-the-mill star located in the outer part of a galaxy that contains a hundred thousand million other stars—and this galaxy but one of millions already on the records?

Is life thus restricted? Of course not. We are not alone. And we can accept life's wide dispersion still more confidently when our third argument is indicated.

To put it briefly: biochemistry and microbiology, with the assistance of geophysics, astronomy and other sciences, have gone so far in bridging the gap between the inanimate and the living that we can no longer doubt but that whenever the physics, chemistry and climates are right on a planet's surface, life will emerge and persist.

This consequence has long been suspected by scientists, but the many researches of the past few years in the field of macromolecules have made it unnecessary any longer to postulate miracles and the supernatural for the origin of life.

The astronomical demonstration of the great number of stars, and therefore the abundance of life opportunities, naturally leads to the belief that countless planets have had long and varied experience with biochemical evolution. Thousands of kinds of terrestrial animals are known to develop neurotic complexes, that is "intelligence." It comes naturally. No higher animal is without it in high degree. Could it be otherwise on another life-bearing planet?

And here we must end with the simple but weighty proposal: There is no reason in the world to believe that our own mental stature has not been excelled by that of sentient beings elsewhere. I am not suggesting, however, that *Homo* is repeated. There are a million variations on the animal theme.

In conclusion, I need not emphasize the possible relevance to philosophy and perhaps to religion of this fourth adjustment in man's view of himself in the material universe.

The Golden Alphabet
LOREN EISELEY

A creature without memory cannot discover the past; one without expectation cannot conceive a future.
—GEORGE SANTAYANA

"Wisdom," the Eskimo say, "can be found only far from man, out in the great loneliness." These people speak from silences we will not know again until we set foot upon the moon. Perhaps our track is somehow rounding evocatively backward into another version of the giant winter out of which we emerged ten thousand years ago. Perhaps it is our destiny to have plunged across it only to re-enter it once more.

Of all the men of the nineteenth century who might be said to have been intimates of that loneliness and yet, at the same time, to have possessed unusual prophetic powers, Henry David Thoreau and Charles Darwin form both a spectacular comparison and a contrast. Both Thoreau and Darwin were voyagers. One confined himself to the ever widening ripples on a pond until they embraced infinity. The other went around the world and remained for the rest of his life a meditative recluse in an old Victorian house in the English countryside. . . .

Both men forfeited the orthodox hopes that had sustained, through many centuries, the Christian world. Yet, at the last, the one transcends the other's vision, or amplifies it. Darwin remains, though sometimes hesitantly, the pragmatic scientist, content with what his eyes have seen. The other turns toward an unseen spring beyond the wintry industrialism of the nineteenth century, with its illusions of secular progress. The two views, even the two lives, can be best epitomized in youthful expressions that have come down to us. The one, Darwin's, is sure, practical and exuberant. The other reveals an exploring, but wary, nature.

Darwin, the empiricist, wrote from Valparaiso in 1834: "I have just got scent of some fossil bones of a MAMMOTH; what they may be I do not know, but if gold or galloping will get them they shall be mine." Thoreau, by nature more skeptical of what can be captured in this world, mused, in his turn, "I cannot lean so hard on any arm as on a sunbeam." It was one of the first of many similar enigmatic expressions that were finally to lead his well-meaning friend, Ellery Channing, to venture sadly, "I have never been able to understand what he meant by his life. . . . Why was he so disappointed with everybody else? Why was he so interested in the river and the woods . . . ? Something peculiar here I judge."

Channing was not wrong. There *was* something peculiar about Thoreau, just as there was something equally peculiar about Darwin. The difference between them lies essentially in the nature of man himself, the creature who persists in drawing sharp, definitive lines across the indeterminate face of nature. Essentially, the problem may be easily put. It is its varied permutations and combinations that each generation finds so defeating, and that our own time is busy, one might say horribly busy, in re-creating. . . .

The whole story of humanity is basically that of a journey toward the Emerald City, and of an effort to learn the nature of Oz, who, perhaps wisely, keeps himself concealed. In each human heart exists the Cowardly Lion and the little girl who was sure that the solution to life lay in just walking far enough. Finally, among our great discoverers are those with precious strawfilled heads who have to make up their own thoughts because each knows he has been made such a little while before, and has stood alone in the fields. Darwin and Thoreau are two such oddly opposed, yet similar, scarecrows. As it turned out, they came to two different cities, or at least vistas. They discovered something of the nature of Oz, and, rightly understood, their views are complementary to each other.

I shall treat first of Darwin and then of Thoreau, because, though contemporaries, they were distinct in temperament. Thoreau, who died young, perhaps trudged farther toward the place which the little girl Dorothy was so sure existed, and thus, in a sense, he may be a messenger from the future. Since futures do not really exist until they are present, it might be more cautious to say that Thoreau was the messenger of a *possible* future in some way dependent upon ourselves.

Neither of the two men ever discovered the nature of Oz himself. The one, Darwin, learned much about his ways—so much, indeed, that I suspect he came to doubt the existence of Oz. The other, Thoreau, leaned perhaps too heavily upon his sunbeam and in time it faded, but not surely, because to the last he clung to the fields and heard increasingly distant echoes. Both men wore spectacles of sorts, for this is a rule that Oz has decreed for all men. Moreover, there are diverse kinds of spectacles.

There are, for example, the two different pairs through which philosophers may look at the world. Through one we see ourselves in the light of the past; through the other, in the light of the future. If we fail to use both pairs of spectacles equally, our view of ourselves and of the world is apt to be distorted, since we can never see completely without the use of both. The historical sciences have made us very conscious of our past, and of the world as a machine generating successive events out of foregoing ones. For this reason some scholars tend to look totally backward in their interpretation of the human future. It is, unconsciously, an exercise much favored in our time.

Like much else, this attitude has a history.

When science, early in the nineteenth century, began to ask what we have previously termed "the terrible questions" because they involved the nature of evil, the age of the world, the origins of man, of sex, or even of language itself, a kind of Pandora's box had been opened. People could classify giraffes and porcupines but not explain them—much less a man. Everything stood in isolation, and therefore the universe of life was bound to appear a little ridiculous to the honestly enquiring mind. What was needed was the kind of man of whom Thoreau had spoken, who could couple two seemingly unrelated facts and reduce the intractable chaos of the world. Such a man was about to appear. In fact, he had already had his forerunners. . . .

The youth who went aboard the *Beagle* in December 1831 was a great deal more clever than his academic record at both Edinburgh and Cambridge might suggest. The ingenuity with which he went about securing his father's permission for the voyage in itself indicates the dedicated persistence with which he could overcome obstacles. There remained in the motherless young man a certain wary reserve, which would finally draw him into total seclusion. In the first edition of the *Origin of Species* he was to write: "When on board H.M.S. *Beagle*, as naturalist, I was much struck with certain facts. . . . These facts seemed to . . . throw light on the origin of species. . . ." The remark is true, but it is also ingenuous. Young Charles's first knowledge of evolution did not emerge spontaneously aboard the *Beagle*, however much that conception was to be strengthened in the wild lands below the equator.

Instead, its genesis in Darwin's mind lies mysteriously back amidst unrecorded nights in student Edinburgh and lost in the tracery of spider tracks over thousands of dusty volumes after his return. For this is the secret of Charles Darwin the naturalist-voyager, the modern Odysseus who came to Circe's island of change in the Galápagos: he was the product of two odysseys, not one. He lives in the public mind partly by the undoubted drama of a great voyage whose purpose, as defined by the chief hydrographer, was the placing of a chain of meridians around the world. While those meridians were being established through Fitzroy's efforts, another set was being posted by Darwin in the haunted corridors of the past.

But the second odyssey, the one most solitary, secretive, and hidden, is the Merlin-like journey which had no ending save at death. It is the groping through webby corridors of books in smoky London—the kind of journey in which men are accountable only to themselves and by which the public is not at all enlivened. No waves burst, no seaman falls from the masthead, no icy continent confronts the voyager. Within the mind, however, all is different. There are ghost fires burning over swampy morasses of books, confusing trails, interceptions of the lost, the endless weaving and unweaving of floating threads of thought drawn from a thousand sources. . . .

The floating threads of all the ideas, all the thinking, all the nightmares of hours spent in the endless galleries of books, meet and are gathered up at last in the great book of 1859—that book termed the *Origin of Species*, which Darwin to the last maintained was only a hasty abstract. . . .

Variation—that subtle, unnoted shifting of the shapes of men and leaves, bird beaks and turtles, that he had pondered over far off in the Circean Galápagos—was now seen to link the seemingly ridiculous and chaotic world of life into a single whole. Selection was the living screen through which all life must pass. No fact could be left a fact; somewhere in the world it was tied to something else. What made a tuft of feathers suddenly appear on a cock's head or induce the meaningless gyrations of a tumbler pigeon? What, in this final world of the fortuitous, the sad eyes questioned, had convinced a tailless ape that he was the object of divine attention? . . .

Thoreau had loved nature as intensely as Darwin and perhaps more personally. He had seen with another set of glasses. He was, in an opposite sense to Darwin, a dweller along the edge of the known, a place where the new begins. Thoreau carries a hint of that newness. He dwelt, without being quite consciously aware of it, in the age after tomorrow. His friends felt universally baffled by Thoreau and labeled him "almost another species." One contemporary wrote: "His eyes slipped into every tuft of meadow or beach grass and went winding in and out of the thickest undergrowth, like some slim, silent, cunning animal." It has been said that he was not a true naturalist. What was he, then? The account just quoted implies a man similar to Darwin, and, in his own way, as powerfully motivated.

Of all strange and unaccountable things. Thoreau admits his efforts at his *Journal* to be the strangest. Even in youth he is beset by a prescient sadness. The companions who beguile his way will leave him, he already knows, at the first turn of the road. He was basically doomed all his life to be the Scarecrow of Oz, and if he seems harsher than that genial figure, it is because the city he sought was more elusive and he did not have even the Cowardly Lion for company. He knew only that by approaching nature he would be consulting, in every autumn-leaf fall, not alone those who had gone before him, but also those who would come after. He was writing before the *Origin of Species*, but someone had sewn amazing eyes upon the Concord Scarecrow.

There is a delicacy in him that is all his own. His search for support in nature is as diligent as that of a climbing vine he had once watched with fascinated attention groping eerily toward an invisible branch. Yet, like Darwin, he had witnessed the worst that nature could do. On his deathbed he had asked, still insatiable, to be lifted up in order that he could catch through the window a glimpse of one more spring.

In one passage in the *Journal* he had observed that the fishers' nets strung across the transparent river were no more intrusive than a cobweb in the sun. "It is," he notes, "a very slight and refined outrage at most." In their symmetry, he realizes, they are a beautiful memento of man's presence in nature, as wary a discovery as the footprint upon Crusoe's isle. Moreover, this little symbol of the fishers' seine defines precisely that delicately woven fabric of human relationships in which man, as a social animal, is so thoroughly enmeshed. There are times when, intellectually, Darwin threshed about in that same net as though trapped by a bird spider in his own forested Brazil.

For the most part, the untraveled man in Concord managed to slip in and out of similar meshes with comparative ease. Like some lean-bodied fish he is there, he is curiously observant, but he floats, oddly detached and unfrightened, in the great stream. "If we see nature as pausing," Thoreau remarks more than once, "immediately all mortifies and decays." In that nature is man, merely another creature in perspective, if one does not come too close, his civilizations like toadstools springing up by the road. Everything is in the flowing, not the past.

Museums, by contrast, are catacombs, the dead nature of dead men.

Thoreau does not struggle so hard as Darwin in his phylogenies to knit the living world together. Unlike the moderns, Thoreau was not constantly seeking nostalgically for men on other planets. He respected the proud solitude of diversity, as when he watched a sparrow hawk amusing itself with aerial acrobatics. "It appeared to have no companion in the universe and to need none but the morning," he remarked, unconsciously characterizing himself. "It was not lonely but it made all the earth lonely beneath it."

Or again, he says plainly, "fox belongs to a different order of things from that which reigns in the village." Fox is alone. That is part of the ultimate secret shared between fox and scarecrow. They are creatures of the woods' edge. One of Thoreau's peculiar insights lies in his recognition of the creative loneliness of the individual, the struggle of man the evolved animal to live "a supernatural life." In a sense, it is a symbolic expression of the equally creative but microcosmic loneliness of the mutative gene. "Some," he remarks, "record only what has happened to them; but others how *they* have happened to the universe."

To this latter record Thoreau devoted the *Journal* that mystified his friends. Though, like Darwin, he was a seeker who never totally found what he sought, he had found a road, though no one appeared to be walking in it. Nevertheless, he seems to have been interiorly informed that it was a way traversed at long intervals by great minds. Thoreau, the physical stay-at-home, was an avid searcher of travel literature, but he was not a traveler in the body. Indeed, there are times when he seems to have regarded that labyrinth—for so he called it—with some of the same feeling he held toward a house—as a place to escape from. The nature we profess to know never completely contained him.

"I am sensible of a certain doubleness," he wrote, "by which I can stand as remote from myself as from another. . . . When the play—it may be the tragedy of life—is over, the spectator goes his way. It was a kind of fiction." This man does suggest another species, perhaps those cool, removed men of a far, oncoming century who can both live their lives and order them like great art. The gift is rare now, and not wholly enticing to earthbound creatures like ourselves.

Once, while surveying, Thoreau had encountered an unusual echo. After days with humdrum companions, he recorded with surprise and pleasure this generosity in nature. He wanted to linger and call all day to the air, to some voice akin to his own. There needs must be some actual doubleness like this in nature, he reiterates, "for if the voices which we commonly hear were all that we ever heard, what then? Echoes . . . are the only kindred voices that I hear."

Here, in Thoreau's question, is the crux, the sum total of the human predicament. This is why I spoke of our figuratively winding our way backward into a spiritual winter, why I quoted an Eskimo upon wisdom. On the eve of the publication of the *Origin of Species,* Thoreau, not by any means inimical to the evolutionary philosophy, had commented: "It is ebb tide with the scientific reports."

In some quarters this has aroused amusement. But what did Thoreau mean? Did he sense amidst English utilitarian philosophy, of which some aspects of Darwinism are an offshoot, an oncoming cold, a muffling of snow, an inability to hear echoes? Paradoxically, Thoreau, who delighted in simplicity of living, was averse to the parsimonious nature of Victorian science. It offended his transcendental vision of man. Lest I seem to exaggerate this conflict, read what Darwin himself admitted of his work in later years:

"I did not formerly consider sufficiently the existence of structures," he confesses, "which as far as we can . . . judge, are neither beneficial nor injurious, and this I believe to be one of the greatest oversights as yet detected in my work. This led to my tacit assumption that every detail of structure was of some special though unrecognized service."

We know that Thoreau already feared that man was becoming the tool of his tools, which can, alas, include ideas. Even now, forgetting Darwin's belated caution, those with the backward-reaching spectacles tell us eagerly, if not arrogantly, in the name of evolution, how we are born to behave and the limitations placed upon us—we who have come the far way from a wood nest in a Paleocene forest. Figuratively, these pronouncements have about them the enlarging, man-destroying evil of the pulsing worm. They stop man at an imagined border of himself. Man suffers, in truth, from a magical worm genuinely enlarged by a certain color of spectacles. It is a part, but not the whole, of the magic of Oz.

Is it not significant, in contrast to certain of these modern prophets, that Thoreau spoke of the freedom he felt to go and come in nature; that what is peculiar to the life of man "consists not in his obedience, but his opposition to his instincts"? The very behavior of the other animals toward mankind, Thoreau knew, revealed that man was not yet the civilized creature he pretended to be.

One must summarize the two philosophies of evolution and then let the Eskimo speak once more. In the Viking Eddas[1] it is written:

> Hard it is on earth . . .
> Ax-time, sword-time . . .
> Wind-time, wolf-time, ere the world falls
> Nor ever shall men each other spare.

Through these lines comes the howl of the world-devouring Fenris-wolf, waiting his moment under the deep-buried rocket silos of today. In the last pages of *Walden* one of Thoreau's wisest remarks is upon the demand

---

[1] Two Icelandic collections of early Norse mythology—the *Poetic* or *Elder Edda* (c. ninth to twelfth centuries) and the *Prose* or *Younger Edda* (early thirteenth century).—EDS.

scientific intellectuals sometimes make, that one must speak so as to be always understood. "Neither men," he says, "nor toadstools grow so." There is a constant emergent novelty in nature that does not lie totally behind us, or we would not be what we are.

Here is where Thoreau's sensitivity to echoes emerges powerfully: It is onflowing man, not past evolutionary man, who concerns him. He wants desperately to know to what degree the human mind is capable of inward expansion. "If the condition of things which we were made for is not yet at hand," he questions anxiously, "what can we substitute?" The echoes he senses are reverberating from the future.

Finally, he compresses into a single passage the answer to the wolf-time philosophy, whether expressed by the Viking freebooters, or by certain of their modern descendants. "After," he says, "the germs of virtue have thus been prevented many times from developing themselves, the beneficent breath of evening does not suffice to preserve them. . . . Then the nature of man does not differ much from that of the brute."

Does this last construction contain the true and natural condition of man? No, Thoreau would contend, for nature lives always in anticipation. Thoreau was part of the future. He walked toward it, knowing also that in the case of man it must emerge from within by means of his own creation. That was why Thoreau saw the double nature of the tool and eyed it with doubt.

The soul of the universe, the Upholder, reported Rasmussen[2] of the Alaskan Eskimo, is never seen. Its voice, however, may be heard on occasion, through innocent children. Or in storms. Or in sunshine. Both Darwin and Thoreau had disavowed the traditional paradise, and it has been said of Thoreau that he awaited a Visitor who never came. Nevertheless, he had felt the weight of an unseen power. What it whispers, said the men of the high cold, is, "Be not afraid of the universe."

Man, since the beginning of his symbol-making mind, has sought to read the map of that same universe. Do not believe those serious-minded men who tell us that writing began with economics and the ordering of jars of oil. Man is, in reality, an oracular animal. Bereft of instinct, he must search constantly for meanings. We forget that, like a child, man was a reader before he became a writer, a reader of what Coleridge[3] once called the mighty alphabet of the universe. Long ago, our forerunners knew, as the Eskimo still know that there is an instruction hidden in the storm or dancing in auroral fires. The future can be invoked by the pictures impressed on a cave wall or in the cracks interpreted by a shaman on the incinerated shoulder blade of a hare. The very flight of birds is a writing to be read. Thoreau strove for its interpretation on his pond, as Darwin,

---

[2] Knud Johan Victor Rasmussen (1879–1933), Danish ethnologist and Arctic explorer.—EDS.

[3] Samuel Taylor Coleridge (1772–1834), British poet.—EDS.

in his way, sought equally to read the message written in the beaks of Galápagos finches.

But the messages, like all the messages in the universe, are elusive.

Some months ago, walking along the shore of a desolate island off the Gulf Coast, I caught a glimpse of a beautiful shell, imprinted with what appeared to be strange writing, rolling in the breakers. Impelled by curiosity, I leaped into the surf and salvaged it. Golden characters like Chinese hieroglyphs ran in symmetrical lines around the cone of the shell. I lifted it up with the utmost excitement, as though a message had come to me from the green depths of the sea.

Later I unwrapped the shell before a dealer in antiquities in the back streets of a seaport town.

"*Conus spurius atlanticus*," he diagnosed for me with brisk efficiency, "otherwise known as the alphabet shell."

But why spurious? I questioned inwardly as I left the grubby little shop, warily refusing an offer for my treasure. The shell, I was sure, contained a message. We *live* by messages—all true scientists, all lovers of the arts, indeed, all true men of any stamp. Some of the messages cannot be read, but man will always try. He hungers for messages, and when he ceases to seek and interpret them he will be no longer man.

The little cone lies now upon my desk, and I handle it as reverently as I would the tablets of a lost civilization. It transmits tidings as real as the increasingly far echoes heard by Thoreau in his last years.

Perhaps I would never have stumbled into so complete a revelation save that the shell was *Conus spurius*, carrying the appellation given it by one who had misread, most painfully misread, a true message from the universe. Each man deciphers from the ancient alphabets of nature only those secrets that his own deeps possess the power to endow with meaning. It had been so with Darwin and Thoreau. The golden alphabet, in whatever shape it chooses to reveal itself, is never spurious. From its inscrutable lettering is created man and all the towering cloudland of his dreams.

5
Final Things

The Good Life

God and Humankind

What Is Reality?

Death

What Is Happiness?

"What Is Man?"

This last section, "Final Things," relates both to ultimate concerns we all share as well as to inescapable conclusions that time or evidence will not alter. A committed Buddhist, Christian, Hindu, or Jew has at least a minimum of absolutes, even though these absolutes may differ within a given belief. In the poem by William Blake, "The Divine Image" is the image of mercy, pity, peace, and love. But in the opening poem, "For Once, Then, Something," Robert Frost can only ask whether he saw truth or a pebble of quartz at the bottom of the well. So some of us ask and some of us answer. All that we can agree upon as editors —and all that many of our writers can agree upon—is that the game of life lacks zest without tossing around the ball of ultimate concerns.

We'd like to note some fascinating aspects of the game as it develops in this section. We begin with several descriptions of "The Good Life": Frost's vision; how a modern historian like Gordon Wright thinks he can go about teaching it; how Socrates conceives and defends it; how Buddha has "even now attained Nirvana"; and how Jesus, "as one having authority," offers promises and makes demands. The five statements move from relativism through the cautious affirmations of a modern liberal, the modest yet firm claim for wisdom by Socrates, the arduous eightfold path of Buddha, to a position that offers the listener everything and requires still more.

These voices, especially those of Buddha and Jesus, prepare us to consider the relationship between "God and Humankind." The universality of a God-centered universe seems much stronger in Psalm 90, in a passage from the Upanishads, in a poem by Ralph Waldo Emerson drawn almost straight from Hindu scriptures, in a curiously doctrinal poem by Walt Whitman, and in Martin Buber's challenging latter-day Judaism. God appears variously both within us and confronting us in an I-Thou relationship.

But is God really in any of these aspects? What is reality? If the existentialists have no solutions in William C. Barrett's view, they at least propose the tough questions and make vivid the sense of crisis; and in "The Allegory of the Cave," written 2,000 years earlier, Socrates tells Glaucon a parable that turns out to be an existential nightmare. Thus humankind deals always with some questions that are never old and never new.

In the group of readings entitled "Death," the psychologist Leslie H. Farber and two great poets, John Donne and Emily Dickinson, remind us just how final death is and how ultimately our common humanity is resolved and affirmed in our common fate.

"What Is Happiness?" William V. Shannon asks, as have philosophers and serious thinkers in every age. His answer is a conservative one, a kind of blend of epicureanism and stoicism. Maybe those who can question and correct the myths of our times can find a fuller happiness, as L. S. Stavrianos implies. Or the secret may be in Denise Levertov's recognition of tasting and seeing "all that lives to the imagination's tongue," or in Joseph Wood Krutch's new world beyond Christianity and science.

Then, "What Is Man?" The lowest animal of Mark Twain and the vain creature of Ecclesiastes? or the riddle of Alexander Pope? or a being only a little lower than the angels and crowned with glory and honor, as the Psalmist sees him? If in the definition of love by St. Paul or in the Divine Image of Blake we have the essence, Thoreau is right to prophesy that "There is more day to dawn."

The Good Life

For Once, Then, Something
ROBERT FROST

Others taunt me with having knelt at well-curbs
Always wrong to the light, so never seeing
Deeper down in the well than where the water
Gives me back in a shining surface picture
Me myself in the summer heaven, godlike,
Looking out of a wreath of fern and cloud puffs.
Once, when trying with chin against a well-curb,
I discerned, as I thought, beyond the picture,
Through the picture, a something white, uncertain,
Something more of the depths—and then I lost it.
Water came to rebuke the too clear water.
One drop fell from a fern, and lo, a ripple
Shook whatever it was lay there at bottom,
Blurred it, blotted it out. What was that whiteness?
Truth? A pebble of quartz? For once, then, something.

History as a Moral Science[1]
GORDON WRIGHT

.... Few people would hold historians solely or principally to blame for the moral transgressions of certain public officials or for the more pervasive ethical confusion that seems to suffuse our age. The fact that some unscrupulous men have made their way into high places and have misused their power is of course not new; nor does it necessarily mean that historians helped put them there, or that historians could somehow have prevented their misdeeds.

We historians might therefore choose to disclaim all responsibility, charging the fault to those in our society who openly profess to be its moral guides, or to the obtuseness of our ex-students who failed to penetrate the message hidden somewhere in our unbiased teaching. But that (as

[1] Excerpted from the author's presidential address to the American Historical Association in December 1975.—EDS.

a fellow Californian liked to say) would be the easy way. Whether we enjoy it or not, we must ask ourselves whether we bear a more diffused kind of responsibility. Some critics assert that we historians, by insisting over the years that moral standards are relative across cultures and over time, have seriously undermined our own capacities (and *a fortiori* those of our students) to make moral judgments of any kind. In eschewing the horrors of moral rhetoric, they say, we have drifted into a moral vacuum; to avoid the charge of moral self-righteousness, we have preferred simply to abdicate.

True, we have clothed our conduct in attractive garb: we speak of detachment, openmindedness, tolerance, understanding. But beneath these euphemisms, the critics say, abdication is the essential reality. . . .

For a long time, of course, historians comforted themselves with the thought that dispassionate, value-free history would at least insure that those who studied it would be led rather automatically to sensible and judicious conclusions.

Thus Henry Charles Lea, after delivering his thunderbolts against Acton, could conclude that "history may and it generally will, convey a moral, but that moral should educe itself from the facts." Most of us today are a bit less sanguine about the automatic nature of the process, yet the idea does persist that the path from raw data to sophisticated judgment needs no guideposts along the route. And even when we are not so sure that the process is easy or automatic, the alternative—guideposts suggested by the historian, functioning as a moral critic as well as a purveyor of facts—continues to be seen as either illegitimate or ineffective. . . .

This recent process of soul-searching has been confined mainly, I suspect, to those of us who find our identity somewhere in the so-called liberal tradition, broadly defined. Our conservative colleagues—at least those who are self-consciously conservative—have had it easier; a good many of them have always been quite openly committed to a system of absolute values, religiously or ethically based, by which the events of the past can be confidently judged without the least embarrassment. On the left, many self-styled radical historians have vigorously asserted the idea of a committed history, either because they too possess a coherent *Weltanschauung*[2] with something like its own absolutes, or because they view history instrumentally, as a tool to achieve social and political change. Both the conservative and the radical positions obviously have their legitimate place in the educational process, so long as neither is imposed as unchallengeable dogma. But the liberals among us—even the "closet liberals" who are reluctant to bear the stigma of a shopworn label—continue to be haunted

---

[2] German, literally "world view"; one's outlook on the nature of the universe.—EDS.

by our pluralistic, skeptical, anti-dogmatic heritage, our rejection of absolutes, our distaste for anything that might look like indoctrination. The result, it seems to me, is that while many students of history may be exposed these days to vigorous and confident expositors of either the conservative or the radical value-system, they rarely receive any clear vision of the past as it appears in the light of liberal values.

I am sometimes tempted to think that we liberals have been re-enacting the charge of the Light Brigade:[3] while cannon volley and thunder to the right and the left of us, we ourselves gallop on in a cloud of dust, unsure just which way is forward, and shouting to those who follow us to study the map and draw their own conclusions. If part of an educator's responsibility is to offer some sort of positive guidance, then perhaps it is true that many of us have unthinkingly abdicated.

True, there are critics who doubt that the abdication has been real—that we have actually practiced the dispassionate objectivity that we preach. "Our smartest radicals," remarked Carl Becker more than 40 years ago, "suspect [the liberal] of being an *agent provocateur* of Capitalism, while conservatives of ancient lineage treat [him] as a Bolshevik masquerading in a rented dress suit." William Appleman Williams, the leading spokesman of the New Left, detects beneath the sham of openmindedness a hidden vice: support of what he calls "the Existing Institution." A talented young American historian, arguing the case of the French *Annales* school, charges that "American historical writing still largely consists of parochial and moralistic studies of events, policies, and individuals," and he proceeds to consign both liberals and Marxists to oblivion as exponents of a dead morality. We liberals thus stand accused in various quarters of violating our own professed standards, and acting in reality (to borrow Heinz Hartmann's phrase) as "hidden preachers."

Whether our real fault is hypocrisy or abdication, those of us in the liberal tradition (a sizable remnant still, though probably an endangered species) do feel most keenly the whiplash of this particular dilemma. Not all of us will be ready to change our ways—to risk giving up our accustomed armor, that somewhat gray and aloof neutrality (or costume of neutrality) that has been so comfortably protective. Some of us will not find it easy to abandon our indulgent fascination for the charismatic rascals and the melodramatic episodes in history—an indulgence that adds some more vivid colors to the basic gray, thus enlivening our prose and awakening our drowsy students.

Nor will all of us readily shake free from the temptation to fix cynically on the flaws and foibles of every leader, nation, age, or professed ideal, to

---

[3] A British brigade, during the Crimean War (on September 20, 1854), knowing the folly of their orders, charged the Russian line and was virtually annihilated. This charge was celebrated in Alfred, Lord Tennyson's poem, "The Charge of the Light Brigade." —Eds.

the point that the very words "moral" and "value" take on ironic overtones. Furthermore, it would be self-defeating if all liberal historians were to forswear the ideal of dispassionate *Wertfreiheit*,[4] for out of that tradition have come (and will doubtless continue to come) some of the most impressive products of our profession.

Nevertheless, I believe that a case can be made for re-legitimizing the writing and teaching of history by liberals whose model is neither the neutral scientist nor the "hidden preacher," but the exponent of a self-conscious and coherent value-system. If one purpose of historical study is to broaden and enrich the minds of students so that they can shape their own values and arrive at their own judgments (as I think they should), that purpose is likely to be best served if they are offered not only raw data and quantified facts, but also broad exposure to various mature interpretations of the past. The liberal interpretation belongs in that spectrum—indeed, perhaps more so today than ever before. In an age of unprecedented complexity, when ideological fanaticism, sporadic bursts of tribal fury, and the advocacy of "realism" in both its crude and its sophisticated form put world stability and even human existence at risk, the liberal temper may offer the nearest thing to a set of guideposts through the minefield. . . .

To argue this case is of course to be immediately suspect. Does it not imply a return to what someone has called "19th-century pieties and platitudes," and to the indoctrination of students through the use of selective evidence, and to a downgrading of the search for truth and understanding as the historian's highest goal? The answer, I think, is that it surely can lead to any or all of these abuses, if misused; but I see no reason to consider such misuse unavoidable.

There are dangers built into all stances toward the teaching and writing of history, including the stance called perfect neutrality. Indeed, the liberal historian who applies his values honestly and consistently will be more likely than any other to take pains to consider all the evidence and all alternative interpretations before advancing and defending his own view of the past. What too many of us have hesitated to do, I believe, is to take that final step—to risk a conclusion, to make a judgment, to advance and defend our view of how things were, and why, and what this meant to people of the time, and what it means to people of today. . . .

It may be the times we live in, or it may be incipient senility, that prods one against his better judgment into reflecting on some of the essentials, and even into wondering, as Carl Becker used to do, "What is the good of history?" A valued French colleague remarked to me not

[4] German, *Wert*, value; *Freiheit*, freedom; that is, the freedom of each historical event to be assessed on its own merits.—EDS.

long ago that such a question is "terribly American," and asserted that so long as there is a market for what we do, the question is irrelevant. Besides, he added, the question reflects the fact that most Americans are much too moralistic; what they need, for their own and the world's repose, is a large dash of cynicism.

He may be right. Yet somehow I remain unregenerate. Perhaps it's a buried aspect of that old liberal heritage, so much maligned in our day; or perhaps it's a surviving spark of an evangelical upbringing. It has not yet driven me to the point of urging that we resurrect the label "moral science" as a category within which our profession might find its proper place. But it does impel me to think that for some of us, at least, our search for truth ought to be quite consciously suffused by a commitment to some deeply held humane values. The efforts to keep these two goals in balance may be precarious; but if we can manage it, perhaps we will be on the way to re-establishing history's role as one—and not the least—of what we might fairly call the moral arts.

The Apology of Socrates
PLATO

Well then, fellow citizens, I must now make my defence, and must try to clear away in this brief time that calumny which you have entertained so long. I would that this might come to pass, if so it should be better for both you and me, and if it profits me to plead. But I think the task to be a hard one, and what its nature is I am, by no means unaware. Still, let the outcome be as it pleases God; the law must be obeyed, and the defence be made.

Let us, then, go back and look at the original accusation from which the slander arose, the slander that gave Meletus his ground for this indictment he has lodged against me. Let us see. Precisely what did the slanderers say when they slandered? We must read their complaint as if it were a legal accusation: "Socrates is wicked; overdoes inquiry into what occurs below the earth and in the heavens; in arguing makes the worse case win; and teaches others to do the same as he." Such is in substance the accusation—what you actually saw in the comedy [the *Clouds*] of Aristophanes, where a man called "Socrates" is swung about, declaring that he treads the air, and sputtering a deal of other nonsense on matters of which I have not one bit of knowledge either great or small. And I do not say so in disparagement of any science such as that, if any one is learned in such matters; I should not wish to be attacked by Meletus upon so grave a charge. But actually, fellow citizens, to me these matters are of absolutely no concern. I call the greater part of you yourselves to witness, and beg all who ever heard me in discussion to tell one another and declare it; many of you are in a position to do this. Declare to one another, therefore, whether any of you ever heard me dealing with such matters either briefly or at length. In that way you will see what all the rest amounts to of what the generality of people say concerning me. . . .

Then perhaps some one of you may be inclined to ask: "But Socrates, what *is* the matter with you? What is the origin of these charges that are made against you? Unless you acted very differently from everybody else, surely no such story and repute would have arisen—if you did not do something other than most people do. Tell us what it is, in order to keep us from rushing to our own conclusion about you."

That, I take it, would be fairly spoken; and I shall try to show you what it is that has given me this name and ill repute. Pray listen. Some of you, perhaps, will take me to be joking, but be assured that I shall tell you the simple truth. The fact is, fellow citizens, that I have got this name through my possession of a certain wisdom. What sort of wisdom is it? A wisdom, doubtless, that appertains to man. With respect to this, perhaps, I actually am wise; whereas those others whom I just now mentioned may possibly be wise with a wisdom more than human, or else I do not know what to say of it; as for me, I certainly do not possess it, and whoever says I do is lying, and seeks to injure me.

And, fellow citizens, do not interrupt me even if I say what seems extravagant, for the statement I shall make is not my own; instead, I shall refer you to a witness whose word can be accepted. Your witness to my wisdom, if I have any, and to its nature, is the god at Delphi. You certainly knew Chaerephon. He was a friend of mine from our youth, and a friend of your popular party as well; he shared in your late exile, and accompanied you on your return. Now you know the temper of Chaerephon, how impulsive he was in everything he undertook. Well so it was when once he went to Delphi, and made bold to ask the oracle this question—and, Gentlemen, please do not make an uproar over what I say; he asked if there was any one more wise than I. Then the Pythian oracle made response that there was no one who was wiser. To this response his brother here will bear you witness, since Chaerephon himself is dead.

Now bear in mind the reason why I tell you this. It is because I am going on to show you whence this calumny of me has sprung; for when I heard about the oracle, I communed within myself: "What can the god be saying, and what does the riddle mean? Well I know in my own heart that I am without wisdom great or small. What is it that he means, then, in declaring me to be most wise? It cannot be that he is lying; it is not in his nature." For a long time I continued at a loss as to his meaning, then finally decided, much against my will, to seek it in the following way.

I went to one of those who pass for wise men, feeling sure that there if anywhere I could refute the answer, and explain to the oracle: "Here is a man that is wiser than I, but you said I was the wisest." The man I went to see was one of our statesmen; his name I need not mention. Him I thoroughly examined, and from him, as I studied him and conversed with him, I gathered, fellow citizens, this impression. This man appeared to me to seem to be wise to others, and above all to himself, but not to be so. And then I tried to show him that he thought that he was wise, but was not. The result was that I gained his enmity and the enmity as well of many of those who were present. So, as I went away, I reasoned with myself: "At all events I am wiser than this man is. It is quite possible that neither one of us knows anything fine and good. But this man fancies that he knows when he does not, while I, whereas I do not know, just so I do not fancy that I know. In this small item, then, at least, I seem to be wiser than he, in that I do not fancy that I know what I do not." Thereafter I went to another man, one of those who passed for wiser than the first, and I got the same impression. Whereupon I gained his enmity as well as that of many more.

Thereafter I went from one man to another, perceiving, with grief and apprehension, that I was getting hated, but it seemed imperative to put the service of the god above all else. In my search for the meaning of the oracle I must go to all who were supposed to have some knowledge. And, fellow citizens, by the God, since I have to tell you the truth, here is pretty much what I encountered. The persons with the greatest reputation seemed to me to be the ones who were well-nigh the most deficient, as I made my search in keeping with the god's intent; whereas others of inferior reputation I found to be men superior in regard to their possession of the truth. I needs must tell you all about my wandering course, a veritable round of toils heroic, which I underwent to prove that the oracle was not to be refuted.

After the statesmen, I went to the poets, tragic, dithyrambic, and the rest. There, I thought, my ignorance would be self-evident in comparison with them. So I took those poems of theirs which seemed to me to have been most carefully wrought by them, and asked the authors what they meant, in order that I might at the same time learn from them. Well, Gentlemen, I am ashamed to tell you the truth; and yet it must be done. The fact is, pretty nearly everybody, so to say, who was present could have spoken better than the authors did about the poems they themselves had written. So here again in a short time I learned this about the poets too, that not by wisdom do they make what they compose, but by a gift of nature and an inspiration similar to that of the diviners and the oracles. These also utter many beautiful things, but understand not one of them. And such, I saw, was the experience of the poets. At the same time I perceived that their poetic gift led them to fancy that in all else, too, they were the wisest of mankind, when they were not. So I went away from them as well, believing that I had the same advantage over them as over the statesmen.

To make an end, I went, then, to the artisans. Conscious that I did not, so to say, know anything myself, I was certain I should find that they knew many things and fine. Nor in that was I deceived; they did indeed know things which I did not, and in that they were wiser than I. But, fellow citizens, these excellent workmen seemed to me to have the same defect as the poets. Because they were successful in the practice of their art, each thought himself most wise about all other things of the highest import, and this mistake of theirs beclouded all that wisdom. So I asked myself the question, for the oracle, whether I preferred to be just what I was, neither wise as they were wise nor ignorant as they were ignorant, or to be both wise and ignorant like them. And my response to myself and the oracle was that it paid me to be as I was.

Such, fellow citizens, was the quest which brought me so much enmity, hatreds so utterly harsh and hard to bear, whence sprang so many calumnies, and this name that is given me of being "wise"; for every time I caught another person in his ignorance, those present fancied that I knew what he did not. But, Gentlemen, in all likelihood it really is the god who is wise, and by that oracle he meant to say that human wisdom is of little worth, or none. And it appears that when he picked out "Socrates," he used my name to take me for an example; it was as if he said: "O race of men, he is the wisest among you, who, like Socrates, knows that in truth his knowledge is worth nothing." So even now I still go about in my search, and, in keeping with the god's intent, question anybody, citizen or stranger, whom I fancy to be wise. And when it seems to me that he is not, in defence of the god I show that he is not. And this activity has left me without leisure either to take any real part in civic affairs or to care for my own. Instead, I live in infinite poverty through my service to the god.

In addition, the young men who of their own accord are my companions, of the class who have most leisure, sons of the very rich—they listen with joy to the men who are examined; they often imitate me, and in turn attempt to test out others. And thereupon, I take it, they find a great abundance of men who imagine they have some knowledge, and yet know little or nothing. And then these men whom they examine get angry, not at them, but at me, and say there is one Socrates, a perfect blackguard, who corrupts the young. Yet when anybody asks them how he does it, and by teaching what, they have nothing to tell, nor do they know. But in order not to seem quite at a loss, they make the usual attacks that are leveled at philosophers, namely, about "things occurring in the heavens and below the earth," "not believing in the gods," and "making the worse case win." What they do not care to utter, I imagine, is the truth: that they have been shown up in their pretence to knowledge when they actually knew nothing. Accordingly, since they are proud, passionate, and numerous, and organized and effective in speaking about me, they have long since filled your ears with their violent calumnies.

From among them have come Meletus, Anytus, and Lycon to attack me;

Meletus aggrieved on behalf of the poets, Anytus on behalf of the artists and the politicians, Lycon on behalf of the rhetoricians. Consequently, as I said at the beginning, I shall be surprised if I succeed, within so short a time, in ridding you of all this swollen mass of calumny.

There, fellow citizens, you have the truth. I hide nothing from you, either great or small, nor do I dissimulate. And yet I know that even by this I stir up hatred, which itself proves that I tell the truth, and that it is precisely this that constitutes the charge against me, and is the cause of it. And whether now or later you investigate the matter, you will find it to be so.

Therewith let me close my defence to you on the charges made against me by my first accusers. . . .

No, fellow citizens, that I am guiltless with respect to Meletus' indictment seems to me to call for no long defence; rather, let this argument suffice. But what I have said before, that much antagonism has arisen against me in the minds of many, rest assured that it is true. And this it is that will undo me, if I am undone, not Meletus nor Anytus, but the slander of the many, and their malice. Many another man, and good ones, has it undone, and, methinks, it will yet undo. There is no danger that the thing may stop with me.

Perhaps some one will say: "Well, Socrates, aren't you ashamed that you pursued a course from which you now are in danger of death?" To that it would be right for me to reply: Good sir, it is not well said if you think that a man of any worth at all ought to calculate his chances of living or dying, and not rather look to this alone, when he acts, to see if what he does is right or wrong, and if his are the deeds of a good man or a bad. By your account, the demigods who fell at Troy would be sorry fellows, all of them, and notably the son of Thetis,[1] who so despised all danger in comparison with any disgrace awaiting him, and with what result? When his mother saw him eager to slay Hector, she, the goddess, addressed him, as I recall, approximately thus: "My child, if you avenge the death of your comrade Patroclus by slaying Hector, then you yourself will die. For you the lot of death," she said, "comes straightway after Hector's." But he, on hearing that, made light of death and danger fearing far more to live a coward and not avenge his loved ones. "Straightway let me die," said he, "once I give the villain his reward, and not continue here, a laughing-stock, beside the hollow ships, a burden to the earth." Do you think that he took heed of death or danger?

That, fellow citizens, is the way things really stand. If any one is stationed where he thinks it is best for him to be, or where his commander has put him, there, as it seems to me, it is his duty to remain, no matter what the risk, heedless of death or any other peril in comparison with disgrace.

[1] Achilles.—EDS.

It would have been dreadful conduct, fellow citizens, had I acted otherwise. When the leaders you had chosen to command me assigned a post to me at Potidaea, at Amphipolis, and at Delium, in the face of death itself I was as steadfast as any one could be in holding the position where they placed me; and when the god, as I believed and understood, assigned to me as my duty that I should live the life of a philosopher, and examine myself and others, it would have been dreadful had I through fear of death, or of anything else whatever, deserted my post. Dreadful indeed would it be, and verily any one would then be justified in bringing me to trial for not believing in gods, when I had disobeyed the oracle, feared death, and thought that I was wise when I was not.

For, Gentlemen, to be afraid of death is nothing else than thinking that one is wise when one is not, since it means fancying that one knows what one does not. Nobody knows, in fact, what death is, nor whether to man it is not perchance the greatest of all blessings; yet people fear it as if they surely knew it to be the worst of evils. And what is this but the shameful ignorance of supposing that we know what we do not? It is there and in that perhaps that I differ, Gentlemen, from the majority of mankind; and if I might call myself more wise than other, it would be in this, that as I do not know enough about what goes on in Hades, so too I do not think that I know. But doing wrong, and disobeying the person who is better than myself, be it god or man, that I know is base and wicked. Therefore never for the sake of evils which I know to be such will I fear or flee from what for all I know may be a good. . . .

All I do is to go about persuading you, both young and old, not to think first of your bodies or your property, nor to be so mightily concerned about them as about your souls, how the spirit shall be at its best; it is my task to tell you that virtue does not spring from wealth, but that wealth and every other good that comes to men in private life or in public proceed from virtue. If it is by saying this that I corrupt the young, then this must be injurious; but any one who holds that I say anything save this says nothing. On that head, fellow citizens, I may assure you that whether you trust Anytus or not, and whether you acquit me or do not acquit me, I shall not alter my course, no matter if I have to die a hundred times.

Now, fellow citizens, do not interrupt, but continue granting my request of you not to cry out at what I may say, but to listen; I do believe that you will profit if you listen. I am, in fact, about to tell you certain other things at which you might possibly protest. Yet please do not. No; for you may rest assured that if you condemn me to death, I being such a person as I say, you will do yourself more harm than you do me. As for me, Meletus will no more hurt me than will Anytus. It does not lie in his power, for in my belief the eternal order does not permit a better man to be harmed by a worse. Oh yes! quite possibly he might kill or banish me, or rob me of my civil rights; and doubtless this man and the next will think that these are major evils. I do not think them such; no, I think it a far greater evil for a man to do what this man now is doing, namely trying to get a man condemned to death unjustly.

So, fellow citizens, at present I am far from making my defence upon my own account, as one might think; I make it for your sake, in order that you may not, by condemning me, do wrong about the gift of the god to you; for if you have me put to death, you will not easily find another of the sort, fastened upon the City by the god, for all the world (if I may use a rather ludicrous comparison) like a gadfly on a great and noble horse that is somewhat sluggish on account of his size and needs the fly to wake him up. So, it seems to me, the god has fastened me like that upon the City, to rouse, exhort, and rebuke each one of you, everywhere besetting you, and never once ceasing all day long. Another one like that, Gentlemen, you will not come by so easily; but if you listen to me, you will take good care of me. You may, however, quite possibly be annoyed, like people awakened from their slumbers, and, striking out at me, may listen readily to Anytus and condemn me to death. Then you would finish out the rest of your life in sleep, unless the god were in mercy to send you some one else to take my place. That it is the deity by whom I, such as I am, have been given to the City you may see from this: it is not like human nature for me to neglect all my own concerns, to put up with a neglected household all these years, and to attend to your affair, ever going to you individually in private, like a father or an elder brother, urging you to care for your moral welfare. And if I got any profit from it all, if these exhortations brought me any pay, there would seem to be some reason in my conduct. As it is, you see for yourselves that my accusers, who, unashamed, have brought so many other charges against me, have yet not had the effrontery to present a witness to allege that I ever took any sort of fee or sought one. Why not? Because, methinks, the witness I present to show that I speak the truth is quite enough—my poverty. . . .

There you have it, Gentlemen. That is pretty much what I might have to say in my defence, that with possibly some additions, to the like effect. Perhaps, however, one or another of you will be angry when he recalls his own experience, in some trial he was engaged in of less gravity than this; if he besought and with many tears implored the judges, and, in order to arouse the greatest pity, brought in his children along with others of his kin and many friends; while, as for me, I shall do nothing of the sort, although I am in danger, as I might suppose, to the last degree of peril. . . .

These things, fellow citizens, it behoves us not to do if we have any reputation whatsoever; and if we do them, you should not allow it. No; you should make this very thing quite clear, that you will far more readily give your vote against the person who drags in these tearful dramas, and makes the City ridiculous, than against the man who argues quietly.

But apart from the question of propriety, Gentlemen, it does not seem right to me to beg the judge for mercy, or, by doing it, to get away, when one ought rather to enlighten and convince him. He does not take his seat for this, the judge, to render justice as a favor, but to decide on what is just. Indeed he took an oath that he would not favor people according to his notion of them, but that he would give judgment in accordance with the laws. And so we should not get you into the habit of perjuring yourselves, nor should you get into it; neither of us should commit impiety. So do not ask me, fellow citizens, to treat you in a way which I take to be dishonorable, wrong, and impious; above all, by Zeus! when I am under accusation of impiety by this Meletus here present; for obviously, if I swayed you and by begging forced you to act against your oath, I would be teaching you not to believe that there are gods, and by my defence would simply accuse myself of not believing in them. But that be far from me! I do believe in them, my fellow citizens, as none of my accusers does; and to you I commend myself, and to the Deity, to judge concerning me what shall be best at once for me and for you. . . .

AFTER HE IS CONDEMNED TO DEATH

For no great thrift in time, my fellow citizens, you will have from those who wish to vilify the City the name and blame of having put to death the wise man, Socrates; for they will call me wise, even if I am not, they who would defame you. If only you had waited for a little while, the thing would have occurred for you in the course of nature; for you can see my age, that I am far along in life, and near to death. I say this, not to all of you, but only to those who voted for my death. And to them I have also to say this as well. It may be, Gentlemen, that you think I lost my cause for lack of arguments of the sort with which I might have won you over, if I had thought that I ought to say and do all things in order to escape the verdict. Far from it. I lost for a lack, but not of arguments; it was for lack of impudence and daring, and for not being ready to say to you the sort of thing it would have given you most pleasure to hear—me weeping and wailing, and doing and saying any and every sort of thing that I hold to be unworthy of me, but you are accustomed to hear from the rest. No, I did not then believe that, to avoid a danger, I ought to do anything unseemly in a freeman, nor do I now regret my manner of defence. No, far rather would I choose this manner of defence, and die, than follow that, and live. Whether in a court of justice or in war neither I nor any other man should seek by using every means conceivable to escape from death; for in battle you very often see that if you throw away your weapons and beg those who are pursuing you for mercy, you may get out of dying. Indeed, in every sort of danger there are various ways of winning through, if one is ready to do and say anything whatever. No, Gentlemen, that is not the hard thing, to escape from death; ah no, far harder is it to escape from sin, for sin is swifter than death. And so I, being old and slow, am overtaken by the slower enemy; while my accusers, who are strong and swift, have been caught by the swifter, namely wickedness.

And so I now depart, by you condemned to pay the penalty of death; and they by the truth convicted of a base injustice. And as I abide the payment, so do they. Who knows? Perhaps it had to be so, and I think that things are as they ought to be.

Touching the future, I desire to make for you who voted to condemn me, a prediction; for I am at the point where men foresee the future best—when they are soon to die. Let me tell you then, you men who have condemned me, that after I am gone there will straightway come upon you a chastisement far heavier, by Zeus, than the death you have set for me. You have now done this in the belief that you have freed yourselves from giving any reckoning for your life; but I tell you the result will be the very opposite for you. There will be more inquisitors to sift you, men whom I now hold in check without your knowing it. And they will be more critical as they are younger, and will annoy you more; for if you think that by putting men to death you will prevent the slur from being cast at you that you do not live aright, you are in error. This way of getting freedom is neither very sure nor fine; no, the finest and readiest way is this, not to interfere with other people, but to render oneself as good a man as possible. There is the prophecy I make for you who voted to condemn me. And of them I take my leave.

With those of you who voted to acquit me I should be glad to talk about this thing that has occurred, while the magistrates are busy and it is not time for me to go to the place where I must die. So, Gentlemen, please wait with me as long as that. There is nothing to keep us from talking to each other as long as it is allowed. To you as to friends I wish to explain the real meaning of what has just happened to me.

Justices, for when I call you that I am naming you aright, the thing that has come to me is wonderful.

My customary warning, by the spirit,[2] in previous times has always, up to now, come to me very often to oppose me, even when a matter was quite important, if ever I was going to do something amiss. But to-day, as you yourselves have witnessed, that thing has happened to me which anybody might suppose, and which is considered, to be the uttermost of evils. Yet neither did the sign from god oppose me when I left my house this morning, nor at the point when I ascended here to the tribunal, nor in my speech at anything I was about to say; though often when I have been talking elsewhere it has stopped me in the middle of a speech. But to-day, with reference to the whole procedure, not once did it oppose me in a thing I did or said. What, then, do I take to be the cause of this? No doubt this thing that has happened to me is good, and it cannot be that our supposition is correct when any of us think that death is a misfortune. For me, the proof of this is telling: it cannot be but that the customary sign would have opposed me, if I had not been about to do a thing that was good. . . .

[2] Demon, or conscience, or the god within.—Eds.

But, Justices, you also it behoves to have good hope with reference to death, and this one thing you must bear in mind as true, that, living or dead, to a good man there can come no evil; nor are his affairs a matter of indifference to the gods. Nor has my destiny now come about by chance; rather, it is clear to me that it was better for me now to die and to be released from my troubles. That is why the sign did not at any point deter me, and why I am not very bitter at those who voted to condemn me, or at my accusers. It is true they did not have this notion in condemning and accusing me; no, they thought to injure me, and therein they merit blame.

One thing, however, I do beg of them. When my sons grow up, then, Gentlemen, I ask you to punish them, you hurting them the same as I hurt you, if they seem to you to care for money, or aught else, more than they care for virtue. And if they pretend to be somewhat when they are nothing, do you upbraid them as I upbraided you, for not regarding as important what they ought to think so, and for thinking they have worth when they do not. If you do that, I shall have received just treatment from you, and my sons as well.

And now the time has come for our departure, I to die, and you to live. Which of us goes to meet the better lot is hidden from all unless it be known to God.

The Sermon at Benares

GAUTAMA BUDDHA

On seeing their old teacher approach, the five bhikkhus agreed among themselves not to salute him, nor to address him as a master, but by his name only. "For," so they said, "he has broken his vow and has abandoned holiness. He is no bhikkhu but Gotama, and Gotama has become a man who lives in abundance and indulges in the pleasures of worldliness."

But when the Blessed One approached in a dignified manner, they involuntarily rose from their seats and greeted him in spite of their resolution. Still they called him by his name and addressed him as "friend Gotama."

When they had thus received the Blessed One, he said: "Do not call the Tathagata by his name nor address him as 'friend,' for he is the Buddha, the Holy One. The Buddha looks with a kind heart equally on all living beings, and they therefore call him 'Father.' To disrespect a father is wrong; to despise him, is wicked."

"The Tathagata," the Buddha continued, "does not seek salvation in austerities, but neither does he for that reason indulge in worldly pleasures, nor live in abundance. The Tathagata has found the middle path."

"There are two extremes, O Bhikkhus, which the man who has given up the world ought not to follow—the habitual practice, on the one hand, of self-indulgence which is unworthy, vain and fit only for the worldly-minded—and the habitual practice, on the other hand, of self-mortification, which is painful, useless and unprofitable.

"Neither abstinence from fish or flesh, nor going naked, nor shaving the head, nor wearing matted hair, nor dressing in a rough garment, nor covering oneself with dirt, nor sacrificing to Agni, will cleanse a man who is not free from delusions.

"Reading the Vedas, making offerings to priests, or sacrifices to the gods, self-mortification by heat or cold, and many such penances performed for the sake of immortality, these do not cleanse the man who is not free from delusions.

"Anger, drunkenness, obstinacy, bigotry, deception, envy, self-praise, disparaging others, superciliousness and evil intentions constitute uncleanness; not verily the eating of flesh.

"A middle path, O Bhikkhus, avoiding the two extremes, has been discovered by the Tathagata—a path which opens the eyes, and bestows understanding, which leads to peace of mind, to the higher wisdom, to full enlightenment, to Nirvana!

"What is that middle path, O Bhikkhus, avoiding these two extremes, discovered by the Tathagata—that path which opens the eyes, and bestows understanding, which leads to peace of mind, to the higher wisdom, to full enlightenment, to Nirvana?

"Let me teach you, O Bhikkhus, the middle path, which keeps aloof from both extremes. By suffering, the emaciated devotee produces confusion and sickly thoughts in his mind. Mortification is not conducive even to worldly knowledge; how much less to a triumph over the senses!

"He who fills his lamp with water will not dispel the darkness, and he who tries to light a fire with rotten wood will fail. And how can anyone be free from self by leading a wretched life, if he does not succeed in quenching the fires of lust, if he still hankers after either worldly or heavenly pleasures. But he in whom self has become extinct is free from lust; he will desire neither worldly nor heavenly pleasures, and the satisfaction of his natural wants will not defile him. However, let him be moderate, let him eat and drink according to the needs of the body.

"Sensuality is enervating; the self-indulgent man is a slave to his passions, and pleasure-seeking is degrading and vulgar.

"But to satisfy the necessities of life is not evil. To keep the body in good health is a duty, for otherwise we shall not be able to trim the lamp of wisdom, and keep our mind strong and clear. Water surrounds the lotus-flower, but does not wet its petals.

"This is the middle path, O Bhikkhus, that keeps aloof from both extremes." . . .

Then the Buddha said:

"He who recognizes the existence of suffering, its cause, its remedy, and its cessation has fathomed the four Noble Truths. He will walk the right path.

"Right views will be the torch to light his way. Right aspirations will be his guide. Right speech will be his dwelling place on the road. His gait will be straight, for it is right behavior. His refreshments will be the right way of earning his livelihood. Right efforts will be his steps: right thoughts his breath; and right contemplation will give him the peace that follows in his footprints.

"Now, this, O Bhikkhu, is the noble truth concerning suffering.

"Birth is attended with pain, decay is painful, disease is painful, death is painful. Union with the unpleasant is painful, painful is separation from the pleasant; and any craving that is unsatisfied, that too is painful. In brief, bodily conditions which spring from attachments are painful.

"Now this, O Bhikkhus, is the noble truth concerning the origin. Verily, it is that craving which causes the renewal of existence, accompanied by sensual delight, seeking satisfaction now here, now there, the craving for the gratification of the passions, the craving for a future life, and the craving for happiness in this life.

"Now this is the noble truth concerning the destruction of suffering: Verily it is the destruction, in which no passion remains, of this very thirst: It is the laying aside of, the being free from, the dwelling no longer upon this thirst.

"Now this is the noble truth concerning the way which leads to the destruction of sorrow. Verily; it is this noble eightfold path; that is to say:

1. right views
2. right aspirations
3. right speech
4. right behavior
5. right livelihood
6. right effort
7. right thoughts
8. right contemplation

"This, then, is the noble truth concerning the destruction of sorrow. By the practice of loving kindness I have attained liberation of heart, and thus I am assured that I shall never return in renewed births. I have even now attained Nirvana."

And when the Blessed One had thus set the royal chariot wheel of truth rolling onward, a rapture thrilled through all the universes.

And when the doctrine was propounded, the venerable Kondanna, the oldest one among the five bhikkhus, discerned the truth with his mental eye, and he said: "Truly, O Buddha, our Lord, thou hast found the truth!"

Then the other bhikkhus, too, joined him and exclaimed: "Truly, thou art the Buddha, thou hast found the truth."

And the Blessed One observed the ways of society and noticed how much misery came from malignity and foolish offenses done only to gratify vanity and self-seeking pride. And the Buddha said: "If a man foolishly does me wrong, I will return to him the protection of my ungrudging love; the more evil comes from him, the more good shall go from me; the fragrance of goodness always comes to me and the harmful air of evil goes to him."

A foolish man, learning that the Buddha observed the principle of great love which commends the return of good for evil, came and abused him. The Buddha was silent, pitying his folly.

When the man had finished his abuse, the Buddha asked him, saying: "Son, if a man declined to accept a present made to him, to whom would it belong?" And he answered: "In that case, it would belong to the man who offered it."

"My son," said the Buddha, "thou hast railed at me, but I decline to accept thy abuse, and request thee to keep it thyself. Will it not be a source of misery to thee? As the echo belongs to the sound, and the shadow to the substance, so misery will overtake the evil-doer without fail."

The abuser made no reply, and Buddha continued: "A wicked man who reproaches a virtuous one is like one who looks up and spits at heaven; the spittle soils not the heaven, but comes back and defiles his own person. The slanderer is like one who flings dust at another when the wind is contrary; the dust does but return on him who threw it. The virtuous man cannot be hurt and the misery that the other would inflict comes back on himself."

The abuser went away ashamed, but he came again and took refuge in the Buddha, the Dharma, and the Sangha.

And Buddha said: "All that we are is the result of what we have thought: it is founded on our thoughts, it is made up of our thoughts. If a man speaks or acts with an evil thought, pain follows him, as the wheel follows the foot of the ox that draws the carriage: If a man speaks or acts with a pure thought, happiness follows him, like a shadow that never leaves him.

" 'He abused me, he beat me, he defeated me, he robbed me'—in those who harbor such thoughts, hatred will never cease; in those who do not harbor such thoughts, hatred will cease. For hatred does not cease by hatred at any time: hatred ceases by love—that is an old rule.

"He who lives looking for pleasures only, his senses uncontrolled, immoderate in his food, idle and weak, will certainly be overthrown by temptation, as the wind throws down a weak tree. He who lives without looking for pleasures, his senses well controlled, moderate in his food, faithful and strong, will certainly not be overthrown, any more than the wind throws down a rocky mountain. . . .

"The thoughtless man, even if he can recite a large portion of the law, but is not a doer of it, has no share in the priesthood, but is like a cowherd counting the cows of others. The follower of the law, even if he can recite only a small portion of the law, but, having forsaken passion and hatred and foolishness, possesses true knowledge and serenity of mind, he, caring for nothing in this world or that to come, has indeed a share in the priesthood. . . .

"As a fletcher makes straight his arrow, a wise man makes straight his trembling and unsteady thought, which is difficult to guard, difficult to hold back. It is good to tame the mind, which is difficult to hold in and flighty, rushing wherever it listeth; a tamed mind brings happiness. Let the wise man guard his thoughts, for they are difficult to perceive, very artful, and they rush wherever they list. . . .

"Knowing that this body is fragile like a jar, and making his thought firm like a fortress, one should attack Mara, the tempter, with the weapon of knowledge, one should watch him when conquered, and should never rest. Before long, alas! this body will lie on the earth, despised; without understanding, like a useless log."

Kisa Gotami had an only son, and he died. In her grief she carried the dead child to all her neighbors, asking them for medicine, and the people said: "She has lost her senses. The boy is dead."

At length, Kisa Gotami met a man who replied to her request: "I cannot give thee medicine for thy child, but I know a physician who can."

And the girl said: "Pray tell me, sir; who is it?" And the man replied "Go to Sakyamuni, the Buddha."

Kisa Gotami repaired to the Buddha and cried: "Lord and Master, give me the medicine that will cure my boy."

The Buddha answered: "I want a handful of mustard-seed." And when the girl in her joy promised to procure it, the Buddha added: "The mustard-seed must be taken from a house where no one has lost a child, husband, parent, or friend."

Poor Kisa Gotami now went from house to house, and the people pitied her and said: "Here is mustard-seed; take it!" But when she asked, "Did a son or daughter, a father or mother, die in your family?" they answered her: "Alas! the living are few, but the dead are many. Do not remind us of our deepest grief." And there was no house but some beloved one had died in it.

Kisa Gotami became weary and hopeless, and sat down at the wayside, watching the lights of the city, as they flickered up and were extinguished again. At last the darkness of the night reigned everywhere. And she considered the fate of men, that their lives flicker up and are extinguished again. And she thought to herself: "How selfish am I in my grief! Death is common to all; yet in this valley of desolation there is a path that leads him to immortality who has surrendered all selfishness."

The Buddha said: "The life of mortals in this world is troubled and brief and combined with pain. For there is not any means by which those that have been born can avoid dying; after reaching old age there is death; of such a nature are living beings. As ripe fruits are early in danger of falling, so mortals when born are always in danger of death. As all earthen vessels made by the potter end in being broken, so is the life of mortals. Both young and adult, both those who are fools and those who are wise, all fall into the power of death; all are subject to death.

"Of those who, overcome by death, depart from life, a father cannot save his son, nor kinsmen their relations. Mark! while relatives are looking on and lamenting deeply, one by one mortals are carried off, like an ox that is led to the slaughter. So the world is afflicted with death and decay, therefore the wise do not grieve, knowing the terms of the world.

"Not from weeping nor from grieving will any one obtain peace of mind; on the contrary, his pain will be the greater and his body will suffer. He will make himself sick and pale, yet the dead are not saved by his lamentation. He who seeks peace should draw out the arrow of lamentation, and complaint, and grief. He who has drawn out the arrow and has become composed will obtain peace of mind; he who has overcome all sorrow will become free from sorrow, and be blessed."

And Punna, wishing to preach the path to enlightenment, sought the Buddha, and the Buddha said, "But, O Punna, the men of that country are violent, cruel and savage. When they become angry at you and do you harm, what will you think then?"

"I shall think them truly good and kind folk, for whilst they speak angry and insolent words, they refrain from striking or stoning me."

"They are very violent folk, Punna. What if they strike or stone you?"

"I shall think them kind and good not to smite me with their staff and sword."

"And what if they do so?"

"I shall think them kind and good indeed who free me from this vile body with so little pain."

"Well said, Punna, well said. With your gift of patience, you may indeed essay this task. Go, Punna, yourself saved, save others."

The Sermon on the Mount
ST. MATTHEW

And seeing the multitudes, he went up into a mountain; and when he was set, his disciples came unto him: and he opened his mouth, and taught them, saying, Blessed are the poor in spirit: for theirs is the kingdom of heaven. Blessed are they that mourn: for they shall be comforted. Blessed are the meek: for they shall inherit the earth. Blessed are they which do hunger and thirst after righteousness: for they shall be filled. Blessed are the merciful: for they shall obtain mercy. Blessed are the pure in heart: for they shall see God. Blessed are the peacemakers: for they shall be called the children of God. Blessed are they which are persecuted for righteousness' sake: for theirs is the kingdom of heaven. Blessed are ye, when men shall revile you, and persecute you, and shall say all manner of evil against you falsely, for my sake. Rejoice, and be exceeding glad: for great is your reward in heaven: for so persecuted they the prophets which were before you.

Ye are the salt of the earth: but if the salt have lost his savour, wherewith shall it be salted? it is thenceforth good for nothing, but to be cast out, and to be trodden under foot of men. Ye are the light of the world. A city that is set on a hill cannot be hid. Neither do men light a candle, and put it under a bushel, but on a candlestick; and it giveth light unto all that are in the house. Let your light so shine before men, that they may see your good works, and glorify your Father which is in heaven. Think not that I am come to destroy the law, or the prophets; I am not come to destroy, but to fulfil. For verily I say unto you, Till heaven and earth pass, one jot or one tittle shall in no wise pass from the law, till all be fulfilled. Whosoever therefore shall break one of these least commandments, and shall teach men so, he shall be called the least in the kingdom of heaven: but whosoever shall do and teach them, the same shall be called great in the kingdom of heaven. For I say unto you, That except your righteousness shall exceed the righteousness of the scribes and Pharisees, ye shall in no case enter into the kingdom of heaven.

Ye have heard that it was said by them of old time, Thou shalt not kill; and whosoever shall kill shall be in danger of the judgment: but I say unto you, That whosoever is angry with his brother without a cause shall be in danger of the judgment: and whosoever shall say to his brother, Raca,[1] shall be in danger of the council: but whosoever shall say, Thou fool, shall be in danger of hell fire. Therefore if thou bring thy gift to the altar, and there rememberest that thy brother hath ought against thee; leave there thy gift before the altar, and go thy way; first be reconciled to thy brother, and then come and offer thy gift. Agree with thine adversary quickly, while thou art in the way with him; lest at any time the adversary deliver thee to the judge, and the judge deliver thee to the officer, and thou be cast into prison. Verily I say unto thee, Thou shalt by no means come out thence, till thou hast paid the uttermost farthing.

Ye have heard that it was said by them of old time, Thou shalt not commit adultery; but I say unto you, That whosoever looketh on a woman to lust after her hath committed adultery with her already in his heart.

---

[1] Emptyhead; a term of hatred and contempt.—EDS.

And if thy right eye offend thee, pluck it out, and cast it from thee: for it is profitable for thee that one of thy members should perish, and not that thy whole body should be cast into hell. And if thy right hand offend thee, cut it off, and cast it from thee: for it is profitable for thee that one of thy members should perish, and not that thy whole body should be cast into hell. It hath been said, Whosoever shall put away his wife, let him give her a writing of divorcement: but I say unto you, That whosoever shall put away his wife, saving for the cause of fornication, causeth her to commit adultery: and whosoever shall marry her that is divorced committeth adultery.

Again, ye have heard that it hath been said by them of old time, Thou shalt not forswear thyself, but shalt perform to the Lord thine oaths: but I say unto you, Swear not at all; neither by heaven; for it is God's throne: nor by the earth; for it is his footstool: neither by Jerusalem; for it is the city of the great King. Neither shalt thou swear by thy head, because thou canst not make one hair white or black. But let your communication be, Yea, yea; Nay, nay: for whatsoever is more than these cometh of evil.

Ye have heard that it hath been said, An eye for an eye, and a tooth for a tooth: but I say unto you, That ye resist not evil: but whosoever shall smite thee on thy right cheek, turn to him the other also. And if any man will sue thee at the law, and take away thy coat, let him have thy cloak also. And whosoever shall compel thee to go a mile, go with him twain. Give to him that asketh thee, and from him that would borrow of thee turn not thou away.

Ye have heard that it hath been said, Thou shalt love thy neighbor, and hate thine enemy. But I say unto you, Love your enemies, bless them that curse you, do good to them that hate you, and pray for them which despitefully use you, and persecute you; that ye may be the children of your Father which is in heaven; for he maketh his sun to rise on the evil and on the good, and sendeth rain on the just and on the unjust. For if ye love them which love you, what reward have ye? do not even the publicans the same? And if ye salute your brethren only, what do ye more than others? do not even the publicans so? Be ye therefore perfect, even as your Father which is in heaven is perfect.

Take heed that ye do not your alms before men, to be seen of them: otherwise ye have no reward of your Father which is in heaven. Therefore when thou doest thine alms, do not sound a trumpet before thee, as the hypocrites do in the synagogues and in the streets, that they may have glory of men. Verily I say unto you, They have their reward. But when thou doest alms, let not thy left hand know what thy right hand doeth: that thine alms may be in secret: and thy Father which seeth in secret himself shall reward thee openly. And when thou prayest, thou shalt not be as the hypocrites are: for they love to pray standing in the synagogues and in the corners of the streets, that they may be seen of men. Verily I say until you, They have their reward. But thou, when thou prayest, enter into thy closet, and when thou hast shut thy door, pray to thy Father, which is in secret; and thy Father which seeth in secret shall reward thee openly. But when ye pray, use not vain repetitions, as the heathen do: for they think that they shall be heard for their much speaking. Be not ye therefore like unto them: for your Father knoweth what things ye have need of, before ye ask him. After this manner therefore pray ye: Our Father which art in heaven, Hallowed be thy name. Thy kingdom come. Thy will be done in earth, as it is in heaven. Give us this day our daily bread. And forgive us our debts, as we forgive our debtors. And lead us not into temptation, but deliver us from evil: for thine is the kingdom, and the power, and the glory, for ever. Amen. For if ye forgive men their trespasses, your heavenly Father will also forgive you: but if ye forgive not men their trespasses, neither will your Father forgive your trespasses.

Moreover when ye fast, be not, as the hypocrites, of a sad countenance: for they disfigure their faces, that they may appear unto men to fast. Verily I say unto you, They have their reward. But thou, when thou fastest, anoint thine head, and wash thy face; that thou appear not unto men to fast, but unto thy Father which is in secret; and thy Father, which seeth in secret, shall reward thee openly.

Lay up not for yourselves treasures upon earth, where moth and rust doth corrupt, and where thieves break through and steal: but lay up for yourselves treasures in heaven, where neither moth nor rust doth corrupt, and where thieves do not break through nor steal: for where your treasure is, there will your heart be also. The light of the body is the eye: if therefore thine eye be single, thy whole body shall be full of light. But if thine eye be evil, thy whole body shall be full of darkness. If therefore the light that is in thee be darkness, how great is that darkness! No man can serve two masters: for either he will hate the one, and love the other; or else he will hold to the one, and despise the other. Ye cannot serve God and mammon. Therefore I say unto you, Take no thought for your life, what ye shall eat, or what ye shall drink; nor yet for your body, what ye shall put on. Is not the life more than meat, and the body than raiment? Behold the fowls of the air: for they sow not, neither do they reap, nor gather into barns; yet your heavenly Father feedeth them. Are ye not much better than they? Which of you by taking thought can add one cubit unto his stature? And why take ye thought for raiment? Consider the lilies of the field, how they grow; they toil not, neither do they spin: and yet I say unto you, That even Solomon in all his glory was not arrayed like one of these. Wherefore, if God so clothe the grass of the field, which to day is, and to morrow is cast into the oven, shall he not much more clothe you, O ye of little faith? Therefore take no thought, saying, What shall we eat? or, What shall we drink? or, Wherewithal shall we be clothed? (For after all these things do the Gentiles seek:) for your heavenly Father knoweth that ye have need of all these things. But seek ye first the kingdom of God, and his righteousness; and all these things shall be added unto you. Take therefore no thought for the morrow: for the morrow shall take thought for the things of itself. Sufficient unto the day is the evil thereof.

Judge not, that ye be not judged. For with what judgment ye judge, ye shall be judged: and with what measure ye mete, it shall be measured to you again. And why beholdest thou the mote that is in thy brother's eye, but considerest not the beam that is in thine own eye? Or how wilt thou say to thy brother, Let me pull out the mote out of thine eye; and behold, a beam is in thine own eye? Thou hypocrite, first cast out the beam out of thine own eye; and then shalt thou see clearly to cast out the mote of thy brother's eye.

Give not that which is holy unto the dogs, neither cast ye your pearls before swine, lest they trample them under their feet, and turn again and rend you. Ask, and it shall be given you; seek and ye shall find; knock, and it shall be opened unto you: for every one that asketh receiveth; and he that seeketh findeth; and to him that knocketh it shall be opened. Or what man is there of you, whom if his son ask bread, will he give him a stone? Or if he ask a fish, will he give him a serpent? If ye then, being evil, know how to give good gifts unto your children, how much more shall your Father which is in heaven give good things to them that ask him? Therefore all things whatsoever ye would that men should do to you, do ye even so to them: for this is the law and the prophets.

Enter ye in at the strait gate: for wide is the gate, and broad is the way, that leadeth to destruction, and many there be which go in thereat: because strait is the gate, and narrow is the way, which leadeth unto life, and few there be that find it. Beware of false prophets, which come to you in sheep's clothing, but inwardly they are ravening wolves. Ye shall know them by their fruits. Do men gather grapes of thorns, or figs of thistles? Even so every good tree bringeth forth good fruit; but a corrupt tree bringeth forth evil fruit. A good tree cannot bring forth evil fruit, neither can a corrupt tree bring forth good fruit. Every tree that bringeth not forth good fruit is hewn down, and cast into the fire. Wherefore by their fruits ye shall know them. Not every one that saith unto me, Lord, Lord, shall enter into the kingdom of heaven; but he that doeth the will of my Father which is in heaven. Many will say to me in that day, Lord, Lord, have we not prophesied in thy name? And in thy name have cast out devils? and in thy name done many wonderful works? And then will I profess unto them, I never knew you: depart from me, ye that work iniquity. Therefore whosoever heareth these sayings of mine, and doeth them, I will liken him unto a wise man, which built his house upon a rock: and the rain descended, and the floods came, and the winds blew, and beat upon that house; and it fell not: for it was founded upon a rock. And every one that heareth these sayings of mine, and doeth them not, shall be likened unto a foolish man, which built his house upon the sand: and the rain descended, and the floods came, and the winds blew, and beat upon that house; and it fell: and great was the fall of it. And it came to pass, when Jesus had ended these sayings, the people were astonished at his doctrine: For he taught them as one having authority, and not as the scribes.

God and Humankind

Psalm 90: Man and the Providence of God

LORD, thou hast been our dwelling place in all generations.
Before the mountains were brought forth,
Or ever thou hadst formed the earth and the world,
Even from everlasting to everlasting, thou *art* God.
Thou turnest man to destruction;
And sayest, Return, ye children of men.
For a thousand years in thy sight
Are but as yesterday when it is past,
And *as* a watch in the night.
Thou carriest them away as with a flood; they are *as* a sleep:
In the morning *they are* like grass *which* groweth up.
In the morning it flourisheth, and groweth up;
In the evening it is cut down, and withereth.
For we are consumed by thine anger,
And by thy wrath are we troubled.
Thou hast set our iniquities before thee,
Our secret *sins* in the light of thy countenance.
For all our days are passed away in thy wrath:
We spend our years as a tale *that is told.*
The days of our years *are* threescore years and ten;
And if by reason of strength *they be* fourscore years,
Yet *is* their strength labor and sorrow;
For it is soon cut off, and we fly away.
Who knoweth the power of thine anger?
Even according to thy fear, *so is* thy wrath.
So teach *us* to number our days,
That we may apply *our* hearts unto wisdom.
Return, O LORD, how long?
And let it repent thee concerning thy servants.
O satisfy us early with thy mercy;
That we may rejoice and be glad all our days.
Make us glad according to the days *wherein* thou hast afflicted us,
And the years *wherein* we have seen evil.
Let thy work appear unto thy servants,
And thy glory unto their children.
And let the beauty of the LORD our God be upon us:
And establish thou the work of our hands upon us;
Yea, the work of our hands establish thou it.

The Upanishads: Svetasvatara

> OM . . .
> With our ears may we hear what is good.
> With our eyes may we behold thy righteousness.
> Tranquil in body, may we who worship thee find rest.
> OM . . . Peace—peace—peace.
> OM . . . Hail to the supreme Self!

Disciples inquire within themselves:

What is the cause of this universe?—is it Brahman? Whence do we come? Why do we live? Where shall we at last find rest? Under whose command are we bound by the law of happiness and its opposite?

Time, space, law, chance, matter, primal energy, intelligence—none of these, nor a combination of these, can be the final cause of the universe, for they are effects, and exist to serve the soul. Nor can the individual self be the cause, for, being subject to the law of happiness and misery, it is not free.

The seers, absorbed in contemplation, saw within themselves the ultimate reality, the self-luminous being, the one God, who dwells as the self-conscious power in all creatures. He is One without a second. Deep within all beings he dwells, hidden from sight by the coverings of the gunas—*sattwa*, *rajas*, and *tamas*. He presides over time, space, and all apparent causes.

This vast universe is a wheel. Upon it are all creatures that are subject to birth, death, and rebirth. Round and round it turns, and never stops. It is the wheel of Brahman. As long as the individual self thinks it is separate from Brahman, it revolves upon the wheel in bondage to the laws of birth, death, and rebirth. But when through the grace of Brahman it realizes its identity with him, it revolves upon the wheel no longer. It achieves immortality.[1]

He who is realized by transcending the world of cause and effect, in deep contemplation, is expressly declared by the scriptures to be the Supreme Brahman. He is the substance, all else the shadow. He is the imperishable. The knowers of Brahman know him as the one reality behind all that seems. For this reason they are devoted to him. Absorbed in him, they attain freedom from the wheel of birth, death, and rebirth.

The Lord supports this universe, which is made up of the perishable and the imperishable, the manifest and the unmanifest. The individual soul, forgetful of the Lord, attaches itself to pleasure and thus is bound. When it comes to the Lord, it is freed from all its fetters.

Mind and matter, master and servant—both have existed from beginningless time. The Maya which unites them has also existed from begin-

---

[1] Here appears for the first time in extant Hindu literature the image of the wheel as applied to birth, death, and rebirth.—EDS.

ningless time. When all three—mind, matter, and Maya—are known as one with Brahman, then is it realized that the Self is infinite and has no part in action. Then is it revealed that the Self is all.

Matter is perishable. The Lord, the destroyer of ignorance, is imperishable, immortal. He is the one God, the Lord of the perishable and of all souls. By meditating on him, by uniting oneself with him, by identifying oneself with him, one ceases to be ignorant.

Know God, and all fetters will be loosed. Ignorance will vanish. Birth, death, and rebirth will be no more. Meditate upon him and transcend physical consciousness. Thus will you reach union with the Lord of the universe. Thus will you become identified with him who is One without a second. In him all your desires will find fulfillment.

The truth is that you are always united with the Lord. But you must *know* this. Nothing further is there to know. Meditate, and you will realize that mind, matter, and Maya (the power which unites mind and matter) are but three aspects of Brahman, the one reality.

Fire, though present in the firesticks, is not perceived until one stick is rubbed against another. The Self is like that fire: it is realized in the body by meditation on the sacred syllable OM.

Let your body be the stick that is rubbed, the sacred syllable OM the stick that is rubbed against it. Thus shall you realize God, who is hidden within the body as fire is hidden within the wood.

Like oil in sesame seeds, butter in cream, water in the river bed, fire in tinder, the Self dwells within the soul. Realize him through truthfulness and meditation.

Like butter in cream is the Self in everything. Knowledge of the Self is gained through meditation. The Self is Brahman. By Brahman is all ignorance destroyed.

To realize God, first control the outgoing senses and harness the mind. Then meditate upon the light in the heart of the fire—meditate, that is, upon pure consciousness as distinct from the ordinary consciousness of the intellect. Thus the Self, the Inner Reality, may be seen behind physical appearance.

Control your mind so that the Ultimate Reality, the self-luminous Lord, may be revealed. Strive earnestly for eternal bliss.

With the help of the mind and the intellect, keep the senses from attaching themselves to objects of pleasure. They will then be purified by the light of the Inner Reality, and that light will be revealed.

The wise control their minds, and unite their hearts with the infinite, the omniscient, the all-pervading Lord. Only discriminating souls practice spiritual disciplines. Great is the glory of the self-luminous being, the Inner Reality.

Hear, all ye children of immortal bliss, also ye gods who dwell in the high heavens: Follow only in the footsteps of the illumined ones, and by continuous meditation merge both mind and intellect in the eternal Brahman. The glorious Lord will be revealed to you.

Control the vital force. Set fire to the Self within by the practice of meditation. Be drunk with the wine of divine love. Thus shall you reach perfection.

Be devoted to the eternal Brahman. Unite the light within you with the light of Brahman. Thus will the source of ignorance be destroyed, and you will rise above karma.[2]

Sit upright, holding the chest, throat, and head erect. Turn the senses and the mind inward to the lotus of the heart. Meditate on Brahman with the help of the syllable OM. Cross the fearful currents of the ocean of worldliness by means of the raft of Brahman—the sacred syllable OM.

With earnest effort hold the senses in check. Controlling the breath, regulate the vital activities. As a charioteer holds back his restive horses, so does a persevering aspirant hold back his mind.

Retire to a solitary place, such as a mountain cave or a sacred spot. The place must be protected from the wind and rain, it must have a smooth, clean floor, free from pebbles and dust. It must not be damp, and it must be free from disturbing noises. It must be pleasing to the eye and quieting to the mind. Seated there, practice meditation and other spiritual exercises.

As you practice meditation, you may see in vision forms resembling snow, crystals, smoke, fire, lightning, fireflies, the sun, the moon. These are signs that you are on your way to the revelation of Brahman.

As you become absorbed in meditation you will realize that the Self is separate from the body and for this reason will not be affected by disease, old age, or death.

The first signs of progress on the path of yoga are health, a sense of physical lightness, clearness of complexion, a beautiful voice, an agreeable odor of the person, and freedom from craving.

As a soiled piece of metal, when it has been cleaned, shines brightly, so the dweller in the body, when he has realized the truth of the Self, loses his sorrow and becomes radiant with bliss.

The yogi experiences directly the truth of Brahman by realizing the light of the Self within. He is freed from all impurities—he the pure, the birthless, the bright.

He is the one God, present in the north, the east, the south, and the west. He is the creator. He enters into all wombs. He alone is now born as all beings, and he alone is to be born as all beings in the future. He is within all persons as the Inner Self, facing in all directions.

---

[2] "The force generated by a person's actions that is held in Hinduism and Buddhism to be the motive power for the round of rebirths and deaths endured by him until he has achieved spiritual liberation and freed himself from the effects of such force."
—*Webster's Third New International Dictionary*.—EDS.

Let us adore the Lord, the luminous one, who is in fire, who is in water, who is in plants and trees, who pervades the whole universe.

The one absolute, impersonal Existence, together with his inscrutable Maya, appears as the divine Lord, the personal God, endowed with manifold glories. By his divine power he holds dominion over all the worlds. At the periods of creation and dissolution of the universe, he alone exists. Those who realize him become immortal.

The Lord is One without a second. Within man he dwells, and within all other beings. He projects the universe, maintains it, and withdraws it into himself.

His eyes are everywhere; his face, his arms, his feet are in every place. Out of himself he has produced the heavens and the earth, and with his arms and his wings he holds them together.

He is the origin and support of the gods. He is the Lord of all. He confers bliss and wisdom upon those who are devoted to him. He destroys their sins and their sorrows.

He punishes those who break his laws. He sees all and knows all. May he endow us with good thoughts!

O Lord, clothed in thy most holy form, which is calm and blissful, and which destroys all evil and ignorance, look upon us and make us glad.

O Lord, thou hast revealed thy sacred syllable OM, which is one with thee. In thy hands it is a weapon with which to destroy ignorance. O protector of thy devotees, do not conceal thy benign person.

Thou art the supreme Brahman. Thou art infinite. Thou hast assumed the forms of all creatures, remaining hidden in them. Thou pervadest all things. Thou art the one God of the universe. Those who realize thee become immortal.

Said the great seer Svetasvatara:

I have known, beyond all darkness, that great Person of golden effulgence. Only by knowing him does one conquer death. There is no other way of escaping the wheel of birth, death, and rebirth.

There is nothing superior to him, nothing different from him, nothing subtler or greater than he. Alone he stands, changeless, self-luminous; he, the Great One, fills this universe.

Though he fills the universe, he transcends it. He is untouched by its sorrow. He has no form. Those who know him become immortal. Others remain in the depths of misery.

The Lord God, all-pervading and omnipresent, dwells in the heart of all beings. Full of grace, he ultimately gives liberation to all creatures by turning their faces toward himself.

He is the innermost Self. He is the great Lord. He it is that reveals the purity within the heart by means of which he, who is pure being, may be reached. He is the ruler. He is the great Light, shining forever.

This great Being, assuming a form of the size of a thumb, forever dwells in the heart of all creatures as their innermost Self. He can be known directly by the purified mind through spiritual discrimination. Knowing him, men become immortal.

This great Being has a thousand heads, a thousand eyes, and a thousand feet. He envelops the universe. Though transcendent, he is to be meditated upon as residing in the lotus of the heart, at the center of the body, ten fingers above the navel.

He alone is *all this*—what has been done and what shall be. He has become the universe. Yet he remains forever changeless, and is the Lord of immortality.

His hands and feet are everywhere; his eyes and mouths are everywhere. His ears are everywhere. He pervades everything in the universe.

Without organs of sense, yet reflecting the activities of the senses, he is the Lord and ruler of all.

He is the friend and refuge of all.

He resides in the body, the city of nine gates. He sports in the world without in innumerable forms. He is the master, the ruler, of the whole world, animate and inanimate.

He moves fast, though without feet. He grasps everything, though without hands. He sees everything, though without eyes. He hears everything, though without ears. He knows all that is, but no one knows him. He is called the Supreme, the Great One.

Subtler than the subtlest, greater than the greatest, the Self is hidden in the heart of all creatures. Through his grace a man loses his cravings, transcends grief, and realizes him as Brahman Supreme.

Brahma[1]

RALPH WALDO EMERSON

If the red slayer think he slays,
   Or if the slain think he is slain,
They know not well the subtle ways
   I keep, and pass, and turn again.

Far or forgot to me is near;
   Shadow and sunlight are the same;
The vanished gods to me appear;
   And one to me are shame and fame.

---

[1] In *New England Quarterly*, 33 (1960), 506–512, K. R. Chandrasekharan has identified the key terms: "Brahma" (properly Brahman), the Absolute or Universal Soul; "red slayer," Siva the Destroyer; "strong gods," devas or celestial beings akin to angels; "sacred Seven," sages who sought God through austerities and penance; "meek lover," the yogi who through simple piety realizes Brahman. For further refinements, see Andrew M. McLean, *New England Quarterly*, 42 (1969), 115–122.—EDS.

They reckon ill who leave me out;
    When me they fly, I am the wings;
I am the doubter and the doubt,
    And I the hymn the Brahmin sings.

The strong gods pine for my abode,
    And pine in vain the sacred Seven;
But thou, meek lover of the good!
    Find me, and turn thy back on heaven.

Chanting the Square Deific
WALT WHITMAN

Chanting the square[1] deific, out of the One advancing, out of the sides,
Out of the old and new, out of the square entirely divine,
Solid, four-sided, (all the sides needed), from this side Jehovah am I,
Old Brahm I, and I Saturnius am;
Not Time affects me—I am Time, old, modern as any,
Unpersuadable, relentless, executing righteous judgments,
As the Earth, the Father, the brown old Kronos, with laws,
Aged beyond computation, yet ever new, ever with those mighty laws rolling,
Relentless I forgive no man—whoever sins dies—I will have that man's life;
Therefore let none expect mercy—have the seasons, gravitation, the appointed days, mercy? no more have I,
But as the seasons and gravitation, and as all the appointed days that forgive not,
I dispense from this side judgments inexorable without the least remorse.

Consolator most mild, the promis'd one advancing,
With gentle hand extended, the mightier God am I,
Foretold by prophets and poets in their most rapt prophecies and poems,
From this side, lo! the Lord Christ gazes—lo! Hermes I—lo! mine is Hercules' face,
All sorrow, labor, suffering, I, tallying it, absorb in myself,
Many times have I been rejected, taunted, put in prison, and crucified, and many times shall be again,
All the world have I given up for my dear brothers' and sisters' sake, for the soul's sake,
Wending my way through the homes of men, rich or poor, with the kiss of affection,

---

[1] Whitman here uses "square" as a noun, modified by the adjective "deific."—EDS.

For I am affection, I am the cheer-bringing God, with hope and all-
  enclosing charity,
With indulgent words as to children, with fresh and sane words, mine only,
Young and strong I pass knowing well I am destin'd myself to an early
  death;
But my charity has no death—my wisdom dies not, neither early nor late,
And my sweet love bequeath'd here and elsewhere never dies.

Aloof, dissatisfied, plotting revolt,
Comrade of criminals, brother of slaves,
Crafty despised, a drudge, ignorant,
With sudra face and worn brow, black, but in the depths of my heart,
  proud as any,
Lifted now and always against whoever scorning assumes to rule me,
Morose, full of guile, full of reminiscences, brooding, with many wiles,
(Though it was thought I was baffled and dispel'd, and my wiles done,
  but that will never be,)
Defiant, I, Satan, still live, still utter words, in new lands duly appearing,
  (and old ones also,)
Permanent here from my side, warlike, equal with any, real as any,
Nor time nor change shall ever change me or my words.

Santa Spirita, breather, life,
Beyond the light, lighter than light,
Beyond the flames of hell, joyous, leaping easily above hell,
Beyond Paradise, perfumed solely with mine own perfume,
Including all life on earth, touching, including God, including Saviour
  and Satan,
Ethereal, pervading all, (for without me what were all? what were God?)
Essence of forms, life of the real identities, permanent, positive, (namely
  the unseen,)
Life of the great round world, the sun and stars, and of man, I, the
  general soul,
Here the square finishing, the solid, I the most solid,
Breathe my breath also through these songs.

God and the Spirit of Man[1]
MARTIN BUBER

If philosophy is here set in contrast to religion, what is meant by religion is not the massive fullness of statements, concepts, and activities

[1] "God and the Spirit of Man" is the substance of a lecture delivered by Buber at a number of American universities in 1951.—Eds.

that one customarily describes by this name and that men sometimes long for more than for God. Religion is essentially the act of holding fast to God. And that does not mean holding fast to an image that one has made of God, nor even holding fast to the faith in God that one has conceived. It means holding fast to the existing God. The earth would not hold fast to its conception of the sun (if it had one), nor to its connections with it, but to the sun itself.

In contrast to religion so understood, philosophy is here regarded as the process, reaching from the time when reflection first became independent to its more contemporary crisis, the last stage of which is the intellectual letting go of God.

This process begins with man's no longer contenting himself, as did the pre-philosophical man, with picturing the living God, to whom one formerly only called—with a call of despair or rapture which occasionally became his first name—as a Something, a thing among things, a being among beings, an It.

The beginning of philosophizing means that this Something changes from an object of imagination, wishes, and feelings to one that is conceptually comprehensible, to an object of thought. It does not matter whether this object of thought is called "Speech" (*Logos*), because in all and each one hears it speak, answer, and directly address one; or "the Unlimited" (*Apeiron*), because it has already leapt over every limit that one may try to set for it; or simply "Being," or whatever. If the living quality of the conception of God refuses to enter into this conceptual image, it is tolerated alongside of it, usually in an unprecise form, as in the end identical with it or at least essentially dependent on it. Or it is depreciated as an unsatisfactory surrogate, helpful to men incapable of thought.

In the progress of its philosophizing, the human spirit is ever more inclined to fuse characteristically this conception, of the Absolute as an object of an adequate thought, with itself, the human spirit. In the course of this process, the idea which was at first noetically[2] contemplated finally becomes the potentiality of the spirit itself that thinks it, and it attains on the way of the spirit its actuality. The subject, which appeared to be attached to being in order to perform for it the service of contemplation, asserts that it itself produced and produces being. Until, finally, all that is over against us, everything that accosts us and takes possession of us, all partnership of existence, is dissolved in free-floating subjectivity.

The next step already takes us to the stage familiar to us, the stage that understands itself as the final one and plays with its finality: the human spirit, which adjudges to itself mastery over its work, annihilates conceptually the absoluteness of the absolute. It may yet imagine that it, the spirit, still remains there as bearer of all things and coiner of all values;

---

[2] That is, apprehended only by the intellect.—EDS.

in truth, it has also destroyed its own absoluteness along with absoluteness in general. The spirit can now no longer exist as an independent essence. There now exists only a product of human individuals called spirit, a product which they contain and secrete like mucus and urine.

In this stage, there first takes place the conceptual letting go of God because only now philosophy cuts off its own hands, the hands with which it was able to grasp and hold him.

But an analogous process takes place on the other side, in the development of religion itself (in the usual broad sense of the word).

From the earliest times, the reality of the relation of faith, man's standing before the face of God, world-happening as dialogue, has been threatened by the impulse to control the power yonder. Instead of understanding events as calls which make demands on one, one wishes oneself to demand without having to hearken. "I have," says man, "power over the powers I conjure." And that continues, with sundry modifications, wherever one celebrates rites without being turned to the Thou and without really meaning its Presence.

The other pseudo-religious counterpart of the relation of faith, not so elementally active as conjuration but acting with the mature power of the intellect, is unveiling. Here one takes the position of raising the veil of the manifest, which divides the revealed from the hidden, and leading forth the divine mysteries. "I am," says the man, "acquainted with the unknown, and I make it known." The supposedly divine It that the magician manipulates as the technician his dynamo, the gnostic lays bare— the whole divine apparatus. His heirs are not "theosophies" and their neighbors alone; in many theologies also, unveiling gestures are to be discovered behind the interpreting ones.

We find this replacement of I-Thou by an I-It in manifold forms in that new philosophy of religion which seeks to "save" religion. In it, the "I" of this relation steps ever more into the foreground as "subject" of "religious feeling," as profiter from a pragmatist decision to believe, and the like.

Much more important than all this, however, is an event penetrating to the innermost depth of the religious life, an event which may be described as the subjectivizing of the act of faith itself. Its essence can be grasped most clearly through the example of prayer.

We call prayer in the pregnant sense of the term that speech of man to God which, whatever else is asked, ultimately asks for the manifestation of the divine Presence, for this Presence becoming dialogically perceivable. The single presupposition of a genuine state of prayer is thus the readiness of the whole man for this Presence, simple-turned-towardness, unreserved spontaneity. This spontaneity, ascending from the roots, succeeds time and again in overcoming all that disturbs and diverts. But in this our stage of subjectivized reflection not only the concentration of the one who prays, but also his spontaneity, is assailed. The assailant is consciousness, the overconsciousness of this man here that he is praying, that he is *praying*, that *he* is praying. And the assailant appears to be invincible. The subjective knowledge of the one turning-toward about his turning-toward, this holding back of an I which does not enter into the action with the rest of the person, an I to which the action is an object—all this de-possesses the moment, takes away its spontaneity. The specifically modern man who has not yet let go of God knows what that means: he who is not present perceives no Presence.

One must understand this correctly: this is not a question of a special case of the known sickness of modern man, who must attend his own actions as spectator. It is the confession of the Absolute into which he brings his unfaithfulness to the Absolute, and it is the relation between the Absolute and him upon which this unfaithfulness works, in the midst of the statement of trust. And now he too who is seemingly holding fast to God becomes aware of the eclipsed Transcendence.

What is it that we mean when we speak of an eclipse of God which is even now taking place? Through this metaphor we make the tremendous assumption that we can glance up to God with our "mind's eye," or rather being's eye, as with our bodily eye to the sun, and that something can step between our existence and his as between the earth and the sun. That this glance of the being exists, wholly unillusory, yielding no images yet first making possible all images, no other court in the world attests than that of faith. It is not to be proved; it is only to be experienced; man has experienced it. And that other, that which steps in between, one also experiences, today. I have spoken of it since I have recognized it, and as exactly as my perception has allowed me.

The double nature of man, as the being that is both brought forth from "below" and sent from "above," results in the duality of his basic characteristics. These cannot be understood through the categories of the individual man existing-for-himself, but only through the categories of his existing as man-with-man. As a being who is sent, man exists over against the existing being before which he is placed. As a being who is brought forth, he finds himself beside all existing beings in the world, beside which he is set. The first of these categories has its living reality in the relation I-Thou, the second has its reality in the relation I-It. The second always brings us only to the aspects of an existing being, not to that being itself. Even the most intimate contact with another remains covered over by an aspect if the other has not become Thou for me. Only the first relation, that which establishes essential immediacy between me and an existing being, brings me precisely thereby not to an aspect of it, but to that being itself. To be sure, it brings me only to the existential meeting with it; it does not somehow put me in a position to view it objectively in its being. As soon as an objective viewing is established, we are given only an aspect and ever again only an aspect. But it is also only the relation I-Thou in which we can meet God at all, because of him, in absolute contrast to all other existing beings, no objective aspect can be attained. Even a vision yields no objective viewing, and he who strains to hold fast an afterimage after the cessation of the full I-Thou relation has already lost the vision.

It is not the case, however, that the I in both relations, I-Thou and I-It, is the same. Rather where and when the beings around one are seen and treated as objects of observation, reflection, use, perhaps also of solicitude or help, there and then another I is spoken, another I manifested, another exists than where and when one stands with the whole of one's being over against another being and steps into an essential relation with him. Everyone who knows both in himself—and that is the life of man, that one comes to know both in himself and ever again both—knows whereof I speak. Both together build up human existence; it is only a question of which of the two is at any particular time the architect and which is his assistant. Rather, it is a question of whether the I-Thou relation remains the architect, for it is self-evident that it cannot be employed as assistant. If it does not command, then it is already disappearing.

In our age, the I-It relation, gigantically swollen, has usurped, practically uncontested, the mastery and the rule. The I of this relation, an I that possesses all, makes all, succeeds with all, this I that is unable to say Thou, unable to meet a being essentially, is the lord of the hour. This selfhood that has become omnipotent, with all the It around it, can naturally acknowledge neither God nor any genuine absolute which manifests itself to men as of nonhuman origin. It steps in between and shuts off from us the light of heaven.

Such is the nature of this hour. But what of the next? It is a modern superstition that the character of an age acts as fate for the next. One lets it prescribe what is possible to do and hence what is permitted. One surely cannot swim against the stream, one says. But perhaps one can swim with a new stream whose source is still hidden? In another image, the I-Thou relation has gone into the catacombs—who can say with how much greater power it will step forth! Who can say when the I-It relation will be directed anew to its assisting place and activity!

The most important events in the history of that embodied possibility called man are the occasionally occurring beginnings of new epochs, determined by forces previously invisible or unregarded. Each age is, of course, a continuation of the preceding one, but a continuation can be confirmation and it can be refutation.

Something is taking place in the depths that as yet needs no name. Tomorrow even it may happen that it will be beckoned to from the heights, across the heads of the earthly archons.[3] The eclipse of the light of God is no extinction; even tomorrow that which has stepped in between may give way.

---

[3] Rulers or high officials; specifically, magistrates in ancient Athens.—Eds.

What Is Reality?

Existentialism as a Symptom of Man's Contemporary Crisis
WILLIAM C. BARRETT

Nowadays we speak quite easily and naturally of the crisis through which our civilization is passing. Without questioning the assumption that we are in the midst of a crisis, I should like to ask whether this feeling of crisis is not something inseparable from human life in any historical period. The more closely we examine the past, the more we find that it, too, is uneasy with its own sense of historical crisis and urgency. Sometimes, in retrospect, these crises look illusory, for mankind has survived some of its worst apprehensions; and then we have to remind ourselves that these men and women of the past felt that bygone crisis in their bones, with the same intimate uneasiness with which we feel ours. We begin to suspect that to live itself is to exist in crisis (more or less actual at any moment), and that only in periods of real historic somnolence and lethargy—real decadence, in short—has mankind been without a sense of crisis. No doubt, there are important differences of degree, and one age may be more plainly a period of breakdown than another; it would be folly to neglect such differences of degree, but the thought that crisis, or the sense of it, is a permanent part of human life, does fortify us to see our own contemporary crisis in a much broader light—as a total human condition.

This thought will explain why I prefer to discuss existential philosophy as a symptom, rather than a solution, of our present crisis. For to the degree that we see our crisis as a total and concrete condition, to that degree we shall doubt that any philosophy, no matter how ambitious, can propose itself as the unique path of salvation. Anyone who has had any personal experience of a spiritual crisis will know that recovery does not come through the acquisition of any new abstract ideas. The progress from health to sickness is a change of being, rather than a change in thought. So, if we agree that our civilization is spiritually sick, we should also expect that the recovery will not come through any single set of ideas, or philosophy, but only through a transformation of our whole existence—thus requiring social, economic, and religious change. A new philosophy would be only a necessary *part* of this total change.

Moreover, it is the very characteristic of Existentialism as a philosophy that it must look with irony upon any system of thought that proposes itself as *the* solution for all of life's crises. Let us remember that Kierkegaard,[1] the founder of Existentialism, began to philosophize with the purpose of discovering difficulties, rather than offering easy and readymade solutions. Existentialism as a philosophy attempts to make man aware of certain basic realities of his life. In this sense it seeks to increase, rather than minimize, our human difficulties. The business of finding solutions must come only after a man is aware of the whole depth, import, and, therefore, difficulty, of his human life.

I

This preliminary definition of existential philosophy will be understood better, if we contrast it with the usual kinds of philosophy now taught in our academies. The various schools of philosophy are distinguished from each other by different beliefs. Thus it comes about that a philosophy is understood as a set of beliefs, or propositions, to which a man gives intellectual assent. A man is said to have a philosophy, then, if he has a system of propositions which he holds to be true on purely intellectual or rational grounds. This is the understanding of philosophy that has prevailed particularly in our period of the departmentalization of all human knowledge. But Existentialism seeks to restore a much more primitive sense of the word, "philosophy," than this: namely, the ancient sense of philosophy as a concrete way of life, rather than an abstract set of propositions. Nietzsche,[2] also an Existentialist, pointed out that for ancient man, and even the modern Oriental, the business of achieving a philosophy is one that engaged the whole man, his total being, and was not pursued simply as one specialized department of knowledge among others. Kierkegaard attacked the Hegelian[3] professors of his time as being philosophers without any real philosophic existence: they had a system of propositions to teach, but the system itself was a means of forgetting the concrete realities of human life. For us in America today the philosopher is merely a "professional" savant among many others.

Existentialism, on the contrary, understands philosophy as a thing that is to be lived, and not merely a body of knowledge to be taught to pupils. I have said that Existentialism attempts to bring to human consciousness the basic, even banal, realities of human life: realities such as death, anxiety, choice, love, freedom, guilt, conscience, the willing acceptance of anxiety, etc., etc. In American academic philosophy today these are not the prevailing concepts: philosophers discuss concepts relating to science, knowledge, logic. Existential concepts are thought to belong to literature, perhaps to poetry. This rejection is an evidence of how far one particular tradition among the intellectual elite of our society has tended to set knowledge above life. If the philosopher exists professionally as a member of a

---

[1] Søren Aabye Kierkegaard (1813–1855), Danish philosopher and theologian.—EDS.
[2] Friedrich Wilhelm Nietzsche (1844–1900), German philosopher.—EDS.
[3] Georg Friedrich Wilhelm Hegel (1770–1831), German idealist philosopher.—EDS.

department in a university, and if he accepts his role as one that deals with one special department of knowledge among others, then he is inevitably drawn to devote himself to those very special and technical problems that seem to be the peculiar province of the "expert." Our technological civilization has tended more and more to worship the expert, and the philosopher, assimilated to his civilization, strives more and more to justify his own professional existence by a high technical competence in the special problems of logic and philosophical analysis. The result is that a great deal of modern philosophy has tended to become divorced from life. Hence it is only natural that Existentialism, which struggles against this tendency, is looked on somewhat askance by a great many American philosophers.

All this has been by way of explaining why it seemed preferable to discuss Existentialism as a symptom, rather than a solution, of our contemporary crisis. But there has also been in the background of my remarks another, and much more drastic point, which will be substantiated by my further discussion, but can be announced now: the point, quite simply, that there is never a solution to any of life's crises. This is one of the cardinal points in existential philosophy itself. The word, "solution," belongs to the vocabulary of science and engineering, suggesting some kind of blueprint that would immediately deliver us from the pain and muddle of suffering, when, in fact, we know that our really deep crises in life are precisely those that we have to live through. Our deepest personal problems do not in the least resemble any problem of engineering, and it is the same, we suggest, with the sickness of civilization, even though the "cure" of a sick civilization might require vast exploits of engineering.

II

That movement in thought should be a symptom of its time, is not in the least a condemnation of this movement as a wild or trivial aberration. I am using the word, "symptom," in its simple and unprejudiced sense of a sign—something that instructs us about the state of the organism from which it arises. Thus Existentialism has a great deal to teach us—which we might otherwise not know—about the condition of the Western civilization that has brought it to birth.

Most Americans connect Existentialism with the current French movement, and particularly with the name of its most brilliant publicist, Jean Paul Sartre.[4] Sartre's is an agile and energetic mind, but his doctrine represents, I believe, a dilution of existential philosophy, and in any case does not take us back to its original sources. These lie in the nineteenth century, and the great innovators are Kierkegaard and Nietzsche—though the latter, unlike Kierkegaard, is not fully aware of his existential point of departure. Existential themes are treated in the fiction of Tolstoi and

[4] Jean-Paul Sartre (1905–   ), French philosopher, novelist.—EDS.

Dostoievski.[5] In this century the two most important existential philosophers have been the German professors, Martin Heidegger and Karl Jaspers.[6] To these names we might add the considerable figure of the Spanish philosopher, José Ortega y Gasset,[7] who has described his philosophy as one of "vital reason," though it is fundamentally existential in its directions. These names should indicate that Existentialism is not a momentary intellectual fad, derived from the French, but a much wider and deeper movement in Western thought, having roots indeed in the profound upheavals of this civilization during the past two centuries. To see what these roots are, we may find it more convenient to turn, not to an abstruse text in philosophy, but to a work of literature that takes a simpler and more direct grasp of the issues involved: Tolstoi's great story, "The Death of Ivan Ilyich," which by this time has become something of a basic scripture for existential thought.

The plot of Tolstoi's story is slight and almost negligible. Ivan Ilyich is an amiable and undistinguished bourgeois, who has spent his whole life trying to be like everyone else in his social class: a successful and happy man, where happiness means only the absence of suffering. But one day Ivan Ilyich feels a pain in his side, which resists all treatment by doctors, and as his illness progresses, he suddenly realizes that he is going to die. For the first time in his life death becomes a reality for him. In the face of this awful presence, all his disguises fall away: confronting death for the first time in his life, he is also confronting himself for the first time. Hitherto in his life he had hid from himself amid the routine mechanisms of all his social, official, and familial functions. Now, as he is about to die, he asks himself the questions: Who am I? What has been the meaning of my life? In the end Ivan Ilyich dies content, because he has reached the point of knowing that the life he lived was empty, futile, and meaningless.

What Tolstoi is saying here, to put it now as a general thesis, is that modern life has alienated the individual from himself. The materialistic and rationalistic nineteenth century, with its emphasis upon all the bourgeois routines of life, has so externalized the individual that he has lost the feeling and the passion for his own personal existence. Modern man, Tolstoi is saying, has lost the meaning of life, and, as with Ivan Ilyich, it will take nothing less than the presence of death to restore this sense of life.

The sense of decadence haunts the nineteenth century, even at the moments of its most splendid optimism. There is a widespread uneasiness

---

[5] Count Leo Nikolayevich Tolstoi (or Tolstoy) (1828–1910), Russian writer, philosopher; Feodor Mikhailovich Dostoievski (or Dostoevsky) (1821–1881), Russian novelist.—Eds.

[6] Martin Heidegger (1889–1976) and Karl Jaspers (1883–1969), German philosophers.—Eds.

[7] José Ortega y Gasset (1883–1955), Spanish humanist.—Eds.

that life has lost its passion, intensity, and meaning; that there has been some secret decline in human vitality. Kierkegaard puts it as eloquently and compactly as one could wish:

> Let others complain that times are bad; I complain that they are petty because they lack passion. Men's thoughts are as flimsy as thin ice and men themselves as insignificant as the thin snow that covers it. Their thoughts are too petty to be sinful. A worm might consider such thoughts to be sinful, but not a man created in the image of God. Their pleasures are circumspect and boring; their passions, sleep; these materialistic souls fulfill their duties, but they collect their usury for it; they believe that although our Lord keeps His accounts in good order, they can hand Him counterfeit. Out with them! This is why my soul always hearkens back to Shakespeare and the Old Testament. There one feels that those who speak are men; there they hate; there they love; there they kill the enemy, curse their descendants for generations to come, there they sin.

This passage might almost have been written by Nietzsche, who launches his plea from the diametrically opposite anti-Christian pole. Modern man, says Nietzsche, lacks a goal, and his existence is, therefore, purposeless and nihilistic. Similar themes appear also in such diverse writers as Stendhal and Burckhardt.[8]

The twentieth century has no reason to forget these fears. Our technological civilization has become even more involved with elaborate apparatus to catch and smother the individual. We have gone beyond the nineteenth century in the development of a fantastic mass culture—in radio, movies, and television—that stamps out all individual differences. Modern society has become more and more a mass society. Cities grow larger, crowds become more and more potent factors, and the individual threatened more than ever by anonymity in the mass. The image of modern man lies in T. S. Eliot's line: "Men and bits of paper, whirled by the cold wind."[9] These fears of the nineteenth century turn out to be prophetic for us: amid this general purposelessness of life, this mass drifting, we set ourselves the task of recapturing the sense and the meaning of life.

III

When Tolstoi speaks of a loss of the meaning of life, he is not referring to a loss of some rational explanation. Nor is the meaning that is to be restored an intellectual one, some new fact or discovery of the mind. On the contrary, the disorder in modern man that Tolstoi's story speaks of is a disorder in the more primitive and irrational, or non-rational, parts of man's being. Existentialism as a philosophy seeks to deal with these irra-

---

[8] Stendhal is the pseudonym of Marie Henri Beyle (1783–1842), French writer; Jakob Christoph Burckhardt (1818–1897), Swiss historian.—EDS.

[9] T. S. Eliot, "Burnt Norton," *Collected Poems of T. S. Eliot, 1909–1935* (New York: Harcourt, Brace & World, Inc., 1936), p. 217.

tional parts of our existence in a way that philosophy has never done before, and by so doing gives reason itself a new place in the human hierarchy.

This is why existential philosophy has been frequently—and, I think, unjustly—criticized as anti-rational. One is not against reason, if one insists that the irrational is an inseparable part of life, and that it is precisely with the irrational parts of our being that modern civilization fails to deal adequately. This so-called "anti-rational" tendency in modern philosophy has now had a long history, from Rousseau to Bergson, Whitehead,[10] and Heidegger in our century, and it embraces too many great names to be dismissed out of hand. Any future rationalism worth its salt will have to assimilate a great deal from these thinkers, and we ourselves would be less than rational, if we did not make an earnest effort to understand in detail how the irrational enters human life.

We gain some idea of the irrational character of life, if we turn back again to Tolstoi's "Ivan Ilyich." As death appears to Ivan Ilyich, it presents itself as something altogether unreasonable and incomprehensible. Immersed in the comfortable structure of his life, he sees this strange and dark intruder creep in to destroy everything. Yet, death is a banal fact, and we know that all men have to die; Ivan Ilyich knows all this with his head, but his heart cannot grasp the incomprehensible fact that he, Ivan Ilyich, should have to die. This bewilderment may strike us as childish, but it is Tolstoi's means of showing us how the irrational, like death, may fall upon us in the most incalculable and unpredictable way, upsetting all our plans for life.

Kierkegaard has expounded the presence of the irrational in another area of human life—in the act of choice or decision. We do not doubt that some decisions are more rational than others, and we may even speak of a decision as being the only rational choice under the circumstances. But is a rational choice one from which the irrational is ever completely excluded? Is any choice, however rational it be, free from the uncertain contingencies of risk and adventure? Of course, there are certain trivial choices that we make every day, and that we may reverse the next day, if we are proved wrong. But these are choices that do not commit us deeply, that leave us relatively disengaged from the consequences. As soon, however, as a choice cuts deeply; as soon as it commits our whole life in a certain direction; so soon, then, do the immense difficulties appear, the balance of probabilities becomes harder, and each alternative appears, however we may canvass its possibilities, as a leap into the unknown.

The choice that personally involved Kierkegaard happened to be the question whether or not to marry. Engaged to a young woman in Copen-

---

[10] Jean Jacques Rousseau (1712–1778), Swiss-born French political philosopher; Henri Bergson (1859–1941), French philosopher; Alfred North Whitehead (1861–1947), British mathematician and philosopher.—Eds.

hagen, he desired marriage intensely, but he felt in himself also a certain religious mission that would prevent him from giving himself completely in marriage. The particular psychological facts involved here are important for an understanding of Kierkegaard's biography, but the peculiarly personal difficulties should not obscure for us the fact that the pathos of choice Kierkegaard faced is universal. There are, in short, choices in life that are irreversible. Kierkegaard could not have made an *experimental* choice of marriage, in the expectation that if it "did not work out"— to use the expression that has become common among us these days— he could return to his religious vocation and its tasks, for the vocation might have been lost through his marriage. On the other hand, if he renounced marriage experimentally, he could not hope to return to the young lady, should the other alternative not work out. She might not be there (as in fact she was not) when he returned. Love has to be seized at the moment it is offered; our indecision pollutes and destroys it.

All of this points to the fact that the situation of human choice is not at all a situation of scientific experiment. A situation is experimental in science when certain scientific controls have been established, so that through these controls we can repeat the experiment at any time and place we choose, and indeed repeat it indefinitely. The more precisely scientific the experiment becomes, the more its features of accidental particularity become refined away, and the easier it becomes to repeat it in all its detail. But our fundamental choices in life do not permit us this degree of control, because they do not permit us this degree of detachment. We have to choose here and now, and for the rest of our life, and the alternative we renounce is lost forever. We could be completely experimental about our own lives only if we were immortal, and so could repeat any situation or choice indefinitely.

But as death is real and our lives finite, every choice is also a renunciation, and this is why Kierkegaard speaks of the *pathos* of human choice. It was this sacrificial and pathetic aspect of choice that led Kierkegaard to his great polemic against the excessively rational philosophy of Hegel. The old adage puts the matter quite simply and adequately, "You cannot eat your cake and have it too"; but Hegel devised a sophisticated dialectic by which it was possible to bring together two conflicting alternatives, thesis and antithesis, into a higher synthesis, so that the speculative philosopher, triumphing over life, could both have his cake and eat it, too. Such a reconciling of opposites is indeed possible in knowledge, where a more inclusive theory may embrace two conflicting alternatives; but it is not possible in life, where the suffering of renunciation cannot be altogether eliminated by reason. This opposition between knowledge and life has been one of the chief themes of Existentialism, as well as of a great deal of modern philosophy and literature.

The Allegory of the Cave
PLATO

Next, said I, here is a parable to illustrate the degrees in which our nature may be enlightened or unenlightened. Imagine the condition of men living in a sort of cavernous chamber underground, with an entrance open to the light and a long passage all down the cave.[1] Here they have been from childhood, chained by the leg and also by the neck, so that they cannot move and can see only what is in front of them, because the chains will not let them turn their heads. At some distance higher up is the light of a fire burning behind them; and between the prisoners and the fire is a track[2] with a parapet built along it, like the screen at a puppet-show, which hides the performers while they show their puppets over the top.

I see, said he.

Now behind this parapet imagine persons carrying along various artificial objects, including figures of men and animals in wood or stone or other materials, which project above the parapet. Naturally, some of these persons will be talking, others silent.[3]

It is a strange picture, he said, and a strange sort of prisoners.

Like ourselves, I replied; for in the first place prisoners so confined would have seen nothing of themselves or of one another, except the shadows thrown by the fire-light on the wall of the Cave facing them, would they?

Not if all their lives they had been prevented from moving their heads.

And they would have seen as little of the objects carried past.

Of course.

Now, if they could talk to one another, would they not suppose that their words referred only to those passing shadows which they saw?[4]

Necessarily.

---

[1] The *length* of the "way in" (*eisodos*) to the chamber where the prisoners sit is an essential feature, explaining why no daylight reaches them.

[2] The track crosses the passage into the cave at right angles, and is *above* the parapet built along it.

[3] A modern Plato would compare his Cave to an underground cinema, where the audience watch the play of shadows thrown by the film passing before a light at their backs. The film itself is only an image of "real" things and events in the world outside the cinema. For the film Plato has to substitute the clumsier apparatus of a procession of artificial objects carried on their heads by persons who are merely part of the machinery, providing for the movement of the objects and the sounds whose echo the prisoners hear. The parapet prevents these persons' shadows from being cast on the wall of the Cave.

[4] The prisoners, having seen nothing but shadows, cannot think their words refer to the objects carried past behind their backs. For them shadows (images) are the only realities.

And suppose their prison had an echo from the wall facing them? When one of the people crossing behind them spoke, they could only suppose that the sound came from the shadow passing before their eyes.

No doubt.

In every way, then, such prisoners would recognize as reality nothing but the shadows of those artificial objects.[5]

Inevitably.

Now consider what would happen if their release from the chains and the healing of their unwisdom should come about in this way. Suppose one of them set free and forced suddenly to stand up, turn his head, and walk with eyes lifted to the light; all these movements would be painful, and he would be too dazzled to make out the objects whose shadows he had been used to see. What do you think he would say, if someone told him that what he had formerly seen was meaningless illusion, but now, being somewhat nearer to reality and turned towards more real objects, he was getting a truer view? Suppose further that he were shown the various objects being carried by and were made to say, in reply to questions, what each of them was. Would he not be perplexed and believe the objects now shown him to be not so real as what he formerly saw?

Yes, not nearly so real.

And if he were forced to look at the fire-light itself, would not his eyes ache, so that he would try to escape and turn back to the things which he could see distinctly, convinced that they really were clearer than these other objects now being shown to him?

Yes.

And suppose someone were to drag him away forcibly up the steep and rugged ascent and not let him go until he had hauled him out into the sunlight, would he not suffer pain and vexation at such treatment, and, when he had come out into the light, find his eyes so full of its radiance that he could not see a single one of the things that he was now told were real?

Certainly he would not see them all at once.

He would need, then, to grow accustomed before he could see things in that upper world. At first it would be easiest to make out shadows, and then the images of men and things reflected in water, and later on the things themselves. After that, it would be easier to watch the heavenly bodies and the sky itself by night, looking at the light of the moon and stars rather than the Sun and the Sun's light in the day-time.

Yes, surely.

Last of all, he would be able to look at the Sun and contemplate its nature, not as it appears when reflected in water or any alien medium, but as it is in itself in its own domain.

No doubt.

[5] The state of mind called *eikasia* . . . [See footnote 6.]

And now he would begin to draw the conclusion that it is the Sun that produces the seasons and the course of the year and controls everything in the visible world, and moreover is in a way the cause of all that he and his companions used to see.

Clearly he would come at last to that conclusion.

Then if he called to mind his fellow prisoners and what passed for wisdom in his former dwelling-place, he would surely think himself happy in the change and be sorry for them. They may have had a practice of honouring and commending one another, with prizes for the man who had the keenest eye for the passing shadows and the best memory for the order in which they followed or accompanied one another, so that he could make a good guess as to which was going to come next.[6] Would our released prisoner be likely to covet those prizes or to envy the men exalted to honour and power in the Cave? Would he not feel like Homer's Achilles, that he would far sooner "be on earth as a hired servant in the house of a landless man"[7] or endure anything rather than go back to his old beliefs and live in the old way?

Yes, he would prefer any fate to such a life.

Now imagine what would happen if he went down again to take his former seat in the Cave. Coming suddenly out of the sunlight, his eyes would be filled with darkness. He might be required once more to deliver his opinion on those shadows, in competition with the prisoners who had never been released, while his eyesight was still dim and unsteady; and it might take some time to become used to the darkness. They would laugh at him and say that he had gone up only to come back with his sight ruined; it was worth no one's while even to attempt the ascent. If they could lay hands on the man who was trying to set them free and lead them up, they would kill him.[8]

Yes, they would.

Every feature in this parable, my dear Glaucon, is meant to fit our earlier analysis. The prison dwelling corresponds to the region revealed to us through the sense of sight, and the fire-light within it to the power of the Sun. The ascent to see the things in the upper world you may take as standing for the upward journey of the soul into the region of the intelligible;[9] then you will be in possession of what I surmise, since that is what you wish to be told. Heaven knows whether it is true; but this, at any

---

[6] The empirical politician, with no philosophic insight, but only a "knack of remembering what usually happens" (*Gorg.* 501 A). He has *eikasia* = conjecture as to what is likely (*eikos*). [*Gorg.* refers to Plato's dialogue on rhetoric, *Gorgias*.—EDS.]

[7] This verse, being spoken by the ghost of Achilles, suggests that the Cave is comparable with Hades.

[8] An allusion to the fate of Socrates. [See "The Apology of Socrates" on page 408. —EDS.]

[9] Plato here refers to the real world of spiritual essences as opposed to the visible, unreal world of the senses.—EDS.

rate, is how it appears to me. In the world of knowledge, the last thing to be perceived and only with great difficulty is the essential Form of Goodness. Once it is perceived, the conclusion must follow that, for all things, this is the cause of whatever is right and good; in the visible world it gives birth to light and to the lord of light, while it is itself sovereign in the intelligible world and the parent of intelligence and truth. Without having had a vision of this Form no one can act with wisdom, either in his own life or in matters of state.

Death

O Death, Where Is Thy Sting-a-Ling-a-Ling?
LESLIE H. FARBER

A word about my title—a line from a British soldiers' song, popular in World War I. Clearly it is an irreverent version of a passage from St. Paul, one of the West's early great thanatologists.[1] In his first letter to the Corinthians, St. Paul (adapting a passage from Hosea) writes, "O death, where is thy victory? O death, where is thy sting? The sting of death is sin, and the power of sin is the law. But thanks be to God, who gives us the victory through our Lord Jesus Christ." Perhaps I should quote the entire lyric of the World War I song, so it may be appreciated how little those soldiers cared for St. Paul's solace:

> The bells of hell go ting-a-ling-a-ling
> For you but not for me,
> And the little devils how they sing-a-ling-a-ling
> For you but not for me.
> O death, where is thy sting-a-ling-a-ling?
> O grave, thy victoree?
> The bells of hell go ting-a-ling-a-ling
> For you but not for me.

My own preference is clear. Popular wisdom about finding God in the trenches notwithstanding, the British soldiers in their own mocking way restore the sting to death and victory to the grave. And they do something more: they suggest the impenetrability of the subject and the necessity of some humor to counter man's futile ambitions to pontificate about matters beyond him.

There is a growing conviction today, however, that those ambitions, far from being futile, are honorable—perhaps heroic—and merit our unprejudiced attention and support. I am speaking, of course, of the extraordinary explosion, over roughly the past ten years, of interest in—study of, speaking and writing about—death and dying. This enthusiasm sweeps across professional lines, age boundaries, and personal frontiers of all kinds. Anyone and everyone may—and increasingly large numbers of people apparently must—join the crusade against man's last dread adversary.

Well, perhaps not exactly. It is not so much a crusade *against* death as it is a quest toward it. The aim would seem to be to capture death—to

---

[1] Students of death.—EDS.

tame it, domesticate it, draw it out of its absolute otherness into the realm of the living, where its mystery will be dispelled by the sweet, resolute counsels of enlightenment, and its significance will be revealed as just another, albeit a crucial, experience in life.

To these ends all manner of enterprises proliferate across the land. In forward-looking secondary schools—not just in California, either—students encounter a variety of death-oriented courses woven into the social-studies, psychology, anthropology, history, or English curriculum. They may do research on biological warfare, medieval confessional devices, suicide rates in suburbia; make field trips to hospital wards and embalming schools; read William Faulkner, Edgar Allan Poe, and Shakespeare; and write their own obituaries. Nor is this quite optional. A girl in a Florida high school became depressed and wanted to drop her death course, but was refused permission by her mother. "I can't handle death," the mother explained to the teacher. "My daughter needs to learn how."

Meanwhile, younger siblings of these death students are being introduced to the subject by means of "value-clarification" activities. They draw pictures of what friends or parents would remember about them should they die, or of something they "feel very strongly" about, and would be "willing to give your life" for; they ponder burial and cremation, life after death, and donating their bodies to science; they try out games of multiple choice: I would rather be (a) a hangman, (b) a member of a firing squad, (c) an electrocutioner in a prison; and then after milk and cookies they play fallout shelter: twelve people are trying to get in, there's only room for six, you must decide which, and why.

At the college level, of course, opportunities for serious study abound. I have no doubt you may now major in death through any number of disciplines, and I suppose it's quite possible that death might go interdepartmental and have an academic region all its own. (This has probably already happened. It's an odd feature of the age we live in that most of the things you think are going to happen any day now have been with us for a while already.)

Once out of school, the student may pursue his interest in death into a variety of professions. If he is a doctor, psychologist, social worker, or the like, he may devote his attentions to the dying, the terminally ill, the aged, and/or the families of any of these. If he is a journalist, he will find editors eagerly responsive to new angles on the subject—or fresh turnings on old angles. If he is a photographer or film-maker, galleries will exhibit, publishers will print, and TV networks will air his pictorial musings on the dying. As a researcher, he will be smiled on by the foundations. As a lecturer, he will pack the halls. In other words, death is now the headliner on the culture and pop-culture circuit.

There are also those who stand to benefit from this outpouring of interest—the old, the incurably diseased of all ages. Here, it seems, where the person is most vulnerable, the enterprise becomes least optional. How many, *in extremis,* could resist these blandishments of attention? The question of what other possibilities of the experience of aging and dying are being violated or obliterated to make room for the consolations of enlightenment is not likely to be pondered—certainly not by the dedicated light-engineers themselves, and not often by the possibly light-exhausted subjects.

We might, at this point, ask some general questions about this burgeoning movement—clearly, however extensive it has already become, it is still a massive growth industry on all fronts. While any movement so large will of course encompass a variety of points of view and considerable divergence of opinion on key issues, nevertheless certain fundamental assumptions may be identified that provide a sense of fellowship and a shared momentum.

What do all these scientists, artists, educators, engineers, philosophers hold in common? First, that death is serious and important; second, that it poses a problem for man; third, that serious and important problems can and should be confronted frontally, so to speak, with every human resource available.

With point one it is difficult to disagree. Point two, the identification of death as a *problem,* with that term's implication of a *solution,* is trickier, more dubious, and leads directly to the simple-mindedness of point three. This idea, that all problems, human and otherwise, must submit to direct assault, is hardly a stranger to the modern temper. It might even be said that this perfectly ordinary notion constitutes the central failure of intelligence in our times. It represents intelligence in the act of doing itself in. The first decision intelligence must make is what to think about, then it must choose a mode of inquiry that does not damage or distort the thing being thought about. Physicists, in particular, seem to be more alert on this point than others, having interested themselves for some time in how the act of investigating alters the thing under investigation.

Social scientists, on the whole, seem never to have given the matter a thought. Occasionally someone will mention the possibility that TV news cameras create as much news as they report. And that's about it. The notion that thinking requires discretion—that big things (truth, love, sex, death) and big ideas (truth, love, sex, death) are as fragile as they are powerful, as subject to mutilation as to clarification—this notion doesn't have a lot of currency. For one thing, it would impose serious restraints on our modern determination to mastery of our world and condition—if not by force, by understanding. There must be no secrets, nothing withheld. No aspect of life or experience shall be closed to the prideful probings of the inflated modern will, which claims unlimited privilege over all of existence. Much of the energy of this will goes into exploring and dispelling the ineffable human mysteries—whose dark presence has always been a reminder to man of his majesty as well as his limitations—in the mistaken conceit that everything human will, and should, yield its secrets if exposed to the proper illumination.

Consider, for example, sex, whose emancipation from traditional meaning and constraint is one of the great success stories of our time.

Sex is both an act and a gesture. As a gesture, it is the mightiest symbol we ever had for the mystery of human relation. That is, it *was*—before the sexologists hauled it out of its protective darkness and into the laboratory spotlight, where they worked it over with calipers and litmus paper and rubber gloves. If Masters and Johnson[2] had been better students of Goethe, all this might have been avoided. Goethe long ago warned us on this point. As Erich Heller puts it: "His [Goethe's] science, like his poetry, is founded on the conviction—self-evident to him—that man, if only he exercises *all* his faculties of understanding, is, as he says, 'adequately equipped' to know what he is meant to know about life, without having to put 'nature on the rack'; for there, he says, she remains silent." (I suppose we must stop charging it all up to Masters and Johnson, as though they actually made the mountain they have so boldly scaled in the service of science and the good life. Procedures they invented, yes; they devised new gear. But the path was laid out before them. They had only to seize the *Zeitgeist*[3] by the throat and make their mad dash for the summit.) In any case, sex, too, is now silent on the rack. But with all the click-clack of instruments, and the hum of a busy lab, no one has noticed that.

Now it is death's turn to be hounded out of the shadows and into—not the laboratory but the living room, where it will settle in as a familiar presence, embodied, perhaps, by a dying friend or relative, and invoked by regular family discussion. The procedures used to demystify death will differ somewhat from those applied to sex, of course. But there is a common motive behind both enterprises—to bring these vast "problems" under the control of the will.

It is generally recognized, of course, that death itself cannot be counted on to respond to such maneuvers, and so the will focuses instead on two related areas: dying and the fear of death.

About dying I will have more to say shortly. The fear of death is a prominent issue in this new movement. The most concentrated and simpleminded effort to give ontological distinction to the fear of death is Ernest Becker's *The Denial of Death*, which received the Pulitzer Prize in 1974. Character formation, schizophrenia, depression, neurosis are all seen as creative efforts to contend with mortality "gone astray." Since the advent of psychoanalysis as a science, in which Freud overruled the traditional prime mover—which was, of course, the individual will—every new school

---

[2] William H. Masters and Virginia E. Johnson, authors of a widely read study of sexuality in men and women.—Eds.

[3] The spirit of the times (German).—Eds.

of psychology has had to smuggle in a substitute for the will. Freud's own prime mover was libido, Jung's the racial unconscious, Harry Stack Sullivan's anxiety; other doctrines have stressed aggression, dependence, power, sado-masochism, inferiority, and so on. Now comes Becker with the "fear of death"—and it functions in exactly the same way, and shares with these other substitutes for responsible individual will the reduction of thought and action to unconscious motive. Becker sees the fear of death as the molder of character; he sees all inspirations, ambitions, and enterprises as efforts to refute death's imperative. Not everyone would follow Becker to this bitter end, but most practitioners of the new thanatology in all its forms appear to believe that the fear of death is a central concern in the course and conduct of our lives.

For myself, I am not so sure. I do not doubt that it is present from time to time. Certainly during life-threatening illnesses and disabilities. And, I believe with Martin Buber,[4] when one is in the grip of guilt. "Here," says Buber, "there rules the one penetrating insight—the one insight capable of penetrating into the impossibility of recovering the original point of departure and the irreparability of what has been done, and that means the real insight into the irreversibility of lived time, a fact that shows itself unmistakably in the starkest of all human perspectives, that concerning one's own death. From no standpoint is time so perceived as a torrent as from the vision of the self in guilt."

In addition, I think death may be feared occasionally in maturity when life seems to have been unlived, when death would be seen as premature.

Presumably, and according to received current doctrine, the threat of death in the form of a seriously disabling illness should seriously alter one's life. In an article in the *New York Times*, the late psychologist, Abraham Maslow, following a heart attack, referred to his life thereafter as his "postmortem life." "Everything," he wrote, "gets doubly precious. You get stabbed by the very act of living, of walking and breathing and eating and having friends. Every single moment of every day is transformed." I knew Dr. Maslow slightly, and my memory of our few conversations is that he was easily given to such operatic overstatements. I recall a similar rhapsody of his over my wife's pregnancy and the excitement of childbirth that lay ahead for her. Let us remember, after all, he was the person responsible for such expressions as "self-actualization" and "peak moments." I am suggesting that far from being "transformed" by his coronary attack, he instead assimilated that harsh event to fit his customary hyperbolic style.

My own first brush with possibly terminal illness was during medical school when a mole that was removed from my leg was diagnosed as melanoma. I will omit the medical details of exploration and diagnosis because they do not bear on the issue. Suffice it to say that I was convinced

---

[4] Theologian and philosopher. See "Notes on Authors" at the end of this book. —EDS.

by all concerned that my chances of survival were, at best, problematical. I recall keenly my realization that my situation was very possibly tragic. I looked at myself in the mirror and thought, "My God, you're too young to die!" And crossing to the window, "If you have only a brief time left, shouldn't you squeeze every drop from the life remaining to you?" Embarrassed by my address to myself in the second person, even after turning away from the mirror, I sought a more dignified way of contending with this poignant moment. Now in the first person, I thought, "Why should I go on with medical school, when I have little chance of surviving to practice as a doctor? There must be another way for me to heighten my remaining time on this earth." Travel? (No money.) Disappear? (No money.) Write a novel? (Too hard, might as well go to medical school.) Nothing both dramatic and feasible occurred to me. Meanwhile the days went by and I continued to attend my classes—if only because I couldn't think of anything better to do. It became increasingly difficult to focus on my tragedy because my studies required a degree of concentration that didn't seem to allow for the kind of posturing I thought fitting. Occasionally when fellow students talked of narrow escapes, I would trot out my own story, which for a while easily took the prize in such competitions. By the time the insurance companies decided I had re-earned my right to be a proper risk, I had worn my confession out, or it had worn me out.

My second brush with death was more recent. That posturing of my youth still remains a possibility. There are times when I am struck once again by the thought that I may fall dead at any moment—even now. And I think of my family, whom I do not wish to leave behind. What happens to these sorrowful reveries? I don't know. I suppose they give way to the exigencies and claims of my ongoing life, so that, as in my youth, I continue, one might say, to attend my classes. There are other times when, I must confess, what I want most is to leave my family behind. Death then seems like a vacation.

I have mentioned these encounters with the image of my own death to suggest that each of us will have something specific, personal, and unique to say about the fear of death. Life serves up different conditions and lays different claims on all of us in every way—why should this not be true as well of our relation to our own death? Some people appear to be death-haunted throughout their lives—sometimes by circumstance, sometimes by inner necessity, sometimes by choice. Others seem to be, again for varying reasons, relatively untouched by a concern with death. For still others—for most of us, I would guess—images of death come and go as the outer or inner weather determines, and we make of them what we will, and we deal with them as we can. Who is to say that these various—and fluid—responses to the shifting issue and image of death are not, by and large, appropriate? Who is to say that there is not perhaps some wisdom in the unwilled waxing and waning of interest in—or fear of—death, experienced in the course of life by most of us? The new thanatologists, that's who. They are busy calling us to order across the land, exhorting us to put aside our timidity, to rise up from our indolence and get down to the business of doing business with death.

What is it that they want from us? Or, we may ask, what is it they want to do for us? Their aim would appear to be twofold. First, they hope to familiarize us with death so that we may contemplate and, when the time comes, face our own deaths and those of our loved ones with acceptance and calm. Two obvious assumptions operate here: one, we are all destructively afraid of death (that is, we all *need* to be cured of the fear of death); and two, we *can be cured* (that is, death need not be frightening). I'm sure it will come as no surprise if I say that both these assumptions—in the broad diagnostic and prescriptive way they are embraced—strike me as questionable.

The second aim of the death counselors concerns the appreciation of life. In order that we may value our precious gift of life more intensely, they urge us to focus on it from the perspective of death. Again, I think there is something questionable about this project; I suspect that the kind of enhancement of the present moment that is produced by this eerie backlighting is not without its hazards. Every moment doubly precious? Not a few just singly precious? And some not so precious? And none at all pure dross? I fear this sort of enhancement works at the expense of discrimination, and in the absence of discrimination experience is flattened—the high intensity level merely renders this flattening more grotesque—and is, thus, inflated and reduced at the same time.

Life, in full ordinariness, provides a rich variety of conditions and occasions for questions of meaning to arise. The meanings that reveal themselves in response to this sort of questioning will be particular and specific. They will emerge out of the immediate ground of living and will in turn nourish that ground. A death perspective, with its wholesale poignancy, cherishing everything temporal, therefore cherishing everything, will swallow up these meanings in an all-purpose "significance" which, valuing everything, cheapens all.

The issue of death also serves a rhetorical function which is not without its attractions both to the theorist and to the person absorbed by the question. For the theorist to invoke death is to announce that he is talking about serious and profound matters. What could be more serious than death? The subject carries more weight than the notion that all is vanity. Similarly for me. If I fall to brooding about my finitude as a mortal, in a mood of apprehension or despondency, I am resorting to an overblown, even hysterical, device for evading the claims of this moment in favor of the claims of eternity. My participation in the moment may require some examination of my duties or my limitations, some act or gesture of a particular, specific nature; my participation in eternity requires merely that I die, and my awe in the face of that injunction can, if I choose to be overwhelmed by it, quite drive out of mind my immediate responsibilities —as writer, psychologist, mate, parent.

In an article in the University of Chicago *Magazine* (Spring 1976), entitled "Courage, Creativity, and Enhancement of Life" and subtitled "Development Value of Fear of Death," Professor Salvatore R. Maddi states that injury and illness are not the only opportunities life affords to come to terms with death. There are milder events which "constitute confrontations with death, if properly understood." For example, "Whenever something ends that you did not want to end (e.g., someone stops loving you while you still love them), or whenever you are overwhelmed by the insufficiency of time and energy to do all you sincerely wish to do, . . . or whenever events are monotonous. . . ." The experience "that things are beyond one's control" or "whenever your conventional values are contradicted by events, . . . when virtue is not rewarded (e.g., a valued colleague who has made a sincere commitment to teaching does not receive tenure), when a situation turns out not to be what it seemed (e.g., it becomes apparent that you are loved for your money, not your personality [drop dead, Rockefellers])," even when "a President acts in an un-American fashion"—all these are "small confrontations with death." In other words, frustration of one's will, disappointment, failure. Professor Maddi summarizes:

> It is important to recognize that unwanted endings, insufficiency of time and energy, monotony, and disproved ideals, though milder than the direct physical threat of death, are similar to it in demonstrating the real fact of our limited control over events, and the naïveté of the conventional values we are all educated to and fall into so easily. In this, such events are legitimate reminders of physical death because they directly threaten psychological death, that chronic state of meaninglessness and powerlessness that I have elsewhere called existential sickness.

His conclusion is not the modest one that one learns from failure. Rather it is that in order to learn from failure one must confront death, if not actually, then metaphorically. The end is a happy one: ". . . frequent experience of small (and for that matter actual) threats of death can have positive developmental value. . . . The person will perceive life as challenging, and find his satisfaction in being equal to the task. . . ."

To some extent, the problem is one of language. Note that terms like loss of control, monotony, powerlessness, even meaninglessness, express varying types of discomfort belonging to life—as if anything short of the full life, whatever that may be, is not merely a reminder of the limitations of mortality, but a "small confrontation with death."

A problem of language? What is served by calling all manner of unhappiness a "confrontation with death"? On the one hand, unhappiness of whatever nature is inflated by such metaphorical shoddiness into the ultimate infringement of life—namely death itself. On the other hand, such inflated rhetoric quite obscures the specific misfortune with its particular measure of guilt, responsibility, and so on. Thus, again, "death" both inflates and reduces.

While I have been chiding the theorists and practitioners in this new field of thanatology for insisting on an immersion in the subject of death that seems to me of doubtful merit, I wish also to point out that this movement—for all that it owes to the blasphemies and excesses of the modern will—did not spring uncaused upon the cultural scene. Surely it was inspired by a situation—particularly, if not exclusively, in America—in which death had been ruled out of existence. The dying were isolated in terminal wards in hospitals, doctors and nurses lied to them; many of them no doubt were (as David Hendin, in his book, *Death as a Fact of Life,* claims) brutalized by the insistent implorings of their families that they recover; and survivors were surely crippled in their efforts to deal with their grief and loss by their refusal to foresee and face the reality of death. Once death occurred, the morticians took over, and bodies were got up in fancy dress to resemble peaceful sleepers for the funeral. In effect, dying was denied to the dying, and death to the dead.

Jessica Mitford was one of the first to sound the alarm in response to these absurdities. In *The American Way of Death,* published in 1963, she focused on the aesthetic and economic grip the morticians held on death. For extravagant prices the funeral home offered a small-scale production of last rites: casket, music, limousines, and artful embalming which, with the help of cosmetics, putty, etc., offered a "lifelike" representation of the deceased. For the moment of the funeral the ravages of decay were disguised, so that the bereaved relatives and friends could see that death was merely a form of sleep in which the dead relative slid painlessly into a different kingdom, with no trace of decomposition to disturb the illusion.

A few years ago I passed by my father's casket, opened for the mourners, and looked briefly at a peculiar dummy I knew was meant to be my father. However splendid the morticians's art may have been, the illusion of life did not capture me. Instead I glimpsed—as briefly as possible—a cadaver painted up to resemble the man I had known. The effect was more macabre than that of the shrunken, bloated cadaver I dissected in medical school. After the services, as my mother and I were walking away, a special hoisting machine began to lift the casket and lower it into the grave. Glancing back at this operation, I saw that the casket was slipping off the machine, the lid falling open. My glance cannot have lasted more than a few seconds, yet the whole scene appeared to me in slow motion: the casket plunging into the grave and my father's poor prettified mummy falling out of its enclosure so that it landed on its head, the neck twisting awry. A glance was enough; I knew the crew would have no trouble stuffing the remains back into the box. I may have underestimated my mother, but I thought she could do without this vision, so

I quickly engaged her in conversation about who would share our limousine until we had put the scene well behind us. No doubt the funeral director was chagrined at this collapse of his enterprise, but he offered no rebate. Nor did I ask for one. Obviously the memory has remained with me—more for certain cinematic features than for any enlightenment on the death of my father. Similarly, the memory of that rouged creature stays with me, but it stays separate from my memories of his life and death.

He died quickly of a heart attack at a ripe old age. Had he died, as my younger brother did, a lingering death, his pain and our pain would have been prolonged, but I do not know that our talk and ruminations in the manner now prescribed would have left us any wiser. Although his death was only a few years ago, it still occurred in the days before our new death doctrines had taken hold. Now that hardly a week goes by that I am not exposed to a new publication from the field of thanatology, I wonder how it would have been today, particularly if this dying had been protracted. Would he have been visited by the staff psychiatrist, fresh from a special course in counseling the dying, and urged to join a group for terminal patients, and would the family have been advised of a group for the relatives of the dying? Would we all have been supplied with the standard texts in the field, and given special "hot-line" phone numbers to use in case difficulties arose? Would his grandchildren, fresh from their values-clarification projects and high-school seminars, have come to the bedside full of stimulating questions? Perhaps one of them might have done a special project just on him—a live one in the bag, so to speak.

Becoming an American had demanded so many adjustments for him, some painful, against the grain, so that his life in Russia became more difficult to recapture. And now at the end there would be further instructions about the stages he was to go through as he died. He would, I imagine, have raised no noisy opposition to this final phase of his Americanization. Would he have been scolded for his docility, for his failure to go through Elisabeth Kübler-Ross's celebrated stages of denial, anger, bargaining, depression, and, finally, acceptance, or would one of the young thanatologists have argued for his maturity in so quickly accepting his fate? I think, regardless of how bizarre all this might have sounded to him, he would have liked being told he was a good patient, if that was how he understood the young man congratulating him on achieving acceptance so readily. I doubt that he would have made much of Kübler-Ross's pronouncement: "The stages of dying are not really about dying but the way we come to grips with the crisis of loss, any loss—you cannot possibly be afraid." At this, I imagine, he would have figuratively shrugged his shoulders and wondered why he shouldn't be afraid of death—if not death, what? Clearly, there was no end to the difficulties of becoming an American. Perhaps he would have contrasted his state with that of his son, who went out in a towering rage, and I think he might have envied the vigor of his son's departure.

We both know and do not know that we will die. We believe that we will and we believe that we won't. Both these beliefs are true, for each belongs to a separate mode of consciousness.

On the one hand, we can hardly withhold our assent to the general truth of Socrates' proposition: all men are mortal, I am a man, therefore I am mortal. If you ask me whether I shall die someday, I will answer, Indeed I shall, possibly even someday soon, though of course I hope not. I answer thus because, in addition to being mortal, I am also rational, even, on occasion, reasonable, and I can figure out the syllogisms on the wall as well as the next man. In this sense I "know" I will die, and this "knowledge" is always available to my consciousness, though it is certainly not always present. Your question will invoke it, so may a passage in a book, an unexpected turn of experience, a visiting memory. My acknowledgment of this "knowledge" may be perfunctory and detached, or it may be accompanied by any of a variety of feelings—dismay, terror, rage, awe, grief, calm. I must admit this "knowledge" into consciousness whenever something causes me to raise my head above the present moment, so to speak, to conceive of the interpenetration of my life and times as a linear event, beginning at my birth, threading through my successive days and years, ending at my death, an image of which I must, in this moment, include in my vision of my life. To some degree this vision, with its harsh imperatives, removes me from the present moment—or drains some of the present out of me. It may, of course, feed back into the present a poignancy, a condition of urgency it previously lacked. This is the famous "enhancement of life" that a cultivation of awareness of death does indeed provide—but not, as we have seen, without penalty.

On the other hand, there is much experience of the present in which my "knowledge" of death plays little or no part. This experience has to do with my acceptance of a cyclical principle operating in my life. Evidence abounds. My body belongs to nature and participates in its recurring rhythms. Days arrive one after another, and to some degree routine repeats itself. Weeks, months, years unfold in this manner. Changes occur, with their indications of development or decay; some projects prosper, some falter. But the images and reminders of renewal and repetition that constitute a natural portion of my awareness tend to persuade me that fatigue will yield to rest, and darkness—of day or spirit—to light; they persuade me that I am a creature who obeys the seasonal principle on a multitude of levels, that I am a renewing and enduring being.

I am not suggesting that this "knowledge" of endurance stands as a contradiction to my other "knowledge"—of my mortality. In the light of the latter, all my seasonal comings and goings fall into place on the birth-death continuum, and all directions in my life fold into a single arrow pointing to the end. But with this "knowledge" of mortality in abeyance, the other truth emerges: my life has been full of directions, they have led to and away from a variety of places, they have not—as I experienced them

—all been pointing along the one line that points to death. From one point of view my life is a single vector in time, but that is not the point of view which informs most of my experience of it. My ordinary pursuit of the present does not constitute an orderly march down the corridor of past-future; it is more like a rummaging in time, to light—or lighten—the one ever-changing moment that is always in part, where I am. It is in this —mood, if you will, that I understand not that death has no claim on me, but that its claim is limited. If death is the great Other, which will fall across my life and extinguish it when it will, then my life is Other to that Other, and knows it not. My life will yield to death, but is not aimed at it.

Of course, if this is all I know about death, I am at best a fool, at worst a menace to myself and others. If I begin to believe that because there is truth in forgetting about death, then there is no death, my life is in some trouble. As David T. Bazelon has said, "Death means the score is real." If I succeed in forgetting about death to the point where the score appears unreal—something we all do from time to time—my life will become a shallow, trivial undertaking. On the other hand, if I refuse to forget death for a moment, if I insist on playing the whole game right under the big shadow, the score will be at least inflated—which is another version of the unreal.

I have said that we both believe and do not believe that we are going to die, and that both beliefs are true. Not only are they both true, they are both necessary. They move around each other freely in our minds, now far apart, now nearly touching. Thanks to the freedom of this give-and-take, thanks to our trust in both truths, the moment we are in—which is all we are ever in—is not imprisoned in the present, nor is it imprisoned in eternity. It remains open and responsive to whatever depth and complexity of meaning we, in our deep and complicated humanness, are able to discover—or provide.

Meditation XVII[1]

JOHN DONNE

Nunc lento sonitu dicunt, morieris[2]

Perchance he for whom this bell tolls may be so ill as that he knows not it tolls for him; and perchance I may think myself so much better than I am as that they who are about me and see my state may

---

[1] From *Devotions upon Emergent Occasions* by John Donne (London, 1624).
[2] Now this bell tolling softly says, you must die.

have caused it to toll for me, and I know not that. The church is catholic, universal, so are all her actions; all that she does belongs to all. When she baptizes a child, that action concerns me; for that child is thereby connected to that body which is my head too and ingrafted into that body whereof I am a member. And when she buries a man, that action concerns me. All mankind is of one author, and is one volume; when one man dies, one chapter is not torn out of the book, but translated into a better language; and every chapter must be so translated. God employs several translators; some pieces are translated by age, some by sickness, some by war, some by justice; but God's hand is in every translation, and his hand shall bind up all our scattered leaves again for that library where every book shall lie open to one another. As therefore the bell that rings to a sermon calls not upon the preacher only but upon the congregation to come, so this bell calls us all; but how much more me who am brought so near the door by this sickness! There was a contention as far as a suit— in which piety and dignity, religion and estimation, were mingled—which of the religious orders should ring to prayers first in the morning; and it was determined that they should ring first that rose earliest. If we understand aright the dignity of this bell that tolls for our evening prayer, we would be glad to make it ours by rising early, in that application, that it might be ours as well as his, whose indeed it is. The bell doth toll for him that thinks it doth; and though it intermit again, yet from that minute that that occasion wrought upon him he is united to God. Who casts not up his eye to the sun when it rises? but who takes off his eye for a comet when that breaks out? Who bends not his ear to any bell which upon any occasion rings? but who can remove it from that bell which is passing a piece of himself out of this world? No man is an island entire of itself; every man is a piece of the continent, a part of the main. If a clod be washed away by the sea, Europe is the less, as well as if a promontory were, as well as if a manor of thy friend's or of thine own were. Any man's death diminishes me, because I am involved in mankind, and therefore never send to know for whom the bell tolls; it tolls for thee. Neither can we call this a begging of misery or a borrowing of misery, as though we were not miserable enough of ourselves but must fetch in more from the next house, in taking upon us the misery of our neighbors. Truly it were an excusable covetousness if we did, for affliction is a treasure, and scarce any man hath enough of it. No man hath affliction enough that is not matured and ripened by it and made fit for God by that affliction. If a man carry treasure in bullion or in a wedge of gold and have none coined into current money, his treasure will not defray him as he travels. Tribulation is treasure in the nature of it, but it is not current money in the use of it, except we get nearer and nearer our home, heaven, by it. Another man may be sick too, and sick to death, and this affliction may lie in his bowels as gold in a mine and be of no use to him; but this bell that tells me of his affliction digs out and applies that gold to me, if by this consideration of another's danger I take mine own into contemplation and so secure myself by making my recourse to my God, who is our only security.

Because I Could Not Stop for Death
EMILY DICKINSON

Because I could not stop for Death—
He kindly stopped for me—
The Carriage held but just Ourselves—
And Immortality.

We slowly drove—He knew no haste
And I had put away
My labor and my leisure too,
For His Civility—

We passed the School, where Children strove
At Recess—in the Ring—
We passed the Fields of Gazing Grain—
We passed the Setting Sun—

Or rather—He passed Us—
The Dews drew quivering and chill—
For only Gossamer, my Gown—
My Tippet—only Tulle—

We paused before a House that seemed
A Swelling of the Ground—
The Roof was scarcely visible—
The Cornice—in the Ground—

Since then—'tis Centuries—and yet
Feels shorter than the Day
I first surmised the Horses Heads
Were toward Eternity—

What Is Happiness?

What Is Happiness?
WILLIAM V. SHANNON

In the Declaration of Independence, Thomas Jefferson proclaimed "the pursuit of happiness" as one of man's unalienable rights. This has become a famous but much misunderstood phrase.

In their new book, *The American Testament,* William Gorman and his colleague Mortimer Adler, long known for their work in editing and teaching the "Great Books" program, have written a close, textual analysis of three great state papers, the Declaration of Independence, the Preamble to the Constitution, and the Gettysburg Address. This lean, carefully reasoned work is the most intellectually nourishing book of this Bicentennial year.

The authors point out that when Jefferson wrote of happiness, his choice of words was no accident. Previously, the common term in the 17th and 18th centuries among liberal philosophers was "property." Thus, John Locke regularly wrote of "life, liberty and property" as man's basic rights.

Jefferson was not opposed to private property—he owned a lot of it himself—but as a philosopher, he wanted his declaration to have a universal relevance and he recognized that man could be happy without property. Property is only secondary and incidental in the pursuit of happiness.

When he used the word happiness, Jefferson had in mind something nobler and more difficult than mere pleasure-getting or status seeking. He wrote in terms of the traditional philosophical conception of happiness deriving from the ancient Greeks. Happiness is "a life well lived or a good life as a whole."

True happiness depends upon the possession of moral values that are normally within an individual's power to acquire. "If he fails to acquire them, he alone is to blame. No organized society or instituted government can confer moral virtue upon him or make him a man of good moral character," Messrs. Gorman and Adler observe.

If the attainment of happiness depends on a person's interior moral disposition, it follows that society or government can do no more than provide the external conditions that facilitate each person's pursuit of happiness.

But how, we might ask, can government assist everybody's pursuit since happiness consists in what each individual wants and what you want may conflict with what I want?

The answer is that, contrary to the current belief, the pursuit of happiness is not the equivalent of today's popular expression: "Let everybody do his own thing." Happiness is not the fulfillment of the lecher's insatiable lust nor the robber baron's greed. This is why we instinctively recoil from Hugh Hefner's empty Playboy "Philosophy" and from the mental picture of Robert Vesco or Howard Hughes hiding out in some Caribbean country with his bodyguards and his untold millions.

Nor is political revolution the sure answer. From the prison camps of the Soviet Union, hero victims daily teach us how false is the Marxist notion that human happiness can be assured by reorganizing class and property relationships on a socialist basis. Alas, the good life, the happy life, is not so easily achieved.

Each of us has to realize his own potentialities and cope with the special circumstances of his own life. In a more fundamental sense, however, as the authors of *The American Testament* stress, the goal each of us is striving to achieve—the good human life—"is not distinctly individual but humanly common."

"The happy or good life is essentially the same for all human beings. Whatever things are really good for any human being are really good for all other human beings; and so if happiness consists in a life enriched by all the things that are really good for a man, happiness is the same for all men."

If we think of happiness in its common human dimensions rather than as an adventure in individual selfishness, the limited things government can do to promote happiness become clear. They are well stated in the Preamble to the Constitution—"establish justice, insure domestic tranquility, provide for the common defense, promote the general welfare, and secure the blessings of liberty."

Within this social framework, happiness depends upon the practice of moral virtues. If we have children, are we prepared to stay home and see to their upbringing and their moral nurture? If we have aged parents, are we prepared to sacrifice our own pleasures and conveniences to care for them in their declining years as they cared for us in our infancy and early childhood?

Or are we a people eager to abandon our children to day care centers and our elderly to "leisure villages" and nursing homes? If we have marriages and families, are we willing to devote ourselves to them and to their strengthening? Or do we regard the family as the human equivalent of the disposable diaper and the throw-away beer can?

Our liberties as well as our happiness are inseparable from our virtues. Only by our moral performance as a people can we make good on our political promises to ourselves.

Myths of Our Time
L. S. STAVRIANOS

"I am just as convinced as can be," states the geochemist Harrison Brown of the California Institute of Technology, "that man has it within his power today to create a world in which people the world over can lead free and abundant and even creative lives. . . . I am convinced that we can create a world which will pale the Golden Age of Pericles into nothingness."

Very few Americans share this optimism. Unlike our forefathers, we look to the future with apprehension rather than expectation—and this at a time when, as Harrison Brown correctly notes, the human race enjoys unprecedented power and potentiality.

One reason for this paradox is that we have become the prisoners of paralyzing myths. These myths depict various problems as being inherently insoluble, whereas actually they are basically socio-political in nature, and their solutions can and are being found.

Three of the most basic and widespread of these myths have to do with allegedly perverse human nature, allegedly uncontrollable population increase, allegedly malignant technological growth.

Let us take a look at each of these in turn.

The "human nature" myth holds that *Homo sapiens* is a singularly disagreeable creature—selfish, covetous and bellicose. But when we examine the record of our paleolithic ancestors, whose history comprises some 80 percent of total human experience, we find that they were the precise opposite of this "human nature" stereotype. The proof of this is the dramatic discovery in 1971 of the Tasaday—a tribe of twenty-seven Stone Age tribesmen who had been living in complete isolation in southern Mindanao Island of the Philippines for at least six centuries.

Their outstanding characteristic is a complete lack of aggressiveness. They have no words for weapons, hostility, anger or war. They have eagerly adopted the long Filipino knife, the bolo, as it is much superior to their stone tools for gathering food, chopping wood and slashing through jungle growth. But they have rejected the spear and the bow and arrow as inefficient tools for gathering food. And all the food they collect (yams, fruit, berries, flowers, fish, crabs, frogs) they divide equally with scrupulous care among all members of the band.

We may conclude, then, that human beings are not born with an inherited instinct for aggression and selfishness. "Human nature" concludes Prof. Albert Bandura of Stanford University, a psychologist, "is a vast potentiality that can be fashioned by social influences into a variety of forms . . . aggression is not an inevitable or unchangeable aspect of man but a product of aggression-promoting conditions within society."

The second great myth of our times is that population growth is uncontrollable and that the human race is doomed to decimation by mass starvation or war. But again this is a case of perceiving an insoluble Malthusian predicament in a soluble socio-political problem.

In demographic matters, as in others, people act according to their best interests as they perceive them. In societies with gross inequities in income distribution and with little opportunity for social mobility and economic security, parents naturally resort to the only available insurance: a large number of children. Conversely, in more egalitarian societies that offer mass education, social mobility and employment opportunities to women, the number of children per family tends to fall.

Hence the substantial decline of birth rates in Taiwan, Sri Lanka and China, as against the soaring rates in India, Indonesia and South America. Dissemination of birth-control information and devices is not enough. Families must be provided with the *motivation* as well as the *means* to limit births. As soon as this has been done, birth rates in country after country have slowed down and populations have stabilized at manageable levels.

The third myth concerns technology, which is considered a Frankenstein monster that forces human beings to be the servants of soulless machines. But the historical record shows that this simply is not so. Each major technological breakthrough in the past has been accompanied by a corresponding breakthrough in mass assertiveness and participation rather than in mass subjugation and submissiveness.

Aristotle perceived this fact when he stated: "There is only one condition in which we can imagine managers not needing subordinates, and masters not needing slaves. This condition would be that each [inanimate] instrument could do its own work . . . as if a shuttle should weave of itself."

Aristotle's observation points up the trap in which all pre-modern civilizations were caught: Technological backwardness promoted slavery, and slavery perpetuated technological backwardness by reducing incentive for experimentation and invention. The great historic contribution of the West was to spring this trap.

The first Industrial Revolution (a labor-*saving* revolution with its machines and steam power) and the second Industrial Revolution (a labor-*replacing* revolution with its computers and automation) have opened new horizons for mankind everywhere.

They are primarily responsible for the pervasive demand for self-management, as expressed by the movements for women's *lib*, minority rights, student activism and worker control. The current technological revolution, like the earlier ones, is leading not to a new age of the pharaohs but to a new level of humanity—to the transcendence of *Homo sapiens* to *Homo humanus*.

The problems of humankind, despite our popular myths, are not insoluble. They can, and are, being solved by peoples capable of social innovation. Those who oppose such innovation view the future with foreboding, but those who welcome it share the buoyancy of Harrison Brown, and also of Cesar Chavez, leader of the United Farm Workers, who declares: "You know what I really think? I really think that one day the world will be great. I really believe the world gonna be great one day."

O Taste and See
DENISE LEVERTOV

The world is
not with us enough.
O *taste and see*

the subway Bible poster said,
meaning *The Lord*, meaning
if anything all that lives
to the imagination's tongue,

grief, mercy, language,
tangerine, weather, to
breathe them, bite,
savor, chew, swallow, transform

into our flesh our
deaths, crossing the street, plum, quince,
living in the orchard and being

hungry, and plucking
the fruit.

A Really New World
JOSEPH WOOD KRUTCH

Our prophets often describe the "new world" which lies just ahead when atomic power has been harnessed to peaceful uses; when we can travel across space instead of merely through air; or even when the work week has been reduced to twenty-five hours. But there is in actual fact nothing really *new* about this new world. It would be merely one which had taken another step in the direction which many previous steps had taken. New worlds never were and never will be created except by new ideas, or aims, or desires, or convictions. Christianity created a new world and so did the seventeenth century's new faith that a knowledge of the laws of nature could change rapidly and radically mankind's condition. To some slight extent our own age is still part of the new world Christianity created and it is still very much part of the new world which faith in science created. But there will be no newer world as long as there is no idea or ideal newer than that of the seventeenth century.

If we should ever decide that we do want a new world we shall have to find first the faith which could make it. As long as we believe that the only human reality is the human condition there will be no fundamental change in that condition. If we should become convinced again that man has a nature and that the greatest of his needs is to create a condition suited to it, then a really new world might come gradually into being.

"What Is Man?"

Psalm 8: The Strength and Glory of Man

O LORD our Lord,
How excellent *is* thy name in all the earth!
Who hast set thy glory above the heavens.
Out of the mouth of babes and sucklings hast thou ordained strength
Because of thine enemies,
That thou mightest still the enemy and the avenger.
When I consider thy heavens, the work of thy fingers,
The moon and the stars, which thou hast ordained;
What is man, that thou art mindful of him?
And the son of man, that thou visitest him?
For thou hast made him a little lower than the angels,
And hast crowned him with glory and honor.
Thou madest him to have dominion over the works of thy hands;
Thou hast put all *things* under his feet:
All sheep and oxen,
Yea, and the beasts of the field;
The fowl of the air, and the fish of the sea,
And whatsoever passeth through the paths of the seas.
O LORD our Lord,
How excellent *is* thy name in all the earth!

The Stoic Code
MARCUS AURELIUS

Begin the morning by saying to thyself, I shall meet with the busybody, the ungrateful, arrogant, deceitful, envious, unsocial. All these things happen to them by reason of their ignorance of what is good and evil. But I who have seen the nature of the good that it is beautiful, and of the bad that it is ugly, and the nature of him who does wrong, that it is akin to me, not [only] of the same blood or seed, but that it participates in [the same] intelligence and [the same] portion of the divinity, I can neither be injured by any of them, for no one can fix on me what is ugly, nor can I be angry with my kinsman, nor hate him. For we are made for co-operation, like feet, like hands, like eyelids, like the rows of the upper and lower teeth. To act against one another then, is contrary to nature; and it is action against one another to be vexed and to turn away.

2. Whatever this is that I am, it is a little flesh and breath, and the ruling part. Throw away thy books; no longer distract thyself: it is not allowed; but as if thou wast now dying, despise the flesh; it is blood and bones and a network, a contexture of nerves, veins, and arteries. See the breath also, what kind of a thing it is; air, and not always the same, but every moment sent out and again sucked in. The third, then, is the ruling part; consider thus: Thou art an old man; no longer let this be a slave, no longer be pulled by the strings like a puppet to unsocial movements, no longer be either dissatisfied with thy present lot, or shrink from the future.

3. All that is from the gods is full of providence. That which is from fortune is not separated from nature or without an interweaving and involution with the things which are ordered by providence. From thence all things flow; and there is besides necessity, and that which is for the advantage of the whole universe, of which thou art a part. But that is good for every part of nature which the nature of the whole brings, and what serves to maintain this nature. Now the universe is preserved, as by the changes of the elements so by the changes of things compounded of the elements. Let these principles be enough for thee; let them always be fixed opinions. But cast away the thirst after books, that thou mayest not die murmuring, but cheerfully, truly, and from thy heart thankful to the gods.

4. Remember how long thou hast been putting off these things, and how often thou hast received opportunity from the gods, and yet dost not use it. Thou must now at last perceive of what universe thou art a part, and of what administrator of the universe thy existence is an efflux, and that a limit of time is fixed for thee, which if thou dost not use for clearing away the clouds from thy mind, it will go and thou wilt go, and it will never return.

5. Every moment think steadily as a Roman and a man to do what thou hast in hand with perfect and simple dignity, and feeling of affection, and freedom, and justice, and to give thyself relief from all other thoughts. And thou wilt give thyself relief if thou doest every act of thy life as if it were the last, laying aside all carelessness and passionate aversion from the commands of reason, and all hypocrisy, and self-love, and discontent with the portion which has been given to thee. Thou seest how few the things are, the which if a man lays hold of, he is able to live a life which flows in quiet, and is like the existence of the gods; for the gods on their part will require nothing more from him who observes these things.

6. Do wrong to thyself, do wrong to thyself, my soul; but thou wilt no longer have the opportunity of honoring thyself. Every man's life is sufficient. But thine is nearly finished, though thy soul reverences not itself, but places thy felicity in the souls of others.

7. Do the things external which fall upon thee distract thee? Give thyself time to learn something new and good, and cease to be whirled around. But then thou must also avoid being carried about the other way; for those too are triflers who have wearied themselves in life by their activity, and yet have no object to which to direct every movement, and, in a word, all their thoughts.

8. Through not observing what is in the mind of another a man has seldom been seen to be unhappy; but those who do not observe the movements of their own minds must of necessity be unhappy.

9. This thou must always bear in mind, what is the nature of the whole, and what is my nature, and how this is related to that, and what kind of a part it is of what kind of a whole, and that there is no one who hinders thee from always doing and saying the things which are according to the nature of which thou art a part.

10. Theophrastus,[1] in his comparison of bad acts—such as a comparison as one would make in accordance with the common notions of mankind—says, like a true philosopher, that the offences which are committed through desire are more blamable than those which are committed through anger. For he who is excited by anger seems to turn away from reason with a certain pain and unconscious contraction; but he who offends through desire, being overpowered by pleasure, seems to be in a manner more intemperate and more womanish in his offences. Rightly, then, and in a way worthy of philosophy, he said that the offence which is committed with pleasure is more blamable than that which is committed with pain; and on the whole the one is more like a person who has been first wronged and through pain is compelled to be angry; but the other is moved by his own impulse to do wrong, being carried towards doing something by desire.

11. Since it is possible that thou mayest depart from life this very moment, regulate every act and thought accordingly. But to go away from among men, if there are gods, is not a thing to be afraid of, for the gods will not involve thee in evil; but if indeed they do not exist, or if they have no concern about human affairs, what is it to me to live in a universe devoid of gods or devoid of providence? But in truth they do exist, and they do care for human things, and they have put all the means in man's power to enable him not to fall into real evils. And as to the rest, if there was anything evil, they would have provided for this also, that it should be altogether in a man's power not to fall into it. Now that which does not make a man worse, how can it make a man's life worse? But neither through ignorance, nor having the knowledge but not the power to guard against or correct these things, is it possible that the nature of the universe has overlooked them; nor is it possible that it has made so great a mistake, either through want of power or want of

---

[1] Greek philosopher (*c.* 371–287 B.C.), leader of the Peripatetic School of philosophy; successor to Aristotle.—EDS.

skill, that good and evil should happen indiscriminately to the good and the bad. But death certainly, and life, honor and dishonor, pain and pleasure,—all these things equally happen to good men and bad, being things which make us neither better nor worse. Therefore they are neither good nor evil.

12. How quickly all things disappear,—in the universe the bodies themselves, but in time the remembrance of them. What is the nature of all sensible things, and particularly those which attract with the bait of pleasure or terrify by pain, or are noised abroad by vapory fame; how worthless, and contemptible, and sordid, and perishable, and dead they are, —all this it is the part of the intellectual faculty to observe. To observe too who these are whose opinions and voices give reputation; what death is and the fact that, if a man looks at it in itself, and by the abstractive power of reflection resolves into their parts all the things which present themselves to the imagination in it, he will then consider it to be nothing else than an operation of nature; and if any one is afraid of an operation of nature, he is a child. This, however, is not only an operation of nature, but it is also a thing which conduces to the purposes of nature. To observe too how man comes near to the Deity, and by what part of him, and when this part of man is so disposed.

13. Nothing is more wretched than a man who traverses everything in a round, and pries into the thing beneath the earth, as the poet says, and seeks by conjecture what is in the minds of his neighbors, without perceiving that it is sufficient to attend to the daemon[2] within him, and to reverence it sincerely. And reverence of the daemon consists in keeping it pure from passion and thoughtlessness, and dissatisfaction with what comes from gods and men. For the things from the gods merit veneration for their excellence; and the things from men should be dear to us by reason of kinship; and sometimes even, in a manner, they move our pity by reason of men's ignorance of good and bad; this defect being not less than that which deprives us of the power of distinguishing things that are white and black.

14. Though thou shouldest be going to live three thousand years, and as many times ten thousand years, still remember that no man loses any other life than this which he now lives, nor lives any other than this which he now loses. The longest and shortest are thus brought to the same. For the present is the same to all, though that which perishes is not the same; and so that which is lost appears to be a mere moment. For a man cannot lose either the past or the future: for what a man has not, how can any one take this from him? These two things then thou must bear in mind; the one, that all things from eternity are of like forms and come round in a circle, and that it makes no difference whether a man shall see the same things during a hundred years, or two hundred, or an infinite

---

[2] In Greek mythology, an attendant spirit or genius.—Eds.

time; and the second, that the longest liver and he who will die soonest lose just the same. For the present is the only thing of which a man can be deprived, if it is true that this is the only thing which he has, and that a man cannot lose a thing if he has it not. . . .

16. The soul of man does violence to itself, first of all, when it becomes an abscess, and, as it were, a tumor on the universe, so far as it can. For to be vexed at anything which happens is a separation of ourselves from nature, in some part of which the natures of all other things are contained. In the next place, the soul does violence to itself when it turns away from any man, or even moves towards him with the intention of injuring, such as are the souls of those who are angry. In the third place, the soul does violence to itself when it is overpowered by pleasure or by pain. Fourthly, when it plays a part, and does or says anything insincerely and untruly. Fifthly, when it allows any act of its own and any movement to be without an aim, and does anything thoughtlessly and without considering what it is, it being right that even the smallest things be done with reference to an end; and the end of rational animals is to follow the reason and the law of the most ancient city and polity.

17. Of human life the time is a point, and the substance is in a flux, and the perception dull, and the composition of the whole body subject to putrefaction, and the soul a whirl, and fortune hard to divine, and fame a thing devoid of judgment. And, to say all in a word, everything which belongs to the body is a stream, and what belongs to the soul is a dream and vapor, and life is a warfare and a stranger's sojourn, and after-fame is oblivion. What then is that which is able to conduct a man? One thing, and only one, philosophy. But this consists in keeping the daemon within a man free from violence and unharmed, superior to pains and pleasures, doing nothing without a purpose, not yet falsely and with hypocrisy, not feeling the need of another man's doing or not doing anything; and besides, accepting all that happens, and all that is alloted, as coming from thence, wherever it is, from whence he himself came; and, finally, waiting for death with a cheerful mind, as being nothing else than a dissolution of the elements of which every living being is compounded. But if there is no harm to the elements themselves in each continually changing into another, why should a man have any apprehension about the change and dissolution of all the elements? For it is according to nature, and nothing is evil which is according to nature.

I Corinthians 13: Love
ST. PAUL

If I speak in the tongues of men
and of angels, but have not love,
I am a noisy gong or a clanging cymbal.
And if I have prophetic powers, and
understand all mysteries and all
knowledge, and if I have all faith,
so as to remove mountains, but have
not love, I am nothing. If I give
away all I have, and if I deliver
my body to be burned, but have not
love, I gain nothing.

Love is patient and kind; love is
not jealous or boastful; it is not
arrogant or rude. Love does not
insist on its own way; it is not
irritable or resentful; it does not
rejoice at wrong, but rejoices in
the right. Love bears all things,
believes all things, hopes all things,
endures all things.

Love never ends; as for prophecies,
they will pass away; as for tongues,
they will cease; as for knowledge,
it will pass away. For our knowledge
is imperfect and our prophecy is
imperfect; but when the perfect comes,
the imperfect will pass away. When
I was a child, I spoke like a child,
I thought like a child, I reasoned
like a child; when I became a man,
I gave up childish ways. For now
we see in a mirror dimly, but then
face to face. Now I know in part;
then I shall understand fully, even
as I have been fully understood.
So faith, hope, love abide, these
three; but the greatest of these is
love.

The Lowest Animal[1]
MARK TWAIN

In August, 1572, similar things were occurring in Paris and elsewhere in France. In this case it was Christian against Christian. The Roman Catholics, by previous concert, sprang a surprise upon the unprepared and unsuspecting Protestants, and butchered them by thousands—both sexes and all ages. This was the memorable St. Bartholomew's Day. At Rome the Pope and the Church gave public thanks to God when the happy news came.

During several centuries hundreds of heretics were burned at the stake every year because their religious opinions were not satisfactory to the Roman Church.

In all ages the savages of all lands have made the slaughtering of their neighboring brothers and the enslaving of their women and children the common business of their lives.

Hypocrisy, envy, malice, cruelty, vengefulness, seduction, rape, robbery, swindling, arson, bigamy, adultery, and the oppression and humiliation of the poor and the helpless in all ways have been and still are more or less common among both the civilized and uncivilized peoples of the earth.

For many centuries "the common brotherhood of man" has been urged —on Sundays—and "patriotism" on Sundays and weekdays both. Yet patriotism *contemplates the opposite of a common brotherhood.*

Woman's equality with man has never been conceded by any people, ancient or modern, civilized or savage.

I have been studying the traits and dispositions of the "lower animals" (so-called), and contrasting them with the traits and dispositions of man. I find the result humiliating to me. For it obliges me to renounce my allegiance to the Darwinian theory of the Ascent of Man from the Lower Animals; since it now seems plain to me that that theory ought to be vacated in favor of a new and truer one, this new and truer one to be named the *Descent* of Man from the Higher Animals.

In proceeding toward this unpleasant conclusion I have not guessed or speculated or conjectured, but have used what is commonly called the scientific method. That is to say, I have subjected every postulate that presented itself to the crucial test of actual experiment, and have adopted it or rejected it according to the result. Thus I verified and established each step of my course in its turn before advancing to the next. These experiments were made in the London Zoological Gardens, and covered many months of painstaking and fatiguing work.

[1] This was to have been prefaced by newspaper clippings which, apparently, dealt with religious persecutions in Crete. The clippings have been lost. They probably referred to the Cretan revolt of 1897.

Before particularizing any of the experiments, I wish to state one or two things which seem to more properly belong in this place than further along. This in the interest of clearness. The massed experiments established to my satisfaction certain generalizations, to wit:

1. That the human race is of one distinct species. It exhibits slight variations—in color, stature, mental caliber, and so on—due to climate, environment, and so forth; but it is a species by itself, and not to be confounded with any other.
2. That the quadrupeds are a distinct family, also. This family exhibits variations—in color, size, food preferences and so on; but it is a family by itself.
3. That the other families—the birds, the fishes, the insects, the reptiles, etc.—are more or less distinct, also. They are in the procession. They are links in the chain which stretches down from the higher animals to man at the bottom.

Some of my experiments were quite curious. In the course of my reading I had come across a case where, many years ago, some hunters on our Great Plains organized a buffalo hunt for the entertainment of an English earl—that, and to provide some fresh meat for his larder. They had charming sport. They killed seventy-two of those great animals; and ate part of one of them and left the seventy-one to rot. In order to determine the difference between an anaconda and an earl—if any—I caused seven young calves to be turned into the anaconda's cage. The grateful reptile immediately crushed one of them and swallowed it, then lay back satisfied. It showed no further interest in the calves, and no disposition to harm them. I tried this experiment with other anacondas; always with the same result. The fact stood proven that the difference between an earl and an anaconda is that the earl is cruel and the anaconda isn't; and that the earl wantonly destroys what he has no use for, but the anaconda doesn't. This seemed to suggest that the anaconda was not descended from the earl. It also seemed to suggest that the earl was descended from the anaconda, and had lost a good deal in the transition.

I was aware that many men who have accumulated more millions of money than they can ever use have shown a rabid hunger for more, and have not scrupled to cheat the ignorant and the helpless out of their poor servings in order to partially appease that appetite. I furnished a hundred different kinds of wild and tame animals the opportunity to accumulate vast stores of food, but none of them would do it. The squirrels and bees and certain birds made accumulations, but stopped when they had gathered a winter's supply, and could not be persuaded to add to it either honestly or by chicane. In order to bolster up a tottering reputation the ant pretended to store up supplies, but I was not deceived. I know the ant. These experiments convinced me that there is this difference between man and the higher animals: he is avaricious and miserly, they are not.

In the course of my experiments I convinced myself that among the animals man is the only one that harbors insults and injuries, broods over them, waits till a chance offers, then takes revenge. The passion of revenge is unknown to the higher animals.

Roosters keep harems, but it is by consent of their concubines; therefore no wrong is done. Men keep harems, but it is by brute force, privileged by atrocious laws which the other sex were allowed no hand in making. In this matter man occupies a far lower place than the rooster.

Cats are loose in their morals, but not consciously so. Man, in his descent from the cat, has brought the cat's looseness with him but has left the unconsciousness behind—the saving grace which excuses the cat. The cat is innocent, man is not.

Indecency, vulgarity, obscenity—these are strictly confined to man; he invented them. Among the higher animals there is no trace of them. They hide nothing; they are not ashamed. Man, with his soiled mind, covers himself. He will not even enter a drawing room with his breast and back naked, so alive are he and his mates to indecent suggestion. Man is "The Animal that Laughs." But so does the monkey, as Mr. Darwin pointed out; and so does the Australian bird that is called the laughing jackass. No— Man is the Animal that Blushes. He is the only one that does it—or has occasion to.

At the head of this article we see how "three monks were burnt to death" a few days ago, and a prior "put to death with atrocious cruelty." Do we inquire into the details? No; or we should find out that the prior was subjected to unprintable mutilations. Man—when he is a North American Indian—gouges out his prisoner's eyes; when he is King John, with a nephew to render untroublesome, he uses a red-hot iron; when he is a religious zealot dealing with heretics in the Middle Ages, he skins his captive alive and scatters salt on his back; in the first Richard's time he shuts up a multitude of Jew families in a tower and sets fire to it; in Columbus's time he captures a family of Spanish Jews and—but *that* is not printable; in our day in England a man is fined ten shillings for beating his mother nearly to death with a chair, and another man is fined forty shillings for having four pheasant eggs in his possession without being able to satisfactorily explain how he got them. Of all the animals, man is the only one that is cruel. He is the only one that inflicts pain for the pleasure of doing it. It is a trait that is not known to the higher animals. The cat plays with the frightened mouse; but she has this excuse, that she does not know that the mouse is suffering. The cat is moderate— unhumanly moderate: she only scares the mouse, she does not hurt it; she doesn't dig out its eyes, or tear off its skin, or drive splinters under its nails—man-fashion; when she is done playing with it she makes a sudden meal of it and puts it out of its trouble. Man is the Cruel Animal. He is alone in that distinction.

The higher animals engage in individual fights, but never in organized masses. Man is the only animal that deals in that atrocity of atrocities,

War. He is the only one that gathers his brethren about him and goes forth in cold blood and with calm pulse to exterminate his kind. He is the only animal that for sordid wages will march out, as the Hessians did in our Revolution, and as the boyish Prince Napoleon did in the Zulu war, and help to slaughter strangers of his own species who have done him no harm and with whom he has no quarrel.

Man is the only animal that robs his helpless fellow of his country—takes possession of it and drives him out of it or destroys him. Man has done this in all the ages. There is not an acre of ground on the globe that is in possession of its rightful owner, or that has not been taken away from owner after owner, cycle after cycle, by force and bloodshed.

Man is the only Slave. And he is the only animal who enslaves. He has always been a slave in one form or another, and has always held other slaves in bondage under him in one way or another. In our day he is always some man's slave for wages, and does that man's work; and this slave has other slaves under him for minor wages, and they do *his* work. The higher animals are the only ones who exclusively do their own work and provide their own living.

Man is the only Patriot. He sets himself apart in his own country, under his own flag, and sneers at the other nations, and keeps multitudinous uniformed assassins on hand at heavy expense to grab slices of other people's countries, and keep *them* from grabbing slices of *his*. And in the intervals between campaigns he washes the blood off his hands and works for "the universal brotherhood of man"—with his mouth.

Man is the Religious Animal. He is the only Religious Animal. He is the only animal that has the True Religion—several of them. He is the only animal that loves his neighbor as himself, and cuts his throat if his theology isn't straight. He has made a graveyard of the globe in trying his honest best to smooth his brother's path to happiness and heaven. He was at it in the time of the Caesars, he was at it in Mahomet's time, he was at it in the time of the Inquisition, he was at it in France a couple of centuries, he was at it in England in Mary's day, he has been at it ever since he first saw the light, he is at it today in Crete—as per the telegrams quoted above—he will be at it somewhere else tomorrow. The higher animals have no religion. And we are told that they are going to be left out, in the Hereafter. I wonder why? It seems questionable taste.

Man is the Reasoning Animal. Such is the claim. I think it is open to dispute. Indeed, my experiments have proven to me that he is the Unreasoning Animal. Note his history, as sketched above. It seems plain to me that whatever he is he is *not* a reasoning animal. His record is the fantastic record of a maniac. I consider that the strongest count against his intelligence is the fact that with that record back of him he blandly sets himself up as the head animal of the lot: whereas by his own standards he is the bottom one.

In truth, man is incurably foolish. Simple things which the other animals easily learn, he is incapable of learning. Among my experiments was this. In an hour I taught a cat and a dog to be friends. I put them in a cage. In another hour I taught them to be friends with a rabbit. In the course of two days I was able to add a fox, a goose, a squirrel and some doves. Finally a monkey. They lived together in peace; even affectionately.

Next, in another cage I confined an Irish Catholic from Tipperary, and as soon as he seemed tame I added a Scotch Presbyterian from Aberdeen. Next a Turk from Constantinople; a Greek Christian from Crete; an Armenian; a Methodist from the wilds of Arkansas; a Buddhist from China; a Brahman from Benares. Finally, a Salvation Army Colonel from Wapping. Then I stayed away two whole days. When I came back to note results, the cage of Higher Animals was all right, but in the other there was but a chaos of gory odds and ends of turbans and fezzes and plaids and bones and flesh—not a specimen left alive. These Reasoning Animals had disagreed on a theological detail and carried the matter to a Higher Court.

One is obliged to concede that in true loftiness of character, Man cannot claim to approach even the meanest of the Higher Animals. It is plain that he is constitutionally incapable of approaching that altitude; that he is constitutionally afflicted with a Defect which must make such approach forever impossible, for it is manifest that this defect is permanent in him, indestructible, ineradicable.

I find this Defect to be *the Moral Sense*. He is the only animal that has it. It is the secret of his degradation. It is the quality *which enables him to do wrong*. It has no other office. It is incapable of performing any other function. It could never have been intended to perform any other. Without it, man could do no wrong. He would rise at once to the level of the Higher Animals.

Since the Moral Sense has but the one office, the one capacity—to enable man to do wrong—it is plainly without value to him. It is as valueless to him as is disease. In fact, it manifestly *is* a disease. *Rabies* is bad, but it is not so bad as this disease. Rabies enables a man to do a thing which he could not do when in a healthy state: kill his neighbor with a poisonous bite. No one is the better man for having rabies. The Moral Sense enables a man to do wrong. It enables him to do wrong in a thousand ways. Rabies is an innocent disease, compared to the Moral Sense. No one, then, can be the better man for having the Moral Sense. What, now, do we find the Primal Curse to have been? Plainly what it was in the beginning: the infliction upon man of the Moral Sense; the ability to distinguish good from evil; and with it, necessarily, the ability to *do* evil; for there can be no evil act without the presence of consciousness of it in the doer of it.

And so I find that we have descended and degenerated, from some far ancestor—some microscopic atom wandering at its pleasure between the mighty horizons of a drop of water perchance—insect by insect, animal by animal, reptile by reptile, down the long highway of smirchless innocence, till we have reached the bottom stage of development—namable as the Human Being. Below us—nothing. Nothing but the Frenchman.

There is only one possible stage below the Moral Sense; that is the Immoral Sense. The Frenchman has it. Man is but little lower than the angels. This definitely locates him. He is between the angels and the French.

Man seems to be a rickety poor sort of a thing, any way you take him; a kind of British Museum of infirmities and inferiorities. He is always undergoing repairs. A machine that was as unreliable as he is would have no market. On top of his specialty—the Moral Sense—are piled a multitude of minor infirmities; such a multitude, indeed, that one may broadly call them countless. The higher animals get their teeth without pain or inconvenience. Man gets his through months and months of cruel torture; and at a time of life when he is but ill able to bear it. As soon as he has got them they must all be pulled out again, for they were of no value in the first place, not worth the loss of a night's rest. The second set will answer for a while, by being reinforced occasionally with rubber or plugged up with gold; but he will never get a set which can really be depended on till a dentist makes him one. This set will be called "false" teeth—as if he had ever worn any other kind.

In a wild state—a natural state—the Higher Animals have a few diseases; diseases of little consequence; the main one is old age. But man starts in as a child and lives on diseases till the end, as a regular diet. He has mumps, measles, whooping cough, croup, tonsilitis, diphtheria, scarlet fever, almost as a matter of course. Afterward, as he goes along, his life continues to be threatened at every turn: by colds, coughs, asthma, bronchitis, itch, cholera, cancer, consumption, yellow fever, bilious fever, typhus fevers, hay fever, ague, chilblains, piles, inflammation of the entrails, indigestion, toothache, earache, deafness, dumbness, blindness, influenza, chicken pox, cowpox, smallpox, liver complaint, constipation, bloody flux, warts, pimples, boils, carbuncles, abscesses, bunions, corns, tumors, fistulas, pneumonia, softening of the brain, melancholia and fifteen other kinds of insanity; dysentery, jaundice, diseases of the heart, the bones, the skin, the scalp, the spleen, the kidneys, the nerves, the brain, the blood; scrofula, paralysis, leprosy, neuralgia, palsy, fits, headache, thirteen kinds of rheumatism, forty-six of gout, and a formidable supply of gross and unprintable disorders of one sort and another. Also—but why continue the list? The mere names of the agents appointed to keep this shackly machine out of repair would hide him from sight if printed on his body in the smallest type known to the founder's art. He is but a basket of pestilent corruption provided for the support and entertainment of swarming armies of bacilli—armies commissioned to rot him and destroy him, and each army equipped with a special detail of the work. The process of waylaying him, persecuting him, rotting him, killing him, begins with his first breath, and there is no mercy, no pity, no truce till he draws his last one.

Look at the workmanship of him, in certain of its particulars. What are his tonsils for? They perform no useful function; they have no value. They have no business there. They are but a trap. They have but the one office, the one industry: to provide tonsilitis and quinsy and such things for the possessor of them. And what is the vermiform appendix for? It has no value; it cannot perform any useful service. It is but an ambuscaded enemy whose sole interest in life is to lie in wait for stray grapeseeds and employ them to breed strangulated hernia. And what are the male's mammals for? For business, they are out of the question; as an ornament, they are a mistake. What is his beard for? It performs no useful function; it is a nuisance and a discomfort; all nations hate it; all nations persecute it with the razor. And because it is a nuisance and a discomfort, Nature never allows the supply of it to fall short, in any man's case, between puberty and the grave. You never see a man bald-headed on his chin. But his hair! It is a graceful ornament, it is a comfort, it is the best of all protections against certain perilous ailments, man prizes it above emeralds and rubies. And because of these things Nature puts it on, half the time, so that it won't stay. Man's sight, smell, hearing, sense of locality—how inferior they are. The condor sees a corpse at five miles; man has no telescope that can do it. The bloodhound follows a scent that is two days old. The robin hears the earthworm burrowing his course under the ground. The cat, deported in a closed basket, finds its way home again through twenty miles of country which it has never seen.

Certain functions lodged in the other sex perform in a lamentably inferior way as compared with the performance of the same functions in the Higher Animals. In the human being, menstruation, gestation and parturition are terms which stand for horrors. In the Higher Animals these things are hardly even inconveniences.

For style, look at the Bengal tiger—that ideal of grace, beauty, physical perfection, majesty. And then look at Man—that poor thing. He is the Animal of the Wig, the Trepanned Skull, the Ear Trumpet, the Glass Eye, the Pasteboard Nose, the Porcelain Teeth, the Silver Windpipe, the Wooden Leg—a creature that is mended and patched all over, from top to bottom. If he can't get renewals of his bric-a-brac in the next world, what will he look like?

He has just one stupendous superiority. In his intellect he is supreme. The Higher Animals cannot touch him there. It is curious, it is noteworthy, that no heaven has ever been offered him wherein his one sole superiority was provided with a chance to enjoy itself. Even when he himself has imagined a heaven, he has never made provision in it for intellectual joys. It is a striking omission. It seems a tacit confession that heavens are provided for the Higher Animals alone. This is matter for thought; and for serious thought. And it is full of a grim suggestion: that we are not as important, perhaps, as we had all along supposed we were.

Know Then Thyself[1]
ALEXANDER POPE

Know then thyself, presume not God to scan;
The proper study of mankind is Man.
Placed on this isthmus of a middle state,
A being darkly wise, and rudely great:
With too much knowledge for the skeptic side,
With too much weakness for the Stoic's pride,
He hangs between; in doubt to act, or rest,
In doubt to deem himself a god, or beast;
In doubt his mind or body to prefer,
Born but to die, and reasoning but to err;
Alike in ignorance, his reason such,
Whether he thinks too little, or too much:
Chaos of thought and passion, all confused;
Still by himself abused, or disabused;
Created half to rise, and half to fall;
Great lord of all things, yet a prey to all;
Sole judge of truth, in endless error hurled:
The glory, jest, and riddle of the world!

More Day to Dawn[1]
HENRY D. THOREAU

The life in us is like the water in the river. It may rise this year higher than man has ever known it, and flood the parched uplands; even this may be the eventful year, which will drown out all our muskrats. It was not always dry land where we dwell. I see far inland the banks which the stream anciently washed, before science began to record its freshets. Every one has heard the story which has gone the rounds of New England, of a strong and beautiful bug which came out of the dry leaf of an old table of apple-tree wood, which had stood in a farmer's kitchen for sixty years, first in Connecticut, and afterward in Massachusetts,—from an egg deposited in the living tree many years earlier still, as appeared by counting the annual layers beyond it; which was heard gnawing out for several

---

[1] From *An Essay on Man, Epistle II. Of the Nature and State of Man With Respect to Himself, as an Individual* (1733).

[1] From *Walden* (1854).

weeks, hatched perchance by the heat of an urn. Who does not feel his faith in a resurrection and immortality strengthened by hearing of this? Who knows what beautiful and winged life, whose egg has been buried for ages under many concentric layers of woodenness in the dead dry life of society, deposited at first in the alburnum of the green and living tree, which has been gradually converted into the semblance of its well-seasoned tomb,— heard perchance gnawing out now for years by the astonished family of man, as they sat round the festive board,—may unexpectedly come forth from amidst society's most trivial and handselled furniture, to enjoy its perfect summer life at last!

I do not say that John or Jonathan will realize all this; but such is the character of that morrow which mere lapse of time can never make to dawn. The light which puts out our eyes is darkness to us. Only that day dawns to which we are awake. There is more day to dawn. The sun is but a morning star.

Ecclesiastes 12:1-8
Remember Now Thy Creator

Remember now thy Creator in the days of thy youth, while the evil days come not, nor the years draw nigh, when thou shalt say, I have no pleasure in them; While the sun, or the light, or the moon, or the stars, be not darkened, nor the clouds return after the rain: In the day when the keepers of the house shall tremble, and the strong men shall bow themselves, and the grinders cease because they are few, and those that look out of the windows be darkened, And the doors shall be shut in the streets, when the sound of the grinding is low, and he shall rise up at the voice of the bird, and all the daughters of musick shall be brought low; Also when they shall be afraid of that which is high, and fears shall be in the way, and the almond tree shall flourish, and the grasshopper shall be a burden, and desire shall fail: because man goeth to his long home, and the mourners go about the streets: Or ever the silver cord be loosed, or the golden bowl be broken, or the pitcher be broken at the fountain, or the wheel broken at the cistern. Then shall the dust return to the earth as it was: and the spirit shall return unto God who gave it.

Vanity of vanities, saith the preacher; all is vanity.

The Divine Image[1]
WILLIAM BLAKE

To Mercy, Pity, Peace, and Love,
All pray in their distress:
And to these virtues of delight
Return their thankfulness.

For Mercy, Pity, Peace, and Love,
Is God, our father dear:
And Mercy, Pity, Peace, and Love,
Is Man, his child and care.

For Mercy has a human heart,
Pity, a human face:
And Love, the human form divine,
And Peace, the human dress.

Then every man of every clime,
That prays in his distress,
Prays to the human form divine,
Love, Mercy, Pity, Peace.

And all must love the human form,
In heathen, Turk, or Jew.
Where Mercy, Love, & Pity dwell,
There God is dwelling too.

[1] From *Songs of Innocence* (1789).

Notes on Authors

James Agee (1909–1955), American author, native of Tennessee, was educated at Exeter and Harvard. He wrote *Let Us Now Praise Famous Men* (1941); *Agee on Film, I* (1958) and *Agee on Film, II* (1960), collections of his film criticism; and the screenplay *The African Queen*. *A Death in the Family*, published posthumously in 1957, won a Pulitzer Prize.

Lydia R. Aguirre (1933–   ) is a member of the Social Work Program of the University of Texas at El Paso. She has helped to edit *Social Casework*.

Muhammad Ali (1942–   ), world's champion heavyweight boxer, is a native of Louisville, Kentucky, where he began his career as a fighter. He won the Olympic championship in 1960 and the world championship in 1963. Originally named Cassius Clay, he changed his name when he became a convert to the Black Muslim religion.

Marcus Aurelius Antoninus (121–180), Roman emperor and philosopher, was one of the greatest Stoics. His *Meditations*, written in Greek, consists of twelve books of sage advice on conduct and living. Though learned and gentle, he still opposed Christianity, even to the extent of persecuting Christians.

Robert Ardrey (1908–   ), American author, is a lecturer and consultant on human behavior. Among his many books are *African Genesis* (1961), *The Territorial Imperative* (1966), *The Social Contract* (1970), and *The Hunting Hypothesis* (1976).

Kenneth J. Arrow (1921–   ), American economist, was educated at the City College of New York and Columbia University. He taught at the University of Chicago before becoming Professor of Economics at Harvard. He is also a consultant of the Rand Corporation, and has received many academic honors in the United States and abroad. Among his writings are *Social Choice and Individual Values* (1951), *Essays on the Theory of Risk Bearing* (1971), and *The Limits of Organization* (1974).

Mary Austin (1868–1924) began her pioneering studies of American Indian life and literature as a young woman. Some of her best-known books are *The Land of Little Rain* (1903), *American Rhythm* (1923), and her autobiography, *Earth Horizon* (1932).

Russell Baker (1925–   ), author and newsman, was educated at Johns Hopkins University. For many years he has written for *The New York Times*. Among his books are *An American in Washington* (1961), *All Things Considered* (1965), and *Poor Russell's Almanac* (1972).

William C. Barrett (1913–   ), formerly editor of *Partisan Review*, is a member of the Department of Philosophy at New York University. He has taught at the University of Illinois and at Brown University. Besides contributing to periodicals, he has written *What is Existentialism?* (1947), *Irrational Man* (1958), and *Philosophy in the Twentieth Century* (1961).

Edward Bellamy (1850–1898), American novelist and social reformer, was the author of *Looking Backward: 2000–1887* (1888), an immensely popular and influential novel that established him as a leader of the socialist movement in America. Among other reforms, Bellamy advocated national ownership of transportation and communications. He also anticipated many aspects of present-day social planning.

Claude Bernard (1813–1878), French scientist, investigated the effect of chemicals on nerves. He propounded the important theory of "interior environment" and discovered the function of the vasomotor nerves. He wrote *An Introduction to Experimental Medicine* (1863) and *General Physiology* (1872).

Leonard Bernstein (1918–   ), conductor and composer, was educated at Harvard University and the Curtis Institute of Music. Lifetime Laureate Conductor of the New York Philharmonic Orchestra, he has also conducted most major American and European orchestras, the opera at La Scala in Milan, the Metropolitan Opera in New York, the Vienna State Opera, and a popular series of "Young People's Concerts" for television. Among his compositions are *Seven Anniversaries for Piano* (1942), *Symphony No. 2—The Age of Anxiety* (1949), *Trouble in Tahiti* (1952), and *West Side Story* (1957). Two of his books are *The Joy of Music* (1959) and *The Infinite Variety of Music* (1966).

William Blake (1757-1827), English artist, mystic, and poet, wrote *Songs of Innocence* (1789), *Songs of Experience* (1794), and a series of visionary "prophetic books." His water colors and engravings, *Illustrations of the Book of Job*, for example, are scarcely less original than his poems.

Harold Bloom (1930–   ), literary critic and scholar, was educated at Cornell, Cambridge, and Yale universities. He is now Professor of English at Yale. Among his writings are *Shelley's Mythmaking* (1959), *The Visionary Company* (1961), *Blake's Apocalypse* (1963), and *Yeats: A Study in Romanticism* (1968).

William Warren (Bill) Bradley (1943–   ) was educated at Princeton and Oxford universities. He recently retired as a professional basketball player with the New York Knicks. He is the author of *Life on the Run: A Career in Basketball* (1976).

Kingman Brewster, Jr. (1919–   ), a lawyer, was president of Yale University before he became ambassador to Great Britain. He was educated at Harvard University and at Yale Law School, where he later taught for many years. He has frequently served in various governmental advisory capacities. Brewster has been widely honored by American colleges and universities, and is the author of *Anti-Trust and American Business Abroad* (1959) and *Law of International Transactions and Relations* (1960).

Jacob Bronowski (1908-1974), British mathematician, scientist, philosopher, and author, was born in Poland. He taught at Oxford University and gave popular lectures on the B.B.C. Among his books are *The Western Intellectual Tradition from Leonardo to Hegel* (1960), *Technology: Man Remakes His World* (1964), *The Identity of Man* (1965), *William Blake and the Age of Revolution* (1965), and *The Ascent of Man* (1973).

Dee Brown (1908–   ), author and librarian, was educated at George Washington University and the University of Illinois. He has been librarian and a professor at the University of Illinois. Among his many books dealing with American history are *The Gentle Tamers: Women of the Old West* (1958), *They Went Thataway* (1960), *Showdown at Little Big Horn* (1964), *Bury My Heart at Wounded Knee* (1971), and *The Westerners* (1974).

Susan Brownmiller (1935–   ), journalist and feminist, wrote *Against Our Will* (1975).

Martin Buber (1878-1965), Jewish theologian and philosopher, was a native of Vienna. He did much to interpret Judaism to contemporary America. Among his books are *I and Thou* (1923), *Israel and the World* (1948), *Good and Evil* (1952), *Pointing the Way* (1957), *I and Thou* (1958), *Hasidism and Modern Man* (1958), and *The Origin and Meaning of Hasidism* (1960).

Gautama Buddha (c.563–c.483 B.C.), founder of one of the great religions of the world, was born a prince in India but renounced his royal status about 533 B.C. Thereafter he taught throughout northern India. According to tradition, his spiritual emancipation and enlightenment came to him at Buddh Gaya, from which his name ("the Enlightened One") derives.

Josiah Bunting III (1939–   ) is president of Hampden-Sydney College in Virginia. He was educated at Virginia Military Institute and at Oxford and Columbia universities.

Bruce Catton (1899–   ) studied at Oberlin College. For many years a newspaperman, he turned to writing of the Civil War in the late 1940s, producing a series of volumes that have won him many awards and honorary degrees. A *Stillness at Appomattox* (1953) won a Pulitzer Prize.

Kenneth Clark (1903–   ), British art critic, was created a life peer in 1969.

He was educated at Winchester School and at Trinity College, Oxford. A protégé of Bernard Berenson, with whom he studied at Florence, he has been director of the National Gallery in London. He narrated two famous television series, "Civilisation" (1969) and "Romantic Versus Classic Art" (1973). He is the author of many books, among them *Landscape into Art* (1949), *Rembrandt and the Italian Renaissance* (1966), *Civilisation* (1969), and *Looking at Pictures* (1973).

Eldridge Cleaver (1935–   ), American author, is a native of Arkansas. Formerly a spokesman for the Black Panthers, Cleaver fled the United States under indictment and lived abroad for several years before voluntarily returning. He is author of *Soul on Ice* (1968) and *Post-Prison Writings and Speeches* (1969), and he has been assistant editor of *Ramparts*.

Aaron Copland (1900–   ) is the composer of symphonies, sonatas, concertos, film scores, and operas. Among his musical works are *Tender Land* (1954), *Piano Fantasy* (1957), and *Music for the Great City* (1964). His books include *What to Listen for in Music* (1939) and *Music and the Imagination* (1952).

Stephen Crane (1871–1900), American novelist and short-story writer, was educated at Lafayette College and Syracuse University. He became a newspaper reporter, war correspondent, and free-lance writer. He is the author of *The Red Badge of Courage* (1895) and other works.

Charles Darwin (1809–1882), English scientist and naturalist, studied the flora and fauna of many lands, especially the Galápagos archipelago. His publication of *On the Origin of Species by Means of Natural Selection* in 1859 was epochal in its revolutionary ramifications. He also wrote *The Descent of Man* (1871), which aroused tremendous controversy.

Emily Dickinson (1830–1886), New England poet, wrote more than 1,700 poems, of which only a few appeared (by accident) in her lifetime. But she recognized her own poetic powers and saved and revised her poems and "published" them in letters to a circle of friends. A small and, in her later life, exceedingly shy woman, she wrote her concentrated verse on great subjects: the natural world, the seasons, love, self-reliance, and the "flood subject," death.

John Donne (1573–1631), the famous Dean of St. Paul's Cathedral and metaphysical poet, was born a Roman Catholic. After his conversion to the Anglican Church, he took holy orders at the suggestion of King James I, who was pleased to grant him several preferments in the church, culminating in the deanship of St. Paul's. Though Donne in early youth was worldly and wrote some of the most passionate love poetry in English literature, he became fervent in spirit and zealous for the Lord. His sermons, many of them preached before Charles I, are among the most eloquent in all English pulpit oratory. His *Devotions*, occasioned by a grave illness, were written in 1623. Many critics consider Donne one of the greatest of English prose writers.

Frederick Douglass (c.1817–1895), abolitionist, orator, and journalist, was born a slave in Maryland, the son of an unknown white father and a slave mother. He escaped to New Bedford, Massachusetts, in 1838, where he was influenced by William Lloyd Garrison, the abolitionist. In 1845 he published *Narrative of the Life of Frederick Douglass* and became active in the abolitionist movement; he also edited *North Star*, a journal advocating freedom for slaves. During the Civil War he advised President Abraham Lincoln. After the war he was U.S. minister to Haiti and became active in the women's suffrage movement.

Peter F. Drucker (1909–   ), author and economics consultant, is a native of Austria. He was educated at the University of Frankfurt in Germany and has received many honorary doctoral degrees. He is Professor of Social Sciences at Claremont Graduate School in California. A few of his books are *The Future of Industrial Man* (1941), *The Practice of Management* (1954), *Managing for Results* (1962), *The Effective Executive* (1967), and *Management: Tasks, Practices, Responsibilities* (1974).

René Dubos (1901–   ), bacteriologist, was born in France. He is on the faculty of the Rockefeller Institute. Among his books are *The White Plague: Tuberculosis, Man, and Society* (1952), *Bio-chemical Determinants of Microbial Diseases* (1954), *The Unseen World* (1962), *Health and Disease* (1965), and *Man Adapting* (1965).

Loren Eiseley (1907–1977), anthropologist and historian of science, was Benjamin Franklin Professor of Anthropology at the University of Pennsylvania. Among his books are *The Immense Journey* (1957), *Darwin's Century* (1958), *The Mind as Nature* (1962), and *All the Strange Hours* (1975). He was also a prolific contributor to scientific journals.

T[homas] S[tearns] Eliot (1888–1965), American poet, dramatist, and critic, was born in St. Louis and educated at Harvard University. He became a British subject in 1927. Two of his major poems are *The Waste Land* (1922) and *Four Quartets* (1936–1942). Among his plays, perhaps the best known are *Murder in the Cathedral* (1935) and *The Cocktail Party* (1950). He was awarded the Nobel Prize for literature in 1948.

Ralph Waldo Emerson (1803–1882), New England poet, lecturer, philosopher, and "friend of those who would live in the spirit," is famous for his essays—which call for an American language and literature—and for his often difficult poetry. His influence—on Henry D. Thoreau, Walt Whitman, and Emily Dickinson, for example—was profound, and it persists in American literature and philosophy. Called "the sage of Concord," he was the leader of the Transcendentalist literary and philosophical movement centered in New England in the nineteenth century.

Erik H. Erikson (1902–   ), psychoanalyst, was born in Germany of Danish parents. He is Professor Emeritus of Human Development at the Harvard School of Medicine. Among his books are *Identity and the Life Cycle* (1959) and *Identity: Youth and Crisis* (1968).

Gerald Eskenazi (1936–   ), a sports reporter for *The New York Times* since 1963, was born in New York City. He contributes to *New York*, *Sport*, and *The New York Times Magazine* and has written nine books. He has also taught at St. John's University in New York. His interests include hiking and rocketry.

Oriana Fallaci, distinguished Italian author, is known especially for her interviews with political figures, including Henry Kissinger, Golda Meir, and the Shah of Iran. Among her books are *Nothing, and So Be It* (1972), *Interview with History* (1975), and *Letter to a Child Never Born* (1976).

Leslie H. Farber (1912–   ) is a practicing psychoanalyst whose most recent book is *Lying, Despair, Jealousy, Envy, Sex, Suicide, Drugs, and the Good Life* (1976).

Dennis Farney (1941–   ), White House correspondent for *The Wall Street Journal*, grew up on a Kansas wheat and cattle farm, was educated at the University of Kansas, and began his newspaper career with the *Kansas City Star*. He has been with *The Wall Street Journal* since 1966. He has also contributed articles to *The Atlantic*, *Smithsonian Magazine*, and *Reader's Digest*. His interests include gardening, hiking, and prairie restoration.

Cheryl M. Fields (1944–   ) is senior editor of *The Chronicle of Higher Education*, for which she writes on major issues affecting colleges and universities in the United States.

Abraham Flexner (1866–1959), physician and educator, directed the Institute for Advanced Studies in Princeton, New Jersey. Associated with the General Education Board, he wrote many books about medical education and higher education in the United States and Europe.

Charles Frankel (1917–   ), American philosopher, was educated at Columbia University, where he now is Old Dominion Professor of Philosophy and Public Affairs. Among his writings are *The Case for Modern Man* (1956), *The Democratic Prospect* (1962), *The Love of Anxiety and Other Essays* (1965), and *The Pleasures of Philosophy* (1968).

Benjamin Franklin (1706–1790), American statesman and author, was by trade a printer in Philadelphia. He published *Poor Richard's Almanack* and an *Autobiography* which ends just as he entered prominence as a public figure. A signer of the Declaration of Independence and a member of the Constitutional Convention, he also served as ambassador to France. Interested in science, he experimented with electricity and invented bifocal eyeglasses, the Franklin stove, and lightning rods.

Robert Frost (1874–1963), American poet, though born in California, lived in New England, mainly in New Hampshire and Vermont, the setting for many of his poems. A distinguished American poet of his time, he was showered with honors, including reading his poem "The Gift Outright" at the inaugural of President John F. Kennedy in 1961. His poems are among the most popular in contemporary America. He was awarded the Pulitzer Prize in 1924, 1931, 1937, and 1943.

Northrop Frye (1912–), literary critic, was educated at Toronto and Oxford. He has been University Professor of English at the University of Toronto since 1967. Among his influential books are *Fearful Symmetry: A Study of William Blake* (1947); *Anatomy of Criticism* (1957); *The Educated Imagination* (1963); *The Well-Tempered Critic* (1963); *Fools of Time* (1967); and *A Study of English Romanticism* (1968).

John Kenneth Galbraith (1908–), American economist, is a native of Canada. He was educated at the University of Toronto, the University of California, and Cambridge University. In addition to a distinguished teaching career at Harvard, he has served as ambassador to India and has frequently advised presidents and government agencies on economic matters. Among his books are *The Great Crash* (1955), *The Affluent Society* (1958), and *Money: Whence It Came, Where It Went* (1975).

Robert Geroch (1942–), physicist, is a professor at the Enrico Fermi Institute of the University of Chicago.

A. Bartlett Giamatti (1938–), Professor of English and Comparative Literature at Yale University, was also educated at Yale. He is author of *The Earthly Paradise and the Renaissance Epic* (1966) and *A Variorum Commentary on the Poems of John Milton* (1970).

Walker Gibson (1919–), Professor of English at the University of Massachusetts, is a past president of the National Council of Teachers of English. Among his books are *The Limits of Language* (1962), *Tough, Sweet, and Stuffy: An Essay on Modern American Prose Styles* (1965), and *Persona* (1969).

William M. Gibson (1912–), author and teacher, was educated at Princeton University and the University of Chicago. Professor of American Literature at the University of Wisconsin, he has taught at the University of Chicago, Williams College, and New York University. Among his books are *The Mark Twain–Howells Letters* (1960, with H. N. Smith) and *The Art of Mark Twain* (1975).

Paul Goldberger (1950–), architecture critic for *The New York Times*, is a member of the Board of Directors of the Parks Council and a member of the Society of Architectural Historians and of the Architectural League of New York. He enjoys opera, good food, wandering around the neighborhoods of New York, and bicycle riding in Central Park.

William Golding (1911–), English novelist, is a graduate of Brasenose College, Oxford. Among his many novels, *Lord of the Flies* (1954) is most widely known and read.

Ellen Goodman (1909–), psychologist, was educated at Moravian College and Lehigh University. She practices diagnostic and counseling psychology in Pennsylvania.

Robert Graves (1895–), English poet and novelist, was born near London and educated at Charterhouse. He fought through the entire First World War and was once even reported killed in action; *Goodbye to All That* (1929) is his autobiographical record of the war. After the war he continued his education at Oxford University, to which he returned as Professor of Poetry in 1961. Since the late 1920s he has lived in Majorca, Spain. Among his historical novels are *I, Claudius* (1934), *Claudius the God* (1934), and *Hercules, My Shipmate*

(1945). His philosophy of poetic myth is stated in *The White Goddess* (1948).

Clement Greenberg (1909–   ), art critic, has written books on many major modern artists, including Joan Miró, Henri Matisse, and Jackson Pollock. His *Art and Culture*, a collection of critical essays, appeared in 1961.

Germaine Greer (1939–   ), a native of Australia, was educated at Melbourne, Sydney, and Cambridge universities, before beginning her career as a teacher and writer. Her best-known work, *The Female Eunuch*, was published in the United States in 1971.

Donald Hall (1928–   ), Professor of English at the University of Michigan (Ann Arbor), is an award-winning poet. He has edited and written many books, among them *A Poetry Sampler* (1962), *A Concise Encyclopedia of English and American Poets and Poetry* (1963), *A Choice of Whitman's Verse* (1968), *Man and Boy* (1968), *The Modern Stylists* (1968), and *Pleasures of Poetry* (1971).

Learned Hand (1872–1961), famous American jurist, was educated at Harvard University and Harvard Law School. He received honorary doctorates from many universities. Admitted to the New York bar in 1897, he enjoyed a distinguished legal career in New York before his appointment as judge of the U.S. Circuit Court (New York) in 1921. In his long career on the bench (1921–1951) he made many notable decisions.

Thomas Jefferson (1743–1826), third President of the United States (1801–1809), composed his own epitaph: "Here was buried Thomas Jefferson, Author of the Declaration of American Independence, of the Statute of Virginia for Religious Freedom, and Father of the University of Virginia."

John Keats (1795–1821), major English poet, was the son of a livery-stable keeper. He was educated in medicine but did not enter practice. His early death in Italy from tuberculosis is one of the greatest tragedies in literature. Yet he crowned his short life with four great odes which will live with the English language: "Ode on Melancholy," "Ode on a Grecian Urn," "Ode to a Nightingale," and "To Autumn."

Parton Keese (1926–   ), sports writer for *The New York Times*, is also the author of *The John Newcombe Family Tennis Book*.

X. J. [Joseph C.] Kennedy (1929–   ), poet, scholar, and teacher, has been Professor of English at Tufts University since 1973. He is author of *Nude Descending a Staircase* (1961), *Mark Twain's Frontier* (1963), *Growing into Love* (1969), *and Introduction to Poetry* (3rd edition, 1974). He frequently contributes to *The New Yorker, Paris Review*, and other magazines.

John Maynard Keynes (1883–1946), influential British economist, was educated at Eton and Cambridge University. He served the British government as economic adviser and was a director of the Bank of England and a governor of the International Bank for Reconstruction and Development. His *Treatise on Money* (1930) is a landmark in the development of modern economics. He also wrote *The End of Laissez-Faire* (1926) and *The General Theory of Employment, Interest, and Money* (1936).

Martin Luther King, Jr. (1929–1968), was a black American churchman who became a political leader during the civil rights movement, president of the Southern Christian Leadership Conference, and winner of the Nobel Peace Prize in 1964. He was assassinated by a white gunman in 1968. He was the author of *Stride Toward Freedom* (1958), *Strength to Love* (1963), and *Why We Can't Wait* (1964).

Arthur Koestler (1905–   ), novelist and essayist, is a native of Hungary. He became a British citizen after World War II. Among his books are *Darkness at Noon* (1941), *The Lotus and the Robot* (1960), *The Act of Creation* (1964), and *Janus, or The Ambiguity of Man* (1966).

Michael Korda (1933–   ), author and publisher, was born in England and educated at Magdalen College, Oxford. He writes film reviews for *Glamour* magazine and is a member of the National Society of Film Critics. He is author of

Male Chauvinism! How It Works (1973) and *Power! How to Get It, How to Use It* (1975).

Joseph Wood Krutch (1893–   ), journalist, teacher, and scholar, was educated at Columbia University. While on the staff of *The Nation*, he taught journalism at Columbia, where he later became Brander Matthews Professor of Dramatic Literature. Among his many books are *The Modern Temper* (1929), *Is the Common Man Too Common?* (1954), *The Great Chain of Life* (1957), *Grand Canyon: Today and All Its Yesterdays* (1958), and *Human Nature and the Human Condition* (1959).

R[onald] D[avid] Laing (1927–   ), psychiatrist, a native of Scotland, took his M.D. degree at the University of Edinburgh and has been director of the Langham Clinic in London. Among his books are *The Divided Self* (1960), *Interpersonal Perception* (1966), *Self and Others* (1970), and *Knots* (1972).

Susanne K. Langer (1895–   ), American philosopher, was educated at Radcliffe and taught at Connecticut College. Among her books are *Philosophy in a New Key* (1942) and its sequel *Feeling and Form* (1953), *Philosophical Sketches* (1962), and *Mind: An Essay on Human Feeling* (1972).

Roy Larson (1929–   ), American journalist, is religion editor of the *Chicago Sun-Times*. He was educated at Augustana College in Illinois and the Garrett Theological Seminary.

Aldo Leopold (1886–1948), American naturalist, pioneered in applying ecological principles to wildlife management. His books, *A Sand County Almanac* (1949) and *Round River* (1953), contain philosophical essays about the need for wilderness and for careful conservation practices.

Denise Levertov (1923–   ), English-born American poet, lives in New York City. She contributes poetry to magazines, and among her books are *Jacob's Ladder* (1961) and *O Taste and See* (1964).

Niccolò Machiavelli (1469–1527), Florentine statesman and political philosopher, wrote *The Prince* (1513), a widely influential book proclaiming the doctrine of the superiority of expediency over morality in an absolutist theory of government. His ideas have also had many applications to organizations other than governments.

Archibald MacLeish (1892–   ), American poet, was educated at Hotchkiss School, Yale University, and Harvard Law School. After serving in World War I, he practiced law for a time, but since 1923 has devoted himself to poetry. During World War II he was Librarian of Congress and headed several wartime government agencies. In more recent years he has been Boylston Professor of English Rhetoric at Harvard University. Among his books are *J.B.*, a verse play on the Book of Job (1958); *Poetry and Experience* (1961); and *Herakles* (1967). He won the Pulitzer Prize for poetry in 1933 and 1953, and for drama (*J.B.*) in 1959.

André Malraux (1901–1976), French novelist, fought against fascism in the Spanish Civil War as an aviator and actively assisted General Charles de Gaulle in the French Resistance during World War II. He later served as minister of cultural affairs in France's Fifth Republic. Among his books are *The Royal Road* (1930), *The Human Condition* (1933), *Days of Hope* (1937), and *The Voices of Silence* (1951).

Marcus Aurelius. *See* Antoninus

St. Matthew (1st century A.D.), one of the twelve disciples of Jesus Christ, is believed to be the author of The Gospel According to St. Matthew, one of the first biographies of Jesus and the first book of the New Testament.

Margaret Mead (1901–   ), American anthropologist, was educated at Columbia University. She has long been affiliated with the American Museum of Natural History and is now its curator of ethnology emeritus. She has taught at Fordham and Columbia universities and has led expeditions to New Guinea and Bali. Among her many books are *Coming of Age in Samoa* (1928), *Growing up in New Guinea* (1930), *Sex and Temperament in Three Primitive Societies* (1935), *And Keep Your Powder*

Dry (1942), *Male and Female* (1949), *People and Places* (1959), and *Anthropologists and What They Do* (1965).

Gilbert Millstein is a writer who is familiar to readers of *The Saturday Evening Post* and *The New York Times*. He writes most frequently about the theater.

Ellen Moers (1928–   ), literary critic and teacher, was educated at Vassar College and Harvard and Columbia universities. She teaches English at Brooklyn College and the City University of New York. She has written *The Dandy: Brummel to Beerbohm* (1960), *The Two Dreisers* (1969), and *Literary Women* (1960).

N. Scott Momaday (1934–   ), author and teacher, is Professor of English at Stanford University and has also taught at the University of California at Berkeley. He has written *House Made of Dawn* (1968), *The Way to Rainy Mountain* (1969), and *Angle of Geese and Other Poems* (1973).

Marianne Moore (1887–1972) is an important modern American poet whose unpretentious verse, much of which deals with animals, has had wide influence on other poets, among them Elizabeth Bishop, Ted Hughes, Robert Lowell, and T. S. Eliot. She was born in St. Louis and educated at Bryn Mawr College. Among her works are *Collected Poems* (1951), which won a Pulitzer Prize; *Like a Bulwark* (1956); and *O To Be a Dragon* (1959).

J. Mitchell Morse (1912–   ), Professor of English at Temple University, has written *The Sympathetic Alien* (1959), *Matters of Style* (1968), *The Irrelevant English Teacher* (1972), and other works.

Norman C. Murphy is a psychologist in the Grant Wood Area Education Agency in Cedar Rapids, Iowa.

Edwin Newman (1919–   ), news commentator, was educated at the University of Wisconsin and Louisiana State University. A member of the N.B.C. (National Broadcasting Company) staff since 1961, he has received the highest awards in journalism and broadcasting and has been president of the Association of Radio-Television News Analysts. He frequently contributes articles to periodicals and has written *Strictly Speaking* (1974) and *A Civil Tongue* (1976).

Robert Oppenheimer (1904–1967), American physicist, as director of the Los Alamos Scientific Laboratory (1943–1945), presided over the development and production of the first atomic bomb. Educated at Harvard, Cambridge, and Göttingen universities, he taught at the University of California and the California Institute of Technology. He was director of the Institute for Advanced Study in Princeton, New Jersey, from 1947 to 1966.

George Orwell is the pseudonym used by Eric Blair (1903–1950), British essayist, novelist, and political satirist. His best-known works are *Animal Farm* (1945) and *1984* (1949).

Alan L. Otten (1920–   ) received degrees from the City College of New York and Columbia University. Associated with *The Wall Street Journal* since 1946, he is now senior national correspondent at the Washington Bureau.

St. Paul (c. 1 A.D.–c. 64), Christian apostle to the Gentiles, was born a Jew in Tarsus and originally named Saul. After his conversion to Christianity he went on missionary expeditions, founded churches, and wrote the Pauline Epistles, a part of the New Testament. He was martyred at Rome after long imprisonment there. He is widely credited with formulating Christian theology.

Ralph J. Perrotta (1937–   ) is executive director of the New York Center for Ethnic Affairs.

Iver Peterson (1942–   ) is a correspondent for *The New York Times*, for which he has covered education and the New York State legislature. He was previously a part-time correspondent for the Saigon bureau of the *Times*.

Plato (c. 427–c. 347 B.C.), Greek philosopher, was a disciple of Socrates. He spent most of his life teaching in Athens, his native city. He wrote *The Dialogues*, based on the teachings of Socrates, who figures largely in them as the initiator of the discussions.

Alexander Pope (1688–1744) was an English poet, critic, editor of Shakespeare (1725), and translator of Homer (1726). Literary arbiter of his day, he also wrote the famous *Essay on Criticism* (1711) and *The Dunciad* (1728–1743), in the latter of which he decimated his enemies and critics.

David Raymond is a high-school student in Connecticut.

Adrienne Rich (1920–   ), a graduate of Radcliffe College, has published many volumes of poetry since *A Change of World* appeared in the Yale Younger Poet series in 1951. Recent volumes are *Diving into the Wreck* (1973) and *Poems Selected and New, 1950–1974* (1975).

Jeffrey Schrank is the editor of *Media Mix Newsletters* and a contributing editor of *Media & Methods*. He is the author of *Teaching Human Beings: 101 Subversive Activities for the Classroom* (1972).

William W. Serrin, a Detroit journalist, is currently working on a book about housing and land use in the United States.

William Shakespeare (1564–1616), greatest English dramatist and poet, was born at Stratford-on-Avon. During his career in London he wrote many dramatic masterpieces including *Hamlet, Othello, King Lear, Macbeth, A Midsummer Night's Dream, Twelfth Night, Henry IV, Richard III, Julius Caesar, Antony and Cleopatra, As You Like It, The Tempest,* and *Henry V*. His plays, issued individually during his life, were first collected and published in folio in 1623. His sonnets, first printed in 1609, are considered among the finest ever written.

William V. Shannon (1927–   ), a member of *The New York Times* editorial board, has written, among other books, *The American Irish* (1966) and *The Heir Apparent* (1966), the latter a book on Robert Kennedy.

Harlow Shapley (1885–1972), American astronomer, was Paine Professor of Astronomy at Harvard University and director of the Harvard Observatory from 1921 to 1952. Educated at the University of Missouri, Princeton, and Harvard, he was president of the American Association for the Advancement of Science. Among his books are *Of Stars and Men* (1958), *The View from a Distant Star* (1964), and *Beyond the Observatory: Through Rugged Ways to the Stars* (1969).

Stephen Spender (1909–   ), English poet, was educated at Oxford University. During the Spanish Civil War he sympathized with the Left. A prominent member of the London literary establishment, he has been coeditor of two important periodicals, *Horizon* and *Encounter*. He is Professor of English Literature at University College, London. His *Collected Poems* appeared in 1954.

L[eften] S[tavros] Stavrianos (1913–   ), historian, teaches at Northwestern University. Among his books are *A Global History of Man* (1962), *The Balkans, 1815–1914* (1963), and *The Middle East* (1966).

Walter [Seager] Sullivan (1918–   ), science editor of *The New York Times*, won the International Nonfiction Book Award in 1965 for his *We Are Not Alone*. He frequently publishes articles in magazines and newspapers.

Studs Terkel (1912–   ), American author and radio-television interviewer, was born in New York City and educated at the University of Chicago. He has written *Giants of Jazz* (1956), *Amazing Grace* (1959), *Hard Times* (1970), and *Working* (1974).

Lewis Thomas (1913–   ) is a physician and a member of the Department of Anesthesiology at Washington University. He is author of *The Lives of a Cell* (1974).

Henry D[avid] Thoreau (1817–1862) called himself "a mystic, a transcendental philosopher, and a natural philosopher to boot." His dominant individualism is evident in his most famous book, *Walden* (1854). It also appears, but tempered by a belief in acting collectively "according to the spirit of our institutions," in the three John Brown speeches (1859–

1860) and *Life Without Principle* (1863) as well as in the paragraphs printed here.

James Thurber (1894–1961), American humorist and cartoonist, was educated at Ohio State University. During much of his career he was on the staff of *The New Yorker* magazine, for which he wrote and drew frequently. Among his books are *My Life and Hard Times* (1933), *Let Your Mind Alone* (1937), *The Male Animal*, a play written with Elliot Nugent (1940), *Fables for Our Time* (1940), and *My World—and Welcome to It* (1942).

Mark Twain is the pseudonym of Samuel L. Clemens (1835–1910), a major American novelist. He was born in Missouri, spent his boyhood in Hannibal on the Mississippi River, left school at about the age of twelve, learned the printer's trade, became a riverboat pilot, prospected in Nevada, and wrote for a newspaper in Virginia City, before finally settling in Hartford, Connecticut. He is the author of *Roughing It* (1872), *The Adventures of Tom Sawyer* (1876), *Life on the Mississippi* (1883), and *Adventures of Huckleberry Finn* (1884), among many other works.

Walt Whitman (1819–1892), Manhattan journalist and revolutionary poet, was stimulated by the example of Ralph Waldo Emerson and perhaps by the sacred writings of the East to produce *Leaves of Grass* (1855–1892), a highly original book of poetry. It was essentially his life's work, which he revised and expanded through some nine editions. It is read in English and in translation all over the world.

Joseph M. Winski (1943–   ) graduated from Ohio State University and has a master's degree in journalism from the University of Illinois. A staff reporter on *The Wall Street Journal* since 1972, he previously taught English and drama in secondary schools.

Mary Wollstonecraft (1759–1797) was an English feminist author whose *A Vindication of the Rights of Woman* (1792) made her one of the earliest advocates of women's liberation. She was married to William Godwin, an author and social philosopher. She died giving birth to Mary, who became the second wife of the poet Percy Bysshe Shelley.

Peregrine [Gerald] Worsthorne (1923–   ) is deputy editor of the London *Sunday Telegraph*. He is author of *The Socialist Myth* (1972).

Gordon Wright (1912–   ), is William H. Bonsall Professor of History at Stanford University. Among his books are *France in Modern Times: 1760 to the Present* (1960) and *The Ordeal of Total War, 1939–1945* (1968).

ACKNOWLEDGMENTS (continued from page iv)

Writing, Language, and Style

"Language and Thought" by Susanne K. Langer. Reprinted from *Fortune* (January 1944) by permission of the author and of *Fortune* Magazine.

"Politics and the English Language" by George Orwell. From *Shooting an Elephant and Other Essays* by George Orwell, copyright, 1945, 1946, 1949, 1950 by Sonia Brownell Orwell; copyright, 1973, 1974, by Sonia Orwell. Reprinted by permission of Harcourt Brace Jovanovich, Inc. By permission of Mrs. Sonia Brownell Orwell and Martin Secker & Warburg.

"Fedgush" by Russell Baker, from *The New York Times*, June 1, 1975. © 1975 by the New York Times Company. Reprinted by permission.

"Baffle-Gab Thesaurus" from *Time* (September 13, 1968). Reprinted by permission from TIME, The Weekly Newsmagazine; Copyright Time Inc. 1968.

"Viable Solutions" by Edwin Newman. First published in *Esquire* magazine. Reprinted by permission.

"The Language Barrier: Why Students Can't Write" by A. Bartlett Giamatti. Reprinted with permission from the January 1976 issue of the *Yale Alumni Magazine*; copyright by Yale Alumni Publications, Inc.

"Being Serious Without Being Stuffy" by Walker Gibson. From *Tough, Sweet and Stuffy: An Essay on Modern American Prose Styles* by Walker Gibson. Copyright © 1966 by Indiana University Press. Reprinted by permission of the publisher.

"An Ethic of Clarity" by Donald Hall. Reprinted with permission of Macmillan Publishing Co., Inc. from *The Modern Stylists* by Donald Hall. Copyright © 1968 by Donald Hall.

Attainment

"Animula" by T. S. Eliot. From *Collected Poems 1909–1962* by T. S. Eliot, copyright, 1936, by Harcourt Brace Jovanovich, Inc.; copyright © 1963, 1964 by T. S. Eliot. Reprinted by permission of Harcourt Brace Jovanovich, Inc. Reprinted by permission of Faber and Faber Ltd. from *Collected Poems 1909–1962* by T. S. Eliot.

"Experience of the Average·Girl: Coming of Age in Samoa" by Margaret Mead. Reprinted by permission of William Morrow and Company, Inc. from *Coming of Age in Samoa* by Margaret Mead. Copyright © 1928, 1955, 1961 by Margaret Mead.

"Working" by Studs Turkel. From *Working: People Talk About What They Do All Day and How They Feel About What They Do*, by Studs Turkel. Copyright © 1972, 1974 by Studs Turkel. Reprinted by permission of Pantheon, a Division of Random House, Inc.

"Us and Them" by R. D. Laing. From *The Politics of Experience* (London: Penguin, 1967), pp. 65–83. Copyright © R. D. Laing, 1967. Reprinted by permission of Penguin Books Ltd.

"Piercing the Veil of the Commonplace" by Charles Frankel. Reprinted with permission of The Chronicle of Higher Education, May 3, 1976. Copyright © 1976 by Editorial Projects for Education, Inc.

"Getting Smart" by Josiah Bunting, III. Reprinted by permission of the author.

"Secrets of the Evergreen People" by Roy Larson, from *The Chicago Sun-Times*, January 25, 1976. Reprinted by permission of The Chicago Sun-Times.

"I Think Continually of Those Who Were Truly Great" by Stephen Spender. Copyright 1934 and renewed 1962 by Stephen Spender. Reprinted from *Selected Poems* by Stephen Spender, by permission of Random House, Inc. Copyright 1934 by Stephen Spender. Renewal copyright 1961 by Stephen Spender. Reprinted by permission of the Harold Matson Co., Inc.

2. SOCIETY

Politics and Economics

"A Plea for the Freedom of Dissent" by Learned Hand, from *The New York Times Magazine*, Feb. 6, 1955. © 1955 by the New York Times Company. Reprinted by permission.

"The New Inequality" by Peregrine Worsthorne. Copyright 1972 by the Sunday Telegraph of London. Reprinted by permission of the author.

"How a Prince Should Keep His Word" by Niccolò Machiavelli. From Machiavelli's *The Prince*, translated and edited by Mark Musa. Copyright © 1964 by St. Martin's Press, Inc. Reprinted by permission of St. Martin's Press, Inc.

". . . None Will Sweat But for Promotion . . ." by Michael Korda. From *Power: How to Get It, How to Use It*, by Michael Korda. Copyright © 1975 by Michael Korda and Paul Gitlin, Trustee for the Benefit of Christopher Korda. Reprinted by permission of Random House, Inc.

"Benighted Nations" by Russell Baker, from *The New York Times*, Nov. 30, 1975. © 1975 by The New York Times Company. Reprinted by permission.

"I Have a Dream" by Martin Luther King, Jr. Reprinted by permission of Joan Daves. Copyright © 1963 by Martin Luther King, Jr.

"Somehow, It Has Overcome" by Kenneth J. Arrow, from *The New York Times*, March 26, 1973. © 1973 by The New York Times Company. Reprinted by permission.

"Oh! We've Been Trojan-Horsed!" by Peter F. Drucker, from *The New York Times*, June 4, 1976. © 1976 by The New York Times Company. Reprinted by permission.

"Directive" by Robert Frost. From *The Poetry of Robert Frost* edited by Edward Connery Lathem. Copyright 1923, 1947, © 1969 by Holt, Rinehart and Winston. Copyright 1951 by Robert Frost. Copyright © 1975 by Lesley Frost Ballantine. Reprinted by permission of Holt, Rinehart and Winston, Publishers.

War

"The Hot Gates" by William Golding. © 1962 by William Golding. Abridged from his essay "The Hot Gates" in *The Hot Gates and Other Occasional Pieces* by permission of Harcourt Brace Jovanovich, Inc. Reprinted by permission of Faber and Faber Ltd. from *The Hot Gates and Other Occasional Pieces* by William Golding.

"The Persian Version" by Robert Graves, from *Poems 1938–1945* by Robert Graves. Reprinted by permission of Curtis Brown, Ltd. Copyright © 1946, 1955, 1958, 1961, 1965 by Robert Graves.

"Appomattox" by Bruce Catton. Selection from *This Hallowed Ground* by Bruce Catton. Copyright © 1955, 1956 by Bruce Catton. Reprinted by permission of Doubleday & Company, Inc.

"War Memories" by Stephen Crane. From *Tales of War* edited by Fredson Bowers, with an introduction by James B. Colvert (Charlottesville, Va.: The University Press of Virginia, 1970). Reprinted by permission of The University Press of Virginia.

"The War Prayer" in *Europe and Elsewhere* by Mark Twain. Copyright, 1923, 1951 by The Mark Twain Company. By permission of Harper & Row, Publishers, Inc.

"A Salutation-Speech from the 19th Century to the 20th" by Mark Twain. From *The Art of Mark Twain* by William M. Gibson (New York: Oxford University Press, 1976).

"On History, Foolishness and Vietnam" by John Kenneth Galbraith, from *The New York Times*, July 12, 1975. © 1975 by The New York Times Company. Reprinted by permission.

Sports

"Billie Jean King: An Attitude, Instinct, and Sense of Urgency" by Parton Keese, from *The New York Times*, Jan. 14, 1976. © 1976 by The New York Times Company. Reprinted by permission.

"O. J. Simpson: Speed, Balance, and E.S.P." by Gerald Eskenazi, from *The New York Times*, Jan. 12, 1976. © 1976 by The New York Times Company. Reprinted by permission.

"Life on the Run" by Bill Bradley. Copyright © 1976 by Bill Bradley. Reprinted by permission of Quadrangle/The New York Times Book Co. from *Life on the Run* by Bill Bradley.

"Why Ali Whipped Patterson" by Muhammad Ali, from *The New York Times*, Sept. 18, 1975. © 1975 by Muhammad Ali/Courtesy of the New York Times. From *The Greatest—My Own Story* by Muhammad Ali with Richard Durham. Copyright © 1975 by Muhammad Ali, Herbert Muhammad and Richard Durham. Reprinted by permission of Random House, Inc.

Minorities

"The Grass on the Mountain" translated by Mary Austin. From *The American Rhythm* (Houghton Mifflin, 1923, 1970). Reprinted by permission of Houghton Mifflin Company.

"Wounded Knee" by Dee Brown. From *Bury My Heart at Wounded Knee* by Dee Brown. Copyright © 1970 by Dee Brown. Reprinted by permission of Holt, Rinehart and Winston, Publishers.

"The Feast of San Diego at Jemez" by N. Scott Momaday. From pp. 128–137 in *The Names: A Memoir*, by N. Scott Momaday. Copyright © 1976 by N. Scott Momaday. Copyright © 1976 by N. Scott Momaday. By permission of Harper & Row, Publishers, Inc.

"The Meaning of the Chicano Movement" by Lydia Aguirre, from *Social Casework* (May 1971). Reprinted by permission of the publisher, Family Service Association of America.

"Why I Left the U.S. and Why I Am Returning" by Eldridge Cleaver, from *The New York Times*, Nov. 18, 1975. © 1975 by the New York Times Company. Reprinted by permission.

Women

"The Stereotype" by Germaine Greer. Abridged from *The Female Eunuch* by Germaine Greer. Copyright 1970, 1971 by G. Greer. Used with permission of McGraw-Hill Book Company. Reprinted by permission of the publisher, MacGibbon Kee Limited/Granada Publishing Limited.

"Rape, But That Has Changed" by Susan Brownmiller, from *The New York Times*, Oct. 1, 1975. © 1975 by The New York Times Company. Reprinted by permission.

"Two-Career Couples" by Alan L. Otten, from *The Wall Street Journal*, July 29, 1976. Reprinted with permission of The Wall Street Journal, © Dow Jones & Company, Inc. 1976. All Rights Reserved.

"Why I Never Married" by Oriana Fallaci. Reprinted by permission of the author.

"Life Without Father" by Ellen Goodman, from *The Washington Post*, Jan. 8, 1977. © 1977, The Boston Globe Newspaper Company. Reprinted with permission.

500   Acknowledgments

"Planetarium" by Adrienne Rich. "Planetarium" is reprinted from *The Will to Change, Poems, 1968–1970*, by Adrienne Rich, Copyright © 1971 by W. W. Norton & Company. Inc. Footnotes by Barbara C. Gelpi and Albert Gelpi, from *Adrienne Rich's Poetry*, A Norton Critical Edition, Edited by Barbara C. Gelpi and Albert Gelpi, Copyright © 1975 by W. W. Norton & Company, Inc. By permission of W. W. Norton & Company, Inc.

3. THE ARTS

Film and Television

"Who Killed King Kong?" by X. J. Kennedy, from *Dissent* (Spring 1960). Reprinted by permission of the author and *Dissent*.

"The New *King Kong*, or A Great Ape Double-Crossed" by X. J. Kennedy. By permission of the author.

"Henry V" by James Agee. From *Agee on Film*, Volume I by James Agee. Copyright © 1958 by The James Agee Trust. Used by permission of Grosset & Dunlap, Inc.

"There Are No Mass Media: All We Have Is Television" by Jeffrey Schrank. Copyright © 1977 by Jeffrey Schrank. Reprinted from *Snap, Crackle, and Popular Taste* by Jeffrey Schrank by permission of the publisher, Dell Publishing Co., Inc. A Delta Original.

Music, Painting, and Architecture

"Why Don't You Run Upstairs and Write a Nice Gershwin Tune?" by Leonard Bernstein. From *The Joy of Music* by Leonard Bernstein. Copyright © 1954, 1955, 1956, 1957, 1958, 1959 by Leonard Bernstein. Reprinted by permission of Simon & Schuster, a Division of Gulf & Western Corporation.

"How We Listen" by Aaron Copland. From *What To Listen For In Music*. Copyright 1957 by McGraw-Hill, Inc. Used with permission of McGraw-Hill Book Company.

"As Picasso Said" by André Malraux. From *Picasso's Mask* (*La Tête D'Obsidienne*) by André Malraux. Copyright © 1974 by Editions Gallimard. English translation © 1975 by Holt, Rinehart and Winston. Translated by June Guicharnaud with Jacques Guicharnaud. Reprinted by arrangement with Holt, Rinehart and Winston.

"The Case for Abstract Art" by Clement Greenberg. Reprinted by permission of the author.

"The School of 'Messy Vitality' " by Dennis Farney, from *The Wall Street Journal*, Jan. 4, 1974. Reprinted with permission of The Wall Street Journal, © Dow Jones & Company, Inc. 1974. All Rights Reserved.

"Chicago's Stunning Architecture" by Paul Goldberger, from *The New York Times*, Sept. 14, 1976. © 1976 by The New York Times Company. Reprinted by permission.

Literature

"The Macbeth Murder Mystery" by James Thurber. Copyright © 1942 James Thurber. Copyright © 1970 Helen W. Thurber and Rosemary Thurber Sauers. From *My World—and Welcome to It*, published by Harcourt Brace Jovanovich, Inc. Originally printed in *The New Yorker*.

"Ars Poetica" by Archibald MacLeish, from *Collected Poems 1917–1952*. Copyright 1952 by Archibald MacLeish. Reprinted by permission of Houghton Mifflin Company.

"The Use of Poetry" by Harold Bloom, from *The New York Times*, Nov. 12, 1975. © 1975 by The New York Times Company. Reprinted by permission.

"On Reading a Poem" by William M. Gibson. Reprinted from *The Psychology of Reading* by Eleanor J. Gibson and Harry Levin by permission of the M.I.T. Press, Cambridge, Massachusetts. Copyright © 1975, M.I.T. Press.

"Nat Pine" by Gilbert Millstein, from *The New York Times Book Review*, Feb. 13, 1977. © 1977 by The New York Times Company. Reprinted by permission.

"The Keys to Dreamland" by Northrop Frye. From *The Educated Imagination* by Northrop Frye, copyright © 1964 by Indiana University Press. Reprinted by permission of the publisher and of the author.

"The Literary Life: Some Representative Women" by Ellen Moers. From *Literary Women* by Ellen Moers. Copyright © 1963, 1972, 1973, 1974, 1975, 1976 by Ellen Moers. Reprinted by permission of Doubleday & Company, Inc.

Art and Life

"Expressiveness" by Susanne K. Langer. Reprinted from *Problems of Art* by Susanne K. Langer with the permission of Charles Scribner's Sons. Copyright © 1957 Susanne K. Langer.

"Cultural Snobbery" by Arthur Koestler. Reprinted by permission of A. D. Peters & Company.

"The Quest for Civilisation" by Kenneth Clark. From pp. 344–347 (under the title "The Quest for Civilisation") in *Civilisation: A Personal View* by Kenneth Clark. Copyright © 1969 by Kenneth Clark. Reprinted by permission of Harper & Row, Publishers, Inc.

4. SCIENCES

Science and Scientists

"The Usefulness of Useless Knowledge" by Abraham Flexner. From *Harper's*, 179 (October 1939), 544–550 (with omissions). Copyright © 1939 by *Harper's* Magazine. Copyright © renewed 1966 by Harper's Magazine. Reprinted by permission of Eleanor Flexner and Jean Flexner Lewinson.

"On Albert Einstein" by Robert Oppenheimer. Reprinted with permission from *The New York Review of Books*. Copyright © 1966 Nyrev, Inc.

"Newton the Man" by John Maynard Keynes. Reprinted by permission of the publisher, Horizon Press, from *Essays In Biography* by John Maynard Keynes, copyright 1951.

Of Life

"The Territorial Imperative" by Robert Ardrey. From *The Territorial Imperative* by Robert Ardrey. Copyright © 1966 by Robert Ardrey. Reprinted by permission of Atheneum Publishers.

"The Ladder of Creation" by Jacob Bronowski. From *The Ascent of Man* by Jacob Bronowski, by permission of Little, Brown and Company. Copyright © 1973 by J. Bronowski. By permission of BBC Publications, The British Broadcasting Corporation.

"Natural Science" by Lewis Thomas. From *The Lives of a Cell* by Lewis Thomas. Copyright © 1973 by The Massachusetts Medical Society. Reprinted by permission of The Viking Press.

"Carbon Monoxide Poisoning" by Claude Bernard, from *An Introduction to the Study of Experimental Medicine* by Claude Bernard. Copyright 1927 by Abelard-Schumann, Ltd. Reprinted by permission of Thomas Y. Crowell Company, Inc.

"The Music of *This* Sphere" by Lewis Thomas. From *The Lives of a Cell* by Lewis Thomas. Copyright © 1971 by The Massachusetts Medical Society. Reprinted by permission of The Viking Press.

"To a Snail" by Marianne Moore. Reprinted with permission of Macmillan Publishing Co., Inc. from *Collected Poems* by Marianne Moore. Copyright 1935 by Marianne Moore, renewed 1963 by Marianne Moore and T. S. Eliot.

Ecology

"Monsieur Tocqueville! Oh, Get Some Water—He's Fainted!" by William W. Serrin, from *The New York Times*, Jan. 2, 1976. © 1976 by The New York Times Company. Reprinted by permission.

"Trying to Restore a Sea of Grass" by Dennis Farney, from *The Wall Street Journal*, June 6, 1975. Reprinted with permission of The Wall Street Journal, © Dow Jones & Company, Inc. 1975. All Rights Reserved.

"Bees and Ecology" by Joseph M. Winski, from *The Wall Street Journal*, Nov. 7, 1974. Reprinted with permission of The Wall Street Journal, © Dow Jones & Company, Inc. 1974. All Rights Reserved.

"Wilderness" by Aldo Leopold. From *A Sand County Almanac, With Other Essays on Conservation from Round River* by Aldo Leopold. Copyright © 1949, 1953, 1966, 1977, by Oxford University Press, Inc. Reprinted by permission.

Some Problems

"Why Can't Computers Be More Like Us?" by Lewis Thomas, from *The Saturday Evening Post* (October 1976). Reprinted with permission © 1976 The Saturday Evening Post Company.

"What Physicists Do: Neaten Up the Cosmos" by Robert Geroch, from *The New York Times*, June 12, 1976. © 1976 by The New York Times Company. Reprinted by permission.

"Molecular Astronomy: The Great Void Is Alive" by Walter Sullivan, from *The New York Times*, Sept. 28, 1975. © 1975 by The New York Times Company. Reprinted by permission.

Some Adjustments

"Trend Is Not Destiny" by René Dubos, from *The New York Times*, Nov. 10, 1975. © 1975 by The New York Times Company. Reprinted by permission.

"On Growth" by René Dubos, from *The New York Times*, Nov. 11, 1975. © 1975 by The New York Times Company. Reprinted by permission.

"Who Should Control Recombinant DNA?" by Cheryl M. Fields. Ms. Fields is a senior editor for The Chronicle of Higher Education. Reprinted by permission.

"Man's Fourth Adjustment" by Harlow Shapley. Reprinted from *The American Scholar*, Volume 25, Number 4 (Autumn 1956). Copyright © 1956 by the United Chapters of Phi Beta Kappa. By permission of the publishers.

"The Golden Alphabet" by Loren Eiseley. Abridged from *The Unexpected Universe*, copyright © 1969, by Loren Eiseley. Reprinted by permission of Harcourt Brace Jovanovich, Inc.

5. FINAL THINGS

The Good Life

"For Once, Then, Something" by Robert Frost. From *The Poetry of Robert Frost* edited by Edward Connery Lathem. Copyright 1923, 1947, © 1969 by Holt, Rinehart and Winston. Copyright 1951 by Robert Frost. Copyright © 1975 by Lesley Frost Ballantine. Reprinted by permission of Holt, Rinehart and Winston, Publishers.

"History as a Moral Science" by Gordon Wright. Excerpted from a longer essay in *The American Historical Review* (February 1976). Reprinted with permission of The Chronicle of Higher Education, February 23, 1976. Copyright © 1976 by Editorial Projects for Education, Inc.

"The Apology of Socrates" by Plato. Reprinted from Lane Cooper (translator):

Plato on the Trial and Death of Socrates. Copyright © 1941 by Lane Cooper. Used by permission of Cornell University Press.

God and Humankind

"The Upanishads," from *The Upanishads: Breath of the Eternal,* translated by Swami Prabhavananda and Frederick Manchester, a Mentor book from New American Library. Copyright 1948, 1957 by Vedanta Society of Southern California, Hollywood, California.

"God and the Spirit of Man" by Martin Buber, from *Eclipse of God* by Martin Buber. Copyright 1952 by Harper & Row, Publishers, Inc. Reprinted by permission of the publisher.

What Is Reality?

"Existentialism as a Symbol of Man's Contemporary Crisis" by William C. Barrett, from *Spiritual Problems in Contemporary Literature* edited by Stanley Romaine Hopper. Copyright 1952 by The Institute for Religious and Social Studies. Reprinted by permission of Harper & Row, Publishers, Inc.

"The Allegory of the Cave" by Plato. From *The Republic of Plato* translated by F. M. Cornford and published by Oxford University Press (1941). Reprinted by permission of the publisher.

Death

"O Death, Where Is Thy Sting-a-Ling-a-Ling?" by Leslie H. Farber. Reprinted from *Commentary,* by permission; copyright © 1977 by the American Jewish Committee.

"Because I Could Not Stop for Death" by Emily Dickinson. Reprinted by permission of the publishers and the Trustees of Amherst College from *The Poems of Emily Dickinson,* edited by Thomas H. Johnson, Cambridge, Mass.: The Belknap Press of Harvard University Press, Copyright © 1951, 1955 by the President and Fellows of Harvard College.

What Is Happiness?

"What Is Happiness?" by William V. Shannon, from *The New York Times,* July 5, 1976. © 1976 by The New York Times Company. Reprinted by permission.

"Myths of Our Time" by L. S. Stavrianos, from *The New York Times,* May 8, 1976. © 1976 by The New York Times Company. Reprinted by permission.

"O Taste and See," from Denise Levertov, *O Taste and See.* Copyright © 1964 by Denise Levertov Goodman. Reprinted by permission of New Directions Publishing Corporation.

"A Really New World" by Joseph Wood Krutch. From *Baja California and the Geography of Hope* by Joseph Wood Krutch (San Francisco: The Sierra Club, 1969). Reprinted by permission.

What Is Man?

"I Corinthians 13: Love" by St. Paul. From the Revised Standard Version of the Bible, copyrighted 1946, 1952, © 1971, 1973.

"The Lowest Animal" by Mark Twain, in Mark Twain, *Letters from the Earth,* edited by Bernard DeVoto. Copyright © 1962 by The Mark Twain Company. Reprinted by permission of Harper & Row, Publishers, Inc.

Index of Authors and Titles

Adolescence, 12
Agee, James: *Henry V*, 217
Aguirre, Lydia R.: Meaning of the Chicano Movement, The, 176
Ali, Muhammad: Why Ali Whipped Patterson, 162
Allegory of the Cave, The, 447
Animula, 62
Apology of Socrates, The, 408
Appomattox, 133
Ardrey, Robert: Territorial Imperative, The, 333
Arrow, Kenneth J.: Somehow, It Has Overcome, 120
Ars Poetica, 260
As Italian as Apple Pie and Baseball, 188
As Picasso Said, Why Assume That To Look Is To See? A Talk Between Malraux and the Master, 238
Aurelius, Marcus: Stoic Code, The, 471
Austin, Mary (trans.): Grass on the Mountain, The, 165

Baffle-Gab Thesaurus, 43
Baker, Russell: Benighted Nations, 112; Fedgush, 41
Barrett, William C.: Existentialism as a Symptom of Man's Contemporary Crisis, 440
Because I Could Not Stop for Death, 464
Bees and Ecology, 361
Being Serious Without Being Stuffy, 52
Bellamy, Edward: Looking Backward, 2000–1887, 117
Benighted Nations, 112
Bernard, Claude: Carbon Monoxide Poisoning, 349
Bernstein, Leonard: Why Don't You Run Upstairs and Write a Nice Gershwin Tune? 227
Bill of Rights, The, 103
Billie Jean King: An Attitude, Instinct, and Sense of Urgency, 150
Blake, William: Divine Image, The, 486
Bloom, Harold: Use of Poetry, The, 261
Bradley, Bill: Life on the Run, 157
Brahma, 433
Brewster, Kingman, Jr.: Should Colleges Retain Tenure? 19
Bronowski, Jacob: Ladder of Creation, The, 337
Brown, Dee: Wounded Knee, 165
Brownmiller, Susan: Rape, But That Has Changed, 194
Buber, Martin: God and the Spirit of Man, 435

Buddha, Gautama: Sermon at Benares, The, 417
Bunting, Josiah, III: Getting Smart, 84

Carbon Monoxide Poisoning, 349
Case for Abstract Art, The, 242
Catton, Bruce: Appomattox, 133
Chanting the Square Deific, 434
Chicago's Stunning Architecture, 254
Clark, Kenneth: Quest for Civilisation, The, 299
Cleaver, Eldridge: Why I Left the U.S. and Why I Am Returning, 185
Copland, Aaron: How We Listen, 233
I Corinthians 13: Love, 476
Crane, Stephen: War Memories, 138
Cultural Snobbery, 292

Darwin, Charles: Struggle for Existence, The, 329
Declaration of Independence, 98
Dickinson, Emily: Because I Could Not Stop for Death, 464
Directive, 126
Divine Image, The, 486
Donne, John: Meditation XVII, 462
Douglass, Frederick: Meaning of July Fourth for the American Negro, The, 180
Drucker, Peter F.: Oh! We've Been Trojan-Horsed! 124
Dubos, René: On Growth, 382; Trend Is Not Destiny, 380

Ecclesiastes 12:1–8: Remember Now Thy Creator, 485
Eiseley, Loren: Golden Alphabet, The, 392
Eliot, T. S.: Animula, 62
Emerson, Ralph Waldo: Brahma, 433
Erikson, Erik H.: Adolescence, 12
Eskenazi, Gerald: O. J. Simpson: Speed, Balance, and E.S.P., 154
Ethic of Clarity, An, 57
Existentialism as a Symptom of Man's Contemporary Crisis, 440
Experience of the Average Girl: Coming of Age in Samoa, 63
Expressiveness, 285

Fallaci, Oriana: Why I Never Married, 200
Farber, Leslie H.: O Death, Where Is Thy Sting-a-Ling-a-Ling? 451
Farney, Dennis: School of "Messy Vitality," The, 249; Trying to Restore a Sea of Grass, 359

505

Index of Authors and Titles

Feast of San Diego at Jemez, The, 170
Fedgush, 41
Fields, Cheryl M.: Who Should Control Recombinant DNA? 383
Flexner, Abraham: Usefulness of Useless Knowledge, The, 308
Football Phenomenon on Campus, The, 4
For Once, Then, Something, 404
Frankel, Charles: Piercing the Veil of the Commonplace, 80
Franklin, Benjamin: Learning to Write, 24; Speech in the Constitutional Convention at the Conclusion of Its Deliberations, September 17, 1787, 101
Frost, Robert: Directive, 126; For Once, Then, Something, 404
Frustrations of the Gifted, 17
Frye, Northrop: Keys to Dreamland, The, 267

Galbraith, John Kenneth: On History, Foolishness, and Vietnam, 145
Gautama Buddha: Sermon at Benares, The, 417
Geroch, Robert: What Physicists Do: Neaten up the Cosmos, 375
Getting Smart, 84
Giamatti, A. Bartlett: Language Barrier, The: Why Students Can't Write, 48
Gibson, Walker: Being Serious Without Being Stuffy, 52
Gibson, William M.: On Reading a Poem, 263
God and the Spirit of Man, 435
Goldberger, Paul: Chicago's Stunning Architecture, 254
Golden Alphabet, The, 393
Golding, William: Hot Gates, The, 128
Goodman, Ellen: Life Without Father, 202
Grass on the Mountain, The, 165
Graves, Robert: Persian Version, The, 132
Greenberg, Clement: Case for Abstract Art, The, 242
Greer, Germaine: Stereotype, The, 192

Hall, Donald: Ethic of Clarity, An, 57
Hand, Learned: Plea for the Freedom of Dissent, A, 94
Henry V, 217
History as a Moral Science, 404
Hot Gates, The, 128
How a Prince Should Keep His Word, 106
How We Listen, 233

I Have a Dream, 114
I Think Continually of Those Who Were Truly Great, 88

Jefferson, Thomas: Declaration of Independence, 98

Keats, John: Ode on a Grecian Urn, 302
Keese, Parton: Billie Jean King: An Attitude, Instinct, and Sense of Urgency, 150
Kennedy, X. J.: New King Kong, or A Great Ape Double-Crossed, The, 214; Who Killed King Kong? 211
Keynes, John Maynard: Newton the Man, 320
Keys to Dreamland, The, 267
King, Martin Luther, Jr.: I Have a Dream, 114
Know Then Thyself, 484
Koestler, Arthur: Cultural Snobbery, 292
Korda, Michael: ". . . None Will Sweat But for Promotion . . ." 108
Krutch, Joseph Wood: Really New World, A, 469

Ladder of Creation, The, 337
Laing, R. D.: Us and Them, 77
Langer, Susanne K.: Expressiveness, 285; Language and Thought, 26
Language and Thought, 26
Language Barrier, The: Why Students Can't Write, 48
Larson, Roy: Secrets of the Evergreen People, 86
Learning to Write, 24
Leopold, Aldo: Wilderness, 364
Levertov, Denise: O Taste and See, 469
Life on the Run, 157
Life Without Father, 202
Literary Life, The: Some Representative Women, 275
Looking Backward, 2000–1887, 117
Love (I Corinthians 13), 476
Lowest Animal, The, 477

Macbeth Murder Mystery, The, 257
Machiavelli, Niccolò: How a Prince Should Keep His Word, 106
MacLeish, Archibald: Ars Poetica, 260
Malraux, André: As Picasso Said, Why Assume That To Look Is To See? A Talk Between Malraux and the Master, 238
Man's Fourth Adjustment, 389
Mead, Margaret: Experience of the Average Girl: Coming of Age in Samoa, 63
Meaning of July Fourth for the American Negro, The, 180
Meaning of the Chicano Movement, The, 176
Meditation XVII, 462

Index of Authors and Titles

Millstein, Gilbert: Nat Pine, 265
Moers, Ellen: Literary Life, The: Some Representative Women, 275
Molecular Astronomy: The Great Void Is Alive, 377
Momaday, N. Scott: Feast of San Diego at Jemez, The, 170
Monsieur Tocqueville! Oh, Get Some Water—He's Fainted! 356
Moore, Marianne: To a Snail, 355
More Day to Dawn, 484
Morse, J. Mitchell: Nothing Is True, Nothing Is False, 8
Murphy, Norman C.: Frustrations of the Gifted, 17
Music of *This* Sphere, The, 351
Myths of Our Time, 467

Nat Pine, 265
Natural Science, 347
New Inequality, The, 104
New *King Kong*, or A Great Ape Double-Crossed, The, 214
Newman, Edwin: Viable Solutions, 43
Newton the Man, 320
". . . None Will Sweat But for Promotion . . ." 108
Nothing Is True, Nothing Is False, 8

O Death, Where Is Thy Sting-a-Ling-a-Ling? 451
O Taste and See, 469
Ode on a Grecian Urn, 302
Oh! We've Been Trojan-Horsed! 124
O. J. Simpson: Speed, Balance, and E.S.P., 154
On Albert Einstein, 315
On Being 17, Bright, and Unable to Read, 15
On Growth, 382
On History, Foolishness, and Vietnam, 145
On Reading a Poem, 263
Oppenheimer, Robert: On Albert Einstein, 315
Orwell, George: Politics and the English Language, 31
Otten, Alan L.: Two-Career Couples, 197

Perrotta, Ralph J.: As Italian as Apple Pie and Baseball, 188
Persian Version, The, 132
Peterson, Iver: Football Phenomenon on Campus, The, 4
Piercing the Veil of the Commonplace, 80
Planetarium, 204
Plato: Allegory of the Cave, The, 447; Apology of Socrates, The, 408

Plea for the Freedom of Dissent, A, 94
Politics and the English Language, 31
Pope, Alexander: Know Then Thyself, 484
Psalm 8: The Strength and Glory of Man, 471
Psalm 90: Man and the Providence of God, 428

Quest for Civilisation, The, 299

Rape, But That Has Changed, 194
Raymond, David: On Being 17, Bright, and Unable to Read, 15
Really New World, A, 469
Remember Now Thy Creator (Ecclesiastes 12:1-8), 485
Rich, Adrienne: Planetarium, 204

St. Matthew: Sermon on the Mount, The, 422
St. Paul: I Corinthians 13: Love, 476
Salutation-Speech from the 19th Century to the 20th, A, 145
School of "Messy Vitality," The, 249
Schrank, Jeffrey: There Are No Mass Media: All We Have Is Television, 220
Secrets of the Evergreen People, 86
Sermon at Benares, The, 417
Sermon on the Mount, The, 422
Serrin, William W.: Monsieur Tocqueville! Oh, Get Some Water—He's Fainted! 356
Shakespeare, William: Sonnet 55: Not marble, nor the gilded monuments, 261
Shannon, William V.: What Is Happiness? 465
Shapley, Harlow: Man's Fourth Adjustment, 389
Should Colleges Retain Tenure? 19
Somehow, It Has Overcome, 120
Sonnet 55: Not marble, nor the gilded monuments, 261
Speech in the Constitutional Convention at the Conclusion of Its Deliberations, September 17, 1787, 101
Spender, Stephen: I Think Continually of Those Who Were Truly Great, 88
Stavrianos, L. S.: Myths of Our Time, 467
Stereotype, The, 192
Stoic Code, The, 471
Struggle for Existence, The, 329
Sullivan, Walter: Molecular Astronomy: The Great Void Is Alive, 377

Terkel, Studs: Working, 70
Territorial Imperative, The, 333

There Are No Mass Media: All We Have Is Television, 220
Thomas, Lewis: Music of *This* Sphere, The, 351; Natural Science, 347; Why Can't Computers Be More Like Us? 373
Thoreau, Henry D.: More Day to Dawn, 484
Thurber, James: Macbeth Murder Mystery, The, 257
To a Snail, 355
Trend Is Not Destiny, 380
Trying to Restore a Sea of Grass, 359
Twain, Mark: Lowest Animal, The, 477; Salutation-Speech from the 19th Century to the 20th, A, 145; War Prayer, The, 142
Two-Career Couples, 197

Us and Them, 77
Use of Poetry, The, 261
Usefulness of Useless Knowledge, The, 308
Upanishads, The: Svetasvatara, 429

Viable Solutions, 43
Vindication of the Rights of Woman, A, 190

War Memories, 138
War Prayer, The, 142
What Is Happiness? 465
What Physicists Do: Neaten up the Cosmos, 375
Whitman, Walt: Chanting the Square Deific, 434
Who Killed King Kong? 211
Who Should Control Recombinant DNA? 383
Why Ali Whipped Patterson, 162
Why Can't Computers Be More Like Us? 373
Why Don't You Run Upstairs and Write a Nice Gershwin Tune? 227
Why I Left the U.S. and Why I Am Returning, 185
Why I Never Married, 200
Wilderness, 364
Winski, Joseph M.: Bees and Ecology, 361
Wollstonecraft, Mary: Vindication of the Rights of Woman, A, 190
Working, 70
Worsthorne, Peregrine: New Inequality, The, 104
Wounded Knee, 165
Wright, Gordon: History as a Moral Science, 404